2015-2016
SEPTEMBER–AUGUST

NIV®

Standard LESSON COMMENTARY®

NEW INTERNATIONAL VERSION®

Edited by
Ronald L. Nickelson

Jim Eichenberger,
Senior Editor

Volume 22

Standard®
PUBLISHING

Cincinnati, Ohio

IN THIS VOLUME

Fall Quarter 2015 (page 1)
THE CHRISTIAN COMMUNITY COMES ALIVE

Lesson Development . . . . David C. Robinson (1), A. Eugene Andrews (2), Kenneth L. Boles (3, 4),
. . . . Tom Thatcher (5–8), Mark S. Krause (9–13)
Verbal Illustrations . . . Charles R. Boatman (1–7), James B. North (8, 9), Douglas C. Schmidt (10, 11)
. . . . Vicki Edwards (12, 13)
Involvement Learning . . . . Cheryl Frey (1–3), Teresa D. Welch (4), Ronald G. Davis (5–8),
. . . . Wendy Guthrie (9–13)
What Do You Think? . . . . .Lloyd Ludwick (1, 2), Corey Auen (3, 4), A. Eugene Andrews (5–8),
. . . . Kenneth L. Boles (9–13)

Winter Quarter 2015–2016 (page 113)
SACRED GIFTS AND HOLY GATHERINGS

Lesson Development . . . . Douglas Redford (1–3), Jon Weatherly (4), Mark S. Krause (5–9),
. . . . Lloyd M. Pelfrey (10–13)
Verbal Illustrations . . . . . Charles R. Boatman (1–7), Candace M. Wood (8, 9), Vicki Edwards (10, 11),
. . . . James B. North (12–13)
Involvement Learning . . . . .Cheryl Frey (1–4), Ronald G. Davis (5–7), Teresa D. Welch (8, 9),
. . . . Wendy Guthrie (10–13)
What Do You Think? . . . . Lloyd Ludwick (1–7), A. Eugene Andrews (8–13)

Spring Quarter 2016 (page 225)
THE GIFT OF FAITH

Lesson Development . . . . Jon Weatherly (1, 2), Corey Auen (3), Kelvin Jones (4),
. . . . Tom Thatcher (5–8), Mark S. Krause (9–13)
Verbal Illustrations . . . . James B. North (1, 2), Douglas C. Schmidt (3), Vicki Edwards (4),
. . . . . Candace M. Wood (5), Ronald L. Nickelson (5), Laura L. Wood (6), Charles R. Boatman (7–13)
Involvement Learning . . . . Ronald G. Davis (1–4), Teresa D. Welch (5–8), Cheryl Frey (9–13)
What Do You Think? . . . . .Lloyd Ludwick (1–11), Richard Koffarnus (12, 13)

Summer Quarter 2016 (page 337)
TOWARD A NEW CREATION

Lesson Development . . . . Douglas Redford (1–3), Jon Weatherly (4–7), Mark S. Krause (8–13)
Verbal Illustrations . . . . Charles R. Boatman (1–7), James B. North (8, 9), Laura L. Wood (10),
. . . . Douglas C. Schmidt (11), Vicki Edwards (12, 13)
Involvement Learning . . . . Ronald G. Davis (1–3), Teresa D. Welch (4–7), Cheryl Frey (8–13)
What Do You Think? . . . . Douglas Redford (1–3), Jon Weatherly (4–7), Mark S. Krause (8–12),
. . . . Truitt F. Evans Sr. (13)

INDEX OF PRINTED TEXTS

The printed texts for 2015–2016 are arranged here in the order in which they appear in the Bible.

REFERENCE	PAGE
Genesis 29:15-30	153
Exodus 12:1-14	193
Exodus 13:13b-15	137
Exodus 20:8-11	121
Exodus 31:12-16	121
Leviticus 16:11-19	209
Leviticus 22:17-25	129
Leviticus 22:31-33	129
Leviticus 23:15-22	201
Leviticus 23:33-43	217
Song of Songs 6:4-12	161
Hosea 1:1-11	169
Zephaniah 1:4-6	345
Zephaniah 1:14-16	345
Zephaniah 2:3	345
Zephaniah 3:1-8	353
Zephaniah 3:9-14	361
Zephaniah 3:20	361
Matthew 23:2-12	145
Mark 9:14-29	233
Mark 10:16	321
Mark 10:17-31	241
Mark 12:38-44	145
Mark 14:26-31	249
Mark 14:66-72	249
Mark 16:1-8	257
Luke 2:22-32	137
Luke 7:1-10	265
Luke 7:36-50	273
Luke 8:26-36	281
Luke 15:11-24	289

REFERENCE	PAGE
Luke 17:1-10	297
Luke 17:11-19	305
Luke 18:9-14	313
Luke 18:15-17	321
Luke 19:1-10	329
John 2:1-12	177
John 11:38-44	185
Acts 4:23-31	9
Acts 4:34-37	17
Acts 5:1-10	17
Acts 5:27-29	25
Acts 5:33-42	25
Acts 7:2-4	33
Acts 7:8-10	33
Acts 7:17	33
Acts 7:33, 34	33
Acts 7:45-47	33
Acts 7:52, 53	33
Acts 8:9-24	41
Acts 9:19b-31	49
Acts 10:24-38	57
Acts 11:1-18a	65
Acts 12:1-11	73
Acts 15:1-12	81
Acts 16:1-5	89
Acts 16:8-15	89
Acts 17:1-4	97
Acts 17:10-12	97
Acts 17:22-25	97
Acts 17:28	97
Acts 18:1-11	105

REFERENCE	PAGE
Acts 18:18-21a	105
Romans 1:18-32	369
Romans 2:17-29	377
Romans 3:9-20	385
Romans 3:21-31	393
Romans 5:1-11	401
Romans 6:1-4	409
Romans 6:12-14	409
Romans 6:17-23	409
Romans 8:28-39	417
Romans 9:6-18	425
Romans 11:11-24	433
Romans 12:1, 2	441
Romans 13:8-10	441

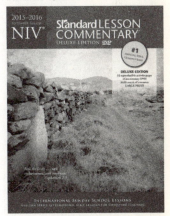

NIV Deluxe Edition

DVD-ROM AVAILABLE!

The *Standard Lesson Commentary®* is available on DVD in the deluxe editions. The DVD contains the full text of both the *NIV® Standard Lesson Commentary®* and the *KJV Standard Lesson Commentary®* powered by QuickVerse® from WORDsearch® Bible Study Software, additional study aids, and a collection of presentation helps that can be projected or reproduced as handouts. Order 020080215 (NIV, pictured above) or 020090215 (KJV). Additional books and resources are available by FREE download from www.wordsearchbible.com/products/free.

For questions regarding the installation, registration, or activation of the DVD, contact WORDsearch Customer Service at 800.888.9898 or 512.615.9444, Mon–Fri, 8 a.m. to 8 p.m.; or Sat, 10 a.m. to 5 p.m. (Central Time). For problems with the DVD, contact WORDsearch Technical Support at 888.854.8400 or 512.835.6900, Mon–Fri, 9 a.m. to 5 p.m. (Central Time); or by e-mail Support@wordsearchBible.com.

Logos Bible Software users! You can purchase the *Standard Lesson eCommentary* as a download from www.logos.com/standard. This is a separate purchase from the print edition.

Cumulative Index

A cumulative index for Scripture passages used in the Standard Lesson Commentary *for September 2010–August 2016 is provided below.*

REFERENCE	YEAR	PAGE
Ge 2:18-25	2013-14	17
Ge 3:8-17	2013-14	25
Ge 3:21	2013-14	25
Ge 3:23	2013-14	25
Ge 9:1	2013-14	33
Ge 9:3-6	2013-14	33
Ge 9:8-17	2013-14	33
Ge 11:1-9	2013-14	41
Ge 12:1-9	2011-12	121
Ge 15:1-6	2011-12	129
Ge 15:5-21	2013-14	49
Ge 15:12-18	2011-12	129
Ge 17:15-17	2013-14	57
Ge 18:9-15	2013-14	57
Ge 21:1-7	2013-14	57
Ge 21:12-14	2013-14	65
Ge 21:17-21	2013-14	65
Ge 22:1-14	2011-12	137
Ge 26:2-5	2013-14	65
Ge 26:12, 13	2013-14	65
Ge 28:1a	2013-14	73
Ge 28:10-22	2013-14	73
Ge 29:15-30	2015-16	153
Ge 39:7-21a	2011-12	153
Ge 41:37-46	2011-12	161
Ge 41:50-52	2011-12	161
Ge 45:3-15	2011-12	169
Ge 50:15-26	2011-12	177
Ex 3:1-6	2010-11	9
Ex 3:7-17	2013-14	81
Ex 3:13-15	2010-11	9
Ex 12:1-14	2013-14	89
Ex 12:1-14	2015-16	193
Ex 13:13b-15	2015-16	137
Ex 14:13, 14	2013-14	97
Ex 14:21-30	2013-14	97
Ex 15:1-5	2011-12	185

REFERENCE	YEAR	PAGE
Ex 15:19-26	2011-12	185
Ex 20:1-11	2010-11	17
Ex 20:8-11	2015-16	121
Ex 23:1-9	2011-12	345
Ex 31:12-16	2015-16	121
Ex 32:1-10	2010-11	25
Ex 34:1-10	2010-11	33
Ex 40:16-30	2013-14	105
Ex 40:34	2013-14	105
Ex 40:38	2013-14	105
Lev 16:11-19	2015-16	209
Lev 19:9-18	2011-12	353
Lev 19:18	2013-14	329
Lev 19:33-37	2011-12	353
Lev 22:17-25	2015-16	129
Lev 22:31-33	2015-16	129
Lev 23:15-22	2015-16	201
Lev 23:33-43	2015-16	217
Lev 25:8-12	2011-12	361
Lev 25:25	2011-12	361
Lev 25:35-40	2011-12	361
Lev 25:47, 48	2011-12	361
Lev 25:55	2011-12	361
Dt 6:4-9	2013-14	329
Dt 6:13-16	2013-14	305
Dt 10:12-22	2011-12	369
Dt 16:18-20	2011-12	369
Jos 1:1-6	2010-11	345
Jos 1:7-18	2010-11	353
Jos 2:2-9	2010-11	361
Jos 2:15, 16	2010-11	361
Jos 2:22-24	2010-11	361
Jos 6:2-4	2010-11	369
Jos 6:12-20	2010-11	369
Jos 7:1	2010-11	377

REFERENCE	YEAR	PAGE
Jos 7:10-12	2010-11	377
Jos 7:22-26	2010-11	377
Jos 11:16-23	2010-11	345
Jdg 2:11-19	2010-11	385
Jdg 3:15-25	2010-11	393
Jdg 3:29, 30	2010-11	393
Jdg 7:2-4	2010-11	401
Jdg 7:13-15	2010-11	401
Jdg 8:22-26a	2010-11	401
Jdg 10:10-18	2010-11	409
Jdg 11:4-6	2010-11	409
Jdg 11:32, 33	2010-11	409
Jdg 13:1-8	2010-11	417
Jdg 13:24, 25	2010-11	417
Ru 1:8-18	2010-11	425
Ru 2:8-18	2010-11	433
Ru 4:1-10	2010-11	441
1Sa 7:3-17	2011-12	377
2Sa 7:4-16	2013-14	233
2Sa 23:1-7	2011-12	385
1Ki 3:16-28	2011-12	393
2Ki 8:1-6	2011-12	401
1Ch 18:14	2011-12	385
2Ch 9:8	2011-12	393
2Ch 19:4-11	2011-12	409
Ezr 3:1-7	2012-13	377
Ezr 3:8-13	2012-13	385
Ezr 6:13-22	2012-13	393
Ezr 7:6-10	2012-13	401

REFERENCE	YEAR	PAGE	REFERENCE	YEAR	PAGE	REFERENCE	YEAR	PAGE
Ezr 8:21-23	2012-13	401	Pr 3:1-12	2011-12	9	Isa 53:3-8	2013-14	297
Ezr 8:24-35	2012-13	409	Pr 4:10-15	2011-12	17	Isa 56:6, 7	2013-14	273
			Pr 4:20-27	2011-12	17	Isa 59:15-21	2014-15	409
Ne 8:2, 3	2012-13	417	Pr 8:22-35	2011-12	233	Isa 61:1-3	2013-14	313
Ne 8:13-18	2012-13	417	Pr 15:21-33	2011-12	25	Isa 65:17-25	2012-13	369
Ne 9:2	2012-13	425	Pr 25:1-10	2011-12	33			
Ne 9:6, 7	2012-13	425	Pr 29:16-27	2011-12	41	Jer 7:1-15	2014-15	417
Ne 9:9, 10	2012-13	425				Jer 7:9-11	2013-14	273
Ne 9:30-36	2012-13	425	Ecc 9:13-18	2011-12	49	Jer 23:1-6	2011-12	433
Ne 12:27-38	2012-13	433	Ecc 10:1-4	2011-12	49	Jer 23:5, 6	2013-14	281
Ne 12:43	2012-13	433	Ecc 11:9, 10	2011-12	57	Jer 30:1-3	2014-15	9
Ne 13:10-12	2012-13	441	Ecc 12:1-7	2011-12	57	Jer 30:18-22	2014-15	9
Ne 13:15-22	2012-13	441	Ecc 12:13	2011-12	57	Jer 31:31-37	2014-15	17
						Jer 32:1-9	2014-15	25
Job 19:1-7	2014-15	49	SS 4:8-16	2011-12	65	Jer 32:14, 15	2014-15	25
Job 19:23-29	2014-15	49	SS 5:1a	2011-12	65	Jer 33:1-11	2014-15	33
Job 24:1	2014-15	57	SS 6:4-12	2015-16	161	Jer 33:14-18	2011-12	433
Job 24:9-12	2014-15	57						
Job 24:19-25	2014-15	57	Isa 6:1-8	2012-13	345	Eze 18:1-13	2014-15	425
Job 42:1-10	2014-15	65	Isa 9:1-7	2011-12	425	Eze 18:30-32	2014-15	425
			Isa 9:6, 7	2010-11	137	Eze 34:23-31	2011-12	441
Ps 8	2010-11	41	Isa 9:6, 7	2013-14	241	Eze 43:1-12	2014-15	73
Ps 19:7-14	2010-11	49	Isa 11:1-8	2010-11	137	Eze 43:13-21	2014-15	81
Ps 46:1-7	2010-11	57	Isa 12	2012-13	353	Eze 47:1-12	2014-15	89
Ps 46	2012-13	17	Isa 29:9-16	2012-13	361	Eze 47:13-23	2014-15	97
Ps 47	2010-11	65	Isa 40:1-8	2010-11	121			
Ps 63	2010-11	73	Isa 40:25, 26	2010-11	121	Da 1:5	2014-15	185
Ps 66:1-12	2010-11	81	Isa 40:29-31	2010-11	121	Da 1:8-17	2014-15	185
Ps 89:35-37	2013-14	241	Isa 41:8-10	2010-11	129	Da 7:1-3	2012-13	233
Ps 90:1-12	2010-11	89	Isa 41:17-20	2010-11	129	Da 7:9-14	2012-13	233
Ps 91:1-6	2010-11	97	Isa 42:1-4	2010-11	129	Da 8:1	2012-13	249
Ps 91:9-16	2010-11	97	Isa 42:9	2010-11	129	Da 8:15-26	2012-13	249
Ps 95:1-7a	2014-15	129	Isa 43:1-7	2010-11	145	Da 9:4-14	2012-13	241
Ps 104:5-9	2013-14	9	Isa 43:10-12	2010-11	145	Da 9:17	2012-13	241
Ps 104:24-30	2013-14	9	Isa 44:21-28	2010-11	153			
Ps 110:1-4	2013-14	249	Isa 45:14-25	2010-11	161	Hos 1:1-11	2015-16	169
Ps 139:1-6	2010-11	105	Isa 48:12-22	2010-11	169	Hos 6:1-3	2013-14	289
Ps 139:13-16	2010-11	105	Isa 49:1-7	2010-11	177			
Ps 139:23, 24	2010-11	105	Isa 52:1, 2	2014-15	105	Am 2:4-8	2014-15	345
Ps 146	2011-12	417	Isa 52:7-12	2014-15	105	Am 5:14, 15	2014-15	353
			Isa 53:1-12	2010-11	185	Am 5:18-27	2014-15	353

REFERENCE	YEAR	PAGE	REFERENCE	YEAR	PAGE	REFERENCE	YEAR	PAGE
Am 6:4-8	2014-15	361	Mt 6:16-18	2014-15	185	Lk 6:12, 13	2013-14	169
Am 6:11-14	2014-15	361	Mt 6:25-34	2011-12	105	Lk 6:17-31	2013-14	169
Am 8:1-6	2014-15	369	Mt 14:22-36	2014-15	145	Lk 7:1-10	2015-16	265
Am 8:9, 10	2014-15	369	Mt 15:1-11	2013-14	321	Lk 7:36-50	2015-16	273
			Mt 15:15-20	2013-14	321	Lk 8:26-36	2015-16	281
Mic 2:4-11	2014-15	377	Mt 21:1-11	2013-14	265	Lk 10:25-37	2014-15	193
Mic 3:5-12	2014-15	385	Mt 23:2-12	2015-16	145	Lk 11:1-13	2014-15	153
Mic 6:3-8	2014-15	393	Mt 25:31-46	2014-15	201	Lk 14:7-18a	2013-14	177
Mic 7:14-20	2014-15	401	Mt 28	2010-11	289	Lk 14:21-24	2013-14	177
						Lk 15:11-24	2015-16	289
Hab 2:1-5	2014-15	41	Mk 8:27-38	2010-11	193	Lk 16:19-31	2013-14	185
Hab 3:17-19	2014-15	41	Mk 9:1	2010-11	193	Lk 17:1-10	2015-16	297
			Mk 9:2-13	2010-11	201	Lk 17:11-19	2015-16	305
Zep 1:4-6	2015-16	345	Mk 9:14-29	2015-16	233	Lk 18:9-14	2015-16	313
Zep 1:14-16	2015-16	345	Mk 10:16	2015-16	321	Lk 18:15-17	2015-16	321
Zep 2:3	2015-16	345	Mk 10:17-31	2015-16	241	Lk 19:1-10	2015-16	329
Zep 3:1-8	2015-16	353	Mk 10:35-45	2010-11	209	Lk 22:14-30	2012-13	257
Zep 3:9-14	2015-16	361	Mk 11:1-11	2010-11	281	Lk 24:1-12	2013-14	289
Zep 3:20	2015-16	361	Mk 11:1-11	2014-15	257	Lk 24:13-21	2012-13	265
			Mk 11:15-19	2013-14	273	Lk 24:25-27	2013-14	297
Hag 1:1-11	2013-14	341	Mk 12:28-34	2013-14	329	Lk 24:28-35	2012-13	265
Hag 1:12-15	2013-14	349	Mk 12:38-44	2015-16	145	Lk 24:36-53	2012-13	273
Hag 2:1-9	2013-14	349	Mk 13:14-27	2010-11	217	Lk 24:44-47	2013-14	297
Hag 2:10-19	2013-14	357	Mk 13:31	2010-11	217			
Hag 2:23	2013-14	365	Mk 14:26-31	2015-16	249	Jn 1:1-5	2012-13	145
			Mk 14:66-72	2015-16	249	Jn 1:1-14	2011-12	241
Zec 4:1-3	2013-14	365	Mk 16:1-8	2015-16	257	Jn 1:14	2012-13	145
Zec 4:6-14	2013-14	365				Jn 1:29-34	2014-15	217
Zec 6:9-15	2013-14	281				Jn 2:1-12	2011-12	249
Zec 7:8-14	2014-15	433	Lk 1:26-40	2013-14	121	Jn 2:1-12	2015-16	177
Zec 9:9, 10	2013-14	265	Lk 1:46-55	2011-12	145	Jn 2:13-22	2011-12	281
			Lk 1:46-56	2013-14	129	Jn 3:11-21	2011-12	257
Mal 3:1-10	2014-15	441	Lk 1:57, 58	2013-14	137	Jn 4:7-15	2011-12	289
			Lk 1:67-79	2013-14	137	Jn 4:21-30	2011-12	289
			Lk 2:1-7	2011-12	145	Jn 6:22-35	2011-12	305
Mt 1:18-23	2013-14	241	Lk 2:1-17	2013-14	145	Jn 9:1-17	2011-12	297
Mt 1:21-23	2010-11	137	Lk 2:8-20	2014-15	137	Jn 10:7-18	2011-12	313
Mt 4:1-11	2013-14	305	Lk 2:21, 22	2013-14	153	Jn 11:17-27	2011-12	321
Mt 5:1-12	2011-12	73	Lk 2:22-32	2015-16	137	Jn 11:38-44	2015-16	185
Mt 5:17-26	2011-12	81	Lk 2:25-38	2013-14	153	Jn 11:41-44	2011-12	321
Mt 5:38-48	2011-12	89	Lk 4:14-21	2013-14	313	Jn 14:1-14	2011-12	329
Mt 6:5-15	2011-12	97	Lk 6:1-11	2013-14	161			

REFERENCE	YEAR	PAGE	REFERENCE	YEAR	PAGE	REFERENCE	YEAR	PAGE
Jn 14:15-26	2014-15	233	Ac 16:8-15	2015-16	89			
Jn 16:4b-15	2014-15	241	Ac 17:1-4	2015-16	97	2Co 1:3-11	2013-14	413
Jn 17:6-21	2014-15	161	Ac 17:10-12	2015-16	97	2Co 1:23, 24	2013-14	421
Jn 18:28-38	2011-12	265	Ac 17:22-25	2015-16	97	2Co 2:1-11	2013-14	421
Jn 19:1-5	2013-14	281	Ac 17:28	2015-16	97	2Co 4:1-15	2013-14	428
Jn 20:1-10	2011-12	273	Ac 18:1-11	2015-16	105	2Co 6:1-13	2013-14	435
Jn 20:19, 20	2011-12	273	Ac 18:18-21a	2015-16	105	2Co 7:1-4	2013-14	435
Jn 20:19-23	2014-15	249	Ac 26:19-32	2012-13	81	2Co 8:1-14	2013-14	442
			Ac 27:1, 2	2012-13	89			
Ac 2:1-7	2014-15	321	Ac 27:33-44	2012-13	89	Gal 2:15-21	2011-12	193
Ac 2:1-16	2012-13	281	Ac 28:1-10	2012-13	97	Gal 3:1-14	2011-12	201
Ac 2:12	2014-15	321	Ac 28:16, 17	2012-13	105	Gal 3:15-18	2011-12	209
Ac 2:22-27	2013-14	249	Ac 28:23-31	2012-13	105	Gal 4:1-7	2011-12	209
Ac 2:29-32	2013-14	249				Gal 5:22-26	2011-12	217
Ac 4:23-31	2015-16	9	Ro 1:18-32	2015-16	369	Gal 6:1-10	2011-12	217
Ac 4:34-37	2015-16	17	Ro 2:17-29	2015-16	377			
Ac 5:1-10	2015-16	17	Ro 3:9-20	2015-16	385	Eph 1:3-14	2012-13	121
Ac 5:27-29	2015-16	25	Ro 3:21-31	2015-16	393	Eph 2:11-22	2012-13	129
Ac 5:33-42	2015-16	25	Ro 5:1-11	2015-16	401	Eph 4:1-16	2012-13	137
Ac 6:8-15	2012-13	49	Ro 6:1-4	2015-16	409	Eph 5:1, 2	2012-13	145
Ac 7:1, 2a	2012-13	49	Ro 6:12-14	2015-16	409	Eph 5:6-14	2012-13	145
Ac 7:2-4	2015-16	33	Ro 6:17-23	2015-16	409	Eph 5:18-33	2012-13	153
Ac 7:8-10	2015-16	33	Ro 8:28-39	2015-16	417	Eph 6:1-4	2012-13	153
Ac 7:17	2015-16	33	Ro 9:6-18	2015-16	425	Eph 6:10-20	2014-15	209
Ac 7:22	2012-13	49	Ro 11:11-24	2015-16	433			
Ac 7:33, 34	2015-16	33	Ro 12:1, 2	2015-16	441	Php 1:12-26	2012-13	161
Ac 7:44a	2012-13	49	Ro 13:8-10	2015-16	441	Php 2:1-11	2010-11	297
Ac 7:45-47	2015-16	33				Php 2:1-13	2012-13	169
Ac 7:45b-49	2012-13	49	1Co 1:10-17	2013-14	373	Php 3:1-11	2012-13	177
Ac 7:51-60	2012-13	57	1Co 3:4-9	2013-14	373	Php 3:12-21	2012-13	185
Ac 7:52, 53	2015-16	33	1Co 6:12-20	2013-14	381	Php 4:1	2012-13	185
Ac 8:1	2012-13	57	1Co 8	2013-14	389			
Ac 8:9-24	2015-16	41	1Co 10:6-22	2013-14	397	Col 1:12-23	2012-13	193
Ac 8:9-25	2012-13	65	1Co 12:1-11	2014-15	305	Col 2:6-15	2012-13	201
Ac 8:26-39	2012-13	73	1Co 12:12-31	2014-15	313	Col 3:5-17	2012-13	209
Ac 9:19b-31	2015-16	49	1Co 13	2012-13	41	Col 4:2-17	2012-13	217
Ac 10:24-38	2015-16	57	1Co 13	2014-15	329			
Ac 11:1-18a	2015-16	65	1Co 14:13-26	2013-14	405	1Th 4:13-18	2012-13	289
Ac 12:1-11	2015-16	73	1Co 14:13-19	2014-15	321	1Th 5:1-11	2012-13	289
Ac 15:1-12	2015-16	81	1Co 15:1-11	2014-15	265			
Ac 16:1-5	2015-16	89	1Co 15:20-22	2014-15	265	2Th 2:1-4	2012-13	297

REFERENCE	YEAR	PAGE	REFERENCE	YEAR	PAGE	REFERENCE	YEAR	PAGE
2Th 2:8-17	2012-13	297	Heb 13:1-3, 6	2012-13	41	1Jn 4:13-21	2014-15	281
						1Jn 5:1-5	2014-15	281
1Ti 2	2010-11	233	Jas 1:19-27	2013-14	193			
1Ti 3	2010-11	241	Jas 2:1-13	2013-14	201	2Jn	2014-15	289
1Ti 4:6-16	2010-11	249	Jas 2:14-26	2013-14	209			
1Ti 5:1-8	2010-11	257	Jas 3:1-12	2013-14	217	3Jn	2014-15	297
1Ti 5:17-22	2010-11	257	Jas 5:13-18	2014-15	177			
						Jude 17-25	2010-11	273
2Ti 2:8-19	2010-11	265	1Pe 1:3-16	2012-13	305			
			1Pe 4:1-11	2012-13	321	Rev 4	2010-11	305
Heb 1:1-9	2014-15	121				Rev 5:5-13	2013-14	257
Heb 4:14-16	2014-15	169	2Pe 1:2-15	2012-13	313	Rev 7:9-17	2010-11	313
Heb 5:1-10	2014-15	169	2Pe 1:20, 21	2012-13	313	Rev 21:1-8	2010-11	321
Heb 10:19-31	2012-13	9	2Pe 3:3-15a	2012-13	329	Rev 21:22-27	2010-11	321
Heb 11:1-6	2012-13	17	2Pe 3:18	2012-13	329	Rev 22:1-9	2010-11	329
Heb 12:1-11	2012-13	25				Rev 22:13-17	2010-11	329
Heb 12:18-29	2012-13	33	1Jn 3:11-24	2014-15	273			

Notes:

THE CHRISTIAN COMMUNITY COMES ALIVE

Special Features

		Page
Quarterly Quiz		2
Quarter at a Glance	Mark S. Krause	3
Get the Setting	Tom Thatcher	4
This Quarter in the Word (Daily Bible Readings)		5
Lesson Cycle Chart		7
Bad Teaching I Have Seen (Teacher Tips)	Richard Koffarnus	8
Student Activity Reproducible Pages (annual Deluxe Edition only)		449
Student Activity Reproducible Pages (free download)	www.standardlesson.com	
In the World (weekly online feature)	www.standardlesson.com/category/in-the-world	

Lessons
Unit 1: Seeds of New Growth

September 6	Praying for Boldness	Acts 4:23-31	9
September 13	Sharing with Sincerity	Acts 4:34–5:10	17
September 20	Speaking Up for God	Acts 5:27-29, 33-42	25
September 27	Standing Firm Against Opposition	Acts 7:2-4, 8-10, 17, 33, 34, 45-47, 52, 53	33

Unit 2: Giving Bold Testimony

October 4	Simon Is Rebuked	Acts 8:9-24	41
October 11	Saul Begins to Preach	Acts 9:19b-31	49
October 18	Peter Preaches to Gentiles	Acts 10:24-38	57
October 25	Peter Defends His Actions	Acts 11:1-18a	65

Unit 3: Spreading the Gospel

November 1	God Rescues Peter	Acts 12:1-11	73
November 8	Saved by Grace	Acts 15:1-12	81
November 15	From Derbe to Philippi	Acts 16:1-5, 8-15	89
November 22	Thessalonica, Berea, and Athens	Acts 17:1-4, 10-12, 22-25, 28	97
November 29	Teaching God's Word	Acts 18:1-11, 18-21a	105

QUARTERLY QUIZ

Use these questions as a pretest or as a review. The answers are on page iv of This Quarter in the Word.

Lesson 1

1. David is quoted to have asked, "Why do the nations _____?" *Acts 4:25*

2. Being filled with the Holy Spirit led to speaking God's Word with boldness. T/F. *Acts 4:31*

Lesson 2

1. Barnabas was from the tribe of _____ and the island of _____. *Acts 4:36*

2. Why did Ananias die? (stole money, lied to the Holy Spirit, cursed Peter?) *Acts 5:3*

Lesson 3

1. Which Pharisee advised leaving the apostles alone? (Gamaliel, Caiaphas, Saul?) *Acts 5:34, 38*

2. The apostles rejoiced that they escaped suffering by the Sanhedrin. T/F. *Acts 5:41*

Lesson 4

1. Abraham _____ his son Isaac on the eighth day of Isaac's life. *Acts 7:8*

2. King _____ originally built a house for the Lord. *Acts 7:47*

Lesson 5

1. Simon refused to be baptized. T/F. *Acts 8:13*

2. Simon offered the apostles _____ for the power to give the Holy Spirit by laying on hands. *Acts 8:18*

Lesson 6

1. Saul first fellowshipped with Christian disciples in the city of _____. *Acts 9:19*

2. How did Saul escape a plot to kill him? (tunnel, basket, disguise?) *Acts 9:24, 25*

3. When the converted Saul first came to Jerusalem, he was warmly received. T/F. *Acts 9:26*

Lesson 7

1. When Cornelius first met Peter, he fell down at Peter's feet. T/F. *Acts 10:25*

2. How did Cornelius learn about Peter? (man in shining clothes, rumor, Scripture?) *Acts 10:30*

Lesson 8

1. Peter traveled from the city of _____ to Caesarea to meet with Cornelius. *Acts 11:5, 13*

2. How many "brothers" accompanied Peter to Caesarea? (none, three, six?) *Acts 11:12*

Lesson 9

1. Who was the first of the apostles to be executed? (John, Andrew, James?) *Acts 12:2*

2. What was Peter doing when the angel came to rescue him? (praying, singing, sleeping?) *Acts 12:6, 7*

Lesson 10

1. Who insisted that Gentiles had to be circumcised? (Pharisees, Sadducees, Paul?) *Acts 15:5*

2. Peter claimed that Gentiles were purified by what? (prayer, faith, law?) *Acts 15:9*

Lesson 11

1. Timothy's mother was Jewish, but his father was not. T/F. *Acts 16:1*

2. What was the name of the woman Paul met in Philippi? (Eunice, Mary, Lydia?) *Acts 16:14*

Lesson 12

1. The Jews of _____ are described as being "more noble." *Acts 17:10, 11*

2. The place called the Areopagus (Mars' Hill) was located in the city of _____. *Acts 17:22*

Lesson 13

1. Who was the husband of Priscilla? (Apollos, Aquila, Claudius?) *Acts 18:2*

2. Crispus, the synagogue leader in Corinth, opposed Paul. T/F. *Acts 18:8*

3. Why did Paul shave his head? (vow, injury, convenience?) *Acts 18:18*

QUARTER AT A GLANCE

by Mark S. Krause

IN MANY CITIES one can find a bewildering variety of churches. Some are large, some are small. Some meet in elaborate buildings, some meet in homes. Some are governed by boards of members, some are directed by a senior minister who calls most of the shots. Why are churches so different? That is a tough question, so an easier (and perhaps better one) might be, "How are churches alike?" In other words, what are the core things that makes a church a church?

What Makes a Church a Church?

The great reformer John Calvin (1509–1564) taught that the church exists where the gospel is faithfully preached and the Lord's Supper and baptism are correctly observed. Most would agree with this, although there are surely many viewpoints regarding specifics. But how did Calvin come up with this formula? What makes a church a church?

Calvin and other leaders in church history turned to the New Testament to answer this question. They believed the first-century church as described in the New Testament reflected the will of Christ himself. Every book in the New Testament describes the first-century church in some way, but a marvelous resource for understanding this topic is the book of Acts.

Acts tells the stories of real people in real churches in many locations. Acts presents first-century church leaders confronting the challenges posed by opponents both external and internal to the church. In Acts, we see the sweet fellowship enjoyed by the members of the persecuted church. We also see conflicts and resolutions regarding circumcision, the gift of the Holy Spirit, etc.

Acts shows us the gospel confronting paganism, and how the message of hope was both accepted and rejected. Acts helps us understand how the church expanded from its beginning in Jerusalem to make its way to the capital city of the Roman Empire. Acts shows us conversions in a real-life manner, not as a doctrinal abstraction.

Acts: Not Just Patterns

When we study Acts, we need to be careful to avoid *the fallacy of patternism*. Patternism proposes that all the positive things we find in the churches of Acts should be replicated in modern churches. The problem with full-orbed patternism is that it fails to recognize practices that were matters of expediency for addressing issues of a specific place and time. For example, should churches today turn to the church in Jerusalem for resolution of controversies (lesson 10)? No, that church ceased to exist when the city was destroyed in AD 70 (or

> Acts helps us understand how the church expanded . . . to make its way to the capital city of the Roman Empire.

before), and the Christian community of modern Jerusalem is not seen as specially authoritative.

Even so, Acts does give us some great precedents to follow. For example, who can doubt the need to search the Scriptures, as the Bereans did (lesson 12), to see if teachers are telling the truth?

Acts: Not Mere History

Yes, Acts is history. But it is "holy history" in that it tells the story of God and his people. Stephen's defense before the Sanhedrin demonstrated that he knew the importance of holy history as he retold the story of the nation of Israel from a Christian perspective (lesson 4); his presentation acknowledged the history of the people of God as continuing with his church.

That story continues to be written today, and this quarter's lessons provide much to ponder in that regard. As you gain insights from the book of Acts, keep in mind that the history of the twenty-first-century church will be *your* history as well!

GET THE SETTING

by Tom Thatcher

THE CHURCH is a divine institution, established by Jesus himself (Matthew 16:18). Even so, the church from its earliest days has borne, for good or for ill, various imprints of the human culture around it. These imprints are also seen in the church's immediate predecessor: the Judaism of the Greco-Roman world.

Whether living within the historic boundaries of the holy land or elsewhere in the Roman Empire, Jews of the first century AD had been influenced by Greco-Roman culture for centuries. As Jews became Christians, they brought those influences with them into the church. Four social units seem to have been particularly influential in the development of the church's community life.

The Household

The primary social unit in the Roman world was the individual household. Roman households typically included family members of three generations and sometimes of different social classes (servants). Households were overseen by the *paterfamilias*, the senior male who carried the family name and who was legally responsible for the well-being of his spouse, children, parents, and servants. Since early churches met primarily in households, this form of community became an important backdrop for the church, which is often portrayed as a family and as "members of his [God's] household" (Ephesians 2:19; compare Galatians 6:10).

The Synagogue

The first Christians were Jews. As such, they were accustomed to gathering in weekly synagogue meetings. These assemblies included opportunities for socializing, but centered on group prayer, study of Scripture, and worship. Since all the apostles were of Jewish background, the synagogue's emphasis on teaching, worship, and benevolent care provided a natural model for the new Christian communities. The importance of the synagogue is seen in the nearly 70 occurrences of that word in the New Testament.

The Societies

Voluntary societies were a feature of Roman social life. Clubs formed around common religious and commercial interests, the former uniting devotees of a patron god and the latter particularly including trade guilds (compare Acts 19:25). Club life was characterized by a spirit of common purpose and mutual support. Gentiles who had participated in such societies doubtless brought these values with them into the church when they converted to Christianity. This fostered a strong sense of mission, loyalty, and mutual support.

The School

The word *school* in this context refers not to public education, which did not exist in Roman society, but rather to small groups of people dedicated to the study and practice of the teachings of an intellectual figure (compare Acts 17:18; 19:9). Philosophical schools were also characterized by a strong sense of lifestyle accountability among members and by a spirit of unity that dissolved normal social barriers—since all were pursuing the same path of wisdom, all were equal. While it is unclear how many philosophers or their disciples actually became part of the first-century church (compare Acts 17:34), this model was well known in the world of Peter and Paul and easily adaptable to the new congregations of Christians.

Result: Focused Community

Drawing from these four, we see in first-century Christianity an emphasis on the family of believers, meetings for worship, a sense of common purpose, and a dedication to the teachings of its founder, Jesus. His life and message was the central event in history, and the earliest churches lived that fact in every way possible.

THIS QUARTER IN THE WORD

Mon, Aug. 31	Prayer of Humility	Matthew 6:9-15
Tue, Sep. 1	Prayer of Gratitude	2 Chronicles 6:1-15
Wed, Sep. 2	Openhearted Life	2 Corinthians 6:1-13
Thu, Sep. 3	Greater Things Through Prayer	John 14:11-13
Fri, Sep. 4	No One Else	Acts 4:1-12
Sat, Sep. 5	No Other Authority	Acts 4:13-22
Sun, Sep. 6	Praying with Boldness	Acts 4:23-31
Mon, Sep. 7	Rescuing the Weak	Psalm 82
Tue, Sep. 8	Living Blamelessly	Psalm 26
Wed, Sep. 9	Sharing Generously	1 Timothy 5:11-19
Thu, Sep. 10	Sharing with All	Isaiah 1:15-18
Fri, Sep. 11	Sharing Troubles	Philippians 4:1-14
Sat, Sep. 12	Sharing Out of Abundance	Luke 3:10-16
Sun, Sep. 13	Sharing All Things	Acts 4:34–5:10
Mon, Sep. 14	The Cause of Truth	Psalm 45:1-7
Tue, Sep. 15	The Life of Truth	Proverbs 14:22-29
Wed, Sep. 16	The Power of Truth	Luke 4:14-19
Thu, Sep. 17	Avoid Foolishness; Live Truthfully	2 Timothy 2:14-16, 22-26
Fri, Sep. 18	Trustworthy and True	Revelation 22:1-7
Sat, Sep. 19	Prevailing Truth	Acts 4:5-12
Sun, Sep. 20	Witnessing to the Truth	Acts 5:27-29, 33-42
Mon, Nov. 16	Creator God	Deuteronomy 32:1-12
Tue, Nov. 17	Promises of God for All	Genesis 9:8-17
Wed, Nov. 18	Blessing of God for All	Genesis 12:1-4
Thu, Nov. 19	Majesty of God	Psalm 8
Fri, Nov. 20	Goodness of God	Psalm 33:13-22
Sat, Nov. 21	Reign of God	Psalm 47
Sun, Nov. 22	Different People, Different Approaches	Acts 17:1-4, 10-12, 22-25, 28
Mon, Nov. 23	Learning from God	Psalm 25:8-12, 20, 21
Tue, Nov. 24	Living with God	Psalm 27:4, 5, 8, 9, 11-14
Wed, Nov. 25	Wisdom from God	Proverbs 16:19-24
Thu, Nov. 26	Commissioned to Teach	Matthew 28:16-20
Fri, Nov. 27	Teach Me Your Ways	Exodus 33:12-18
Sat, Nov. 28	Apollos Grows in Ministry	Acts 18:24-28
Sun, Nov. 29	Paul's Ministry Partners	Acts 18:1-11, 18-21a

Answers to the Quarterly Quiz on page 2

Lesson 1—1. rage. 2. true. **Lesson 2**—1. Levi, Cyprus. 2. lied to the Holy Spirit. **Lesson 3**—1. Gamaliel. 2. false. **Lesson 4**—1. circumcised. 2. Solomon. **Lesson 5**—1. false. 2. money. **Lesson 6**—1. Damascus. 2. basket. 3. false. **Lesson 7**—1. true. 2. man in shining clothes. **Lesson 8**—1. Joppa. 2. six. **Lesson 9**—1. James. 2. sleeping. **Lesson 10**—1. Pharisees. 2. faith. **Lesson 11**—1. true. 2. Lydia. **Lesson 12**—1. Berea. 2. Athens. **Lesson 13**—1. Aquila. 2. false. 3. vow.

Mon, Sep. 21	Remembering God's Commands	Deuteronomy 7:1-11
Tue, Sep. 22	Remembering God's Love	Psalm 31:1-5, 19-24
Wed, Sep. 23	Remembering God's Word	Psalm 119:89-94
Thu, Sep. 24	Remembering God's Grace	1 Corinthians 1:1-9
Fri, Sep. 25	Remembering God's Will	1 Thessalonians 5:16-25
Sat, Sep. 26	Responding to God's Faithfulness	Acts 6:7-15
Sun, Sep. 27	Remembering God's Faithfulness	Acts 7:2-4, 8-10, 17, 33, 34, 45-47, 53
Mon, Sep. 28	Never Moved	
Tue, Sep. 29	Be Content	Psalm 15
Wed, Sep. 30	Stand Firm	Hebrews 13:5-10
Thu, Oct. 1	Stand Boldly	Ephesians 6:14-18
Fri, Oct. 2	Stand Regardless	Acts 13:52–14:3
Sat, Oct. 3	Stand Ready	Acts 8:1-8
Sun, Oct. 4	The Spirit Is Not for Sale	Acts 8:26-40
Mon, Oct. 5	God's Perfect Way	Acts 8:9-24
Tue, Oct. 6	God's Trustworthy Way	Psalm 18:20-30
Wed, Oct. 7	God's Holy Way	Psalm 112:1, 2, 6-9
Thu, Oct. 8	God's Awesome Way	1 Peter 1:16-19
Fri, Oct. 9	God's Surprising Way	Luke 11:30-37
Sat, Oct. 10	God's Unconventional Way	Acts 9:1-9
Sun, Oct. 11	Saul Earns Credibility	Acts 9:10-19a
Mon, Oct. 12	God's Love Prevails	Acts 9:19b-31
Tue, Oct. 13	Peter Takes a Risk	Romans 8:31-39
Wed, Oct. 14	Lord of the Sabbath	Matthew 14:22-33
Thu, Oct. 15	Peter Is Stretched	Matthew 12:1-8
Fri, Oct. 16	Peter Follows Through	Acts 10:1-16
Sat, Oct. 17	God for All	Acts 10:17-23
Sun, Oct. 18	Peter Takes Another Risk	Acts 10:39-48
Mon, Oct. 19	A Light to the Nations	Isaiah 49:5-7
Tue, Oct. 20	Water for Everyone	John 4:3-14
Wed, Oct. 21	A Gentle Defense	1 Peter 3:13-18
Thu, Oct. 22	Strangers Become Heaven's Citizens	Ephesians 2:11-22
Fri, Oct. 23	Good Examples to Follow	Philippians 3:17-21
Sat, Oct. 24	Called Christians	Acts 11:19-26
Sun, Oct. 25	Trusting the Spirit	Acts 11:1-18
Mon, Oct. 26	The Rock That Saves	Psalm 18:1-9
Tue, Oct. 27	The Shepherd Who Restores	Psalm 80:1-3, 7, 17-19
Wed, Oct. 28	God Saves Daniel	Daniel 6:19-24
Thu, Oct. 29	The Faithful God	Daniel 6:25-28
Fri, Oct. 30	God Saves Paul	Acts 27:14-25
Sat, Oct. 31	The Freeing God	Acts 12:12-18
Sun, Nov. 1	God Delivers Peter	Acts 12:1-11
Mon, Nov. 2	Thanking God	Romans 1:8-15
Tue, Nov. 3	The Forgiving God	Nehemiah 9:6-21
Wed, Nov. 4	Abundant Grace	Romans 16:25-27
Thu, Nov. 5	The Accessible God	Hebrews 4:12-16
Fri, Nov. 6	God Is Making All Things New	Revelation 21:1-5
Sat, Nov. 7	Grace for Gentiles	Galatians 3:6-14
Sun, Nov. 8	God Makes No Distinction	Acts 15:1-12
Mon, Nov. 9	The Way We Should Go	Jeremiah 26:1-6
Tue, Nov. 10	Boundless Riches of Christ	Ephesians 3:7-12
Wed, Nov. 11	Generosity of God	Ezekiel 36:22-30
Thu, Nov. 12	Cost of Following	Matthew 8:18-22
Fri, Nov. 13	Paul and Silas in Prison	Acts 16:16-24
Sat, Nov. 14	Paul and Silas Escape	Acts 16:25-40
Sun, Nov. 15	Mission to Macedonia	Acts 16:1-5, 8-15

LESSON CYCLE CHART

International Sunday School Lesson Cycle, September 2010–August 2016

Year	Fall Quarter (Sep, Oct, Nov)	Winter Quarter (Dec, Jan, Feb)	Spring Quarter (Mar, Apr, May)	Summer Quarter (Jun, Jul, Aug)
2010–2011	The Inescapable God (Exodus, Psalms)	Assuring Hope (Isaiah, Matthew, Mark)	We Worship God (Matthew, Mark, Philippians, 1 & 2 Timothy, Jude, Revelation)	God Instructs His People (Joshua, Judges, Ruth)
2011–2012	Tradition and Wisdom (Proverbs, Ecclesiastes, Song of Songs, Matthew)	God Establishes a Faithful People (Genesis, Exodus, Luke, Galatians)	God's Creative Word (John)	God Calls for Justice (Pentateuch, History, Psalms, Prophets)
2012–2013	A Living Faith (Psalms, Acts, 1 Corinthians, Hebrews)	Jesus Is Lord (John, Ephesians, Philippians, Colossians)	Undying Hope (Daniel, Luke, Acts, 1 & 2 Thessalonians, 1 & 2 Peter)	God's People Worship (Isaiah, Ezra, Nehemiah)
2013–2014	First Things (Genesis, Exodus, Psalm 104)	Jesus and the Just Reign of God (Luke, James)	Jesus' Fulfillment of Scripture (Pentateuch, 2 Samuel, Psalms, Prophets, Gospels, Acts, Revelation)	The People of God Set Priorities (Haggai, Zechariah, 1 & 2 Corinthians)
2014–2015	Sustaining Hope (Job, Isaiah, Jeremiah, Ezekiel, Habakkuk)	Acts of Worship (Psalms, Daniel, Matthew, Luke, John, Ephesians, Hebrews, James)	The Spirit Comes (Mark, John, Acts, 1 Corinthians, 1–3 John)	God's Prophets Demand Justice (Isaiah, Jeremiah, Ezekiel, Amos, Micah, Zechariah, Malachi)
2015–2016	The Christian Community Comes Alive (Acts)	Sacred Gifts and Holy Gatherings (Pentateuch, Song of Songs, Hosea, Micah, Gospels)	The Gift of Faith (Mark, Luke)	Toward a New Creation (Zephaniah, Romans)

"God"	"Hope"	"Worship"	"Community"	"Tradition"	"Faith"	"Creation"	"Justice"

BAD TEACHING I HAVE SEEN

Teacher Tips by Richard Koffarnus

THE February 11, 1957, edition of *Life* magazine shocked America when it labeled Sunday school "the most wasted hour in the week," because it was supposed to teach people the Bible but failed to do so. Well, *Life* is now defunct, while Sunday school survives, but the magazine was correct about one thing: Americans, then as now, are largely biblically illiterate.

Of course, much of that illiteracy stems from lack of involvement in the church. Nevertheless, some of the blame lies at the feet of Bible teachers whose poor teaching methods have wasted the precious, God-given opportunity to pass on important Bible knowledge to willing students.

I have been a Sunday school teacher for nearly 30 years, so I have witnessed (and been guilty of) lots of bad teaching. Here are two prime examples of teaching mistakes that waste learning time.

Failing to Focus on the Students

One of the most common mistakes made by Bible teachers is to think they are teaching a lesson rather than teaching students. That error can lead to a focus on finishing the material rather than drawing the students into the lesson to experience new ideas and skills.

For instance, some teachers read the lesson verbatim to the class, rarely interacting with the students. However, the lesson commentary is designed for the teacher's *preparation*, to help you understand the Bible text and see its significance and application, not for reading to the class!

The way to involve your students is to use discussion questions and learning activities, such as those provided with these lessons, to help them discover God's Word and truth for themselves. My older adult students aren't always comfortable with some learning activities, such as role plays or small group studies, but they react well to short Bible quizzes and discussion questions. Experiment with different learning activities, and challenge your students to learn more by doing more. It will be time well spent.

Failing to Answer Questions

Rarely a week goes by in my Bible class when I don't get a thoughtful, challenging question from a student. For example, a wheelchair-bound woman once asked me, "Why doesn't God heal me after I prayed so hard and so long?" There was total silence in my class of 50-some students as I tried to answer her question both scripturally and compassionately. While such questions can be very difficult to deal with, they provide an excellent opportunity to apply the Bible to your students' real life concerns.

Unfortunately, some teachers shy away from those opportunities. Author D. R. Silva notes, "Christians are famous for telling people to be 'childlike,' and yet one of the greatest qualities of a child (the never-ending list of questions) is often discouraged." Why discourage questions from students? Sometimes teachers think questions distract from the lesson. Rather, they usually indicate where the lesson is taking the class. Be prepared to go there with them.

You run two risks by doing this. One risk is that you will get a question that is totally off the subject; the other risk is that you will get a question you cannot answer. In the first case, I compliment the student on an interesting question and suggest that I can better discuss an answer one-on-one with him or her after class. In the second case, I admit that I don't know, but promise to have an answer by next Sunday's class. Both can lead to great teaching opportunities.

Waste No More!

Whether or not Sunday school is a wasted hour depends greatly on faithful teachers using good tools and methods. Are your students growing in the faith as Ephesians 4:13-16 requires?

PRAYING FOR BOLDNESS

DEVOTIONAL READING: Matthew 6:9-15
BACKGROUND SCRIPTURE: Acts 4:1-31

ACTS 4:23-31

²³ On their release, Peter and John went back to their own people and reported all that the chief priests and the elders had said to them. ²⁴ When they heard this, they raised their voices together in prayer to God. "Sovereign Lord," they said, "you made the heavens and the earth and the sea, and everything in them. ²⁵ You spoke by the Holy Spirit through the mouth of your servant, our father David:

"'Why do the nations rage
    and the peoples plot in vain?
²⁶ The kings of the earth rise up
    and the rulers band together
against the Lord
    and against his anointed one.'

²⁷ Indeed Herod and Pontius Pilate met together with the Gentiles and the people of Israel in this city to conspire against your holy servant Jesus, whom you anointed. ²⁸ They did what your power and will had decided beforehand should happen. ²⁹ Now, Lord, consider their threats and enable your servants to speak your word with great boldness. ³⁰ Stretch out your hand to heal and perform signs and wonders through the name of your holy servant Jesus." ³¹ After they prayed, the place where they were meeting was shaken. And they were all filled with the Holy Spirit and spoke the word of God boldly.

KEY VERSE

After they prayed, the place where they were meeting was shaken. And they were all filled with the Holy Spirit and spoke the word of God boldly. —**Acts 4:31**

THE CHRISTIAN COMMUNITY COMES ALIVE

Unit 1: Seeds of New Growth

LESSONS 1–4

LESSON AIMS

After participating in this lesson, each learner will be able to:

1. List key elements of the apostles' prayer.

2. Explain the apostles' reaction to threats by the Jewish leadership.

3. Write a prayer asking God for boldness in witness for the week ahead.

LESSON OUTLINE

Introduction
  A. Useless Axiom
  B. Lesson Background
 I. Release (ACTS 4:23)
 II. Prayer (ACTS 4:24-30)
  A. Praising the Creator (v. 24)
  B. Remembering Christ (vv. 25-28)
    Raging Against God
  C. Requesting Help (vv. 29, 30)
III. Results (ACTS 4:31)
  A. On the Structure (v. 31a)
    Transformational Shakings
  B. On Those Gathered (v. 31b)
Conclusion
  A. Do We Have Not Because We Ask Not?
  B. Prayer
  C. Thought to Remember

Introduction

A. Useless Axiom

A sarcastic axiom of warfare is, "There are old soldiers, and there are bold soldiers, but there are no old, bold soldiers." Even as we recognize that that is simply false in an absolute sense, we acknowledge more than a kernel of truth to be present, since the majority of bestowals of the Medal of Honor—the highest award for valor in America's armed forces—are posthumous.

But does even that kernel of truth help us in our Christian walk? Not at all. The axiom suggests a way for one not to have his or her life ended prematurely, but a long earthly life is not the ultimate goal of the Christian. The ultimate goal, rather, is eternal life for ourselves and for as many others as we can influence for Christ as possible. To influence others in this way requires boldness, the subject of today's lesson.

B. Lesson Background

The nine verses of today's lesson come at the very end of the larger textual section of Acts 3:1–4:31. The chain of events in this larger section occurs within a two-day time frame (note particularly the time references "because it was evening, they put them in jail until the next day" and "the next day" in Acts 4:3, 5). These events were preceded, of course, by the birth of the church on the Day of Pentecost in AD 30, related in Acts 2:1-41.

Following that birth, Acts 2:42-47 describes the pattern of fellowship that developed. The indefinite time references "every day" and "daily" in verses 46, 47 and "one day" that opens chapter 3 mean that we are unable to calculate how much time elapsed between the Day of Pentecost and the chain of events of Acts 3:1–4:31. It may be tempting to suggest a time frame based on the growth of the church from "about three thousand" on the Day of Pentecost (2:41) to "the number of men . . . grew to about five thousand" (4:4), but such efforts are speculative.

The first link in the chain of events that leads up to our lesson text is the healing miracle of Acts 3:1-10, which took place in the temple precincts.

That miracle resulted in an opportunity to teach the crowd that gathered (3:11-26). Peter's gospel message did not sit well with "the priests and the captain of the temple guard and the Sadducees" (4:1). So they arrested Peter and John, holding them in custody to answer to the Jewish religious authorities the next day (4:3, 5, 6). Those authorities constituted "the Sanhedrin" (4:15).

Referring to the miracle described in Acts 3:6-8, the question the council posed to the two apostles was straightforward: "By what power or what name did you do this?" (Acts 4:7). The bold response by the two "unschooled, ordinary men" was startling (4:13). The fact that the man who had been healed was standing right there was an enormous complication for the Sanhedrin (4:14-16, 21, 22)!

The best the members of the council could do was to order Peter and John "not to speak or teach at all in the name of Jesus" (Acts 4:18). Peter and John, however, already had received orders that superseded those of the council, and they fearlessly said so (4:19, 20). The end of the council proceedings brings us to today's text.

I. Release

(ACTS 4:23)

23. On their release, Peter and John went back to their own people and reported all that the chief priests and the elders had said to them.

After being released by the Jewish authorities, it is significant that *Peter and John* report everything *to their own people.* This group consists of the other apostles and believers, and Peter and John hide nothing from them. There is no sugar coating! The first recorded persecution of the new church has just occurred, and with it the first recorded resistance by the apostles. The new believers need to know what lies ahead. Jesus had forewarned his apostles of persecution for his name's sake (John 15:18-21).

One has to wonder if that warning is yet to sink in for the apostles at this point, let alone for the newer converts. Jesus had told the apostles about various things that they failed to grasp until later,

and prediction of persecution may be among those. Now they have actually experienced it.

Tellingly, Peter and John do not run from persecution and hide (contrast Matthew 26:56b, 69-75; John 20:19; etc.). But neither do they just go right back to preaching and healing. Something else must come first: reporting to their fellow believers *all that the chief priests and the elders had said to them.* We do not know how many of the 3,000 new converts of Acts 2:41 are still in the city at this time. Many Jewish visitors who were in the city for Pentecost undoubtedly have departed for home. But the group of believers in Jerusalem probably numbers many more than the 120 of Acts 1:15.

Many people today who consider themselves Christians seem to have no use for the church, but such an outlook would be incomprehensible for the apostles! After being detained overnight and grilled before the authorities, Peter and John need interaction with fellow believers. Those two are not ashamed of what has happened to them, and it is not necessary or appropriate to keep anything hidden from the rest. This is an important facet of genuine fellowship—the open sharing of experiences, whether good or bad. The result is mutual encouragement and strengthening of our faith.

What Do You Think?
What are your church's policies and practices for sharing various kinds of information? What can be done to help people and share their issues?
Talking Points for Your Discussion
- Regarding praises
- Regarding challenges being or to be faced
- Other

II. Prayer
(ACTS 4:24-30)
A. Praising the Creator (v. 24)
24a. When they heard this, they raised their voices together in prayer to God.

After the group receives the report about what has happened to Peter and John, the first reaction is to pray. They do not first have a brainstorming session to figure out their next move. They do not call in experts to advise them as to how they should proceed under such circumstances. No, they turn to God *in prayer*.

Whether one person leads in this prayer or several people voice spontaneous prayer is unknown and unimportant. What is vital is their unity as they pray *together*. This unity has its roots in the fellowship described in Acts 2:42-47.

24b. "Sovereign Lord," they said, "you made the heavens and the earth and the sea, and everything in them.

The prayer does not begin by asking for God's help. Rather, it begins by acknowledging God's place in the universe. The imageries in this part of the prayer are quite familiar to those of Jewish background (see Exodus 20:11; Psalm 146:6; contrast Acts 17:22-26). It is God who has made all that is. He is the Creator, and ultimately the one in control. No matter what has happened to Peter and John—or is yet to happen to any believer—God is still in control. When facing difficult and disheartening times, a return to that fundamental truth is vital. God is still on the throne. He has not relinquished control to the forces opposed to his kingdom, nor will he ever do so.

What Do You Think?

How does recognition of God's sovereignty influence how you pray?

Talking Points for Your Discussion

- Concerning a terminal illness
- Concerning a natural disaster
- Concerning a personal tragedy
- Concerning a national tragedy
- Other

B. Remembering Christ (vv. 25-28)

25a. "You spoke by the Holy Spirit through the mouth of your servant, our father David:

This half verse introduces Psalm 2:1, 2 to be part of the prayer. Even though there is no part of that psalm that names David as its author, the text before us clearly identifies it as such. David wrote by inspiration of the Holy Spirit, as Mark 12:36 and Acts 1:16 establish. The mechanics of the inspiration are not described, but the source is clear: God. He is the ultimate author of all Scrip-

ture. Peter will leave no doubt about this when he pens the words of 2 Peter 1:20, 21 many years later.

25b. "'Why do the nations rage
and the peoples plot in vain?
26. The kings of the earth rise up
and the rulers band together
against the Lord
and against his anointed one.'

In the original setting of Psalm 2, the reference is probably to the enthronement of the king and the opposition faced from enemies. As the apostles and their fellow believers consider this passage, they see clear parallels with the actions of those who set themselves in opposition to Jesus, the Christ. We note that the latter part of Psalm 2:2 speaks of actions "against his anointed." The Greek word *Christ* means "anointed one," a connection seen further in our next verse.

❧ RAGING AGAINST GOD ❧

In September 2013, members of a motorcycle gang surrounded an SUV in New York City, brought it to a halt, and started smashing its windows. Bikers dragged the driver out onto the street as his wife and 2-year-old child watched in horror. Several assailants were arrested for the attack, including an undercover detective who was riding with the gang. This incident of road rage apparently was touched off by a minor collision between the SUV and one of the motorcycles; the rage escalated when a more serious collision occurred as the nervous SUV driver tried to drive off.

The incident seems to be part of a pattern that has become a feature of modern life. Unruly demonstrations over economic issues in America and other countries, violent political riots in the Muslim world, deadly attacks by deranged gunmen in schools, and lack of civility generally tell us something is seriously wrong in our world. Yet this is nothing new; we are just more aware of rage incidents because modern technology allows them to be reported instantly. And if evil people will rage against their fellow humans, why should they not rage against God as well?

We cannot control anyone else's rage, but we can control our response to it. The first-century Christians responded by looking to God and acknowledging his sovereignty in such situations. So can we. —C. R. B.

27. "Indeed Herod and Pontius Pilate met together with the Gentiles and the people of Israel in this city to conspire against your holy servant Jesus, whom you anointed.

The identities of the Lord's enemies in Psalm 2:1, 2 are now specified. *Herod* Antipas, tetrarch of Galilee and Perea, and *Pontius Pilate,* Roman governor or procurator of Palestine, had been key players in the condemnation of Jesus (Luke 23:1-25). It was the Romans (*the Gentiles*), persuaded by *the people of Israel,* who had crucified Jesus. To put an innocent man to death at any time is an atrocity; to have done so to Jesus, the Lord's anointed, borders on the incomprehensible!

But even as this psalm is applied to Jesus, the believers also see its relevance to their own circumstances since the same people are in authority. Can Christ's followers expect to be treated any differently than Christ himself was?

28. "They did what your power and will had decided beforehand should happen.

HOW TO SAY IT

Elymas	*El*-ih-mass.
Ephesians	Ee-*fee*-zhunz.
Gentiles	*Jen*-tiles.
Herod Antipas	*Hair*-ud *An*-tih-pus.
Jerusalem	Juh-*roo*-suh-lem.
Pentecost	*Pent*-ih-kost.
Pontius Pilate	*Pon*-shus (or *Pon*-tee-us) *Pie*-lut.
Sanhedrin	*San*-huh-drun or San-*heed*-run.
Thessalonians	*Thess*-uh-*lo*-nee-unz
	(*th* as in *thin*).

The culprits in verse 27 have acted according to their own free will. But when all is said and done, they act to bring about what God in his foreknowledge and sovereignty had *decided beforehand should happen.* God had not lost control of the situation when Jesus was crucified.

Several books popular in the last century proposed that the crucifixion and resurrection of Jesus were reactions by God to a situation that had spun out of control, the resurrection being God's attempt to make the best of a bad situation. As we can see in this verse and Acts 2:23, nothing could be further from the truth! God is always in complete control, and the death of his Son was planned from the beginning. Jesus is indeed the "Lamb who was slain from the creation of the world" (Revelation 13:8).

C. Requesting Help (vv. 29, 30)

29. "Now, Lord, consider their threats and enable your servants to speak your word with great boldness.

Again, it is important to note that the part of the prayer requesting God's help is not the first part! Acknowledgement of God's power, authority, foreknowledge, etc., comes first.

Also interesting is what the believers do *not* pray for: they do not pray for future deliverance from such persecution. Nor do they pray condemnation on those who have attacked Peter and John so unfairly. Instead, they pray for *great boldness* to go on speaking God's word. In a way, they pray that God will help them get right back into the same kind of situation that Peter and John have just escaped from!

The word translated *boldness* occurs a dozen times in Acts in noun and verb forms, with two of those dozen in today's lesson text: here and in verse 31. (Compare other occurrences in Acts 2:29; 4:13; 9:27, 28; 13:46; 14:3; 18:26; 19:8; 26:26; 28:31.) A majority of the uses in Acts describes Paul's preaching. Elsewhere, Paul specifically requests prayer "that whenever I speak, words may be given me so that I will fearlessly make known the mystery of the gospel, for which I am an ambassador in chains. Pray that I may declare it fearlessly, as I should" (Ephesians 6:19, 20).

Visual for
Lesson 1

Keep this map posted as you study lessons 1–10 to give your learners a geographical perspective.

That later request by Paul is very much in harmony with the group's request that we see in the text before us. More than anything else in this first experience of persecution, they ask God to enable them to continue speaking forthrightly so that the progress of the gospel will not be slowed by any fear on their part.

What Do You Think?

How do we know when we should pray for boldness rather than deliverance and vice versa?

Talking Points for Your Discussion

- Matthew 26:39, 42
- Colossians 4:3
- 2 Thessalonians 3:1, 2
- Other

---

30. "Stretch out your hand to heal and perform signs and wonders through the name of your holy servant Jesus."

In addition to the request for boldness, the group asks God to continue to do what he is already doing regarding *signs and wonders.* These miracles, which include healing, confirm the message of the gospel for receptive audiences. The miracles are going to be done *through the name of your holy servant Jesus,* the very name the Jewish authorities have just forbidden to be preached (Acts 4:18). It is apparent that the Father and the Son are working together, which is entirely consistent with the claims of Jesus in the Gospels (example: John 5:19-23).

When we consider the numerous healings in the Gospels and in the book of Acts, we see a couple of motives for performing these. The first and most obvious is simple compassion (example: Matthew 20:34). But in addition to compassion, Jesus and the apostles also perform miraculous healings as signs of the authority of the message they bring. The miraculous display of compassion opens hearts to accept the truth of the gospel.

III. Results
(ACTS 4:31)
A. On the Structure (v. 31a)

31a. After they prayed, the place where they were meeting was shaken.

God responds to the prayer in dramatic and powerful ways! The word *shaken* has both figurative and literal applications in the New Testament: figurative uses indicate people are agitated or disturbed in some way (compare Acts 17:13 and 2 Thessalonians 2:2), while literal uses imply a swaying back and forth of physical structures, as if by earthquake or tremor (compare Acts 16:26). The literal is intended here, since the text refers to *the place* where the believers are gathered as being shaken.

The physical shaking is only the introduction to God's response to the prayer, however. The most important part of his response comes next.

❧ *TRANSFORMATIONAL SHAKINGS* ❧

The Ring of Fire is the popular name given to a horseshoe-shaped volcanic zone of the earth's crust. It stretches 25,000 miles from near the tip of South America, up the Pacific coast of that continent and North America, across the Aleutian chain of islands, then down through Japan, the Philippines, and New Zealand. The Ring of Fire features over 75 percent of the world's volcanoes. The seismic forces that trigger volcanic eruptions are at work in earthquakes as well. Thus, not surprisingly, 90 percent of all earthquakes (and 80 percent of the most severe ones) strike along the Ring of Fire.

The city of San Francisco lies on the Ring of Fire, and the 1906 earthquake that struck that city is probably the most famous temblor in American history. On the other side of the Ring of Fire, the earthquake that hit Fukushima, Japan, in 2011 captured worldwide attention. Both quakes, as do many others, exhibited transforming power in a destructive and tragic sense.

The trembling that shook the place where the disciples were gathered was not an impersonal destructive force of nature—just the opposite! Accompanied by filling with the Holy Spirit, it was a personal constructive force of God. As we meditate on this account, let us remember that future shakings by the hand of God are certain, but he and his kingdom cannot be shaken by anything (Hebrews 12:25-29). May this realization give us courage and boldness today.   —C. R. B.

B. On Those Gathered (v. 31b)

31b. And they were all filled with the Holy Spirit and spoke the word of God boldly.

There are five occasions in the book of Acts where individuals or groups of people are described as being *filled with the Holy Spirit.* The first such filling (Acts 2:4) is accompanied by the apostles' being empowered to preach the gospel in other tongues (languages). The second (4:8) is accompanied by Peter's bold address to the Sanhedrin. The third is the verse before us, as accompanied by empowerment to speak *the word of God boldly.*

The fourth (Acts 13:9) is in conjunction with Paul's condemnation of Elymas the sorcerer. The fifth (13:52) is accompanied by the disciples' being filled with joy. (In passing, we may note that 9:17 offers a sixth use of this phrase; this one concerns Saul, with no further explanation, as a requested result of his conversion.)

Analyzing these five, we see that the second and third are the only ones that happen on the same day. God is intensely aware of what is unfolding in this first recorded persecution of the church, and he knows just what to do about it. The gathered believers have prayed the right prayer with the right motives (contrast James 4:3).

The result is that those gathered are and will be given the boldness they need to continue to carry out the commission they have received (Matthew 28:19, 20). Holy Spirit–enabled boldness counteracts fear.

> **What Do You Think?**
> Are there times when boldness in witness would do more harm than good? Why, or why not?
> *Talking Points for Your Discussion*
> - Esther 4:14
> - Ecclesiastes 3:7b
> - Amos 5:13
> - Other

Conclusion

A. Do We Have Not Because We Ask Not?

The church had a radical transforming influence as it spread over the Roman Empire and beyond. Boldness was a critical factor in that success—boldness that often seems to be lacking in the twenty-first-century church. Some may attempt to excuse lack of boldness by asserting that the apostles were filled with the Holy Spirit in a special way. The text indicates, however, that all who were present were empowered by the Spirit to speak with boldness. That empowerment for boldness followed from asking for boldness.

Reflect for a moment on all the prayer requests you hear expressed each week at church. When was the last time you heard a prayer request for boldness?

B. Prayer

Dear Lord, help us put boldness at the very top of our prayer requests! May we ask for this daily and with right motives. In the name of Jesus, for whom we are to be bold, amen.

C. Thought to Remember

God still grants boldness.

VISUALS FOR THESE LESSONS

The visual pictured in each lesson (example: page 14) is a small reproduction of a large, full-color poster included in the *Adult Resources* packet for the Fall Quarter. That packet also contains the very useful *Presentation Tools* CD for teacher use. Order No. 020019215 from your supplier.

INVOLVEMENT LEARNING

Enhance your lesson with NIV® Bible Student (from your curriculum supplier) and the reproducible activity page (at www.standardlesson.com or in the back of the NIV® Standard Lesson Commentary Deluxe Edition).

Into the Lesson

Distribute index cards on which you have printed the following situations, one situation per card: (1) a promotion at work; (2) a serious health problem; (3) an amazing answer to prayer; (4) losing your wallet or billfold. Duplicate cards as necessary so each learner has one. Ask for volunteers who have *situation one* to say whom they would first share the news with and why. Repeat for the other three situations. Keep this moving rapidly; don't let it drag out.

Make a transition by saying, "Whether good news or bad, we usually want to share information right away. The same was true with the apostles Peter and John when they were persecuted for preaching about Jesus. They had friends they wanted to tell! Let's find out who and why."

Into the Word

Form learners into three groups; hand each group one of the following assignments. Give these instructions to all groups: "You will be conducting an interview with one of the characters from today's lesson and its background. Select one person to conduct the interview and another to be interviewed as you work through the assigned passage."

Group 1: Interview of Annas, the high priest. Read Acts 4:1-22 and pose these questions to be answered: 1. "What was it about Peter and John that so disturbed you?" 2. "When you questioned those two, how did Peter respond?" 3. "What was it about those two men that astonished you and your colleagues?" 4. "When you commanded them to stop preaching in the name of Jesus, how did they react?"

Group 2: Interview of John. Read Acts 4:18-31 and pose these questions to be answered: 1. "When the Jewish leaders commanded you and Peter to stop preaching in the name of Jesus, why did you refuse?" 2. "What was the first thing the two of you did when they released you, and what was the reac-

tion?" 3. "Why did you ask God for boldness when it seems that you already demonstrated plenty of that trait?" 4. "What happened then?"

Group 3: Interview of a Christian at the prayer meeting. Read Acts 4:23-31 and pose these questions to be answered: 1. "When you heard Peter and John's report, why did you and the others decide to pray rather than, say, have a strategy session on what to do next?" 2. "Why did the treatment of Peter and John make you and the others think of Psalm 2:1, 2?" 3. "Why did you conclude that the actions of Herod and Pilate were part of God's plan?" 4. "How did the dramatic event at the end of the prayer time affect you personally?"

Allow five to eight minutes for groups to prepare their interviews; then ask the groups in turn to conduct them for the whole class.

Into Life

Begin a discussion by stating, "When Peter and John prayed with their fellow Christians, there were other things they could have asked God to do, but they didn't. What might these have included?" (*Possible responses*: they didn't pray for deliverance from future persecution; they didn't pray against the Jewish leaders; they didn't ask for wisdom or strength.)

Then ask, "What two specific things did they ask God to grant?" (*Expected responses*: boldness when speaking and further "signs and wonders" in Jesus' name.) Then observe: "In fact, they were asking for more of the same things that got them in trouble with the Jewish leaders in the first place! How can this serve as an example of how we should pray?"

Alternative. Distribute copies of the "Parts of the Prayer" and "Improving Your Prayers" activities from the reproducible page, which you can download. Have learners complete as indicated. Encourage use of the resulting prayers in devotional times in the week ahead.

Sharing with Sincerity

Devotional Reading: Isaiah 1:15-18
Background Scripture: Acts 4:32–5:11

Acts 4:34-37

[34] There were no needy persons among them. For from time to time those who owned land or houses sold them, brought the money from the sales [35] and put it at the apostles' feet, and it was distributed to anyone who had need.

[36] Joseph, a Levite from Cyprus, whom the apostles called Barnabas (which means "son of encouragement"), [37] sold a field he owned and brought the money and put it at the apostles' feet.

Acts 5:1-10

[1] Now a man named Ananias, together with his wife Sapphira, also sold a piece of property. [2] With his wife's full knowledge he kept back part of the money for himself, but brought the rest and put it at the apostles' feet.

[3] Then Peter said, "Ananias, how is it that Satan has so filled your heart that you have lied to the Holy Spirit and have kept for yourself some of the money you received for the land? [4] Didn't it belong to you before

it was sold? And after it was sold, wasn't the money at your disposal? What made you think of doing such a thing? You have not lied just to human beings but to God."

[5] When Ananias heard this, he fell down and died. And great fear seized all who heard what had happened. [6] Then some young men came forward, wrapped up his body, and carried him out and buried him.

[7] About three hours later his wife came in, not knowing what had happened. [8] Peter asked her, "Tell me, is this the price you and Ananias got for the land?"

"Yes," she said, "that is the price."

[9] Peter said to her, "How could you conspire to test the Spirit of the Lord? Listen! The feet of the men who buried your husband are at the door, and they will carry you out also."

[10] At that moment she fell down at his feet and died. Then the young men came in and, finding her dead, carried her out and buried her beside her husband.

Key Verse

There were no needy persons among them. For from time to time those who owned land or houses sold them, [and] brought the money from the sales. —**Acts 4:34**

THE CHRISTIAN COMMUNITY COMES ALIVE

Unit 1: Seeds of New Growth

LESSONS 1–4

LESSON AIMS

After participating in this lesson, each learner will be able to:

1. Summarize the attitude toward possessions of the disciples after the Day of Pentecost.

2. Contrast the mind-set of Ananias and Sapphira with that of Barnabas and the other disciples.

3. Contribute monetary support sacrificially to a ministry project in the week ahead.

LESSON OUTLINE

Introduction
   A. To Whom Much Is Given . . .
   B. Lesson Background
 I. Sincere Givers (ACTS 4:34-37)
   A. Needs Met (vv. 34, 35)
      Utopian Movements
   B. Notable Example (vv. 36, 37)
 II. Insincere Givers (ACTS 5:1-10)
   A. Deceit Planned (vv. 1, 2)
   B. Deceiver Ananias Confronted (vv. 3, 4)
      Motives for Giving
   C. Deceit's Result, Part 1 (vv. 5, 6)
   D. Deceiver Sapphira Confronted (vv. 7, 8)
   E. Deceit's Result, Part 2 (vv. 9, 10)
Conclusion
   A. Much Is Required
   B. Prayer
   C. Thought to Remember

Introduction

A. To Whom Much Is Given . . .

It was the late 1970s, and my small-town church of about 80 people was facing a big challenge: major repairs were needed to the roof of the educational building. The cost was to be $4,000 (about $15,000 in today's money). That was a hefty burden for that church, located as it was in an area with a somewhat depressed economy. The church board, with some reluctance, decided on a Tuesday night to move forward with the project. The concern was where we would get the money, but we stepped out on faith.

The next night at Bible study, a dear saint came up to me and asked if I could stop by her house the next afternoon. So on Thursday I did. That's when she told me that she had just sold some family land and wanted to give 10 percent to the church. She wondered if there was a special project that needed funding. She had received $40,000 for the sale of the land, and 10 percent of that was the exact amount needed for our project.

Is it mere coincidence that such things happen? No! These are "God incidents," when he blesses his faithful people to be a blessing in turn. The old adage, "You can't outgive God" is proven true time and again. This is a lesson I learned early in my ministry life. As he sees faithfulness in those he blesses, he turns right around and blesses them anew.

B. Lesson Background

The number of disciples had been steadily increasing since the birth of the church on the Day of Pentecost (Acts 2:47; 4:4). Threats from the Jewish authorities (see last week's lesson) did not deter the preaching of the gospel; the apostles knew their higher calling to be obedience to the command of God.

As a result of their faithful witness, God blessed the Jerusalem church with unity (Acts 4:32). Satan had been unsuccessful in using outside opposition to stop the spread of the gospel message (4:1-31), so he changed strategies: he attempted to use something positive that was happening within the church to derail its growth and influence.

I. Sincere Givers
(ACTS 4:34-37)

A. Needs Met (vv. 34, 35)

34. There were no needy persons among them. For from time to time those who owned land or houses sold them, brought the money from the sales

Despite threats by the Jewish authorities (Acts 4:17, 21), the believers continue their practice of sharing possessions with fellow Christians who are in need (compare 2:45). A spirit of liberality and community fills the Jerusalem church.

A good way to understand the word *community* is "common unity." Acts 2:44 notes that the believers have "everything in common." Jesus had declared that when needs are met, it is just as if the help provided is done for Christ himself (Matthew 25:40). Those today whose money runs out before the end of the month know the emotional pressure this can cause. How much worse this kind of stress can be in the first century, an era without government "safety nets," etc.

The believers in Jerusalem realize that if one part of the body hurts, the others hurt with it. Seeing needs, those not lacking in resources are willing to help. Their selling of *land or houses* to help others is misunderstood in various ways today. Some use this passage to promote the view that Christians should own nothing—selling all and distributing the proceeds in a manner that results in all Christians' being equal in an economic sense (with further support claimed from Luke 18:22; 2 Corinthians 8:13-15). This interpretation presumes that a procedure of the first-century church is the same as a New Testament command.

At the other extreme are those who contend that the practice in the passage before us is not applicable for the church today where governments take care of these types of situations. This allows the church (so the claim goes) to use most of its resources for spiritual issues of evangelism, etc.

A middle-ground view is that the procedure we see here is not a mandatory precedent but an example of what believers can do to help fellow Christians who are in need. Such an example risks being ignored in a modern culture where home ownership is seen as almost "a right" and the accumulation of assets seen as a mark of good Christian stewardship. We keep in mind that this passage is written not to defend a culture's economic system but to demonstrate the need for generosity.

What Do You Think?

What extraordinary or unique benevolence campaigns have you seen or participated in? How did things turn out?

Talking Points for Your Discussion
- Christian benevolence campaigns
- Secular benevolence campaigns

❧ *UTOPIAN MOVEMENTS* ❧

Of the many attempts to build utopian communities in America, the "most Christian" may well have been the Shakers. Officially known as the United Society of Believers in Christ's Second Appearing, a group of Shakers came to America from England in 1774, establishing their first settlement in New York state.

Shakers believed in common property, mandatory attendance at Sunday services, pacifism, and celibacy (the latter meaning that community growth was limited to conversions and adoptions). The term *Shaker* originated from the spontaneous dance that worshippers often engaged in during Sunday services.

The Shakers eventually experienced the same problems as other utopian communities: young people moved away, older members died, and converts ceased to join as the novelty and idealism of the movement dissipated. Further, the industrial revolution meant that demand for handcrafted Shaker goods declined, undermining economic sustainability. By the early 1900s, almost all Shaker settlements in America had ceased to exist.

Christian utopian movements frequently take at least some of their inspiration from Acts 4:32-35. The church has long wrestled with a question this text raises: Do these verses mandate the community described, or do they simply present a congenial result of a temporary situation? Even assuming only the latter, the actions of those earliest believers should challenge the temptation to selfishness that is never far from us. —C. R. B.

35. and put it at the apostles' feet, and it was distributed to anyone who had need.

Not only is the church in its earliest days an example of marvelous community and generosity, it also demonstrates organizational qualities. In Acts 2:44, 45 earlier, the sharing of resources seems to have been done directly between those having and those needing. The text before us, however, indicates gifts now being directed through the apostles for them to oversee distribution *to anyone who had need*.

This may be an example of how the first-century church adjusts its methods as it grows and learns better ways of doing things. If that is the case, then Acts 6:1-4 may indicate further improvements in organizational effectiveness and efficiency later as the apostles establish a system to meet needs while they devote themselves "to prayer and the ministry of the word" (v. 4).

> **What Do You Think?**
> How can you help enhance your church's ministry of matching needs with people or organizations that have resources to meet those needs?
> *Talking Points for Your Discussion*
> - Regarding needs to be addressed locally
> - Regarding needs best addressed by partnering with organizations that specialize in doing so
> - Applicability of 2 Thessalonians 3:10
> - Other

B. Notable Example (vv. 36, 37)

36, 37. Joseph, a Levite from Cyprus, whom the apostles called Barnabas (which means "son of encouragement"), sold a field he owned and brought the money and put it at the apostles' feet.

A certain *Joseph* is a notable example of generosity. His actions speak to this, and his attitude is evident in the nickname he is given by the apostles: *Barnabas (which means "son of encouragement").* The Greek word translated *encouragement* is also rendered "comfort" (see 2 Corinthians 1:3-7; 7:7) and "exhortation" (see Hebrews 13:22) in

the New Testament. All three translations point to this man's being very much a "people person" (compare Acts 9:26, 27; 11:19-26).

His concern for others is demonstrated in the actions described here. He knows that what he owns is not something to hold on to at this point. In Israelite history, Levites are the ones who receive tithes (see Numbers 18:21, 24; Nehemiah 10:37) and in turn render tithes themselves (Numbers 18:26). But Barnabas, a Levite himself, seems to realize that that covenantal procedure is now eclipsed since what he brings is not a tithe (10 percent), but the entire proceeds of his sale of land.

If the land Barnabas owns is back in his home area of *Cyprus,* then selling that piece of property may involve a round trip of about 500 miles over land and sea (since Cyprus is an island) to complete the transaction. To make such an arduous trip would indicate considerable dedication to the cause of Christ!

Another mark of Barnabas's character is that he does not seek a different procedure by viewing himself as special in some way. (We note his leadership designations and actions in Acts 9:27; 11:22; 14:14; etc.) He merely lays his gift *at the apostles' feet* as does everyone else.

> **What Do You Think?**
> When should givers be identified publicly rather than remaining anonymous? Why?
> *Talking Points for Your Discussion*
> - Considering Matthew 5:16 in relation to 6:1-4
> - Considering the desires of the giver
> - Other

II. Insincere Givers
(ACTS 5:1-10)
A. Deceit Planned (vv. 1, 2)

1, 2. Now a man named Ananias, together with his wife Sapphira, also sold a piece of property. With his wife's full knowledge he kept back part of the money for himself, but brought the rest and put it at the apostles' feet.

With the introduction of *Ananias* and *Sapphira,* we see two of the same actions we saw regarding Barnabas: *a piece of property* is *sold* and money from the sale subsequently is placed *at the apostles' feet.* But the similarities end there.

The word translated *kept back* is used in the Greek version of the Old Testament (called *the Septuagint*) only in Joshua 7:1. There it is translated "took" in describing Achan's sin. Luke, the author of Acts, apparently wants the reader to see the connection. Both that passage and the one before us teach sobering lessons about deceit.

What Do You Think?
What issues should couples discuss when deciding how best to support God's work financially?
Talking Points for Your Discussion
- Regarding support for their local church
- Regarding support for parachurch organizations
- Regarding gifts that yield no tax deductions
- Other

B. Deceiver Ananias Confronted (vv. 3, 4)

3. Then Peter said, "Ananias, how is it that Satan has so filled your heart that you have lied to the Holy Spirit and have kept for yourself some of the money you received for the land?

Last week's lesson showed us the apostles' reaction to a threat from outside the church; our passage today shows us Peter's reaction to an internal threat. Ananias and Sapphira are pretenders, deceivers. They pretend to have donated all *of the money . . . received for the land* they have sold, while actually holding back part. Their motives for doing so are unstated, but they have allowed *Satan* to influence them so that they seem to have no qualms with their plot—it is premeditated, not spur of the moment.

If these two had allowed the Holy Spirit to be the dominant influence in their lives, they would

HOW TO SAY IT

Achan	*Ay*-kan.
Ananias	An-uh-*nye*-us.
Barnabas	*Bar*-nuh-bus.
Cyprus	*Sigh*-prus.
Levite	*Lee*-vite.
Sapphira	Suh-*fye*-ruh.
Septuagint	Sep-*too*-ih-jent.

not have cooked up this deceit in the first place. Lying to fellow believers is bad enough (Colossians 3:9); attempting to lie *to the Holy Spirit* is to presume that one has the power to deceive him. Such presumption is blasphemy!

4. "Didn't it belong to you before it was sold? And after it was sold, wasn't the money at your disposal? What made you think of doing such a thing? You have not lied just to human beings but to God."

The property Ananias and Sapphira sold was their own. The two could have kept either the property or all the money from its sale. They could have chosen to donate a portion of the proceeds while openly keeping the remainder for themselves. Owning property, making money from the sale of assets, and deciding how much to give to the work of God's kingdom are all personal matters.

Even so, the choices people make in this regard have a way of revealing the nature of their relationship with God. God so closely identifies himself with those created in his image that the way someone treats others is indicative of how that person relates to God. We see this in David's lamenting his sin of adultery. When he confessed that sin, he said it was a sin against God only (Psalm 51:4). In Matthew 25, Jesus identifies the good deeds and the lack of good deeds done for others as actions done or left undone to him. Ananias thinks he is lying *just to human beings* (the apostles), but that is not true. Ultimately, he is lying *to God.*

We would dearly love to hear Ananias's answer to the question *What made you think of doing such a thing?* for that could reveal his motives. But punishment comes so swiftly that the question remains unanswered.

❧ MOTIVES FOR GIVING ❧

A study of a few years ago analyzed how giving patterns differed among Americans of various economic levels. Within the mountain of data and charts that resulted was this interesting nugget: those in the lowest income class directed more than three-quarters of their donations to religious organizations and organizations devoted to helping meet the basic needs of the poor, while those

No one lacked for anything

Visual for Lesson 2. *Point to this visual as you pose the discussion question that is associated with Acts 4:34, page 19.*

in the highest income class directed less than one-quarter of their donations that way. The latter demographic showed a much greater preference for supporting the arts, education, etc.

We naturally wonder why the difference! Could it be that endowments for high-profile arts and educational organizations result in the wealthiest givers having the satisfaction of "seeing their name in lights" in ways that donations to religious organizations do not?

When a need to assist the church's poor of the first century presented itself, many members accepted the challenge. However, the gift from Ananias and Sapphira seems to have been prompted by a desire for recognition, not by compassion for those in need. To what extent is this a problem in the church of today? —C. R. B.

C. Deceit's Result, Part 1 (vv. 5, 6)

5. When Ananias heard this, he fell down and died. And great fear seized all who heard what had happened.

The Scripture does not tell us whether Ananias is in any way remorseful or even if he has time to be so (compare Acts 12:23; contrast Joshua 7:20, 21; Acts 8:18-24). All that is said is that *he fell down and died.*

We may wonder how many are present to witness this act of divine judgment. Since the tainted gift has been laid "at the apostles' feet" (v. 2, above), it seems that at least one other apostle

besides Peter is there. Beyond that, verse 6 (next) indicates "some young men" to be in close proximity. The fact that *great fear* comes on all who hear *what had happened* implies eyewitnesses to the event (or at least to the result) to spread the news (compare Acts 5:11, not in today's text).

This fear can have more than one component: being personally convicted that one has not always been truthful, fear of Peter personally, etc. Most likely it includes a dawning awareness of how serious God is about his church and her purity. The need for such purity is probably the very reason God takes such a drastic action as we see here. He wants people to see their role in maintaining the purity of the church.

God's judgmental action in that regard corresponds with the way he interacted with the Israelites as they entered the promised land. Because of the sin of Achan, God declared that "Israel has sinned; they have violated my covenant, which I commanded them to keep. They have taken some of the devoted things; they have stolen, they have lied, they have put them with their own possessions" (Joshua 7:11). The death penalty resulted there too (7:19-26).

6. Then some young men came forward, wrapped up his body, and carried him out and buried him.

There is no record of a funeral, words of explanation or exhortation by Peter, or eulogy. Attempts to undermine the purity of the church place the perpetrator at the gravest of risks—the wrath of God. Those who so perish leave no good memory.

D. Deceiver Sapphira Confronted (vv. 7, 8)

7. About three hours later his wife came in, not knowing what had happened.

Perhaps the "young men" of verse 6 (above) have tried to contact Sapphira in the intervening *three hours* but have been unable to do so. Perhaps Peter has instructed them to stay put and keep their mouths shut—we don't know; the text does not say. There are no cell phones, Twitter, or Facebook at the time to get information out. Since Sapphira shows up *not knowing what had happened,* she has exactly the same chance to come clean by truthfully answering Peter's question that we see in the next verse.

8. Peter asked her, "Tell me, is this the price you and Ananias got for the land?"

"Yes," she said, "that is the price."

Throughout Bible history, we see that God is as much or even more interested in the attitude of the giver as he is in the gift itself (examples: Psalm 51:17; Hosea 6:6; Matthew 9:13; 2 Corinthians 8:12). But some do not learn this lesson; ulterior motives in giving still exist today. Those who are clever in this regard can fool others, since the Holy Spirit may choose not to reveal the sin. If the impure motive is for recognition or an attempt to get one's way, these ends may be realized. The reality, though, is that such deceivers receive only that recognition as the reward (see Matthew 6:2).

But the Holy Spirit *is* revealing the sin in the case at hand. If Sapphira answers Peter's question honestly, she may have a chance to extricate herself from the web of deception she has helped spin. Sadly, she chooses to maintain the charade. In so doing, she reaps the reward of her deception.

What Do You Think?

How have the examples of others taught you to be a better giver? (Be careful about using real names.)

Talking Points for Your Discussion
- Positive examples, Christian and secular
- Negative examples, Christian and secular

E. Deceit's Result, Part 2 (vv. 9, 10)

9. Peter said to her, "How could you conspire to test the Spirit of the Lord? Listen! The feet of the men who buried your husband are at the door, and they will carry you out also."

Immediately after Sapphira's lie, Peter reveals that he knows all about the conspiracy *to test the Spirit of the Lord*. A temptation to sin is not what is in view (as it is in Matthew 4:1-11). The idea, rather, is a testing of the Holy Spirit. Testing God is forbidden (Matthew 4:7 [quoting Deuteronomy 6:16]; 1 Corinthians 10:9). Yet challenging authority seems to be part of human nature. Children test parents by stepping as close to boundaries as possible. Throughout the Old Testament, we see the nation of Israel testing the patience of God time and again (example: Exodus 17:1-7).

To attempt to test the Lord is actually to test ourselves—a test that one always fails. Sapphira is about to experience divine punishment for her own failure in this regard.

10. At that moment she fell down at his feet and died. Then the young men came in and, finding her dead, carried her out and buried her beside her husband.

As with her husband Ananias, there appears to be no opportunity for Sapphira to respond to the accusation Peter has just made. It's too late for that. The judgment of God is immediate and irrevocable.

This is a foreshadowing of the final judgment. At that time it will be too late to repent. Before that time comes, however, God will accept those with broken and contrite hearts (Psalm 51:17) who turn to his Son for forgiveness (John 3:16; 14:6). But time is running out.

Conclusion

A. Much Is Required

God, the giver of every good gift, desires that those who receive from him be faithful in their stewardship of those gifts. When we hear that word *stewardship,* we naturally may think of how we manage our finances, give back to God, etc. But biblical stewardship involves something much more foundational: the giving of our hearts to him. When we do, we will be faithful in all other aspects of stewardship (1 Corinthians 4:2). To conduct ourselves with godly sincerity is vital (2 Corinthians 1:12). Today's text serves as a cautionary tale in that regard.

B. Prayer

Generous God, help us to be genuine and sincere givers, giving to you our hearts first. As we do, we will respond to the needs around us for your glory, not ours. In Jesus' name, amen.

C. Thought to Remember

Sincere generosity glorifies God.

INVOLVEMENT LEARNING

Enhance your lesson with NIV® Bible Student (from your curriculum supplier) and the reproducible activity page (at www.standardlesson.com or in the back of the NIV® Standard Lesson Commentary Deluxe Edition).

Into the Lesson

To four learners, distribute four name tags and accompanying pairs of statements per the following, one set per learner. Adjust the names depending on the male/female makeup of your class.

1a–Adam: I give 15 percent of my income to my church. It's not a hardship at my income level, and it assures me a leadership voice. **1b**–Ben: I give 5 percent of my income to my church. I would really like to give more, but much of my income is needed to care for Mom.

2a–Mario: I gave $100 a month to missions last year. I had more money to give because I decided to get a used car instead of a new one. **2b**–Mykala: I gave $50 a month to missions last year. I could have given more, but I was saving up for an Alaskan cruise.

Ask the first pair (Adam and Ben) to stand and read their first statements only. Then ask the class, "So, who is the 'greater' or 'more sincere' giver of these two?" After a few responses, have the pair read their second statements; then repeat your question. Do the same for Mario and Mykala. Conclude: "It's not always easy to tell who is the more sincere giver since motives may be unknown to us. In today's lesson similar gifts were given but motives differed. Let's see what happened."

Into the Word

Ask a skillful reader (recruited in advance) to help you present the lesson text. In response to the following questions (asked by you or a learner), have the person read the indicated verses from today's text: Why were there no needy Christians in the first-century church in Jerusalem? *(4:34, 35)* / What notable individual sold land in order to help out his fellow Christians? *(4:36, 37)* / Who else sold property? *(5:1)* / What sneaky thing did this couple do? *(5:2)* / What did Peter say to Ananias after he heard his lie? *(5:3, 4)* / What happened to Ananias? *(5:5, 6)* / What happened next? *(5:7, 8)* / What did Peter say to Sapphira? *(5:9)* / What happened to her? *(5:10)*.

Write on the board the words *Similar* and *Different* as titles for two categories. Then ask learners to name things that were similar about Barnabas and the couple of Ananias and Sapphira; jot responses on the board (*expected responses*: each decided to sell land, each decided to give money to help other Christians, each gave money to the apostles, each could have kept all or part of the money for themselves).

Do the same for how they differed (*expected responses*: Barnabas told the truth, but the couple lied; Barnabas gave it all, while the couple kept back some; Barnabas continued to live and serve the Lord, while the couple died and were buried that day). Be sure to make the point that Ananias and Sapphira had every right to keep any part of the money for themselves; they just shouldn't have lied about it.

Option. As a test to see how much learners have retained, distribute copies of the "Truth or Consequences" activity from the reproducible page, which you can download. Challenge learners to complete this very quickly (three minutes or less), Bibles closed. Conduct a whole-class discussion as learners score their own work.

Into Life

Distribute blank index cards and challenge learners to make a list of things they would be willing to sell in order to generate funding to meet the basic needs of other Christians. Assure learners that you will not collect their lists. After a few minutes, ask what the nature of the items one is willing to sell might suggest about generosity.

Alternative. Distribute copies of the "Private Property?" activity from the reproducible page. Form learners into small groups for discussion. Have groups share their conclusions regarding question 3 with the class as a whole.

SPEAKING UP FOR GOD

DEVOTIONAL READING: Revelation 22:1-7
BACKGROUND SCRIPTURE: Acts 5:12-42

ACTS 5:27-29, 33-42

27 The apostles were brought in and made to appear before the Sanhedrin to be questioned by the high priest. 28 "We gave you strict orders not to teach in this name," he said. "Yet you have filled Jerusalem with your teaching and are determined to make us guilty of this man's blood."

29 Peter and the other apostles replied: "We must obey God rather than human beings!"

. . . .

33 When they heard this, they were furious and wanted to put them to death. 34 But a Pharisee named Gamaliel, a teacher of the law, who was honored by all the people, stood up in the Sanhedrin and ordered that the men be put outside for a little while. 35 Then he addressed the Sanhedrin: "Men of Israel, consider carefully what you intend to do to these men. 36 Some time ago Theudas appeared, claiming to be somebody, and about four hundred men rallied to him. He was killed, all

his followers were dispersed, and it all came to nothing. 37 After him, Judas the Galilean appeared in the days of the census and led a band of people in revolt. He too was killed, and all his followers were scattered. 38 Therefore, in the present case I advise you: Leave these men alone! Let them go! For if their purpose or activity is of human origin, it will fail. 39 But if it is from God, you will not be able to stop these men; you will only find yourselves fighting against God."

40 His speech persuaded them. They called the apostles in and had them flogged. Then they ordered them not to speak in the name of Jesus, and let them go.

41 The apostles left the Sanhedrin, rejoicing because they had been counted worthy of suffering disgrace for the Name. 42 Day after day, in the temple courts and from house to house, they never stopped teaching and proclaiming the good news that Jesus is the Messiah.

KEY VERSE

Peter and the other apostles replied: "We must obey God rather than human beings!" —**Acts 5:29**

THE CHRISTIAN COMMUNITY COMES ALIVE

Unit 1: Seeds of New Growth

LESSONS 1–4

LESSON AIMS

After participating in this lesson, each learner will be able to:

1. Describe the apostles' resolve to proclaim Jesus as the Messiah.

2. Contrast the motives of the apostles with those of their opponents.

3. Share the gospel boldly with one unbeliever in the week ahead.

LESSON OUTLINE

Introduction
  A. Someone Has to Speak Up!
  B. Lesson Background
 I. Apostles' Stand (ACTS 5:27-29, 33)
  A. Defiant Refusal (vv. 27-29)
    The Captive Conscience
  B. Furious Response (v. 33)
 II. Gamaliel's Plea (ACTS 5:34-39)
  A. Present Situation (vv. 34, 35)
  B. Previous Examples (vv. 36, 37)
  C. Future Action (vv. 38, 39)
 III. Council's Decision (ACTS 5:40-42)
  A. Strong Warning (v. 40)
  B. Joyful Response (vv. 41, 42)
    Suffering for His Name
Conclusion
  A. Obeying God, Not People
  B. Hearing God's Call Personally
  C. Prayer
  D. Thought to Remember

Introduction

A. Someone Has to Speak Up!

William Wilberforce (1759–1833) became a Christian in 1785. Already a member of the British Parliament, he soon became a vocal opponent of slavery. He saw the need to acknowledge human dignity and decided to speak up for the cause of freedom. He devoted the rest of his life to passing laws that first outlawed the slave trade itself (1807) and then outlawed slavery altogether (1833) throughout most of the British Empire.

Many names come readily to mind when we think of those who have spoken up for worthy causes. For Patrick Henry in the American colonies and for Gandhi in India, the cause was national freedom. For Martin Luther King, Jr., the cause was civil rights. When they saw situations that demanded their voices, they knew they had to speak up!

For Peter and the other apostles, the cause was even greater: their cause was to liberate people from the shackles of sin, to bring the repentant into the heavenly kingdom. The apostles proclaimed Jesus as the Messiah not just because *they* felt strongly about the matter but because *God himself* did. That is why they knew they had to speak up, regardless of the opposition.

B. Lesson Background

The church was born speaking. All the apostles spoke up on the Day of Pentecost, proclaiming the gospel message in many languages. Peter led out as the primary spokesman, convicting the crowd and urging people to repent (Acts 2).

Some time after the Day of Pentecost, Peter and John healed a crippled beggar at the gate of the temple and proclaimed Jesus to the crowd that gathered (Acts 3). When the Sanhedrin seized Peter and John to demand that they stop speaking about Jesus, Peter said, "We cannot help speaking about what we have seen and heard" (4:20). When Peter and John rejoined the other believers, "the place where they were meeting was shaken. And they were all filled with the Holy Spirit and spoke the word of God boldly" (4:31; see lesson 1).

Official opposition mounted as the apostles continued to speak. They were arrested again and thrown into jail, but an angel from God opened the door and sent them back to the temple courts to preach (Acts 5:18-20). When the Jewish religious authorities sent for the prisoners, the jail was discovered to be empty. Soon someone reported that the apostles were preaching again—right back in the same place where they had been arrested! With considerable frustration, the authorities brought them in yet again. What could be done to make these Christians stop talking?

I. Apostles' Stand
(ACTS 5:27-29, 33)
A. Defiant Refusal (vv. 27-29)

27. The apostles were brought in and made to appear before the Sanhedrin to be questioned by the high priest.

The Sanhedrin rules the Jewish nation (under the watchful eye of the Romans). It is led by the high priest and his assistant. There are 69 other members as well, drawn from those of the high priestly family, from the elders of the people, and from the teachers of the law (see Acts 4:5, 6; 5:17; 24:1). The Sanhedrin meets daily, except for Sabbaths and feast days, and functions as something like a modern supreme court. To its members it seems appropriate, therefore, to render a verdict on the preaching of these Jews who are proclaiming that the Messiah has come. The Sanhedrin has brought them in once already and threatened them (Acts 4:18, 21). The apostles, however, went right back to speaking in the temple courtyard about Jesus. The council will now try again to decide what action it should take to make the apostles stop.

28. "We gave you strict orders not to teach in this name," he said. "Yet you have filled Jerusalem with your teaching and are determined to make us guilty of this man's blood."

The high priest (who is Annas; see Acts 4:6) reminds the apostles that they already have been warned in no uncertain terms not to speak or teach in the name of Jesus (4:18). The members of the Sanhedrin conveniently fail to recall that Peter has already told them that he has to listen to God, that he will go on telling of what he has seen and heard from Jesus (4:19, 20).

The apostles' preaching about Jesus makes the Sanhedrin look bad. In words of feigned innocence, the high priest complains that the apostles are intending to bring *this man's blood* on its members. But members of the Sanhedrin surely have not forgotten their role in the death of Jesus! During a trial held in the dark of night, they had hastily condemned him to be "worthy of death" (Matthew 26:66). In the trial before Pilate the next morning, these same leaders had persuaded the people to ask that a murderer be released, but Jesus be crucified (27:20). The leaders and the people had responded to Pilate's objection by affirming "His blood is on us and on our children!" (27:25). These leaders know they are guilty of getting Jesus killed, but they seem to have rationalized away that guilt.

> *What Do You Think?*
> How do those in authority attempt to suppress the Christian message today?
> *Talking Points for Your Discussion*
> - Civil authorities
> - Family members
> - Employers
> - Other

29. Peter and the other apostles replied: "We must obey God rather than human beings!"

Peter and the other apostles do not waver. They know their duty is to speak up for Jesus, and they will not be intimidated by any human authority that says otherwise. The Sanhedrin may be the supreme court over all of Israel, but it is not supreme over God. So the only answer the apostles can give is the one we see here (compare Acts 4:19).

It is important to note that the apostles are simply stating the necessary facts. It is not that they think themselves to be somehow immune from governmental authority (compare Matthew 23:2, 3). The issue is that the demand of the Sanhedrin is directly contrary to a command of God. So the only thing the apostles can do is to reject the Sanhedrin's directive.

❧ THE CAPTIVE CONSCIENCE ❧

On October 31, 1517, Martin Luther nailed his 95 theses to the door of All Saints' Church in Wittenberg, Germany. Those theses set forth Luther's disagreements with certain practices of the Roman Catholic Church of his era. He considered himself to be a loyal priest of the church, but his study of Scripture had given him a new understanding of Christian faith and life.

Despite Luther's avowed loyalty, the result was official persecution by both church and state. He was given a chance to recant his views when he appeared before a general assembly of the estates of the Holy Roman Empire in 1521. Luther replied that he had to take his stand on Scripture. He ensured continued persecution with these words: "I am bound by the Scriptures I have quoted, and my conscience is captive to the Word of God. I cannot and will not recant anything."

Luther's stand serves today as one of the most powerful demonstrations in all of history of a conscience informed by Scripture. But the stand of Peter and John before the Sanhedrin was a precursor. Such stands are possible only when one first takes "captive every thought to make it obedient to Christ" (2 Corinthians 10:5). What progress are you making in that regard?   —C. R. B.

B. Furious Response (v. 33)

33. When they heard this, they were furious and wanted to put them to death.

The members of the Sanhedrin are angry enough to kill the apostles right then and there! They do not have the legal authority to do so (John 18:31), but that fact will not prevent them from killing Stephen by mob action later (Acts 7:57-60). We note that the emotional reaction of being *furious* is the same in both instances (7:54).

The Sanhedrin's reaction should not come as a surprise to the apostles. Jesus already had warned that they would face such persecution; if people hated Jesus, they will also hate his disciples (John 15:18-20). The time will come even when "anyone who kills you will think they are offering a service to God" (16:2).

II. Gamaliel's Plea
(ACTS 5:34-39)

A. Present Situation (vv. 34, 35)

34. But a Pharisee named Gamaliel, a teacher of the law, who was honored by all the people, stood up in the Sanhedrin and ordered that the men be put outside for a little while.

Gamaliel is the most respected Jewish scholar of his time, the grandson of the famous and revered Rabbi Hillel (lived about 110 BC–AD 10). Gamaliel is a member of the Pharisees, a group known for its diligence in keeping the law in every detail. Gamaliel teaches the most promising of the young rabbinical students, including Saul of Tarsus (Acts 22:3). As a leading member of the Sanhedrin, people listen when Gamaliel speaks!

To his credit, Gamaliel is concerned that justice be done. He speaks up, even though it would be safer and easier to say nothing. It seems that most of the Sanhedrin want to kill the apostles, but Gamaliel is not one to rush to judgment. So he calls for the accused to be escorted out of the room while the council discusses the matter further (compare Acts 4:15).

35. Then he addressed the Sanhedrin: "Men of Israel, consider carefully what you intend to do to these men.

The phrase *men of Israel* is a common way to demand the attention of a Jewish audience (see Acts 2:22; 3:12; 13:16; 21:28; the 2011 edition of the NIV has "fellow Israelites" in these four passages, although the Greek is the same as the passage at hand). The phrase reminds listeners of their national heritage and calls them to their duty to act on what they are about to hear.

As Gamaliel continues his address, he advises caution. It's time to hit the pause button and take a look at the bigger picture. This is exactly the kind of caution that will not be exercised in the condemnation of Stephen later (Acts 7:54-58).

B. Previous Examples (vv. 36, 37)

36. "Some time ago Theudas appeared, claiming to be somebody, and about four hundred men rallied to him. He was killed, all his followers were dispersed, and it all came to nothing.

Gamaliel proceeds to illustrate why caution is indicated. First, he reminds his colleagues of an uprising that had been fomented by a certain Theudas following the death of Herod the Great in 4 BC. The first-century Jewish historian Josephus describes that era as being one of "ten thousand other disorders in Judea, which were like tumults, because a great number put themselves into a warlike posture, either out of hopes of gain to themselves, or out of enmity to the Jews." It was in that time of political turmoil that Theudas had gathered around himself *about four hundred men,* seeing a chance to revolt against the Roman overlords.

The rebellion of Theudas did not gain traction, however, and soon failed. The lesson Gamaliel draws from that episode is this: insurrections come and go, usually without permanent damage to the public peace and safety, so it's important not to overreact. Gamaliel may also be implying that the Sanhedrin should let the Romans handle such problems.

HOW TO SAY IT

Essenes	*Eh*-seenz.
Gamaliel	Guh-*may*-lih-ul or Guh-*may*-lee-al.
Judas	*Joo*-dus.
Pharisees	*Fair*-ih-seez.
Pilate	*Pie*-lut.
rabbi	*rab*-eye.
rabbinical	ruh-*bin*-ih-kul.
Sadducees	*Sad*-you-seez.
Sanhedrin	San-huh-drun or San-*heed*-run.
Theudas	*Thoo*-dus.

37. "After him, Judas the Galilean appeared in the days of the census and led a band of people in revolt. He too was killed, and all his followers were scattered.

For a second example, Gamaliel reminds his colleagues of the incident involving a certain *Judas the Galilean.* That man's attempt at revolt came a few years after the one by Theudas, around AD 6, according to Josephus. He describes Judas of Galilee as "a teacher of a peculiar sect of his own, . . . not at all like the rest of those their leaders" and as being the author "of the fourth sect of Jewish philosophy," the other three being Pharisees, Sadducees, and Essenes.

The spark that ignited this revolt was a tax imposed on Judea by the governor of Syria. An even larger number of men participated in this rebellion, determined to win independence for their nation. This revolt failed as well.

C. Future Action (vv. 38, 39)

38. "Therefore, in the present case I advise you: Leave these men alone! Let them go! For if their purpose or activity is of human origin, it will fail.

So now, what should be done with these noisy, troublesome disciples of Jesus? Probably to the surprise of his colleagues, Gamaliel recommends that the council merely ignore them. His reasoning is that this uprising, even though its followers already number in the thousands (Acts 4:4), could very well prove to be just another knee-jerk human enterprise. If so, it will collapse of its own accord. Then the trouble will be over, and the Sanhedrin will have no blood on its hands.

39. "But if it is from God, you will not be able to stop these men; you will only find yourselves fighting against God."

Gamaliel recognizes that there is another possibility: this new movement could actually be inspired by God. If—as the Christians claim—it is indeed of God, then the Sanhedrin will not be able to overthrow it. To attempt to do so will only place the council in the unenviable, no-win position of fighting God!

Even though the Sanhedrin properly appears in a very negative light in this situation, it must be conceded that its members do not want to oppose God. They wish to oppose here only Jesus' followers, who in the minds of the council members are not on the side of God.

Gamaliel speaks up not in defense of the Christians but in defense of practicality. To do nothing might just work out in the Sanhedrin's favor.

> **What Do You Think?**
> How can we discern whether a person or idea is "of God" today? What do we do with our conclusions?
>
> *Talking Points for Your Discussion*
> - Matthew 7:15-20
> - Titus 1:6-16
> - 1 John 4:1-3
> - Jude 4, 8
> - Revelation 2:14, 15, 20

III. Council's Decision
(ACTS 5:40-42)

A. Strong Warning (v. 40)

40. His speech persuaded them. They called the apostles in and had them flogged. Then they ordered them not to speak in the name of Jesus, and let them go.

Gamaliel's argument is convincing. Endeavors of human origin are wont to fail; council members hope this is one such. Divine initiatives, for their part, are not to be resisted. So the logical course of action is to do nothing. The Sanhedrin will wait and watch.

Even so, the council members are not entirely passive: they summon the apostles back into the assembly and have them flogged. The severity of the beating is not stated, but it may consist of up to 40 lashes for each apostle (Deuteronomy 25:1-3; compare 2 Corinthians 11:24). Perhaps, in spite of Gamaliel, council members think they can hurry matters along and trigger the collapse of what they see as merely a human insurgence by discouraging its leaders.

As before, the council members demand that the apostles stop speaking *in the name of Jesus* (compare Acts 4:17, 18). Hoping that this will take care of the problem, the authorities *let them go.*

B. Joyful Response (vv. 41, 42)

41. The apostles left the Sanhedrin, rejoicing because they had been counted worthy of suffering disgrace for the Name.

Bloodied and bruised, the apostles make their exit. But while their bodies are beaten, their spirits are not—just the opposite! To have been lashed for speaking up simply shows that they have been *counted worthy of suffering disgrace* for the name of Jesus. The disgrace, however, is not in anything they have done; by speaking up and by suffering for a noble cause, the apostles have done nothing disgraceful. The disgraceful thing, rather, is in how their own religious leaders have treated them. Whatever pain the apostles endure is worth it!

Later, the apostle Paul will himself become no stranger to suffering after he had been one to inflict it (Acts 7:54–8:3; 2 Corinthians 11:23-27; 12:8-10). Like the other apostles, he will come to consider it a privilege to suffer for the name of Jesus. As he later informs fellow believers, "it has been granted to you on behalf of Christ not only to believe in him, but also to suffer for him" (Philippians 1:29).

> **What Do You Think?**
> If a Christian is never persecuted, does that say anything negative or cautionary about the genuineness of his or her faith? Explain.
>
> *Talking Points for Your Discussion*
> - Reasons why it may
> - Reasons why it might not
> - Considering definition of "persecution"

❧ *SUFFERING FOR HIS NAME* ❧

In his foreword to the 2013 book *Persecuted: The Global Assault on Christians*, Eric Metaxas asserts that "Christians are the single most widely persecuted religious group in the world today." Many sources, including the highly respected Pew Research Center, offer evidence leading to this conclusion. So far in this century, the targeting of Christians for church burnings, torture, and outright murder has occurred in Kenya, Egypt, Pakistan, Syria, and Indonesia, among other places.

Yet such persecution is not a new phenomenon, as today's text reveals. Neither is it a surprise, since Jesus had predicted it (Matthew 24:9). The Sanhedrin not only demanded that the apostles quit proclaiming the gospel, it had them beaten to make sure they got the message!

We are to obey governing authorities (Romans 13:1-5), but that obedience must turn to disobedience when such authorities attempt to silence the gospel. Will you be ready to suffer in that regard when the time comes? And what can you do right now to support those currently being persecuted for the name of Christ? —C. R. B.

42. Day after day, in the temple courts and from house to house, they never stopped teaching and proclaiming the good news that Jesus is the Messiah.

Now it's back to work as usual (compare Acts 2:46). The apostles clearly are not intimidated by their treatment at the hands of the authorities. The apostles cannot stop speaking up! This becomes the pattern for the first-century church. At every opportunity Christ is proclaimed. When persecution becomes so intense that "all except the apostles" flee Jerusalem (Acts 8:1), the message spreads farther still (8:4). Nothing can silence the gospel.

> *What Do You Think?*
> In what contexts have you found it most difficult to maintain your Christian witness? Why?
> *Talking Points for Your Discussion*
> - Workplace situations
> - Family gatherings
> - Public places (praying in restaurants, etc.)
> - Other

Conclusion

A. Obeying God, Not People

Throughout history, Christians have been challenged to obey the call of God and do the will of God. They have often been called to stand against popular opinion and speak out against violations of God's will. They have opposed slavery, tyranny, child labor, substance abuse, the international sex trade, etc. They have worked to shine the light of

Visual for
Lessons 3 & 6

Have learners sing all four stanzas, then discuss which of the four was most meaningful and why.

truth into darkness, to feed the hungry, to heal the sick, to lift up the fallen, to care for the downtrodden, to bring peace.

Speaking up in the name of Jesus begins with telling the good news of salvation and continues with proclaiming whatever is consistent with the redeemed life. Wherever there is any situation that falls short of what God intends for humanity, Christians must speak up.

B. Hearing God's Call Personally

If someone ought so speak up, who should that someone be? Logically, it should be the same person who sees the problem and knows that it needs to be addressed. It should be the person who prays daily, "Your will be done, on earth as it is in heaven" (Matthew 6:10). It should be the person who knows that Jesus is the only Savior of the world and that lives are to be lived in his footsteps. Christians seeing a need are not to wait for someone else to do something; they themselves should step up and speak up!

C. Prayer

Dear God, help us to follow the example of the earliest Christians in not failing to speak up. Give us opportunities to share our faith, and give us the boldness we need to do so. In Jesus' name, amen.

D. Thought to Remember

Speak up for Christ, no matter what.

INVOLVEMENT LEARNING

Enhance your lesson with NIV® Bible Student (from your curriculum supplier) and the reproducible activity page (at www.standardlesson.com or in the back of the NIV® Standard Lesson Commentary Deluxe Edition).

Into the Lesson

Pair off learners to discuss when they would or wouldn't speak up in various situations. Allow 30 to 60 seconds for discussing each of the following as you write them on the board: (1) a good friend has a visible stain on a blouse or shirt; (2) your college professor mocks Christianity; (3) your boss often uses profanity in your presence.

Allow time for the pairs to share their decisions in whole-class discussion. Then say, "It's easier to speak up in some situations than others. In lesson 1, we saw the results of the apostles having been warned and threatened for preaching Jesus, and in today's lesson we will see them confronted with another decision in that regard."

Into the Word

Summarize the Lesson Background to set the stage for study of the lesson text proper. Emphasize the apostles' determination to keep preaching Jesus no matter what. Then ask four learners to read aloud the lesson text; assign verses in this way: narrator (verses 27, 29a, 33-35a, 40-42), high priest (verses 28), Peter (verse 29b), and Gamaliel (verses 35b-39). *Alternative*: Instead of an audible reading of the text, distribute copies of the "Read the Headlines!" activity from the reproducible page, which you can download. Have learners work in pairs to complete as indicated. Announce a time limit of four minutes to encourage speed.

Distribute to study pairs or small groups handouts featuring two columns that are headed *Reasons to Keep Silent* and *Reasons to Speak Out*. Down the left-hand side have three rows that are labeled *The Apostles, Gamaliel*, and *The Sanhedrin*, one designation per row. Assign each pair or group to work on one of the rows. (If you have more than three pairs/groups, make duplicate assignments.) Say, "Try to come up with as many reasons as you can that your assigned person or group would have had for keeping silent and for speaking out."

As pairs/groups work, write the column headings and row labels on the board. Enter learners' ideas within this matrix during the ensuing whole-class discussion of groups' conclusions. *Expected and possible reasons to keep silent*: fear of persecution (apostles); fear that his advice would be rejected (Gamaliel); potentially going against God (Sanhedrin). *Expected and possible reasons to speak out*: desire to be obedient to God (apostles); keep the council from going against God (Gamaliel); control the situation to ensure their continuing in power (Sanhedrin).

Note that some possible reasons are speculative. While listing responses on the board, pay special attention to the apostles' reasons for speaking out in spite of threats.

Into Life

Using the lesson's Introduction, verbally sketch the story of William Wilberforce regarding his lifelong efforts to end slavery in the British Empire. Then say, "Wilberforce was able to have a great influence on the world of his time because of his willingness to speak out against slavery and his refusal to be dissuaded by all the forces that opposed him. What evils exist in our day that we need to speak up about?"

Expect learners to mention issues such as abortion, human trafficking, and pornography. For any areas that seem to strike a chord with your learners, probe deeper as you call for ways your class can help address the problem by speaking out or otherwise taking action. Then remind the class that speaking out for Jesus and the eternal salvation he offers is the most important thing. Ask learners to suggest ways to bring the gospel into their active opposition of the issues they just mentioned.

Option or alternative. Distribute copies of the "To Speak or Not to Speak" activity from the reproducible page to be completed privately and reflectively during the last five minutes of class.

STANDING FIRM
AGAINST OPPOSITION

DEVOTIONAL READING: 1 Corinthians 1:1-9
BACKGROUND SCRIPTURE: Acts 7:1-53

ACTS 7:2-4, 8-10, 17, 33, 34, 45-47, 52, 53

2 To this he replied: "Brothers and fathers, listen to me! The God of glory appeared to our father Abraham while he was still in Mesopotamia, before he lived in Harran. 3 'Leave your country and your people,' God said, 'and go to the land I will show you.'

4 "So he left the land of the Chaldeans and settled in Harran. After the death of his father, God sent him to this land where you are now living."

. . . .

8 "Then he gave Abraham the covenant of circumcision. And Abraham became the father of Isaac and circumcised him eight days after his birth. Later Isaac became the father of Jacob, and Jacob became the father of the twelve patriarchs.

9 "Because the patriarchs were jealous of Joseph, they sold him as a slave into Egypt. But God was with him 10 and rescued him from all his troubles. He gave Joseph wisdom and enabled him to gain the goodwill of Pharaoh king of Egypt. So Pharaoh made him ruler over Egypt and all his palace."

. . . .

17 "As the time drew near for God to fulfill his promise to Abraham, the number of our people in Egypt had greatly increased."

. . . .

33 "Then the Lord said to him, 'Take off your sandals, for the place where you are standing is holy ground. 34 I have indeed seen the oppression of my people in Egypt. I have heard their groaning and have come down to set them free. Now come, I will send you back to Egypt.'"

. . . .

45 "After receiving the tabernacle, our ancestors under Joshua brought it with them when they took the land from the nations God drove out before them. It remained in the land until the time of David, 46 who enjoyed God's favor and asked that he might provide a dwelling place for the God of Jacob. 47 But it was Solomon who built a house for him."

. . . .

52 "Was there ever a prophet your ancestors did not persecute? They even killed those who predicted the coming of the Righteous One. And now you have betrayed and murdered him— 53 you who have received the law that was given through angels but have not obeyed it."

KEY VERSE

Heaven is my throne, and the earth is my footstool. What kind of house will you build for me? says the Lord. Or where will my resting place be? —**Acts 7:49**

The Christian Community Comes Alive

Unit 1: Seeds of New Growth

Lessons 1–4

Lesson Aims

After participating in this lesson, each learner will be able to:

1. Summarize the faith and failure of ancient Israel.

2. Compare and contrast Stephen's persecutors with the forefathers who killed the prophets.

3. Write a note of encouragement to a missionary serving in a hostile field.

Lesson Outline

Introduction
    A. What's Your Story?
    B. Lesson Background
  I. Story of Faith (Acts 7:2-4)
    A. God's Call (vv. 2, 3)
    B. Abraham's Response (v. 4)
  II. Story of Betrayal (Acts 7:8-10)
    A. Covenant (v. 8)
    B. Betrayal (v. 9a)
    C. Rescue (vv. 9b, 10)
  III. Story of Deliverance (Acts 7:17, 33, 34)
    A. People's Status (v. 17)
    B. God's Plan (vv. 33, 34)
      Visual Reminders, Visual Cautions
  IV. Story of Victory (Acts 7:45-47)
    A. Taking the Land (v. 45)
    B. Building the Temple (vv. 46, 47)
  V. Story of Murder (Acts 7:52, 53)
    A. Bold Accusation (v. 52)
    B. Tragic Guilt (v. 53)
      Murdering for God?
Conclusion
    A. Remember Your Identity
    B. Remember Your Task
    C. Prayer
    D. Thought to Remember

Introduction

A. What's Your Story?

Each of us has a story. That story explains who we are and how we came to be who we are. The story includes the tragedies and victories that have shaped us. Perhaps you can trace your story back through many generations. Parts of your story may make you swell with pride (whether of the godly or ungodly kind); parts of your story may make you cringe with shame. But whatever the details, your story makes you who you are.

As Christians, the most important part of our story is that we have chosen to follow Jesus. We remember that our sins have been forgiven; we realize that we have a future in Heaven. Our individual stories are chapters within the greater story of all the people of God. Part of our chapter is the call to stand firm. Today's lesson involves an example of one who did just that.

B. Lesson Background

As today's text opens, thousands already had become followers of Christ in the earliest days of the church (Acts 2:41; 4:4). Even many Jewish priests had become believers (6:7). The first-century church had taken seriously the call to be a genuine fellowship (2:42, 46) and to share with those in need (2:45; 4:32). Caring for widows was part of this; one of the seven men chosen to serve the church in that regard was Stephen (6:1-6).

Stephen was involved not only in the church's benevolence ministry, he also "performed great wonders and signs among the people" (Acts 6:8). He spoke out boldly for Christ, so much so that unbelievers became hostile. A source of this hostility was "the Synagogue of the Freedmen" (6:9). There were more than 400 synagogues in Jerusalem at that time, and the membership of this one was made up largely of former slaves who had gained their freedom.

False accusations began to flow when Stephen's opponents were unable to refute the wisdom and spirit with which he spoke. Ultimately, Stephen found himself being hauled up before the Sanhedrin (the ruling Jewish council) to answer these (Acts 6:11-14).

I. Story of Faith

(ACTS 7:2-4)

The high priest, who presides over the Sanhedrin's proceedings, has invited Stephen to make his defense against the charge of blasphemy (Acts 7:1). Addressing the council, Stephen begins to recount the story of Israel—their story and his own. It is a long story, but one that patriotic Jews love to hear.

A. God's Call (vv. 2, 3)

2. To this he replied: "Brothers and fathers, listen to me! The God of glory appeared to our father Abraham while he was still in Mesopotamia, before he lived in Harran.

The story had its beginning about 2,000 years earlier, in the distant land of Mesopotamia (Iraq and eastern Syria today). There, in the ancient city of Ur, God had called Abraham to follow his leading to relocate (Genesis 11:31; 12:1); Ur was where Abraham lived *before he lived in Harran* (see commentary on v. 4, below). His obedience to the call meant that henceforth all Israelites would look to him as their common ancestor, the father of their nation (John 8:39, 53; etc.).

3. "'Leave your country and your people,' God said, 'and go to the land I will show you.'

Genesis 12:1 is the reference. Even though Abraham was already 75 years old (12:4), God had called him to pull up stakes to begin a new chapter in his life's story (12:5). Abraham was given only a hint of how the journey would end; he was to trust God with the result.

HOW TO SAY IT

Abraham	*Ay*-bruh-ham.
Canaan	*Kay*-nun.
Chaldeans	Kal-*dee*-unz.
Gentiles	*Jen*-tiles.
Harran	*Hair*-run.
Mesopotamia	*Mes*-uh-puh-*tay*-me-uh.
Midian	*Mid*-ee-un.
Potiphar	*Pot*-ih-far.
Sanhedrin	*San*-huh-drun or San-*heed*-run.
Syria	*Sear*-ee-uh.
Ur	Er.

What Do You Think?
What did you have to "leave behind" to follow Christ? Which was the most difficult? Why?
Talking Points for Your Discussion
- Friendships
- Habits
- Attitudes
- Other

B. Abraham's Response (v. 4)

4. "So he left the land of the Chaldeans and settled in Harran. After the death of his father, God sent him to this land where you are now living."

Abraham had accompanied his father, Terah, from Ur to Harran, a distance of over 600 miles traveling west-northwest within what we call the Fertile Crescent (11:31). Abraham (named Abram at the time) lived in Harran until his father died (11:32), then was called to resume the epic journey. So he traveled southwest to the land of Canaan. His trip to Bethel (12:8) involved a distance of another 500 difficult miles as he passed through unknown lands for the destination of God's choosing. Thus did Abraham go out "even though he did not know where he was going" (Hebrews 11:8), but trusting the plan of God. The nation of Israel was born out of that trust.

II. Story of Betrayal

(ACTS 7:8-10)

Acts 7:5-7 (not in today's text) draws on Genesis 12:7; 13:15; 15:13, 14; and 24:7. Stephen uses these passages to add detail to his review of Israel's history.

A. Covenant (v. 8)

8. "Then he gave Abraham the covenant of circumcision. And Abraham became the father of Isaac and circumcised him eight days after his birth. Later Isaac became the father of Jacob, and Jacob became the father of the twelve patriarchs.

God's covenant with Abraham began with a promise to make that man a great nation and to

Visual for
Lesson 4

Point to this visual and ask, "How are the stands we are called to take like and unlike that of Stephen's?"

bless all the families of the earth through him (Genesis 12:2, 3). The covenant included the land of Palestine (13:14, 15). Some time later, the covenant was formalized with a blood sacrifice, and the promise was added that Abraham's innumerable descendants would live in a foreign country for 400 years (15:9-13). Some 25 years after the initial promise, God added to the covenant the requirement of circumcision. Throughout the history of the Israelites to come, every male baby was to be circumcised *eight days after his birth* (17:10-14).

Just as God promised, Abraham and Sarah had a baby boy in their old age (Genesis 17:17; 18:11; 21:1-5). The covenant relationship with God was passed on to that child, Isaac, and then to his son Jacob, from whose sons came the 12 tribes of Israel. The fulfillment of the promise that Abraham would be the father of a great nation was slowly gaining momentum.

Also gaining momentum is the plan Stephen has for his speech before the council. He is not telling them anything they don't know. What he *is* doing, rather, is laying the foundation for leveling countercharges. He is charged with blasphemy (Acts 6:11-14), but he plans to turn the tables.

B. Betrayal (v. 9a)

9a. "Because the patriarchs were jealous of Joseph, they sold him as a slave into Egypt.

There was sibling rivalry among the 12 sons of Jacob concerning Joseph, the eleventh of the 12

(Genesis 37:1-11). His resentful brothers plotted to kill him (37:19, 20), but ultimately decided to sell him to slave traders who were on their way to Egypt (37:23-28). Thus began a pattern in the story of the Israelite people. Driven by jealousy and resentment, they often challenged the man God had raised up to lead them (example: Judges 8:1, 2, 6). It happened several times in the life of Moses —at least once by his own siblings (Numbers 12:1, 2). It even happened when God sent his own Son.

C. Rescue (vv. 9b, 10)

9b, 10. "But God was with him and rescued him from all his troubles. He gave Joseph wisdom and enabled him to gain the goodwill of Pharaoh king of Egypt. So Pharaoh made him ruler over Egypt and all his palace."

In spite of the conspiracy against Joseph, *God was with him.* That meant rescue from the troubles of the young man's slavery. First, Joseph was favored in the eyes of Potiphar and made chief steward over all his house. Then after he was unjustly thrown in prison, God *gave Joseph wisdom and enabled him to gain the goodwill of Pharaoh* (Genesis 39–41). When Joseph was able to interpret Pharaoh's dreams and warn him to prepare for coming years of famine, the grateful ruler put him in charge of managing all Egypt. Joseph was even put in charge of the palace, and all Pharaoh's people had to answer to Joseph (41:39, 40).

The one rejected and scorned by his brothers was lifted by God to be a ruler; this is symbolic of what happened to Jesus (Acts 5:30, 31). The pattern begins with Joseph: those whom the people reject are subsequently exalted by God. This is a point that Stephen especially wants to impress upon the members of the Sanhedrin.

What Do You Think?
How has God delivered you from afflictions or other disasters?
Talking Points for Your Discussion
▪ In matters of faith
▪ In matters of others' envy
▪ In matters of your own insecurity or immaturity
▪ Other

III. Story of Deliverance

(ACTS 7:17, 33, 34)

In Acts 7:11-16 (not in today's text), Stephen summarizes facts found in Genesis 41:54–50:13 regarding Joseph and the 75 members of his extended family in Egypt. This sets the stage for another observation about Abraham.

A. People's Status (v. 17)

17. "As the time drew near for God to fulfill his promise to Abraham, the number of our people in Egypt had greatly increased."

Famine in the promised land had forced Joseph's brothers to come to Egypt for food; they eventually brought all their family members to live there. They may not have realized it at the time, but two specific predictions were being fulfilled: the descendants of Abraham were multiplying (Genesis 15:5), and the 400-year sojourn in a foreign land was beginning (15:13). The Israelites were on their way to becoming a great nation (12:2).

As Stephen summarizes Exodus 1:1–3:6 in Acts 7:18-32 (not in today's text), circumstances changed for the worse for God's covenant people. By the end of the 400-year period, the Israelites had been reduced in position from that of honored guests to slaves. But God raised up a deliverer: Moses. That leads to Stephen's next observation.

B. God's Plan (vv. 33, 34)

33. "Then the Lord said to him, 'Take off your sandals, for the place where you are standing is holy ground.

Stephen quotes Exodus 3:5. Moses had spent 40 years of his life as a shepherd in Midian, staying as far from Egypt as possible because of a murder charge against him there. Then one day he saw a burning bush—a bush that flamed, but was not consumed. When he went near to investigate, he heard the voice of the Lord as Stephen quotes here.

❧ VISUAL REMINDERS, VISUAL CAUTIONS ❧

Tourists in Europe are often awestruck at the sight of the great cathedrals that dot the continent. The cathedral is the most significant historic structure in many of Europe's great cities. Visitors to Paris, for example, never forget the sight of the Notre-Dame Cathedral, which is situated on an island in the middle of the Seine River.

Sadly, however, many of those great cathedrals and churches are nearly empty of worshippers. Europe has drifted far from its once-dominant Christian roots, and the great structures, now little more than tourist attractions, stand as mute cautions to that fact.

The burning bush that caught the eye of Moses was a passing phenomenon. It cannot be visited today as cathedrals can. Even so, it lives on in the pages of Scripture and in countless stained-glass treatments as a reminder of that man's call and faith. When others look at our spiritual track record, do they see a reminder or a caution?

—C. R. B.

> *What Do You Think?*
> Are there places today that qualify as holier than others? Why, or why not?
> *Talking Points for Your Discussion*
> ▪ Regarding physical structures
> ▪ Regarding historic places
> ▪ Other

34. "'I have indeed seen the oppression of my people in Egypt. I have heard their groaning and have come down to set them free. Now come, I will send you back to Egypt.'"

Stephen next quotes Exodus 3:7, 8, 10. Wow—does Stephen know the Scriptures! But Stephen is not demonstrating his mastery of the facts of history to show how smart he is. Rather, he is sketching the pattern of rebellion among God's people in defiance of divine saving actions.

This pattern is fleshed out in Acts 7:35-43 (not in today's text), where Stephen summarizes Exodus 2:14; 3:2, 3; 14:21; 19:1-6; 20:1-7; Numbers 14:3; Amos 5:25-27; etc. Most significant of all, Stephen quotes the prophecy in Deuteronomy 18:15 that God would someday raise up a prophet like Moses himself, one that the people must hear (Acts 7:37). This prophet-like-Moses has turned out to be Jesus, and the recent rejection of him by members of the Sanhedrin is at the heart of Stephen's countercharge, as we shall see.

IV. Story of Victory
(ACTS 7:45-47)

The tabernacle referred to below is described briefly in Acts 7:44 (not in today's text), per Exodus 26.

A. Taking the Land (v. 45)

45. "After receiving the tabernacle, our ancestors under Joshua brought it with them when they took the land from the nations God drove out before them. It remained in the land until the time of David,

After the 40 years of wilderness wandering, a generation was finally ready to trust God and allow Joshua to lead them into the promised land. The land was possessed at the time by the people of Canaan with whom God was so displeased (Leviticus 18:24-27). God therefore drove them out, giving victory after victory to the armies of Israel. By *the time of David* some 400 years later, the Israelites were well established in the promised land.

B. Building the Temple (vv. 46, 47)

46. "who enjoyed God's favor and asked that he might provide a dwelling place for the God of Jacob.

David, a man after God's own heart (1 Samuel 13:14; Acts 13:22), wanted to build a permanent house for God. It was not right, David reasoned, that he should live in a beautiful palace—"a house of cedar"—while the ark of God's covenant was still "in a tent" (2 Samuel 7:2). *The God of Jacob* had always been faithful to the covenant, and he certainly deserved to be given David's best.

47. "But it was Solomon who built a house for him."

But David was not permitted to build the temple for God (1 Chronicles 22:8). Instead, the builder of the temple was to be his son Solomon. The beautiful temple that Solomon built became a source of great pride for the nation of Israel, as did the temple that replaced it (Mark 13:1).

Since Stephen stands accused of saying that Jesus would destroy the temple (Acts 6:13, 14), it is appropriate to honor the place of the temple in Israel's history. The false accusation against Stephen had also been lodged against Jesus himself (Matthew 26:59-61; compare John 2:19-21).

V. Story of Murder
(ACTS 7:52, 53)

Quoting Isaiah 66:1, 2, Stephen has more to say about the temple in Acts 7:48-50 (not in today's text). Following that, he shifts into accusation mode in Acts 7:51, drawing on imagery from Exodus 32:9; 33:3, 5; Isaiah 63:10; etc.

A. Bold Accusation (v. 52)

52. "Was there ever a prophet your ancestors did not persecute? They even killed those who predicted the coming of the Righteous One. And now you have betrayed and murdered him—

Sharp words indeed! But Stephen speaks facts regarding the persecution of the prophets (2 Chronicles 36:16), and Jesus had spoken much the same (Matthew 23:31). Those prophets had predicted the coming of the Messiah, *the Righteous One,* the just man who would do God's will. Then when he did come, the members of the Sanhedrin had him killed. Just as Peter and the other apostles had harshly accused the council (Acts 5:30), so also does Stephen. He stands firm and speaks the truth boldly. They are guilty of condemning an innocent man—God's Son.

B. Tragic Guilt (v. 53)

53. "you who have received the law that was given through angels but have not obeyed it."

The rulers are tragically guilty of everything Stephen says. They know the law of God, so they should know what is right and what is their duty.

The law has been entrusted to them since given by God through angels (see also Galatians 3:19; Hebrews 2:2). But those rulers have failed to keep the law, just as so many earlier generations had failed. Sanhedrin members are more interested in maintaining their positions by pleasing the Romans than they are in pleasing God (John 11:48).

What Do You Think?
What are some aspects of keeping "the law of Christ" (Galatians 6:2)?
Talking Points for Your Discussion
- Concerning what we are to do
- Concerning what we are not to do

The remainder of Acts 7 reveals that Stephen's speech enrages the members of the Sanhedrin. He has stood firm for the truth, but they cannot endure it. So they stone him to death. Thus Stephen becomes the first Christian martyr.

❧ *Murdering for God?* ❧

Killing others in the name of God has a long history and shows no signs of abating. A relatively recent example is the violence of early 2014 between two branches of Islam in Iraq. Also a sad, never-ending reality is killings of Christians by those of non-Christian religions.

But before pointing too many fingers at non-Christians, we should pause to reflect on the fact that killing in the name of Christ also has a sordid history. Prime examples in that regard are the Crusades and the Inquisition of centuries gone by. The former involved waging "holy war" to retake Palestine from "infidels"; the latter involved attempts to root out heresy within Christendom, with punishment as severe as being burned at the stake. Those claiming the name of Christ have sometimes played into the hands of skeptics by hating enemies, real and imagined, instead of loving them as Jesus commanded.

Stephen boldly accused the members of the Sanhedrin of complicity in religious murder. Just as their ancestors had killed prophets who spoke God's truth, the council members had killed Jesus, the Messiah whom God had sent. The Sanhedrin proved Stephen's point by killing him as well. If you were accused of having the same inclinations as those who instigated the Crusades and/or the Inquisition, how would you respond? —C. R. B.

Conclusion
A. Remember Your Identity

Many of us can remember from childhood the parental caution *Always remember who you are!* The same imperative applies to us as Christians as we face the daily challenges and temptations of life. And just who are we as Christians? Being of Christ, we are children of Abraham, the man of faith (see Galatians 3:29). As we cherish the story of Moses, we pledge our lives to the greater prophet Jesus (Acts 7:37), the Son of God who leads us in our exodus from sin-slavery.

B. Remember Your Task

We know that the story of God's people has not always been an easy one. We know that we do not wrestle against mere flesh and blood, but "against the powers of this dark world and against the spiritual forces of evil in the heavenly realms" (Ephesians 6:12). We win the ultimate victory in this battle as we stand firm. We resist the devil, not God's Spirit.

As we do, we join our story to the story of Christians through the centuries. The challenge is to recognize that we must stand firm in all occasions of life. Think of opposition to God in government, rejection of God in academia, or when acquaintances want to relax the standards of what is right. Whatever difficulty may arise, we are to be ready to take part in the age-old story of standing firm. There will be opposition, but standing firm for God is always the right thing to do.

C. Prayer

Dear God, thank you for inspiring the heroes of old to stand firm in the face of opposition. Forgive us when we have faltered, but strengthen us so that their victory stories may be repeated in our own times. In the name of Jesus, amen.

D. Thought to Remember

Stand for God and he will stand with you.

INVOLVEMENT LEARNING

Enhance your lesson with NIV® Bible Student (from your curriculum supplier) and the reproducible activity page (at www.standardlesson.com or in the back of the NIV® Standard Lesson Commentary Deluxe Edition).

Into the Lesson

Write the following on the board: "A gentle answer turns away wrath" (Proverbs 15:1). Say, "Think about times you have faced opposition. How did you know which situations called for a 'gentle answer' rather than a response that was confrontational?" Encourage open discussion, but caution learners not to share details that would be inappropriate for your class setting. (*Option*: you can depersonalize this by asking about experiences of Christians in general rather than experiences of your learners in particular.) Discuss how emotions can interfere with making the right decision in this regard (but don't let this drag out).

Make a transition by saying, "As we consider the kinds of responses God expects us to make in the face of opposition, we can gain insight from how his people in Bible times did so. Stephen's case is as an example."

Option. Before class begins, place in chairs copies of the "Responding in a Crisis" activity from the reproducible page, which you can download. Learners can begin working on this as they arrive.

Into the Word

Summarize for the class the nature and source of the opposition to Stephen according to the Lesson Background. Then say, "Let's begin our study of Stephen's defense with the end in view" as you have a learner read dramatically the last two verses of the lesson text, Acts 7:52, 53. Then say, "Now let's work our way through Stephen's defense from the beginning to see how his observations led up to his countercharge in those last two verses."

Work through the text in terms of the verse groupings of the Lesson Outline, pausing after each segment is read to ask, "How is this segment preparatory to Acts 7:52, 53?" Jot responses on the board. Use the commentary to offer hints. (*Alternative*: cover the entirety of Acts 7:2-50 in this way, with additional verse groupings as required.)

Use the following discussion questions to wrap up this segment: 1. How can opposition serve to strengthen faith in God? 2. What incidents from the Bible help you know how to stand firm in the face of opposition? [The "Responding in a Crisis" activity mentioned above notes some possibilities.] 3. Under what circumstances, if any, is a believer today justified in confronting religious or secular leaders as strongly as did Stephen? Why?

Option. Follow the study above by forming learners into three small groups to consider the following passages: *Group 1*—Exodus 2:11-14; 6:6-9; 14:10-12. *Group 2*—Exodus 15:22-24; 16:1-3; 17:1, 2. *Group 3*—Numbers 12:1, 2; 14:1-4; 16:1-3. Have the passages listed on handouts along with these instructions: "Scan these passages and summarize the opposition Moses faced from God's chosen people. How do these oppositions compare and contrast with the opposition to Stephen? Does Stephen's accusation in Acts 7:53 place the members of the Sanhedrin, who have 'received the law [of Moses],' as opponents of Moses? Why, or why not?" Have groups share conclusions in a whole-class discussion.

Into Life

Say, "Many missionaries serve on difficult, even hostile, mission fields. Let's take a few minutes to write a note to one of these." Come prepared with the names of one or more missionaries. Distribute paper or stationery for writing. If learners seem stuck on what to write, you can suggest that they can remind the missionary or missionaries that they are not forgotten and that God's peace and comfort are always a prayer away. As learners finish, offer to collect the notes to mail or convert into e-mail, recognizing that learners may wish to do so themselves.

Option. Distribute copies of the "Persecuted Christians" activity from the reproducible page. Allow time to complete and discuss as indicated.

SIMON IS REBUKED

DEVOTIONAL READING: Hebrews 13:5-10
BACKGROUND SCRIPTURE: Acts 8:9-25

ACTS 8:9-24

9 Now for some time a man named Simon had practiced sorcery in the city and amazed all the people of Samaria. He boasted that he was someone great, 10 and all the people, both high and low, gave him their attention and exclaimed, "This man is rightly called the Great Power of God." 11 They followed him because he had amazed them for a long time with his sorcery. 12 But when they believed Philip as he proclaimed the good news of the kingdom of God and the name of Jesus Christ, they were baptized, both men and women. 13 Simon himself believed and was baptized. And he followed Philip everywhere, astonished by the great signs and miracles he saw.

14 When the apostles in Jerusalem heard that Samaria had accepted the word of God, they sent Peter and John to Samaria. 15 When they arrived, they prayed for the new believers there that they might receive the Holy Spirit, 16 because the Holy Spirit had not yet come on any of them; they had simply been baptized in the name of the Lord Jesus. 17 Then Peter and John placed their hands on them, and they received the Holy Spirit.

18 When Simon saw that the Spirit was given at the laying on of the apostles' hands, he offered them money 19 and said, "Give me also this ability so that everyone on whom I lay my hands may receive the Holy Spirit."

20 Peter answered: "May your money perish with you, because you thought you could buy the gift of God with money! 21 You have no part or share in this ministry, because your heart is not right before God. 22 Repent of this wickedness and pray to the Lord in the hope that he may forgive you for having such a thought in your heart. 23 For I see that you are full of bitterness and captive to sin." 24 Then Simon answered, "Pray to the Lord for me so that nothing you have said may happen to me."

KEY VERSE

Repent of this wickedness and pray to the Lord in the hope that he may forgive you for having such a thought in your heart. —**Acts 8:22**

THE CHRISTIAN COMMUNITY COMES ALIVE

Unit 2: Giving Bold Testimony

LESSONS 5–8

LESSON AIMS

After participating in this lesson, each learner will be able to:

1. Retell the story of Simon the sorcerer.

2. Explain the circumstances and significance of the mission to Samaria.

3. Write a prayer that asks God for good motives for ministry.

LESSON OUTLINE

Introduction
  A. More Than a Name
  B. Lesson Background
I. Simon's Salvation (ACTS 8:9-13)
  A. Sorcerer's Fame (vv. 9-11)
  B. Evangelist's Impact (vv. 12, 13)
II. Apostles' Actions (ACTS 8:14-17)
  A. Traveling to Samaria (v. 14)
  B. Praying for Believers (vv. 15-17)
    Evidence of Conversion
III. Simon's Sin (ACTS 8:18-24)
  A. Request (vv. 18, 19)
  B. Rebuke (vv. 20-23)
    Buying Power?
  C. Remorse (v. 24)
Conclusion
  A. The Two Simons
  B. Prayer
  C. Thought to Remember

Introduction

A. More Than a Name

Many people have had their names become famous (or infamous) by their accomplishments, but in some cases the name outlives the person in a different way. For example, Jules Léotard (1838–1870) is now largely forgotten as the father of the modern trapeze act, but his name lives on as the designation of the one-piece, skintight acrobatics outfit that he popularized.

Our lesson today features a person who lives on in infamy because his name has given us the English word *simony*. This refers to the practice of purchasing favors from, or even offices of power within, the church. Still today, attempts to buy or sell anything of a distinctly spiritual nature is liable to be condemned as simony, an illustration of the fact that some sins can outlive the sinner.

B. Lesson Background

Just before ascending to Heaven, Jesus told the apostles that they were to testify about him "in Jerusalem, and in all Judea and in Samaria, and to the ends of the earth" (Acts 1:8). Acts 2–7 covers the first stage of the plan as the apostles took the lead in proclaiming Christ in Jerusalem; the result was that thousands accepted Jesus as Messiah (2:41; 4:4; 6:7).

During this time, two nonapostles by the names Stephen and Philip rose to prominence as Spirit-filled leaders. Initially, these two were included in the group of seven appointed to manage the church's benevolence ministry (Acts 6:1-6). Both were also active as evangelists, and this work led to persecution: Stephen's death by stoning and Philip's departure from Jerusalem (7:59, 60; 8:1b-5).

These circumstances resulted in Philip's being a key figure in the spread of the gospel. Leaving Jerusalem, he "went down to a city in Samaria" (Acts 8:5), where he found a receptive audience (8:6-8). Since the death of King Solomon in about 931 BC, the tribes of Israel had been divided into two groups, with the 10 northern tribes following kings who eventually ruled in a city of Samaria (1 Kings 12:25-30; 16:23-29; etc.). The rift between the two groups widened after many in the northern tribes were taken into exile in 722 BC and their territory recolonized with non-Israelites (2 Kings 17:1-6, 24). That situation resulted in intermarriages, leading "pure blood" Jews to view their Samaritan neighbors as spiritually and racially impure (Ezra 4:1-5; Nehemiah 4:1, 2).

Looking past historical differences, Philip followed the example of Jesus in outreach to the Samaritans (see John 4:1-42). Philip's message was confirmed with miraculous displays of power that included exorcisms and healings (Acts 8:6, 7). Through the power of Christ, the long-awaited messianic age had finally come even to Samaritans.

I. Simon's Salvation
(ACTS 8:9-13)

A. Sorcerer's Fame (vv. 9-11)

9. Now for some time a man named Simon had practiced sorcery in the city and amazed all the people of Samaria. He boasted that he was someone great,

Following a brief account of Philip's success, Luke (the author of Acts) reveals that the Samaritans are already accustomed to displays of supernatural power. A sorcerer *named Simon* has been active, amazing the people in that regard. Those today who are familiar with Las Vegas–style illusionists might assume that Simon is simply a sleight-of-hand charlatan. But Luke assumes (as certainly do the Samaritans as well) that Simon's power is real and of supernatural origin (compare Exodus 7:11, 22; 8:7).

HOW TO SAY IT

Gentiles	*Jen*-tiles.
Herod	*Hair*-ud.
Judea	Joo-*dee*-uh.
Judeans	Joo-*dee*-unz.
Messiah	Meh-*sigh*-uh.
messianic	mess-ee-*an*-ick.
Moses	*Mo*-zes or *Mo*-zez.
Nehemiah	*Nee*-huh-**my**-uh.
Samaria	Suh-*mare*-ee-uh.
Samaritans	Suh-*mare*-uh-tunz.
simony	*sy*-muh-nee.

Put another way, Simon is not a "magician" in the modern sense, but rather is a shaman who uses occult rituals to perform seemingly impossible tasks. The outcome of the story suggests that he uses these skills for profit; this is a widely recognized trade in the ancient world (compare Acts 16:16-19).

What Do You Think?

Is it ever a good idea to watch TV shows or movies that feature sorcery, witchcraft, etc.? What about reading fiction books by Christian authors who use descriptions of magic to teach Christian values? Explain.

Talking Points for Your Discussion
- Issues of cultural awareness or engagement
- Issues of susceptibility to temptation
- Issues of setting an example
- Other

10, 11. and all the people, both high and low, gave him their attention and exclaimed, "This man is rightly called the Great Power of God." They followed him because he had amazed them for a long time with his sorcery.

Luke now addresses the scope of Simon's influence. People of all social classes (*both high and low*) affirm his power and acknowledge a divine source. It is difficult to determine the precise value of Simon's title *the Great Power of God*. Since this takes place in Samaria, home to ancient Israelite tribes, *God* here may refer to the true God of Israel. If this is the case, the Samaritans perhaps have come to view Simon as a powerful prophet like Elijah, or perhaps even as a physical manifestation of God's power.

By the first century AD, however, Samaria has been colonized by Gentiles and is heavily influenced by paganism. Herod the Great had built an imperial temple in the province's capital city and had transformed Samaria into a Roman administrative center. If Luke is thinking primarily of the Gentile population, then Simon's title may simply stress the magnitude of his occult skill (*Great Power*) without suggesting specifically that the people think him to be empowered by the God of Israel.

In any case, the Samaritans' reaction to Simon and his power is more typical of paganism than of traditional Jewish faith since that reaction demonstrates admiration of an individual whose actions are condemned by the Law of Moses (Deuteronomy 18:9-13; contrast Acts 14:11-13; 28:1-6).

B. Evangelist's Impact (vv. 12, 13)

12. But when they believed Philip as he proclaimed the good news of the kingdom of God and the name of Jesus Christ, they were baptized, both men and women.

The effect of Philip's work is clear: impressed by his signs and heeding his message, many Samaritans accept his claims about Jesus. Their submission in baptism indicates their desire to be cleansed of sin. Throughout the book of Acts, water baptism is portrayed as the typical conclusion to episodes in which individuals come to faith in Christ (see Acts 2:41; 9:18; 10:47, 48; 19:5).

Here as elsewhere in the Bible, *the name of Jesus Christ* symbolizes his person and power, identifying Christ as the source of Philip's ability to work miracles. Philip likely pronounces Jesus' name in the context of healings and exorcisms, a practice that can easily lead people to compare and contrast him with Simon. Since any supernatural power Simon possesses is undoubtedly demonic in origin, we rightly doubt that he performs any exorcisms, given what Jesus says in Luke 11:17-20.

13. Simon himself believed and was baptized. And he followed Philip everywhere, astonished by the great signs and miracles he saw.

At first glance it seems that Simon's story will have a happy ending. Like the others, and apparently showing much humility, he accepts Christ and is baptized.

What Do You Think?

How do we help the less spiritually mature from becoming enamored with certain preachers and their methods rather than with Christ himself?

Talking Points for Your Discussion

- Regarding indicators that a problem exists
- Regarding various corrective approaches
- Regarding resource personnel who can help
- Other

II. Apostles' Actions
(ACTS 8:14-17)

A. Traveling to Samaria (v. 14)

14. When the apostles in Jerusalem heard that Samaria had accepted the word of God, they sent Peter and John to Samaria.

The stoning of Stephen touched off a persecution against Christians in Jerusalem, the result being that "all except the apostles were scattered throughout Judea and Samaria" (Acts 8:1). We naturally wonder why the apostles—*Peter and John* being two of that group—do not flee the city as well.

One proposal is that only Jewish Christians who are "the Hellenistic Jews" rather than "the Hebraic Jews" (see the distinction in Acts 6:1) are subject to persecution at this point. But the word *all* in Acts 8:1 works against this theory. Taking that fact into account, we might theorize that after a brief period of time the persecution ebbs to the point that some Christians feel it's safe to return to Jerusalem as long as they keep a low profile; seeing that happen, the apostles remain to help keep the believers unified. But this is just a theory; the text doesn't say.

B. Praying for Believers (vv. 15-17)

15, 16. When they arrived, they prayed for the new believers there that they might receive the Holy Spirit, because the Holy Spirit had not yet come on any of them; they had simply been baptized in the name of the Lord Jesus.

On their arrival, Peter and John realize that the new Samaritan believers have not yet received *the Holy Spirit*. Luke clearly is not referring to the indwelling of the Spirit that all Christians experience, since the Samaritans' baptisms *in the name of the Lord Jesus* matches the plea and promise "be baptized, every one of you, in the name of Jesus Christ for the forgiveness of your sins. And you will receive the gift of the Holy Spirit" in Acts 2:38.

But if not that, then what? Two theories are worthy of mention. One proposal is that Luke is referring to the forthcoming bestowal of the Holy Spirit by laying on of the apostles' hands (v. 17, next) in terms of imparting spiritual gifts for service or otherwise empowering believers to testify about Christ. Seen to be supporting this proposal are Acts 4:8, 31; 6:10; 7:54-56; 19:1-6; 20:23; Romans 1:11; etc.

The other proposal is that Luke is referring to a more dramatic manifestation of the Spirit's presence, such as experienced at Pentecost (Acts 2:1-4) and to be experienced again when Peter takes the gospel to Gentiles (10:44-46). Taken in such a light, the text before us would indicate that even though the Samaritans believe in Christ and have been baptized, they have not yet received any visible manifestation of or by the Spirit that would indicate God's approval of extending the gospel to non-Jews. This proposal is said to be supported by the prophesied spread of the gospel according to the stages established in Acts 1:8, and by what Simon sees and how he reacts in Acts 8:18-24 (below).

Under either alternative, a prayer of consecration on the part of Peter and John is called for.

17. Then Peter and John placed their hands on them, and they received the Holy Spirit.

To follow a prayer of consecration with a laying on of hands is also noted in Acts 6:5, 6; 13:3. The practice is doubtless based on Old Testament precedent, where laying on of hands is sometimes mentioned in the context of blessings and prayers of preparation for a specific task (see Genesis 48:14-16; Numbers 8:10, 11; 27:23).

The apostles do not possess any inherent ability to bestow the Holy Spirit—only God can do that, just as the choice to accept Samaritans into the church rests with him alone. Here he honors both the faith of the Samaritans and the prayer of the apostles by granting that bestowal.

What Do You Think?

What are some ways the presence of the Holy Spirit should be evident in Christians' lives?

Talking Points for Your Discussion

▪ In the lives of new Christians

▪ In the lives of spiritually mature Christians

❧ *EVIDENCE OF CONVERSION* ❧

There's an old story about a man who moved to a new community and started attending a church there. However, there was a problem: that church expected prospective members to tell impressive stories of their conversion experiences, but the man had no such to relate. Having been brought up in a Christian home and attending Sunday school from an early age, he had simply grown up in the faith and had never strayed from it.

So what should he do? Time after time, he watched as others described startling, even miraculous, conversion experiences, after the telling of which they were warmly accepted into church membership. Finally, he concocted a bogus story, told it, and was accepted into membership as well.

Then his conscience began working on him. After confessing his deceit, he was kicked out of the church. He observed dryly, "When I lied, they accepted me, but when I told the truth, they rejected me!" Today's lesson and lesson 7 describe conversions that were accompanied by supernatural manifestations. But many conversions in Acts are described without such signs (see lessons 11–13). Absent those, what outward evidence affirms your own identity to be genuinely *Christian*?

—C. R. B.

III. Simon's Sin

(ACTS 8:18-24)

A. Request (vv. 18, 19)

18, 19. When Simon saw that the Spirit was given at the laying on of the apostles' hands, he offered them money and said, "Give me also this ability so that everyone on whom I lay my hands may receive the Holy Spirit."

Simon has already seen "great signs and miracles" (Acts 8:13). The fact that he now sees something even more marvelous indicates that the bestowal of the Spirit is indeed accompanied by some kind of visible manifestation. This may be empowerment for the Samaritans to speak in other tongues (compare 2:4; 10:46; 19:6), although this is conjecture since the text doesn't say.

For Peter, John, and Philip, the point of what is happening is clear, but Simon reads things through the lens of his own experiences. To be able to perform displays of power, as Simon has done, is one thing; to be able to empower others to perform amazing displays is quite another!

For a person like Simon, skilled in all kinds of occult rituals that involve touching people in various ways, the act of empowering *at the laying on of the apostles' hands* must seem like one more magical technique he can obtain. How much will people be willing to pay if he can enable them, simply by prayer and touch, to perform miracles themselves?

B. Rebuke (vv. 20-23)

20. Peter answered: "May your money perish with you, because you thought you could buy the gift of God with money!

Peter's response indicates his awareness both of Simon's motives and the seriousness of what the man is attempting. Simon seems unaware that God's gifts, including salvation and all that the Spirit can bring to a person's life, are not for sale. They come to us as free expressions of God's grace, not at the whim of human beings. This being the case, Peter cannot sell to Simon the ability he seeks, simply because it isn't Peter's to sell. Bestowal of the Spirit is by God's decision alone.

Simon has doubtless accumulated substantial wealth during his career as a sorcerer, and he is in a position to pay well. Peter's strong response indicates that his motives are entirely opposite those of Simon.

> **What Do You Think?**
> How do we decide which religious errors call for a strong response rather than a gentle one, or even no response at all?
> *Talking Points for Your Discussion*
> - Considering the nature of the error
> - Considering the one voicing the error
> - Considering the context in which the error is expressed
> - Other

21. "You have no part or share in this ministry, because your heart is not right before God.

Peter's condemnation of Simon here can serve as a model for addressing situations of serious moral failure. Two main points are evident. First, Peter clearly notes the root of the problem: Simon's *heart is not right before God*. Simon does not desire

to help people, but rather seeks to enhance his own status. As is often the case, a wrong attitude is accompanied by an essential doctrinal problem: a failure to understand how God operates, as evident from Simon's belief that God's gifts are for sale. Such thinking calls for stern rebuke, not only to correct Simon but also to break his hold over the Samaritans who admire his magical skills (Acts 8:9-11, above).

❧ BUYING POWER? ❧

Some years ago, a certain wealthy man was providing significant financial support to a Christian college. He made sure that "the right people" knew this, and he parlayed his reputation into power and influence regarding the direction the school should take. After a disagreement one day with the administration, he demanded to speak at a meeting of the college's board of directors. There he said, "I am the single largest contributor to this institution, and that gives me the right to a say in how it is run."

If we think that simony is no longer an issue of the church, we should think again! The worldly philosophy that *money is power* still leaks over into the Lord's work. But the world's idea of power and God's idea of power are vastly different. It's vital that God's people understand that difference!

By the way, there was something that neither the wealthy donor nor the board members of that college knew: the wife of one of the school's administrators worked in the college's financial office, and she regularly returned her paychecks to the school. Her quiet, regular gifts totaled more than the proud donor's occasional large gifts! He wasn't the biggest donor after all. —C. R. B.

22, 23. "Repent of this wickedness and pray to the Lord in the hope that he may forgive you for having such a thought in your heart. For I see that you are full of bitterness and captive to sin."

Second, while Peter does not minimize the seriousness of Simon's sin, he does not close the door on him either. While verses 21 and 23 pull no punches, verse 22 offers Simon a way out of the situation: he can change his thinking (*repent*) and confess his sin to God; if he does so, God will forgive him. This point is critical to any attempt to rescue someone from the clutches of sin. Sin cannot be overlooked, but the goal of any rebuke of sin should be to lead the erring one to repentance.

C. Remorse (v. 24)

24. Then Simon answered, "Pray to the Lord for me so that nothing you have said may happen to me."

Perhaps surprisingly, Peter's rebuke seems successful. With Simon's motives now exposed, that man apparently realizes that Philip and the apostles are not merely stronger wizards than he, but rather are people driven by a desire to please God and to help others.

Challenged and perhaps inspired by Peter's example, Simon asks Peter to pray for him to be forgiven. While Simon's reaction does not match Peter's direction that Simon be the one to do the praying, it shows considerable improvement over Simon's earlier, selfish request (compare James 5:16).

Conclusion

A. The Two Simons

Visitors to the Vatican in Rome may be surprised to see an unusual painting that depicts a struggle between two men. One of the men seems to be levitating in the air while the other, standing on the ground in a crowd of people, points his hands toward Heaven. The painting reflects an early Christian legend that holds less hope for Simon the sorcerer than Acts 8 might allow.

According to the legend, Simon founded a heretical sect and moved to Rome to propagate his teachings by continuing to practice sorcery. Simon Peter, hearing of the sorcerer's growing influence,

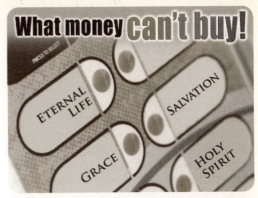

Visual for Lesson 5. *Start a discussion as you point to this visual and ask, "What are some other things money cannot buy?"*

went to Rome to challenge him yet again. Rather than repenting on this occasion, Simon attempted to prove his superior power by flying through the air. The apostle Simon Peter supposedly responded by calling on God to expose the man's wickedness, which resulted in Simon's falling from the sky and breaking his leg, an injury that led to his death.

Of course, there is little reason to believe this legend, and the true ending of Simon the sorcerer's story cannot be known. But that does not detract from seeing two very different approaches to the gifts and power of God in today's text: that of Simon the sorcerer, who sought to use God to serve his own purposes, and that of Simon Peter the apostle, who did the exact opposite.

The legacy of Simon Peter is that of a foundational figure who was instrumental not only in helping birth the church but also in protecting her purity. The selfishness of the other Simon, by contrast, has made his name a lasting symbol of greed and false motives. What's your legacy?

B. Prayer

Father, please help us keep our motives pure in our service to you. Let us never seek personal glory for any aspect of our faith as we keep one another accountable in working together for your kingdom. In Jesus' name, amen.

C. Thought to Remember

Bold witness includes bold confrontation.

INVOLVEMENT LEARNING

Enhance your lesson with NIV® Bible Student (from your curriculum supplier) and the reproducible activity page (at www.standardlesson.com or in the back of the NIV® Standard Lesson Commentary Deluxe Edition).

Into the Lesson

As learners arrive, have the question *What do you know about sorcery?* written on the board. Encourage several minutes of sharing, which may include personal experiences. This question will allow you to "take the temperature" of your class on this subject before beginning the lesson proper.

Option. Place in chairs copies of the "Of Sorcerers and Sorcery" activity from the reproducible page, which you can download, for learners to work on as they arrive. This will help set the biblical framework for the lesson.

Into the Word

Have four learners take turns reading the 16 verses of the lesson text audibly, changing readers with every verse. After they finish, say, "I am going to pull some objects out of my hat to see how you associate them with the text."

Begin pulling from a hat the following items: a large numeral *1*, a battery, two small calendars, a crown or tiara, a bride and groom wedding cake topper, a small stop sign, a big plastic ear, a pair of white gloves, play money, a tombstone, a small plastic heart, praying hands emblem, and toy handcuffs. *Option*: For any of the above items that you don't have access to, you can use pictures of them as found on the Internet.

As you reveal each item, ask, "How can you relate this to today's story of Simon the sorcerer?" Affirm any reasonable connection that learners offer; for suggestions that seem to be too much of a stretch, ask for clarification. Here are some associations you can offer if learners do not do so: *large numeral 1*—Simon was thought of as "someone great" (v. 9); *battery*—reflects power attributed to Simon (v. 10); *calendars*—the long time Simon had been impressing people (v. 11); *crown/tiara*—reflects the kingdom of God (v. 12a); *cake topper*—both men and women believed and were baptized (v. 12b); *stop sign*—signs that the apostle

impressed Simon (v. 13); *ear*—Christians in Jerusalem heard from a distance (v. 14); *white gloves*—the laying on of the apostles' hands (vv. 15-17); *money*—Simon's offer (v. 18); *tombstone*—Simon and his money perishing (v. 20); *heart*—Simon's heart was not right with God (v. 21); *praying hands*—Peter telling Simon to repent and pray and Simon asking Peter to pray for him (vv. 22, 24); *handcuffs*—the fact Simon was held captive by his sin (v. 23). *Option*: reveal items randomly rather than in verse order.

Wrap up the segment by asking, "Are there any objects that you think I should have used but did not? If so, what and why?"

Into Life

Distribute index cards on which the following are printed, one entry per card: singing ability, signing ability, speaking ability, servant's heart, skill at handling money, leadership ability, artistic ability, teaching ability, prayer warrior, evangelistic skill, organizational ability, information technology skills.

As you give the cards to individuals, pairs, or small groups (depending on the size of your class), say, "Wrong motives are still with us regarding what we wish we had or are working toward. How could the skills or abilities on your cards be used for human glory instead of God's glory? How about the other way around?" After discussion, close with prayer that each learner would have right motives in desiring and using God's gifts.

Option. Distribute copies of the "Of Motives and Ministry" activity from the reproducible page. Allow a few minutes at the end of class for quiet reflection for learners to complete as indicated.

Option. If your learning space has Internet access, show a YouTube® video segment of five minutes or less from Ben Alexander and his Exposing Satan's Power ministry. Some videos are quite lengthy; thus you will need to be selective.

SAUL BEGINS TO PREACH

DEVOTIONAL READING: Psalm 18:20-30
BACKGROUND SCRIPTURE: Acts 9:19b-31

ACTS 9:19B-31

19b Saul spent several days with the disciples in Damascus. 20 At once he began to preach in the synagogues that Jesus is the Son of God. 21 All those who heard him were astonished and asked, "Isn't he the man who raised havoc in Jerusalem among those who call on this name? And hasn't he come here to take them as prisoners to the chief priests?" 22 Yet Saul grew more and more powerful and baffled the Jews living in Damascus by proving that Jesus is the Messiah.

23 After many days had gone by, there was a conspiracy among the Jews to kill him, 24 but Saul learned of their plan. Day and night they kept close watch on the city gates in order to kill him. 25 But his followers took him by night and lowered him in a basket through an opening in the wall.

26 When he came to Jerusalem, he tried to join the disciples, but they were all afraid of him, not believing that he really was a disciple. 27 But Barnabas took him and brought him to the apostles. He told them how Saul on his journey had seen the Lord and that the Lord had spoken to him, and how in Damascus he had preached fearlessly in the name of Jesus. 28 So Saul stayed with them and moved about freely in Jerusalem, speaking boldly in the name of the Lord. 29 He talked and debated with the Hellenistic Jews, but they tried to kill him. 30 When the believers learned of this, they took him down to Caesarea and sent him off to Tarsus.

31 Then the church throughout Judea, Galilee and Samaria enjoyed a time of peace and was strengthened. Living in the fear of the Lord and encouraged by the Holy Spirit, it increased in numbers.

KEY VERSE

At once he began to preach in the synagogues that Jesus is the Son of God. —**Acts 9:20**

THE CHRISTIAN COMMUNITY COMES ALIVE

Unit 2: Giving Bold Testimony
LESSONS 5–8

LESSON AIMS

After participating in this lesson, each learner will be able to:

1. List the special challenges faced by the apostle Paul in the earliest days of his ministry as Saul.

2. Explain the role of Barnabas in the earliest days of Paul's ministry and why that role was important.

3. Role-play a conversation among early believers who were skeptical of Paul (Saul).

LESSON OUTLINE

Introduction
  A. The Leopard Has His Spots Changed
  B. Lesson Background
I. Preaching in Damascus (ACTS 9:19b-25)
  A. Success (vv. 19b-22)
    Saul, the Epileptic Mystic?
  B. Persecution (vv. 23, 24)
  C. Escape (v. 25)
II. Preaching in Jerusalem (ACTS 9:26-30)
  A. Success (vv. 26, 27)
    Encouragers Still Needed!
  B. Persecution (vv. 28, 29)
  C. Escape (v. 30)
III. The Church Flourishes (ACTS 9:31)
Conclusion
  A. Returning to the Scene of the Crime
  B. Prayer
  C. Thought to Remember

Introduction

A. The Leopard Has His Spots Changed

When we are suspicious that someone will behave as badly as always, we may predict it by citing the proverb, "A leopard can't change his spots." Many who are familiar with this saying are perhaps unaware of its source: the prophet Jeremiah. Frustrated by the depravity of his people and predicting their imminent judgment, Jeremiah said that they had become so wicked that it would be no more possible for them to change their preference for evil than for a leopard to change its spots. So they might as well get ready for punishment (Jeremiah 13:23).

Even so, God can change the spots that a leopard cannot! Likewise, God can change the heart of those who repent. This is one of the most distinct features of Christianity. God's grace is so magnificent and his love so powerful that even the most desperate sinner can turn to him and be forgiven. Put another way, the genius of the gospel lies in the foundational premise that even the most hardened sinner can be changed by God's power.

The premier example of this principle is the subject of our lesson today: the apostle Paul, initially known as Saul. (Since he does not become known as Paul until Acts 13:9, the name Saul will usually be used in our lesson.) His life was one of radical conversion; the skeptical reactions to this unfortunately illustrate also the fact that people are not as forgiving as God is.

The issue is not so much whether a leopard can change its spots as it is whether those spots can be changed—somehow, some way—by any outside intervention. When we don't believe that other people can be transformed, we make it difficult for God's grace to be effective in them. Fortunately for the world, God connected Saul with people who believed in him.

B. Lesson Background

Today's lesson explores the beginning of the missionary career of the apostle Paul. He is rightly regarded as the Lord's point man in the expansion of the gospel outside the fold of historic Judaism. As seen in previous lessons, the church at first focused its evangelistic efforts on Jerusalem and the surrounding area. The success of these efforts, combined with lingering hostility toward Jesus himself, led the Jewish religious authorities to oppose the church and its message (see Acts 4:1-3, 13-21; 5:17, 18, 40).

The situation became more oppressive, however, by an event that took place within four years of Jesus' death. While many Jewish Christians, including the apostles, regularly met and prayed at the temple (Acts 3:1; 5:12-14), others took the debate to synagogues that were frequented by Jews who had migrated to Jerusalem (6:9). The result was the martyrdom of Stephen (7:54-60). The Jewish authorities seemed concerned that the new teaching would get out of hand, so the high priest commissioned a zealous young Pharisee from Tarsus to take the lead in investigating the situation in Damascus, some 150 miles to the north of Jerusalem (9:1, 2; 26:12; compare 7:58; 8:1-3).

Luke (the author of the book of Acts) tells us that Saul "began to destroy the church. Going from house to house, he dragged off both men and women and put them in prison" (Acts 8:3). The perpetrator himself admits that he "put many of the Lord's people in prison, and when they were put to death, I cast my vote against them" (26:10; compare 22:4). Other than that, we don't know much about Saul's investigative and interrogation tactics (compare 22:19).

HOW TO SAY IT

Ananias	An-uh-*nye*-us.
Arabia	Uh-*ray*-bee-uh.
Aretas	*Air*-ih-tas.
Barnabas	*Bar*-nuh-bus.
Caesarea Maritima	Sess-uh-*ree*-uh Mar-uh-*tee*-muh.
Caesarea Philippi	Sess-uh-*ree*-uh Fih-*lip*-pie or *Fil*-ih-pie.
Damascenes	*Da*-muh-*scenes*.
Damascus	Duh-*mass*-kus.
Messiah	Meh-*sigh*-uh.
Pharisee	*Fair*-ih-see.
synagogue	*sin*-uh-gog.
Tarsus	*Tar*-sus.

As Christians fled Jerusalem, Saul apparently followed them. Reflecting on this time in his life years later, he described himself as having been unusually zealous in his desire to protect traditional Jewish beliefs, noting the violence of his efforts to suppress the new movement (Galatians 1:13, 14; Philippians 3:6; compare Acts 22:5, 19) and characterizing himself as the "worst" of sinners in light of the severity of his actions (1 Timothy 1:15). A careful review of information from Acts and the epistles suggests that his reign of terror lasted perhaps as long as a full year before his departure for Damascus. Everything changed, however, on a road outside that city one day.

Having learned of Christians in Damascus, Saul was on his way to find them when he had a remarkable encounter with Christ. While the apostle's letters do not elaborate the details of this experience, Acts includes three accounts of the incident: Acts 9:3-9; 22:6-11; and 26:12-18 (the latter two quote Saul/Paul himself). The accounts differ slightly in detail, but each stresses the common point that Jesus appeared personally to call Saul to be his witness to both Jews and, especially, Gentiles (9:15; 22:21; 26:20, 23). The year was about AD 34. Our text for today picks up three days after Saul's encounter with Christ and immediately after Saul was ministered to by a certain Ananias (9:10-19a; compare 22:12).

I. Preaching in Damascus
(ACTS 9:19b-25)
A. Success (vv. 19b-22)

19b, 20. Saul spent several days with the disciples in Damascus. At once he began to preach in the synagogues that Jesus is the Son of God.

The sudden and complete change in Saul's attitude toward Jesus and Christians is profound! Saul had left Jerusalem several days earlier with authorization from the high priest to arrest any Christians he found in the Damascus synagogues (Acts 9:1, 2; 22:5). Imagine the surprise of the synagogue leaders who allow Saul to address their gatherings, only to realize that he is preaching *for* Jesus rather than against him!

Visual for
Lessons 3 & 6

Point to this visual as you ask, "How does Saul's stand compare with that of Stephen in lesson 3?"

Luke says little at this point about the content of Saul's message. Later we learn that the messages included exhortations "that they should repent and turn to God and demonstrate their repentance by their deeds" (Acts 26:20), but we wonder how much Saul, being a brand-new Christian, really knows about Jesus at this early stage.

Clues elsewhere in the New Testament help us answer this. First, Saul has substantial experience interrogating Christians by this point (see the Lesson Background). These experiences have allowed him ample opportunity to learn the foundational facts of Jesus' life and ministry and the main arguments Christians use in defense of their faith.

Second, the extended account of one of the apostle's synagogue sermons in Acts 13:15-41 reveals that his message to Jews focuses less on the details of Jesus' life than it does on how that life fits within the bigger picture. Beginning with the promises to Abraham and David, the apostle rehearses prophecies that point to the coming of the Messiah and proclaims that Jesus' resurrection demonstrates him to be the one of whom the prophets had spoken. Being highly trained in Jewish customs and beliefs (Acts 22:3; Galatians 1:14; Philippians 3:4-6), Saul is already well-prepared to discuss the biblical prophecies that point to the risen one he has seen.

Third, the apostle himself notes that "the gospel I preached is not of human origin. I did not receive it from any man, nor was I taught it; rather, I received it by revelation from Jesus Christ" (Galatians 1:11, 12). Whether this revelation came to Saul all at once on the road to Damascus or piece by piece over a period of time—perhaps during his time in Arabia (1:17)—we cannot say.

❧ SAUL, THE EPILEPTIC MYSTIC? ❧

Mental health professionals have long been interested in the religious conversion experiences of their patients. Some of those professionals think many such experiences to be delusional; their articles in scholarly journals occasionally take that tack in analyzing such experiences among the mentally ill.

For example, one article looked at conclusions of a previous study regarding "schizophrenia-like psychoses of epilepsy" in which "mystical delusional experiences were 'remarkably common.'" The same piece made reference to a previous article titled "Was the Apostle Paul an Epileptic?"

Another study examined the conversions of 22 religious professionals who had received psychoanalytical treatment for mental disorders. The breakdown (pun unavoidable!) was that "Two were diagnosed as paranoid schizophrenia, 3 were suffering from psycho-neurotic depression, 7 were obsessive-compulsive reactions, and the remaining 10 had personality disorders." This could imply that most if not all religious conversion experiences are explainable as mental illness.

Festus apparently held that position regarding the man formerly known as Saul (Acts 26:24). But consider Saul's behavior both before and after his conversion experience. Did not his changed behavior indicate he had adopted correct thinking? And shouldn't ours as well? —C. R. B.

21. All those who heard him were astonished and asked, "Isn't he the man who raised havoc in Jerusalem among those who call on this name? And hasn't he come here to take them as prisoners to the chief priests?"

Hearing the content of Saul's message, the audiences are shocked at its source! How can a person who has done what Saul has done say what he is now saying? Perhaps the synagogue leaders assume at first that Saul is using a trick to endear himself to suspected Christians so that he can lure them out of hiding.

What Do You Think?
What stories of conversion inspire you most in your service for Christ? Why?

Talking Points for Your Discussion
- Biblical conversion accounts
- Modern conversion accounts of high-profile individuals
- Conversions in which you participated
- Others

22. Yet Saul grew more and more powerful and baffled the Jews living in Damascus by proving that Jesus is the Messiah.

The confusion of *the Jews living in Damascus* grows. Their initial surprise at Saul's message becomes an embarrassing realization that he is in fact identifying himself with those who acknowledge Jesus to be the promised Messiah. Synagogue leaders are no match for Saul in debating Scripture (compare Acts 17:1-4), and doubtless they do not know how to respond to his claims that he has seen the risen Christ personally.

B. Persecution (vv. 23, 24)

23. After many days had gone by, there was a conspiracy among the Jews to kill him,

As on later occasions, the local Jewish authorities eventually resort to violence in their attempts to defeat this opponent (compare Acts 13:50; 14:5, 19; 17:5; etc.; see further comments on 9:24, below). Luke's indefinite reference to this deadly plot being hatched *after many days* is supplemented by the apostle's remarks in Galatians 1:17, 18.

24. but Saul learned of their plan. Day and night they kept close watch on the city gates in order to kill him.

Luke's wording in and of itself might lead one to conclude that the Jewish authorities seek to deal with Saul all by themselves. But the apostle's comments on the situation point to a bolder strategy: "In Damascus the governor under King Aretas had the city of the Damascenes guarded in order to arrest me" (in 2 Corinthians 11:32). It is difficult to imagine that a pagan king like Aretas is prompted to act by some kind of religious conviction as he sides with the local Jews against Saul. But it is easy to imagine that the leading Jews of Damascus convince Aretas that Saul is a troublemaker who is stirring up rebellion (compare Luke 23:14; Acts 24:5).

The strategy of the Jews of Damascus and its failure (see below) become typical of Saul's later experience as an evangelist and church planter. On entering a new city, he usually will find a local synagogue in which to preach. But the synagogue rulers will become alarmed when Jews and converts to Judaism are swayed by the gospel message, so those rulers will first try to refute the apostle with argumentation. After those attempts fail, the local Jewish religious authorities will attempt to silence him by force (see 2 Corinthians 11:24, 25). Ironically, this tactic will have the effect of spreading the Christian message even farther, as the apostle moves on to city after city in search of new audiences.

What Do You Think?
How should we respond when hatred of the gospel presents itself today?

Talking Points for Your Discussion
- Regarding hatred directed toward the gospel message itself
- Regarding hatred directed toward a gospel messenger other than ourselves
- Regarding hatred directed toward us personally

C. Escape (v. 25)

25. But his followers took him by night and lowered him in a basket through an opening in the wall.

Providentially, some believers learn of the plot against Saul's life and help him leave the city. Adding a bit of detail is 2 Corinthians 11:33, which says the escape is "in a basket from a window in the wall." Certain private residences within ancient cities have a section of the city's wall as part of their own structure, and that may be the case here (compare Joshua 2:15). Since the guards at the gate are watching for him, Saul must use the cover of darkness to make good his escape.

II. Preaching in Jerusalem
(Acts 9:26-30)
A. Success (vv. 26, 27)

26. When he came to Jerusalem, he tried to join the disciples, but they were all afraid of him, not believing that he really was a disciple.

Galatians 1:17, 18 tells us that three years pass between Acts 9:19 and 9:26. Even so, the believers in Jerusalem have not forgotten Saul's earlier actions. The distrust is so profound that *all* are *afraid of him*. Whatever rumors they have heard about his conversion are disbelieved. Perhaps some think those stories to be a ruse—a ploy to win their confidence and gain access to their meetings.

27. But Barnabas took him and brought him to the apostles. He told them how Saul on his journey had seen the Lord and that the Lord had spoken to him, and how in Damascus he had preached fearlessly in the name of Jesus.

Barnabas first appears in Acts 4:36, 37 as an example of one who cares for the needs of others (see lesson 2). How and when he meets Saul is unknown, but Barnabas clearly lives up to his reputation on this occasion. The very fact that he is in a position to arrange a private meeting between Saul and *the apostles* shows not only his complete faith in Saul but also the respect and trust he has earned among the highest circles of leadership in the Jerusalem church.

Barnabas is perhaps one of the most important of the often overlooked heroes of the Bible and, indeed, of Western history in general. Since his initiative here lays the groundwork for Saul's missionary journeys (as Paul), how would this world

be different had Barnabas not been willing to vouch for his conversion?

❧ *Encouragers Still Needed!* ❧

In 2013, the University of Akron's graduation rate was only 40 percent for first-time, full-time students. So the school began a pilot program to assist "emergent students," which is an elegant way of describing those at risk of dropping out because of being unprepared for the rigors of college academics. The program involves hiring part-time staff members as "academic encouragers."

Humanity in general and Christianity in particular can use more encouragers! Barnabas is an example. We see this facet of his personality as he interceded on Saul's behalf with the suspicious disciples and again in Acts 15:36-39, where he refused to write off John Mark as a lost cause.

What it takes to be an encourager is a heart to help and a willingness to take a risk. Those traits come more naturally to some than to others, but everyone can be an encourager on some level. Are you growing in Christ in that regard? —C. R. B.

B. Persecution (vv. 28, 29)

28, 29. So Saul stayed with them and moved about freely in Jerusalem, speaking boldly in the name of the Lord. He talked and debated with the Hellenistic Jews, but they tried to kill him.

Saul's experiences in Jerusalem and Damascus are parallel. Now in the company of the leaders of the church and enjoying their endorsement, he continues his work of preaching (presumably in synagogues). The fact that he is opposed by Jews who have adopted the Greek language and customs (*the Hellenistic Jews*) may indicate that he preaches to them specifically. But the one who had persecuted Christians again finds himself targeted for death. We readily imagine that the authorities are only too eager to make an example of their once-zealous disciple turned traitor.

C. Escape (v. 30)

30. When the believers learned of this, they took him down to Caesarea and sent him off to Tarsus.

Luke refers here not to Caesarea Philippi (Matthew 16:13) but to Caesarea Maritima. This is the port city on the Mediterranean coastline that serves as a Roman administrative center and military headquarters. About 60 miles from Jerusalem, this city figures prominently in the narrative of Acts (10:1, 24; 11:11; 12:19; 18:22; 21:8; 23:33; etc.).

More than 300 miles due north of Caesarea Maritima across the sea is the city of Tarsus. It is Saul's hometown (Acts 9:11; 21:39; 22:3). As such, it is both familiar and distant enough to allow Saul some level of safety. Barnabas will travel there later in order to bring him to Antioch to work with the growing Christian movement for "a whole year" in that city (11:25, 26).

III. The Church Flourishes

(Acts 9:31)

31. Then the church throughout Judea, Galilee and Samaria enjoyed a time of peace and was strengthened. Living in the fear of the Lord and encouraged by the Holy Spirit, it increased in numbers.

This verse provides an accurate, if somewhat awkward (for Saul), assessment of the situation after Saul's departure. His persecutions had ravaged the church, and his return had initiated a period of suspicion. The situation was further aggravated when he began preaching in Jerusalem, thereby drawing the attention of the authorities.

His departure, by contrast, is connected with a period of spiritual and numerical growth. Several times the book of Acts notes that periods of turmoil are followed by prosperity as the result of successful resistance to persecution or resolution of intra-church conflict (4:32-37; 5:12-16, 42; 6:7; 12:24).

Conclusion

A. Returning to the Scene of the Crime

The depth of Saul's repentance—the extent to which this leopard had his spots changed—is indicated by a small detail in today's text that is easily overlooked. Acts 9:29 indicates that Saul, after returning to Jerusalem and being accepted by the church, began to preach to Greek-speaking Jews —those who probably had moved to Jerusalem from elsewhere in the Roman Empire. At one level, Saul's selection of them as his target audience only makes sense: as a native of Tarsus and himself fluent in Greek (Acts 21:37), he naturally may have felt drawn to Jews of similar background.

A closer look, however, suggests a deeper motive. Saul first appears in Acts at the stoning of Stephen, who was killed after he had preached to Jews from Greek-speaking areas (Acts 6:8-14). Stephen had worked among those from Cilicia (6:9), the Roman province in which Tarsus, Saul's hometown, was located. This fact can explain his own involvement in Stephen's death (8:1) and the urgency of his desire to stamp out what he saw as heresy (8:3).

If this is the case, then Acts 9:29 may be telling us that Saul not only changed his outlook on Christ but also continued Stephen's work among his (Saul's) fellow expatriates as he tried to undo his earlier damage. By returning to the scene of his earlier crime against Christ, Saul's conversion was truly complete.

B. Prayer

Lord, help us change what we need to change about ourselves and the grace to accept changes you have worked in others. In Jesus' name, amen.

C. Thought to Remember

God still changes people. Expect it!

INVOLVEMENT LEARNING

Enhance your lesson with NIV® Bible Student (from your curriculum supplier) and the reproducible activity page (at www.standardlesson.com or in the back of the NIV® Standard Lesson Commentary Deluxe Edition).

Into the Lesson

Put this coded message on display: *E PIRSUN CEN BI CHENGID BY THI PUWIR UF GUD!* Before anyone has a chance to decode the message, ask for a show of hands for those who believe this affirmation. As learners exhibit confusion, ask someone to decode the message. *Solution*: after each E, I, O, or U is replaced by the vowel preceding it in the alphabet, the affirmation is *A person can be changed by the power of God!* Note that this is the key truth regarding Saul in today's study.

Into the Word

Say that you want to talk about "the ABC's of Saul's change." Note that Acts 9:10-31 features a significant *A* and a significant *B* in Saul's change. Ask, "Can you find the *A* and the *B*?" Allow learners time to be confused, to look in the text, and to ponder. If they need a clue, say, "You will find these as proper names." This should result in someone identifying Ananias (vv. 10-18) and Barnabas (vv. 26-30). Then affirm, "The *C* stands for *Christians* in a more general sense, whom today's text calls *disciples* (vv. 19b, 25). Though change comes through the power of God, it is also fostered by the encouraging support of fellow believers."

Continue by noting that change involves overcoming barriers. Say, "As I read today's lesson text, look for barriers that Saul faced both in Damascus and in Jerusalem." Call for discoveries after reading the text. Barriers noted may include (1) the difficulty of Saul's convincing others that his change was genuine, (2) opposition and threats from former colleagues who had become enemies, (3) building new relationships with those who previously saw him as an enemy, and (4) developing a new viewpoint and reevaluating previous assumptions.

Ask, "How could the Christians of Damascus and of Jerusalem know that Saul was really changed?" Assign three people to role-play a possible scenario in a Christian community either in Damascus or Jerusalem. Assign the roles of (1) Ananias or Barnabas, (2) a skeptic, and (3) a believer in Saul's change. Direct the skeptic to begin the conversation with an expression of doubts. Let the three develop the arguments as others observe. Note at the end, "Change is confirmed by the observations of honest witnesses."

Pull the thoughts of this segment together by recapping that (1) though change comes by the power of God, it is also fostered by the encouraging support of other Christians; (2) change involves overcoming barriers; and (3) change is confirmed by the observations of honest witnesses. *Option*: If time allows, ask for examples of all three being present in other Bible characters who changed.

Option. Distribute copies of the "More Than an *S* and a *P*" activity from the reproducible page, which you can download, to be completed by pairs or small groups. This will allow a more thorough look at the changes in Saul's life and future.

Into Life

Give each learner a copy of the following personal evaluation exercise, which you have prepared on index cards or slips of paper. Use this heading: *"Therefore, if anyone is in Christ, the new creation has come: The old has gone, the new is here!" (2 Corinthians 5:17).* Include the following entries, leaving space for writing after each one: 1. I am helping new believers be accepted and grow. 2. I am identifying and overcoming barriers to acceptance. 3. I am looking for and accepting evidence that lives have been changed for Christ.

Say, "Give yourself a letter grade from *A* to *F* in each area. Also make a note of how you intend to improve." With either this activity or the alternative below, assure learners that this is for their personal use only; you will not collect them.

Alternative. Distribute copies of the "A Leopard and Its Spots" activity from the reproducible page. Allow a few minutes for completion.

PETER PREACHES TO GENTILES

DEVOTIONAL READING: Romans 8:31-39
BACKGROUND SCRIPTURE: Acts 10:1-44

ACTS 10:24-38

24 The following day he arrived in Caesarea. Cornelius was expecting them and had called together his relatives and close friends. 25 As Peter entered the house, Cornelius met him and fell at his feet in reverence. 26 But Peter made him get up. "Stand up," he said, "I am only a man myself."

27 While talking with him, Peter went inside and found a large gathering of people. 28 He said to them: "You are well aware that it is against our law for a Jew to associate with or visit a Gentile. But God has shown me that I should not call anyone impure or unclean. 29 So when I was sent for, I came without raising any objection. May I ask why you sent for me?"

30 Cornelius answered: "Three days ago I was in my house praying at this hour, at three in the afternoon. Suddenly a man in shining clothes stood before me 31 and said, 'Cornelius, God has heard your prayer and remembered your gifts to the poor. 32 Send to Joppa for Simon

who is called Peter. He is a guest in the home of Simon the tanner, who lives by the sea.' 33 So I sent for you immediately, and it was good of you to come. Now we are all here in the presence of God to listen to everything the Lord has commanded you to tell us."

34 Then Peter began to speak: "I now realize how true it is that God does not show favoritism 35 but accepts from every nation the one who fears him and does what is right. 36 You know the message God sent to the people of Israel, announcing the good news of peace through Jesus Christ, who is Lord of all. 37 You know what has happened throughout the province of Judea, beginning in Galilee after the baptism that John preached— 38 how God anointed Jesus of Nazareth with the Holy Spirit and power, and how he went around doing good and healing all who were under the power of the devil, because God was with him."

KEY VERSES

Then Peter began to speak: "I now realize how true it is that God does not show favoritism but accepts from every nation the one who fears him and does what is right." —**Acts 10:34, 35**

THE CHRISTIAN COMMUNITY COMES ALIVE

Unit 2: Giving Bold Testimony
LESSONS 5–8

LESSON AIMS

After participating in this lesson, each learner will be able to:

1. State why Peter was hesitant to share the gospel with Gentiles.

2. Explain why Peter changed his viewpoint regarding sharing the gospel with Gentiles.

3. Identify a cultural assumption that hinders the spread of the gospel and make a plan to overcome it in his or her life.

LESSON OUTLINE

Introduction
  A. Crossing the Line Together
  B. Lesson Background
 I. Following God's Instructions (ACTS 10:24-26)
  A. Expectation (vv. 24, 25)
  B. Correction (v. 26)
 II. Addressing the Gathering (ACTS 10:27-29)
  A. Facts (vv. 27, 28)
  B. Question (v. 29)
 III. Recounting the Vision (ACTS 10:30-33)
  A. What Cornelius Witnessed (vv. 30-32)
    "Who You Gonna Call?"
  B. What Cornelius Did (v. 33)
 IV. Perceiving the Truth (ACTS 10:34-38)
  A. Facts About God (vv. 34-36)
    The Scandal of Unfairness
  B. Facts About Christ (vv. 37, 38)
Conclusion
  A. Their Courage, and Ours
  B. Prayer
  C. Thought to Remember

Introduction

A. Crossing the Line Together

The number *42* became famous for its key role in the popular novel *A Hitchhiker's Guide to the Galaxy*. But sports fans associate that number with a real-world figure: Jackie Robinson (1919–1972). Wearing number *42* while playing for the Brooklyn Dodgers in 1947, Robinson became major-league baseball's very first rookie of the year. More significantly, he became the first African-American to play major league baseball in the modern era.

That fact brought with it racial slurs and physical abuse during Robinson's playing career. His success as a player spoke for itself, but his skill on the field never seemed to make him immune from racial hostility. One of his more famous sayings epitomizes his responses to these challenges: "I'm not concerned with your liking or disliking me; all I ask is that you respect me as a human being."

Robinson's memory now has that respect, and in 1997 the number *42* became the first player-number to be retired officially by an entire professional league—no major league baseball team allows any player to wear that number today. The exception is April 15 of each year, when *every* player walks onto the diamond wearing number *42*.

Robinson was not alone in breaking baseball's color barrier. Branch Rickey, general manager and part owner of the Dodgers, had been looking for prospects within the "Negro League" for several years, seeking a player who could both perform well on the field and handle the intense pressure that would come with the position. His determination to eliminate segregation in baseball gave Robinson his opportunity.

Lesson 5 highlighted the first-century church's crossing of a racial and cultural divide; today's lesson involves another such crossing as salvation through Jesus was extended to Gentiles in the historic meeting between Peter and Cornelius. The shock waves that resulted from that meeting have reverberated across the centuries—and still do.

B. Lesson Background

Today's passage is an excerpt from a longer story that extends from Acts 10:1 to 11:18. The length of this episode, about 6.2 percent of the book of Acts, reflects its significance as a major turning point in spiritual—even world—history.

Just before his ascension, Jesus declared that the apostles would be his witnesses "in Jerusalem, and in all Judea and Samaria, and to the ends of the earth" (Acts 1:8). The apostles didn't seem to comprehend this to mean extension of the gospel to Gentiles, given the surprise expressed in Acts 10:45; 11:18. As observant Jews, the apostles had been brought up to view Gentiles as unclean pagans, who might endanger the apostles' own religious and moral purity.

As such, the apostles probably interpreted Christ's words in Matthew 28:19, 20 and Acts 1:8 geographically rather than ethnically: surely Jesus meant that they were to preach to *Jews* who lived in all nations. A divine correction to this misunderstanding was needed!

That correction began with two visions that occurred about 21 hours apart: the first to a Roman centurion named Cornelius (Acts 10:1-6) and the second to the apostle Peter (10:9-16). The respective locations were the cities of Caesarea Maritima and Joppa, about 30 miles apart, on the Mediterranean coastline. Before his vision, Cornelius had developed a reputation of being "a righteous and God-fearing man, . . . respected by all the Jewish people" (10:22).

There is no indication, however, that Cornelius had fully converted to Judaism. Luke (the author of Acts) refers to individuals like Cornelius as "God-fearing" or "who worship God" (Acts 10:2; 13:16, 26) and/or being "devout" (10:2), in contrast with those who had converted to Judaism fully (2:11; 6:5; 13:43). Even so, God, recognizing the sincerity of Cornelius's faith, chose this man to be the starting point for extending the gospel to Gentiles. God's initiative began when he sent an angel to Cornelius to tell him to send for Peter (10:3-8).

At the time Peter received his own vision, he had "stayed in Joppa for some time" (Acts 9:43). Peter had been summoned there on behalf of a dead woman for whom he performed a resurrection (9:36-41). One day he became hungry while praying on a rooftop (10:9, 10), and that's when he experienced a strange vision of "a large sheet" being lowered from Heaven (10:11).

The sheet was filled with all kinds of unclean creatures, whose meat was not to be eaten according to Leviticus 11. Three times a voice from Heaven told Peter to "kill and eat" (Acts 10:13, 16); Peter insisted each time that he could not do so, stressing that he had "never eaten anything impure or unclean" (10:14). The voice responded each time, "Do not call anything impure that God has made clean" (10:15). Although Jesus had declared "all foods clean" (Mark 7:19), nobody at the time seemed to realize the significance of this pronouncement in setting aside the dietary laws. So Peter had continued to adhere to them.

Thus Peter was troubled by the experience. What could it mean? The answer came quickly as the delegation from Cornelius arrived while Peter was still pondering (Acts 10:17). Prompted by the Holy Spirit, Peter agreed to accompany them back to their master's house (10:19-23). The company of 10—Peter, "six brothers" (11:12; see next week's lesson), and the delegation of "three men" from Cornelius (10:19)—remained the night before setting out for Caesarea Maritima (10:23).

I. Following God's Instructions
(ACTS 10:24-26)
A. Expectation (vv. 24, 25)

24. The following day he arrived in Caesarea. Cornelius was expecting them and had called together his relatives and close friends.

Luke's reference to *the following day* is important in setting the context of the events to follow. The 60-mile round-trip from Caesarea Maritima to Joppa and back requires a few days, and that gives Cornelius time to call *together his relatives and close friends*—certainly Gentiles like Cornelius himself.

We easily imagine Cornelius to be stunned beyond belief to have learned from an angel that his prayers and alms have "come up as a memorial offering before God" (Acts 10:4). He has been told to summon Peter (10:5), but has not been told exactly why. Cornelius apparently has decided that whatever Peter has to say must be shared with others firsthand!

25. As Peter entered the house, Cornelius met him and fell at his feet in reverence.

The magnitude of Cornelius's expectation is evident by his response on seeing Peter. This response of obeisance reflects Cornelius's pagan upbringing. In the ancient world, religious figures are revered as shamans who can secure special favors from the gods, if they are not gods themselves (compare Acts 14:11-13). This expectation is doubtless enhanced by the fact that Cornelius has never met Peter, probably knowing of him only as the man mentioned in the vision.

B. Correction (v. 26)

26. But Peter made him get up. "Stand up," he said, "I am only a man myself."

Peter immediately corrects the well-intentioned Cornelius (compare Acts 14:14, 15; Revelation 19:10; 22:8, 9). Christ had modeled the humility his followers were to display (John 13:3-17), insisting that they not revel in holding power over others (Matthew 20:20-28; 23:8-12; Mark 10:35-45; Luke 22:24-27). Peter's comment is therefore in sharp contrast with the practice of the Roman military system, which honors the emperor as a god and attributes almost superhuman qualities to great generals. Peter does not aspire to, nor will he accept, such reverence.

II. Addressing the Gathering
(ACTS 10:27-29)

A. Facts (vv. 27, 28)

27, 28. While talking with him, Peter went inside and found a large gathering of people. He said to them: "You are well aware that it is against our law for a Jew to associate with or visit a Gentile. But God has shown me that I should not call anyone impure or unclean.

These two verses put a sharp point on the lesson that God wants Peter, and the readers of Acts, to learn from this incident. The centurion's family and friends seem to have no qualms about meeting with a Jew. But such a situation is normally unacceptable to devout Jews such as Peter. They view Gentiles as unclean people, contact with whom will transfer the uncleanness.

Following the custom of the day, Cornelius likely has planned a banquet in Peter's honor. But for a Jew to dine with Gentiles would be a serious moral failure (compare Acts 11:2, 3). Certainly, interactions with Gentiles had angered God in the past, as associating with pagans had led to intermarriages and idolatry (Deuteronomy 7:3, 4; 1 Kings 11:1-9; Ezra 9:1-10:4; Nehemiah 13:23-30). So we easily imagine Peter's discomfort as he crosses the threshold of the house. The apostle even reminds those gathered that Jewish law forbids him from associating with Gentiles in any way.

But verse 28 also reveals that the point of Peter's earlier vision has not been lost on him—at least not this time (contrast Galatians 2:11-13). He realizes that God was not instructing him literally to eat unclean animals, but rather was informing him not to avoid anyone when it comes to gospel outreach (Acts 10:15).

B. Question (v. 29)

29. "So when I was sent for, I came without raising any objection. May I ask why you sent for me?"

The delegation from Cornelius already has informed Peter of the purpose of their mission and of their master's unique experience (Acts 10:21, 22). The 30-mile trip from Joppa has allowed many hours for further discussion. But Peter wants to hear it all from Cornelius personally. So Peter asks Cornelius the reason for the meeting.

III. Recounting the Vision
(Acts 10:30-33)

A. What Cornelius Witnessed (vv. 30-32)

30, 31. Cornelius answered: "Three days ago I was in my house praying at this hour, at three in the afternoon. Suddenly a man in shining clothes stood before me and said, 'Cornelius, God has heard your prayer and remembered your gifts to the poor.

Cornelius commences to relate the context and content of his visionary experience (see Acts 10:2-4), beginning with what he was doing at the time. Luke is showing us that God has not selected Cornelius at random; this man is in many respects the ideal Gentile to approach with the gospel. He not only fears Israel's God (10:2, 22) but also observes key Jewish devotional activities: he fasts, as Jews do (compare Luke 18:12; Acts 13:2); he prays to God *at three in the afternoon,* the standard Jewish time of prayer (compare Acts 3:1); he provides *gifts to the poor,* a typical mark of Jewish piety (compare Matthew 6:2; Acts 10:2). Cornelius seems to be a better Jew than many Jews are (compare Luke 7:6-9)!

> **What Do You Think?**
> What attitudes and/or behaviors contribute to an effective prayer life? What can hinder it?
> *Talking Points for Your Discussion*
> - 1 Chronicles 5:20
> - 2 Chronicles 30:27
> - Lamentations 3:44
> - James 4:3
> - 1 Peter 3:7
> - Other

As God extends his grace to everyone, the facts of Cornelius's devoutness will pose problems for Jewish Christians who might question his salvation or standing before God. Were this man an idolater and blatant sinner, Jewish Christians could more easily doubt the validity of Peter's judgment and the reality of his vision. But since Cornelius is just as faithful as most Jews, though not a convert (see the Lesson Background), then why should he be excluded from God's kingdom merely on the basis of ethnicity, which no one can control?

⅍ *"WHO YOU GONNA CALL?"* ⅍

Three psychologists lose their research grant for the study of paranormal phenomena, so they start a business removing ghosts for anyone troubled by them. Eventually, a hotel manager hires the team to capture a ghost that is haunting the building, the first of hundreds of ghosts eventually found to be troubling New York City. Many plot twists later, the team ends up saving the city by sealing a portal to the spirit world.

The above is a thumbnail description of the 1984 movie *Ghostbusters.* Intended as a comedy, the movie also reflects a point on the time line of our culture's fascination with "the spirit world," an interest that has not abated in the three decades since the movie's release. Such interest is a reverse image of biblical spirituality: as the former grows in popularity, the latter is increasingly rejected.

The Bible allows (and encourages) only one method of contact with the heavenly realm, and that one method is prayer to God Almighty. That is the path that Cornelius chose, and God in turn honored that choice by responding in the way the text describes. The example of this Roman centurion still speaks to us today. When seeking truth, there is only one ultimate source, and it is to him we direct our requests.   —C. R. B.

32. "'Send to Joppa for Simon who is called Peter. He is a guest in the home of Simon the tanner, who lives by the sea.'

As Cornelius summarizes the vision, we detect a note of irony in the fact that Peter has been staying *in the home of Simon the tanner.* A tanner works with animal skins; thus Peter has been staying at a house that exposes him to carcasses that Jews know cause defilement (Leviticus 11).

Even so, Peter's reaction to his own vision (Acts 10:14) and opening statement to those gathered here (10:28) shows that he is conscientious. What Peter is hearing Cornelius say Peter will relay when called to explain his own actions (11:13, 14).

B. What Cornelius Did (v. 33)

33. "So I sent for you immediately, and it was good of you to come. Now we are all here in the presence of God to listen to everything the Lord has commanded you to tell us."

Both Cornelius and Peter have obeyed the messages in their respective instructions. Peter can scarcely ask for a more receptive audience, and doubtless he would be elated to hear the words *we are all here in the presence of God to listen to everything the Lord has commanded you to tell us* from the lips of any of his fellow Jews! Hearing them from a Gentile must be startling, to say the least.

IV. Perceiving the Truth
(ACTS 10:34-38)

A. Facts About God (vv. 34-36)

34. Then Peter began to speak: "I now realize how true it is that God does not show favoritism

Evaluating the sequence of events, Peter now realizes that his own vision, disturbing as it was, has been timed to coincide perfectly with the vision to Cornelius. He can draw no conclusion

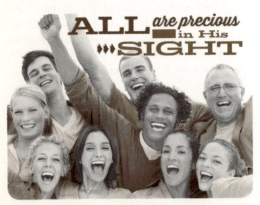

Visual for Lesson 7. *Point to this visual as you pose the discussion question that is associated with verse 34, top of the next column.*

other than *that God does not show favoritism*—that he intends the gospel for everyone.

What Do You Think?
What hinders Christians from viewing people as God does? How do we make progress here?
Talking Points for Your Discussion
- Hindrances at the level of the individual
- Hindrances at the level of one's regional culture
- Hindrances at the level of the congregation
- Other

35. "but accepts from every nation the one who fears him and does what is right.

Here, *nation* does not refer to political identity but to ethnic and religious background. People everywhere who fear God and who demonstrate that fear by obeying him are welcome. If this seems obvious to us after 2,000 years of Christian history, it is shocking to Peter and his first-century Jewish compatriots (compare Acts 10:45; 11:17, 18). We can imagine Peter's surprise to hear these words coming from his own mouth! The verses that follow mark the first time that an Israelite offers Gentiles the opportunity to become full members of the covenant community without requiring circumcision (compare Acts 15:1-21; Galatians 2:2-5).

36. "You know the message God sent to the people of Israel, announcing the good news of peace through Jesus Christ, who is Lord of all.

Acts 10:36-43 probably constitutes a concise summary of a sermon that may go on for hours, perhaps with many pauses to answer questions. Some see in these eight verses a highly condensed version of the four Gospels.

Despite the nature of his current audience, Peter does not hide the fact that Jesus' ministry focused almost exclusively on *the people of Israel*. But at the same time Peter notes that Jesus, who was the anticipated Messiah of the Jews, is now the *Lord of all* people. The *peace* Jesus preached refers primarily to peace between God and sinners. But in the context of Peter's sermon, it also includes peace between divided people groups (Gentiles and Jews) that is now possible through common faith in Christ.

The list of political scandals grows longer by the year. One of the most notorious examples of such corruption in U.S. history was the Teapot Dome scandal of the 1920s. The issue involved favoritism on the part of Secretary of the Interior Albert B. Fall in leasing oil reserves at Teapot Dome in the state of Wyoming. The fact that this was done without competitive bidding led to a congressional investigation.

The resulting trial revealed that Fall had received today's equivalent of more than $5 million for his role in the shady deal. Fall became the first member of a president's cabinet to be sent to prison.

People want life to be fair. Most are outraged when power is used to enrich oneself at the expense of others. Most are aghast at the idea of special treatment for certain classes of people—except perhaps when they belong to the favored class! The truth that God does not show favoritism dawned on Peter in the course of being sent to Cornelius, an encounter that taught the apostle that he had to change his perceptions and practices. History tells us that the church still has improvements to make in this regard! What will be your part in making that happen?

—C. R. B.

B. Facts About Christ (vv. 37, 38)

37, 38. "You know what has happened throughout the province of Judea, beginning in Galilee after the baptism that John preached —how God anointed Jesus of Nazareth with the Holy Spirit and power, and how he went around doing good and healing all who were under the power of the devil, because God was with him."

HOW TO SAY IT

Caesarea Maritima	Sess-uh-*ree*-uh Mar-uh-*tee*-muh.
centurion	sen-*ture*-ee-un.
Cornelius	Cor-*neel*-yus.
Gentiles	*Jen*-tiles.
Joppa	*Jop*-uh.
Mediterranean	*Med*-uh-tuh-*ray*-nee-un.
Samaria	Suh-*mare*-ee-uh.

The declaration *you know what has happened throughout the province of Judea* indicates prior knowledge on the part of the Gentile audience (compare Acts 26:26). But there is still more to learn, so Peter focuses on Jesus' healings and exorcisms, signs of supernatural power that marked Christ's divine authority.

As Peter speaks, the Holy Spirit comes upon the gathered Gentiles, empowering them to speak in tongues (Acts 10:44-46, not in today's text), just as the apostles had experienced at Pentecost (2:1-4; 11:15). If the Jewish Christians with Peter have any lingering objections regarding his openness to Gentiles, they can scarcely criticize him after seeing this clear sign of God's acceptance.

> **What Do You Think?**
> In what ways can (and should) you speak of Christ's work in your own life personally?
> *Talking Points for Your Discussion*
> - Regarding spiritual blessings
> - Regarding physical provisions
> - Regarding situational provisions
> - Other

Conclusion
A. Their Courage, and Ours

Crossing long-established barriers requires courage. Having been brought up in a culture that had taught people for centuries to avoid interacting with foreigners, Peter found his worldview changed within a period of 48 hours. A courageous spirit of openness to God's leading impelled the first-century church to do what was needed to extend its mission. Is that spirit ours as well?

B. Prayer

Lord, we all have biases that can be very hard to overcome. Help us to see beyond our own attitudes to the calling you have for us. Make us willing to do what we must to fulfill your mission. In the name of Jesus, who did just that, amen.

C. Thought to Remember

"Problems are the price you pay for progress."
—Branch Rickey (1881–1965)

INVOLVEMENT LEARNING

Enhance your lesson with NIV® Bible Student (from your curriculum supplier) and the reproducible activity page (at www.standardlesson.com or in the back of the NIV® Standard Lesson Commentary Deluxe Edition).

Into the Lesson

Before learners arrive, use masking tape to create a very noticeable line on the floor across the threshold of your classroom's doorway. Also post one or more signs prominently that read *Do not cross this line!* As learners arrive and hesitate, assure them, "Oh, it's OK. Come on in!"

When it's time to begin class, ask learners what they first thought when they saw the line and the command. After brief discussion, say, "Today's study is about crossing lines that people once thought should not be crossed. Let's see what God's Word has to teach us in that regard."

Into the Word

Distribute handouts of the lesson text, Acts 10:24-38, then form learners into four small groups or pairs. Give each group/pair one of these designations: *Brothers from Joppa* (from Acts 10:23b, just prior to today's text) / *Peter* / *Cornelius* / *The assembly in Cornelius's house*.

Say, "In about five minutes, I'm going to ask you what you saw, according to your group designation. Use those five minutes to read through the text and circle important elements in that regard." After the five minutes are up, ask, "What did you see?" as you cycle through the groups, asking for only one response before moving on to the next group. Some expected responses among many are "I/we saw a house full of Gentiles!" (*Brothers* or *Peter* groups); "I saw a Roman centurion fall at my feet!" (*Peter* group); "I/we saw a common Jewish man approaching!" (*Assembly* group); "I saw a man I thought I should bow before!" (*Cornelius* group).

Repeat cycling through the groups until there are no more responses. Use the commentary to discuss the significance of what groups saw.

Option. Distribute to study pairs copies of the "Cornelius or Peter?" activity from the reproducible page, which you can download. You can make this a contest to see which pair can finish fastest as they complete as indicated. Discuss especially anything learners find surprising.

Have a learner read aloud Mark 7:24-30 and another read John 12:20-26. Ask, "What could or should Peter have learned on these occasions about Jesus' attitude toward non-Jews, if anything?" Encourage free discussion. Note that a specific revelation was necessary for Peter to change his mind about the proper audience for the gospel. Follow up by asking, "What specific revelation from God in his Word has caused you to change your mind about a long-held belief?" This will allow easy transition to the Into Life segment.

Into Life

Say, "As Peter retold the events of Acts 10 to believers in Jerusalem later, he asked a profound rhetorical question in Acts 11:17: 'Who was I to think that I could stand in God's way?' What tends to stand in God's way when it comes to sharing the gospel today?" Jot responses on the board. Follow up by asking, "What steps can we take to eliminate those barriers to the gospel?" Encourage free discussion as you continue to enter responses on the board.

Alternative. Distribute copies of the "Personal Inventory on Bias" activity from the reproducible page. Allow a few minutes of quiet reflection at the end of class for completion. Assure your learners that you will not collect them when completed. Depending on the nature of your class, some may be willing to share their results, but don't put anyone on the spot to do so. Be prepared to share the results of your own inventory.

End class by peeling up the masking tape "barrier" from the floor. Tear it into smaller pieces and distribute them to class members as they depart. Challenge learners to affix their pieces of the "barrier" to the outside covers of their Bibles as a reminder of today's lesson in private devotional times in the week ahead.

PETER DEFENDS HIS ACTIONS

DEVOTIONAL READING: 1 Thessalonians 1:1-7
BACKGROUND SCRIPTURE: Acts 11:1-18

ACTS 11:1-18A

[1] The apostles and the believers throughout Judea heard that the Gentiles also had received the word of God. [2] So when Peter went up to Jerusalem, the circumcised believers criticized him [3] and said, "You went into the house of uncircumcised men and ate with them."

[4] Starting from the beginning, Peter told them the whole story: [5] "I was in the city of Joppa praying, and in a trance I saw a vision. I saw something like a large sheet being let down from heaven by its four corners, and it came down to where I was. [6] I looked into it and saw four-footed animals of the earth, wild beasts, reptiles and birds. [7] Then I heard a voice telling me, 'Get up, Peter. Kill and eat.'

[8] "I replied, 'Surely not, Lord! Nothing impure or unclean has ever entered my mouth.'

[9] "The voice spoke from heaven a second time, 'Do not call anything impure that God has made clean.' [10] This happened three times, and then it was all pulled up to heaven again.

[11] "Right then three men who had been sent to me from Caesarea stopped at the house where I was staying. [12] The Spirit told me to have no hesitation about going with them. These six brothers also went with me, and we entered the man's house. [13] He told us how he had seen an angel appear in his house and say, 'Send to Joppa for Simon who is called Peter. [14] He will bring you a message through which you and all your household will be saved.'

[15] "As I began to speak, the Holy Spirit came on them as he had come on us at the beginning. [16] Then I remembered what the Lord had said: 'John baptized with water, but you will be baptized with the Holy Spirit.' [17] So if God gave them the same gift he gave us who believed in the Lord Jesus Christ, who was I to think that I could stand in God's way?"

[18] When they heard this, they had no further objections and praised God.

KEY VERSE

"So if God gave them the same gift he gave us who believed in the Lord Jesus Christ, who was I to think that I could stand in God's way?" —**Acts 11:17**

THE CHRISTIAN COMMUNITY COMES ALIVE

Unit 2: Giving Bold Testimony
LESSONS 5–8

LESSON AIMS

After participating in this lesson, each learner will be able to:

1. Summarize Peter's explanation of his actions and why that explanation was important.

2. Outline the steps the church took to assess the validity of the mission to Gentiles.

3. Interview a missionary regarding how he or she assessed God's call to that particular mission field.

LESSON OUTLINE

Introduction
    A. The Original Rules of Order
    B. Lesson Background
  I. Objection to Gentiles (Acts 11:1-3)
    A. Report Heard (v. 1)
    B. Peter Criticized (vv. 2, 3)
      Power of the Grapevine
  II. Consideration of Evidence (Acts 11:4-17)
    A. Vision (vv. 4-10)
    B. Witnesses (vv. 11-14)
      The Message in Words
    C. Outcome (vv. 15-17)
  III. Acceptance of Gentiles (Acts 11:18a)
Conclusion
    A. I Will, but I Won't Like It
    B. Prayer
    C. Thought to Remember

Introduction

A. The Original Rules of Order

Those who have served on church boards, as trustees of civic organizations, etc., are doubtless aware of *Robert's Rules of Order*. These "rules" are widely recognized in North America as the standard guidelines for parliamentary procedure—that is, as the proper way to run a meeting.

The rules were first formulated in 1863 by Henry Robert, a colonel in the U.S. Army. Robert did not, however, develop these with a view to military application. The genesis of his rules arose from more mundane circumstances: he was asked to preside at a church meeting, and he realized that he did not know how to keep things moving in an orderly and fair manner (compare 1 Corinthians 14:40). Later he came to realize that meetings were conducted differently in various parts of the country, thus seeing the need for a universal standard.

Robert's first attempt at formulating such a standard was released as a book in 1876. Now in its eleventh (2011) edition, *Robert's Rules of Order* sets forth widely accepted principles such as addressing the chair of the meeting (rather than the entire gathering) and limiting the length of debate. All this emerged from Robert's desire to run a more orderly session of his church board.

Our passage today, while not formulated as "rules of order," reveals how the unexpected behavior of a church leader was handled in a meeting of the first-century church. As such, it may have something to say about how to go about addressing important issues in the church of the twenty-first century.

B. Lesson Background

As we saw in last week's lesson, the earliest Christians were Jews, who had been taught to remain separate from pagan Gentiles (Acts 10:28). Gentiles might be welcome to observe and learn at synagogue meetings, but they could not be accepted fully until they had rejected their ancestral gods and (for men) received circumcision, the sign of Abraham's covenant (Genesis 17:9-14; compare Exodus 12:48; Ezekiel 44:9). The first followers of Jesus, being Jews, seemed to have assumed that the same would be true in their new religious movement. They expected Jesus, the promised Messiah of the Old Testament, to return one day to judge the world and destroy the powers of evil (that is, the Gentiles). As a result, the earliest Christians did not attempt to evangelize Gentiles at first (Acts 11:19). God, however, had a different idea. As was often the case, he set his plan in motion in an unexpected way.

Acts 2:1–6:7 shows the church growing exponentially in Jerusalem and Judea as the gospel was proclaimed, being verified by miraculous signs. All this brought the church into conflict with the Jerusalem authorities, eventually leading to the first Christian martyrdom (6:8–7:60). A widespread persecution, led by Saul of Tarsus, immediately followed. Many Christians fled Jerusalem for safety (8:1-3; 11:19). As they traveled, they continued to spread the good news about Jesus.

The result was that Samaritans (lesson 5) and Gentiles (lesson 7) began to learn about Christ—a classic instance of God's bringing good from tragedy. The leaders of the first-century church needed new thinking—God's thinking—to see the inclusiveness that he intended for the gospel.

I. Objection to Gentiles
(Acts 11:1-3)
A. Report Heard (v. 1)
1. The apostles and the believers throughout Judea heard that the Gentiles also had received the word of God.

Rumors always seem to spread quickly, even in cultures without modern electronic commu-

HOW TO SAY IT

Abraham	*Ay*-bruh-ham.
Caesarea Maritima	Sess-uh-*ree*-uh Mar-uh-*tee*-muh.
Cornelius	Cor-*neel*-yus.
Gentiles	*Jen*-tiles.
Joppa	*Jop*-uh.
Judea	Joo-*dee*-uh.
Messiah	Meh-*sigh*-uh.
Pharisees	*Fair*-ih-seez.

nication. Luke (the author of Acts) refers here to the events of Acts 10 (last week's lesson), which tells the story of the conversion of a Roman military officer named Cornelius, along with family and friends, that resulted from a meeting with the apostle Peter.

How *the apostles and the believers* back in Jerusalem and Judea learn of this is not stated, but it seems very doubtful that Cornelius and his companions are the source. It is more likely that Jewish Christians in the vicinity of Caesarea Maritima (Acts 10:1), possibly concerned that Peter has stepped out of line, have sent or taken reports to Jerusalem regarding what has happened. The events that follow make clear that the believers back there do indeed know, but lack some vital details.

B. Peter Criticized (vv. 2, 3)
2. So when Peter went up to Jerusalem, the circumcised believers criticized him

The circumcised believers in Jerusalem are Jewish Christians. Of course, all male Jewish Christians had been circumcised prior to accepting Christ. So the phrase *the circumcised* seems to point to a Judaizing outlook that Paul will confront later (Acts 15:1-29; Galatians 2:11-14). This viewpoint insists that pagans need to acknowledge and adhere to the Law of Moses for acceptance of Christ to mean anything (Acts 15:5). Some of the circumcised believers will abandon this outlook (Acts 11:18, below) and some will not (Galatians 6:12, 13; Titus 1:10).

3. and said, "You went into the house of uncircumcised men and ate with them."

The accusation of the circumcision party is consistent with their religious outlook. Devout Jews, especially priests and Pharisees, view pagan Gentiles as unclean people, and therefore Jews can eat nothing at a Gentile's table (compare Acts 10:28).

These sensitivities should not be confused with modern concerns about unsanitary dining conditions. Ancient peoples are unaware of microorganisms or of the connection between bacteria and physical illness. From the Jewish point of view, eating or touching unclean things is a clear violation of the Law of Moses. Peter's act of eating with Cornelius, a Gentile, is considered to be a serious breach of law and a moral failure. Obviously, Peter's critics do not have the whole story!

❧ POWER OF THE GRAPEVINE ❧

I teach at a Christian university, and I am often amazed at the way communication happens (or doesn't happen) on our campus. When staff members want to advertise a particular event, they put up posters, make announcements in chapel, put messages in student mailboxes, etc. Even so, some students will claim ignorance of the event, that they were never told about it.

On the other hand, sometimes communication happens in informal ways ("through the grapevine") that defy understanding. Some years ago, budgetary considerations forced the administration to let three faculty members go. The faculty members affected were informed of this late on a Friday afternoon, months before the actual termination of their contracts. Other faculty members got wind of the fact that some of their colleagues were being let go, but they didn't know exactly who. Yet by Sunday evening students in the dorm not only knew of the dismissals, they also knew the identity of the three faculty members involved —even before the rest of the faculty did!

The proverbial grapevine is an amazing thing, but also a dangerous thing. Spreading partial information can do great harm, even if that partial information is completely true in and of itself. And too often *grapevine* equates to *gossip*, so we do well to know the difference. You can insert your own cautionary tale in that regard here!
—J. B. N.

II. Consideration of Evidence
(ACTS 11:4-17)
A. Vision (vv. 4-10)

4. Starting from the beginning, Peter told them the whole story:

This verse and the 13 that follow set forth the issues that Peter brings to the table in defense of his interactions with some Gentiles. This section summarizes Acts 10:9-48 while adding a bit more information, as we shall see.

5a. "I was in the city of Joppa praying, and in a trance I saw a vision.

There are two visions from God that are key elements to the story: one to Cornelius (Acts 10:3) and one to Peter (10:10). Peter begins his testimony by rehearsing the facts of his own vision (see 10:9-20). It occurred *in the city of Joppa*, where he had performed a resurrection (9:36-41). This miracle opened many hearts to receive the gospel (9:42), so "Peter stayed in Joppa for some time" (9:43). Joppa is an ancient seaport (compare 2 Chronicles 2:16; Jonah 1:3). Its modern name is Jaffa.

5b. "I saw something like a large sheet being let down from heaven by its four corners, and it came down to where I was.

Peter's description regarding *a large sheet . . . four corners* matches precisely the wording in Acts 10:11 in both English and Greek.

6, 7. "I looked into it and saw four-footed animals of the earth, wild beasts, reptiles and birds. Then I heard a voice telling me, 'Get up, Peter. Kill and eat.'

The sheet Peter affirms having seen contained many and varied creatures. In this light, the command for Peter to *kill and eat* presented a big problem for the apostle since the Law of Moses is specific regarding "clean" creatures that may serve as food for the Israelites and "unclean" creatures that may not. Although some *four-footed animals of the earth, wild beasts,* and *birds* are allowed per Leviticus 11, to eat any "creature that moves along the ground," such as *reptiles,* is expressly forbidden (11:41-43). Even eating "clean" animals is forbidden if the blood has not been drained (17:10-14).

Peter's Jewish audience is undoubtedly puzzled. Why would God tell a Jew to do something that violates the law that he (God) had given to Moses himself?

8. "I replied, 'Surely not, Lord! Nothing impure or unclean has ever entered my mouth.'

Peter assures his audience of Jewish Christians that he knows the rules. Demonstrating how incredible the content of this vision seems to his fellow Jews, Peter stresses that he had resisted the voice's command. While Jesus had been criticized for failing to observe Jewish purity customs and for allowing his disciples to ignore them (see Mark 7:1-5), he never specifically advised his followers to eat food that was forbidden by the Law of Moses (compare 7:19). Peter thus is on common ground with his audience: he shares their concerns —or at least he had shared them up to the point of the vision.

> **What Do You Think?**
> What convictions seem hardest for people to abandon or replace? Why is that?
> *Talking Points for Your Discussion*
> - Regarding convictions that were once valid but no longer are
> - Regarding convictions based in emotion
> - Other

9. "The voice spoke from heaven a second time, 'Do not call anything impure that God has made clean.'

Now Peter begins to discuss the meaning of the vision. The vision has not been left to Peter's own interpretation, and Acts 10:17 establishes that the meaning was very quick in coming. In this particular case, God has made it clear that he alone —not Peter, the Pharisees, etc.—has the authority to determine what is *clean* or *impure*.

10. "This happened three times, and then it was all pulled up to heaven again.

The vision follows the principle of "two or three witnesses" (Deuteronomy 19:15; Matthew 18:16; 2 Corinthians 13:1). The fact that God had rehearsed both the vision itself and its interpretation *three times* sets aside any doubt for Peter that the experience actually happened.

B. Witnesses (vv. 11-14)

11. "Right then three men who had been sent to me from Caesarea stopped at the house where I was staying.

Peter's puzzlement regarding the vision's application had been resolved quickly by the concurrent arrival of *three men . . . from Caesarea* by Cornelius (Acts 10:17). Peter had made the connection immediately: the vision had nothing to do with food, but rather was a lesson about associating with people thought to be unclean—Gentiles (10:28). God was calling for a change in outlook.

12. "The Spirit told me to have no hesitation about going with them. These six brothers also went with me, and we entered the man's house.

Acts 10:23b, 45 note that fellow believers had accompanied Peter on the trip from Joppa to Caesarea Maritima. But now an additional detail emerges: the fellow believers were six in number; that's triple the number of witnesses required by Deuteronomy 19:15. While *these six brothers* had not experienced Peter's vision personally, all had met Cornelius and those gathered in his house. The six witnessed the outcome of that meeting firsthand, and they can vouch for the accuracy of Peter's account. They are available to testify about what God has done.

> **What Do You Think?**
> How can we be sure that it is the Holy Spirit who is calling us to a task?
> *Talking Points for Your Discussion*
> - Role of Scripture
> - Role of motives
> - Role of subjectivity (feelings, etc.)
> - Role of objective verification
> - Other

13, 14. "He told us how he had seen an angel appear in his house and say, 'Send to Joppa for Simon who is called Peter. He will bring you a message through which you and all your household will be saved.'

Peter now rehearses the main points of Cornelius's testimony, thus adding yet another witness to the mix. Cornelius, a Roman centurion stationed in Judea, had come to accept the God of

Israel through his encounters with Jews (Acts 10:1, 2; see also lesson 7). Being pleased with Cornelius, God had sent an angel to instruct him to send *for Simon who is called Peter.*

The first account of Cornelius's vision does not specify why he was to do so (Acts 10:5, 6). Here the reason is given: Peter had the message that could tell Cornelius how to *be saved.* Jesus had declared that "salvation is from the Jews" (John 4:22), and Peter ended up being God's spokesman in that regard to this particular group of Gentiles.

❧ THE MESSAGE IN WORDS ❧

Today the simple preaching of the gospel is no longer considered "cool" by many. To communicate to the modern generation, we are encouraged to use charts, pictures, video clips, PowerPoint®, etc. I'm not opposed to all that. But I have concerns that sometimes the message is in danger of being overwhelmed by the medium as we lose sight of simple communication via the spoken word.

When Peter recounted the story that Cornelius told him, the apostle quoted the message of the angel given via the centurion that Peter would "bring you a message through which you and all your household will be saved." Simple, straightforward preaching was powerfully effective in conveying the message.

Francis of Assisi is quoted as saying, "Preach the gospel at all times—if necessary use words." That sounds cute, but there is no evidence that Francis actually said it. It sounds more like a modern exaltation of fuzzy do-goodism at the expense of verbal communication. The use of words will never be supplanted as the foundational medium by which people receive the gospel.   —J. B. N.

C. Outcome (vv. 15-17)

15. "As I began to speak, the Holy Spirit came on them as he had come on us at the beginning.

There has been a multitude of witnesses to this point: Peter himself, the threefold voice of God within Peter's vision, Cornelius (in absentia), and the six brothers who had accompanied Peter. Now Peter mentions yet another witness: *the Holy*

Spirit. As Peter was telling the story of Christ to Cornelius and the other Gentiles gathered at his house, the Spirit of God overcame them, and they began to speak in tongues, or foreign languages (Acts 10:44-46).

Bible students debate the significance of this event, especially in view of its timing: Did Cornelius receive the Spirit before he believed or after? Why was Cornelius baptized (Acts 10:48) when he already had received the Spirit? Did Cornelius receive the permanent, indwelling gift of the Spirit at the moment described here, or did he receive only the ability to speak in tongues?

These questions should not distract us from the clear and immediate significance for the discussion at hand: God was treating Gentiles (*them*) the same way that he had treated Jews (*us*). *The beginning* here clearly refers to Acts 2:1-4, when the Holy Spirit came upon the apostles at Pentecost, empowering them to speak in tongues. That miracle symbolized that the gospel would be proclaimed to people of all nations. But the apostles apparently did not realize at the time that God was thinking not only of Jews who lived in those countries, but also of their Gentile neighbors.

16. "Then I remembered what the Lord had said: 'John baptized with water, but you will be baptized with the Holy Spirit.'

Peter refers to Jesus' promise recorded in Acts 1:5. John the Baptist himself had said as much, telling his own disciples and his enemies that the one to follow him would baptize "with the Holy Spirit" (Mark 1:8; John 1:33).

> *What Do You Think?*
>   At what times are you most likely to recall a passage of Scripture? How has that recall aided you in those times?
> *Talking Points for Your Discussion*
> ▪ Positive situations (unexpected blessings, etc.)
> ▪ Negative situations (temptations, tragedies, etc.)

17. "So if God gave them the same gift he gave us who believed in the Lord Jesus Christ, who was I to think that I could stand in God's way?"

Peter closes with a statement that both defends his own actions and points to an inevitable conclusion: his critics can debate with him, but how can they debate with God? Since at least seven Jewish Christians (Peter plus his six companions) had seen Cornelius and other Gentiles speaking in tongues, it is impossible to deny that God has now set his seal on these people and, thereby, has shown approval of Peter's preaching to them. Since there can be no doubt of God's intentions, any further debate will be pointless at best and sinfully rebellious at worst.

III. Acceptance of Gentiles
(Acts 11:18a)

18a. When they heard this, they had no further objections and praised God.

This verse brings the episode to its proper end. The ardent Jewish Christians, initially opposed to Peter's actions, switch from criticism to praise after carefully reviewing the evidence.

What Do You Think?
What will be your role in helping your church welcome those of backgrounds or situations not shared or experienced by its members?
Talking Points for Your Discussion
- Via small or midsize groups
- Via modifications on how worship is expressed (music styles, etc.)
- Via increased sensitivity to physical limitations and impairments
- Other

Conclusion
A. I Will, but I Won't Like It

When my children were younger, they would often resist our instructions or try to avoid doing what we had told them to do (they still do so, incidentally). After realizing that resistance was futile, they would sometimes give in with an angry, "I'll do it, but I won't like it!" Talking with other parents, we've learned that our children weren't particularly original here—most do the same. And it's been even more interesting to realize, through

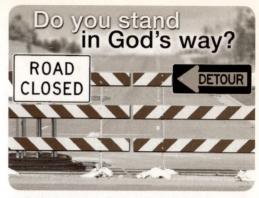

Visual for Lesson 8. *Start a discussion by pointing to this visual as you ask, "What can we do to avoid standing in God's way?"*

many experiences at work and at church, that adults often adopt the same kind of attitude: give in only when you have to, but don't change your viewpoint even then. Unfortunately, this attitude can spread to a point where it becomes crippling for an organization.

Today's passage reminds us that such a posture has no place in the church. As we've seen, Acts 11 tells the story of a highly controversial event that touched on significant doctrinal concerns, provoking strong emotions in the process. Yet the story doesn't end with one group holding a grudge and stomping off mad, or another group gloating over winning a close vote. Rather, the text shows the church carefully considering the evidence and, in the end, conceding to what God himself had done. If this is not the typical outcome of church disputes in our own experience, we can perhaps understand why the church in its very earliest days expanded rapidly, both in numbers and geographically, while divided churches today dwindle and die.

B. Prayer

Lord, keep our minds open to the truth and to your leading. Let us never put our personal preferences and biases before the will of your Son. It is in his name we pray; amen.

C. Thought to Remember

"To avoid criticism, do nothing, say nothing, and be nothing." —Elbert Hubbard (1856–1915)

INVOLVEMENT LEARNING

Enhance your lesson with NIV® Bible Student (from your curriculum supplier) and the reproducible activity page (at www.standardlesson.com or in the back of the NIV® Standard Lesson Commentary Deluxe Edition).

Into the Lesson

Bring pictures of a variety of foods. As you reveal each in turn, call for a show of hands regarding who would not eat it. Ask, "Is there any reason other than taste for your refusal?" Discuss.

Alternative. Distribute copies of the "Would You Eat It?" activity from the reproducible page, which you can download. Have learners work on this in pairs or groups of three.

After either of the above, make a transition by saying, "The vision recalled in today's study was not about food—though at first Peter thought it was. It was about people."

Into the Word

Use the lesson text as the basis for a fictitious courtroom setting per the script below. Recruit in advance three learners to play the parts of Peter, a prosecuting attorney (PA), and jury foreman. You will play the part of the judge; others are jurors.

ల ల ల

Judge: Members of the jury, today we decide the case of Peter of Galilee. He is accused of associating with Gentiles, who are unclean according to God's law. Prosecutor, you may begin.

PA: Peter, word has it that you associated with—even ate with—Gentiles. Is this true?

Peter: It began one day while I was praying . . .

PA (interrupting): Get on with it, Peter! How do you plead? Did you or did you not break the law by associating with Gentiles?

Peter: That question cannot be answered with a simple *yes* or *no*, since events convinced me that that law has been set aside.

PA (sputtering): What? Of all the . . .

Judge: Let's hear the whole story.

Peter: [Summarizes Acts 11:5-14.]

PA: But Peter, surely you know that claims of personal visions can't be verified, even though you had six fellow Israelites with you!

Peter: But my vision *was* verified—verified by the Holy Spirit himself with many witnesses present. [Summarizes Acts 11:15-17.]

PA (at a loss for words): No further questions.

Judge: Members of the jury, you have heard the testimony. What is your decision?

Foreman of the Jury: Your Honor, we the jury find the defendant guilty—guilty of obeying the Lord! And we want to do likewise.

ల ల ల

Use the following questions to lead a discussion about the text: 1. Why was it so shocking to Jewish believers for Peter to have entered the home of a Gentile? 2. What did the vision of the unclean animals have to do with Peter's decision to go to see Cornelius? 3. What parts of Peter's story helped convince those in Judea that salvation through Jesus was also available to the Gentiles? 4. Is there a group of people nearby to whom we might be reluctant to reach out with the message of salvation? If so, why?

Into Life

Conduct an interview with a Christian who has moved to a different cultural setting to communicate the gospel. An in-class interview with a missionary home on furlough or retired would be ideal. If not possible, you might be able to arrange for the interview to happen via Internet video (such as Skype™). Another possibility is an interview via e-mail correspondence, conducted ahead of time, that you print out and bring to class.

The key question in the interview should be, "How did you determine that God wanted you where you are?" Include related questions such as, "Whom have you seen accept the gospel when some thought it unlikely that he or she would do so?" Encourage whole-class discussion as appropriate.

Alternative. Distribute copies of the "The Universal Gospel" activity from the reproducible page for pairs or small groups to complete as indicated. Do advance research regarding areas greatest in need of the gospel (the "10/40 window," etc.) so you can correct misconceptions in the ensuing discussion.

GOD RESCUES PETER

DEVOTIONAL READING: Psalm 18:1-9
BACKGROUND SCRIPTURE: Acts 12:1-24

ACTS 12:1-11

¹ It was about this time that King Herod arrested some who belonged to the church, intending to persecute them. ² He had James, the brother of John, put to death with the sword. ³ When he saw that this met with approval among the Jews, he proceeded to seize Peter also. This happened during the Festival of Unleavened Bread. ⁴ After arresting him, he put him in prison, handing him over to be guarded by four squads of four soldiers each. Herod intended to bring him out for public trial after the Passover.

⁵ So Peter was kept in prison, but the church was earnestly praying to God for him.

⁶ The night before Herod was to bring him to trial, Peter was sleeping between two soldiers, bound with two chains, and sentries stood guard at the entrance. ⁷ Suddenly an angel of the Lord appeared and a light shone in the cell.

He struck Peter on the side and woke him up. "Quick, get up!" he said, and the chains fell off Peter's wrists.

⁸ Then the angel said to him, "Put on your clothes and sandals." And Peter did so. "Wrap your cloak around you and follow me," the angel told him. ⁹ Peter followed him out of the prison, but he had no idea that what the angel was doing was really happening; he thought he was seeing a vision. ¹⁰ They passed the first and second guards and came to the iron gate leading to the city. It opened for them by itself, and they went through it. When they had walked the length of one street, suddenly the angel left him.

¹¹ Then Peter came to himself and said, "Now I know without a doubt that the Lord has sent his angel and rescued me from Herod's clutches and from everything the Jewish people were hoping would happen."

KEY VERSE

So Peter was kept in prison, but the church was earnestly praying to God for him. —**Acts 12:5**

THE CHRISTIAN COMMUNITY COMES ALIVE

Unit 3: Spreading the Gospel
LESSONS 9–13

LESSON AIMS

After participating in this lesson, each learner will be able to:

1. Explain why Herod intended to execute Peter.

2. Relate the purpose and power of prayer to Peter's miraculous rescue.

3. Pray for one Christian whose life is endangered because of his or her witness for Christ.

LESSON OUTLINE

Introduction
  A. Praying for Miracles
  B. Lesson Background
I. Herod's Oppression (ACTS 12:1-5)
  A. James Killed (vv. 1, 2)
  B. Peter Imprisoned (vv. 3, 4)
  C. Church Praying (v. 5)
    Bring an Umbrella?
II. Peter's Rescue (ACTS 12:6-11)
  A. Heavily Guarded (v. 6)
  B. Dramatically Freed (vv. 7, 8)
  C. Divinely Escorted (vv. 9, 10)
    Our Part
  D. Eventually Aware (v. 11)
Conclusion
  A. Praying for Release
  B. Prayer
  C. Thought to Remember

Introduction

A. Praying for Miracles

Our modern world, scientific and rational as it is, leaves no place for the power of the miraculous that comes through prayer. Christians may tacitly adopt this viewpoint in failing to appeal to God for his supernatural intervention. We may see this in failing to pray that God would rescue believers who are in peril because of their witness for truth.

Today's lesson looks at a time when Peter, the leader of the apostles, was within hours of execution. How would the church be different today if his life had ended that early? We can't answer that question, but we know the result of his continued life: he ministered for another two decades, preaching and teaching the gospel of Christ.

B. Lesson Background

The book of Acts is "volume two" of the books written by Luke, a companion of Paul (Colossians 4:14; 2 Timothy 4:11). There is great value in comparing the stories of Acts with the accounts of the Gospel of Luke (the "former book," per Acts 1:1), for they were intended to be read together.

Acts 12 relates the last of the big stories in the book's presentation of events centered on and around the first-century Jerusalem church. Jerusalem is revisited in Acts 15 (next week's lesson) and in chapters 21–23, but those sections focus on the results of Paul's travels rather than on the Jerusalem church as such.

The actions in today's lesson occur within the time frame AD 41–44, more than a decade after the great Day of Pentecost. Two facts allow us to compute this. First, Acts 11:28 refers to a famine during the time of Emperor Claudius, who reigned AD 41–54. Second, Acts 12:23 notes the death of Herod Agrippa I, which occurred in AD 44.

By the time of today's lesson, the church had weathered the crises of the imprisonments of its apostles (Acts 4, 5) and the death of Stephen (chaps. 6 and 7). It had expanded the reach of the gospel to Samaria (chap. 8), to Damascus (chap. 9), to Gentiles in Caesarea Maritima (chap. 10), and to the regional capital of Antioch in Syria (chap. 11). We can surmise that the Jerusalem church was still the hub of Christian activities and the home of most of the apostles (see Acts 8:1b). By the time of today's lesson, the apostles were veteran leaders and experienced teachers.

Acts 12 presents a historical event in three parts. First is the arrest and execution of James, the brother of John. Second is the arrest and near-execution of Peter, leader of the apostles. Third is the cautionary conclusion of the death story of prideful Herod Agrippa I, grandson of the King Herod of Matthew 2:1 and Luke 1:5.

There are several Herods in the New Testament. The one in our lesson had been sent to Rome as a child and raised in the imperial court with young Claudius. Herod was a reckless youth, and apparently fled Rome to escape creditors. He returned to Judea and eventually gained control of much of the territory previously ruled by his grandfather.

I. Herod's Oppression
(Acts 12:1-5)
A. James Killed (vv. 1, 2)

1. It was about this time that King Herod arrested some who belonged to the church, intending to persecute them.

This time is the early AD 40s, and *King Herod* is Herod Agrippa I (see the Lesson Background). The prophesied famine of Acts 11:28 undoubtedly causes problems for him. Perhaps he seeks to divert the discontent of his Jewish subjects by persecuting the church. Although the church is populated with Jews, there is great animosity directed toward it by Jews loyal to synagogue and temple. The word *some* may indicate action against others besides James and Peter (next two verses).

What Do You Think?
Is it proper to label all forms of opposition to Christianity as *persecution*? Why, or why not?
Talking Points for Your Discussion
- Considering the source of the opposition
- Considering the nature of the opposition
- Considering the extent of the opposition
- Considering self-inflicted difficulties
- Other

---

2. He had James, the brother of John, put to death with the sword.

Herod's first choice of Christian victims is James, one of the famous "sons of thunder" (Mark 3:17); he is always mentioned either second or third in the lists of Jesus' disciples (Matthew 10:2-4; Mark 3:16-19; Luke 6:13-16; Acts 1:13). The fact that he is *the brother of John* keeps us from confusing him with the other men named James (compare Matthew 10:3; 13:55).

We are not told whether there is any sort of trial or merely an execution with the appearance of being legal. The following story of Peter gives the impression that James is arrested and held in jail before being executed. His death *with the sword* probably refers to beheading (compare Matthew 14:10), but there are other ways to kill someone with a sword. At any rate, death by sword is much quicker than crucifixion.

What Do You Think?
What purposes might God have in allowing some of his messengers to be killed but not others? How is your faith affected by this?
Talking Points for Your Discussion
- Jeremiah 26:20-24
- Acts 7:59–8:4
- Hebrews 11:36-40; 12:4
- Revelation 6:9-11
- Other

B. Peter Imprisoned (vv. 3, 4)

3. When he saw that this met with approval among the Jews, he proceeded to seize Peter also. This happened during the Festival of Unleavened Bread.

The death of the apostle James results in quick approval by the opponents of Christianity. Although this takes place more than a decade after the crucifixion of Jesus and the stoning of Stephen, some Jews in Jerusalem are still pleased by this sort of murderous behavior by government officials. Why?

One suggestion is that the Antioch church's practice of allowing Gentiles to become part of the church without circumcision has become a flash point for the Jews in Jerusalem (compare Acts

Visual for Lesson 9. As you discuss verse 5, point to this visual and ask learners about their experiences with church-wide prayer campaigns.

11:20, 26). Under this theory, a rivalry between synagogue and church has moved into deadly territory, with great animosity emanating from the rank and file members of Jerusalem synagogues (compare 6:9).

Another suggestion is that the phrase *the Jews* is a shorthand reference to the Jewish leaders in Jerusalem who are associated with the temple, not a general reference to Jewish people in the city. Herod Agrippa, ever the politician, is therefore seen to be more concerned with currying favor with those leaders than with the general populace.

Luke (the author of Acts) includes the detail that this happens during *the Festival of Unleavened Bread*, the weeklong celebration that includes Passover. This fact brings to mind the occasion of Jesus' death (see Luke 22:1). In so doing, it portends an ominous "history repeating itself" outcome for Peter.

4. After arresting him, he put him in prison, handing him over to be guarded by four squads of four soldiers each. Herod intended to bring him out for public trial after the Passover.

Any Roman ruler like Herod has a network of informers. So he is able to ascertain that Peter is the most important Christian leader in Jerusalem and also determine his whereabouts. Peter is therefore apprehended efficiently by Herod's agents and thrown into prison.

Herod assigns Peter's custody to a total of 16 soldiers to guard the apostle. This does not mean that all 16 guard Peter constantly. A likely configuration is that each squad serves a shift of three hours' duration. Two soldiers would be with Peter personally during each shift while two others guard the doors (v. 6, below). Herod seems to fear a rescue attempt.

The prison where Peter is held is nothing like the clean, brightly lighted halls and cells of "correctional facilities" that we have today. Prisons in Roman days are in the lowest basements of buildings, filthy dungeons with no windows, with dank, oppressive air.

Luke does not specify this prison's location, but a possibility is the Fortress Antonia. This is a military garrison complex built by Herod the Great, sited just outside the northwest corner of the temple walls. Incarceration here would mean that Peter is in a secure facility, guarded by specially assigned soldiers, within a military complex that is fortified and patrolled by guards.

Unlike Pilate's treatment of Jesus during the Passover week, Herod has the political shrewdness to wait until *after the Passover* to carry out the execution. The religious festivities will be over and not be a distraction for Herod's murderous actions. The execution of Peter will thus be the biggest show in town, a political triumph for Herod.

C. Church Praying (v. 5)

5. So Peter was kept in prison, but the church was earnestly praying to God for him.

Herod's decision to delay buys some time—time for the church to mount a prayer campaign on Peter's behalf. We don't know how long he is *kept in prison,* but it is likely no more than a few days. Peter's fellow believers do not see this as a time for despair, but as a time for action. The author characterizes them as *earnestly praying to God for him.*

At least some of those praying remember that Peter had been rescued miraculously from imprisonment some 10 years earlier (see Acts 5:17-20). That situation was not as dangerous, however, for it involved the temple police and death was less likely. This time the situation involves Roman soldiers and a maximum-security prison; Peter's execution seems all but certain, given what has just happened to James.

We may assume that the church folks are praying for Peter's spiritual strength so he can face this trial with boldness (see Acts 4:29). Everyone is aware that Peter had denied Jesus when Peter's life was at risk before (see Luke 22:54-62), a story that Peter himself has likely retold many times. Even if God chooses not to rescue Peter (as has been the case with James), those praying on his behalf surely ask God that Peter not shrink back and deny the Lord again.

❧ *Bring an Umbrella?* ❧

Some years ago I heard the story (probably one of those made-up "preacher stories") of an agricultural area that was experiencing severe drought. If the farmers didn't get a good rain soon, there would be no crops.

So the local church decided to hold a prayer meeting, specifically to pray for rain. Yet everyone was shocked when one young girl came to the prayer meeting with an umbrella! (Another version of the story has the preacher standing up and saying, "We've all gathered here to pray for rain, but how many of you brought your umbrellas?" No one had.)

Everyone knows that prayer and church go hand in hand, but often the relationship seems superficial. Of course we pray at church. We have an invocation, prayer for the communion, prayer for the offering, a benediction, and in the middle somewhere perhaps a pastoral prayer. But if we're not careful, all of this may end up being just a hollow routine that we follow every Sunday. Hollow routine certainly is not the impression we get of the Jerusalem church as the pray "earnestly" to God on behalf of Peter.

Even so, Acts 12:13-16 may reveal a bit of a "no umbrellas" state of mind as those praying end up being astonished at how things turned out. Whenever we're astonished at God's answer to prayer, we should remind ourselves that he is able to do abundantly more than we ask!

—J. B. N.

II. Peter's Rescue
(ACTS 12:6-11)
A. Heavily Guarded (v. 6)

6. The night before Herod was to bring him to trial, Peter was sleeping between two soldiers, bound with two chains, and sentries stood guard at the entrance.

Zero hour approaches, for the execution likely is to take place in the early morning. Peter is as secure as a prisoner can be, *between two soldiers, bound with two chains*. Perhaps the chains are fastened to the wall or to the soldiers. Furthermore, sentries are standing *guard at the entrance* of the place. The author relates these details to make sure the readers do not see what is about to happen to be the result of sloppy security.

B. Dramatically Freed (vv. 7, 8)

7. Suddenly an angel of the Lord appeared and a light shone in the cell. He struck Peter on the side and woke him up. "Quick, get up!" he said, and the chains fell off Peter's wrists.

What follows gives us the impression that both Peter and the guards are in a deep, supernaturally induced slumber, for none of them react to the appearance of *an angel of the Lord*. The dark dungeon is illuminated by the angel's presence, yet neither Peter nor the guards awaken.

The angel's physical nature—temporary though it is—is shown by his ability to whack *Peter on the side* to wake him. The angel also speaks audibly as he helps Peter get to his feet. The angel's words convey the need for urgency, wanting to get Peter to safety without delay. Chains prove to be no problem for the divinely sent messenger, of course (see Acts 16:26)!

HOW TO SAY IT

Antioch	*An*-tee-ock.
Antonia	An-*toe*-nee-uh or
	An-*toe*-nyuh.
Caesarea Maritima	Sess-uh-*ree*-uh
	Mar-uh-*tee*-muh.
Damascus	Duh-*mass*-kus.
Herod Agrippa	*Hair*-ud Uh-*grip*-puh.
Jerusalem	Juh-*roo*-suh-lem.
Syria	*Sear*-ee-uh.

8. Then the angel said to him, "Put on your clothes and sandals." And Peter did so. "Wrap your cloak around you and follow me," the angel told him.

The angel continues to give directions to Peter, who is probably still half-asleep. The angel does not explain the need to be fully clothed, but simply instructs Peter to follow him. This is a time to trust, and these directions must be both bewildering and comforting at the same time.

C. Divinely Escorted (vv. 9, 10)

9. Peter followed him out of the prison, but he had no idea that what the angel was doing was really happening; he thought he was seeing a vision.

The obedient Peter follows the angel, but thinks the experience to be unreal, part of *a vision*. The apostle already has experienced both a vision (Acts 10:9-16; 11:5-10, last week's lesson) and an actual angelic rescue from prison (5:19). But lingering sleepiness may be preventing him from comprehending that what is happening is "actual." This verse in particular gives the impression that the author is passing along the results of a firsthand conversation he later has with Peter.

10. They passed the first and second guards and came to the iron gate leading to the city.

WHY IS MY NIV DIFFERENT?

It opened for them by itself, and they went through it. When they had walked the length of one street, suddenly the angel left him.

The angel continues to lead Peter out of the prison, which probably is very dark and may seem to be a confusing maze. The duo passes two more levels of security, *the first and second* guard stations. The guards manning these probably are sleeping as well, a divinely induced sleep to guarantee Peter's safe escape (compare Matthew 28:4).

The iron gate leading to the city, the last barrier to freedom, is finally reached. There is no guard here, but this gate should be locked, openable only with the appropriate key. (Archaeologists have recovered many simple but effective keys used by the Romans.) The angel does not produce such a key; instead the gate opens by itself, allowing access to the city streets. Wasting no time and giving no further instructions, the angel merely departs—probably walking away quickly, but perhaps simply vanishing.

❧ *OUR PART* ❧

The miraculous elements in today's text naturally catch our eye. The appearance of the angel, the dropping of the chains from Peter' wrists, the guards who are kept from awakening, the iron gate opening by itself—all these are marvels, to be sure. But there is also the human, nonmiraculous side of the story that is also important.

Consider the angel's instructions for Peter to get dressed. One would think that if the angel had the power to drop the chains and open an iron gate without touching it, he also had the power to keep Peter warm during a midnight stroll through the city, right? Further, the angel could have bodily transported Peter out of the prison in the blink of an eye (compare Acts 8:39). But that's not what happened. Instead, Peter walked through the prison, out the gate, and down one block before the angel left him.

Sometimes we think that if the Lord is going to do something, then he can very well do it all by himself. When William Carey, who is considered to be the father of modern missions, was concerned about converting the pagans, a well-meaning church leader told him, "When God pleases to convert the pagans, he will do it without your aid." All too often we act the same way. We pray for our church to grow, then we wait for God to do it. We hope the church will find adults to lead the youth groups, but we never think about becoming involved. God wants to work through us (see Ezekiel 22:30). He is ready to do great things in our midst, if we will only get up and walk. —J. B. N.

What Do You Think?
What are some ways that God might use us as rescuers instead of sending an angel?
Talking Points for Your Discussion
- Regarding spiritual dangers and needs
- Regarding physical dangers and needs

D. Eventually Aware (v. 11)

11. Then Peter came to himself and said, "Now I know without a doubt that the Lord has sent his angel and rescued me from Herod's clutches and from everything the Jewish people were hoping would happen."

For Peter to come to himself means he eventually is awake fully. We wonder how long this takes at this point—five seconds? five minutes? The text doesn't say, but it is only now that Peter concludes that this is not a vision or dream. He actually has escaped death through divine intervention. He himself had nothing by which to release the chains, cause the guards to sleep, or open the gate. It is God who has orchestrated everything about the escape.

Peter understands the implications: he is safe *from Herod's clutches* and from the murderous desires of *the Jewish people*. He is still in a dangerous situation, but he is confident that God is protecting him. Very shortly he will take the precaution of leaving the area, keeping himself safe and not endangering those who might hide him (Acts 12:17).

The serious and confounding nature of this divine escape is shown in what happens at the prison the next day. The prison staff search the place thoroughly for Peter, thinking he must be hiding inside. They cannot believe he got past the secure iron gate. Herod, probably thinking that Peter's escape can have occurred only with insider assistance, orders that the guards involved be executed for their dereliction of duty (Acts 12:19; contrast Matthew 28:11-14).

What Do You Think?
What can we do to increase our trust in God?
Talking Points for Your Discussion
- Before needing a deliverance or rescue
- While needing a deliverance or rescue
- After receiving a deliverance or rescue

Conclusion

A. Praying for Release

How much time do you typically spend in daily prayer? a minute? five minutes? The believers in Jerusalem pulled an all-nighter as they prayed "earnestly" for Peter while he was in prison. Theirs were not quick prayers, sentence prayers, small prayers. If you read the rest of the story, you will find that many were praying when Peter showed up at the door of the house where they were gathered (Acts 12:12). They were praying so hard that they seem to have been annoyed at the interruption of Peter's knock on the door!

We may not know of someone who is in prison for his or her faith, but we do know of other ways that people are locked up in their lives. Do you need to be released from something that has put you in spiritual prison? Do you have a friend or relative who needs spiritual freedom? Are you willing to pray fervently for that person, just as the church prayed for Peter? God hears and answers prayers. God has the power to release us from all kinds of bondages.

B. Prayer

God, there is no prison so strong that you cannot free its captives. There is no situation so dire that you cannot provide relief. There is no life so ruined that you cannot restore it. May we trust you to save and protect us, to deliver us from evil and the valley of the shadow of death. We pray this in the name of our Savior, Jesus Christ; amen.

C. Thought to Remember

Miracles can result from prayer.

INVOLVEMENT LEARNING

Enhance your lesson with NIV® Bible Student (from your curriculum supplier) and the reproducible activity page (at www.standardlesson.com or in the back of the NIV® Standard Lesson Commentary Deluxe Edition).

Into the Lesson

Challenge learners to recall events from the life of Peter as recorded in the Gospels; jot responses on the board. (*Possible responses among others*: walked on water with Jesus, witnessed Jesus' transfiguration, cut off an ear of a servant of the high priest, denied Jesus three times.) After learners have exhausted their memories, say, "Today we will study another event in Peter's life. This event is found in Acts 12."

Into the Word

Randomly distribute the following statements, printed in large letters on strips of poster board. (Do not include the enumeration you see here.)

1–Herod arrested various Christians, including James. 2–Herod had James put to death. 3–Herod arrested Peter and put him in prison. 4–The church prayed diligently for Peter. 5–Peter was asleep between two guards. 6–An angel came to Peter in prison. 7–The angel hit Peter to wake him up. 8–The angel instructed Peter to get up and get dressed. 9–As Peter followed the angel, he thought he was having a vision. 10–The angel led Peter past the guards, out of prison, and out of the gate to the street. 11–The angel suddenly disappeared. 12–Peter knew God had sent the angel to rescue him from Herod and the Jewish people.

If your class has fewer than 12 learners, some will receive more than one statement. If you have more than 12 learners, create additional, different statements from the lesson text. Call on learners in alphabetical order by first names to read their strips aloud, come forward to affix them to the board (be sure to bring masking tape for them to do so) in proper chronological order in relation to other strips previously placed.

When all strips are placed, ask a volunteer to read Acts 12:1-11 aloud slowly. As the volunteer reads, have another learner check the statement order to make sure it is correct. Then say, "Now

that we've worked through the text, let's go back to the beginning: Why did God rescue Peter but allow James to be killed?" Learner responses will be speculative since the text doesn't say. But this question undoubtedly will be on the minds of many, so it's worthwhile to bring it out into the open for discussion.

To wrap up this part, mention that tradition holds that Peter was crucified in Rome. Thus Peter didn't escape martyrdom; his was only delayed (compare John 21:18).

Option. Distribute copies of the "Divine Rescue" activity from the reproducible page, which you can download. Use this as a closed Bible post-test to gauge learners' retention; have them score their own tests when finished.

Make a transition by saying, "While we may not understand why God allowed James to be killed and Peter to escape, we can follow the example of the church during this time of persecution: they prayed."

Into Life

Display a list of missionaries or nationals whom your church supports. Relate facts of persecution or potential persecution as you discuss the situation and ministry of each. If such a list cannot be created, present instead results of your own Internet research regarding Christians who are currently in prison for their faith.

Say, "To end our time together, we are going to follow the example of the first-century church and spend some time in prayer for fellow Christians who are experiencing persecution, or are in danger of persecution, for their faith." Use one of your two lists above as the basis of class prayers. Give everyone a chance to pray.

Option. Distribute copies of the "Earnest Prayer" activity from the reproducible page. Encourage learners to fill this out as indicated and keep it as a prayer reminder.

SAVED BY GRACE

DEVOTIONAL READING: Revelation 21:1-5
BACKGROUND SCRIPTURE: Acts 15:1-35

ACTS 15:1-12

¹ Certain people came down from Judea to Antioch and were teaching the believers: "Unless you are circumcised, according to the custom taught by Moses, you cannot be saved." ² This brought Paul and Barnabas into sharp dispute and debate with them. So Paul and Barnabas were appointed, along with some other believers, to go up to Jerusalem to see the apostles and elders about this question. ³ The church sent them on their way, and as they traveled through Phoenicia and Samaria, they told how the Gentiles had been converted. This news made all the believers very glad. ⁴ When they came to Jerusalem, they were welcomed by the church and the apostles and elders, to whom they reported everything God had done through them.

⁵ Then some of the believers who belonged to the party of the Pharisees stood up and said, "The Gentiles must be circumcised and required to keep the law of Moses."

⁶ The apostles and elders met to consider this question. ⁷ After much discussion, Peter got up and addressed them: "Brothers, you know that some time ago God made a choice among you that the Gentiles might hear from my lips the message of the gospel and believe. ⁸ God, who knows the heart, showed that he accepted them by giving the Holy Spirit to them, just as he did to us. ⁹ He did not discriminate between us and them, for he purified their hearts by faith. ¹⁰ Now then, why do you try to test God by putting on the necks of Gentiles a yoke that neither we nor our ancestors have been able to bear? ¹¹ No! We believe it is through the grace of our Lord Jesus that we are saved, just as they are."

¹² The whole assembly became silent as they listened to Barnabas and Paul telling about the signs and wonders God had done among the Gentiles through them.

KEY VERSES

God, who knows the heart, showed that he accepted them by giving the Holy Spirit to them, just as he did to us. He did not discriminate between us and them, for he purified their hearts by faith. —**Acts 15:8, 9**

The Christian Community Comes Alive

Unit 3: Spreading the Gospel
Lessons 9–13

Lesson Aims

After participating in this lesson, each learner will be able to:

1. State the issues that resulted in the Jerusalem Council.

2. Explain why keeping the Law of Moses is unnecessary for salvation.

3. Role-play a modern situation in which believers meet to resolve differences.

Lesson Outline

Introduction
  A. Turning Points in History
  B. Lesson Background
 I. Conflict Defined (Acts 15:1-3)
  A. Demand by Hardliners (v. 1)
  B. Challenge by Paul and Barnabas (v. 2a)
  C. Journey to Jerusalem (vv. 2b, 3)
    Conflict and Resolution
 II. Council Convened (Acts 15:4-6)
  A. Delegation Proclaims (v. 4)
  B. Pharisees Contend (v. 5)
  C. Council Considers (v. 6)
III. Judaizers Overruled (Acts 15:7-12)
  A. No Difference in People (vv. 7-9)
  B. Salvation Through Grace (vv. 10, 11)
  C. Proof by Miracles (v. 12)
    Mergers and Biases
Conclusion
  A. Lasting Impact of the Jerusalem Council
  B. Prayer
  C. Thought to Remember

Introduction

A. Turning Points in History

On January 1, 1863, President Abraham Lincoln issued the Emancipation Proclamation. It took many years for the proclamation to be enforceable, but it was a bold step nonetheless. It was a turning point in the history of the country, and because the U.S. was the largest slave-holding nation on earth at the time, it was a turning point in the history of the world.

Historians can point to many events that were turning points, events that forced changes in the course of history. Today's lesson is about one such: the decision of the Jerusalem Council, which set the course of church history. If the decision of that council had gone another way, it is likely that most of those studying this lesson would not be Christians today—and not studying this lesson!

B. Lesson Background

The Jerusalem Council was convened in about AD 51, some 20 years after the resurrection of Jesus and the birth of the church on the Day of Pentecost. Much had happened in those two decades, and a focus of the book of Acts is the expansion of Christianity beyond the Jewish people.

Many Gentiles were at least tolerated by Jews with whom they interacted. Some Gentiles, like the centurion of Luke 7:1-10, had established positive relationships with local synagogues. But while such Gentiles might be seen as friends of the synagogue, and even recognized as "devout" or "God-fearers" (see the Lesson Background of lesson 7), they were not considered to be "children of Abraham" by Jews (Acts 13:26; contrast Galatians 3:7).

There were also Gentiles who chose to embrace Judaism fully; these were *converts* (Acts 6:5; 13:43). Male converts were required to be circumcised—a painful, even dangerous surgical procedure in the days of rudimentary anesthetics and no antibiotics. They were also expected to keep the Law of Moses, not least of which were the dietary laws. Both of these were big issues for Gentiles. No adult male would easily agree to be circumcised, and pork was a favorite meat of the Greeks and Romans, preferred by some over beef or mutton (compare Deuteronomy 14:8).

The book of Acts records the advance of the church geographically, and this had implications for the nature of its membership. The first Christians—the 3,000 baptized on the Day of Pentecost—were all Jews and converts to Judaism (Acts 2:5, 11). The gospel then spread to Samaria (8:5). The Samaritans were not full-blood Jews and did not worship at the Jerusalem temple (John 4:20-22; also see the Lesson Background to lesson 5), but they practiced circumcision and kept the food laws, so that was not much of a stretch.

But then Peter was impelled by the Holy Spirit to preach to and baptize the Roman centurion Cornelius and other Gentiles (Acts 10:9–11:18, lesson 7). After Peter answered criticism in that regard, the church leaders in Jerusalem approved his actions (11:18, lesson 8). Further inclusion of Gentiles happened in Antioch, where the gospel was preached freely to Greeks (11:19-21). This in turn led to the first missionary journey of Paul and Barnabas (12:25–14:28), with many Gentiles coming to faith as a result (13:44-48; 14:1, 27). When Paul's preaching to Gentiles was criticized by the Jews of local synagogues, he made a deliberate move to turn his ministry focus to Gentiles (13:46; compare 18:6).

From the perspective of historical hindsight, the divinely directed events recorded in Acts were pushing Jewish Christians to accept Gentiles into full fellowship of the church. But this was not so evident at the time. Yet even as Peter, Paul, and others were winning Gentiles to Christ, a teaching that had to be addressed was that access to Christ and salvation was impossible without first going through the synagogue and the Law of Moses. The need to settle this issue resulted in a gathering of Christian leaders in Jerusalem, the famous Jerusalem Council of today's lesson.

I. Conflict Defined
(ACTS 15:1-3)
A. Demand by Hardliners (v. 1)

1. Certain people came down from Judea to Antioch and were teaching the believers: "Unless you are circumcised, according to the custom taught by Moses, you cannot be saved."

As is often the case in heated controversies, the complexities might be boiled down to a single issue. In this case, it is circumcision. Even so, the single issue of circumcision has profound implications for continued application of other tenets of the Law of Moses. The absolutist group of *certain people [who] came down from Judea* (and therefore from Jerusalem) *to Antioch* (Acts 14:26-28) demands circumcision for all Gentile men who are part of the church. This demand is reinforced with a threat: no circumcision, no salvation.

This group sees Christianity as a type of superlative Judaism. Yes, the Messiah had come. Yes, God had raised him from the dead. But other than that, nothing had changed much. Christians, like Jews, are to keep the law. After all, Jesus was the Jewish Messiah. If one wants to enjoy the blessings of being a Christian, then one needs to accept his Jewishness as one's own. It is possible for a Gentile to become a Christian, this group proposes, but the Gentile must first embrace the Law of Moses by converting to Judaism.

B. Challenge by Paul and Barnabas (v. 2a)

2a. This brought Paul and Barnabas into sharp dispute and debate with them.

Paul, never afraid to defend the gospel (compare Galatians 1:6-10), does not let this Judaizing viewpoint go unchallenged. He and Barnabas

HOW TO SAY IT

Cornelius	Cor-*neel*-yus.
Judas Barsabbas	*Joo*-dus *Bar*-sab-bus.
Judas Iscariot	*Joo*-dus Iss-*care*-ee-ut.
Matthias	Muh-*thigh*-us (*th* as in *thin*).
Phoenicia	Fuh-*nish*-uh.
Samaria	Suh-*mare*-ee-uh.
Samaritans	Suh-*mare*-uh-tunz.
Sidon	*Sigh*-dun.
Silas	*Sigh*-luss.
synagogue	*sin*-uh-gog.
Tyre	Tire.

see in Jesus a path that transcends their own Jewish heritage. They see that the salvation offered by Jesus is not just for Jews and converts to Judaism. As John the Baptist said, Jesus is "the Lamb of God, who takes away the sin of the world!" (John 1:29), not just the sins of the Jews. So Paul and Barnabas see no need for a Gentile to become a Jew before becoming a Christian.

What Do You Think?
How do we know when to take a firm stand on an issue and risk disunity in the process?
Talking Points for Your Discussion
- Matthew 17:24-27
- Acts 15:36-41
- Romans 16:17
- 1 Corinthians 15:1-4, 58; 16:13
- Titus 3:10
- Other

C. Journey to Jerusalem (vv. 2b, 3)

2b. So Paul and Barnabas were appointed, along with some other believers, to go up to Jerusalem to see the apostles and elders about this question.

The church in Antioch seems to be thriving by this time. But Jerusalem is home base for *the apostles and elders,* who are the most influential Christian leaders of the day. So the unidentified leaders in Antioch send there a delegation to get the definitive answer. Paul seems to be writing about this in Galatians 2, where he mentions Titus, who "was a Greek," as one of the travelers (2:3). This means that the delegation includes a respected Gentile from the Antioch church.

❧ CONFLICT AND RESOLUTION ❧

A minister accused the chairman of the elders of being divisive and prideful, and the minister asked the board to discipline him. Instead, they put the matter up for a church vote. All those on the ministerial staff said they would resign if the church voted to retain the chairman. The congregation did so, and the staff quit as promised.

There has been conflict within the church almost since day one as the apostles found their efforts challenged. We see this in today's text, and it certainly was not to be the last such squabble. One might think that conflict would be less likely in the church because it is ultimately God's endeavor. But given the fact of Satan's opposition, conflict within the church should not surprise us.

When conflict comes, the example of the apostles is instructive: they provided an appropriate forum for people to express their opinions. Debate was not suppressed. Then the leaders simply made a decision on the next course of action. There are times and circumstances to encourage discussion, but also times and circumstances that call for the opposite (see Titus 1:10, 11). May we be ready and willing to lead or be led in both cases.   —D. C. S.

3. The church sent them on their way, and as they traveled through Phoenicia and Samaria, they told how the Gentiles had been converted. This news made all the believers very glad.

The distance between Jerusalem and Antioch is about 300 miles, and the group apparently goes overland rather than taking any part of the trip by sea. In so doing, the travelers pass through the territory of Phoenicia, which features the well-known cities of Tyre and Sidon (compare Luke 6:17; 10:13). The route also takes them through Samaria, the quasi-Jewish region that received the gospel several years earlier (lesson 5).

The journey seems not to be taken at a fast pace, since Paul and the others have time to speak along the way of *how the Gentiles had been converted.* Mention of *all the believers* implies the existence of churches, and the message is received very positively in these. It is possible that Paul and Barnabas are collecting more attendees along the way for the meeting in Jerusalem.

What Do You Think?
What occasions in your life as a Christian have brought you the greatest joy? Why?
Talking Points for Your Discussion
- Regarding times of personal spiritual victory
- Regarding times of progress by your church
- Other

II. Council Convened
(ACTS 15:4-6)

A. Delegation Proclaims (v. 4)

4. When they came to Jerusalem, they were welcomed by the church and the apostles and elders, to whom they reported everything God had done through them.

The initial reception of the Antioch delegation is positive, as Paul and Barnabas are given a forum to state their position. They do not do this by doctrinal or scriptural argumentation (contrast Acts 28:23), but by telling their story. The focus is on results (compare 15:12). The direction of God in including the Gentiles into the church is undeniable. The presence of Titus may also be a powerful witness to the appropriateness of the Gentile ministry (see comment on 15:2b, above).

B. Pharisees Contend (v. 5)

5. Then some of the believers who belonged to the party of the Pharisees stood up and said, "The Gentiles must be circumcised and required to keep the law of Moses."

As persuasive as Paul's story is to us today, it does not win over the hardliners in the Jerusalem church. These are not Jewish laymen; they are Pharisees—Jewish Christians who retain their identity as defenders of *the law of Moses* in all its intricacies. There is a certain irony in this, because Paul is also a Pharisee (Acts 23:6; Philippians 3:5). These men demand a requirement to keep the law in general and circumcision in particular.

C. Council Considers (v. 6)

6. The apostles and elders met to consider this question.

The presentation by Paul and Barnabas and the rebuttal by the Pharisees are preliminary to the main session, for now *the apostles and elders* convene *to consider this question*. We know the identities of the apostles; they are the original 12 chosen by Jesus, minus Judas Iscariot, plus Matthias (Acts 1:26), minus James, brother of John (12:2), for a total of 11. Paul and Barnabas are called *apostles* in Acts 14:14, but since they are presenters they might not be included as deciders.

We are less certain who the elders are. The James who is the brother of Jesus eventually joins Peter in articulating the decision of the group (Acts 15:13). Some think him to be an additional apostle per Galatians 1:19, but that interpretation is not certain. So he might be seen as the leader of the elder group. It is likely that Judas Barsabbas and Silas are part of this eldership (Acts 15:22).

> **What Do You Think?**
> Is the procedure we see here a precedent for deciding doctrinal questions today? Why, or why not?
>
> *Talking Points for Your Discussion*
> - Considering the nature of the office of apostle
> - Considering the nature of the doctrine at issue
> - Considering the fallibility of human interpretation
> - Other

The leaders of the Jerusalem church have made organizational adjustments over the two decades since the Day of Pentecost. In Acts 6, a group was appointed to oversee food distribution, probably the beginning of deacons (although that term is not used there). Elders, a feature of the Jewish synagogues, are older and spiritually mature leaders recognized by the community. The continuation of this role can be seen by the appointment of elders by Paul and Barnabas in the churches they already have founded at this point (Acts 14:23).

III. Judaizers Overruled
(ACTS 15:7-12)

A. No Difference in People (vv. 7-9)

7. After much discussion, Peter got up and addressed them: "Brothers, you know that some time ago God made a choice among you that the Gentiles might hear from my lips the message of the gospel and believe.

We cannot imagine a person with greater moral authority than Simon Peter, whose name is first in all listings of the apostles (Matthew 10:2-4; Mark 3:16-19; Luke 6:13-16; Acts 1:13). This close associate of Jesus preached the first gospel sermon on Pentecost and is surely a dominant personality two decades later. For him to rise to voice his

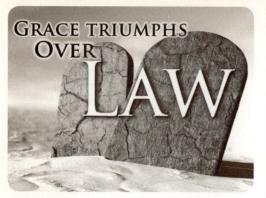

GRACE TRIUMPHS OVER LAW

Visual for Lesson 10. *Point to this visual as you ask, "What happens when we allow this statement to become a reality for us personally?"*

viewpoint is therefore not surprising. We might think of him as first among equals.

Peter begins by referring to his experience with Cornelius, a story told in Acts 10 and repeated in chapter 11 (see lessons 7 and 8). This is its third telling, a significant detail since authors emphasize the importance of events by retelling (compare Acts 9:1-19 with 22:1-21 and 26:9-23).

Peter lifts up two things from the Cornelius account. First, Peter understands this to have been God's choice, not his own. Indeed, Peter had been sent to Cornelius almost unwillingly. God was persistent, though, using visionary experiences and coincidences that can be understood only as divine in origin.

Second, Peter emphasizes that Cornelius and the other Gentiles came to faith after hearing the gospel preached by himself. Some details of this are given in Acts 10:34-48, with no word concerning circumcision or keeping the Law of Moses.

8, 9. "God, who knows the heart, showed that he accepted them by giving the Holy Spirit to them, just as he did to us. He did not discriminate between us and them, for he purified their hearts by faith.

The final confirmation came when the Holy Spirit descended on the believing Cornelius and his people in a manner reminiscent of the great outpouring of the Spirit on the Day of Pentecost (Acts 2:4; 10:44-46; 11:15). At that time, Peter interpreted what was happening as fulfillment of

prophecy (2:16-18). With Cornelius, Peter understands the phenomenon to have been God's sign that uncircumcised Gentiles are acceptable candidates for baptism and inclusion in the people of God (10:47, 48; 11:16, 17).

Peter repeats his conclusion from that day in Caesarea: that God does *not discriminate between us and them* (compare Acts 10:34, 35). True cleansing is not by ritual, but internally, in the heart. For both Jew and Gentile, this can be done only by God as a result of faith.

B. Salvation Through Grace (vv. 10, 11)

10. "Now then, why do you try to test God by putting on the necks of Gentiles a yoke that neither we nor our ancestors have been able to bear?

Peter then challenges the Pharisee position directly. He asks, in effect, why they are so eager to burden the Gentiles with a system that the Jews themselves have failed to maintain. Circumcision may be the flash point of the day, but it represents a larger issue: a way of relating to God that the Jews have not *been able to bear*. The Pharisees are an elitist group that takes pride in adherence to the law. But Jesus criticized the Pharisees for legalistic behavior that lacked hearts of love and faith (see Matthew 23:23-28).

11. "No! We believe it is through the grace of our Lord Jesus that we are saved, just as they are."

This is one of the most important verses not only in Acts but in the entire Bible. There is only one way of salvation, and that is the way of *grace*. We cannot earn salvation by keeping the law—eating the right foods, circumcising boys and men, etc. Salvation is through grace, the grace extended to all of humanity by *our Lord Jesus*. It works the same way for Jew and Gentile alike.

The letters of Paul, written after the Jerusalem Council, echo this view of salvation in many places (example: Ephesians 2:5-9). Paul bases his argument for salvation by grace through faith on key texts from the Jewish Scriptures, demonstrating there is only one way to be saved (example: Habakkuk 2:4 quoted in Romans 1:17; Galatians 3:11). Both Peter and Paul understand that the demand of these Pharisees has to be defeated, lest Christ's death be rendered valueless (see Galatians 2:21).

> **What Do You Think?**
> How can we better live the life of grace?
> *Talking Points for Your Discussion*
> - In our private thoughts
> - In interacting with fellow believers
> - In interacting with unbelievers
> - Other

C. Proof by Miracles (v. 12)

12. The whole assembly became silent as they listened to Barnabas and Paul telling about the signs and wonders God had done among the Gentiles through them.

Luke does not give the words of *Barnabas and Paul* at this point. He just offers the impression that they are allowed to speak at length for the whole assembly, telling what happened during their recent missionary journey. Their preaching was accompanied by *signs and wonders* that can be understood only as acts of God.

Everyone should come to the conclusion that God has approved of the message of salvation to the Gentiles (compare Hebrews 2:4). Once this hurdle is overcome, history tells us that the church grows like wildfire among the Gentiles.

> **What Do You Think?**
> In the church, when should we keep silent and allow others to have their say, and when should we insist on being heard? Why?
> *Talking Points for Your Discussion*
> - Regarding issues of doctrine
> - Regarding matters of expediency
> - Titus 1:10, 11
> - Other

Acts 15:13-35 tells us that the argument of Paul, Barnabas, and Peter wins the day. The decision of the council, voiced by James (v. 13), is that Gentiles do not have to be circumcised. The way of salvation does not go through Moses. Becoming a Christian does not require converting to Judaism first.

The 90-year-old church was "graying out" and dying. But the leaders were not ready to give up, so they approached another church in a nearby town and asked to merge with them as a satellite campus. After six months of prayer and respectful dialogue, the two churches voted unanimously to merge. Today the once-dying congregation has young families filling the pews, with most of those older, graying folks holding their babies.

The first-century church experienced a type of merger between established Jewish Christians and new Gentile believers. This was the great mystery that Paul wrote about in Ephesians 3—that God would exclude no one, regardless of ethnic heritage, who desired to be reconciled with him. Even so, the merger was not a smooth process. Peter, who explained his own support for Gentile inclusion, still had his own biases to overcome, biases that Paul confronted publicly (Galatians 2:11-21).

God continues to call us to purposeful inclusion. James, brother of Jesus, later warned against exercising favoritism in the church (James 2:1-12). When we sense an old prejudice rising to the surface, it's time to reflect and repent.   —D. C. S.

Conclusion

A. Lasting Impact of the Jerusalem Council

Ever since the Jerusalem Council in AD 51, there still have been those within the church who have tried to make salvation contingent on rules that must be kept. It cannot be that way. Just like Peter and Paul, we are saved through the grace of the Lord Jesus Christ. This truth we live!

B. Prayer

Holy God, source of grace and truth, you have loved us when we were unlovely. You have welcomed us when we were ungrateful. You have offered peace when we rebelled. May we come to you, offering our hearts as we receive your grace. We pray in the name of the one who died for us, Jesus our Lord, amen.

C. Thought to Remember

Embrace grace!

INVOLVEMENT LEARNING

Enhance your lesson with NIV® Bible Student (from your curriculum supplier) and the reproducible activity page (at www.standardlesson.com or in the back of the NIV® Standard Lesson Commentary Deluxe Edition).

Into the Lesson

Write this definition on the board: *a point at which a significant change occurs.* Ask who knows what concept this definition represents. After someone answers "turning point," say, "Nations, organizations, and individuals all experience turning points—sometimes for the better, sometimes for the worse. Today we will study one of the most significant turning points in the history of the church."

Into the Word

Ask four learners to take turns reading the text aloud, three verses each. Then set the context for the lesson by covering the information in the Lesson Background. Use a map (or sketch one on the board) to illustrate the progress of the gospel over the course of 20 years since the Day of Pentecost.

Next, draw on the board two columns headed *Major / Minor*, one heading each. Ask, "What are some problems or challenges the church underwent in those 20 years, up to the point of today's text?" As learners respond, write the problem or challenge mentioned down the left-hand side of the board and ask, "How big a problem was that —major or minor?" Issues learners may mention are persecutions by Jewish authorities (lessons 1, 3), deceivers within the church (lesson 2), and how to deal with former enemies (lesson 6).

Shift focus by writing the lesson title, "Saved by Grace," as the last entry on the left-hand side of the board. Ask, "How many think this was a major problem? How many think it was a minor problem?" Count the hands raised after each question and enter each tally in the appropriate column. Ask for justification in each case.

It is quite possible that no one will believe that this was a minor problem. For greater depth of discussion, secretly recruit in advance one of your sharper learners to take the "it was minor" position and be prepared to argue for it firmly if no one else does. This should challenge those of the "it was major" position to muster their best evidence in response. Wrap up with a good-natured confession regarding your prearranged plan.

Next, write this phrase on the board, from Acts 15:1b: "Unless you _____, according to . . . Moses, you cannot be saved." Ask, "What might the opponents of Paul and Barnabas have put in the blank other than the text's 'are circumcised' to make essentially the same point?" (*Potential responses*: eat kosher foods, observe the annual feasts, keep the Sabbath, tithe, etc.) Say, "What we see here is that the issue is bigger than circumcision in and of itself. The issue is salvation by law-keeping, which is an unendurable yoke according to verse 10 [*option*: display picture of a yoke] versus salvation by grace according to verse 11."

Alternative. In place of having the text read aloud to open this segment, use the "The Jerusalem Council" activity from the reproducible page, which you can download, to depict the text dramatically. You can recruit actors in advance so they can look over the script ahead of time, or simply distribute copies of the activity to be used at the appropriate time (memorization not expected).

Into Life

Ask volunteers to role-play how conflict could be resolved regarding one or both of these scenarios: (1) someone has left $100,000 to the church and strong opinions are forming regarding how to spend the money, and (2) church leaders are thinking it's time to go from one worship service to two on Sunday, but some oppose this change.

Wrap up by asking, "How was this different in substance from what we see in today's text?" Learners should see the critical distinction between issues of faith and doctrine (in the text) and issues of expediency (in the role plays). Brainstorm how disagreements in these two should be approached differently.

FROM DERBE TO PHILIPPI

DEVOTIONAL READING: Matthew 8:18-22
BACKGROUND SCRIPTURE: Acts 16:1-15

ACTS 16:1-5, 8-15

¹ Paul came to Derbe and then to Lystra, where a disciple named Timothy lived, whose mother was Jewish and a believer but whose father was a Greek. ² The believers at Lystra and Iconium spoke well of him. ³ Paul wanted to take him along on the journey, so he circumcised him because of the Jews who lived in that area, for they all knew that his father was a Greek. ⁴ As they traveled from town to town, they delivered the decisions reached by the apostles and elders in Jerusalem for the people to obey. ⁵ So the churches were strengthened in the faith and grew daily in numbers.

. . . .

⁸ So they passed by Mysia and went down to Troas. ⁹ During the night Paul had a vision of a man of Macedonia standing and begging him, "Come over to Macedonia and help us." ¹⁰ After Paul had seen the vision, we got ready at once to leave for Macedonia, concluding that God had called us to preach the gospel to them.

¹¹ From Troas we put out to sea and sailed straight for Samothrace, and the next day we went on to Neapolis. ¹² From there we traveled to Philippi, a Roman colony and the lead-ing city of that district of Macedonia. And we stayed there several days.

¹³ On the Sabbath we went outside the city gate to the river, where we expected to find a place of prayer. We sat down and began to speak to the women who had gathered there. ¹⁴ One of those listening was a woman from the city of Thyatira named Lydia, a dealer in pur-

ple cloth. She was a worshiper of God. The Lord opened her heart to respond to Paul's message. ¹⁵ When she and the members of her house-hold were baptized, she invited us to her home. "If you con-sider me a believer in the Lord," she said, "come and stay at my house." And she persuaded us.

KEY VERSE

After Paul had seen the vision, we got ready at once to leave for Macedonia, concluding that God had called us to preach the gospel to them. —**Acts 16:10**

THE CHRISTIAN COMMUNITY COMES ALIVE

Unit 3: Spreading the Gospel

LESSONS 9–13

LESSON AIMS

After participating in this lesson, each learner will be able to:

1. List the significant events in Paul's travels through Derbe, Lystra, Troas, and Philippi.

2. Compare and contrast Paul's decision to circumcise Timothy with Paul's opposite decision regarding Titus (Galatians 2:1-5).

3. Identify a short-term mission trip in which to participate and plan to do so.

LESSON OUTLINE

Introduction
  A. Macedonian Call
  B. Lesson Background
I. New Helper (ACTS 16:1-3)
  A. Timothy's Pedigree (vv. 1, 2)
  B. Paul's Decision (v. 3)
    Building Bridges
II. Renewed Strength (ACTS 16:4, 5)
  A. Message (v. 4)
  B. Growth (v. 5)
III. New Mission Field (ACTS 16:8-15)
  A. Vision in Troas (vv. 8, 9)
  B. Journey to Macedonia (vv. 10-12)
    Sensing God's Leading
  C. Woman of Faith (vv. 13-15)
Conclusion
  A. Worldwide Evangelism Today
  B. Prayer
  C. Thought to Remember

Introduction

A. Macedonian Call

Many churches use the words *Macedon* or *Macedonian* in naming classes, ministries, or publications. The phrase *Macedonian call* has come to designate a summons to be a missionary. The idea comes from Acts 16:9, which is part of today's text.

Some claim that the era of foreign missions is over. But mission opportunities definitely still exist, given that more than 4 billion people worldwide do not claim Christ as Savior! Although we should not expect to receive a call in a vision as the apostle Paul did, today's lesson will help us understand the heart and challenges of a person whose life was dedicated to cross-cultural evangelism.

B. Lesson Background

Paul's second missionary journey (Acts 16:1–18:22) was prefaced by his desire to revisit the churches he planted during his first journey (15:36). He needed to communicate the decision of the Jerusalem Council: Gentiles were not expected to keep the Jewish law in order to be part of the church (last week's lesson).

This expedition was almost blown apart at the outset when Paul and Barnabas had a tense disagreement over the advisability of taking along John Mark, a relative of Barnabas (Colossians 4:10). John Mark had abandoned them on the first journey (Acts 12:25; 13:5, 13), and Barnabas wanted to give him a second chance (15:37). But Paul would have none of it (15:38). Therefore, they divided into two teams: Barnabas and John Mark returned to the island of Cyprus (15:39), the home territory of Barnabas (4:36), while Paul recruited Silas, a respected church leader (15:22), to accompany him (15:40, 41). The year was about AD 52.

I. New Helper

(ACTS 16:1-3)

A. Timothy's Pedigree (vv. 1, 2)

1, 2. Paul came to Derbe and then to Lystra, where a disciple named Timothy lived, whose mother was Jewish and a believer but whose

father was a Greek. The believers at Lystra and Iconium spoke well of him.

Paul's route on his first missionary journey had taken him through Pisidian Antioch, Iconium, Lystra, and Derbe, in that order (Acts 13:3–14:21a). To return to Syrian Antioch, Paul had retraced his steps back through those cities (14:21b, 26). On this journey, however, the visitations begin in Derbe. Why the difference?

Tracing the two trips on a map reveals that the route of the first involved a sea voyage to Perga on the mainland via the island of Cyprus (Acts 13:13). There is no need for Paul to return to Cyprus to achieve the goal of Acts 15:36 since that island is the destination of Barnabas and John Mark (15:39). Instead of boarding a ship, Paul and Silas travel overland from Syrian Antioch to Derbe, perhaps stopping at Tarsus, Paul's hometown, on the way (compare 22:3). This is a more direct route.

The author's interest this time is not in the churches of Derbe and Lystra as much as it is in a person in Lystra: a certain *Timothy*. He is depicted in five ways.

HOW TO SAY IT

Aegean	Uh-*jee*-un.
Bithynia	Bih-*thin*-ee-uh.
Cyprus	*Sigh*-prus.
Derbe	*Der*-be.
Egnatian	Egg-*nay*-shun.
Galatia	Guh-*lay*-shuh.
Iconium	Eye-*ko*-nee-um.
Lystra	*Liss*-truh.
Macedon	*Ma*-seh-dawn (*a* as in *mad*).
Macedonia	Mass-eh-*doe*-nee-uh.
Mysia	*Mish*-ee-uh.
Neapolis	Nee-*ap*-o-lis.
Perga	*Per*-gah.
Philippi	Fih-*lip*-pie or *Fil*-ih-pie.
Phrygia	*Frij*-ee-uh.
Pisidian Antioch	Pih-*sid*-ee-un *An*-tee-ock.
Samothrace	Sam-o-*thrace*.
Syrian Antioch	*Sear*-ee-un *An*-tee-ock.
Timothy	*Tim*-o-thee (*th* as in *thin*).
Troas	*Tro*-az.

First, Timothy's name means "one who honors God." Names in the ancient world have transparent meaning, and this man is marked as coming from a religious family. Second, he is referred to as *a disciple*, meaning he believes in Jesus and is an active member of the church at Lystra.

Third, his mother is described as *Jewish* but also as *a believer*; so she too is a Christian and a part of the church. Fourth, the fact that Timothy's father is *a Greek* implies that he is neither a Christian nor a Jew. Fifth, Timothy is presented as having a positive reputation among the Christians in not only Lystra but also in Iconium, which is about 15 miles to the north-northeast.

We know from 2 Timothy 1:5 that Eunice and Lois are the names of Timothy's mother and grandmother, respectively. But there is no mention of a father in that text, perhaps because of death, divorce, or abandonment. Any of these possibilities may indicate that Timothy has grown up without the benefit of a father to oversee his spiritual development, leaving Eunice and Lois to be the ones to ensure he knows the Jewish Scriptures, our Old Testament (2 Timothy 3:15). Even so, the father must have been involved in Timothy's life at least in the beginning, otherwise Eunice would have had Timothy circumcised (next verse).

B. Paul's Decision (v. 3)

3. Paul wanted to take him along on the journey, so he circumcised him because of the Jews who lived in that area, for they all knew that his father was a Greek.

We do not know how old Timothy is, but perhaps he is in his late teens (1 Timothy 4:12). Paul wants to take him along, and this is apparently agreeable to both Timothy and his mother. But there is one item of unfinished business: Timothy's circumcision. At first, this may seem ironic, even inconsistent, given Paul's recent struggle against requiring circumcision (Acts 15, last week's lesson). Why does he take out his knife a few months later to circumcise a fellow believer?

We are told that this is *because of the Jews who lived in that area, for they all knew that his father was a Greek*. Paul's strategy is still to seek out the synagogue in any new city he visits and begin his evangelistic work among Jews (see Acts 17:1, 10; 18:4). It is one thing to abide by the edict of the Jerusalem Council that Gentiles do not need circumcision; it is another thing to tell Jews that circumcision is optional. This has nothing to do with Timothy's standing as a Christian (he is already recognized as "a disciple" in Acts 16:1). It has to do, rather, with his Jewish identity. Paul simply does not want the distraction of controversy over an uncircumcised Jewish companion.

What Do You Think?

What are some concessions or accommodations that we might need to make in order to minimize distractions to the gospel message?

Talking Points for Your Discussion
- Within the local church as a whole
- In our individual lives
- In our patterns of family life
- Other

In performing the circumcision, Paul acts as Timothy's proper Jewish father caring for his son in a traditional and honorable way. The bond between these two becomes so strong that Paul later refers to Timothy as his "true son in the faith" (1 Timothy 1:2). By contrast, Paul adamantly refused to have Titus, a Greek, circumcised (Galatians 2:3). This distinction is entirely consistent with Paul's presentation at the Jerusalem Council and the council's decision (Acts 15).

❧ *BUILDING BRIDGES* ❧

Jack and Betty have been working with a tribe in Papua New Guinea for over 12 years on translating the New Testament. The couple insists on involving tribal members so that they will have a sense of ownership in the project. Tribal involvement helps Jack and Betty maintain awareness of cultural sensitivities, a vital factor in their ministry success.

Paul recognized the profound danger of the pressure for new Gentile believers to be circumcised, and he opposed that pressure successfully (last week's lesson). But Timothy's case was different: it was wise for that young Jewish man to be circumcised in order to avoid being a distraction to reaching fellow Jews with the gospel. Jesus had no problem causing offense when a stand for truth demanded it (example: Matthew 15:1-14). But he also exercised sensitivity when he agreed to pay the temple tribute, even though he was exempt, "so that we may not cause offense" (Matthew 17:24-27).

Neither Jesus nor Paul ever compromised on the essentials of the faith. But they also took identical paths when it came to conceding on the smaller issues of cultural sensitivities. Are we as sensitive as we should be to the cultural expectations that new Christians or potential new Christians bring with them? —D. C. S.

II. Renewed Strength
(ACTS 16:4, 5)
A. Message (v. 4)

4. As they traveled from town to town, they delivered the decisions reached by the apostles and elders in Jerusalem for the people to obey.

The traveling band now includes Paul, Silas, and Timothy, a dynamic threesome. Without specifics, Luke (the author of this narrative) tells us that the team continues to visit the cities where Paul has already planted churches, a main purpose being to communicate *the decisions* of the Jerusalem Council, which are noted in Acts 15:23-29.

B. Growth (v. 5)

5. So the churches were strengthened in the faith and grew daily in numbers.

Those decisions are good news! They remove any thought—at least for the time being (compare Galatians 3:1-12)—that the way to Christ and salvation goes through the synagogue. The result is spiritual and numeric growth.

What Do You Think?

What barriers limit our church's spiritual and numeric growth? What can we do about these?

Talking Points for Your Discussion
- Regarding "out front" ministries
- Regarding "behind the scenes" ministries
- Regarding collaboration with other churches
- Other

III. New Mission Field
(ACTS 16:8-15)

A. Vision in Troas (vv. 8, 9)

8. So they passed by Mysia and went down to Troas.

Paul and his group leave the area of Lystra and travel northwest through Phrygia and Galatia (Acts 16:6, not in today's text). These are regional descriptions, so we do not know the cities visited. Paul may intend to go to Ephesus, one of the largest cities in the empire, but any plans in that regard are overruled by the Holy Spirit (16:6b). By unknown means, the Spirit also overrules the group's attempt to turn north into Bithynia (16:7).

So instead they arrive in the port city of Troas, at the northern extremity of the Aegean Sea. This city is about 10 miles from the site of ancient Troy, and the name *Troas* is reminiscent of that storied place. Since this city is in the district of Mysia, then *passed by Mysia* indicates the group does not stay there.

There is no mention of any church planting in Troas at this time, even though there are believers there when Paul preaches in Troas at a later date (Acts 20:5-12). Perhaps there is already a church in the city when Paul arrives. Luke seems to join the group here (see comment on 16:10), so perhaps he is a leader in the Troas church, if it exists.

9. During the night Paul had a vision of a man of Macedonia standing and begging him, "Come over to Macedonia and help us."

The Bible generally differentiates dreams from visions, although both are used by God to communicate special messages. As the man in the vision communicates verbally, his presence must seem very real to Paul! The phrase *begging him* indicates an earnest request. The request is simple: *Come over to Macedonia and help us.* The dramatic and emotional power of this vision is evident. This is not an angel thundering a decree from God, but a man, like Paul, pleading for help. It now makes sense to Paul why he has been forbidden to go in two other directions (Acts 16:6, 7).

Paul knows exactly what help is needed: spiritual help. All of Macedonia—a territory to the west, across the Aegean Sea—needs the gospel that Paul can bring. This lets us sense the urgent need for foreign missionaries today. It is not so much our churches saying, "Go, they need you," but the unevangelized in other countries saying, "Come, we desperately need you."

What Do You Think?
How should we evaluate what seem to be God's directional calls today?
Talking Points for Your Discussion
- Regarding biblical tenets
- Regarding the weight to be given to subjective impressions (feelings, etc.)
- Regarding the seeking of objective viewpoints (input from others, etc.)
- Other

B. Journey to Macedonia (vv. 10-12)

10. After Paul had seen the vision, we got ready at once to leave for Macedonia, concluding that God had called us to preach the gospel to them.

Troas is a port in which the party can find a ship to cross the Aegean Sea and enter the Greek peninsula. Paul wastes no time in preparing to do so, but we are left to wonder how this is accomplished from a financial standpoint. Booking passage on a ship requires money, and Paul's travel seems to be lightly funded (Acts 18:3; 1 Corinthians 9:3-18).

A clue to where the money comes from might be in the change of pronouns from *they* to *we* in this verse. This change indicates that Luke, the author of Acts, has now joined the group without fanfare. Elsewhere, we know that Luke is a physician (Colossians 4:14), and his inclusion may provide a source of funding for this sea voyage. Paul, Silas, Timothy, and Luke—all committed and eager to take the gospel to Macedonia.

❧ SENSING GOD'S LEADING ❧

Emma was certain that the Lord was calling her to southern Israel to serve Kurdish refugees fleeing political oppression. The church leaders, convinced of the Lord's leading in this matter, committed to supporting her. Emma returned home when the political tensions eased. She turned 84 during that 18-month mission.

Visual for Lesson 11. *Keep this map posted as you study lessons 11–13 to give your learners a geographical perspective.*

God still calls people to mission work today, and like Emma, we may get a strong impression that the Lord wants us to go to a particular place. If this happens, we should not move forward in isolation. There is safety and wisdom in bringing to mature believers our subjective sense of God's leading. They can help evaluate the legitimacy of the need and our preparedness for helping to meet it.

Positive affirmations in these areas are likely God's confirmation that this is indeed his leading. Then it's time to get moving!   —D. C. S.

11. From Troas we put out to sea and sailed straight for Samothrace, and the next day we went on to Neapolis.

Samothrace is an island about 45 miles northwest of Troas, and the ship stops there for the night. The next day it arrives in Neapolis, which is about 70 miles from Samothrace. This is a quick passage, reinforcing the impression that God is directing Paul's movements. Neapolis is the seaport for the more substantial city of Philippi, located about 10 miles inland.

Even though this is a rather short trip (two days and 115 miles), there is a historical issue here that we should notice. By going from Troas to Neapolis, Paul is moving into Europe. While there undoubtedly are Christians in some parts of Europe by this time (about AD 52), it is likely that most cities of Macedonia and the rest of the Greek peninsula are untouched by the gospel.

12. From there we traveled to Philippi, a Roman colony and the leading city of that district of Macedonia. And we stayed there several days.

Philippi is a city with a long history. Its name is from Philip II of Macedon, who established it in 356 BC. That same year, his son known to us as Alexander the Great was born. About 94 years before Paul's visit, Philippi had been the site of a decisive battle in a Roman civil war, the city subsequently being made into a Roman colony. Veterans of the Roman legions were then allowed to retire there, usually after 20 years of service.

Philippi is an important Roman commercial and administrative center in the heart of the Greek world. It is on the Egnatian Way, the primary Roman highway that carried huge amounts of trade traffic across the region.

C. Woman of Faith (vv. 13-15)

13. On the Sabbath we went outside the city gate to the river, where we expected to find a place of prayer. We sat down and began to speak to the women who had gathered there.

Paul's preferred tactic of presenting the gospel first in a local synagogue doesn't work here since there doesn't seem to be a synagogue in Philippi. Instead, Paul encounters a group of women *on the Sabbath* near a river that is a suitable *place of prayer*. By Jewish tradition, it takes 10 Jewish men (over age 12) to constitute a proper synagogue. Yet not even one man is mentioned as being present, only women. But that is no hindrance to Paul!

> *What Do You Think?*
> Where are your favorite places to pray? Why?
> *Talking Points for Your Discussion*
> ▪ Places with minimal distractions
> ▪ Places having certain visual aids
> ▪ Other

14. One of those listening was a woman from the city of Thyatira named Lydia, a dealer in purple cloth. She was a worshiper of God. The Lord opened her heart to respond to Paul's message.

A woman . . . named Lydia is present. She is not described as being Jewish (contrast Acts 16:1), but as *a worshiper of God.* Since she is here on a Sabbath, she may be in the same category as Cornelius: a Gentile attracted to Judaism, but not a full convert (see the Lesson Background of lesson 7).

Lydia's hometown of Thyatira is a substantial city on the other side of the Aegean, about 100 miles southeast of Troas (compare Revelation 2:18-29). She is presented as *a dealer in purple cloth,* a luxury item that can yield substantial income. Thyatira is a known source of purple dye, and she may have homes both there and in Philippi—a city that is an ideal outlet for her goods on the Roman highway.

What is most important is her reaction to the gospel message: she is touched deeply and is willing to accept Jesus. The fact that the Lord opens her heart may indicate that he removes mistaken conceptions that would prevent her from accepting a crucified Messiah.

What Do You Think?
How can you help your church enhance ministry to its members whose occupations keep them on the road a lot?
Talking Points for Your Discussion
▪ Regarding needs assessment
▪ Regarding prayer support
▪ Other

---

15. When she and the members of her household were baptized, she invited us to her home. "If you consider me a believer in the Lord," she said, "come and stay at my house." And she persuaded us.

Lydia's decision is followed by baptism, and this includes *the members of her household.* We are given the impression that this happens quickly, the same day. The river that is a peaceful prayer retreat may also become a baptistery for several new believers. An act of hospitality follows as Lydia welcomes the travelers into her home. Given her status as a successful merchant, this is likely a comfortable home, perhaps the first such lodging Paul has enjoyed for many weeks.

There is a certain irony in that the first evangelistic success in Europe is not with "a man of Macedonia," but with a woman of Asia! Paul's obedient response to the Macedonian call has resulted in success as God intends, with more to come.

Conclusion
A. Worldwide Evangelism Today

The Joshua Project identifies over 7,000 of the more than 16,000 people groups in the world today as "unreached." This means that less than 2 percent of their populations are evangelical Christians, or that less than 5 percent are Christians of any type.

Missions experts contend that these unreached people groups will never be evangelized without intentional, strategic, cross-cultural missions efforts. Christians must be sent to them with the gospel. What other hope is there where no churches exist? But there are millions of unevangelized people within the "reached" groups as well. We need intentional outreach in both categories.

There is no question that this is a mighty challenge! Successful cross-cultural evangelism requires dedicated missionaries having proper training and support. The work is sacrificial, causing hardships for families—hardships often unrecognized and unappreciated by supporting churches.

Many churches today have turned inward, choosing to support only local ministries. These worthy organizations need support, that is true, but there are billions who remain without hope, without salvation. They are calling, "Come help us!" When we answer this Macedonian call with a resounding, "Yes, we will!" we bring eternal salvation to modern Lydias and their families. May we be bold in our faith and generous in our support of reaching the world's unreached.

B. Prayer

Lord, how can they hear without a preacher? Give us urgency and commitment for the task of taking the gospel to the lost throughout the world. We pray in the name of Jesus, the one who commanded us to make disciples of all nations; amen.

C. Thought to Remember
Listen for God's call and heed it.

INVOLVEMENT LEARNING

Enhance your lesson with NIV® Bible Student (from your curriculum supplier) and the reproducible activity page (at www.standardlesson.com or in the back of the NIV® Standard Lesson Commentary Deluxe Edition).

Into the Lesson

Distribute blank index cards. Say, "On your card, define the word *missionary*. No fair using your smartphone or tablet to look up a definition online. You have 30 seconds—*Go!*" After you call time, ask for volunteers to read their definitions. Differences can lead to lively discussion, but don't let this drag out.

Make a transition as you say, "We could almost say that the travels of the apostle Paul to foreign lands make him the touchstone for defining the word *missionary*. Today's lesson finds him in a region known as Macedonia. It is from today's text that we get the phrase *Macedonian call*, which has become a term used for the call to be a foreign missionary."

Option. Before learners arrive, place in chairs copies of the "Finding the Way" activity from the reproducible page, which you can download. Learners can begin working on this as they arrive.

Into the Word

Assign the following six segments from Acts 16 to be read by volunteers: verses 1, 2 / verse 3 / verses 4, 5 / verses 8, 9 / verses 10-13 / verses 14, 15. After a segment is read, pose discussion questions and ask learners to respond in a way that goes deeper than what is obvious on a surface reading of the text; you're seeking implications, not just bare facts. Below are *just a few samples* in this regard; use this as a pattern to create further discussion questions.

Verses 1, 2: What do these two verses tell us about Timothy? (*Obvious answer*: he was a disciple; *implication*: he had been converted as a result of Paul's previous missionary journey, not the journey now being studied.)

Verse 3: Why did Paul circumcise Timothy? (*Obvious answer*: "because of the Jews who lived in that area"; *implication*: Timothy needed to be circumcised for the sake of his Jewish heritage so

he would not be a distraction as Paul presented the gospel to fellow Jews.)

Verses 4, 5: What was Paul doing on his revisit of various cities? (*Obvious answer*: delivering the decisions of the Jerusalem Council; *implication*: a missionary not only works to share the gospel with those who have never heard it, but also to correct any doctrinal misunderstandings.)

Verses 8, 9: What happened in Troas? (*Obvious answer*: Paul received a vision of a man of Macedonia; *implication*: a turning point in world history as the gospel spread into Europe.)

Verses 10-13: What did Paul do on the Sabbath in Philippi? (*Obvious answer*: went to the riverside; *implication*: Philippi did not have a strong enough Jewish presence to form a synagogue.)

Verses 14, 15: What do we know about Lydia's occupation? (*Obvious answer*: she was "a dealer in purple cloth"; *implication*: dealing in a luxury item indicates that Lydia was not a poor person.)

Into Life

Say, "Taking the gospel to those who have never heard it is the most important thing we can ever do. Some of us already have had the opportunity to go on a short-term mission trip or have supported others who did so. Whatever the circumstances, sharing God's message of salvation is part of Jesus' commands to us."

Ask learners who have been on short-term mission trips to share their experiences. Discuss the logistics for such trips. Identify class members who will plan such a short-term trip and gain approval and input from church leadership.

Alternative. Distribute copies of the "Macedonian Call" activity from the reproducible page as a take-home. Encourage learners to research the website noted and commit to praying for Christians to heed God's missionary calls. (*Option*: If your learning space has Internet access, take a few minutes to introduce that site to your learners.)

THESSALONICA, BEREA, AND ATHENS

DEVOTIONAL READING: Psalm 47
BACKGROUND SCRIPTURE: Acts 17:1-32

ACTS 17:1-4, 10-12, 22-25, 28

1 When Paul and his companions had passed through Amphipolis and Apollonia, they came to Thessalonica, where there was a Jewish synagogue. 2 As was his custom, Paul went into the synagogue, and on three Sabbath days he reasoned with them from the Scriptures, 3 explaining and proving that the Messiah had to suffer and rise from the dead. "This Jesus I am proclaiming to you is the Messiah," he said. 4 Some of the Jews were persuaded and joined Paul and Silas, as did a large number of God-fearing Greeks and quite a few prominent women.

. . . .

10 As soon as it was night, the believers sent Paul and Silas away to Berea. On arriving there, they went to the Jewish synagogue. 11 Now the Berean Jews were of more noble character than those in Thessalonica, for they received the message with great eagerness and examined the Scriptures every day to see if what Paul said was true. 12 As a result, many of

them believed, as did also a number of prominent Greek women and many Greek men.

. . . .

22 Paul then stood up in the meeting of the Areopagus and said: "People of Athens! I see that in every way you are very religious. 23 For as I walked around and looked carefully at your objects of worship, I even found an altar with this inscription: TO AN UNKNOWN GOD. So you are ignorant of the very thing you worship—and this is what I am going to proclaim to you.

24 "The God who made the world and everything in it is the Lord of heaven and earth and does not live in temples built by human hands. 25 And he is not served by human hands, as if he needed anything. Rather, he himself gives everyone life and breath and everything else."

. . . .

28 "'For in him we live and move and have our being.' As some of your own poets have said, 'We are his offspring.'"

KEY VERSE

"As I walked around and looked carefully at your objects of worship, I even found an altar with this inscription: TO AN UNKNOWN GOD. So you are ignorant of the very thing you worship—and this is what I am going to proclaim to you." —**Acts 17:23**

THE CHRISTIAN COMMUNITY COMES ALIVE

Unit 3: Spreading the Gospel
LESSONS 9–13

LESSON AIMS

After participating in this lesson, each learner will be able to:

1. Retell the events that led up to Paul's dramatic speech in Athens.

2. Contrast Paul's approach to those who did not accept the authority of Hebrew Scriptures with his approach to those who did.

3. Explain how he or she will present the gospel to a friend who rejects the authority of the Bible.

LESSON OUTLINE

Introduction
    A. Searching the Scriptures
    B. Lesson Background
I. In Thessalonica (ACTS 17:1-4)
    A. Three Sabbaths, Usual Proof (vv. 1-3)
    B. Some Jews, Many Gentiles (v. 4)
    Reading It, and Reading It Rightly
II. In Berea (ACTS 17:10-12)
    A. Usual Proof, Noble Listeners (vv. 10, 11)
    Milo
    B. Many Jews, Many Gentiles (v. 12)
III. In Athens (ACTS 17:22-25, 28)
    A. Unique Venue, Changed Proof (vv. 22, 23)
    B. Creator Facts, Creation Facts (vv. 24, 25, 28)
Conclusion
    A. The Gospel in All Contexts
    B. Prayer
    C. Thought to Remember

Introduction

A. Searching the Scriptures

Why are the Scriptures so important to the church? Why are certain words on a page (or screen) more important than others? What is the best use of Scripture? These questions are all related to the nature of authority when it comes to certain works of literature, the concept of using the writings of others as guides for our lives.

This great Jewish heritage of Scriptures, sacred writings that have authority in the community and in the lives of individuals, has passed to Christians. We believe that God speaks through the books of the Bible, written by men but inspired by the Holy Spirit (2 Timothy 3:16; 2 Peter 1:21).

Part of today's lesson concerns the Bereans, synagogue members who searched the Scriptures diligently to see if the claims of Paul about Jesus were true. May we never forget that God's truth resides in the Scriptures, and that like those noble Bereans, we can search them ourselves to learn things of utmost, eternal importance.

B. Lesson Background

The background to last week's lesson applies to this week's, so that information need not be repeated here. A new element, however, concerns the city of Athens. Surely, one of the most interesting stories in Acts about Paul is his experience there. That Greek city was famous for having been the home base of noteworthy philosophers in centuries gone by. Athens' legendary reputation is summed up nicely by Robert P. Conway:

> Athens reached its zenith under Pericles (495–429 BC), who built the Parthenon, numerous temples, and other splendid buildings. Literature, philosophy, science, and rhetoric flourished; and Athens attracted intellectuals from all over the world. In Paul's day, its prestige was challenged by Alexandria [compare Acts 18:24] and Tarsus [compare Acts 21:39; 22:3], but not in popular opinion.

A factor often overlooked today is that ancient Athens was also a religious center (Acts 17:22, part of today's study). The dividing line between philosophy and religion that is drawn by many today was unknown in the ancient world (and surely the two cannot be separated even now). That context meant that Paul's preaching of the gospel outside the synagogue (17:17) required a different strategy than he used in Thessalonica, Berea, etc.

I. In Thessalonica
(ACTS 17:1-4)

Last week's lesson saw Paul and companions in Philippi, the leading city in the northern region of the Greek peninsula known as Macedonia. After nearly causing a riot in Philippi, Paul and Silas were flogged, imprisoned, and ultimately asked to leave town (Acts 16:16-40). Time to move on!

A. Three Sabbaths, Usual Proof (vv. 1-3)

1. When Paul and his companions had passed through Amphipolis and Apollonia, they came to Thessalonica, where there was a Jewish synagogue.

The "we" of Acts 16:10-12, 16 changes back to *they* (compare 16:4, 7, 8), so we assume that Luke (the author of Acts) is no longer accompanying Paul, Silas, and Timothy. The trio proceeds westward along the Egnatian Way, passing through the cities of *Amphipolis and Apollonia*. The trip from Philippi to Amphipolis is about 33 miles, from Amphipolis to Apollonia about 28 miles. Each segment is thus a single day's journey by horse, but we do not know the band's method of transportation.

Amphipolis (meaning "a city pressed on all sides") is a Roman administrative center. From

HOW TO SAY IT

Areopagus	Air-ee-*op*-uh-gus.
Amphipolis	Am-*fip*-o-liss.
Apollonia	Ap-uh-*low*-nee-uh.
Athenian	Uh-*thin*-e-un.
Athens	*Ath*-unz.
Egnatian	Egg-*nay*-shun.
Epimenides	Ep-ih-*men*-ih-deez.
Crete	Creet.
Messiah	Meh-*sigh*-uh.
Parthenon	*Par*-thuh-non (*th* as in *thin*).
Silas	*Sigh*-luss.
Thessalonica	*Thess*-uh-lo-**nye**-kuh (*th* as in *thin*).

Apollonia (meaning "pertaining to Apollo"), the highway connects to Thessalonica, another 30 miles or so distant. Paul does not seem to linger in either Amphipolis or Apollonia, probably because there are no synagogues and he cannot find a gathering of Jewish people like the one he found in Philippi. However, there is *a Jewish synagogue* in Thessalonica.

> *What Do You Think?*
> How should Paul's apparent decision not to linger in Amphipolis or Apollonia inform our church-planting strategies today, if at all? Why?
> *Talking Points for Your Discussion*
> - Issue of a larger plan
> - Issue of divine direction
> - Issue of evaluating soil suitable for the gospel
> - Other

2. As was his custom, Paul went into the synagogue, and on three Sabbath days he reasoned with them from the Scriptures,

Paul employs his usual strategy when beginning ministry in a new city: he joins fellowship with the local synagogue (compare Acts 9:20; 13:5; 17:10, 17; etc.). The fact that he teaches there for *three Sabbath days* means he is in town for no less than two full weeks. We cannot determine how much longer he stays than that because he may remain in town for quite some time even after he can no longer teach in the synagogue. In such a setting it is most appropriate to use *the Scriptures* in presenting the case for Jesus.

A few months later, Paul will write the two letters we call 1 and 2 Thessalonians to the church that results from his evangelistic efforts here. The nature of these letters shows that while the recipients have embraced Paul's message about Jesus as Messiah, they remain unsettled concerning several areas of doctrine. In particular, they are confused about the nature of Christ's second coming (1 Thessalonians 4:13–5:11; 2 Thessalonians 2:1-12), and this causes friction within the church.

Paul's stay in Thessalonica is a long enough time to cover this area of doctrine (2 Thessalonians 2:5). But teaching something once is often not enough. People need reminders.

3. explaining and proving that the Messiah had to suffer and rise from the dead. "This Jesus I am proclaiming to you is the Messiah," he said.

Paul uses Scripture to make two points above all: the necessity of Jesus' suffering (a reference to his death) and his rising *from the dead*. First-century Jews expect the Christ (Messiah) to come, but they are looking for a powerful military-style leader who will reestablish Israel as a great nation (compare Acts 1:6). They do not expect a Messiah who is killed by the Romans and then rises from the grave.

Paul works through their (and his) own Scriptures in a way that shows his audience that those things were indeed prophesied. (This is likely an exposition of Isaiah 53 and similar texts.) After working through the appropriate texts, Paul is able to claim that Jesus has fulfilled the prophecies. Therefore Jesus is the Messiah, the long-awaited Christ. This is Paul's method of teaching in Jewish settings (compare Acts 9:22).

B. Some Jews, Many Gentiles (v. 4)

4. Some of the Jews were persuaded and joined Paul and Silas, as did a large number of God-fearing Greeks and quite a few prominent women.

Paul's presentation is undoubtedly powerful, but the results are uneven in a surprising direction: whereas *a large number* of Greeks (Gentiles) believe, only *some of the Jews* do. Since Paul, himself a Jew and an expert in the Law of Moses, reasons from the Jewish Scriptures, one would expect those results to be flipped the other way around! On the significance of the description *God-fearing* regarding these Greeks, see the Lesson Background of lesson 7. The *prominent women* may be wives of leading male citizens.

❧ READING IT, AND READING IT RIGHTLY ❧

I am blessed to know a few Christians who have converted from Judaism, and I have asked them about one thing that has always confused me: since there is so much prophecy about the Messiah in the Old Testament, how can it be hard for Jews to believe in Jesus? I especially wondered how someone could read the book of Isaiah and not see Jesus, since it contains so much messianic prophecy. When I ask about this, I usually hear the same answer: Isaiah isn't read in synagogues. The focus instead is often on the first five books of the Bible. It's not that they aren't reading Isaiah rightly, it's that they aren't reading Isaiah at all!

The Jews whom Paul addressed had expectations of what the Messiah would be and do. But Paul showed them how their expectations differed from what Scripture said. The result: only "some of the Jews were persuaded." Why not many, most, or all? Perhaps what held back the unconvinced majority were preconceptions or misconceptions that prevented them from reading the Word rightly, from seeing and accepting what the Word actually said.

That's a warning to us all. We must turn to the light of the Word with our minds open to its truths. When we approach the Word with our minds already made up or thinking we already know what it says, we close ourselves off to what God may want us to see. —V. E.

II. In Berea
(ACTS 17:10-12)

Hostility again forces Paul to move on (Acts 17:5-9, not in today's text). Ironically, the disbelieving Jews who start the trouble in Thessalonica use as their justification "Caesar's decrees" (17:7). The Jewish opponents of Jesus had done something similar (John 19:12, 15).

A. Usual Proof, Noble Listeners (vv. 10, 11)

10. As soon as it was night, the believers sent Paul and Silas away to Berea. On arriving there, they went to the Jewish synagogue.

Paul and Silas are secreted away during the night from the mortal dangers of Thessalonica *to Berea*, a thriving city about 50 miles to the west. Timothy is apparently left in Thessalonica, but he will join Paul and Silas in Berea shortly (Acts 17:14). Paul wastes no time in repeating his usual strategy: approaching his fellow Jews in *the Jewish synagogue* in order to tell them about Jesus.

11. Now the Berean Jews were of more noble character than those in Thessalonica, for they received the message with great eagerness and

examined the Scriptures every day to see if what Paul said was true.

The word translated *noble* usually refers to one's social status, as it does in Luke 19:12 and 1 Corinthians 1:26. But here it signifies "better disposition." The implication is that the Bereans are more fair-minded. Even if they disagree with Paul, they will not seek to have him jailed or try to kill him. They do not allow vested interests to interfere (contrast John 11:48). Instead, they listen to what Paul teaches and then verify his message by reading the Scriptures with great care. They do not automatically accept Paul's interpretation, but check his claims against the highest authority: the Word of God, not allowing preconceived positions to determine the truth.

What Do You Think?
When, if ever, is it appropriate to praise one group over another by name today? Explain.
Talking Points for Your Discussion
- Within Christianity
- Outside Christianity

❧ MILO ❧

My in-laws lived most of their lives near Kansas City. When they traveled to visit family, they often spent much of their drive time in rural areas. Frequently my mother-in-law would ask, "I wonder what that is?" referring to the crop growing in fields alongside the highway. My father-in-law nearly always gave the same response: "milo."

In their later years, however, a conversation about agriculture revealed that he had no idea what milo looked like! My mother-in-law could not believe her ears. For years she had believed what he said to be true. Now when we believe we are hearing malarkey, we refer to it as *milo.*

In Dad's defense, everyone knew he was not a farmer or a crop expert. He was simply answering a casual question with a casual response or best guess. Those asking questions should realize that they have to go to a proper source to ensure an accurate answer. The Bereans seemed to know that. As Paul was teaching them, they took their questions directly to the Scripture to evaluate his interpretations—they tested the information

properly. We who live in an age rich with both information and disinformation must do the same as we listen to sermons and lessons. God's Word is still our standard.   —V. E.

B. Many Jews, Many Gentiles (v. 12)

12. As a result, many of them believed, as did also a number of prominent Greek women and many Greek men.

In contrast with "some" Jewish converts to Christ in Thessalonica (Acts 17:4, above), *many of* the Berean Jews believe Paul's message; his message that Jesus is the Christ passes the scriptural test. Further, *many Greek men* (Gentiles) believe as well. Some of these Gentiles may be associated with the synagogue, but it is likely that the good news brought by Paul is also embraced by outsiders who have no connections with Judaism.

The stay in Berea does not end happily, however. While the Bereans themselves process Paul's claims in a thoughtful manner, agitators from Thessalonica show up and a dangerous situation ensues (Acts 17:13, not in today's text). So Paul leaves Berea, while Silas and Timothy remain behind for the time being (17:14). Some Bereans are dedicated enough to escort Paul all the way to Athens, about 300 miles to the south (17:15).

III. In Athens
(ACTS 17:22-25, 28)

Paul explores the city of Athens alone (Acts 17:14, 16) until Silas and Timothy can join him. He finds a synagogue (17:17) and teaches there, but he is startled by the sight of many temples in the city that are dedicated to various Greek deities. It seems to Paul that the city is "full of idols" (17:16). Although he grew up in the Greek city of Tarsus, he seems not to have encountered *this* level of idolatry before!

But that problem is also an opportunity for evangelism, so Paul presents the gospel not only "in the synagogue with both Jews and God-fearing Greeks" but also "in the marketplace day by day" (Acts 17:17). His efforts regarding the latter are noticed by some philosophers (17:18), who take him to a meeting of their guild at an open-air forum known as "the Areopagus" (or "Mars' hill" in older translations; see 17:19). This is located on a rocky hilltop near the city's temple to the goddess Athena, the famed Parthenon.

A. Unique Venue, Changed Proof (vv. 22, 23)

22. Paul then stood up in the meeting of the Areopagus and said: "People of Athens! I see that in every way you are very religious.

Paul uses a different approach in his presentation of the gospel *in the meeting of the Areopagus.* It would be useless to appeal to Jewish Scriptures as Paul does in synagogues, because the authority of those writings is not acknowledged by this audience of Greek philosophers (Acts 17:18). Therefore, Paul constructs a message that will receive a hearing in this pagan, non-Jewish context.

He begins by noting that the citizens of Athens *are very religious.* This acknowledges that the Athenians are concerned about spiritual matters and therefore curious about spiritual truths. Paul is saying, in effect, "You are religious, and so am I, so let's talk about religion. I have some very important things to tell you." This establishes common ground.

> **What Do You Think?**
> Under what circumstances would public proclamation or debate as Paul engaged in be an appropriate way to present the gospel today? When would it not? Why?
> *Talking Points for Your Discussion*
> - Considering media technology
> - Considering what persuades audiences today
> - Other

23. "For as I walked around and looked carefully at your objects of worship, I even found an altar with this inscription: TO AN UNKNOWN GOD. So you are ignorant of the very thing you worship—and this is what I am going to proclaim to you.

In touring the city of Athens, Paul has seen dozens, perhaps hundreds, of altars for the worship of pagan deities. One in particular has caught his eye: the one *TO AN UNKNOWN GOD.* Its existence seems to witness to the Athenians' desire to avoid

overlooking any gods or goddesses. The numerous altars in the city may not be sufficient. Better to offer a token of worship to a deity they have not identified than to risk offending him!

Another possible reason for this altar is that the Greeks are always concerned about how a god might be able to benefit them. Maybe it would be good to offer a little homage to a neglected deity, because then the deity might bless the worshipper out of gratitude. Either way, the Athenians do not want to take any chances, so they have an altar of contingency. Paul's message is, "You are right! You missed one! Let me to tell you about him."

> **What Do You Think?**
> What features of today's culture are similar to those of Thessalonica, Berea, and/or Athens? Why is this question important?
> *Talking Points for Your Discussion*
> - Positive similarities
> - Negative similarities

B. Creator Facts, Creation Facts (vv. 24, 25, 28)

24. "The God who made the world and everything in it is the Lord of heaven and earth and does not live in temples built by human hands.

Paul continues laying common ground. The philosophers do not believe the world was self-created. They attribute the physical world to an act of creation by divine powers, and they have elaborate myths to tell this story.

Even so, some philosophers of this period are beginning to question the idea of a multiplicity of gods, especially in the realm of creation. And while some of the common folk might actually believe that a god lives in a temple, these sophisticated men do not believe this. Paul's logic is that it would be preposterous for a deity to live in a humanly built structure, no matter how glorious (compare 1 Kings 8:27). The ancient Parthenon, one of the most magnificent temples of antiquity, is clearly visible to the group, just a couple hundred yards away. We can even imagine Paul gesturing to it and the other temples of the Acropolis as he speaks.

25. "And he is not served by human hands, as if he needed anything. Rather, he himself gives everyone life and breath and everything else."

Since the Creator *gives everyone life and breath and everything else*, that logically implies that he is self-sustaining and independent. For the human mind to imagine a creator-god who requires human worship for sustenance is ridiculous! The true Creator-God is not dependent on humans; rather, we are dependent on him.

28. "'For in him we live and move and have our being.' As some of your own poets have said, 'We are his offspring.'"

Following further comments on humanity's relationship with God (vv. 26, 27, not in today's text), Paul buttresses his argument by quoting two pagan authors. The line *For in him we live and move and have our being* is from Epimenides of Crete, a sixth-century BC philosopher. (Paul also quotes Epimenides in Titus 1:12.) The second quotation, *We are his offspring*, is from Aratus, a third-century BC Greek poet who had spent time in Athens.

In quoting these sources, Paul is not equating the writings of Epimenides or Aratus with Scripture. Rather, he is saying, "Hey, even some of your own guys have figured out this part." By not quoting Genesis 1:1, etc., Paul is thus taking great care to stay on common ground as long as possible (see Acts 17:29, 30, not in today's text).

> *What Do You Think?*
> What common starting points can we draw on today as we lead people to Christ?
> *Talking Points for Your Discussion*
> ▪ Regarding Muslims
> ▪ Regarding Jews
> ▪ Regarding agnostics
> ▪ Other

Where Paul loses some of the philosophers is when he begins to discuss Jesus' resurrection (Acts 17:31, 32), so Paul makes his exit (17:33). Even today, there is really no reason to pursue preaching the gospel to those who refuse to believe in the resurrection (see 1 Corinthians 15:12-19); the gospel without the resurrection of Christ is no gospel at all. Paul continues with those who will listen, and he does have some converts (Acts 17:34), although it seems that no church is planted in Athens.

Visual for Lesson 12. *Have this photograph of the Parthenon on display as you discuss the logical flow of Paul's argument in verse 24.*

Conclusion
A. The Gospel in All Contexts

Paul was prepared to engage the philosophers of his day. He was not shy about presenting the claims of Christianity in the inner sanctum of the learned—the Areopagus of Athens. Paul believed that truth would withstand any challenge and that it must be proclaimed and defended. When he worked with Jews with whom he shared a common understanding of the authority of Scripture, his appeal was on that basis. But when he spoke to Greeks who did not share that belief, he pressed his claims on the basis of logic and quotations from their own writers.

The church needs highly educated Christians who are able to speak its message in all contexts. To be able to debate with philosophers as Paul did is not the calling of every Christian. But we must not settle for putting our faith in a box, apart from our intellectual life.

B. Prayer

Father, in you we live, we move, we have our being. Give us wisdom to speak the truth in clarity and without fear. May we be noble in our study and bold in our proclamation. We pray this in the name of Jesus, who died and rose again; amen.

C. Thought to Remember

Search the Scriptures daily.

INVOLVEMENT LEARNING

Enhance your lesson with NIV® Bible Student (from your curriculum supplier) and the reproducible activity page (at www.standardlesson.com or in the back of the NIV® Standard Lesson Commentary Deluxe Edition).

Into the Lesson

Distribute to three learners one index card each on which you have written a prediction for the near future. Have one prediction be about the stock market, one about a sports team, and one about population change.

Ask one learner to read the prediction on his or her card, then call for a show of hands of those who think the prediction will come true. Follow by asking, "What if I said that the source of this prediction is [name of a reliable source]. Now how many believe it will come true?" After a show of hands, ask, "What if I said that the source of this prediction is [name of an unreliable source]. Now how many believe it will come true?" Follow the same procedure for the second and third predictions, jotting on the board the changing belief tallies as reliable and unreliable sources are mentioned.

Say, "When faced with a decision, a discerning person will evaluate the reliability of the information on which the decision is to be made. This includes noting the credibility of the source of the information. In today's lesson we will examine how three groups did so when they heard the gospel."

Into the Word

Form learners into pairs or groups of three. Distribute identical handouts that feature three blank columns headed *1–Thessalonica / 2–Berea / 3–Athens*, one each. Down the left-hand side have the following as designations for three rows, one each: *A–Paul's source of information / B–Place in the city where information was presented / C–Positive result(s) of information presented*. Have intersection C-3 shaded dark, since it will not be used. Include these instructions: "Take eight minutes to fill out the eight intersections of columns and rows with facts you discover in Acts 17:1-4, 10-12, 22-25, 28."

After you call time, ask one group for its conclusions regarding the proper entry for intersection A-1, then poll the other groups for any improvements. Repeat for all column and row intersections, rotating through your groups. *Expected responses*: A-1, Scripture (v. 2); A-2, Scripture (v. 11); A-3, logic and pagan writers (vv. 24, 25, 28); B-1, synagogue (vv. 1, 2); B-2, synagogue (v. 10); B-3, Areopagus (v. 22); C-1, some Jews and a large number of God-fearing Greeks believed (v. 4); C-2, many Jews and a number of Greeks believed (v. 12).

Option. Leave intersection C-3 unshaded and challenge learners to look elsewhere in Acts 17 for the answer. *Expected response*: "a woman . . . and a number of others" believed (Acts 17:34).

After all intersections are described, pose these two questions (one at a time) for discussion: 1. Why the difference in results between Thessalonica and Berea despite Paul's use of the same source of information in both places? 2. Why did Paul use Scripture as his source of information in synagogues but not at the Areopagus? (This question will serve as a transition to Into Life.)

Into Life

Pose this question for learners to discuss in their previously formed groups or for whole-class brainstorming: "Speaking of the Areopagus, how would you present the gospel to someone who rejects the authority and credibility of the Bible?" If your learners have trouble grappling with this question, offer this hint: "Think in terms of identifying and using the source of authoritative information that the person *does* accept as your launching point."

Option. For deeper study following the above, distribute copies of the "Three Points" activity from the reproducible page, which you can download. Have learners complete as indicated in pairs or groups of three.

Option. Before either of the two activities above, distribute copies of the "Aeropaguses in My Day" from the reproducible page for learners to complete as indicated.

TEACHING GOD'S WORD

DEVOTIONAL READING: Matthew 28:16-20
BACKGROUND SCRIPTURE: Acts 18

ACTS 18:1-11, 18-21A

¹ After this, Paul left Athens and went to Corinth. ² There he met a Jew named Aquila, a native of Pontus, who had recently come from Italy with his wife Priscilla, because Claudius had ordered all Jews to leave Rome. Paul went to see them, ³ and because he was a tentmaker as they were, he stayed and worked with them. ⁴ Every Sabbath he reasoned in the synagogue, trying to persuade Jews and Greeks.

⁵ When Silas and Timothy came from Macedonia, Paul devoted himself exclusively to preaching, testifying to the Jews that Jesus was the Messiah. ⁶ But when they opposed Paul and became abusive, he shook out his clothes in protest and said to them, "Your blood be on your own heads! I am innocent of it. From now on I will go to the Gentiles."

⁷ Then Paul left the synagogue and went next door to the house of Titius Justus, a worshiper of God. ⁸ Crispus, the synagogue leader, and his entire household believed in the Lord;

and many of the Corinthians who heard Paul believed and were baptized.

⁹ One night the Lord spoke to Paul in a vision: "Do not be afraid; keep on speaking, do not be silent. ¹⁰ For I am with you, and no one is going to attack and harm you, because I have many people in this city." ¹¹ So Paul stayed in Corinth for a year and a half, teaching them the word of God.

. . . .

¹⁸ Paul stayed on in Corinth for some time. Then he left the brothers and sisters and sailed for Syria, accompanied by Priscilla and Aquila. Before he sailed, he had his hair cut off at Cenchreae because of a vow he had taken. ¹⁹ They arrived at Ephesus, where Paul left Priscilla and Aquila. He himself went into the synagogue and reasoned with the Jews. ²⁰ When they asked him to spend more time with them, he declined. ²¹ But as he left, he promised, "I will come back if it is God's will."

KEY VERSES

One night the Lord spoke to Paul in a vision: "Do not be afraid; keep on speaking, do not be silent. For I am with you, and no one is going to attack and harm you, because I have many people in this city."

—Acts 18:9, 10

The Christian
Community Comes Alive

Unit 3: Spreading the Gospel
Lessons 9–13

Lesson Aims

After participating in this lesson, each learner will be able to:

1. List the names of those who supported Paul during his ministry in Corinth.

2. Compare and contrast Paul's ministries in Corinth and Athens.

3. Participate in a mock debate on the proposal that all missionary endeavors should follow Paul's "tentmaker" model.

Lesson Outline

Introduction
  A. Displacement for Ministry
  B. Lesson Background
 I. New Connection (Acts 18:1-4)
  A. Making Tents (vv. 1-3)
    Policy Writing for God
  B. Presenting Christ (v. 4)
 II. Renewed Connection (Acts 18:5-11)
  A. Turning to the Gentiles (vv. 5, 6)
    He Sends Help
  B. Baptizing Jews and Gentiles (vv. 7, 8)
  C. Receiving a Vision (vv. 9-11)
 III. New Mission Field (Acts 18:18-21a)
  A. Sailing for Syria (v. 18)
  B. Reasoning in Ephesus (vv. 19-21a)
Conclusion
  A. Adaptability for Ministry
  B. Prayer
  C. Thought to Remember

Introduction

A. Displacement for Ministry

I am now living in the seventh state for which I have had a driver's license. Each move has involved joining a different church with different ministry involvements. My wife and I can attest to the fact that it is sometimes difficult to make such adjustments. It is not only hard to make new friends, but also hard to find one's niche in the programs of a new church.

Even so, we have had it easy compared with the apostle Paul. There were no churches in the towns he visited—he had to start them! Indeed, planting churches was his task. But it seems that no sooner had he gotten started in doing so than he would be run out of town by opponents. This happened time after time.

Today's lesson offers us an exception in that Paul was able to stay in Corinth for about 18 months, his longest period of located ministry in a church he planted up until that time. But a year and a half still isn't very long! Yet that was the nature of Paul's ministry vocation. He was driven by his desire to spread the gospel and directed by the Holy Spirit to be on the move.

B. Lesson Background

We are able to date Paul's time in Corinth more precisely than any other point in his ministry. Acts 18:12 mentions that Gallio was "proconsul of Achaia" (the Roman province in southern Greece) at the time. Archaeologists have discovered an inscription that allows us to date Gallio's tenure in Corinth to be AD 51–53, meaning that Paul's 18 months there overlapped that span of time in some way.

Corinth at the time was large and important. The Romans had destroyed the city in 146 BC but planted a Roman colony in the same place 102 years later, in 44 BC. That effort recognized the area's strategic location on a narrow strip of land that connected the Peloponnesian Peninsula to the south with the larger Greek Peninsula to the north. This isthmus, less than five miles wide at its narrowest, had been improved with the *diolkos*: a stone pavement and a carved track for cartwheels or wooden skids that allowed ships to be plucked from the waters of the Ionian Sea to the west, transported overland, and refloated in the Aegean Sea to the east (or vice versa). This procedure eliminated hundreds of miles of dangerous sailing around the Peloponnesian Peninsula.

The city of Corinth controlled this operation and reaped substantial income from it. This made Corinth a center of trade, with a very diverse and cosmopolitan citizenry as a result. The fact that Paul could spend 18 months there and then move on for reasons other than fear of life and limb certainly distinguished this mission field from others he had encountered to that point!

I. New Connection
(ACTS 18:1-4)
A. Making Tents (vv. 1-3)
1. After this, Paul left Athens and went to Corinth.

Paul does not linger in Athens (last week's lesson) as he heads to the next big city: Corinth. Reliable population estimates for cities in antiquity are notoriously difficult to come by. But population density studies suggest Corinth's inhabitants to

HOW TO SAY IT

Achaia	Uh-*kay*-uh.
Aquila	*Ack*-wih-luh.
Aegean	Uh-*jee*-un.
Berea	Buh-*ree*-uh.
Caesarea Maritima	Sess-uh-*ree*-uh Mar-uh-*tee*-muh.
Cenchreae	*Sen*-kree-uh.
diolkos (Greek)	*dih*-all-kos (*o* as in *cost*).
Gallio	*Gal*-ee-o.
Gamaliel	Guh-*may*-lih-ul or Guh-*may*-lee-al.
Ionian	Eye-*owe*-nee-un.
Nazirite	*Naz*-ih-rite.
Peloponnesian	Peh-luh-puh-*nee*-shun.
Thessalonica	*Thess*-uh-lo-*nye*-kuh (*th* as in *thin*).
Titius	*Tish*-us (*i* as in *dish*).

number at least 95,000. Other studies propose a number as much as three times that figure—we just don't know. In any case, Corinth is one of the largest cities in the Roman Empire, about 50 miles west of smaller Athens.

2. There he met a Jew named Aquila, a native of Pontus, who had recently come from Italy with his wife Priscilla, because Claudius had ordered all Jews to leave Rome. Paul went to see them,

Paul is without his fellow travelers Timothy and Silas (see v. 5, below), but he finds companionship nonetheless. Aquila is originally from the region of Pontus (see Acts 2:9), which is on the southern shore of the Black Sea. Pontus has a strong trading relationship with Rome, and Aquila seems to be a successful businessman.

Claudius is emperor from AD 41 to 54. His edict of AD 49 for the expulsion of all Jews from the city of Rome appears to have been prompted by violent fighting, perhaps mob-led killings, between the Christian and non-Christian Jews in the city. Claudius was not interested in sorting out this controversy with an eye to justice, so he apparently just kicked all Jews out of the city wholesale. This married couple seems to have been able to relocate their business to Corinth and become established there.

Luke (the author of Acts) does not say that Aquila and Priscilla are Christians when Paul meets them, but they seem to function that way in this chapter. Perhaps they became Christians while in Rome. That would have been entirely possible if those from Rome who were present on the Day of Pentecost (Acts 2:10) had spread the gospel message in that city on their return. In any case, this couple had to leave town when Jews were expelled.

3. and because he was a tentmaker as they were, he stayed and worked with them.

Paul joins this couple in a way we have not seen of him to this point in Acts: working at a trade for a living. (First Thessalonians 2:9 and 2 Thessalonians 3:7-10, portions of two letters Paul will write while in Corinth, indicate that he had worked to support himself previously while in Thessalonica.) All three are tentmakers, a new piece of personal information about Paul. He has been trained to be a rabbi by the famous Gamaliel (Acts 22:3), and all rabbis of this period have a professional skill—they are carpenters, bakers, etc.

A tentmaker of this era does not work with the canvas or lightweight nylon fabrics of modern camping gear, but with heavy material such as leather or woven goat hair. The tents being sold in Corinth are durable products used in semipermanent situations. Construction of such tents requires arduous handwork, using palm guards and hefty needles as pieces are stitched together with leather straps. It is a skilled profession with a ready market, thus allowing Paul to earn a living.

The importance of Paul's willingness to support himself in this manner will be seen when he writes to the church in Corinth several years hence (see 1 Corinthians 4:12; 9:1-18; compare Acts 20:34). The accommodations that Paul shares with Aquila and Priscilla may serve as personal lodging, tent factory, and sales shop concurrently. Skilled craftsmen such as Paul are in demand in a commercial center like Corinth, and he probably is able to make these arrangements quickly.

> *What Do You Think?*
> Is Paul's self-supporting approach a precedent for mission funding today? Why, or why not?
> *Talking Points for Your Discussion*
> ▪ Contexts where it is advantageous today
> ▪ Contexts where it is disadvantageous today
> ▪ 1 Corinthians 9:4-14

❧ *Policy Writing for God* ❧

Though raised by a Christian mother, my step-dad has been an agnostic for most of his life. He has a strong work ethic and is very good to our family, but the topic of faith used to be poorly tolerated.

Then one day came bad news: after more than 20 years of marriage, my mother was diagnosed with cancer. My sister, herself a cancer survivor, told my stepdad that it was her faith in Christ that got her through the long rounds of chemotherapy and radiation. She minced no words in insisting that he attend church with our mother as part of his support for her.

He agreed (or complied at least). There were many churches from which to choose, but the decision was not difficult since he already had a personal relationship with one of the ministers. The reason that a professed agnostic had a minister as a friend? That minister was also his insurance agent and an active member of a local service organization. My stepfather already had grown to respect the man's integrity and lifestyle.

Although my mother's cancer has been in remission for years, my stepfather still attends church regularly, is open to family prayers, and is more open-minded in discussions about God than ever before. I, for one, am very grateful to those who serve as modern "tentmakers" as they let their love for God and people permeate all they do.   —V. E.

B. Presenting Christ (v. 4)

4. Every Sabbath he reasoned in the synagogue, trying to persuade Jews and Greeks.

Although Sabbath-keeping is not an issue under the new covenant (Colossians 2:16), Paul likely does not work at his trade on this day of the week. Taking it as time-off serves two purposes: (1) it prevents a distraction of being seen as violating the Law of Moses, and (2) it allows the apostle to speak of Jesus *in the synagogue* on *every Sabbath*.

Here, as in the synagogues of other Greek cities visited, Paul reasons with both Jews and the non-Jewish Greeks (Gentiles) who have some relationship with the synagogue. The word translated *reasoned* is the source of our word *dialogue*, indicating Paul's method is give-and-take discussion.

> *What Do You Think?*
> How would you begin to share your faith with a new neighbor who moved to your street?
> *Talking Points for Your Discussion*
> ▪ Timing considerations
> ▪ Common ground considerations
> ▪ Cautions to consider
> ▪ Other

II. Renewed Connection

(ACTS 18:5-11)

A. Turning to the Gentiles (vv. 5, 6)

5. When Silas and Timothy came from Macedonia, Paul devoted himself exclusively to preaching, testifying to the Jews that Jesus was the Messiah.

After Paul has been in Corinth for several weeks (or months), *Silas and Timothy* rejoin him (see lessons 11 and 12; 1 Thessalonians 3:1-5). This reunion seems to energize the apostle, and he begins to press his claims about Jesus. Paul's earlier method of dialogue seems to progress to testifying, meaning he is now preaching about Jesus openly and powerfully. This is primarily *to the Jews*, who need to be convinced that their own Scriptures are fulfilled by the life story of Jesus.

❧ *HE SENDS HELP* ❧

Charles G. Finney (1792–1825) has been called the father of modern revivalism. He led meetings that produced revivals in the northeastern U.S. primarily from 1825 to 1835 as part of what is called the Second Great Awakening in America.

Finney did not work alone. He had men who traveled to towns days ahead of scheduled meetings to conduct intercessory prayer. Two such men were Daniel Nash and Abel Clary. Often Nash would even miss the meetings themselves because he was so focused on praying for them. Finney said, "I did the preaching altogether, and brother Nash gave himself up almost continually to prayer"; regarding Clary, "He never, that I could learn, appeared in public, but gave himself wholly to prayer." Finney attributed much of the response to his preaching to his faithful intercessors.

Although called by Christ personally to preach the gospel, even the great apostle Paul did his work with the encouragement and support of other godly people by his side. Christian collaboration bears great fruit yet today—ours is not a "lone ranger" calling! Give thanks for those whom God has given to journey alongside you! —V. E.

6. But when they opposed Paul and became abusive, he shook out his clothes in protest and said to them, "Your blood be on your own heads! I am innocent of it. From now on I will go to the Gentiles."

Paul's new tactic is not well received. He stirs up opposition, and this leads to a parting of ways. Unable to refute his arguments, opponents attack him on a personal level in some way, committing blasphemy in the process (compare Acts 13:45).

In response to the personal attacks, the feisty Paul dramatically shakes *his clothes* as if he is ridding himself of even the dust of this hostile synagogue (compare Luke 9:5; Acts 13:51). The dire warning *Your blood be on your own heads!* reminds us of God's call to the prophet Ezekiel to be a "watchman." If the watchman doesn't sound a warning when he should, then he is accountable for resulting bloodshed; but if the watchman does fulfill his duty to warn, then any resulting bloodshed is on the heads of those who do not heed the warning (Ezekiel 33:1-9). Paul's meaning is clear: the Jews of Corinth who reject his message reject Jesus, and they will be held responsible for this decision (compare Acts 17:31).

So Paul has fulfilled his duty. There is nothing more he can do for these obstinate Jews, so he makes a pronouncement he has made before (Acts 13:46) and will make again (28:28): *I will go to the Gentiles.* In the larger picture of Acts, this is fulfilling the commission he received from Jesus himself (see 22:21; 26:17).

What Do You Think?
  Under what circumstances is Paul's giving up on
    certain people a model for us today, if ever?
Talking Points for Your Discussion
  ▪ Considering circumstances of overt hostility
  ▪ Considering best use of time
  ▪ Considering cases of apostasy
  ▪ Other

B. Baptizing Jews and Gentiles (vv. 7, 8)

7. Then Paul left the synagogue and went next door to the house of Titius Justus, a worshiper of God.

The events that follow are both ironic and surprising. Ironically, Paul does not go far from the synagogue when he leaves; he sets up his ministry headquarters right next door! The fact that *Titus Justus,* the resident of *the house,* worships God indicates that he is a Gentile who has a relationship with the Jews in the adjacent synagogue (compare Acts 13:16; 16:14).

8. Crispus, the synagogue leader, and his entire household believed in the Lord; and many of the Corinthians who heard Paul believed and were baptized.

The surprising part is the move made by *Crispus, the synagogue leader.* Not everyone in the synagogue rejects Paul's claims. Crispus and *his entire household* commit themselves fully to Paul and his message. This is a bold decision, because Acts 18:17 implies that Crispus loses his synagogue position to another as a result. But he is willing to forsake that position to follow Christ (Luke 14:33). As elsewhere in Acts, belief in Jesus is followed by baptism (Acts 2:38, 41; 8:12, 36; 10:48; 16:14, 15, 30-33).

C. Receiving a Vision (vv. 9-11)

9, 10. One night the Lord spoke to Paul in a vision: "Do not be afraid; keep on speaking, do not be silent. For I am with you, and no one is going to attack and harm you, because I have many people in this city."

Rejection is undoubtedly distressing for Paul. He longs for his beloved fellow Jews to believe his saving message about Jesus as the Messiah

Visual for Lesson 13. *For deeper discussion, ask simply, "Why baptism?" as you address the implications of verse 8.*

(see Romans 9:3). Fellow Jews had posed a threat recently in Thessalonica and Berea, resulting in a hasty exit in each place. Will the same happen here in Corinth?

At just the right time, the Lord speaks *to Paul in a vision.* This is the risen Christ, the one who met Paul (as Saul) on the road to Damascus (Acts 9:5). The Lord's message has two parts. First, Paul is encouraged to keep speaking. The rejection by certain Jews of Corinth is only that, not a sign of God's displeasure or the need for a change of message. Paul is doing the right thing and must continue. No harm will come to him, as proven later by the unsuccessful attack of Acts 18:12-16 (not in today's text).

Second, Paul is granted insight into the real nature of the situation in Corinth. He is dealing with a small drama, the synagogue and its Gentile friends. This may involve a few hundred people. But the Lord reveals that he has *many people in this city.* Who are they? We are not told (and, apparently, neither is Paul). But the point is that we cannot assume that any place is so unredeemedly pagan that God has no witness there. God has been in Corinth before Paul, making hearts receptive.

11. So Paul stayed in Corinth for a year and a half, teaching them the word of God.

The vision achieves its intended effect of giving Paul the courage to remain in Corinth, so he stays for eighteen months. These many months allow him to develop deep and lasting relationships among the Corinthians as he teaches *them the word of God.* We can see the nature of these relationships in the two letters Paul writes to this church while he was on the third missionary journey (1 and 2 Corinthians).

III. New Mission Field
(ACTS 18:18-21a)
A. Sailing for Syria (v. 18)

18. Paul stayed on in Corinth for some time. Then he left the brothers and sisters and sailed for Syria, accompanied by Priscilla and Aquila. Before he sailed, he had his hair cut off at Cenchreae because of a vow he had taken.

Paul's time in Corinth is done when he decides to return to Syria. This means he is headed back to Antioch of Syria, his sending church. He will also spend time in Jerusalem on the way to Antioch (Acts 18:22). He has taken a vow of some kind, and this is accompanied by shaving his head.

This is not explained, but Paul may have taken a Nazirite vow at some time in the past (Numbers 6:5, 18); this may be related to his discouraging time in Corinth earlier, a humbling of himself to be used as a vessel for God's service (see 2 Timothy 2:21). The shaving of the hair is the end of part of the vow, a preparation for visiting the temple in Jerusalem (compare Acts 21:24). Paul, Priscilla, and Aquila leave from Cenchreae, the eastern port of Corinth that services its Aegean Sea trade.

> **What Do You Think?**
> What things are important enough for you to take a vow for, if any? Why?
> *Talking Points for Your Discussion*
> ▪ Regarding what you intend to defend
> ▪ Regarding what you intend to quit
> ▪ Regarding what you intend to accomplish
> ▪ Considering Numbers 30:2
> ▪ Other

B. Reasoning in Ephesus (vv. 19-21a)

19. They arrived at Ephesus, where Paul left Priscilla and Aquila. He himself went into the synagogue and reasoned with the Jews.

The sea voyage from Cenchreae to Ephesus is one of about 250 miles. On arrival, Paul may have to wait a few days for another ship to take him all the way to Caesarea Maritima, on the coast of Palestine. Never one to waste an opportunity, Paul makes contact with the Jews of Ephesus to present the gospel to them. The phrase *Paul left Priscilla and Aquila* speaks to Paul's parting company from them; verses 20, 21a (next) indicate why he needs to move on without them.

20, 21a. When they asked him to spend more time with them, he declined. But as he left, he promised, "I will come back if it is God's will."

The interests of Paul and the Ephesian Jews coincide: they desire that he *spend more time with them*, and Paul wants to do so. But Paul is on a tight schedule, so he must budget his time carefully (compare Acts 20:16). Furthermore, the Holy Spirit previously had denied Paul a ministry in Asia, where Ephesus is located (16:6), so the apostle is careful to make a promise to return only *if it is God's will*. In the meantime, the Ephesians can learn from Aquila, Priscilla, and (later) Apollos (18:18, 19, 24-26).

> **What Do You Think?**
> Why is learning to say *no* an important part of the Christian's life? How have you grown spiritually in this regard?
> *Talking Points for Your Discussion*
> ▪ Regarding issues of rest
> ▪ Regarding issues of keeping promises
> ▪ Regarding issues of prior commitments
> ▪ Other

Conclusion

A. Adaptability for Ministry

A great many words can be used to describe the apostle Paul. One of the best is surely *adaptable*. In his own words, "To the Jews I became like a Jew, to win the Jews. . . . To those not having the law I became like one not having the law (though I am not free from God's law but am under Christ's law), so as to win those not having the law. To the weak I became weak, to win the weak. I have become all things to all people so that by all possible means I might save some" (1 Corinthians 9:20-22).

How adaptable will you choose to be for the sake of the gospel?

B. Prayer

Lord, strengthen us when we are discouraged and challenge us to be adaptable for your work. Bless our ministries for you, whether big or small. We pray this in the name of Jesus; amen.

C. Thought to Remember

Be a Paul to someone today!

INVOLVEMENT LEARNING

Enhance your lesson with NIV® Bible Student *(from your curriculum supplier)* and the reproducible activity page *(at www.standardlesson.com or in the back of the* NIV® Standard Lesson Commentary Deluxe Edition*).*

Into the Lesson

Pose this question: "What's it like to move to a place where you don't know anyone and the surroundings are unfamiliar?" Encourage several responses, but don't let this drag out. Make a transition by saying, "Today we will explore this question in a segment of the apostle Paul's life."

Option. As a review of the five lessons of this unit, place in chairs copies of the "Who Am I?" crossword puzzle from the reproducible page, which you can download. Learners can begin working on this as they arrive.

Into the Word

Have volunteers take turns reading aloud the last five verses of last week's text (that is, Acts 17:22-25, 28) followed by all verses of this week's text. After the reading, say, "Close your Bibles, and let's see how much you remember."

Distribute the following sentences in very large lettering on strips of poster board, one each: A–Paul quoted Gentile writers to introduce an audience in this city to the one true God. B–Paul supported himself here by working at his trade of tentmaking. C–Paul arrived here by sea voyage. D–Paul found in this city a couple with whom he could live and work. E–A named synagogue official of this city believed Paul's message. F–Paul made reference in this city to a pagan altar inscribed TO AN UNKNOWN GOD. G–Paul stayed here a year and a half. H–Paul received encouragement from the Lord in a vision while here. I–Paul got a haircut in this city. J–Although Jews in this city wanted Paul to stay longer, he declined. K–Paul delivered a message at the Areopagus (Mars' hill) in this city. L–Paul had an acrimonious parting of the ways with Jews of this city.

Draw on the board four columns having the following headings, one each: *Athens / Corinth / Cenchreae / Ephesus.* Ask the learner with sentence strip A to read it aloud, then come forward and affix it under the proper heading (provide tape). Invite agreements and disagreements; discuss as appropriate. Repeat the procedure with the remaining strips. (*Expected responses:* A, F, K for Athens; B, D, E, G, H, L for Corinth; I for Cenchreae; and C, J for Ephesus.)

After all the strips have been affixed in correct columns on the board, discuss the differences in Paul's methodology in Athens and Corinth, given the differing natures of his audiences. Also use strips as starting points to offer insights from the commentary in this verse-order sequence: D–verses 1, 2; B–verse 3; L–verses 4-7; E–verse 8; H–verses 9, 10; G–verse 11; I–verse 18; C–verses 18, 19; J–verses 20, 21a.

Into Life

Say, "In today's text, we see Paul working at a secular trade to support himself while he ministered in Corinth. This has been called the 'tent-making model,' since that's what Paul was doing. Let's find out if that's always the best way for mission work to be financed."

Ask two learners to come forward to engage each other in a mock pro-and-con debate on this proposal: *All missionary endeavors should follow Paul's "tentmaker" model.* You should recruit your debaters several days in advance so they have time to prepare. It will be important for your debaters to consider 1 Corinthians 9:3-18; 2 Corinthians 11:7-9; 1 Thessalonians 2:9; and 2 Thessalonians 3:7-10 in their argumentation. Allow each two minutes to state the position, then one minute each for rebuttal. Discuss results.

Option. Display the name of a missionary (or other person in full-time Christian service) your church supports; then give each learner one or more copies of the "Encouragement!" activity from the reproducible page. Allow two minutes for completion before collecting notes for delivery to the intended recipients.

SACRED GIFTS AND HOLY GATHERINGS

Special Features

		Page
Quarterly Quiz		114
Quarter at a Glance	Douglas Redford	115
Get the Setting	Lloyd M. Pelfrey	116
This Quarter in the Word (Daily Bible Readings)		117
Israelite Observances (Chart Feature)		119
Why Study the Old? (Teacher Tips)	Richard Koffarnus	120
Student Activity Reproducible Pages (annual Deluxe Edition only)		465
Student Activity Reproducible Pages (free download)	www.standardlesson.com	
In the World (weekly online feature)	www.standardlesson.com/category/in-the-world	

Lessons

Unit 1: What We Bring to God

December 6	The Sabbath Day	Exodus 20:8-11; 31:12-16	121
December 13	Acceptable Offerings	Leviticus 22:17-25, 31-33	129
December 20	Dedication of the Firstborn	Exodus 13:13b-15; Luke 2:22-32	137
December 27	A Generous Gift	Matthew 23:2-12; Mark 12:38-44	145

Unit 2: Four Weddings and a Funeral

January 3	A Bride Worth Waiting For	Genesis 29:15-30	153
January 10	The Most Beautiful Bride	Song of Songs 6:4-12	161
January 17	An Unfaithful Bride	Hosea 1:1-11	169
January 24	A Wedding in Cana	John 2:1-12	177
January 31	The Death of a Friend	John 11:38-44	185

Unit 3: Holy Days

February 7	Passover	Exodus 12:1-14	193
February 14	Festival of Weeks	Leviticus 23:15-22	201
February 21	Day of Atonement	Leviticus 16:11-19	209
February 28	Festival of Tabernacles	Leviticus 23:33-43	217

QUARTERLY QUIZ

Use these questions as a pretest or as a review. The answers are on page iv of This Quarter in the Word.

Lesson 1
1. Which day of the week is the Sabbath? (first, sixth, seventh?) *Exodus 20:10*
2. The Sabbath was designed by God to be a day of _____. *Exodus 31:15*

Lesson 2
1. For the ancient Israelites, acceptable animals for sacrifices included goats. T/F. *Leviticus 22:19*
2. Animals for what kind of offering could be blemished? (freewill, burnt, peace?) *Leviticus 22:23*

Lesson 3
1. The Israelites were to sacrifice the firstborn male animals of their flocks. T/F. *Exodus 13:15*
2. Holding the baby Jesus in the temple, a man named _____ praised God. *Luke 2:25, 28*

Lesson 4
1. Jesus proclaimed that the teachers of the law and Pharisees sat in whose seat? (Satan's, Samuel's, Moses'?) *Matthew 23:2*
2. Whom did Jesus use as an example of true giving? (a Pharisee, a Gentile, a widow?) *Mark 12:43*

Lesson 5
1. Jacob's two wives were named Rachel and _____. *Genesis 29:23*
2. Jacob loved his two wives equally. T/F. *Genesis 29:30*

Lesson 6
1. The hair of Solomon's beloved is compared with a flock of _____. *Song of Songs 6:5*
2. The beauty of Solomon's beloved inspired him like what? (archers, chariots, slingshots?) *Song of Songs 6:12*

Lesson 7
1. The woman Hosea was to take as a wife worked as a seamstress. T/F. *Hosea 1:2*

2. One of Hosea's children was named Maher-shalal-hash-baz. T/F. *Hosea 1:4, 6, 9*

Lesson 8
1. The wedding in Cana had problems when it ran out of what? (cake, roast lamb, wine?) *John 2:3*
2. After the miracle at Cana, Jesus went to Capernaum. T/F. *John 2:12*

Lesson 9
1. One of the sisters of Lazarus was named Martha. T/F. *John 11:39*
2. Lazarus was bound with what when he emerged from the grave? (ropes, strips of linen, nothing?) *John 11:44*

Lesson 10
1. The animal to be sacrificed for Passover could be a goat. T/F. *Exodus 12:5*
2. On the original Passover night, the Lord struck down the firstborn in homes not marked with olive oil. T/F. *Exodus 12:13*

Lesson 11
1. The Festival of Weeks (Pentecost) was to occur _____ days after Passover. *Leviticus 23:16*
2. Harvesters were not to leave any part of a field unharvested. T/F. *Leviticus 23:22*

Lesson 12
1. The implement that held burning coals was called a _____. *Leviticus 16:12*
2. The procedure on the Day of Atonement involved the blood of how many kinds of animals? (two, three, seven?) *Leviticus 16:11, 14, 15, 18.*

Lesson 13
1. The Festival of Tabernacles was held in the seventh month. T/F. *Leviticus 23:34*
2. The Festival of Tabernacles was a solemn seven-day observance. T/F. *Leviticus 23:40*

QUARTER AT A GLANCE

by Douglas Redford

THE THEME OF TRADITION is the focal point of this quarter of studies, entitled "Sacred Gifts and Holy Gatherings." In that regard, the lessons provide a look at some of the God-ordained traditions that became an integral part of the life of his people in biblical times.

The word *tradition* often draws negative reactions. Some view traditions as practices that are adhered to for no reason other than "we've always done it that way." Thinking people, so it is said, don't blindly accept traditions; such people are prepared to think and act "outside the box."

There is, however, great value in staying "inside the box" if God is the one who has designed the box! Traditions instituted by God merit our respect and our observance. Traditions (even those not specifically authorized by God) can offer order and structure in a world characterized by the chaotic disorder of sin.

Keeping Traditions

God gave the ancient Israelites a series of directives for instituting what could be called traditions. These included observances such as the weekly Sabbath (lesson 1) and the annual Day of Atonement (lesson 12). Requirements that accompanied their observances (along with the punishment for any violations) were made very clear.

The presentation of various offerings formed part of the Israelites' worship tradition, but not just anything could be brought as an acceptable offering (lesson 2). God's requirements were designed in part to keep the tradition of giving from being mindlessly or carelessly observed.

Three annual pilgrimage festivals (lessons 10, 11, and 13) were also instituted by God. These were special occasions for Israelites to come together to mark their identity as God's people and celebrate his faithfulness to them. One should note that the Festival of Tabernacles was to consist of seven days of rejoicing (Leviticus 23:40). Traditions need not be dreary, burdensome rituals that are devoid of joy.

Kept by Traditions

The aforementioned traditions were part of the Israelites' spiritual calendar, to which they were to give top priority. Elsewhere in this quarter's studies, we will think more in terms of traditions that are part of the social framework, specifically the traditions of weddings and funerals. Sadly, these traditions have been stripped of spiritual meaning in many cases today. Yet within God's plan both weddings and funerals can be vital teaching tools and means of witnessing to unbelievers of the significance of Christian faith.

Consider what weddings and funerals represent. A wedding highlights the greatest act of unity that is possible to experience on a human level. A funeral, by contrast, marks the greatest experience of separation that we endure on planet Earth. There is perhaps no tradition as joyous as a wedding and none as heartbreaking as a funeral.

> There is . . . great value in staying "inside the box" if God is the one who has designed the box!

If any two traditions have potential for Christian witness to an unbelieving world, it is these!

We keep a proper perspective amidst these highest of highs and lowest of lows by first of all maintaining a relationship with God, the creator of marriage and the one whose Son died and rose again to defeat death. Second, we keep perspective by maintaining relationships with the special people whom God places in our lives. Without these two ingredients, traditions of any kind can deteriorate into nothing more than lifeless ritual. But with these ingredients, we will come to understand an important principle: as we keep traditions, traditions will keep us. And therein lies their power.

GET THE SETTING

by Lloyd M. Pelfrey

THE STUDIES for the next three months have *Traditions* as the overall theme, and various aspects of Israel's religious customs are explored. It is sometimes alleged that Israel's festivals and sacrificial practices were borrowed from the traditions of neighboring nations. Do the facts support this accusation, which would discredit the divine origin of Israelite worship practices?

Similarities in Traditions

A tradition has been defined as "a custom or practice that continues to be followed by succeeding generations." Traditions often are based on significant historical events. One universal tradition among ancient cultures was that of animal sacrifice. The biblical perspective is that Abel demonstrated this in Genesis 4:4. Noah and his family form a critical point in this tradition. They are the progenitors of all humanity after the flood, and their sacrifices after leaving the ark became an example that resulted in many variations (Genesis 8:20).

Differences in Traditions: Babylonia

When Abram journeyed from Babylonia to Canaan, did he bring Babylonian religious traditions with him? Babylon's most famous festival celebrated the arrival of spring. It also became a festival of the new year, and its elaborate features involved the king's submission to Marduk, a Babylonian god. Abram's sacrifices are totally dissimilar (Genesis 12:7, 8; 13:18; 15:9, 10). The arrival of spring was celebrated throughout the Middle East, but not by the patriarchs or in Israel. The Israelites kept the Passover in the spring, but the emphasis was redemption from Egypt.

Differences in Traditions: Egypt

Given that the Israelites were in Egypt for 430 years (Exodus 12:40, 41), it would be logical that the religious customs of the Egyptians would be reflected in Israelite practices. But that is not the case. The people of Egypt loved to celebrate—any god, goddess, or Pharaoh. Regional and national holidays totaled over 30 percent of the Egyptian calendar. By contrast, Israel's calendar devoted less than 6 percent of the year for divinely directed festivals and observances. Egyptians sacrificed cattle, goats, antelopes, and geese; the latter two were not sacrificed in Israel. Egyptians sometimes decorated animals with finery before sacrificing them, but the Israelites never followed suit.

Differences in Traditions: Canaan

The ruins of the ancient city of Ugarit were discovered in 1929 in northern Syria. The clay tablets unearthed there reveal a language similar to Hebrew, and both use similar terms for various types of sacrifices. But rather than propose that the Israelites borrowed Ugaritic vocabulary and customs, it is reasonable to conclude that similarities are based on a common agrarian lifestyle. The sacrificial animals are ones that are important to the people in that region, and it is a "sacrifice" to give valuable animals to a deity.

One tradition of the Canaanites was that of boiling a kid (young goat) in its mother's milk. The Law of Moses definitely prohibits this (Exodus 23:19; 34:26; Deuteronomy 14:21). The ancient rabbis speculated much on the reason, and archaeology provides the answer: it seems that the Lord did not want his people to imitate this Canaanite practice (see also Deuteronomy 18:9).

Given by God!

The testimony of the Bible is clear: Israel did not borrow its traditions from other nations. Israelite festivals were not attempts to entice blessings from fickle gods. Rather, the festivals were vivid, memorable events designed to recall the hardships, deliverances, and miracles that formed part of God's faithfulness when he brought his people into the land promised to the patriarchs.

THIS QUARTER IN THE WORD

Mon, Nov. 30	Very Good	Genesis 1:28—2:3
Tue, Dec. 1	Day of Atonement	Leviticus 16:29-34
Wed, Dec. 2	Finding in God a Refuge	Psalm 62:1, 2, 5-9
Thu, Dec. 3	Promised Rest	Hebrews 4:1-11
Fri, Dec. 4	Eternal Rest	Revelation 14:12, 13; 21:1-5
Sat, Dec. 5	Work, Then Rest	Exodus 16:22-26
Sun, Dec. 6	A Day of Rest	Exodus 20:8-11; 31:12-16
Mon, Dec. 7	Living Sacrifice	Psalm 40:1-8
Tue, Dec. 8	Contrite Sacrifice	Psalm 51:15-19
Wed, Dec. 9	Loving Sacrifice	Mark 12:28-34a
Thu, Dec. 10	Complete Sacrifice	Romans 12:1-8
Fri, Dec. 11	Faithful Sacrifice	Hebrews 11:4-16
Sat, Dec. 12	Perfect Sacrifice	1 John 4:9-16
Sun, Dec. 13	Acceptable Sacrifice	Leviticus 22:17-25, 31-33
Mon, Dec. 14	Separate for a Purpose	Leviticus 20:7, 8, 22-24
Tue, Dec. 15	God's Heart and Dedication	2 Chronicles 30:5-12
Wed, Dec. 16	Dedication of Samson	Judges 13:2-5, 24, 25
Thu, Dec. 17	Dedication of Samuel	1 Samuel 1:11, 20, 24-28
Fri, Dec. 18	Dedication of David	1 Samuel 16:10-13
Sat, Dec. 19	Dedication of Firstborn	Leviticus 12
Sun, Dec. 20	Dedication of Jesus	Exodus 13:13b-15; Luke 2:22-32

Mon, Feb. 15	Perfect Atonement	Hebrews 2:10-17
Tue, Feb. 16	Appointed for Atonement	Hebrews 3:1-6
Wed, Feb. 17	Completed Atonement	Romans 3:21-26
Thu, Feb. 18	Preparation and Atonement	Exodus 30:1-10
Fri, Feb. 19	Obedience and Atonement	Leviticus 8:30-36
Sat, Feb. 20	Sin Offering for Atonement	Leviticus 16:1-10
Sun, Feb. 21	A Clean Slate	Leviticus 16:11-19
Mon, Feb. 22	God of the Journey	Psalm 68:5-10
Tue, Feb. 23	The Journey Begins	Exodus 3:1-6
Wed, Feb. 24	The Journey Falters	Deuteronomy 1:29-33
Thu, Feb. 25	Remember the Journey	Deuteronomy 8:1-11
Fri, Feb. 26	Jesus and the Journey	John 3:14-21
Sat, Feb. 27	Stephen and the Journey	Acts 7:30-42a
Sun, Feb. 28	Heritage and Hope	Leviticus 23:33-43

Answers to the Quarterly Quiz on page 114

Lesson 1—1. seventh. 2. rest. **Lesson 2**—1. true. 2. freewill. **Lesson 3**—1. true. 2. Simeon. **Lesson 4**—1. Moses'. 2. a widow. **Lesson 5**—1. Leah. 2. false. **Lesson 6**—1. goats'. 2. chariots. **Lesson 7**—1. false. 2. false. **Lesson 8**—1. wine. 2. true. **Lesson 9**—1. true. 2. strips of linen. **Lesson 10**—1. true. 2. false. **Lesson 11**—1. 50. 2. false. **Lesson 12**—1. censer. 2. two. **Lesson 13**—1. true. 2. false.

Mon, Dec. 21	Modeled Generosity	John 1:10-18
Tue, Dec. 22	Gracious Generosity	Ephesians 2:1-10
Wed, Dec. 23	Excellent Generosity	2 Corinthians 8:3-9
Thu, Dec. 24	Wise Generosity	Colossians 3:12-17
Fri, Dec. 25	Loving Generosity	Romans 12:6-13
Sat, Dec. 26	Humble Generosity	Matthew 6:1-6
Sun, Dec. 27	Generous Even in Poverty	Matthew 23:2-12; Mark 12:38-44

Trustworthy Lives

Mon, Dec. 28	Honesty: The Best Policy	Proverbs 11:9-13
Tue, Dec. 29	Wisdom More Than Strength	Proverbs 12:19-26
Wed, Dec. 30	Judged Faithful	Proverbs 24:3-7, 13, 14
Thu, Dec. 31	The Lord Is Present	1 Timothy 1:12-17
Fri, Jan. 1	Welcome Home	Genesis 28:15-22
Sat, Jan. 2	One Groom, Two Brides	Genesis 29:9-14
Sun, Jan. 3		Genesis 29:15-30
Mon, Jan. 4	A Perfect Woman	Proverbs 31:10, 11, 20, 25, 26
Tue, Jan. 5	The Perfect Shepherd	John 10:1-6
Wed, Jan. 6	The Good Shepherd	John 10:7-15
Thu, Jan. 7	The Eternal Shepherd	John 10:22-30
Fri, Jan. 8	The Most Perfect Love	Song of Songs 4:9-15
Sat, Jan. 9	The Most Handsome Groom	Song of Songs 5:9-16
Sun, Jan. 10	The Most Beautiful Bride	Song of Songs 6:4-12
Mon, Jan. 11	A Clean and Faithful Heart	Psalm 51:6-12
Tue, Jan. 12	The Faithful God	Psalm 89:24-29
Wed, Jan. 13	Faithful to Truth	Psalm 119:25-32
Thu, Jan. 14	Free in the Spirit	Galatians 5:16-25
Fri, Jan. 15	Unfaithful Israel	Hosea 4:1-6
Sat, Jan. 16	Faithful God	Hosea 2:18-23
Sun, Jan. 17	An Unfaithful Bride	Hosea 1

ii

Mon, Jan. 18	The Mighty Deeds of God	Psalm 77:11-15
Tue, Jan. 19	The Resurrected Messiah	Acts 2:22-28
Wed, Jan. 20	The Gift of Sight	John 9:1-11
Thu, Jan. 21	The Gift of Health	Matthew 15:29-38
Fri, Jan. 22	The Clean Gift	Matthew 5:21-26
Sat, Jan. 23	The Healing Mission of Jesus	Luke 4:16-24
Sun, Jan. 24	Water to Wine	John 2:1-12

Trust in Facing Death — Psalm 56

Mon, Jan. 25	Life Eternal	Isaiah 25:6-10
Tue, Jan. 26	Darkness Dispelled	Matthew 4:12-17
Wed, Jan. 27	For God's Glory	John 11:1-6
Thu, Jan. 28	I Am Life	John 11:17-27
Fri, Jan. 29	Jesus Wept	John 11:28-37
Sat, Jan. 30	Alive Again	John 11:38-44
Sun, Jan. 31	Young Jesus and the Passover	Luke 2:41-49
Mon, Feb. 1	Jesus' Last Passover	Matthew 26:20-30
Tue, Feb. 2	Plague of Flies	Exodus 8:20-29
Wed, Feb. 3	Plague of Locusts	Exodus 10:12-20
Thu, Feb. 4	Detailed Instructions	Numbers 9:1-4, 13
Fri, Feb. 5	When Your Children Ask	Joshua 4:1-7
Sat, Feb. 6	Preparing for Passover	Exodus 12:1-14
Mon, Feb. 8	Praise the Lord	Psalm 147:1-11
Tue, Feb. 9	Thanks Be to God	1 Chronicles 17:16-27
Wed, Feb. 10	In All Things, Thanks	Ephesians 5:15-20
Thu, Feb. 11	In Spite of Everything, Thanks	Romans 7:14-25
Fri, Feb. 12	Increasing Thanks	2 Corinthians 4:7-15
Sat, Feb. 13	In the End, Thanks	Revelation 11:15-19
Sun, Feb. 14	Praise for a Bountiful Harvest	Leviticus 23:15-22

iii

ISRAELITE OBSERVANCES

MONTH	DAY(S)	FEAST	OLD TESTAMENT REFERENCES (PARTIAL)
NISAN (OR ABIB) MARCH—APRIL	14	PASSOVER	EXODUS 12:6, 43-49; LEVITICUS 23:5; NUMBERS 28:16; DEUTERONOMY 16:1, 2
	15-21	FEAST OF UNLEAVENED BREAD	EXODUS 12:15-20; 23:15; LEVITICUS 23:6, 9-14; NUMBERS 28:17; DEUTERONOMY 16:3, 4
SIVAN MAY—JUNE	6	PENTECOST - ALSO KNOWN AS —FEAST OF WEEKS —DAY OF FIRSTFRUITS —FEAST OF HARVEST	EXODUS 23:16a; 34:22a; LEVITICUS 23:15-21; NUMBERS 28:26-31; DEUTERONOMY 16:9-12, 16
TISHRI (OR ETHANIM) SEPTEMBER—OCTOBER	1	FEAST OF TRUMPETS	LEVITICUS 23:23-25; NUMBERS 29:1-6
	10	DAY OF ATONEMENT	LEVITICUS 16; 23:26-32; NUMBERS 29:7-11
	15-21	FEAST OF TABERNACLES - ALSO KNOWN AS —FEAST OF BOOTHS —FEAST OF INGATHERING	EXODUS 23:16b; 34:22b; LEVITICUS 23:33-36a, 39-43; NUMBERS 29:12-34; DEUTERONOMY 16:13-17; 31:10
	22	ASSEMBLY OF THE EIGHTH DAY	LEVITICUS 23:36b; NUMBERS 29:35-38
ADAR FEBRUARY—MARCH	14-15	FEAST OF PURIM	ESTHER 9:20-32

WHY STUDY THE OLD?

Teacher Tips by Richard Koffarnus

DURING A STUDY of an Old Testament book, one of my students asked, "Why do we have to cover the Old Testament? I thought we were a New Testament church!" That was a fair question deserving of a fair answer.

Reason 1

First, familiarity with the Old Testament is essential to fullest understanding of the New Testament in general and Jesus in particular. One conservative estimate notes 295 Old Testament passages quoted and over 600 alluded to in the New. That means that over 10 percent of New Testament verses include Old Testament material! Some scholars think the percentage to be much higher, depending on how broadly one defines *alluded to*. In any case, if we want to understand fully the New Testament and Jesus as it presents him to us, then we had better know the Old!

Reason 2

Second, Jesus studied the Old Testament. A popular question in recent years is, "What would Jesus do?" Well, we know what Jesus did with the Old Testament: he learned it inside and out. When challenged on his doctrine or behavior, he often responded by quoting Scripture. When he appeared to two disciples on the road to Emmaus after his resurrection, Jesus reviewed "Moses and all the Prophets" in explaining "what was said in all the Scriptures concerning himself" (Luke 24:27). If Jesus thought it important to know the Old Testament, shouldn't we?

Reason 3

Third, the Old Testament continued to be recognized as Scripture by the first-century church both before and while the New Testament was being written. Peter opened the church doors on Pentecost (Acts 2) with a sermon based on Joel 2, Psalm 16, and Psalm 110. Toward the end of his life, with the church well established, Peter was still quoting the Old Testament in his letters that we call 1 and 2 Peter—at least 13 times total. Being a New Testament church is to recognize the importance of the Old Testament.

Reason 4

Fourth, the Old Testament provides vital details about our past as well as promises concerning our future. From the Old Testament we learn who we are in relation to God and the rest of creation, how we got here, why we are here, and what our destiny holds. We learn how God has prepared a way of salvation and why we need it. To be sure, the New Testament addresses all these topics as well. But the Old Testament offers insightful details that the New Testament presumes, and we are much the poorer for not studying those details.

Reason 5

Fifth, the Old Testament provides us with valuable character studies. The "Hall of Faith" in Hebrews 11 offers biographical sketches of numerous Old Testament heroes who can serve as examples of vital faith for Christians today. But as good as that exposition is, it is only a highly condensed summary, as the writer himself notes in verse 32. For fullest understanding of the spiritual triumphs and failures of those heroes, we should let Hebrews 11 impel us to study the entirety of their stories as recorded in the Old Testament.

Summary, Courtesy of Paul

We can scarcely do better than allow the apostle Paul to offer the concluding remarks of our brief investigation.

> For everything that was written in the past was written to teach us, so that through the endurance taught in the Scriptures and the encouragement they provide we might have hope (Romans 15:4; compare 1 Corinthians 10:6, 11).

THE SABBATH DAY

DEVOTIONAL READING: Hebrews 4:1-11
BACKGROUND SCRIPTURE: Exodus 16:23; 20:8-11; 31:12-18;
Deuteronomy 5:12-15; Leviticus 23:3-8; Matthew 12:1-14; Acts 13:42

EXODUS 20:8-11

⁸ "Remember the Sabbath day by keeping it holy. ⁹ Six days you shall labor and do all your work, ¹⁰ but the seventh day is a sabbath to the LORD your God. On it you shall not do any work, neither you, nor your son or daughter, nor your male or female servant, nor your animals, nor any foreigner residing in your towns. ¹¹ For in six days the LORD made the heavens and the earth, the sea, and all that is in them, but he rested on the seventh day. Therefore the LORD blessed the Sabbath day and made it holy."

EXODUS 31:12-16

¹² Then the LORD said to Moses, ¹³ "Say to the Israelites, 'You must observe my Sabbaths. This will be a sign between me and you for the generations to come, so you may know that I am the LORD, who makes you holy.

¹⁴ "'Observe the Sabbath, because it is holy to you. Anyone who desecrates it is to be put to death; those who do any work on that day must be cut off from their people. ¹⁵ For six days work is to be done, but the seventh day is a day of sabbath rest, holy to the LORD. Whoever does any work on the Sabbath day is to be put to death. ¹⁶ The Israelites are to observe the Sabbath, celebrating it for the generations to come as a lasting covenant.'"

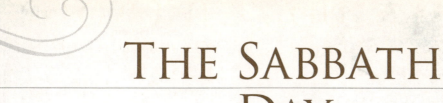

KEY VERSE

Remember the Sabbath day by keeping it holy. —**Exodus 20:8**

Photo: CharlieAJA / iStock / Thinkstock

Sacred Gifts and Holy Gatherings

Unit 1: What We Bring to God

LESSONS 1–4

Lesson Aims

After participating in this lesson, each learner will be able to:

1. List requirements for observing the Sabbath and penalties for failing to do so.

2. Explain the significance of the Sabbath as a sign.

3. Suggest a specific action or routine that can serve as a sign of his or her belief in the holiness of God.

Lesson Outline

Introduction
  A. Time-out
  B. Lesson Background
I. Sabbath's Institution (Exodus 20:8-11)
  A. Command Given (vv. 8-10)
  B. Command Explained (v. 11)
    The Power of Example
II. Sabbath's Importance (Exodus 31:12-16)
  A. Sacred Sign (vv. 12, 13)
    Someone Special
  B. Strict Punishment (vv. 14, 15)
  C. Steadfast Observance (v. 16)
Conclusion
  A. Rest for the Week
  B. Rest for the Weak
  C. Prayer
  D. Thought to Remember

Introduction

A. Time-out

The significance of the word *time-out* varies by setting. In sporting events, players often welcome a time-out for rest or to plan a critical play. On the other hand, no child wants to hear *time-out* from a parent, because it means that the child must take some quiet time alone after having disobeyed or becoming too rowdy.

Today's Scripture highlights God's command to his people Israel to "remember the Sabbath." The Sabbath (which means "ceasing") was God's weekly time-out for his children of the Old Testament era. It was not for discipline of bad behavior, but to encourage them to remember their Creator and to imitate him in the important area of rest.

B. Lesson Background

Since the theme of this quarter's lessons is *tradition*, some observations about that concept are in order. Often the word *tradition* carries negative connotations. For example, *traditionalist* may refer to someone who is rigidly tied to certain beliefs or practices and is unwilling to change them.

Traditions, however, can assist nations, cities, churches, and families in remembering their roots and respecting their heritage. Yes, traditions can become stale and routine; but properly handled, traditions can achieve worthwhile purposes. Such was God's intent in instituting Sabbath observances as an ongoing tradition for ancient Israel.

The first part of today's text is taken from the Ten Commandments, which God gave to his people at Mount Sinai after their exodus from Egypt (Exodus 19:1, 2). The second part of our text comes from Exodus 31 at the conclusion of the instructions regarding the construction of the tabernacle (which begin in chapter 25).

I. Sabbath's Institution

(Exodus 20:8-11)

The first three of the Ten Commandments are concerned with proper respect or reverence for the Lord himself (Exodus 20:3-7). The fourth commandment, our area of study today, comes next.

A. Command Given (vv. 8-10)

8. "Remember the Sabbath day by keeping it holy.

The fourth commandment deals with the issue of time. God, of course, is eternal (Deuteronomy 33:27; Psalm 90:2; Habakkuk 1:12). He transcends time. For human beings, however, time is very much woven into the fabric of our lives. (Try keeping track of how often you look at a watch or clock or ask what time it is on any given day!)

The concept of a *Sabbath day* was impressed upon the Israelites before this commandment was issued. Exodus 16:1-3 records how the Israelites began to grumble about their lack of food only a month and a half after the Lord had miraculously provided their deliverance from bondage in Egypt. God responded by promising to "rain down bread from heaven" (v. 4), which the people called "manna" (v. 31).

In instructing the people regarding the manna, God told them to gather just enough to meet their daily needs on the first through the fifth days of each week. On the sixth day (Friday), they were to gather twice as much as they needed so that on the seventh day (Saturday) they would not have to gather any. The seventh day was to be recognized as "a holy sabbath to the Lord" (Exodus 16:23), a day of rest (v. 30).

God's provision of manna eventually ceases (Joshua 5:12), but Sabbath observance for the ancient Israelites does not. With his decree of the fourth commandment, God makes observance of the Sabbath an enduring part of their religious life. They are to keep this day holy. The explanation of how to do so follows.

9, 10. "Six days you shall labor and do all your work, but the seventh day is a sabbath to

HOW TO SAY IT

Aaron	*Air*-un.
Deuteronomy	Due-ter-*ahn*-uh-me.
Habakkuk	Huh-*back*-kuk.
Jonah	*Jo*-nuh.
Nineveh	*Nin*-uh-vuh.
Noah	*No*-uh.
Sinai	*Sigh*-nye or *Sigh*-nay-eye.

the Lord your God. On it you shall not do any work, neither you, nor your son or daughter, nor your male or female servant, nor your animals, nor any foreigner residing in your towns.

The schedule that accompanied the provision of the manna again offers a helpful illustration of the fourth commandment in wider application. The people labor to gather manna on each of the first six days of any given week; on the seventh day they rest and gather none. (They cannot gather any on the seventh day even if they want to, since no manna is provided on that day.) This is how all work is to be structured. The first six days of any week are workdays for the people; *but the seventh day is a sabbath to the Lord your God.*

We can note at this point that this commandment also establishes that work is something approved and mandated by God. When God created man in his image, he gave him work to do. "The Lord God took the man and put him in the Garden of Eden to work it and take care of it" (Genesis 2:15). God's pronouncement concerning work after the fall was not a curse on work itself; rather, the pronouncement addressed the conditions under which work would be carried out. Work was to become a demanding, sweat-producing effort (Genesis 3:17-19). The Sabbath provides a respite from that part of the consequences of the first sin.

The Sabbath's observance applies to all members of a household, whether children or servants. One cannot command that a servant work on the Sabbath, for the servant must be given the opportunity to rest as well. This also applies to *any foreigner residing in your towns,* referring to someone who is not a native-born Israelite. Such a person may be a traveler passing through who lodges temporarily with an Israelite family. Or the individual could be someone from another people-group who has chosen to identify with the covenant people permanently. In the New Testament, this person is sometimes referred to as one who fears and worships God (Acts 10:1, 2; 13:16, 26).

Not only is Sabbath-rest to be observed by humans, it is also to be granted to livestock. Such a requirement highlights the comprehensive nature of the command. Not working *your animals* means that the Israelites are not to engage in their primary livelihood, since they are an agricultural people. Humane treatment of animals is a biblical principle (Proverbs 12:10).

Granting rest even to animals is probably more than just a way of acknowledging that they are God's creation and should be treated with care and respect, although this is certainly true. The Scriptures teach that all creation is subject to the consequences of human sin in Eden (Romans 8:19-23). God's covenant with Noah following the flood included all living creatures (Genesis 9:8-17). The tenth plague on Egypt (the death of the firstborn) included "the firstborn of the cattle" (Exodus 11:4, 5). We can further note that the nationwide repentance produced in Nineveh through the preaching of Jonah involved animals as well as humans (Jonah 3:6-8).

What Do You Think?

Since observing special days is a personal matter in the New Testament era (Romans 14:5-8), what benefits and dangers are there for a church to encourage its members to do so?

Talking Points for Your Discussion

- Regarding Christmas
- Regarding Easter
- Regarding Good Friday
- Other

B. Command Explained (v. 11)

11. "For in six days the LORD made the heavens and the earth, the sea, and all that is in them, but he rested on the seventh day. Therefore the LORD blessed the Sabbath day and made it holy."

Here we see the basis for the Israelites' observance of the Sabbath. Remembering to rest *on the seventh day* is to follow a precedent set by the Creator himself; it is to bring the week under his lordship. Ultimately, Sabbath observance recognizes that the Israelites' time is not their own; it is a gift from God, to be used by following the pattern established by the giver.

The fact that the Lord rested on the seventh day does not imply sleep on his part, since God (unlike humans) has no need of it (Psalm 121:4). Rather,

this verse is saying that God rested on the seventh day because his work of creating was finished. For that reason he *blessed,* or set apart as holy, the Sabbath Day; his people are to do the same as they go about creating their livelihoods.

❧ THE POWER OF EXAMPLE ❧

We're all indebted to Charles F. Kettering (1876–1958) for inventing the electric starter for cars. He also invented Freon®, the gas that made air conditioning possible. He is less known for an important bit of parental advice: "Every father should remember that one day his son will follow his example instead of his advice." It's another way of stating the old proverb, "Like father, like son."

Many parents have learned the truth of this the hard way! Research shows that the moods our children pick up from us have the effect of "wiring" them to respond to the world in the same way we do.

God's establishment of Sabbath observance was modeled on his own behavior. He was not saying, "Do as I say, not as I do" (compare Matthew 23:3). If he found it appropriate to rest from labor, who are we to think that we need not do so as well? We are in great peril whenever we fail to follow an example God has set for us to emulate. See John 13:15, 34.   —C. R. B.

What Do You Think?

How do you make sure you get adequate rest?

Talking Points for Your Discussion

- Regarding sleep
- Regarding time off
- "I'd rather burn out than rust out"
- Other

II. Sabbath's Importance
(EXODUS 31:12-16)

Exodus 31 begins with God telling Moses of certain men (vv. 2, 6a) who are to "make everything I have commanded you" (v. 6b) concerning the tabernacle and the items associated with it. This includes the clothing to be worn by the high priest Aaron and his sons (vv. 7-11). An additional reminder of the Sabbath's importance that occurs just after these instructions is noteworthy: not even the construction of something as sacred as the tabernacle is to keep the Israelites from observing the Sabbath! They must not say, "We're doing an important, God-given task; we don't have time to rest." The appointed day of rest must be maintained faithfully.

A. Sacred Sign (vv. 12, 13)

12, 13. Then the Lord said to Moses, "Say to the Israelites, 'You must observe my Sabbaths. This will be a sign between me and you for the generations to come, so you may know that I am the Lord, who makes you holy.

Circumcision is considered a covenant sign between God and his people (Genesis 17:9-11), but that rite is limited to males. Keeping the Lord's Sabbaths, by contrast, is something that applies to all Israelites. Exodus 20:8 speaks of keeping the Sabbath holy; here the emphasis is on the holiness of the Sabbath-keeper: *I am the Lord, who makes you holy.* To be made holy is to be sanctified (compare 1 Corinthians 1:2). Prior to giving Israel the Ten Commandments, God had established his covenant with the people, calling them "a kingdom of priests and a holy nation" (Exodus 19:6).

What Do You Think?
What function, if any, should signs have in the New Testament era? How do you apply your conclusions to your life?
Talking Points for Your Discussion
- Regarding unbelievers
- Regarding fellow believers

❧ SOMEONE SPECIAL ❧

Unrequited love is a recurring theme in popular music. One song puts a Christmas twist on that theme as the singer laments the fact that she fell in love with someone the previous Christmas, but the object of her affection treated it so lightly that he was soon gone from her life. The singer vows that this Christmas she'll be more selective and won't make the same mistake. Instead, she'll look for "someone special" to fall in love with. (If only falling in love worked that way!)

The theme of that song offers a certain parallel to spiritual allegiances: people keep giving their hearts to the gods of human imagination, only to be disappointed when those fictitious gods do not return the affection. Such gods are never there when expected.

All the while the true God keeps calling to us. The ancient Israelites were to respond to that call by keeping his commandments (see Exodus 20:6; Deuteronomy 5:10; 7:9; etc.); we are to do so as well (see John 14:15). It is keeping the commands of Jesus that declares the heart's intent. That declaration is that we have found love for the world to be unsatisfying, and only the holy God is that "someone special" to whom we must cling (John 15:19).   —C. R. B.

B. Strict Punishment (vv. 14, 15)

14. "'Observe the Sabbath, because it is holy to you. Anyone who desecrates it is to be put to death; those who do any work on that day must be cut off from their people.

The holiness of the Sabbath is further reinforced by the strict punishment to be administered in the case of disobedience: *anyone who desecrates* the Sabbath by doing *any work on that day must be cut off from their people.* No work is permitted on the Sabbath under penalty of death.

What Do You Think?
Which daily spiritual disciplines help you most in living a life of greater holiness? Why?
Talking Points for Your Discussion
- When out in public
- When alone

Numbers 15:32-36 records the only instance in the Old Testament where someone incurred the death penalty because he was discovered working on the Sabbath. (He was gathering wood, presumably to use for cooking; compare Exodus 35:3.) In light of that account, perhaps it is more understandable why some Jews in Jesus' day see him as a Sabbath-breaker and as one who encourages others to do the same by, for example, telling someone to carry his bed on the Sabbath (John 5:10-18).

The incident in Numbers 15:32-36 should be considered in light of what verses 30, 31 say about sinning "defiantly" and despising the Lord's command. Apparently, a rebellious, arrogant attitude characterized the individual who was gathering wood on the Sabbath, and he was swiftly punished for defying a clear command of the Lord.

By Jesus' time, however, groups such as the Pharisees focused so closely on the actions of a person during the Sabbath that they paid no attention to the motive behind the act. In their eyes and according to their definition, Jesus frequently broke the Sabbath. But as Jesus noted, calling a good act evil simply because of the day on which it is done makes keeping the Sabbath more important than helping someone in need. Such an attitude does not fit with the divine purpose for providing the Sabbath. As Jesus puts it, "The Sabbath was made for man, not man for the Sabbath" (Mark 2:27).

15. "For six days work is to be done, but the seventh day is a day of sabbath rest, holy to the LORD. Whoever does any work on the Sabbath day is to be put to death.

This verse reiterates the emphasis of the previous one and highlights the fact that God is the Lord of the Israelite calendar. He allots six days for work; on the seventh, work is prohibited. His people must plan their schedules accordingly.

What Do You Think?

What would be involved in promoting observance of a Sabbath principle instead of a Sabbath day?

Talking Points for Your Discussion

- Mark 2:27
- Colossians 2:16
- Hebrews 4:9
- Other

C. Steadfast Observance (v. 16)

16. "'The Israelites are to observe the Sabbath, celebrating it for the generations to come as a lasting covenant.'"

The Sabbath forms part of the covenant between the Lord and the ancient Israelites. Some believe that this covenant, being *lasting,* still remains in effect; thus they continue to worship on the seventh day (Saturday). But the New Testament points to the first day of the week (Sunday) as the day Christians are to gather in worship (Acts 20:7; 1 Corinthians 16:1, 2; compare Colossians 2:16, 17). This is only fitting since Jesus' resurrection occurred on the first day of the week.

As used in the verse before us and the wider context of Scripture, the word *lasting* does not denote "absolutely never ending," but rather refers to something that will endure only as long as God's covenant remains in effect with Israel. Similar language is used of other items associated with worship under the old covenant that comes to an end when the church is established (example: the tabernacle's "incense will burn regularly . . . for the generations to come" [Exodus 30:8]).

Conclusion
A. Rest for the Week

At first blush, the idea of ceasing work may seem appropriate for the ancient Israelites, but not for us today, since life in our "24/7" culture is so much more complex. Just think how things on our to-do lists remain undone for weeks and weeks! The state of the economy pressures many people to work more than one job. The situation seems especially difficult for single-parent families. A weekly day of rest seems like an impossibility for many.

So how should Christians view the fourth commandment? How does it apply, if at all, to us? Does God expect modern Christians to rest the way he expected the people of ancient Israel to rest on their Sabbath?

While the New Testament provides a precedent for setting aside the first day of the week as the Lord's Day (Acts 20:7; Revelation 1:10), it does not specifically require us to abstain from work as the Israelites were required under the old covenant. Nowhere in Acts or the Epistles do we find any discussion of this particular issue. Perhaps the closest thing to it is Paul's instruction to the Christians in Rome concerning certain days being regarded as sacred or special, but he clearly sees this as a matter of personal conviction (Romans 14:5-8).

Ideally, not having to work on Sunday at one's regular job is a blessing. Some individuals, like David Green, the founder and CEO of the Hobby Lobby chain, have committed themselves to keeping their businesses closed on Sunday to give employees time for worship and family. But many Christians who would greatly appreciate not having to work on Sunday do not have this option. Some occupations by nature require work on Sunday (example: firefighters).

Even so, it is important that the spiritual purpose behind observance of the Lord's Day be given its due in some way. Observing the Sabbath reminded the Israelites of God's role as Creator not only of the world (Exodus 20:11) but also of their nation when he delivered them from Egyptian bondage (Deuteronomy 5:15). Christians give special attention on the Lord's Day to remember their deliverance from the spiritual bondage of sin through Jesus' death and resurrection. Sabbath observance in Old Testament times focused on the old creation; Lord's Day observance in New Testament times focuses on the new creation in Christ (2 Corinthians 5:17; Galatians 6:15).

If one's work schedule does not allow attendance at worship on Sunday morning, then the remembrance should occur, if possible, at some other time on Sunday. This could be a Sunday evening worship service (if available) or, in a more private setting, worship with a smaller group of believers who also have to work on Sunday.

We live in a time when it is all too easy to let Sunday be treated as "just another day" on the calendar. Is reserving the Lord's Day for worship a priority for you? May we not let either business or "busy-ness" distract us from this priority!

B. Rest for the Weak

While the previous section addressed the necessity of spiritual renewal, the benefit of physical rest is certainly worth considering as well. Following a series of very busy and exhausting events, Jesus told his disciples on one occasion, "Come with me by yourselves to a quiet place and get some rest" (Mark 6:31). Jesus recognized the need for some downtime for his disciples. His counsel should be heeded in our world of fran-

Visual for Lesson 1. *Start a discussion by pointing to the caption in this visual as you ask, "What are some ways to make this happen?"*

tic schedules and overcommitments. As Vance Havner (1901–1986) observed, "If you don't come apart, you will come apart!" What he meant was that if one doesn't set aside time for personal rest and rejuvenation, he or she eventually will pay the price for not doing so.

Making time for adequate rest is a matter of stewardship; it is taking proper care of our bodies. Lack of rest reflects poor stewardship, and it detracts from our ability to serve God faithfully and to the best of our ability.

C. Prayer

Father, help us to take seriously the principle of rest that is embedded in the fourth commandment. May we take the time to rest (physically and spiritually) so that our lives can more fully reflect daily the true rest that only Jesus provides. In Jesus' name. Amen.

D. Thought to Remember

If God took a day to rest,
shouldn't we?

VISUALS FOR THESE LESSONS

The visual pictured in each lesson (example: top of this page) is a small reproduction of a large, full-color poster included in the *Adult Resources* packet for the Winter Quarter. That packet also contains the very useful *Presentation Tools* CD for teacher use. Order No. 020029215 from your supplier.

INVOLVEMENT LEARNING

Enhance your lesson with NIV® Bible Student (from your curriculum supplier) and the reproducible activity page (at www.standardlesson.com or in the back of the NIV® Standard Lesson Commentary Deluxe Edition).

Into the Lesson

Before class, take one chair and face it to a corner. Start a discussion by making the sign for time-out (one hand vertical with your other hand on top of it horizontally to form the letter *T*). Ask, "What does it mean when you see someone making this sign during a football game?" After someone responds "time-out," point to the chair in the corner and ask, "When a mother makes this gesture to a child, what does it mean?" After someone responds "time-out as punishment," say, "God used one of the Ten Commandments to tell his people when to take a time-out. Let's see what that involved and why it was important."

Into the Word

Form learners into pairs or groups of three. Depending on the size of your class, give each pair or group one or more of the following statements, which you have reproduced on index cards, one statement per card. *Card A*–The Israelites were to observe the Sabbath and make it holy by taking a half-day off. *Card B*–Only Israelite males were required to keep the Sabbath. *Card C*–Although God wanted the Israelites to honor the Sabbath, he was willing to overlook infractions. *Card D*–God's commandment regarding the Sabbath applied to the Israelites only until they were settled in the promised land.

After you distribute the cards, say, "Each statement has a factual error. Compare the statement on the card with today's text to identify the error." Call for conclusions after a few minutes. *Expected responses:* A–Every indication in the text is that Sabbath observance involved the entire day (Exodus 20:8; 31:15; etc.). B–This commandment applied to everyone and even to the livestock (Exodus 20:10). C–The penalty for defiling the Sabbath or doing any work on it was death (Exodus 31:14, 15). D–The Sabbath was to be a sign between God and the Israelites throughout their generations (Exodus 31:13); it was to be "a lasting covenant" (see commentary on 31:16).

Alternative. Distribute to individuals or pairs of learners seven 8½" x 11" sheets of paper that feature the following seven words, one word per sheet: Sign / Animals / laBor / oBserve / creAtion / deaTh / Holy. The emphasized letters should be as large as possible. Ask recipients to find a reference to their word in today's text, then write out a brief explanation of how this word applies to the Sabbath. After a few minutes for research, call time and ask that the *Sign* sheet be brought forward, the explanation read to the class, and the sheet affixed to the board (bring tape). Be prepared to use the commentary to fill in overlooked information.

Repeat the procedure for the remaining six words, in the order given, with sheets being affixed to the board in a column. When all seven sheets are posted, the emphasized letters will spell *Sabbath* vertically. This activity may work better visually if you prepare the sheets of paper in landscape format (that is, turned sideways).

Into Life

Say, "The Sabbath was a sign that the ancient Israelites were a holy nation, set apart by God for his purposes. In what ways can Sunday serve the same or similar function for Christians?" Encourage free discussion. Expect such answers as "commitment to attending Lord's Day worship is a sign of commitment to Christ," and "Sunday worship recognizes the day of Jesus' resurrection as the distinctive of Christianity."

Option or Alternative 1. Distribute copies of the "Principle Practiced" activity from the reproducible page, which you can download. Ask learners to pair off to discuss the four questions listed.

Option or Alternative 2. Distribute copies of the "Rest Wrestling" activity from the reproducible page. Allow a minute of reflection on the first statement; then call for reactions. Repeat for the second.

ACCEPTABLE OFFERINGS

DEVOTIONAL READING: Hebrews 11:4-16

BACKGROUND SCRIPTURE: Leviticus 22:17-33; 23:9-14, 31-33; Deuteronomy 22:6, 7; Micah 6:6-8; Isaiah 1:10-20; Romans 12:1, 2; 1 Corinthians 10:14-22

LEVITICUS 22:17-25, 31-33

[17] The LORD said to Moses, [18] "Speak to Aaron and his sons and to all the Israelites and say to them: 'If any of you—whether an Israelite or a foreigner residing in Israel—presents a gift for a burnt offering to the LORD, either to fulfill a vow or as a freewill offering, [19] you must present a male without defect from the cattle, sheep or goats in order that it may be accepted on your behalf. [20] Do not bring anything with a defect, because it will not be accepted on your behalf. [21] When anyone brings from the herd or flock a fellowship offering to the LORD to fulfill a special vow or as a freewill offering, it must be without defect or blemish to be acceptable. [22] Do not offer to the LORD the blind, the injured or the maimed, or anything with warts or festering or running sores. Do not place any of these on the altar as a food offering presented to the LORD. [23] You may, however, present as a freewill offering an ox or a sheep that is deformed or stunted, but it will not be accepted in fulfillment of a vow. [24] You must not offer to the LORD an animal whose testicles are bruised, crushed, torn or cut. You must not do this in your own land, [25] and you must not accept such animals from the hand of a foreigner and offer them as the food of your God. They will not be accepted on your behalf, because they are deformed and have defects.'"

[31] "Keep my commands and follow them. I am the LORD. [32] Do not profane my holy name, for I must be acknowledged as holy by the Israelites. I am the LORD, who made you holy [33] and who brought you out of Egypt to be your God. I am the LORD."

KEY VERSE

Keep my commands and follow them. I am the LORD. —Leviticus 22:31

Graphic: Nikolay Kurkin / Hemera / Thinkstock

Sacred Gifts and Holy Gatherings

Unit 1: What We Bring to God

Lessons 1–4

Lesson Aims

After participating in this lesson, each learner will be able to:

1. Summarize the regulations concerning acceptable and unacceptable offerings.

2. Explain the connection between proper sacrifices and hallowing God's holy name.

3. Identify one area in his or her life where less-than-the-best is given to God and make a plan for change.

Lesson Outline

Introduction
  A. Standards Matter
  B. Lesson Background
 I. Specific Requirements (Leviticus 22:17-25)
  A. Expectations (vv. 17-22)
    No Double Standard
  B. Exceptions (v. 23)
  C. Further Expectations (vv. 24, 25)
 II. General Requirements (Leviticus 22:31-33)
  A. An Obedient People (v. 31)
  B. A Holy God (vv. 32, 33)
    Holiness Lost?
Conclusion
  A. Great Expectations
  B. Put Your Heart into It
  C. Prayer
  D. Thought to Remember

Introduction

A. Standards Matter

Some years ago, one of my fellow employees drove across the street to pick up lunch. She got her food at the drive-up window then brought it back to her desk to eat. Imagine her surprise when she found a ring in her salad! (Fortunately, she noticed it before taking a bite.) The ring apparently had slipped off the finger of the individual preparing the salad, and the person had not noticed it was missing. Needless to say, my friend had second thoughts about getting food from *that* place again!

We naturally expect the food we purchase to meet certain quality and health standards. When such standards are not met, we are disappointed and even angry. (Lawsuits have been filed over such lapses.) We do not soon forget these incidents, and we are quick to warn others of our less-than-satisfactory experience.

Today's lesson focuses on God's concern for acceptable offerings. Standards matter to him, for reasons that we will examine more closely in the course of our study.

B. Lesson Background

If a survey were taken of Christians regarding which of the 66 books of the Bible is the least appealing or most confusing, Leviticus would probably rank in the top three. Who knows how many well-meaning individuals have determined to read through the Bible in a year, only to find themselves bogging down when they reach Leviticus! They are bewildered (and perhaps a bit upset) by the constant references to the sacrificing of animals and to blood. Further, regulations about ceremonially clean and unclean foods seem far removed from life in the twenty-first century.

Rather than focusing on the details of the laws and regulations when studying Leviticus, perhaps it is more helpful to consider the book's primary themes of *sacrifice* and *holiness*, both of which play prominent roles in the New Testament as well. *Sacrifice* is important because of Jesus' supreme, once-for-all offering of himself on the cross (Hebrews 9:24-28) and because of the responsibility of his followers to offer themselves as living sacrifices (Romans 12:1). *Holiness* is crucial because the holiness imperative in Leviticus 19:2 is repeated in 1 Peter 1:15, 16 in instructing Christians how to live. Both themes play important parts in today's lesson text, from Leviticus 22.

I. Specific Requirements
(LEVITICUS 22:17-25)
A. Expectations (vv. 17-22)

17. The LORD said to Moses,

The phrase *the Lord said to Moses* or one similar to it occurs dozens of times in Leviticus, emphasizing the divine origin of its contents. The final verse of the book summarizes the contents: "These are the commands the Lord gave Moses at Mount Sinai for the Israelites" (Leviticus 27:34). Thus the Lord reveals to Moses not only the Ten Commandments at Mount Sinai (the source of last week's lesson) but also all the standards for holy living provided within Leviticus as well.

18. "Speak to Aaron and his sons and to all the Israelites and say to them: 'If any of you —whether an Israelite or a foreigner residing in Israel—presents a gift for a burnt offering to the LORD, either to fulfill a vow or as a freewill offering,

Aaron and his sons serve the people of Israel as their priests (Aaron as the high priest), though two of Aaron's four sons died earlier because they "offered unauthorized fire before the Lord" (Leviticus 10:1, 2). That tragedy sets a tone regarding the kinds of offerings that are acceptable and unacceptable to the Lord. Not only must Aaron and his sons be aware of the rules (since they officiate at these sacred occasions), but all who would worship the Lord must understand

HOW TO SAY IT

anthropomorphic	*an*-thruh-puh-***more***-fik.
Deuteronomy	Due-ter-*ahn*-uh-me.
Ecclesiastes	Ik-*leez*-ee-*as*-teez.
Leviticus	Leh-*vit*-ih-kus.
Malachi	*Mal*-uh-kye.
Sinai	*Sigh*-nye or *Sigh*-nay-eye.

what they should and should not bring. We note that these regulations also apply to *a foreigner residing in Israel* who desires to worship the Lord. This is the same group mentioned in last week's study of Exodus 20:10.

The *burnt offering* is the first offering mentioned in this book (Leviticus 1:1-17). It is the most common of all the sacrifices, prepared each morning and evening (Numbers 28:1-8) and offered on holy days as well (28:26–29:40). A burnt offering is one in which the entire animal (except for its skin; see Leviticus 1:6; 7:8) is consumed by the fire on the bronze altar located outside of the Holy Place, in the courtyard of the tabernacle (Exodus 38:1-7). The complete consumption of the offering symbolizes the complete devotion and surrender of the worshipper to the Lord.

The verse before us links presenting a burnt offering with presenting *a gift* to *fulfill a vow or as a freewill offering*. Regulations for making vows are given in Numbers 30 and Deuteronomy 23:21-23; the latter places strong emphasis on keeping one's vow (see also Ecclesiastes 5:4-6). A vow is tied to a particular situation, usually one of desperation, in which one has promised the Lord that he or she will do something for him if he helps the individual in a certain way. A good example is the vow Hannah made concerning her son in 1 Samuel 1:9-11. Bad things happen when vows are made in haste (Judges 11:30-40). A freewill offering, for its part, is given in response to a blessing from God that is unexpected and for which one has not asked.

19, 20. "'you must present a male without defect from the cattle, sheep or goats in order that it may be accepted on your behalf. Do not bring anything with a defect, because it will not be accepted on your behalf.

For a burnt offering, such as the one just described, to be acceptable to the Lord, it must be *a male without defect* (compare 1 Peter 1:19). A certain flexibility is made available in that it can be taken from *the cattle, sheep*, or *goats*. Specific defects that constitute being blemished will be listed in upcoming verses of our text.

Why a male is to be offered for a burnt offering and not a female is not stated. Some suggest practical considerations play a part: the future existence of flocks and herds depends on having a greater number of females than males. Female animals are acceptable for other types of offerings (Leviticus 3:1, 6; 4:27, 28).

> *What Do You Think?*
> How do we make sure we give God our best in ways other than monetary offerings?
> *Talking Points for Your Discussion*
> - Philippians 1:9-11
> - 2 Timothy 2:15
> - Other

The practice of offering blemished or flawed animals for sacrifice becomes an issue centuries later in the time of the prophet Malachi. The Lord points out through that prophet that the people would not think of presenting such offerings to the governor, the human ruler of the people. Why then should they bring defective offerings to the Lord? (See Malachi 1:6-9.)

> *What Do You Think?*
> Since our giving doesn't involve animal sacrifices, how do you ensure that your monetary offerings are without blemish?
> *Talking Points for Your Discussion*
> - Matthew 5:16; 6:1-4
> - Mark 12:41-44
> - 2 Corinthians 8:12; 9:6, 7
> - Other

21. "'When anyone brings from the herd or flock a fellowship offering to the Lord to fulfill a special vow or as a freewill offering, it must be without defect or blemish to be acceptable.

Like a burnt offering, *a fellowship offering* can accompany either a *vow* or *a freewill offering* (see Leviticus 3). The uniqueness of the fellowship offering is found in the meal that concludes its presentation. The priests are allowed to eat certain portions of the sacrificed animal (7:31-34); other portions of the animal are to be eaten by the worshipper according to the regulations given in the law (7:11-21). Because of the nature of this offer-ing (which recognizes fellowship or peace between God and his people, particularly concerning the priests who serve God), it is not to be made using animals having blemishes.

> *What Do You Think?*
> Are vows or pledges of giving (such as in faith-promise campaigns) appropriate today? Why, or why not?
> *Talking Points for Your Discussion*
> - Regarding conditional vows or pledges
> - Regarding unconditional vows or pledges

22. "'Do not offer to the Lord the blind, the injured or the maimed, or anything with warts or festering or running sores. Do not place any of these on the altar as a food offering presented to the Lord.

Listed here are some of the defects that make an animal unacceptable for sacrificial purposes. The words *injured* and *maimed* cover any kind of wound. The deficiencies that follow describe certain skin conditions. *Warts* are growths on the skin; these include tumors. *Festering or running sores* are also noted in Leviticus 21:20, with exact meaning uncertain. Animals with any of these conditions cannot be placed *on the altar as a food offering.* They are not whole or complete, and God requires sacrifices that are without blemish.

A principle found throughout Scripture is that those who come before the holy God must come with their best. For the people to be holy as God desires means that their offerings to him must be holy, without flaws or defects. Such offerings reflect conditions that existed prior to the fall, before sin entered the world and produced the brokenness that has permeated the entire creation ever since. The blemishes found in animals are examples or symptoms of that brokenness.

God's desire for unblemished offerings reflects his intention that his people give something to him that shows its "original" condition—that is, an object not marred by the consequences of being part of a sin-cursed world. He wants his people to give something as free from sin's effects as possible because he himself is fully free from sin. In offering an unblemished animal, the giver is reminded to be holy before God in daily conduct (Leviticus 11:44, 45; quoted in 1 Peter 1:15, 16).

❧ No Double Standard ❧

The month of December sees football season winding down as all college and professional teams finish out their regular-season schedules. Except for teams competing in postseason play after the first of the year, equipment is stowed and "what might have been" scenarios are pondered. The month of December is also a time for football coaches to wonder about their future employment if their teams didn't do well. For example, five head coaches in the National Football League were fired on December 30, 2013, after their teams' performances did not meet expectations.

To have a perfect season is extremely difficult for any team, college or professional. But alumni, fans, and team owners always seem to expect something close to it. Isn't it interesting how we're inclined to expect nothing less than the best from others even though we often fail to attain that standard ourselves?

When God established the rules for Israel's sacrifices, he called for the very best. That was his way of educating Israel about divine standards. One might argue that a perfect animal does not exist; be that as it may, God still wanted Israel to know that they were to give him their best. When Christ came as the ultimate fulfillment of the requirements of the sacrificial system, he showed us that God lives by his own standards in the giving of his Son as the perfect sacrifice. What do we offer God in return?
—C. R. B.

B. Exceptions (v. 23)

23. "'You may, however, present as a freewill offering an ox or a sheep that is deformed or stunted, but it will not be accepted in fulfillment of a vow.

Here an exception to the above regulations is given: *an ox or a sheep that is deformed or stunted* (that is, having one or more deficiencies or deformities that normally disqualify it from being sacrificed) can be used to make *a freewill offering* but not as *fulfillment of a vow.* We have seen in

Visual for Lesson 2. *Point to this visual as you ask, "As Christmas reminds us of God's perfect gift to us, what can we give back to him in gratitude?"*

the previous verses that a freewill offering that is specifically a burnt offering or a fellowship offering must not have any defects; thus the offering described in the verse before us is apparently not in those categories but is simply offered voluntarily to the Lord. Perhaps this allows for the status of poorer worshippers (compare Leviticus 5:7, 11; 12:8; 14:21, 22, 30-32).

This verse also establishes that fulfilling a vow involves a more costly sacrifice than does a freewill offering. One can give a defective animal as a freewill offering, but a vow always demands something of greater value in acknowledgment of a promise to the Lord.

C. Further Expectations (vv. 24, 25)

24, 25. "'You must not offer to the LORD an animal whose testicles are bruised, crushed, torn or cut. You must not do this in your own land, and you must not accept such animals from the hand of a foreigner and offer them as the food of your God. They will not be accepted on your behalf, because they are deformed and have defects.'"

No damage to an animal's testicles is permitted if it is to be presented to the Lord. (In parallel, Leviticus 21:16-23 restricts priests who have a similar condition from serving at the altar before the Lord.) This command therefore forbids offering castrated animals to the Lord as sacrifice. Castration is primarily a pagan practice of the time, and an animal in this state is disqualified from being offered as a sacrifice since it is blemished in the eyes of God.

Verse 25 uses the phrase *the food of your God* to describe the offerings that God's people are to bring to him (see also Leviticus 21:6, 8, 17, 21, 22). Does this mean that the Israelites view God as actually eating their sacrifices? Psalm 50:7-13 speaks decisively against such an idea.

What we are seeing, rather, is figurative terminology to describe offerings that are pleasing to God. Leviticus 1:9, 17; 2:2; 3:5 refer to certain sacrifices as having "an aroma pleasing to the Lord." Yet "God is spirit" (John 4:24), so how can he smell? This kind of language is called *anthropomorphic*, where human characteristics are used of God in order to aid our understanding of how he thinks or reacts to certain matters. Human senses are attributed to God in Scriptures not because he actually uses these senses but because such imagery helps us appreciate how he responds to what humans do.

> **What Do You Think?**
> Under what circumstances, if any, should a church refuse an offering or a gift? Why?
> **Talking Points for Your Discussion**
> - Regarding gifts from Christians
> - Regarding gifts from unbelievers
> - Regarding gifts from organizations

II. General Requirements
(LEVITICUS 22:31-33)
A. An Obedient People (v. 31)

31. "Keep my commands and follow them. I am the LORD.

As this series of instructions concludes, the basics of the Israelites' responsibilities are reemphasized. The people's duties can be summarized with one word: *obedience*. This is what God has always required of his people, in both Old and New Testament times.

B. A Holy God (vv. 32, 33)

32, 33. "Do not profane my holy name, for I must be acknowledged as holy by the Israel-

ites. I am the LORD, who made you holy and who brought you out of Egypt to be your God. I am the LORD."

The foundational event that establishes the Israelites as God's covenant people is the exodus *out of Egypt*. It is as foundational to ancient Israel's identity as the cross and the empty tomb of Jesus are to the identity of Christians.

God's covenant with his people includes many aspects, and one such is not to profane his holy name. Profanity is often thought of in terms of what is said. But when God's chosen, covenant people fail to live holy lives that honor him on a consistent basis, they are profaning the name that marks them as belonging to him. Holiness is to permeate every part of their lives during every part of their days.

Also noteworthy in these closing verses is the phrase *acknowledged as holy*. God desires to have his holiness upheld by his people. But he also says *I am the Lord, who made you holy*. While God commands his people to be holy, as we have seen, holiness is ultimately a privilege bestowed by God upon his people. To be holy is to be set apart, and he has set Israel apart by means of their deliverance from bondage. They must now set themselves apart from their pagan surroundings by living lives of faithful obedience.

❧ HOLINESS LOST? ❧

"Take Time to Be Holy" is an old Christian hymn many of us sang when we were younger (and may still sing today). The hymn urges Christians to spend much time in prayer and Bible study. We are instructed to find our friends among God's people, help those in need, and work at making our conduct so pure that others will see Christ in us. The "take time" counsel that begins each of the four stanzas implies that holiness doesn't come quickly or easily.

We don't seem to hear much about holiness in church these days; in many churches, there's no discussion of holiness at all. And then there's the world, where there is no concept of, let alone concern for, holiness whatsoever—either in personal lifestyle or the respect for God's holy name of which today's text speaks. Think about how casually people, even some Christians, throw God's name around in less-than-holy ways.

So the question is appropriate: Has the concept of holiness been lost? If so, how do we get it back? Our text suggests that holiness starts with an awareness of who God is and of what he has done to rescue his people. Out of this awareness then flow the attitudes and behaviors that make us Christlike. What will you do to get back on (or stay on) the path to greater holiness this week?

—C. R. B.

What Do You Think?
Is God's name ever profaned by something we don't do? Why, or why not?
Talking Points for Your Discussion
- In lack of action when action is called for
- In failing to speak up when doing so is called for

Conclusion

A. Great Expectations

Occasionally we hear or read of a parent who places excessive demands on his or her children. Perhaps the father was a star athlete in high school or college, so he expects his son to follow in his footsteps. The son, however, may have little interest or skill in athletics. But instead of allowing the son the freedom to make his own decision, the father prods the son to make athletics a priority. The result is predictable—frustration for both father and son and a growing alienation from each other as time goes by.

Some who read the requirements that God made of his people in today's text may also be a bit frustrated. Why did an offering have to be perfect if it was going to be burned up anyway? Wouldn't the concept of grace be taught more effectively by accepting offerings with flaws? And aren't God's standards teaching his people to look down on individuals who have certain "flaws," whatever they might be (compare Leviticus 21:16-23)?

One must keep in mind when studying the laws concerning Old Testament offerings that undergirding all of them is the holiness of God. Throughout the book of Leviticus, the principle stated in Leviticus 22:32 in today's text is empha-

sized. It is vital that God's holiness not be compromised in any way and that his people learn to honor that holiness in every detail of their lives.

So the requirements given in the Law of Moses regarding offerings are not there because God is a demanding, ruthless tyrant. Rather, they are there to impress upon those who present offerings the nature of the one being worshipped. And in the bigger picture of humanity's redemption, God's requiring "the best" prepares for how he one day offers his own best—his sinless Son—as the perfect sacrifice to die for imperfect people (1 Peter 1:18, 19).

B. Put Your Heart into It

Under the new covenant, giving is not measured in terms of the kind of animals we offer. The New Testament's teaching on giving is centered more on certain principles, one of which is that the heart or motivation of the giver must be in tune with God's desires. Paul tells the Corinthians, for example, "Each of you should give what you have decided in your heart to give, not reluctantly or under compulsion, for God loves a cheerful giver" (2 Corinthians 9:7). Of course, we should be quick to add that sincere motivation and heartfelt obedience mattered under the old covenant too. As Samuel told King Saul, "To obey is better than sacrifice, and to heed is better than the fat of rams" (1 Samuel 15:22; compare Mark 12:33).

Victor Hugo (1802–1885) wrote, "You can give without loving, but you can never love without giving." If we love God and make obedience to his will a daily priority, the proper kind of giving will follow.

C. Prayer

Father, may we see giving not just in terms of money but also in terms of our daily living—in the things that don't show up on a treasurer's report. And help us to be more mindful each day of all you have freely given us. In the name of your greatest gift, Jesus. Amen.

D. Thought to Remember

Give of your best to the Master.

INVOLVEMENT LEARNING

Enhance your lesson with NIV® Bible Student (from your curriculum supplier) and the reproducible activity page (at www.standardlesson.com or in the back of the NIV® Standard Lesson Commentary Deluxe Edition).

Into the Lesson

Display a box wrapped with Christmas wrapping paper and ask learners to think of one specific person for whom they usually buy a Christmas gift. After a minute of silent reflection, begin removing the following items from the box: a cell phone, a gift card, a diet book, a DVD of a children's movie, and a box of chocolates.

As you reveal each item individually, ask for volunteers to share why that particular gift would or would not be appropriate for the person they have in mind. Talk briefly about what criteria they use when buying Christmas gifts (lifestyle, hobbies, etc.). Then say, "Our gifts often say something about our regard for the other person. In the Old Testament, the Israelites were taught to bring only the best offerings as an indication of their respect for God's holiness. Let's see how and why."

Into the Word

Form three groups of no more than four learners each. Give each group one of the following three assignments, which you have prepared on handouts. (For larger classes, form more groups and give duplicate assignments.)

To Whom, From Whom, and Why—Read Leviticus 22:17-25, 31-33. Surface facts: What individuals and general groups received the message? From whom did the message originate? Deeper implications: How do the facts of verses 31-33 relate to the facts of verses 17, 18? Why are "foreigners" spoken of positively in verse 18 but negatively in verse 25?

The Positive What and Why—Read Leviticus 22:17-25, 31-33. Surface facts: What types of animals could be offered as sacrifices? What qualities were they to have? Deeper implications: If someone did not have or could not find a perfect animal to sacrifice, then what? Why the quality exception in verse 23a?

The Negative What and Why—Read Leviticus 22:17-25, 31-33. Surface facts: What negative qualities would cause the Lord to reject a sacrifice? What is being said about foreigners in verse 25? Deeper implications: Why the quality exception in verse 23a? Why are foreigners spoken of negatively in verse 25 but positively in verse 18?

After several minutes, work through group responses as a class. When you arrive at a question that is duplicated across groups, have one group state its answer, then immediately turn to the other group and say, "Your group has this question as well. Do you agree with what you've just heard?" Disagreements will create opportunities for in-depth study. See the commentary for expected and possible responses.

Option. Distribute copies of the "Nothing Less Than Perfect" skit from the reproducible page, which you can download. Ask six learners to act out their parts, with your best reader/actor playing the part of the priest. (If your class is smaller, you can delete one or more of the non-priest parts or have actors play more than one part.)

Before beginning the skit, ask everyone else to have the lesson text open so they can locate the verses related to what the priest says about each animal as the skit progresses. Since this may result in awkward starting and stopping to locate verses, an alternative is to go through the skit twice—the first time quickly and smoothly, the second time stopping to discover relevant verses.

Into Life

Give each learner a strip of paper featuring these three words: *Time, Talent, Treasure.* Say, "These are the three typical ways we categorize what we have available to offer back to God. Although we can all do better in all three areas, circle the one of the three where you need the most improvement in removing 'blemishes' from what you offer to God." [Pause while learners do so.] Continue: "Take this with you to post in a place where you will see it daily for a week as a prayer reminder."

DEDICATION OF THE FIRSTBORN

DEVOTIONAL READING: 2 Chronicles 30:5-12
BACKGROUND SCRIPTURE: Exodus 13:11-16; Leviticus 12:1-8;
Numbers 3:5-13; Luke 2:21-39

EXODUS 13:13B-15

13b "Redeem every firstborn among your sons.

14 "In days to come, when your son asks you, 'What does this mean?' say to him, 'With a mighty hand the LORD brought us out of Egypt, out of the land of slavery. 15 When Pharaoh stubbornly refused to let us go, the LORD killed the firstborn of both people and animals in Egypt. This is why I sacrifice to the LORD the first male offspring of every womb and redeem each of my firstborn sons.'"

LUKE 2:22-32

22 When the time came for the purification rites required by the Law of Moses, Joseph and Mary took him to Jerusalem to present him to the Lord 23 (as it is written in the Law of the Lord, "Every firstborn male is to be consecrated to the Lord"), 24 and to offer a sacrifice in keeping with what is said in the Law of the Lord: "a pair of doves or two young pigeons."

25 Now there was a man in Jerusalem called Simeon, who was righteous and devout. He was waiting for the consolation of Israel, and the Holy Spirit was on him. 26 It had been revealed to him by the Holy Spirit that he would not die before he had seen the Lord's Messiah. 27 Moved by the Spirit, he went into the temple courts. When the parents brought in the child Jesus to do for him what the custom of the Law required, 28 Simeon took him in his arms and praised God, saying:

29 "Sovereign Lord, as you have promised,
   you may now dismiss your servant in
      peace.
30 For my eyes have seen your salvation,
31   which you have prepared in the sight of
      all nations:
32 a light for revelation to the Gentiles,
   and the glory of your people Israel."

KEY VERSE

When the time came for the purification rites required by the Law of Moses, Joseph and Mary took him to Jerusalem to present him to the Lord. —Luke 2:22

SACRED GIFTS AND HOLY GATHERINGS

Unit 1: What We Bring to God

LESSONS 1–4

LESSON AIMS

After participating in this lesson, each learner will be able to:

1. Match the presentation of the infant Jesus as firstborn with its Old Testament antecedent.

2. Compare and contrast modern baby-dedication ceremonies in the church with the Old Testament dedication of the firstborn.

3. Help plan a service regarding children born in the past year to families in the church.

LESSON OUTLINE

Introduction
  A. "Order, Order!"
  B. Lesson Background
I. Principle Presented (EXODUS 13:13b-15)
  A. The Regulation (v. 13b)
  B. The Reason (vv. 14, 15)
    More on Birth Order
II. Principle Practiced (LUKE 2:22-32)
  A. Everyday Action (vv. 22-24)
  B. Expectant Man (vv. 25-27a)
  C. Extraordinary Words (vv. 27b-32)
    Whose Timing?
Conclusion
  A. When the Firstborn Wasn't Spared
  B. Dedications Today
  C. Prayer
  D. Thought to Remember

Introduction

A. "Order, Order!"

Many studies have been done on the topic of birth order and its influence both on parenting and on child development. The middle child in our family often played "the middle-child card" (and still does!) as a way of creating sympathy for himself. This is because the middle child in a family is believed to be the one who ends up being slighted or ignored. The oldest child may be treated with great fondness simply by being first. The youngest may be treated similarly because that child will be the last to leave the nest and thus may be spoiled more than the others. The middle child gets, well, "caught in the middle."

The position of the firstborn male was a mark of distinction in biblical times. Our lesson today surveys the Old Testament command of God regarding redemption of the firstborn, and our New Testament text shows it being applied to Jesus.

B. Lesson Background

The studies of this quarter examine the concept of *tradition* from three angles: traditions for honoring God (unit 1), for observing special occasions (unit 2), and for celebrating holy times (unit 3). Traditions can provide opportunities to reinforce important foundational truths that a country, a community, a church, a family, or an individual must keep at the forefront of their identity.

The practice of sanctifying by redemption every Israelite firstborn male was so important that it was the second observance commanded of Israel following the exodus from Egypt. (The first was the Passover; see lesson 10.) Exodus 13, from which the first portion of our lesson text is drawn, addresses this. The important role of the firstborn male is further seen in his receiving certain privileges, including leadership responsibilities and a greater share of the family inheritance once the father had passed away (Deuteronomy 21:15-17).

Being a firstborn male Israelite had great significance because of the unique history of the nation. Regarding the infant Jesus, the Gospel of Luke notes as being carried out the redemption that Exodus describes.

I. Principle Presented
(Exodus 13:13b-15)

Exodus 13:11, 12 states that after the Lord brings the people "into the land of the Canaanites," they are to "give over to the Lord the first offspring of every womb. All the firstborn males of your livestock belong to the Lord." In the case of a firstborn donkey, it is to be redeemed with a lamb, perhaps because of the donkey's value as a pack animal (v. 13a). However, if the firstborn donkey is not redeemed, its neck is to be broken. Why such a severe action is to be taken is not clear, but perhaps the severity encourages the act of redemption.

A. The Regulation (v. 13b)

13b. "Redeem every firstborn among your sons.

Similar to this half-verse is Exodus 34:20: "Redeem all your firstborn sons." To *redeem* means to buy back by means of a payment. The specifics are these: "When they are a month old, you must redeem them at the redemption price set at five shekels of silver, according to the sanctuary shekel" (Numbers 18:16; see also Leviticus 27:6; Numbers 3:39-51).

The idea of *ransom*, in which a price is paid so that someone is set free, is tied to this. Jesus used this manner of language to describe the price he would pay at the cross to free us from bondage to sin: "The Son of Man did not come to be served, but to serve, and to give his life as a ransom for many" (Matthew 20:28; see also the parallel Mark 10:45; compare 1 Timothy 2:5, 6).

B. The Reason (vv. 14, 15)

14. "In days to come, when your son asks you, 'What does this mean?' say to him, 'With a mighty hand the LORD brought us out of Egypt, out of the land of slavery.

This verse depicts a scene similar to one that is described in connection with the observance of the Passover (Exodus 12:25-28) and, later, the building of a memorial of stones to commemorate the crossing of the Jordan River into Canaan (Joshua 4:20-24). When he is old enough, a son (perhaps the firstborn son, who has been redeemed) asks what the process of redemption means. Why is it necessary?

Here we see illustrated one of the practical benefits of a practice or tradition, in this case the act of redeeming the firstborn. It provides an opportunity for ancient Israelite parents to explain to their children the historical roots of their faith. The ceremony of redeeming the firstborn son is not a custom of human origin. Rather, the rite is solely at God's initiative: it commemorates the work of his *mighty hand* in bringing the Israelites *out of Egypt, out of the land of slavery.*

> **What Do You Think?**
> How can we help children better understand the release from sin-bondage that undergirds Jesus' birth at Christmas?
> *Talking Points for Your Discussion*
> - When the church gathers
> - At home
> - Other

15. "'When Pharaoh stubbornly refused to let us go, the LORD killed the firstborn of both people and animals in Egypt. This is why I sacrifice to the LORD the first male offspring of every womb and redeem each of my firstborn sons.'"

Here the specific reason for the redemption of the firstborn is given. Its origin lies in the last of the 10 plagues that the Lord brought on Pharaoh and the land of Egypt (Exodus 11).

Because God spared the firstborn of the Israelites in Egypt, each firstborn among the males in Israel in future generations is to be spared by an act of redemption. A price was paid in order to save the Israelites' firstborn from death; that price is to be acknowledged and commemorated by future generations through the redemption of the firstborn males.

We should note that *the firstborn of . . . animals* were affected by the tenth plague: "the Lord struck down all the firstborn in Egypt, . . . and the firstborn of all the livestock as well" (Exodus 12:29). Therefore every firstborn male among the animals must be redeemed as well (Exodus 13:13a).

❧ MORE ON BIRTH ORDER ❧

Imagine three children in the same family. Child X grows up to be a good listener, a mediator, and a people-pleaser, someone who is loyal to friends. Child Y is a playful comic, a charmer, and a risk-taker who challenges the position of others. Child Z is a born leader, a perfectionist, smarter than average, and averse to risks. From those descriptions, can you give their birth order?

Classic birth-order theory was developed by Alfred Adler (1870–1937). Modifications to his theory over the years propose that child X was born second, child Y was born last, and child Z was the firstborn. The theory might have some usefulness in terms of broad generalizations, but our experience tells us there is much more to how personality traits come to be than birth-order theory can account for.

The Bible places importance on birth order almost from the very beginning; there are dozens and dozens of references to the "firstborn,"

HOW TO SAY IT

Canaan	*Kay*-nun.
Deuteronomy	Due-ter-*ahn*-uh-me.
Egypt	*Ee*-jipt.
Gabriel	*Gay*-bree-ul.
Leviticus	Leh-*vit*-ih-kus.
Messiah	Meh-*sigh*-uh.
messianic	mess-ee-*an*-ick.
Moses	*Mo*-zes or *Mo*-zez.
Nunc Dimittis	Nunk Dih-*mit*-us.
Pharaoh	*Fair*-o or *Fay*-roe.
Zechariah	Zek-uh-*rye*-uh.

particularly in the Old Testament (see this lesson's Introduction). This emphasis is not unique to the Judeo-Christian worldview. For example, Pharaoh's firstborn was his heir-apparent in Egyptian culture. In striking down all the firstborn of Egypt, God demonstrated that his power was greater than cultural norms and any fictitious gods behind them. God was in control of Egypt's destiny. Israel, God's firstborn in the Old Testament era (Exodus 4:22), was the one blessed.

God's ultimate blessing, however, belongs to Jesus, God's firstborn in the New Testament era (Colossians 1:15-20; Hebrews 1:6). It is he—the firstborn who was not at all risk-averse, contrary to birth-order theory—who has redeemed us.

—C. R. B.

II. Principle Practiced
(LUKE 2:22-32)

Luke 2 is perhaps the most frequently recited Scripture at this time of year. Usually it is the first 20 verses that draw the most attention since they describe the events surrounding the birth of Jesus. Verse 21 notes Jesus' circumcision on the eighth day, as prescribed by the Law of Moses; at the same time, he is given the name *Jesus* as commanded by the angel Gabriel (Luke 1:31). Assigning a boy's name at the time of circumcision is not prescribed in the law; it is a tradition added later. The same procedure is followed when the son of Zechariah and Elizabeth is named (Luke 1:57-63).

A. Everyday Action (vv. 22-24)

22. When the time came for the purification rites required by the Law of Moses, Joseph and Mary took him to Jerusalem to present him to the Lord

The purification rites for Mary are a separate matter from Jesus' circumcision. Following the birth of a son, a mother has to wait 40 days before presenting the required purification offering. The seven days before her son's circumcision on the eighth day are included as the first part of these 40 days, as Leviticus 12:1-4 makes clear. This ceremony of purification is conducted in the temple in Jerusalem (12:6, 7).

Why would God require purification from an act (childbirth) that he commanded of a man and a woman (Genesis 1:28)? *The Law of Moses* is not entirely clear on this point, but the ceremony may be related to God's declaration following the sin in Eden that the woman's pain would increase during childbirth (Genesis 3:16).

In that light, the purification ceremony may serve to remind the woman (and her husband) of the somber consequences of that sin. Some suggest that the bleeding that accompanies childbirth (referred to three times in Leviticus 12:4, 5, 7) makes a woman ceremonially unclean since the only blood that is permitted to come before God is that of sacrificial animals.

In the final analysis, the Scriptures are often silent about the specific reasoning behind the various laws by which God's people are to live. But in a general sense, the connection is always between the holy nature of God and his desire for his people to be holy as well.

What Do You Think?

How can cultural traditions surrounding births be modified to encourage Christian parenting?

Talking Points for Your Discussion

▪ Regarding baby showers
▪ Regarding birth announcements
▪ Other

23, 24. (as it is written in the Law of the Lord, "Every firstborn male is to be consecrated to the Lord"), and to offer a sacrifice in keeping with what is said in the Law of the Lord: "a pair of doves or two young pigeons."

The actions of Joseph and Mary are explained in light of Exodus 13 and Leviticus 12. The required purification sacrifice is usually a lamb (Leviticus 12:6); but if the mother is too poor to afford a lamb, then the offering of *a pair of doves or two young pigeons* is acceptable (see Leviticus 12:8). That Joseph and Mary bring the alternative offering indicates their poverty.

An offering such as this also helps to confirm that the visit of the wise men does not occur until sometime later (Matthew 2:11). Had Joseph and Mary received the gold from the wise men before

this purification, they likely would provide the costlier purification sacrifice of a lamb.

B. Expectant Man (vv. 25-27a)

25. Now there was a man in Jerusalem called Simeon, who was righteous and devout. He was waiting for the consolation of Israel, and the Holy Spirit was on him.

Here the account of a usual purification practice at the temple takes an unusual turn. We are introduced to Simeon, a man described as *righteous and devout*. For him to be *waiting for the consolation of Israel* has messianic overtones. Many in his day anticipate that consolation primarily in political terms: they expect the Messiah to be someone who delivers Israel from the hated, oppressive rule of the Romans. But Simeon holds a much different (and much more accurate) understanding of the Messiah, as we shall see.

Simeon's better understanding is traced to the presence of *the Holy Spirit* in his life. Even though we are less than 10 percent into the book of Luke at this point, the author already has highlighted the influence of the Holy Spirit in the circumstances surrounding the lives of several individuals: John the Baptist (Luke 1:13-15), Mary (1:35), Elizabeth (1:41), and Zechariah (1:67).

26, 27a. It had been revealed to him by the Holy Spirit that he would not die before he had seen the Lord's Messiah. Moved by the Spirit, he went into the temple courts.

People today sometimes use the term *bucket list* to describe specific goals they would like to achieve before they die (or "kick the bucket," as the idiom goes). *The Holy Spirit* has revealed to Simeon one item for that man's bucket list: he will not die before seeing *the Lord's Messiah*.

The same Spirit who has revealed this fact to righteous and devout Simeon now directs him toward its fulfillment. So Simeon comes *into the temple courts* where Joseph and Mary have brought the infant Jesus.

C. Extraordinary Words (vv. 27b-32)

27b. When the parents brought in the child Jesus to do for him what the custom of the Law required,

Joseph and Mary have come with *the child Jesus* to fulfill what *the custom of the Law* requires according to Leviticus 12. It's safe to presume that they are unaware that another fulfillment is about to take place!

28. Simeon took him in his arms and praised God, saying:

One can only imagine the parents' reaction when a complete stranger approaches them and takes their child *in his arms*! But we must keep in mind that they have already experienced some extraordinary events in connection with their extraordinary child. This episode adds another to that list.

> **What Do You Think?**
> When was an occasion you were in "the right place at the right time" to be a conduit of God's blessing to another? How did things turn out?
> *Talking Points for Your Discussion*
> • Regarding a fellow believer
> • Regarding an unbeliever

29. "Sovereign Lord, as you have promised, you may now dismiss your servant in peace.

The Holy Spirit by this point has informed Simeon that the child who has just been brought into the temple is indeed the promised one—the Lord's Messiah. Having witnessed the fulfillment of the Lord's promise to him, Simeon now views his earthly life as complete. He is ready to be dismissed *in peace* from it. The Latin phrase *Nunc Dimittis* is often attached to Simeon's words; it reflects the first words of his prayer in the Greek text, translated here as *now dismiss*.

❧ WHOSE TIMING? ❧

Helen Small doesn't dream small dreams. She started college in 1939, but dropped out to become a wife and mother. Even so, she never gave up her dream of getting a college education. In 2004, with her unfulfilled desire still nagging at her, she went back to college, learning to use computers and the Internet along the way.

She graduated in 2007, but her dream was even bigger, and she enrolled in graduate school. In 2010, she was awarded a master's degree in psy-

chological sciences—at age 90! Small said she hoped her story would inspire other older people to fulfill their own lifelong dreams.

Simeon's dream of seeing the Messiah before passing on was not something he could just decide to do as Helen Small did. Simeon had to wait for God's timing. What he *could* do, however, was live a just and devout life, which God rewarded by promising that he would live to see the Messiah. Thinking about your own yet-to-be fulfilled dreams of service to God, are you waiting on God's timing to get started, or is he waiting on yours?
—C. R. B.

30, 31. "For my eyes have seen your salvation, which you have prepared in the sight of all nations:

Simeon speaks of the child in his arms as the source of the Lord's salvation. But the salvation in view is far more comprehensive and substantial than any kind of political deliverance. In fact, this child is destined to affect not only Israel but *all nations* (compare Isaiah 40:5; 52:10).

32. "a light for revelation to the Gentiles, and the glory of your people Israel."

Luke 1:54, 55 records the previous words of Mary that highlight God's mercy promised "to Abraham and his descendants." Zechariah, filled with the Spirit (1:67), also praised the Lord for his mercy and his remembrance of his covenant with the descendants of Abraham (1:72-75).

The "good news that will cause great joy" (Luke 2:10) is to be heralded to Jews first, as Jesus directs (Matthew 10:5, 6) and as Paul affirms (Romans 1:16). But the Gospels are also characterized by several accounts and statements of Jesus' intent that his good news is to go "outside the box," to all other nations as Simeon declares (compare Matthew 28:19, 20; Luke 24:47; etc.). The verse before us leaves no doubt regarding the scope of "all nations" in verse 31, above. It's not just all Jews but all Jews and Gentiles—everyone!

No wonder Joseph and Mary marvel at Simeon's words (Luke 2:33, not in today's text). The parents have come to present their son to the Lord, but clearly he is destined for some remarkable accomplishments!

What Do You Think?

What will you do this Christmas season to help reveal Jesus to a lost world?

Talking Points for Your Discussion

- Regarding personal witness
- Regarding the nature of your Christmas decorations
- Other

Conclusion

A. When the Firstborn Wasn't Spared

The joy of the Christmas season may cause us to overlook how Jesus, God's firstborn, was treated. The term *firstborn* in Colossians 1:15 doesn't mean "born first," but highlights Jesus' preeminence as the Son of God and the special privileges that belong to him as a result (compare Exodus 4:22). Yet unlike the firstborn in Israel at the time of the tenth plague, Jesus was not spared from death. He became the substitute for sinful humanity at the cross. He is the Passover lamb who was sacrificed and whose blood now makes it possible for God's judgment and wrath to pass over us (John 1:29; 1 Corinthians 5:7).

Jesus is still the true gift of Christmas, the one that keeps on giving—giving eternal life to those who trust in him. The cross, the place where God did not spare his own firstborn from death, results in our redemption, that we may be called "children of God" (John 1:12; 1 John 3:1, 2).

B. Dedications Today

The Old Testament discusses the sanctifying, redeeming, or setting apart of the firstborn (Exodus 13:2, 12, 13), but what about the New Testament? Quite simply, we are no longer under the ordinances of the law (Colossians 2:13, 14), so this practice is not required of Christian families.

Even so, some churches celebrate annually (or more often, depending on the size of the church) a "Baby Day" on which parents of newborns are encouraged to bring their infants. Such celebrations may include a special service of prayer as parents dedicate their children to the Lord. The congregation, for its part, may take a vow through

responsive reading to pray for the children in that regard.

But wait—is it possible for one human being to dedicate another to the Lord's service? Not really! The child will make his or her own decision in that regard later on. Unique dedication decisions by parents in the Old Testament era should be seen as just that (1 Samuel 1:11; etc.).

What *is* possible, however, is that parents can dedicate themselves to rearing children in the Lord. In that light, a Baby Day service can accomplish much in impressing on parents the fact that parenthood is a genuine ministry. Fathers and mothers must see their families as "congregations" to whom they must minister so that the children can come to know and love the Lord.

No individual like Simeon will show up to make any stunning announcements during Baby Day services. But who knows how God will use the children of parents so dedicated?

C. Prayer

Father, thank you for the special gift of Jesus, the "firstborn over all creation," whom you did not spare from death. May our celebrations at this time of year reflect our gratitude for this daily. In Jesus' name. Amen.

D. Thought to Remember

Although the Israelites' firstborn were spared from death, God's was not.

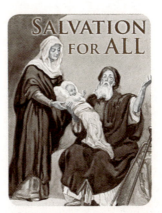

Visual for Lesson 3

Start a discussion by pointing to this visual as you pose the question at the top of this page.

INVOLVEMENT LEARNING

Enhance your lesson with NIV® Bible Student (from your curriculum supplier) and the reproducible activity page (at www.standardlesson.com or in the back of the NIV® Standard Lesson Commentary Deluxe Edition).

Into the Lesson

Pair learners to discuss this question: *How did your birth-order position affect the way your parents treated you?* After a few minutes, switch to a whole-class discussion by answering the question yourself, then encourage others to share their experiences. Make a transition by saying, "While birth order may or may not make any difference today, parents in Bible times had certain responsibilities regarding their firstborn son. Today we see how Jesus' earthly parents honored one such responsibility."

Alternative. Display a nativity scene or other Christmas decoration that has a special significance for you in family tradition and explain it. Then invite learners to talk about how they use their own Christmas decorations to remind themselves of family traditions that help promote the true meaning of Christmas. Make a transition by saying, "God included directives in the Law of Moses that were to become teaching traditions from parent to child. One such involved the redemption of the firstborn. Let's see how it applied to Jesus."

Into the Word

Say, "We're going to begin our study with an open-Bible test. Don't worry—the test has only one question, and it's a true/false question at that. That's not too intimidating, is it?" Ask for absolute silence as you give each learner a handout printed with the following:

True or False: Luke 2:24 specifies or summarizes
  the redemption price for the firstborn that is
  referred to in Exodus 13:13b-15.
(Scriptures you may find helpful in answering this
  question: Leviticus 12; Numbers 18:14-16.)

As learners ponder the question, stress again the need for absolute silence (so the individualized learning experience won't be ruined by someone blurting out an opinion). After learners finish, say, "When you looked up Leviticus 12 and Numbers 18:14-16, you realized the answer was false, right?"

Use learner reactions for deeper study of Exodus 13:13b-15 and Luke 2:22-24, as you include these questions: "When you compare the requirements of Leviticus 12:6, 8 with how Mary and Joseph fulfilled them in Luke 2:24, what should we conclude about their financial status?" *(Expected response: they were too poor to afford a lamb.)* "What else do the actions of this couple tell us about them?" *(Expected response: they were devout and careful to obey all the requirements of the law).*

Read Luke 2:25-32 aloud, then engage learners in a series of compare and contrasts: (1) Simeon's character in Luke 2:25 with those seen in Matthew 1:19; John 12:4-6; Acts 10:22; 17:5; (2) Simeon's expectations in Luke 2:25 with that of Luke 23:51; (3) the Holy Spirit's work in Luke 2:26, 27 with Luke 4:1; 22:3-6; Acts 10:22; (4) the affirmations in Luke 22:30-32 with Isaiah 49:6; Romans 11:11. This can be a small-group activity with groups being given different or identical assignments.

Option. As a closed-Bible posttest, distribute copies of the "Make It True" activity from the reproducible page, which you can download. Discuss results after a few minutes of individualized work.

Into Life

Form learners into teams to plan a *Baby Day* segment of your church's worship service. Assume that this segment will be about 10 minutes in length. Have teams consider the following in their planning: (1) how babies and parents will be introduced, (2) song or hymn, if any, to be sung, (3) charge to be given to the congregation in general, (4) charge to be given to the parents in particular, and (5) Scripture to be used as a basis for a brief devotional thought. Discuss results as a class; pass ideas on to your church's leadership.

Option. Distribute copies of "Honor to Whom Honor Is Due" activity from the reproducible page. Use it to brainstorm ways to honor the "senior saints" in your congregation.

A Generous Gift

Devotional Reading: John 1:10-18
Background Scripture: Matthew 23:1-12; Mark 12:38-44

Matthew 23:2-12

2 "The teachers of the law and the Pharisees sit in Moses' seat. 3 So you must be careful to do everything they tell you. But do not do what they do, for they do not practice what they preach. 4 They tie up heavy, cumbersome loads and put them on other people's shoulders, but they themselves are not willing to lift a finger to move them.

5 "Everything they do is done for people to see: They make their phylacteries wide and the tassels on their garments long; 6 they love the place of honor at banquets and the most important seats in the synagogues; 7 they love to be greeted with respect in the marketplaces and to be called 'Rabbi' by others.

8 "But you are not to be called 'Rabbi,' for you have one Teacher, and you are all brothers. 9 And do not call anyone on earth 'father,' for you have one Father, and he is in heaven. 10 Nor are you to be called instructors, for you have one Instructor, the Messiah. 11 The greatest among you will be your servant. 12 For those who exalt themselves will be humbled, and those who humble themselves will be exalted."

Mark 12:38-44

38 As he taught, Jesus said, "Watch out for the teachers of the law. They like to walk around in flowing robes and be greeted with respect in the marketplaces, 39 and have the most important seats in the synagogues and the places of honor at banquets. 40 They devour widows' houses and for a show make lengthy prayers. These men will be punished most severely."

41 Jesus sat down opposite the place where the offerings were put and watched the crowd putting their money into the temple treasury. Many rich people threw in large amounts. 42 But a poor widow came and put in two very small copper coins, worth only a few cents.

43 Calling his disciples to him, Jesus said, "Truly I tell you, this poor widow has put more into the treasury than all the others. 44 They all gave out of their wealth; but she, out of her poverty, put in everything —all she had to live on."

Key Verse

Those who exalt themselves will be humbled, and those who humble themselves will be exalted.

—**Matthew 23:12**

SACRED GIFTS AND HOLY GATHERINGS

Unit 1: What We Bring to God

LESSONS 1–4

LESSON AIMS

After participating in this lesson, each learner will be able to:

1. Note a godly characteristic to contrast with each of the behaviors or traits that Jesus condemned in the religious leaders.

2. Tell how the poor widow's example can be followed by people of comfortable means today.

3. Identify one attitude or action in need of change and make a plan to do so.

LESSON OUTLINE

Introduction
   A. Definitions from God's Dictionary
   B. Lesson Background
 I. Prideful Prominence (MATTHEW 23:2-7)
   A. Hypocrites as Leaders (vv. 2, 3)
   B. Hypocrites in Setting Standards (v. 4)
   C. Hypocrites for Wanting Attention (vv. 5-7)
   "Sitting in the Catbird Seat"
 II. Humble Servanthood (MATTHEW 23:8-12)
   A. Change of Focus (vv. 8-10)
   B. Greatness Through Service (vv. 11, 12)
   A Call to Humble Service
 III. Cruel Pretenders (MARK 12:38-40)
   A. Gaining Honor (vv. 38, 39)
   B. Devouring Houses (v. 40)
 IV. Trustful Generosity (MARK 12:41-44)
   A. Many Give Much (v. 41)
   B. One Gives All (vv. 42-44)
Conclusion
   A. A Great Contrast
   B. Prayer
   C. Thought to Remember

Introduction

A. Definitions from God's Dictionary

When we want to understand an unfamiliar word, we may consult a dictionary. But definitions therein describe how words are commonly used, and that usage is subject to change. As Christians, we want to know how God defines words—and his definitions do not change.

As we think carefully about today's passage in the context of Jesus' life, we will be able to understand God's definition of *generosity*, a subject of our lesson. So informed, we will then be able to make a better response to God's generosity, reflecting it in our own generosity toward others.

B. Lesson Background

Today's texts from Matthew and Mark follow a series of exchanges between Jesus and his opponents during his final public ministry in Jerusalem. These opponents included Pharisees and teachers of the law. The latter served the vital role of copying Scripture by hand in an era that did not have copy machines, electronic texts, etc. This function resulted in these teachers' being recognized as experts in the Scriptures.

Pharisees, for their part, were advocates of a particular way of interpreting Scripture (compare Acts 23:8). This group believed that God would restore or maintain his favor on the Jewish people only if they kept his law faithfully. To ensure that they did so, the Pharisees "built a fence" around the law by developing oral traditions as legal commentary regarding how to apply God's written ordinances. Pharisees thought that people wouldn't even come close to violating God's written law if they adhered to these oral traditions.

Most Pharisees probably did not believe that God was overly concerned with the minor details of their oral tradition. But they did believe that devout Jews honored God by not violating the law as they followed detailed traditions. Pharisees were held in high esteem by most Jews, even if they did not strictly follow the Pharisees' traditions.

In contrast to these is the widow who appears in the second of our two texts for today. Widows were especially vulnerable in biblical times. Those who lacked sons or other male relatives were essentially left without means of support. They might earn some coins selling handwork, but few could make a living by doing that.

As a result, many widows depended on the generosity of the community to survive. God's law required such generosity (Deuteronomy 24:19-21; compare Acts 6:1; 1 Timothy 5:3), but those needs were easy to overlook. A widow without family or community support was in a desperate situation. She had nowhere to turn but to God (Deuteronomy 10:18; 1 Timothy 5:5).

I. Prideful Prominence
(MATTHEW 23:2-7)

A. Hypocrites as Leaders (vv. 2, 3)

2. "The teachers of the law and the Pharisees sit in Moses' seat.

Speaking "to the crowds and to his disciples" (Matthew 23:1), Jesus affirms the importance of the position of *the teachers of the law and the Pharisees*. The expression *Moses' seat* does not refer to a literal place to sit. Rather, it speaks to the position of those who guide Israel in understanding God's law. Jesus is affirming what the audience believes: these teachers are in a vital position.

Those of us who are familiar with the story line of the Gospels may tend to think of these teachers and the Pharisees as obviously wicked. But for Jesus' audience, they are the most highly respected people. We can better hear the significance of Jesus' harsh words (below) against that background.

3. "So you must be careful to do everything they tell you. But do not do what they do, for they do not practice what they preach.

Jesus has criticized religious leaders previously for teaching certain things (Matthew 15:1-20). The heart of his critique is the difference between what the leaders claim to be and how they actually live.

HOW TO SAY IT

Pharisees	*Fair*-ih-seez.
phylacteries	fih-*lak*-ter-eez.
Zebedee	*Zeb*-eh-dee.

Here Jesus highlights that problem. Those leaders have become prominent because of their expertise in the law. But from positions of prominence they use that expertise to manipulate people and take advantage of them. This is not consistent with the ideal of sitting in Moses' seat: interpreting rightly the law of the God who liberates his lowly people from oppression.

The fact that they *do not practice what they preach* fits a description that Jesus applies elsewhere: *hypocrite* (Matthew 23:13-29; etc.). *Hypocrite* is the Greek word for "actor," and hypocrites are those who appear to be something they are not. This description refers to the religious leaders' claims to honor God when their actions show that they use their teaching to disobey him (example: Mark 7:9-13). The ultimate expression of their hypocrisy is their claim of allegiance to God while rejecting God's very Son, who stands in their midst.

B. Hypocrites in Setting Standards (v. 4)

4. "They tie up heavy, cumbersome loads and put them on other people's shoulders, but they themselves are not willing to lift a finger to move them.

Earlier, Jesus had invited all "who are weary and burdened" to come to him for rest, for he gives a light, easy burden (Matthew 11:28-30). By contrast, the hypocritical leaders *tie up heavy, cumbersome loads* on others while taking none of the burden on themselves. The problem is that the teachers of the law and the Pharisees use their expertise to create interpretations that encumber others while making loopholes for themselves; in so doing, they enhance their own power and prestige. By contrast, Jesus, though greater than others, lowers himself to serve the weak.

C. Hypocrites for Wanting Attention (vv. 5-7)

5. "Everything they do is done for people to see: They make their phylacteries wide and the tassels on their garments long;

Jesus has already affirmed that the true subjects of God's kingdom do their righteous deeds where only God can see (Matthew 6:1-18) so that God is glorified (5:16). This is the righteousness that surpasses that of the Pharisees and teachers of the law (5:20). But the hypocritical religious leaders are focused not on serving God but on receiving honor and prestige from other people.

Jesus drives his point home by citing prominent parts of the Pharisees' appearance. *Phylacteries* are small leather boxes containing pieces of parchment on which are inscribed Scripture passages. This custom probably began with a literal application of the instruction to bind the law on one's hand or forehead (Deuteronomy 6:8; 11:18; compare Exodus 13:9, 16). *The tassels on their garments* are fringes attached to the edges of the shawl worn by devout Jewish men. The strings of the fringe serve as a memory device (Numbers 15:37-40).

Jesus' critique is not of the phylacteries and fringes themselves. (Some think that Jesus himself may have worn the prayer shawl; see Matthew 9:20, 21.) Rather, he is critiquing the pursuit of prominence reflected in ostentatious display. Those who seek the approval of people already have their reward (6:1, 2, 5, 16). They have no standing with God, whom they effectively ignore.

What Do You Think?

What, if anything, does this passage have to say about the way we dress today?

Talking Points for Your Discussion

- For church
- For work
- For leisure
- Other

---

6. "they love the place of honor at banquets and the most important seats in the synagogues;

The religious leaders' quest for prominence extends to their behavior *at banquets*. Many guests might be invited to feasts held in wealthy households, and those guests may include a prominent religious leader. Such a person expects public recognition by being seated at *the place of honor*.

There is a certain parallel of this situation *in the synagogues*. Synagogues in Jesus' day are places for regular gatherings of faithful Jewish people for the reading of Scripture and prayer. In such gatherings, special chairs are set aside for those educated in God's law, who are invited to speak on its practice. (Others mostly sit on benches or the

floor.) Jesus accuses the religious leaders of seeking the prominence that is attached to the *most important seats* at such gatherings. Again, their motive is not to serve God but to gain prestige (compare Luke 14:7-11).

❧ *"Sitting in the Catbird Seat"* ❧

An interesting idiom of a few decades past is "sitting in the catbird seat." Attributed to Brooklyn Dodgers' radio announcer "Red" Barber, it appeared first in print in a 1942 short story of the same title by James Thurber. A character in the story remarked that her boss was "sitting in the catbird seat," which drew on the catbird's known tendency to perch on the highest point to sing. This meant that the boss was in control of his world.

The problem of the religious leaders of Jesus' day is that they viewed their position "in Moses' seat" (v. 2, above) as the same as being "in the catbird seat." To realize that one sits in Moses' seat should bring with it the humility of Moses himself (see Numbers 12:3); for the teachers of the law and Pharisees, the opposite had happened.

Jesus' caution about imitating such leaders (vv. 8-10, below) still applies. Our love for God's Word should always be greater than admiration for those who seem to be authorities on it.—C. R. B.

7. "they love to be greeted with respect in the marketplaces and to be called 'Rabbi' by others."

Open-air markets are among the most public of places in Jesus' world. These are ideal settings for religious leaders to be hailed with special words of praise from many people. *Rabbi* is a term of honor that means "my great one." It is commonly used for a recognized teacher of Israel's Scriptures. It is telling that Jesus says of those he criticizes that they desire *to be called "Rabbi" by others*. Prominence among people, not submission to God, is what they seek.

II. Humble Servanthood

(Matthew 23:8-12)

A. Change of Focus (vv. 8-10)

8. "But you are not to be called 'Rabbi,' for you have one Teacher, and you are all brothers.

Now Jesus explains the heart of the religious leaders' error: their desire for prominence among people is effectively an act of rebellion against divine authority. Since all people bear God's image, then *you are all brothers*—equal to one another. We ultimately live under the authority not of greater, more powerful humans but under the authority of God Almighty. Being a teacher of God's Word is indeed honorable, as Jesus says (vv. 2, 3, above). But to seek prominence and power through that role means pursuing a position that can belong only to God.

9. "And do not call anyone on earth 'father,' for you have one Father, and he is in heaven.

Like the title *Rabbi*, the word *father* can be used to refer to teachers of the law, though it is likely reserved for great figures of the past (Acts 3:13; etc.). Because Israelites refer to God as *Father,* and Jesus himself does so quite often, this term especially highlights the way that those seeking prominence end up trying to usurp God's authority. The one enthroned *in heaven* has authority greater than *anyone on earth.*

What Do You Think?
Under what circumstances, if any, should Christians address one another by title? Why?
Talking Points for Your Discussion
- Regarding religious titles (Reverend, Pastor, etc.)
- Regarding academic titles (Doctor, Professor, etc.)
- Other

10. "Nor are you to be called instructors, for you have one Instructor, the Messiah.

The word *instructors* refers to respected teachers. Again, seeking the prominence implied by such an honorific amounts to displacing divine authority. There is but one ultimate *Instructor*, and he is *the Messiah*. This word means "anointed one," referring to the great king promised by God.

With this turn of phrase, Jesus brings into focus the essence of the issue. Seeking power over others means usurping God's power, but the power of Christ is not the kind that seeks prominence and status. Jesus exercises God's power in a way very unlike that of the prideful religious leaders.

This helps us understand that Jesus is speaking of much more than which terms are appropriate as titles for leaders. It is not a question of what terms we use but what we mean by them. That in turn is a question of how we understand ourselves and how we understand God.

B. Greatness Through Service (vv. 11, 12)

11. "The greatest among you will be your servant.

Jesus made this point previously when the mother of Zebedee's sons asked that they be allowed to sit at his right and left in his kingdom (Matthew 20:20-28). Those who truly honor God will not seek such prominence. They recognize that greatness from God's perspective is the opposite of how people typically view greatness. For God, those who are greatest are those who serve others.

Jesus explained the basis for that different perspective this way: "Just as the Son of Man did not come to be served, but to serve, and to give his life as a ransom for many" (Matthew 20:28). Greatness from God's perspective means serving others because God the Son lowers himself to become human and willingly give his life on the cross for unworthy humanity (compare Mark 9:35; Luke 9:46-48; 22:24-26).

What Do You Think?
How have you seen servant-leadership benefit the church in ways that other leadership styles could not have?
Talking Points for Your Discussion
- In response to a crisis
- When correction was needed
- Regarding issues in the public eye
- Other

❧ A CALL TO HUMBLE SERVICE ❧

Perhaps you do not recognize the name Jorge Bergoglio. Today he is better known as Pope Francis, due to his election to the papacy in March 2013. Many who do not recognize papal authority are nevertheless intrigued by the man's humility as contrasted with some of his predecessors. Francis has instructed the cardinals to think of him as "first among equals" rather than as their boss. He shuns use of the papal limousine. In October 2013, he fired a bishop for having spent $43 million on his personal residence.

Even if we disagree with many aspects of Roman Catholic doctrine, we can still admire Francis's call for humble service and his willingness to model it personally. Since that challenge originated with Jesus, it is for all who call on his name. How will others see this call modeled by you this week?   —C. R. B.

12. "For those who exalt themselves will be humbled, and those who humble themselves will be exalted."

Jesus previously told his followers that God exalts those who humble themselves as children (Matthew 18:4). Jesus also has warned that *those who exalt themselves* are trying to usurp God's authority, which subjects them to his judgment (21:33-46). Those who exalt themselves not only attempt to take God's rightful place, they also ignore and disdain who God truly is: the one who humbles himself to serve his servants!

This reminds us that the humility of which Jesus speaks is more than being modest about one's accomplishments, etc. It is an outlook and lifestyle of serving others because God himself does so in Christ (compare Luke 14:11; 18:14).

III. Cruel Pretenders
(MARK 12:38-40)
A. Gaining Honor (vv. 38, 39)

38. As he taught, Jesus said, "Watch out for the teachers of the law. They like to walk around in flowing robes and be greeted with respect in the marketplaces,

Mark's Gospel gives us a shorter account of Jesus' denunciation of the religious leaders. Its focus is much like that of Matthew's, just considered, but it makes a distinct emphasis as we shall see. (Luke 20:45-47 is also parallel.)

The discourse begins with a condemnation of seeking prominence, similar to that in Matthew. *Flowing robes* refers to the distinctive clothing worn by some religious leaders of the day. Such robes mark them for special honor as they conduct themselves in public. Being *greeted with respect* includes titles of honor and terms of praise.

39. "and have the most important seats in the synagogues and the places of honor at banquets.

These terms closely parallel those in Matthew. The religious leaders focus on their own power, seeking to be first wherever they can.

What Do You Think?
What can churches do to help their leaders avoid the attitudes and motives that Jesus describes?
Talking Points for Your Discussion
- Before the problem occurs
- After the problem has occurred

B. Devouring Houses (v. 40)

40. "They devour widows' houses and for a show make lengthy prayers. These men will be punished most severely."

Making *lengthy prayers* for *show* fits the prior description of the religious leaders. They seek honor from people instead of from God. But here we also see a new idea: those who seek to be great are the very ones who *devour widows' houses*. Such leaders take advantage of vulnerable people. We can imagine prominent religious leaders using their intricate interpretations of the Law of Moses to seize the property of the poor. When one becomes focused on personal power, then others become either obstacles to power or opportunities to gain more power (compare James 2:6).

IV. Trustful Generosity
(MARK 12:41-44)
A. Many Give Much (v. 41)

41. Jesus sat down opposite the place where the offerings were put and watched the crowd putting their money into the temple treasury. Many rich people threw in large amounts.

As Jesus concludes his condemnation of the religious leaders, he takes a seat near *the place where the offerings* for the temple are received (compare 2 Kings 12:9). Historical sources tell us that 13 trumpet-shaped receptacles for this purpose stand in the temple's Court of Israel, where only Jewish men and women are allowed. Mark notes that those who are rich place large offerings in the receptacles. Since all money at the time is minted from metal, a large offering is very obvious because numerous coins clang as they are tossed in.

B. One Gives All (vv. 42-44)

42. But a poor widow came and put in two very small copper coins, worth only a few cents.

By contrast, the offering of *a poor widow* is tiny, only *two very small copper coins*. These Roman coins are *leptons* in the original language, which literally means "thin." We estimate the value of one such coin at $1/128$ of a day's wage. Two such coins would seem to be an insignificant gift.

43. Calling his disciples to him, Jesus said, "Truly I tell you, this poor widow has put more into the treasury than all the others.

But the widow's offering demonstrates something that Jesus' followers must understand. While others may assess her gift as insignificant, Jesus says it is the greatest one! That assessment must puzzle the disciples, until Jesus explains it.

44. "They all gave out of their wealth; but she, out of her poverty, put in everything—all she had to live on."

Now we understand why the widow's offering is greater than that of the rich people. For those with an abundance, a large offering requires minimal trust in God. Those with great resources can still expect to have plenty to meet their needs and even their wants. The widow, however, is destitute. What she has is too little to live on. She has nowhere to turn but to God. Her offering expresses utter trust in and dependence on him.

What Do You Think?
When have you seen in another the kind of giving Jesus commended? How did things turn out?
Talking Points for Your Discussion
- Regarding a contribution to an organization
- Regarding a contribution to an individual
- Regarding help you received
- Other

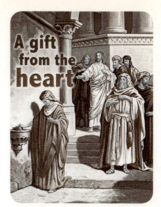

Visual for Lesson 4

Start a discussion by pointing to this visual as you pose the question at the bottom of this page.

Conclusion

A. A Great Contrast

There can be no greater contrast than that between the religious leaders and the poor widow of the first century AD. The leaders sought the approval of people, forgetting God in the process. The widow had been abandoned by people and could trust only in God. The leaders believed that they did great things in the public eye. The widow's great deed was unnoticed by all except Jesus. The leaders' pride left them heartless toward the weak. The widow's need taught her generosity like that of God himself, who gave his Son for us.

Real generosity is not a product of abundance but of humble, lowly trust. The more we know we need God, the more we trust him. The more we trust, the more we realize his generosity. And so we in turn are compelled to be generous with others as he is generous with us.

B. Prayer

O generous God, our Father, help us ever to be mindful of the danger of preferring the approval of people more than reliance on you. Remind us how much we depend on you. Open our eyes to the joy of imitating your generosity. In Jesus' name. Amen.

C. Thought to Remember

Let God's generosity be the model for yours.

INVOLVEMENT LEARNING

Enhance your lesson with NIV® Bible Student (from your curriculum supplier) and the reproducible activity page (at www.standardlesson.com or in the back of the NIV® Standard Lesson Commentary Deluxe Edition).

Into the Lesson

Form learners into four pairs or small groups. Give each group an index card that has one of the following words and its definitions: *gazump (verb):* to raise the price on something after agreeing to a lower price; *pandiculation (noun):* the act of stretching and yawning; *wabbit (adjective):* exhausted, worn out; *snickersnee (noun):* a long knife.

Challenge groups to come up with two other plausible-sounding definitions for the word they have, writing the two false definitions on the card. Collect the cards when groups finish, then pick a card and read aloud its word with the three possible definitions. Ask the groups that did not work on that particular card to decide which definition is correct, with a spokesperson announcing each group's decision. (No fair using smartphones, etc., to look up correct answers!) Do the same for the remaining three cards. Congratulate both the team that had the most correct guesses and the team that stumped the others the most.

Make a transition by saying, "Sometimes we think we know what a word means when we really don't. The teachers of the law and the Pharisees in today's lesson thought they knew what it meant to be *righteous*, but Jesus overturned their definition. Let's see how."

Into the Word

Give each learner a two-column handout titled "Jesus vs. the Religious Leaders." Have the left-hand column headed *Jesus,* underneath which you have listed the following summaries of some of his teachings: 1–He gives his followers light, easy burdens. 2–He taught followers to take care of others. 3–He spoke on the importance of not doing good deeds to gain attention. 4–He taught his disciples the nature of true leadership. 5–He instructed on the nature of sacrificial giving.

Ask learners to work in pairs to read through the two lesson texts to find examples that con-trast with what Jesus taught. Contrasts are to be written in the right-hand column, which you have labeled *Religious Leaders.* Discuss results as a class. *(Expected responses: 1–Matthew 23:4; 2–Mark 12:40; 3–Matthew 23:5-7; Mark 12:38, 39; 4–Matthew 23:8; Mark 12:38; 5–Mark 12:44.)*

Discuss the difference between the religious big shots and Jesus' ideal disciple by posing the following questions, one at a time, for discussion: 1. Why were Jesus' disciples not to seek important titles? 2. Why were the two small coins of the widow much more impressive to Jesus than the large gifts from the rich people? 3. What did the gifts to the temple treasury reveal about attitudes and priorities? 4. What are some things we can do to develop attitudes and behaviors that Jesus commends?

Alternative. Distribute copies of the "Seven Ways to Be a Hypocrite" activity from the reproducible page, which you can download. After learners work in pairs to complete this, call for conclusions to share with the class as a whole. Then distribute copies of the "Four Ways to Be Godly" activity from the reproducible page to be completed as a whole-class exercise.

Into Life

Relate the following story: "Tom Crist of Calgary, Alberta, Canada, won $40 million dollars in a lottery in December 2013. Amazingly, he announced that he was donating all the money to charity because he and his children already had what they needed." After cautioning that this story is not an endorsement to play the lottery, lead a discussion by asking for learners' reactions to Tom Crist's decision. Explore what connections they see between the story and Mark 12:41-44, if any.

Option. Distribute copies of the "One Thing to Change" activity from the reproducible page. Due to its highly personal nature, learners should be encouraged to complete this exercise at home.

A Bride Worth Waiting For

DEVOTIONAL READING: 1 Timothy 1:12-17
BACKGROUND SCRIPTURE: Genesis 28–30

GENESIS 29:15-30

¹⁵ Laban said to him, "Just because you are a relative of mine, should you work for me for nothing? Tell me what your wages should be."

¹⁶ Now Laban had two daughters; the name of the older was Leah, and the name of the younger was Rachel. ¹⁷ Leah had weak eyes, but Rachel had a lovely figure and was beautiful. ¹⁸ Jacob was in love with Rachel and said, "I'll work for you seven years in return for your younger daughter Rachel."

¹⁹ Laban said, "It's better that I give her to you than to some other man. Stay here with me." ²⁰ So Jacob served seven years to get Rachel, but they seemed like only a few days to him because of his love for her.

²¹ Then Jacob said to Laban, "Give me my wife. My time is completed, and I want to make love to her."

²² So Laban brought together all the people of the place and gave a feast. ²³ But when evening came, he took his daughter Leah and brought her to Jacob, and Jacob made love to her. ²⁴ And Laban gave his servant Zilpah to his daughter as her attendant.

²⁵ When morning came, there was Leah! So Jacob said to Laban, "What is this you have done to me? I served you for Rachel, didn't I? Why have you deceived me?"

²⁶ Laban replied, "It is not our custom here to give the younger daughter in marriage before the older one. ²⁷ Finish this daughter's bridal week; then we will give you the younger one also, in return for another seven years of work."

²⁸ And Jacob did so. He finished the week with Leah, and then Laban gave him his daughter Rachel to be his wife. ²⁹ Laban gave his servant Bilhah to his daughter Rachel as her attendant. ³⁰ Jacob made love to Rachel also, and his love for Rachel was greater than his love for Leah. And he worked for Laban another seven years.

KEY VERSE

Jacob made love to Rachel also, and his love for Rachel was greater than his love for Leah. And he worked for Laban another seven years. —**Genesis 29:30**

SACRED GIFTS AND HOLY GATHERINGS

Unit 2: Four Weddings and a Funeral

LESSONS 5–9

LESSON AIMS

After participating in this lesson, each learner will be able to:

1. Describe Jacob's expectation and Laban's deception.

2. Compare and contrast Laban's actions with modern "bait and switch" deceptions.

3. Write a prayer of commitment to honest dealings.

LESSON OUTLINE

Introduction
   A. Marriage Chaos
   B. Lesson Background
 I. Contract Agreed (GENESIS 29:15-20)
   A. Laban's Request (v. 15)
   B. Laban's Daughters (vv. 16, 17)
   C. Jacob's Offer (v. 18)
   D. Laban's Acceptance (vv. 19, 20)
      Perils of a Family Business
 II. Deception Rationalized (GENESIS 29:21-26)
   A. Expectation (vv. 21, 22)
   B. Substitution (vv. 23, 24)
   C. Confrontation (vv. 25, 26)
 III. Contract Modified (GENESIS 29:27-30)
   A. Seven More Years (v. 27)
      Bankruptcies, Fiscal and Otherwise
   B. One More Wife (vv. 28-30)
Conclusion
   A. Mixed Families
   B. Prayer
   C. Thought to Remember

Introduction

A. Marriage Chaos

I was recently in Uganda to do some teaching and was taken off guard when one of my students for the day said that he wondered why American families are so small. When asked how many brothers and sisters he had, he answered, "Thirty." Further questioning revealed that his father, a wealthy Muslim, had four wives. Four wives and 31 children! This was far outside my experience and comfort level, but the other students in the class did not see this as unusual or even exceptional in their country.

Today's lesson is about marriage customs that are outside our comfort level. Jacob, the lesson's focal character, ended up having two wives simultaneously. Or did he? Actually, each wife was given in marriage with a female servant, and these two women ended up serving as secondary wives (concubines) for Jacob. He had children by all four women. There were eventually 12 sons and at least one daughter in the family. None of this is condemned as immoral or seen as unusual in our lesson text, yet few if any Christians in the western world today would find the idea of multiple or secondary wives as acceptable (and we should not).

The value of today's lesson is not in what it teaches us about the ideal structure of a family, however. It is a study in the two characters of Jacob, the father of the nation of Israel, and of Laban, his father-in-law. It is also about the great love Jacob had for Rachel, a tender and romantic account in a time and place where marriage was viewed more as a male-dominated business arrangement than anything else.

B. Lesson Background

The book of Genesis begins with grand, dramatic accounts of worldwide significance: creation of the world, the fall of sinful humanity, and a flood of judgment. Beginning with the concluding verses of Genesis 11, the story line focuses on the person of Abraham (about 2000 BC), who ended up in the land of Canaan with son and heir Isaac.

Isaac's two sons, Esau and Jacob, had a turbulent relationship. With the help of his mother and the blessing of his father, Jacob left home to find a suitable wife from his mother's people (Genesis 28:2). On the way, he had a marvelous, visionary dream of a stairway connecting earth and Heaven, with the Lord at the top. Jacob was promised that his descendants would possess the land of Canaan as a mighty nation, the people of the Lord (Genesis 28:10-15).

Jacob finally arrived in the land of his mother's people, and right away he met Rachel, his uncle Laban's daughter, at a community well. This divinely directed connection placed him in Laban's household, just as Jacob's mother intended. Jacob began to work for Uncle Laban, and that is where this week's lesson begins.

We refer to the men of the second part of Genesis as *patriarchs*. They were the leaders of family clans, which were networks of wives, children, relatives, hired men, and slaves—all operating as semi-autonomous communities. These patriarchal clans made their livelihoods by tending large flocks and herds of livestock. This made the clans nomads in the sense that they would sometimes move so that their livestock would have adequate grazing. The tents the clans lived in were quite substantial in that they could be equipped with rugs, furniture, and cooking equipment.

These clan-communities were surprisingly large. On one occasion, Abraham was able to muster 318 men from his retinue to form a small army to rescue his nephew, Lot (Genesis 14:14). If we include the women and children, this community may have had 1,000 people. This was the social situation both of Isaac's clan (which Jacob left) and of Laban's clan (which Jacob joined).

HOW TO SAY IT

Abraham	*Ay*-bruh-ham.
Bilhah	*Bill*-ha.
Canaan	*Kay*-nun.
Esau	*Ee*-saw.
fait accompli	**fay**-tuh-*kom*-**plee**.
Jacob	*Jay*-kub.
Laban	*Lay*-bun.
patriarchs	*pay*-tree-arks.
Zilpah	*Zil*-pa.

I. Contract Agreed
(Genesis 29:15-20)

A. Laban's Request (v. 15)

15. Laban said to him, "Just because you are a relative of mine, should you work for me for nothing? Tell me what your wages should be."

Jacob has been in the service of Laban for a month by this time (Genesis 29:14). It has become clear that Jacob is more than a visiting relative, and Laban wants to clarify the relationship. Jacob, a strong young man capable of moving the heavy stone that covered the community well (29:10), has doubtlessly proved himself as a hard worker. He is not just a visiting relative who drinks Laban's wine, eats Laban's food, and sleeps late.

Reading the entire story of Jacob and Laban reveals tension throughout their 20-year partnership (see Genesis 31:38-42). If Laban has heard of Jacob's clever maneuver to obtain his brother's birthright (Genesis 25:29-34), then Laban may be distrustful of Jacob. The question of the verse before us may be Laban's way of averting a later, unexpected claim for wages from Jacob.

> *What Do You Think?*
> Under what circumstances, if any, is it unwise to work for a relative? Why?
> *Talking Points for Your Discussion*
> - Regarding temporary situations or specified periods of time
> - Regarding permanent or open-ended situations
> - Regarding Christian vs. non-Christian relatives

B. Laban's Daughters (vv. 16, 17)

16, 17. Now Laban had two daughters; the name of the older was Leah, and the name of the younger was Rachel. Leah had weak eyes, but Rachel had a lovely figure and was beautiful.

Laban has two daughters and (apparently) no sons, since at least one daughter has shepherd duties (Genesis 29:6). The fact that Rachel has *a lovely figure* and is *beautiful* implies that Leah is relatively less endowed with these qualities. Leah's only noted characteristic is her *weak eyes*, but the meaning of this is uncertain. The footnote in the

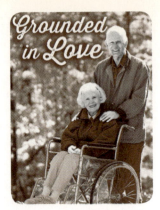

Start a discussion by pointing to this visual as you ask, "How can we make love last a lifetime?"

New International Version says that an alternative translation is "delicate."

Either way, it would be wrong to read all this as a contrast between a homely sister and a gorgeous sister. There is no indication in the story that Jacob is repulsed by Leah; after all, he will end up having six sons and one daughter by her (Genesis 29:31-35; 30:17-21).

Even so, we now begin to see the backdrop of the sibling rivalry that will be evident in Genesis 29:31–30:20. Leah will have to fight for her place as a respected wife.

C. Jacob's Offer (v. 18)

18. Jacob was in love with Rachel and said, "I'll work for you seven years in return for your younger daughter Rachel."

Laban has asked Jacob about proper wages, but Jacob answers with a request for Rachel as a wife. He has no money to pay a bride price, so as a substitute he offers to work for *seven years*. This is a substantial proposal and shows us the depth of Jacob's attraction to Rachel, something that has only grown during his month-long residence in the household of Laban.

D. Laban's Acceptance (vv. 19, 20)

19. Laban said, "It's better that I give her to you than to some other man. Stay here with me."

Laban's agreement helps us understand his character. Jacob's offer is enormous, but in response it

is as if Laban shrugs his shoulders and says, "Well, OK, that's not much, but I'll give you the family discount." Young Jacob has little leverage with which to bargain, so he seems satisfied.

❧ *PERILS OF A FAMILY BUSINESS* ❧

Working in the family business has been a common human experience throughout much of history. This was true even in America well into the twentieth century. An example is the family farm, where succeeding generations took over the tasks of planting, harvesting, animal husbandry, etc.

There are advantages to working in the family business. But there are challenges as well, such as preventing family feuds, keeping nonfamily employees motivated, and not letting emotions ruin the business. Feuding happens when family members do not separate their business and personal lives. Low morale may plague nonfamily employees who realize that their "outsider" status limits advancement opportunities. Ruinous emotions may be sparked when a supervisor takes corrective action for subpar performance by a family member.

We may see some of the above reflected in passages such as Genesis 15:2, 3; Judges 11:1, 2; and John 10:12, 13. We definitely get indications of family-business challenges in today's text and in the outcome recorded in Genesis 30:25–31:55! Much of the problem can be traced to lack of communication, whether intentional or unintentional. As a result, underlying issues went unaddressed, only to create big problems later. The fact that both Laban and Jacob had deceptive sides to their personalities didn't help! Recalling that "everything that was written in the past was written to teach us" (Romans 15:4), what does their relationship teach you?
—C. R. B.

20. So Jacob served seven years to get Rachel, but they seemed like only a few days to him because of his love for her.

This verse describes one of the most romantic and moving episodes in the entire Bible (even in all of literature). If Jacob's attraction to Rachel had been merely physical, those lustful feelings surely would have waned in short order and transferred to another woman.

Jacob's relationship with his future wife allows for frequent contact in the household situation, but this is very guarded and controlled—what we would call "chaperoned" today. He very likely does not have any private moments with her, but he sees her at her best and her worst, on good days and bad days. It is a testimony to her character that Jacob does not become disillusioned over these years. If anything, his love grows stronger.

> **What Do You Think?**
> Under what circumstances, if any, would a very lengthy engagement be a good idea today?
> *Talking Points for Your Discussion*
> - Considering the emotional maturity of those to be married
> - Considering the spiritual maturity of those to be married
> - 1 Corinthians 7:9, 36
> - Other

II. Deception Rationalized
(Genesis 29:21-26)
A. Expectation (vv. 21, 22)

21. Then Jacob said to Laban, "Give me my wife. My time is completed, and I want to make love to her."

While the time passes quickly, Jacob also has been counting the days. He is eager to claim his bride now that the seven years of service is fulfilled. Even after that length of time, Jacob has not shared with her a tent for the night to this point. Even so, Rachel is already his wife in a certain sense because of the nature of betrothals in this culture. Jacob's patience is transformed to impatience now that this long-awaited day has come.

22. So Laban brought together all the people of the place and gave a feast.

Laban follows local protocol and stages a great wedding feast for his daughter and new son-in-law. This is a joyous occasion, planned for weeks, with plenty of food and drink. Many lambs and goats are slaughtered and roasted. Figs, raisins, and other delicacies are served. Wine flows freely. The people of this community are hard workers, not people of leisure, and they join the celebration willingly and heartily.

> **What Do You Think?**
> What are some ways to prepare for a wedding that will honor God and serve as a witness to unbelievers in attendance?
> *Talking Points for Your Discussion*
> - Regarding location
> - Regarding vows
> - Regarding budget
> - Regarding scheduling
> - Other

B. Substitution (vv. 23, 24)

23, 24. But when evening came, he took his daughter Leah and brought her to Jacob, and Jacob made love to her. And Laban gave his servant Zilpah to his daughter as her attendant.

The scenario unfolds something like this: (1) a special "marriage tent" is prepared for the wedding night, (2) Laban delivers his daughter to this tent in her wedding regalia, then (3) Jacob goes in to spend the night with his new wife. But that new wife is Leah, not Rachel! We can imagine that it is after dark, the tent is poorly illuminated, Jacob is at least slightly inebriated, and Leah is wearing robes and a veil. All this makes it difficult for the trusting Jacob to detect that he is spending the night with the wrong sister.

We are also given another detail that explains some later events: Leah comes with a servant named Zilpah. Leah is probably into her 20s by now, and Zilpah is her personal slave, whose ownership is being transferred from Laban to Leah. Zilpah is likely only 10 or 12 years old. She figures into the story later when Leah uses her as a proxy wife to provide more sons for Jacob (Genesis 30:9-13).

C. Confrontation (vv. 25, 26)

25. When morning came, there was Leah! So Jacob said to Laban, "What is this you have done to me? I served you for Rachel, didn't I? Why have you deceived me?"

Daylight reveals Laban's deception. Jacob has spent the night with the older sister! This makes

Leah his wife nonetheless; there is no undoing this. Jacob immediately confronts his father-in-law, reminding him that their deal involved Rachel, not Leah. He speaks plainly and accuses Laban of having cooked up a subterfuge that must have been premeditated.

We can only imagine the sense of rejection that Leah must feel. Even so, she has been a willing part of this deception. There is no attempt by Jacob to dismiss her, however. She will prove to be a loyal (if somewhat jealous) wife who eventually gives him six sons and a daughter, so this is not to be the last night the two spend together. The situation, as it unfolds, will reveal the problems of a plural marriage: a household filled with rivalries and intrigue.

What Do You Think?

What lessons have you learned about healthy relationships with in-laws?

Talking Points for Your Discussion

- Regarding the handling of holidays
- Regarding grandchildren
- Regarding expectations of visits
- Regarding non-Christian in-laws
- Other

26. Laban replied, "It is not our custom here to give the younger daughter in marriage before the older one."

Laban is unapologetic and unrepentant for his trickery. He cites a custom of which Jacob is apparently unaware: daughters must be married in the order of their birth.

But this does not change the fact that Laban substituted Leah for Rachel deceptively. Laban is correct to care about both daughters despite differences in their physical appearances, but his deception is nonetheless dishonorable. Even so, there is no court of appeal above the patriarch himself (in this case, Laban).

In the larger context of Jacob's story, we remember that Jacob deceived his father, Isaac, to steal the father's blessing from brother Esau (Genesis 27:1-36). We sense irony in the fact that Jacob the trickster now has been tricked himself (compare Genesis 31:20).

III. Contract Modified
(GENESIS 29:27-30)
A. Seven More Years (v. 27)

27. "Finish this daughter's bridal week; then we will give you the younger one also, in return for another seven years of work."

Laban already has a plan to resolve this sticky situation: Jacob is welcome to have Rachel too—*for another seven years of work*. Laban includes something to sweeten the deal, something he knows Jacob will be unable to resist: Jacob may have Rachel at the beginning of the additional seven years of service rather than having to wait until the end.

This concession by Laban seems prudent from the aspect of Rachel's age. If Rachel were 16 when the first seven years began, she would be 23 now. Another seven years would make her 30, missing many years of potential childbearing. Laban knows that having both daughters produce sons as soon as possible is to everyone's advantage.

❧ *BANKRUPTCIES, FISCAL AND OTHERWISE* ❧

The city of Detroit, Michigan, filed for bankruptcy in 2013. At the time, it was the largest municipal bankruptcy ever. Many issues were involved in the city's insolvency, but one that received much attention was the inability to pay retiree pensions as had been agreed. Many American cities faced similar problems, with pension plans underfunded by as much as 75 percent. Similar problems were noted with employee healthcare coverage.

State governments had problems as well. For example, Illinois had reserves for less than one-half of its then-current and future pension obligations. In all cases, government entities were trying to revise pension plans—sometimes unilaterally, sometimes through negotiation. Understandably, employee unions resisted the attempts, calling them unfair.

When Jacob completed the agreed upon seven years of labor, he expected to receive what had been promised to him by oral contract. But Laban unilaterally and secretively changed the terms; he had the power to do so, so he simply did it. Jacob was appropriately incensed and demanded an explanation. Whether or not he liked the explanation was irrelevant because his marriage to Leah was a done deal—or in fancier terms, a *fait accompli*. The rest, as they say, is history. The question still open, however, is how much of Laban's ethical bankruptcy we see in ourselves. —C. R. B.

B. One More Wife (vv. 28-30)

28, 29. And Jacob did so. He finished the week with Leah, and then Laban gave him his daughter Rachel to be his wife. Laban gave his servant Bilhah to his daughter Rachel as her attendant.

Jacob quickly agrees to Laban's deal without further bartering. His great love, Rachel, will be his in seven more days, not seven more years. We can imagine that the scheming Laban also takes advantage of the situation to combine the wedding celebrations of his two daughters, thus relieving himself of the responsibility for another expensive gala for Rachel's wedding a few years later!

As with Leah, Rachel comes with a servant, a slave girl named Bilhah. This all seems to be pre-arranged by Laban, and we get the sense that at least Leah and Rachel, if not Zilpah and Bilhah as well, are agreeable to Laban's plans ahead of time since no one tips Jacob off before the first wedding night. Bilhah, like Zilpah, later becomes a surrogate wife and bears two sons for Jacob (Genesis 30:3-8). As Jacob comes to be seen as the father of the nation of Israel, the 12 tribes will be descendants of the sons born to him by his four wives.

30. Jacob made love to Rachel also, and his love for Rachel was greater than his love for Leah. And he worked for Laban another seven years.

This story is completed with two seemingly positive notes: (1) Jacob and Rachel are finally together and (2) Jacob fulfills his agreement to work *for Laban another seven years*. But the fact that Jacob favors Rachel over Leah casts an ominous shadow on this family's future. This favoritism will stoke the flames of rivalry between these two sisters (Genesis 29:31–30:24). The resentment that results will play a big part in the selling of Rachel's son Joseph as a slave (chap. 37).

> **What Do You Think?**
> How can we prevent preferential love in family relationships? Why is it important to do so?
> *Talking Points for Your Discussion*
> ▪ Parent-to-child
> ▪ Grandparent-to-grandchild
> ▪ Sibling-to-sibling
> ▪ Other

Conclusion

A. Mixed Families

When we speak of the "tribe of Judah," we usually don't think about the fact that Judah was a historical figure, a boy who grew up in a confusing home where his brothers had different mothers. Although Jacob loved Rachel most, Judah was a son of Leah; of the 12 sons, he was the ancestor of Jesus the Messiah.

Many families today are "mixed" in some way. They may include a stepfather, a stepmother, half-sisters, and half-brothers. The conflicts that result are not always minor. Yet God worked through Jacob's tangled family situation to create his beloved nation of Israel to usher in the Messiah. God also can work through the varied situations of families in the church to bring stability so children can become faithful followers of Christ.

Committed love in a relationship will help in navigating the many challenges that beset a family. Jacob never stopped loving Rachel, and this love was a sort of glue that seemed to hold the larger household together. In the end, God blessed the entire family in tangible ways. He desires to do so for us as well.

B. Prayer

Heavenly Father, to you we commit ourselves and our families. We are not perfect. We have tensions and issues, disappointments and tragedies. For these we seek your help and blessing that we may serve you best. In Jesus' name. Amen.

C. Thought to Remember

No family is perfect,
but all may be blessed and used by God.

INVOLVEMENT LEARNING

Enhance your lesson with NIV® Bible Student (from your curriculum supplier) and the reproducible activity page (at www.standardlesson.com or in the back of the NIV® Standard Lesson Commentary Deluxe Edition).

Into the Lesson

Write the following actions and behaviors on the board: *doing business with relatives / setting wages / showing favoritism / coming to a day of reckoning / planning and/or hosting a big wedding / using a "bait and switch" tactic / hiding wrongdoing under cover of darkness / complaining / refusing to break tradition / amending a contract / seeing nothing wrong with polygamy.* Pause after you write each one to ask, "What do you know about this one from anywhere in the Bible?"

Encourage responses, but do not add any observations of your own. For any that learners do not have a response, simply say, "Well . . . let's move on. What do you think about this one?" as you write the next. Make a transition by noting that each is an element in today's text.

Alternative. As learners arrive, give each a copy of the "The Last Seven Years" activity from the reproducible page, which you can download. After a few minutes of individual work, invite learners to voice their responses, which you list on the board. Make a transition by saying, "Wow! It seems like only yesterday that this one [point to one] and that one [point to another] happened. Time really does seem to fly, doesn't it? That was no less true in the ancient world, as we shall see."

Into the Word

Have three learners read the text aloud, taking the parts of narrator, Laban, and Jacob. Following that, form learners into five pairs or small groups that are designated as follows: Jacob Group / Laban Group / Leah Group / Rachel Group / Zilpah & Bilhah Group.

Ask each group to examine the text in order to be prepared to (1) summarize for the class the role of the person(s) after whom the group is named and (2) characterize the emotions of the named individual(s). The emotional characterizations can also be based on a general awareness of human psychology—what learners sense would have been true for these real people—as well as the text itself.

Have each group report its conclusions to the class as a whole. At an appropriate point during each group's presentation ask, "Do you think you are evaluating this person through a lens of modern cultural attitudes?" Ask for justification for either a *yes* or a *no* answer. Be prepared to add observations from the commentary that learners seem unaware of; as you do, ask, "Does this fact change your conclusions about [name of Bible character under discussion]?" For negative emotional characterizations such as guilt, ask, "If that person felt guilt because the plan was deceptive, then why did he [or she] go along with it?

Into Life

Write the word *DISHONESTY* on the board. Instruct: "Name some recent nonpolitical news events that had at their core an element of dishonesty concerning a key person in the story." After jotting several responses on the board, assign the following texts to be read aloud: Luke 8:15; Romans 12:17; 2 Corinthians 8:21; 2 Corinthians 13:7; Philippians 4:8; 1 Peter 2:12. After each is read, ask learners to reflect on how a person's character is addressed. Encourage free discussion.

As learners depart, give each a strip of paper on which the following is printed:

A Prayer for Honesty in Personal Relationships
O Lord, the one who deals with us in complete honesty, help me to be fully honest in my dealings with _____. In Jesus' name. Amen.

Say, "During your devotional time each day in the week ahead, pull out this prayer and mentally fill in the blank with the name of a specific individual. Then pray the prayer and see what happens!"

Option. Before distributing the prayer slips, give each learner a copy of the "Waiting for What You Want" activity from the reproducible page. This can be a whole-class brainstorming exercise.

THE MOST BEAUTIFUL BRIDE

DEVOTIONAL READING: John 10:7-15
BACKGROUND SCRIPTURE: John 10:1-11; Song of Songs

SONG OF SONGS 6:4-12

4 You are as beautiful as Tirzah, my darling,
   as lovely as Jerusalem,
   as majestic as troops with banners.
5 Turn your eyes from me;
   they overwhelm me.
Your hair is like a flock of goats
   descending from Gilead.
6 Your teeth are like a flock of sheep
   coming up from the washing.
Each has its twin,
   not one of them is missing.
7 Your temples behind your veil
   are like the halves of a pomegranate.
8 Sixty queens there may be,
   and eighty concubines,
   and virgins beyond number;
9 but my dove, my perfect one, is unique,
   the only daughter of her mother,
   the favorite of the one who bore her.
The young women saw her and called her
      blessed;
   the queens and concubines praised her.
10 Who is this that appears like the dawn,
   fair as the moon, bright as the sun,
   majestic as the stars in procession?

11 I went down to the grove of nut trees
   to look at the new growth in the valley,
to see if the vines had budded
   or the pomegranates were in bloom.
12 Before I realized it,
   my desire set me among the royal char-
      iots of my people.

KEY VERSE

My dove, my perfect one, is unique, the only daughter of her mother, the favorite of the one who bore her.
   —Song of Songs 6:9

SACRED GIFTS AND HOLY GATHERINGS

Unit 2: Four Weddings and a Funeral

LESSONS 5–9

LESSON AIMS

After participating in this lesson, each learner will be able to:

1. Explain the word pictures that describe the bride.

2. Tell how important it is for a husband to express appreciation for his wife.

3. State one way his or her church can help strengthen Christian marriages and offer assistance in doing so.

LESSON OUTLINE

Introduction
   A. Obsession with Appearance
   B. Lesson Background
 I. Overwhelming Beauty (SONG OF SONGS 6:4-7)
   A. Words of Love (vv. 4, 5a)
   B. Description of Loveliness (vv. 5b-7)
     What Is Beauty? It Depends!
II. Blessed Beauty (SONG OF SONGS 6:8-12)
   A. Praised by Others (vv. 8, 9)
     Honored by One's Peers
   B. Sought by Her Beloved (vv. 10-12)
Conclusion
   A. An Issue of Interpretation
   B. Inner and Outer Beauty
   C. Prayer
   D. Thought to Remember

Introduction

A. Obsession with Appearance

On Wilshire Boulevard in Beverly Hills, there are offices for many physicians who specialize in cosmetic surgery. These doctors are commonly called *plastic surgeons*. While they do a variety of procedures for children and adults who are disfigured due to accidents or birth defects, most of their business is servicing folks who want to look better. Lest you think this is just for women, be assured that these doctors do a brisk business in cosmetic surgery for men too.

Beverly Hills and Los Angeles are not the only places you will find these practitioners. There are cosmetic surgeons in every major city in America and Canada. I recently heard of cosmetic surgeons in Istanbul who specialize in transplanting hair from the back of men's necks to their faces so that they may have fuller beards. In that culture, a full beard is considered very manly and attractive to women. These hair-transplant doctors are not lacking for business.

Doubtlessly there are some who are reading or hearing this lesson who have used the services of a cosmetic surgeon, and the intent here is not to demean such folks or make them feel guilty. The point is that this phenomenon (which has been around in some form for centuries) is widespread for a reason: our desire to look good. This is not a bad thing. An appropriate level of concern for one's appearance is a sign of physical and mental health. The two extremes of obsession and total disdain with one's appearance may indicate emotional illness. Our lesson today concerns a woman who looks her best for her suitor.

B. Lesson Background

A neglected book in our Bibles is the last one in the Old Testament section we call the Books of Poetry. The given title for this book is The Song of Songs, Which Is Solomon's. This is often shortened to Song of Solomon or Song of Songs. Some translations use the title Canticles, which is another way of referring to songs.

The book is a challenge to understand, because it is poetic dialogue with various speakers—and the speakers are not identified, as they would be if one were reading, say, a play by Shakespeare. We can assume that the male lead in this poetic drama is King Solomon, but it is difficult to pinpoint a time and place in that man's life where this book fits. Solomon was the third king of Israel, reigning about 970–930 BC. His wealth and accomplishments were amazing. He was the builder of the great temple of the Lord in Jerusalem, as well as of lavish palaces and estates for his own pleasure.

Solomon's life included having 700 wives and 300 concubines (1 Kings 11:3). The book of the Bible at issue today pictures his relationship (or attempted relationship) with a singular woman, a shepherd girl (Song of Songs 1:8). The story behind the poetry seems to be that the king has fallen in love with this shepherdess and wants to bring her to his palace as a wife, but she pines for a boyfriend from her home village.

I. Overwhelming Beauty
(Song of Songs 6:4-7)

A. Words of Love (vv. 4, 5a)

4. You are as beautiful as Tirzah, my darling, as lovely as Jerusalem, as majestic as troops with banners.

This section begins with three comparisons concerning the physical beauty of the woman. Good poetry uses vivid, figurative language drawn from the world of the writer, and these images can be difficult to understand outside the original context. So we must attempt to unravel these perplexing references for understanding in our time.

The first comparison involves a play on words involving a city named *Tirzah*, which means

HOW TO SAY IT

Amminadab *(Hebrew)*	Uh-*min*-uh-dab.
Canaanite	*Kay*-nun-ites.
Canticles	*Kan*-tih-kulls (*i* as in *tip*).
Clairvaux	Kler-*vo*.
Gilead	*Gil*-ee-ud (*G* as in *get*).
Solomon	*Sol*-o-mun.
Tirzah	*Tur*-zuh.

"beauty" or "pleasure." The play on words is as if the man is saying, "She is as beautiful as Beauty-ville." Tirzah is a Canaanite city that was conquered back in the time of Joshua (Joshua 12:24); it later serves as the capital of the northern kingdom of Israel (see 1 Kings 16:8). It is in a jewel-like setting of lush hillsides and flowing streams, so the name is justified.

Second, the woman is compared with *Jerusalem*, a city that undergoes massive, expensive construction projects during Solomon's reign. It is the most magnificent city of the region, crowned by the temple in all its splendor. The city must be breathtaking to the traveler approaching from lower elevations.

The third reference is more difficult, being based on appreciation of *an army* arrayed in battle gear and colorful regalia. This is not the army engaged in gritty battle, but parading with its banners, brightly colored uniforms, and polished, gleaming weaponry. The word picture of this *majestic* sight is that of inspiring awe.

In summary, we might say the woman is praised for her natural beauty (Tirzah), her impeccable grooming (Jerusalem), and her colorful, complementing clothing (parading army).

> *What Do You Think?*
> What are appropriate ways to praise one's spouse's physical appearance?
> *Talking Points for Your Discussion*
> - In public
> - In family settings
> - On special occasions
> - Other

5a. Turn your eyes from me; they overwhelm me.

The man now describes how this woman's beauty affects him emotionally. When she looks at him, he is overcome that such a lovely person would glance his way. He commands as a king might, "Don't look at me, it is more than I can stand! You make my heart race!" These are words of love, for there is much more here than a dispassionate appreciation of beauty. This woman has touched his heart.

B. Description of Loveliness (vv. 5b-7)

5b. Your hair is like a flock of goats descending from Gilead.

The man continues to praise the woman's beauty in terms that are unusual for us. We might think of *a flock of goats* as dirty, smelly, and noisy. But try instead to imagine a large flock of black goats, tightly packed together, moving down a hillside. When viewed from a distance, the flock would appear as a shimmering black wave, like the full black hair of the man's beloved. This is hair that is not covered by a veil or scarf, but bouncing like the incredible hair of the models we see in TV shampoo commercials.

6. Your teeth are like a flock of sheep coming up from the washing.
Each has its twin,
not one of them is missing.

A full set of teeth is a sign of health, and this woman is not missing any. They are as gleaming as newly washed sheep. Since the woman is darker-skinned (Song of Songs 1:5, 6), such bright, white teeth are even more striking and beautiful. This is probably more than an appreciation of dental attributes, though. It is the recognition of a lovely smile.

> **What Do You Think?**
> What unique ways have you seen or heard of someone expressing love for another?
> *Talking Points for Your Discussion*
> - In a marriage proposal
> - At a wedding
> - At a renewal of wedding vows
> - On a birthday
> - Other

7. Your temples behind your veil are like the halves of a pomegranate.

The temples of the woman's head include her cheeks. These are the rosy-pinkish color *of a pomegranate*, which is a luxury fruit in Solomon's day. As with the full set of teeth, this is an appreciation of a healthy appearance as well as of beauty. The man gets but a glimpse of this part of her face, for it is covered by her *veil* of hair, making her even more enticing. See also Song of Songs 4:3b.

❧ *WHAT IS BEAUTY? IT DEPENDS!* ❧

What feminine characteristic is most important when determining beauty? Throughout history, the answer has depended greatly on one's culture. Tattoos and other marks have long been seen as attractive features of beauty in many places. At one time, the feet of Chinese girls were bound so they would not grow; to have small feet was a thing of beauty that also had positive social-class (and negative health) implications.

The elongated, brass-ringed necks of women of the Kayan tribe near the Thailand/Myanmar border exhibit another unique perception of beauty. In a practice now prohibited, Mauritian women at one time were force-fed to make them heavy and more desirable.

Therefore it is not surprising that the writer's description of a beautiful Israelite woman in ancient times seems so strange to us. He uses images that are appropriate to an ancient agrarian culture, and they simply don't "say it" for us. The widely varying beauty standards we observe around the world tell us that physical beauty is a highly subjective matter. It also suggests there is more to real beauty than physical characteristics.
—C. R. B.

II. Blessed Beauty
(SONG OF SONGS 6:8-12)
A. Praised by Others (vv. 8, 9)

8. Sixty queens there may be,
and eighty concubines,
and virgins beyond number;

The man, Solomon, acknowledges that he has 60 wives and 80 *concubines* already. The mention of *virgins beyond number* indicates that there are many future wives and concubines waiting for him.

We are rightly troubled by this seemingly casual and even prideful reference to the multitude of sexual partners that Solomon experiences in his lifetime. Two things should be noted, however. Many of these wives are received as part of political alliances. When a king in the ancient world makes a pact with another king, a daughter might be given in marriage to seal the deal (example: 1 Kings 3:1). These other kings have many wives too, so there is no lack of daughters available for this purpose (compare 2 Chronicles 11:21). While this seems strange to us, it is a normal part of statecraft in Solomon's day (but see warnings in Exodus 34:15, 16; Deuteronomy 7:1-4).

That leads us to the second issue of note: despite his great wisdom, Solomon's collection of wives ultimately proves to be unwise for the king. The religious demands of these non-Israelite women cause him to stumble spiritually (see 1 Kings 11:1-10; Nehemiah 13:26). His desire for many wives is motivated by lust for both power and pleasure (see Ecclesiastes 2:8), and both motivations cause Solomon to lose the favor of the Lord.

9. but my dove, my perfect one, is unique,
the only daughter of her mother,
the favorite of the one who bore her.
The young women saw her and called her
blessed;
the queens and concubines praised her.

This verse celebrates the uniqueness of the beloved woman. She is a dove, a gentle and graceful bird that makes soothing cooing sounds that are most unlike the grating cry of a crow. She has been cherished and nurtured in being *the only daughter* of a loving mother.

The man's rapturous estimation of her is not fantasy, for when she is presented at the royal court, all *the queens and concubines* are likewise impressed by her stunning beauty. *The young women* of the household give her a blessing, and the wives praise her. This is a remarkable reaction from these potential rivals! There are doubtless some great beauties among these women, so the attraction must be more than physical loveliness. The beloved woman perhaps sways them with her humble, gentle demeanor. She is too sweet to despise, even overcoming jealousy that naturally arises.

❧ *Honored by One's Peers* ❧

Thirty-six influential members of the motion picture industry gathered in 1927 to launch the Academy of Motion Picture Arts and Sciences. It was to be a means of honoring outstanding contributors to the production of motion pictures. Membership in the Academy today numbers 6,000 in 17 categories. These disciplines include many behind-the-scenes professionals whose names are seldom seen except on the credits at the end of a film.

On Oscar night, the industry recognizes artists whose work in the past year has been exemplary, the physical appearances of those artists being a non-issue. But the public seems most interested in the physical attractiveness of the actors and actresses who capture media attention on the proverbial red carpet.

When the king's beloved was judged by her peers, the primary consideration seemed to be physical beauty. However, there is a hint that they saw more significant qualities in her. This may remind us of 1 Samuel 16:7: "People look at the outward appearance, but the Lord looks at the heart." May that be our focus as well. —C. R. B.

B. Sought by Her Beloved (vv. 10-12)

10. Who is this that appears like the dawn,
fair as the moon, bright as the sun,
majestic as the stars in procession?

The NIV presents this verse as shifting speakers from the man to "Friends." Other versions propose that this verse continues the man's thoughts. Either way, the woman is depicted as fresh as the new morning. She is fair and lovely as a full moon rising. Her beauty is undimmed, as *bright as the sun,* the most magnificent thing in the sky.

In the final comparison of this verse, the Hebrew wording behind the translation *majestic as the stars in procession* is exactly the same as that translated "as majestic as troops with banners" in verse 4, above. The different translation here is seen necessary to maintain a continuity with the imagery of moon and sun.

> *What Do You Think?*
> How do expressions of love change appropriately at various stages of a couple's relationship? Why?
>
> *Talking Points for Your Discussion*
> - Engaged couples
> - Newlyweds
> - In child-rearing years
> - As empty-nesters
> - Other

11. I went down to the grove of nut trees
to look at the new growth in the valley,
to see if the vines had budded
or the pomegranates were in bloom.

The NIV proposes that we now return to the thoughts of the man; other versions have this verse to be the musing of the woman of his desire. Supporting the idea of Solomon being the speaker is a certain translation of Song of Solomon 6:12 (below). Supporting the idea of the woman's speaking is the similar language of 7:12, given its proximity to 7:10, which says "his desire is for me."

Either way, the verse seems to indicate a break in the flow of thought, as attention turns to the various trees and vines that are in their budding, flowering, and/or spreading stages. Such a period in the agricultural cycle is a time of unmatched beauty in tended groves and vineyards. Thoughts of yearning and desire give way to meditation on the beauty of the natural world, which can have a calming effect.

> *What Do You Think?*
> What is a Christian reaction to the statement "Beauty will save the world" (from a novel)?
> *Talking Points for Your Discussion*
> - Positive reactions
> - Negative reactions

12. Before I realized it,
my desire set me among the royal
chariots of my people.

This has been called one of the most difficult verses in the Bible to interpret, and English translations offer alternatives in their footnotes. Some have interpreted the image of chariots as a way of referring to the wedding bed, but this seems unlikely.

The NIV's translation takes the position that the speaker is Solomon, since he seems to be saying something like, "Ah, now I am *among the royal chariots of my people.*" This proposal fits with verse 11 in describing the calming effect the hike among the groves has on the man. He can imagine his status with his beloved as akin to riding in a magnificent royal chariot to the acclaim of his loving subjects. This is surely a matchless feel-

ing that even the greatest and most popular kings enjoy but rarely.

The alternative translation "among the chariots of the people of the prince," listed in the NIV footnote, causes some to understand the speaker to be female, since princes—one of whom is the object of her *desire*—are male. The other footnoted alternative, "among the chariots of Amminadab," creates further uncertainty, since the word *Amminadab* is a transliteration. Its literal meaning of "my noble people" supports the idea of Solomon speaking. But *Amminadab* can also be a personal name, as in 1 Chronicles 15:11.

> *What Do You Think?*
> What analogies would you suggest for describing inner qualities rather than physical beauty?
> *Talking Points for Your Discussion*
> - 1 Samuel 16:7
> - Isaiah 53:2
> - Galatians 5:22, 23
> - 1 Peter 3:3, 4
> - Other

Conclusion
A. An Issue of Interpretation

From ancient times, the sensual nature of the poetry in the Song of Songs has been offensive to some. On the surface, there is little doctrinal content here. This has caused some to interpret the book figuratively as an expression of the love of God for Israel or as the love of Christ for the church in a prophetic sense.

An extreme example of this is Bernard of Clairvaux (1090–1153), a medieval French abbot who was the most famous preacher of his day. By the time of his death, he had completed 86 sermons on the Song of Solomon, and these took him only into chapter 3—less than half way through the book!

In these sermons, Bernard explores the spiritual idea of the heavenly bridegroom (Christ, the Word) and his relationship with his earthly bride (either the church or the individual believer, see Revelation 19:7). These are powerful, beautiful sermons, but they have little to do with the intended meaning of the Song of Solomon.

This type of figurative interpretation of the Song of Songs still makes itself known in the church today. When we sing, "I am my beloved's and he is mine; his banner over me is love" from Song of Songs 6:3 combined with 2:4, we are not celebrating the human love that those passages indicate, but the love that Christ has for us. When we sing of Christ as the "rose of Sharon" or the "lily of the valley," we are ignoring the original context of Song of Songs 2:1, which speaks of the beauty of a woman.

May we seek to understand the Song of Songs as originally intended: in terms of the powerful language of human love. As we do, we will learn how God intends us to appreciate the beauty of our marriage partners. While these may be uncomfortable as lesson topics for some, there is nothing unseemly here.

B. Inner and Outer Beauty

The woman who is the object of the king's affections in today's lesson was a stunning beauty, to be sure. But what was it about her that drew his attentions so dramatically and in such an obsessively focused way? Surely there were other women of great physical beauty among his household of wives and concubines! Yet none seems to have excited his passions like this one.

It is probably accurate to say that there is more here than meets the eye. Many indications in this book strongly hint that this woman was as lovely in character as she was in physical attributes. She was not a sophisticated courtesan, a product of the royal court and the big city. She was a simple country girl, innocent and pure, and was not overwhelmed by the attentions of the king. While God had blessed her with physical attractiveness that turned the head of the king, she had not cheapened this with pettiness, arrogance, or pride. The book does not describe her spiritually, but a secure relationship with God would have contributed to her attractiveness.

When I perform a wedding, I have a little custom. While I am standing in the front of the church with the groom and the music of the wedding march begins, the bride will appear in the back of the aisle, usually with her father. At that point I always lean over to the groom and say, "Just look at her. She is the most beautiful woman in the

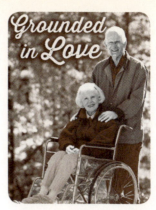

Grounded in Love

Visual for Lessons 5 & 6

Point to this visual as you pose the discussion question on page 165.

world right now, and she has made herself beautiful for you. Don't ever forget this moment."

And she is and she has. And the groom always smiles because he knows that it is true. Even a woman who is unattractive by worldly standards glows with joy and happiness on her wedding day. It is due to more than an expensive dress, the work of a hair stylist, or the craft of a makeup artist. She is truly beautiful because she is committing herself to her beloved and he to her.

May we who are married remember that day. Perhaps the years have not been kind to us when it comes to physical beauty. Try as we might to delay the effects of aging, those effects are relentless and universal. Even the world's greatest cosmetic surgeons can do only so much, and sometimes their work even distorts the handsomeness of an older person. Yet a bright smile, gentle eyes, soft speech, loving words, and a humble spirit are ultimately more attractive than any other features of beauty, no matter what our culture tells us.

C. Prayer

God of both men and women, you created us to be in relationships. Often these are hard, strained, even broken. Give us wisdom and grace to appreciate the inner beauty of character. We pray this in the name of Jesus our beautiful Savior. Amen.

D. Thought to Remember

Praise and celebrate strong marriages.

INVOLVEMENT LEARNING

Enhance your lesson with NIV® Bible Student (from your curriculum supplier) and the reproducible activity page (at www.standardlesson.com or in the back of the NIV® Standard Lesson Commentary Deluxe Edition).

Into the Lesson

Have this partial sentence displayed as your class assembles: *The greatest love song ever written is _____.* Ask learners how they would complete the sentence. After each suggestion, ask, "Why is that your choice?" After several suggestions and reasons are offered, make a transition as you say, "The book of the Bible we look at today, the Song of Songs, could be called the greatest love song ever written. Let's see why."

Alternative. Ask, "How important is it for one person to express appreciation for the other in a dating or wedded relationship?" After a few responses, ask, "Are words enough, or does a love relationship require a more tangible demonstration of affection?" After everyone has had a chance to respond, play a version of the song "Show Me" from *My Fair Lady* (the lyrics and video are readily available online). Then ask if anyone would like to change his or her answer to the second question (expect humorous reactions). Make the transition noted above.

Into the Word

Give each learner a handout featuring the phrases below to complete. Say, "In today's text, Solomon speaks glowingly of the one to whom he is attracted. Complete each of the expressions on your handout with a modern-day compliment."

You are as beautiful as the city of _____ (v. 4).
Your eyes make me _____ (v. 5a).
Your hair has the glossy sheen of _____ (v. 5b).
Your smile makes me think of _____ (v. 6).
Your face has the glow of _____ (v. 7).
When other women see you, they _____ (vv. 8, 9).
Your appearance reminds me of a morning that _____ (v. 10).
When thoughts of you begin to drive me crazy, I go to _____ to regain calm (v. 11).
When I think of you, I feel like _____ (v. 12).

You may need to adjust your directions based on the nature of your class. For example, if your class is women-only, you might say, "Complete these sentences with words you would like to hear."

Option. For deeper discussion regarding the nature of the marriage relationship as God intends, distribute copies of the "Husbands and Wives" activity from the reproducible page, which you can download. One way to use this activity is to read and discuss all 10 passages as a whole-class exercise, but this can be very time-consuming. Another method is to assign the texts to pairs or small groups, half being designated *What to Do* and the other half designated *What Not to Do*; pairs/groups will present summaries of the texts to the class according to those designations. Discuss what connections learners see with today's lesson text.

Into Life

Announce a brainstorming session by saying, "Let's think of ways our church can encourage and strengthen Christian marriages." Before beginning, stress that a brainstorm list accepts all suggestions for initial inclusion, so no negative reactions are allowed for ideas as first offered. Jot all responses on the board.

If the group hesitates or seems stuck, consider using stimulus questions such as the following to get ideas flowing: What could be included in our curriculum for teens and young adults in regard to Christian marriage? What wedding or anniversary gifts would best help couples think about the commitment they make at and in marriage? How could our class provide childcare for parents to have periodic getaways? What about financial planning guidance?

Option. Distribute copies of the "Solomon's Wives" activity from the reproducible page. Depending on the nature of your class and the time available, this can be either a whole-class or small-group activity, to be completed as indicated.

AN UNFAITHFUL BRIDE

DEVOTIONAL READING: Psalm 89:24-29
BACKGROUND SCRIPTURE: Hosea 1–3

HOSEA 1:1-11

¹ The word of the LORD that came to Hosea son of Beeri during the reigns of Uzziah, Jotham, Ahaz and Hezekiah, kings of Judah, and during the reign of Jeroboam son of Jehoash king of Israel:

² When the LORD began to speak through Hosea, the LORD said to him, "Go, marry a promiscuous woman and have children with her, for like an adulterous wife this land is guilty of unfaithfulness to the LORD." ³ So he married Gomer daughter of Diblaim, and she conceived and bore him a son.

⁴ Then the LORD said to Hosea, "Call him Jezreel, because I will soon punish the house of Jehu for the massacre at Jezreel, and I will put an end to the kingdom of Israel. ⁵ In that day I will break Israel's bow in the Valley of Jezreel."

⁶ Gomer conceived again and gave birth to a daughter. Then the LORD said to Hosea, "Call her Lo-Ruhamah (which means "not loved"), for I will no longer show love to Israel, that I should at all forgive them. ⁷ Yet I will show love to Judah; and I will save them—not by bow,

sword or battle, or by horses and horsemen, but I, the LORD their God, will save them."

⁸ After she had weaned Lo-Ruhamah, Gomer had another son. ⁹ Then the Lord said, "Call him Lo-Ammi (which means "not my people"), for you are not my people, and I am not your God.

¹⁰ "Yet the Israelites will be like the sand on the seashore, which cannot be measured or counted. In the place where it was said to them, 'You are not my people,' they will be called 'children of the living God.' ¹¹ The people of Judah and the people of Israel will come together; they will appoint one leader and will come up out of the land, for great will be the day of Jezreel."

KEY VERSE

When the LORD began to speak through Hosea, the LORD said to him, "Go, marry a promiscuous woman and have children with her, for like an adulterous wife this land is guilty of unfaithfulness to the LORD."

—**Hosea 1:2**

SACRED GIFTS AND
HOLY GATHERINGS

Unit 2: Four Weddings and a Funeral

LESSONS 5–9

LESSON AIMS

After participating in this lesson, each learner will be able to:

1. Tell the story of Hosea's unusual family.

2. Explain how the marriage of Hosea and Gomer represented the relationship between the Lord and Israel.

3. Identify one way to improve his or her spiritual fidelity and make a plan to do so.

LESSON OUTLINE

Introduction
  A. Well Begun?
  B. Lesson Background
I. Marriage That Illustrates (HOSEA 1:1-3a)
  A. God Commands (vv. 1, 2)
    The Clarity of 20/20 Hindsight
  B. Hosea Obeys (v. 3a)
II. Names That Symbolize (HOSEA 1:3b-9)
  A. First Child (vv. 3b-5)
  B. Second Child (vv. 6, 7)
  C. Third Child (vv. 8, 9)
    What's in a Name?
III. Vision That Predicts (HOSEA 1:10, 11)
  A. Restored Population (v. 10)
  B. Coming King (v. 11)
Conclusion
  A. Restoring a Damaged Relationship
  B. Prayer
  C. Thought to Remember

Introduction

A. Well Begun?

Some reports claim that the divorce rate among evangelical Christians is the same as the rest of the population (or perhaps even higher). Other analysis claims, however, that the divorce rate for active, churchgoing Christians is significantly lower than that of the general population. Either way, we should agree that the divorce statistics are too high, for Christians or anyone else.

The reasons cited for divorce are familiar: money problems, infidelity, meddling in-laws, personal tragedies, constant fighting—the list goes on and on. Operating under the maxim "Well begun is half done," the best way to minimize these potential obstacles is in-depth premarital counseling. Today's lesson begins with a startling account of premarital counseling by the ultimate counselor: God. His directive counsel to Hosea was for that prophet to take a wife from among the local prostitutes! Could such a marriage possibly succeed?

B. Lesson Background

The opening verse of the book of Hosea dates that prophet's ministry as beginning during the reign of King Uzziah and ending during the reign of King Hezekiah, both of Judah. The date range is thus about 767–687 BC. Hosea is also mentioned in conjunction with King Jeroboam of Israel. He is the second king of that name in the Bible; he is the "son of Jehoash" (2 Kings 14:23-29; Hosea 1:1), not Jeroboam the "son of Nebat," an earlier king (compare 1 Kings 11:26–14:20).

Jeroboam II reigned 793–753 BC, a particularly prosperous time in the northern kingdom of Israel (2 Kings 14:25-27). Hosea does not mention other kings of Israel who followed him, although Hosea surely ministered during their reigns since Hezekiah of Judah did not begin to rule until at least 24 years after the death of Jeroboam II.

Hosea also does not mention the invasion of the northern kingdom of Israel by the Assyrians in 722 BC. That catastrophic event ended Israel's existence as a nation, so Hosea's ministry to that kingdom ended before then. A general time line for Hosea's ministry therefore is 755–725 BC, with its primary focus being the northern kingdom of Israel and its capital city of Samaria. This made Hosea a contemporary with Isaiah, Micah, and Amos. Hosea's name means "salvation" or "he will save."

I. Marriage That Illustrates
(HOSEA 1:1-3a)
A. God Commands (vv. 1, 2)

1. The word of the LORD that came to Hosea son of Beeri during the reigns of Uzziah, Jotham, Ahaz and Hezekiah, kings of Judah, and during the reign of Jeroboam son of Jehoash king of Israel:

These references set the context for the book. Hosea is *son of Beeri*, the father otherwise unidentified. Hosea is contemporary with four kings of Judah: *Uzziah* (also called *Azariah*, see 2 Kings 14:21; 15:1-7; 2 Chronicles 26:1), *Jotham* (2 Kings 15:32-38; 2 Chronicles 27), *Ahaz* (2 Kings 16; 2 Chronicles 28), and *Hezekiah* (2 Kings 18:1–20:21; 2 Chronicles 29:1–32:33). These are all descendants of David, rightful heirs of his royal line. (For the chronology, see the Lesson Background.) This introduction serves to tell the reader that what follows may be a collection of Hosea's prophecies over a period of many years.

It is interesting to note that there is no mention here of kings of northern Israel following

HOW TO SAY IT

Beeri	Be-*ee*-rye.
Canaanites	*Kay*-nun-ites.
Diblaim	Dib-*lay*-im.
Hezekiah	Hez-ih-*kye*-uh.
Hosea	Ho-*zay*-uh.
Issachar	*Izz*-uh-kar.
Jehoash	Jeh-*ho*-ash.
Jehu	*Jay*-hew.
Jeroboam	Jair-uh-*boe*-um.
Lo-Ammi *(Hebrew)*	Lo-*am*-my.
Lo-Ruhamah *(Hebrew)*	Lo-roo-*hah*-muh.
Nebat	*Nee*-bat.
Uzziah	Uh-*zye*-uh.

Jeroboam son of Jehoash, although the names of six kings could be included per 2 Kings 15:8-31; 17:1-6. The silence regarding these six may indicate disapproval, for they were a series of usurpers —men who gained the throne by assassination and intrigue.

2a. When the LORD began to speak through Hosea,

Hosea is one of the first prophets whose oracles are preserved in a book. As such, he sets a pattern for those who follow. While there is a mix of material, the book is primarily messages from God for which the prophet is the voice, not the origin. Those who hear these words are doing more than listening to a human, and those who read the book now are doing more than reading the words of a human. This is the solemn Word of God.

2b. the LORD said to him, "Go, marry a promiscuous woman and have children with her,

The initial word of the Lord is personal, a command to the prophet himself. Hosea's prophetic career begins not with preaching and prophesying but with a symbolic action. He is told to find a wife (contrast Jeremiah 16:2), so we know he is of marriageable age and likely has not been married previously. What is unusual is the segment of the female population from which he is to take a wife: she is to be *promiscuous*, meaning an immoral woman who is probably a prostitute! Such marriages are forbidden for priests (Leviticus 21:7), but we don't know if Hosea is one of those. God can make exceptions to his laws in any case.

The action the prophet is directed to take is certainly not an impersonal thing, like hiding an article of clothing (Jeremiah 13:1-11). Rather, it is a life-changing action, something that must give Hosea pause before he obeys. This contrasts with the situation of Jacob, who was sent on a journey so that he might not select a wife from those considered unacceptable by his family (Genesis 27:46; 28:6).

The offspring resulting from Hosea's marriage will be considered children of a prostitute. This can have serious implications from a family relationship standpoint (compare Judges 11:1, 2).

2c. "for like an adulterous wife this land is guilty of unfaithfulness to the LORD."

Hosea is not on a mission of mercy to redeem a wayward woman. Rather, this is to be an object lesson for the nation, for the people of Israel have been unfaithful to their covenant with the Lord (see Hosea 4:10-13). It is not mere coincidence that the religion of the Canaanites includes temple prostitution, in which paying for the services of a cultic priestess is considered an act of worship. The charge in the verse before us has both symbolic and literal aspects (compare Isaiah 1:21; 57:3; Jeremiah 2:20; 5:7; Ezekiel 16).

> What Do You Think?
> What are some positive ways for our lives to illustrate biblical principles?
> *Talking Points for Your Discussion*
> - In family life
> - In church life
> - In vocation
> - Other

❧ *THE CLARITY OF 20/20 HINDSIGHT* ❧

The Bible is filled with commands and instructions that seem to make sense only in 20/20 hindsight. God told Abram to leave his homeland for a place God would show him. Later, God told him to sacrifice Isaac, the son of promise. God told Jeremiah to buy a field at the very time the Babylonians were laying siege to Jerusalem, a seemingly poor real-estate investment! In the New Testament, Jesus called fishermen to leave their livelihood and follow him.

And then there is this very strange command to Hosea: "Go, marry a promiscuous woman." God's reason for telling Hosea to do so may be equally puzzling: "For like an adulterous wife this land is guilty of unfaithfulness." Wouldn't we be tempted to respond, "Why should I suffer because of what the wider culture is doing?"

Let's shift the question to this: Have you ever experienced a compulsion that seemed as if it could be coming only from God? Perhaps it was to speak to a certain stranger about Christ or to make an unusually generous gift or to sign up for a mission trip. If you did experience such a prompting, what was the end result? The clarity of 20/20 hindsight encourages us to look at the result, but results are only available later, by definition. Until that "later" is available, we walk by faith.
—C. R. B.

B. Hosea Obeys (v. 3a)

3a. So he married Gomer daughter of Diblaim,

Hosea's choice of a wife is a certain Gomer, whose name means "completion." It appears elsewhere in the Bible as a man's name (Genesis 10:2) and that of a people (Ezekiel 38:6). It may be her prostitute nickname, with "completion" taken as something like "ultimate one." Perhaps Hosea decides to marry not just any prostitute but the most infamous and disreputable one in town. She is the complete prostitute, and no one sees her as anything else.

> What Do You Think?
> What are some ways you have been challenged to obey God when doing so was not easy?
> *Talking Points for Your Discussion*
> - Regarding cultural expectations
> - Regarding workplace expectations
> - Regarding expectations of family members
> - Other

II. Names That Symbolize
(HOSEA 1:3b-9)
A. First Child (vv. 3b-5)

3b. and she conceived and bore him a son.

Whatever the prophet's misgivings, Hosea's obedience results in a son for him. This is surely a happy time for the new parents despite the scandalous nature of their marriage. We should expect that this birth is properly celebrated.

4. Then the LORD said to Hosea, "Call him Jezreel, because I will soon punish the house of Jehu for the massacre at Jezreel, and I will put an end to the kingdom of Israel.

The Lord is not finished with Hosea, and the symbolism is pressed further. The name for the new son is *Jezreel,* which means "God sows." Names in the Old Testament have meaning, and these meanings are readily apparent to Hosea's audience. Jezreel is the name of a city in the tribal territory of Issachar (Joshua 19:17-23). Jezreel is also the name of the valley within which that city is located (see the next verse below; also see Joshua 17:16). Its name originally was a reference to its agricultural fertility, farmland that is so productive it seems as if God sows the seeds himself.

But the name Jezreel is better remembered by Israelites in its association with various battles (see Judges 6:33; 1 Samuel 29:1; etc.). For Hosea, the name is more recently connected with the murder of an innocent man (1 Kings 21:1-14) and the retaliation massacre of the royal family and those closely associated with it in about 841 BC (2 Kings 10:1-11; compare 1 Kings 21:15-27; 2 Kings 9:7-26, 30). The name Jezreel has a blood-soaked history!

Combining this history with the meaning "God sows," the total effect may be construed as "God will sow destruction." This is a prediction of his vengeance, punishment for the atrocities of Jezreel where innocents were murdered and the ruthless Jehu became king. Jehu not only had killed all remnants of the line of Ahab, he also had slaughtered 42 emissaries from the king of Judah (2 Kings 10:12-14). God approved Jehu's actions in general (2 Kings 9:1-10; 10:30), but Jehu went too far by shedding more blood than God intended. God has not forgotten this outrage.

5. "In that day I will break Israel's bow in the Valley of Jezreel."

The name of Hosea's son is a way for the Lord to communicate a future promise for Israel: He will break its *bow*, a reference to a weapon in the arsenal of an ancient army. This weapon depends on the springiness of its wood to propel deadly arrows. If broken, a bow is useless. God's promise portends the destruction of Israel's military power, leaving it defenseless against the might of Assyria (see the Lesson Background).

B. Second Child (vv. 6, 7)

6. Gomer conceived again and gave birth to a daughter. Then the LORD said to Hosea, "Call her Lo-Ruhamah (which means "not loved"), for I will no longer show love to Israel, that I should at all forgive them.

The second child born to Hosea and Gomer is a daughter, and she too is given a symbolic name

as directed by the Lord. The name *Lo-Ruhamah* is the combination of two Hebrew words: *Lo* is a word of negation meaning "no" or "not"; *Ruhamah* is a word referring to compassion and can be translated "mercy" or "love."

The combination therefore means "no more mercy" or, as the NIV has it, *"not loved."* This is the signal that the Lord's compassion for Israel has come to an end, for he promises not to show them love or forgiveness. National disaster looms, and the hand of the Lord is behind it (contrast 1 Peter 2:10).

We should not fail to notice the horror of the little daughter's name. It is a sign of rejection. There is nothing cute about it. Naming is the prerogative of the father, and Hosea's obedience to the Lord's command undoubtedly makes heads shake and gossipy tongues wag in his village. We can only imagine the toll this takes on Hosea himself.

7. "Yet I will show love to Judah; and I will save them—not by bow, sword or battle, or by horses and horsemen, but I, the LORD their God, will save them."

In contrast, God's *love to Judah*, the southern kingdom, will continue. It will be saved from the Assyrian menace. This will come about not because of the nation's military might but by the miraculous hand of God himself. This proves true on the night when 185,000 trained warriors of Assyria are destroyed by an act of the Lord (see 2 Kings 19:35).

> *What Do You Think?*
> How does God's heart toward Judah serve as a model, if at all, for how to respond when wounded by another?
> *Talking Points for Your Discussion*
> - Concerning a spouse
> - Concerning a friend
> - Concerning a fellow Christian
> - Other

C. Third Child (vv. 8, 9)

8, 9. After she had weaned Lo-Ruhamah, Gomer had another son. Then the Lord said, "Call him Lo-Ammi (which means "not my

people"), for you are not my people, and I am not your God.

The birth of Hosea's three children seems to happen in rapid sequence as we read this chapter. But verse 8 indicates that the third child is not conceived until the daughter has been weaned (finished her breast-feeding). So we might understand the "family-addition period" of Hosea's message to be of five or six years' duration.

As with the first two children, the third is given a symbolic name, and this one is the most chilling of all. The son is to be called *Lo-Ammi,* another combination of two Hebrew words that are self-explanatory for Hosea's original readers: *Lo* means "not," and *Ammi* means "my people." This is a negation of one of the greatest promises enjoyed by the nation of Israel: that they are God's chosen people (see Deuteronomy 7:6; 14:2).

Although this rejection is reversed later (Hosea 2:23), it must strike a note of terror for the people who understand its implications. This is the father disowning his son (contrast Exodus 4:22), the wayward child being kicked out of the family. The great promise of the covenant is a two-way relationship. The nation of Israel has been chosen to be God's people, and the Lord has agreed to be their God (Leviticus 26:12). The naming of Hosea's third child indicates that this covenant relationship is now breached.

For Hosea's family, this name sounds like, "This boy is not my son." As with the daughter's name,

Visual for Lesson 7

Use this visual as a backdrop for the discussion question on page 175.

this undoubtedly sets tongues wagging, perhaps fueling speculation that Gomer has been unfaithful and the child is not Hosea's. Those who focus only on that are missing the bigger picture.

> **What Do You Think?**
> What "names" would you give to different seasons in the spiritual life of a Christian? How can doing so be useful?
>
> *Talking Points for Your Discussion*
> - Regarding a season of guilt
> - Regarding a season of grief
> - Regarding a season of doubt
> - Regarding a season of victory
> - Other

❧ WHAT'S IN A NAME? ❧

Vermont Connecticut Royster (1914–1996) was named after his paternal grandfather. His strange name did not seem to hinder his success in life; Royster had a distinguished six-decade career with the *Wall Street Journal.* He started as a reporter in 1936, progressed through several positions to become editor, finally ending up as editor emeritus. His name came from a family tradition of using the names of states. He had great-uncles named Arkansas Delaware, Wisconsin Illinois, Oregon Minnesota, and Iowa Michigan Royster. Their unusual names earned them a place in *Ripley's Believe It or Not!*

Whimsical names are a staple of at least two shows on National Public Radio. The credits that close Garrison Keillor's *A Prairie Home Companion®* often include Amanda Reckonwith ("a man to reckon with"). The hosts of NPR's *Car Talk* named their business corporation Dewey, Cheethem & Howe ("Do we cheat 'em? And how!"). The latter is a gag line that has been used by many comedians.

When we come to the names God told the prophet Hosea to give his children, there is no whimsy involved. These names—Jezreel, Lo-Ruhamah, and Lo-Ammi—had serious meanings. They spoke of what had gone wrong between God and his people. Does it make you wonder what names God would give babies today? —C. R. B.

III. Vision That Predicts
(HOSEA 1:10, 11)
A. Restored Population (v. 10)

10. "Yet the Israelites will be like the sand on the seashore, which cannot be measured or counted. In the place where it was said to them, 'You are not my people,' they will be called 'children of the living God.'

Over a period of several years, Hosea delivers a message of coming disaster for Israel. The text now takes a turn to the longer-range vision of future restoration. We are reminded of the promise to Abraham of descendants that will be "as *the sand on the seashore*" (Genesis 22:17). This future day will be more than a readoption of Israel as a people. It will be individualized, for all included persons will be called *children of the living God*. This is a family picture, a remarkable depiction of a coming time of blessing (compare Romans 9:26-28).

B. Coming King (v. 11)

11. "The people of Judah and the people of Israel will come together; they will appoint one leader and will come up out of the land, for great will be the day of Jezreel."

Our lesson ends with a verse that gives a picture of the future that may puzzle the reader. We can understand it if we begin at the end and work backward.

Hosea promises *great will be the day of Jezreel*. Remembering that Jezreel means "God sows," we know this ultimate future is not that of God sowing destruction (the promise of vv. 3, 4). This is a vision, rather, of God sowing blessings. That matches the picture of the people coming *up out of the land*, as if they are a crop sprouting and growing. Furthermore, both Judah and Israel *will come together* when this happens.

This cannot be understood solely as recovery from the Assyrian crisis that Israel is to face a few years after Hosea gives this prophecy. This is a messianic vision, a promise of a coming king who will unite and lead an uncountable number of God's people. This is a vision of Christ and his church, the new people of God. This will be the perfect marriage, the marriage of the Lamb and his bride, the church (see Revelation 19:7-9).

The complete story of Hosea and Gomer's marriage is difficult to piece together, but there seems to be a time of later alienation and reconciliation. Hosea is commanded to redeem her from the life of prostitution to which she returns (Hosea 3:1-3). With God's blessing, their marriage is restored to one of love and mutual respect.

> *What Do You Think?*
> What risks are worth taking and not taking when trying to rebuild a broken relationship? Why?
> *Talking Points for Your Discussion*
> - Considering the nature of the relationship
> - Considering where the fault lies
> - Other

Conclusion
A. Restoring a Damaged Relationship

Marriages between Christians are not immune from trouble and even failure. Divorce is a reality, and there is little to be gained from making divorced persons outcasts or fueling their feelings of guilt. They feel guilty enough already.

On the other hand, the restoration of a damaged marriage should not be considered to be beyond the will or power of God. Hosea's marriage was clouded by sexual unfaithfulness and the undoubted tension arising from the scandalous naming of his children. The thing that saved the marriage was the prophet's willingness to heed God's commands to love Gomer again no matter how much she had hurt Hosea. This is symbolic of the way the Lord loves his people, despite their spiritual adultery.

B. Prayer

Holy God, help us ever to remember that the church, the bride of Christ, must remain pure! Show us our part in keeping her that way and strengthen us to do so. We pray in the name of the bridegroom, Jesus. Amen.

C. Thought to Remember

Stay faithful to God, forsaking all other gods.

INVOLVEMENT LEARNING

Enhance your lesson with NIV® Bible Student (from your curriculum supplier) and the reproducible activity page (at www.standardlesson.com or in the back of the NIV® Standard Lesson Commentary Deluxe Edition*).*

Into the Lesson

Have one of your good oral readers stand before the class and read Hosea 11:1, 3, 4, 8; 13:14; 14:1, 2, 4. Following the reading, ask, "Do you hear anything that you would not expect from God as he reveals himself elsewhere in Scripture?" Comment by reading or quoting 1 John 4:16. Emphasize the truth that "God is love!"

Make a transition by noting that just as parental love includes discipline to keep children on the right path, so too did the heavenly Father's love for the children of Israel.

Alternative. Distribute copies of the "He Loves Me . . . He Loves Me Not" activity from the reproducible page, which you can download. Have learners work in pairs to decide which Scriptures tell about God's love for his people (*expected result: they all do*). Then say, "Although God's Word contains a strong message of his love, the message he had for the Israelites through the naming of Hosea's children was not so pleasant. Let's see how and why."

Into the Word

Draw a five-point scale on the board. Label point five as *Speak, Lord! Your servant is delighted to hear you!* Label point one as *Not in a million years, Lord!* Say, "Let's imagine that anything a person of the Bible might hear directly from God could be put on this scale according to the recipient's reaction. How would you characterize that reaction here: [read Acts 9:4]? Put one or more small check marks on the scale according to learner responses. Repeat the process for Genesis 6:13; Luke 1:31; Judges 6:12, 14; and Hosea 1:2.

After reactions to Hosea 1:2 (saved for last), ask, "Why would God give such a directive?" Note, if no one else does, that God wanted his prophet to present a visually dramatic lesson to his people. This seemed to be an effort to "shake some sense into them," as it were. Comment: "God uses visual aids whenever it is appropriate to do so. What are some other visual aids God used to impress his message on people in the Bible?" Learners may recall Jeremiah's wearing the yoke in Jeremiah 27, Ezekiel's "playing toy soldier" in Ezekiel 4:1-3, and the tongues of fire at Pentecost in Acts 2:3.

Say, "Let's be alert for other visual aids as we read through Hosea 1:1-11." Have two learners do so, switching readers with every verse. Then ask, "What other visual aids did you see?" Learners likely will mention the names of Hosea's three children and the uncountable grains of sand; be sure to do so if they do not. As you explain the significance of the children's names (see the commentary), ask for a modern equivalent (possibilities: *Nine-eleven* for Jezreel, *Ignored* for Lo-Ruhamah, and *Rejected* for Lo-Ammi). Ask learners to speculate on how society would react to such names.

Next, ask learners to focus on the first word of verse 10—*yet.* Say, "That word implies that things will be different in the future." Read aloud verses 10 and 11 and add verse 1 of chapter 2. Say, "Look what was to happen when God reversed the implications of the children's names: the rejected become God's people again; Jezreel becomes a day of victory rather than tragedy; the unloved one is again loved by God! These reversals are a perfect picture of how God wants to work with everyone."

Into Life

Give each learner a strip of paper on which the phrase *A Touch of Gomer* is repeated along its length. Say, "Put this strip where you will see it daily in the week ahead as a challenge to your own temptations to spiritual unfaithfulness. At the end of the week, tear it up to signify your resolve to renewed faithfulness."

Option. Distribute copies of the "Illustrations for Today" activity from the reproducible page. Have learners work in threes, attempting to reach a group consensus. Discuss results as a class.

A WEDDING IN CANA

DEVOTIONAL READING: Matthew 5:12-16
BACKGROUND SCRIPTURE: John 2:1-12

JOHN 2:1-12

¹ On the third day a wedding took place at Cana in Galilee. Jesus' mother was there, ² and Jesus and his disciples had also been invited to the wedding. ³ When the wine was gone, Jesus' mother said to him, "They have no more wine."

⁴ "Woman, why do you involve me?" Jesus replied. "My hour has not yet come."

⁵ His mother said to the servants, "Do whatever he tells you."

⁶ Nearby stood six stone water jars, the kind used by the Jews for ceremonial washing, each holding from twenty to thirty gallons.

⁷ Jesus said to the servants, "Fill the jars with water"; so they filled them to the brim.

⁸ Then he told them, "Now draw some out and take it to the master of the banquet."

They did so, ⁹ and the master of the banquet tasted the water that had been turned into wine. He did not realize where it had come from, though the servants who had drawn the water knew. Then he called the bridegroom aside ¹⁰ and said, "Everyone brings out the choice wine first and then the cheaper wine after the guests have had too much to drink; but you have saved the best till now."

¹¹ What Jesus did here in Cana of Galilee was the first of the signs through which he revealed his glory; and his disciples believed in him.

¹² After this he went down to Capernaum with his mother and brothers and his disciples. There they stayed for a few days.

KEY VERSE

What Jesus did here in Cana of Galilee was the first of the signs through which he revealed his glory; and his disciples believed in him. —**John 2:11**

SACRED GIFTS AND
HOLY GATHERINGS

Unit 2: Four Weddings and a Funeral

LESSONS 5–9

LESSON AIMS

After participating in this lesson, each learner will be able to:

1. Outline the salient features of Jesus' first miracle.

2. Explain the purpose of Jesus' miracles.

3. Explore ways to develop an apologetics ministry in his or her church to help strengthen believers' faith.

LESSON OUTLINE

Introduction
  A. A Daughter Is Married
  B. Lesson Background
 I. Village Wedding (JOHN 2:1, 2)
  A. Mary the Helper (v. 1)
  B. Jesus the Guest (v. 2)
 II. Social Crisis (JOHN 2:3-10)
  A. Running out of Wine (vv. 3-5)
    A Messed-Up Banquet
  B. Filling up Containers (vv. 6-8)
  C. Wondering at Quality (vv. 9, 10)
 III. First Sign (JOHN 2:11, 12)
  A. Revealing Divine Glory (v. 11)
    Whose Glory?
  B. Departing for Capernaum (v. 12)
Conclusion
  A. Miracles and Me
  B. Prayer
  C. Thought to Remember

Introduction

A. A Daughter Is Married

I have performed dozens of weddings in my ministerial career. These have ranged from very simple affairs (one time the bride wore her high school prom dress and the groom wore his work uniform) to elaborate extravaganzas (sit-down reception dinners for more than 200 guests at $80 each). Circumstances were reversed recently, as my oldest daughter married. My wife and I experienced many things as the parents of the bride: great expense, tenseness that everything be "just right," and a strange mixture of sadness and joy as we saw our little girl all grown up and entering into her own family status. "All eyes were on the bride," as they say, and ours certainly were.

Today's lesson is dramatically situated in a wedding, but the focus of the story is not the bride or the groom. In fact, we don't even know their names or anything about them. But that's not important since the wedding serves only as a backdrop to Jesus' first miracle.

B. Lesson Background

The Old Testament is loaded with wedding language. Some of it is literal (example: Genesis 29:22-28, lesson 5), and some is figurative (example: Psalm 19:5). Some is positive (example: Isaiah 62:5), and some is negative (example: Jeremiah 7:34). A wedding was always a big deal in the world of the Bible, and some of Jesus' teachings drew on imagery from wedding celebrations (see Matthew 9:15; 22:2-14; 25:1-3; Luke 12:35, 36; 14:7-11). Jesus used such illustrations because marriage celebrations were a well-known and popular feature of village life, allowing a pause in the grind of a difficult existence that required long hours of work. Weddings were cherished occasions.

There were variations in the way village weddings were celebrated, but a regular feature was a large, festive meal, where the guests were treated to abundant food and drink. Dancing and singing of traditional songs were also staples. The cost of hosting such an event was high, and the bridegroom might hire a coordinator or steward to manage things.

Since customs of honor and status naturally led to comparisons with other wedding celebrations, no bridegroom would have wanted to be seen as miserly for scrimping on this very public event. Villages had long corporate memories! Instead, the tendency was to provide a wedding feast so lavish that the bridegroom would be thought of as a generous person who met his village's expectations in abundant ways.

I. Village Wedding
(JOHN 2:1, 2)
A. Mary the Helper (v. 1)

1. On the third day a wedding took place at Cana in Galilee. Jesus' mother was there,

The phrase *the third day* indicates the elapse of time from the previous incident, the calling of Philip and Nathanael (John 1:43-51). That took place near the Jordan River at a place known as "Bethany on the other side of the Jordan," where John the Baptist was ministering (1:28-43).

Jesus' mother, Mary, is present at this wedding that takes place in the village of *Cana in Galilee*. Her trip from Nazareth, about nine miles due south of Cana, makes it probable that she has a family connection with someone in the wedding party. She may have come early to help out.

There is no mention of Mary's husband, Joseph, making it likely that he has passed away. We thus see her as an independent woman who is not homebound by her widow's status. With Jesus being about age 30 at this time (see Luke 3:23), Mary is in her mid- to late-40s.

B. Jesus the Guest (v. 2)

2. and Jesus and his disciples had also been invited to the wedding.

HOW TO SAY IT

Bethany	*Beth*-uh-nee.
Cana	*Kay*-nuh.
Capernaum	Kuh-*per*-nay-um.
Galilee	*Gal*-uh-lee.
Nathanael	Nuh-*than*-yull (*th* as in *thin*).
Nazareth	*Naz*-uh-reth.

If Mary is related to the bride or the groom, then so too is Jesus. So there may be a family expectation involved in his presence, and he is accompanied by a group of disciples. This is presented like a teacher with his chosen students, as a rabbi with his followers (John 1:35-39). At this early point, this group includes Andrew (1:40), Peter (1:42), Philip (1:43), Nathanael (1:49; known as Bartholomew in the other Gospels), and the unnamed disciple of John the Baptist (1:35-40). The latter has been proposed to be John the Evangelist, author of the fourth Gospel. If he is present, then it is likely that his brother, James, is already part of Jesus' entourage (compare Matthew 4:21, 22). So possibly half of the eventual 12 accompany Jesus to Cana.

Jesus and his band of disciples are collectively invited to participate in this joyous celebration, and they accept. Nathanael is from Cana (John 21:2), so it is likely he is acquainted with the family hosting the wedding.

II. Social Crisis
(JOHN 2:3-10)
A. Running out of Wine (vv. 3-5)

3. When the wine was gone, Jesus' mother said to him, "They have no more wine."

Mary has her finger on the pulse of the event, and she is quickly aware when there is a problem with the wine supply. We see the importance of this fact to her when she turns to her extraordinary son Jesus for help.

The wine supply has been exhausted, and there is *no more*. The likely reason for having run out is that there are more guests than expected. The half dozen or so disciples of Jesus may account for part of this. Perhaps unanticipated guests, even freeloaders, have come and are not turned away. This can indicate that the celebration has been budgeted too tightly, and there is no extra "just in case" wine.

I have been at banquets where the caterers cut things too close and there was not enough food. It is embarrassing. There is not much that can be done except admit the shortfall and hope the guests are forgiving. But in Jesus' day, to run short is a grave social error. The bridegroom and his family have doubtlessly attended other village weddings where there was abundant food and drink. They now fail to reciprocate, and the guests will end up feeling cheated. This lack of hospitality will not be forgotten!

There probably are no ready supplies of wine that can be purchased quickly in a small village like Cana. Even if more wine is available from a larger town a few miles away, several hours will be needed to bring it from there to Cana; by the time it arrives, the banquet will have fizzled—the guests muttering and going home.

This is a crucial moment, and *Jesus' mother* understands what is at stake. So she presents the problem to her son, believing him to be capable of providing a solution. There is much unsaid here, but Mary understands that Jesus is able to provide the fix.

❧ A MESSED-UP BANQUET ❧

I worked in one of my university's educational offices during my time in graduate school. One of my responsibilities was to coordinate a two-week summer academic institute that concluded with a banquet. The academic program flowed without a hitch. Unfortunately, I cannot say the same for the banquet. At the last minute, when it was absolutely impossible to make any additions or adjustments, my supervisor and I discovered that I had neglected to order the selection of beverages commonly provided at these functions.

Describing my embarrassment is just as impossible now as it was then. Any positive feelings I had for the success of the academic program flew out the window as I realized the dissatisfaction I had caused not only to my supervisor but also to the student guests. My supervisor knew it was unintentional on my part, and he never held it against me. Nonetheless, it is a humiliation difficult to forget.

We like to be prepared. We like to know we have done a good job. It is unsettling to feel that we have failed. But perhaps some of those failures and shortcomings can also be ways to remind ourselves of human fallibility. The more such reminders we have, the more we become aware of our need for the infallible Jesus.   —C. M. W.

4. "Woman, why do you involve me?" Jesus replied. "My hour has not yet come."

Jesus' response is difficult to translate in a way that conveys the courteous rebuke that he intends—something like, "Why does this matter to us?" His response to his mother may seem very abrupt to modern sensibilities, almost rude, but there is no disrespect meant. His justification for his tough question to his mother is that his *hour has not yet come* (compare John 7:6-8, 30; 8:20). This means that to intervene miraculously will push up the timetable for Jesus' revealing himself publicly as more than a mere man. Indeed, the eventual result of the forthcoming water-to-wine miracle is a revealing of his glory (see John 2:11, below).

> *What Do You Think?*
> What are ways to respond when put on the spot to do something when the timing seems wrong?
> *Talking Points for Your Discussion*
> ▪ Considering the need that exists
> ▪ Considering the motives of the one asking
> ▪ Considering the options available
> ▪ Considering the consequences of declining
> ▪ Other

5. His mother said to the servants, "Do whatever he tells you."

Rather than respond to Jesus, Mary simply tells *the servants* to follow his instructions. She seems to be sure that he will act and help resolve this embarrassing situation, although she likely does not know how.

> *What Do You Think?*
> What was a situation where you served as a go-between? How did things turn out?
> *Talking Points for Your Discussion*
> ▪ Situation of equipping
> ▪ Situation of rebuke
> ▪ Situation of comfort
> ▪ Other

B. Filling up Containers (vv. 6-8)

6. Nearby stood six stone water jars, the kind used by the Jews for ceremonial washing, each holding from twenty to thirty gallons.

The household has available *six stone water jars.* This description indicates that these have been hewn from limestone, making them more expensive than cheaper pottery vessels. Stone jars hold water for ritual cleansings in the home. Such containers are used in the belief that they help eliminate uncleanness associated with Gentiles or other unclean things (compare Mark 7:3, 4; John 3:25). The presence of such jars indicates that this is a house with some wealth, and that it is an observant household when it comes to religious matters.

The variation *twenty to thirty gallons* regarding capacity is due to the fact that the jars are of different sizes, as would be expected from such hand-crafted items. The total volume potential of these six vessels therefore is in the neighborhood of 150 gallons, give or take 20 gallons.

> **What Do You Think?**
> What do you need to make available for the Lord's use? How will you do so?
> *Talking Points for Your Discussion*
> - Material resources
> - Spiritual gifts
> - Personal abilities
> - Other

7. Jesus said to the servants, "Fill the jars with water"; so they filled them to the brim.

To *fill the jars with water* may take 30 minutes or so, depending on the number of servants available and the distance to the village well. Filling these vessels completely (*to the brim*) indicates that there is no way to add wine later; this will prevent attempts to explain away the miracle that is about to happen as being any kind of sleight of hand.

8. Then he told them, "Now draw some out and take it to the master of the banquet."

They did so,

There is no magic here. No mystical words are spoken. Not even a prayer is recorded as being offered. As soon as the containers are filled, their contents are suitable for testing, for the water has changed into fine wine that will meet anyone's quality standards (see v. 10, below). Before it is offered it to the guests, however, Jesus wants *the*

master of the banquet to taste the newly created wine. This person is the one who has been hired to coordinate the event.

If we pause for a minute here, we can appreciate how lavish and expensive this wedding feast really is. It requires a group of hired servers and the services of an event coordinator. Since the extra wine that Jesus provides totals at least 130 gallons, we can imagine that at least that much has already been consumed. If we assume as much as a half-gallon per guest before Jesus intervenes, this implies approximately 260 adult attendees at a minimum, with at least twice that many being more likely. This helps us understand how damaging to the reputation of the bridegroom and his family a lack of wine would be—and why Mary is so concerned about it.

C. Wondering at Quality (vv. 9, 10)

9. and the master of the banquet tasted the water that had been turned into wine. He did not realize where it had come from, though the servants who had drawn the water knew. Then he called the bridegroom aside

A little plot twist is noted to establish the miracle further. The obedient servants do indeed take a sample of this new wine to *the master of the banquet* as directed by Jesus, but they do not tell him its source.

As soon as the coordinator tastes this new supply, he suspects something is amiss, so he speaks to *the bridegroom* himself. This action in and of itself is highly unusual, for the bridegroom is deeply involved in the festivities, enjoying the greatest day of his life. He is paying this *master of the banquet* to see to the details so that he (the bridegroom) is not bothered.

10. and said, "Everyone brings out the choice wine first and then the cheaper wine after the guests have had too much to drink; but you have saved the best till now."

The coordinator speaks with the experience of one who has overseen many weddings. He gently chides the bridegroom for an apparent mix-up of the wine supplies that the bridegroom has made available to him. Normally, the coordinator points out, better wine is served at the outset of the banquet. Such wine is *choice* in that it is not vinegary. It is costly, and the guests will be pleased with it. Later, *after the guests have had too much to drink,* a thrifty host serves cheaper wine. It does not taste as good, but the guests who by then are slightly "buzzed" will not notice the difference. This is not only a clever way to stretch the banquet budget, it is also socially acceptable and considered normal.

We should note that the phrase *had too much to drink* does not imply that first-century Jewish weddings are drunken galas. Conscientious Jews know the Scripture's warning against drunkenness (Proverbs 23:19-21; etc.), and wine of this era and economic context has an alcohol content of only 2 or 3 percent. By contrast, modern table wine runs 8 to 14 percent alcohol by volume.

In the case at hand, the wine miraculously created by Jesus is considered by the wedding coordinator to be excellent. It is better even than the wine the bridegroom had made available or approved for the initial stages of the banquet.

What Do You Think?

When was a time you were surprised as God did something astonishing by means of something quite ordinary? What did this teach you?

Talking Points for Your Discussion

- Ordinary situation
- Ordinary things
- Other

III. First Sign
(JOHN 2:11, 12)
A. Revealing Divine Glory (v. 11)

11. What Jesus did here in Cana of Galilee was the first of the signs through which he revealed his glory; and his disciples believed in him.

VISUALS FOR THESE LESSONS

The visual pictured in each lesson (example: top of page 183) is a small reproduction of a large, full-color poster included in the *Adult Resources* packet for the Winter Quarter. That packet also contains the very useful *Presentation Tools* CD for teacher use. Order No. 020029215 from your supplier.

This event marks the *first* of Jesus' *signs.* A sign is more than a bare display of supernatural power; it is a miracle with significance, a miracle that points to or signifies something.

Miraculous signs have two closely related purposes. First, they serve as a method for Jesus to reveal *his glory,* meaning to demonstrate his divine nature as the Son of God. When supernatural claims are backed up with supernatural evidence, the second purpose can be achieved: belief. That's the effect we see on the part of Jesus' disciples. Sadly, Jesus' miraculous signs do not have this effect on everyone (John 12:37). Even so, John's recounting of Jesus' miraculous signs is the central purpose of the book, for he hopes this will bring the reader to faith (see John 20:30, 31).

What Do You Think?

In what ways has Christ's work in your life increased your faith in him?

Talking Points for Your Discussion

- Regarding a change in life direction
- Regarding provision in a time of need
- Regarding a healing, physical or spiritual
- Other

❧ WHOSE GLORY? ❧

Brides and their weddings serve as ingredients for so-called reality TV shows. Consider those that match brides to wedding dresses. In most instances, brides, family members, and friends have a price range in mind when they arrive at the dress store to shop. Most of the time, however, budgetary constraints are tossed aside as the bride falls in love with a more expensive fashion.

Creators of TV shows know that *conflict* is the key to attracting a large base of viewers. Therefore, TV shows sensationalize the drama that plays out among brides, family members, and friends as everyone tries to have a say in the selection of the bride's dress. Sometimes things get just plain ugly as clearheaded thinking takes a backseat to emotions. Dreams for a fabulous wedding day turn into nightmares.

Perhaps a way to keep all the drama from happening in the first place is to ask this question up

front: *Who is the main one to be glorified at this wedding, the bride or Jesus?* When this question is asked and properly answered, the selection of the bride's attire might be made easier! Jesus is to be the real glory in every aspect of our lives.
—C. M. W.

B. Departing for Capernaum (v. 12)

12. After this he went down to Capernaum with his mother and brothers and his disciples. There they stayed for a few days.

Jesus will return to Cana to perform another miraculous sign (John 4:46-54), but for now he and his entourage head about 17 miles east-northeast to Capernaum, a fishing village on the Sea of Galilee. The mention of his *brothers* indicates that Jesus' relatives have been in Cana for the wedding.

The reason everyone heads not to Nazareth but to Capernaum for a short stay there of *a few days* is probably because the time for the annual Passover celebration in Jerusalem is at hand (John 2:13; compare 4:45). Capernaum is a convenient point of departure for Galilean travelers who take the traditional route along the Jordan River valley to Jerusalem. Capernaum is also the base for the fishing business of James, John, Simon Peter, and Andrew, who are among the disciples of the traveling band (compare Matthew 4:13, 18-22; Mark 1:16-21; Luke 4:31, 38; 5:1-10). That fact may indicate that Jesus will have a place to stay as these men extend the hospitality of their homes to him.

Jesus will end up using this lakeside village as a type of headquarters for his Galilean ministry. The importance of Capernaum in that regard is seen in its being mentioned 16 times in the Gospels.

Conclusion

A. Miracles and Me

Have you noticed how churches treat claims of miracles differently? Churches that can't seem to say enough about miracles have mottoes like, "Expect a miracle," or "This is a place of miracles." These can be exciting places, where the Spirit of God is said to be moving dynamically and fre-

Visual for Lesson 8

Point to this visual as you pose the discussion question associated with verse 11.

quently. However, some of the members of these churches may feel left out because they are suffering and no miracles come into their lives.

Other churches feel like places where miracles would be unwelcome and embarrassing. Faith is a rational matter in these churches, and the Christian life is based on obedience, not signs and wonders. Don't expect a miracle, because "God helps those who help themselves" (a saying mistakenly attributed to the Bible).

We gain clarity when we understand the purpose of miracles from the Bible's perspective. Miracles were not just Jesus' way of helping the helpless. They were a way for him to show his divine glory and bring unbelievers to faith as a result. Sadly, that did not always happen. Even resurrections did not compel everyone to believe (Luke 16:31; John 11:43-54). Doubtless there were scoffers at the wedding in Cana when the story got out about the water turned to wine. But hearts that acknowledge miracles "belong to those . . . who have faith and are saved" (Hebrews 10:39).

B. Prayer

Lord God, may our lives reveal the glory of Jesus! May we ever invite him in, as he was invited to that wedding so long ago. It is in his abiding name we pray. Amen.

C. Thought to Remember

Believe the signs about Jesus.

INVOLVEMENT LEARNING

Enhance your lesson with NIV® Bible Student (from your curriculum supplier) and the reproducible activity page (at www.standardlesson.com or in the back of the NIV® Standard Lesson Commentary Deluxe Edition).

Into the Lesson

Write this challenge on the board: *Give examples of prayers that are too small for God to answer.* Expect at least some learners to say that there's no such thing. Others may respond with examples such as prayers for good weather on a day planned for an outside activity, for an event to go smoothly, or for the healing of a pet.

Comment: "Some of us might consider something to be insignificant for God to respond to. However, in today's lesson Jesus' mother makes a request of him that may seem 'little' in the great scheme of eternity. And technically it wasn't even a prayer, but a verbal expression of concern to Jesus in person regarding a need. Let's see if we can gain insight about God's nature that was demonstrated in Jesus' first miracle."

Into the Word

Say, "Early in his ministry, Jesus began calling men to follow him. This group, eventually 12 in number, accompanied Jesus to a wedding celebration in Cana in Galilee." Use the Lesson Background to summarize the nature of village weddings of that day. Also point out the location of Cana on a map; draw attention as well to points of interest around that village, such as Nazareth, Capernaum, and the Sea of Galilee.

Divide learners into small groups of three to five and give each these identical instructions: "Read John 2:1-11 in your group. Then make a list of questions that your group has regarding the story as a whole or particular elements of it."

When groups finish, have spokespersons voice their groups' questions. See if members of other groups have satisfactory responses before you, the teacher, answer. (*Option:* Write all the questions on the board before inviting responses.)

Be prepared to provide information from the commentary about the following: the amount of water and wine involved, the quality of the wine created, the likely alcohol content of the wine in Jesus' day compared with wine today, the actions of Mary, the nature of the stone jars, and the position and actions of the master of the banquet.

At an appropriate point, note that an abundance of wine is an Old Testament symbol of the messianic age—the time when the Messiah would come to bring salvation. To demonstrate this, ask five learners to read aloud the following passages, one each: Isaiah 25:6; Jeremiah 31:12; Joel 2:19; Amos 9:13-15; Zechariah 9:15. Then pose this question for discussion: How do these prophecies help us understand the significance of this miracle of wine and the reaction of the disciples to believe in Jesus?

Option. For a broader look at people's reactions to Jesus' miracles, distribute copies of the "More Miracles in the Gospel of John" activity from the reproducible page, which you can download. Have learners complete individually as indicated. (If time is short, form four small groups to take one passage each.) Compare and contrast reactions noted with that of the disciples in John 2:11.

Into Life

Say, "When the disciples witnessed the miraculous provision of wine, they 'believed in him' (John 2:11). What was it that caused you to believe in Jesus?" Encourage a time of sharing; compare and contrast the reasons your learners put faith in Jesus. Expand the discussion by asking what caused others they know to believe in him and what barriers keep people from belief in Jesus. Ask, "What do these facts tell us about good and not-so-good ways to present the gospel to others?"

Option. Distribute copies of the "Beyond Initial Belief" activity from the reproducible page. Allow learners time to complete it in pairs, then discuss how their entries in the lower right quadrant could be combined into a whole-church ministry to strengthen members' faith.

THE DEATH OF A FRIEND

DEVOTIONAL READING: Isaiah 25:6-10
BACKGROUND SCRIPTURE: John 11:1-44

JOHN 11:38-44

³⁸ Jesus, once more deeply moved, came to the tomb. It was a cave with a stone laid across the entrance. ³⁹ "Take away the stone," he said.

"But, Lord," said Martha, the sister of the dead man, "by this time there is a bad odor, for he has been there four days."

⁴⁰ Then Jesus said, "Did I not tell you that if you believe, you will see the glory of God?"

⁴¹ So they took away the stone. Then Jesus looked up and said, "Father, I thank you that you have heard me. ⁴² I knew that you always hear me, but I said this for the benefit of the people standing here, that they may believe that you sent me."

⁴³ When he had said this, Jesus called in a loud voice, "Lazarus, come out!" ⁴⁴ The dead man came out, his hands and feet wrapped with strips of linen, and a cloth around his face.

Jesus said to them, "Take off the grave clothes and let him go."

KEY VERSE

When he had said this, Jesus called in a loud voice, "Lazarus, come out!" —**John 11:43**

SACRED GIFTS AND HOLY GATHERINGS

Unit 2: Four Weddings and a Funeral

LESSONS 5–9

LESSON AIMS

After participating in this lesson, each learner will be able to:

1. Tell how Lazarus was raised from the dead.

2. Compare and contrast the resurrections of Lazarus and Jesus.

3. Share with one other person a hymn, song, or poem that reflects the Christian hope of eternal life.

LESSON OUTLINE

Introduction
  A. Funerals and Faith
  B. Lesson Background
I. Tomb Opened (JOHN 11:38-41a)
  A. Grieving Friend (v. 38)
  B. Worried Sister (vv. 39-41a)
    Opportunities to Trust
II. Lazarus Emerges (JOHN 11:41b-44)
  A. Preparing with Prayer (vv. 41b, 42)
    A Boy Named Dennis
  B. Commanding to Come Forth (vv. 43, 44)
Conclusion
  A. The Hope of Resurrection
  B. Prayer
  C. Thought to Remember

Introduction

A. Funerals and Faith

"God's finger touch'd him, and he slept." So wrote Alfred, Lord Tennyson when reflecting on his friend Arthur Henry Hallam, who died suddenly in 1833, at age 22. This line is part of the poem, "In Memoriam A.H.H." It contains other memorable lines, and it was widely read and admired in the nineteenth century. It was a favorite of Queen Victoria, who found great comfort in reading it after the death of her beloved Prince Albert. The poem has been mentioned as among the greatest poetic works of its century.

Tennyson explores the topic of death in many ways, but always from the perspective of faith. He ends the extremely long poem of 2900 lines by describing his beloved colleague as "That friend of mine who lives in God" (line 2896). Tennyson's faith was challenged but remained unshaken by this death of one so dear. Tennyson believed the Lord to be the master of the living and of the dead. Therefore his dead friend was in fellowship with the same God whom he, Tennyson, continued to worship while still living.

Funerals tell us a lot about how the family and friends of the departed view death. For Christians, there is sometimes a celebratory mood that almost becomes a blissful denial of the death. This is usually not satisfactory, for the loss of a loved one is sad even for believers. Funerals for unbelievers can only be described as awkward since there are few words of comfort for those who die without the hope of resurrection to eternal life with Jesus.

Last week's lesson was about a village wedding, one of the most joyous events in rural life. This lesson's setting is a village funeral, also a major event but with a completely different tone. It was a time of wailing instead of dancing. Both events were significant in the life of a village. And in both cases Jesus intervened to change a dire situation into a happy ending.

B. Lesson Background

The household of siblings Mary, Martha, and Lazarus was in the village of Bethany. Bethany was on the outskirts of Jerusalem, on the lower eastern slope of the Mount of Olives. This mountain is situated directly east of the temple area in Jerusalem, across the Kidron Valley. To travel between Bethany and Jerusalem, one would skirt the southern flank of this mountain, a walk of about two miles (see John 11:18). Bethany also was located on the Jericho Road. Thus pilgrims from Galilee would pass through the village as they made the final ascent from the valley of the Jordan River to Jerusalem.

Jesus may have used the household of Mary, Martha, and Lazarus as a convenient base when he visited Jerusalem (see Mark 11:11). The two-mile walk, 30 minutes each way, was inconsequential in a society where everyone was accustomed to walking. Martha, Mary, and Lazarus are described as "loved" by Jesus (John 11:5). Luke records a story about the sisters (not mentioning Lazarus) that involved another visit by Jesus in their home (Luke 10:38-42). This story shows a familiarity with Jesus similar to that which he had with his chosen 12. The home may have been large and comfortable, although we have no information regarding the household's source of income (note Mary's possession of expensive ointment in John 12:1-5).

When a person died in that time and place, the interment of the body followed very quickly. Embalming was not practiced by the Jews of Jesus' day (contrast Genesis 50:1-3, 26), so a decaying corpse would soon begin to smell of decomposition —thus the urgency to have the body entombed.

Nonetheless, the body would be washed, wrapped in linen shrouds, and perhaps have spices and various sweet-smelling concoctions included in the wrappings to mask bad odors (compare John 19:39, 40). After the body was placed in a ready tomb, the entrance would be sealed using a stone carved for this purpose (compare Matthew 27:60). That is all very different from the modern custom of using a casket and concrete vault, digging a suitably deep hole, and marking the spot with a headstone in a community cemetery. In Bethany, there would be no burial in the sense of shoveled dirt filling a hole. Family tombs in places like Bethany were ready to be used on short notice.

Today's lesson is prefaced by what may seem to be curious inactions by Jesus. While he was some distance from Bethany and Jerusalem, Jesus received word that his friend Lazarus was gravely ill and that the man's sisters wanted Jesus to come (John 11:1-3). But without apparent reason, Jesus delayed (11:6), arriving days after the interment (11:17). Yet comparing the time frames of John 11:6 with 11:17 leads to the conclusion that Lazarus would have died even if Jesus had started toward Bethany immediately. Even so, Jesus could have healed Lazarus from a distance (compare Matthew 8:5-13), so why didn't he?

Jesus explained that the death of Lazarus was to result in faith (John 11:15). Indeed, the question he asked Martha after he arrived was "Do you believe this?" (11:26). Her confession of faith contrasted with the voices of skepticism (11:37), leading into today's text.

I. Tomb Opened
(JOHN 11:38-41a)
A. Grieving Friend (v. 38)

38. Jesus, once more deeply moved, came to the tomb. It was a cave with a stone laid across the entrance.

Jesus is experiencing heavy emotions, described as his being *deeply moved*. We should remember that while Jesus was God in the flesh (John 1:14), he was also a man. He experienced human emotions.

Jesus arrives at *the tomb*, which is outside the village. The place of interment is *a cave* that is probably located in some stone outcropping on the lower eastern side of the Mount of Olives. This is likely an area of other family tombs, caves that have been prepared to be suitable as underground rooms for the remains of the dead.

HOW TO SAY IT

Bethany	*Beth*-uh-nee.
Galilee	*Gal*-uh-lee.
Jairus	*Jye*-rus or *Jay*-ih-rus.
Jericho	*Jair*-ih-co.
Kidron	*Kid*-ron.
Lazarus	*Laz*-uh-rus.

Visual for Lesson 9. *Start a discussion by pointing to this visual as you ask, "What makes you believe the truth of this statement?"*

As are other area tombs, the entrance to the resting place of Lazarus's body is covered by *a stone* carved for this purpose. Ancient family tombs have been found having disk-like stones, three or four feet in diameter, that are rolled on a track across the entrance.

However, not all tomb-caves have upright entrances. Sometimes such caves descend vertically rather than extend back horizontally. This may be the case here, and artists sometimes portray Lazarus's subsequent exit from the tomb as coming up a stairway that has been chiseled out of the stony ground.

B. Worried Sister (vv. 39-41a)

39. "Take away the stone," he said.

"But, Lord," said Martha, the sister of the dead man, "by this time there is a bad odor, for he has been there four days."

To open a tomb is a serious matter. Such action can be construed as a desecration of the grave, so it must be ordered by a family member. That may be why Martha is the one to respond when Jesus says *Take away the stone*. She seems to be the older of the sisters, now in charge of the family's business following the death of her brother, Lazarus.

Martha's response indicates that she is not eager to grant Jesus' request. Four days have passed since the death of Lazarus, and she assumes that his body is in its smelliest phase of decomposition. What we observe are the limits of faith. Mar-

tha fully believes that Jesus could have healed Lazarus of his sickness and prevented his death (John 11:21) as does her sister, Mary (11:32), but their faith cannot imagine what is about to happen. For them, resurrection is a future event, a promised time when all of God's righteous people will be raised from the dead (11:24). Have the two not heard of the raising of the widow's son at Nain (Luke 7:11-17) or that of Jairus's daughter (8:40-56)?

> **What Do You Think?**
> How can we make sure we are "on the same wavelength" with God as we ponder what his will for us might be?
> *Talking Points for Your Discussion*
> ▪ Regarding use of material resources
> ▪ Regarding use of time
> ▪ Other

❧ OPPORTUNITIES TO TRUST ❧

The classic movie *It's a Wonderful Life* is loaded with lessons that can be relearned with each viewing. One such lesson is that the unexpected twists and turns of life can call for agonizing decisions. George Bailey, the movie's main character, initially resists his father's desire that George join him at Bailey Building and Loan Association. George has other ideas, as he dreams of becoming a world traveler.

Those plans change as a result of the unexpected death of George's father. Using every excuse and defense imaginable, George tries to avoid taking over his father's position at the building and loan, but he eventually gives in. Subsequent events take George on a life journey he never anticipated.

George Bailey is a fictional character, but Martha is not. Dealing with the dark event of the death of her brother, she initially resisted Jesus' request to have the stone removed. But her ultimate willingness to trust Jesus led her to experience an event that redirected her life and strengthened her faith. Each of life's unexpected turns is an opportunity to trust Jesus. When those turns come, will we focus on our doubts or focus on him?

—C. M. W.

40. Then Jesus said, "Did I not tell you that if you believe, you will see the glory of God?"

In response, Jesus reminds Martha of their earlier conversation. His challenge to her was that the one who believes in him will never die (John 11:26). Death is sad, but it is not the end for those who trust in Jesus. This is a crucial point, for the tomb might not be opened if Martha's faith falters. Her faith is challenged by the trauma of being asked to have a beloved relative's grave disturbed.

We are reminded of John's later conversation with the risen Christ, who declares himself to hold "the keys of death and Hades" (Revelation 1:18); he is capable of breaking the hold that death has over humanity. To believe in and understand Jesus' power over death is to be aware of the glory of God, and this glory is about to be revealed to Martha in the resurrection of her dead brother.

In the Old Testament, *the glory of God* is synonymous with God's presence, something that was observed at Sinai (Exodus 24:17), at the tabernacle (Exodus 40:34), and in the temple (2 Chronicles 7:1). God is present in the person of Jesus, and this was revealed earlier in glorious fashion at the Transfiguration (see Matthew 17:2; compare 2 Peter 1:16, 17). Although what has unfolded thus far in our text may seem little more than a humble human drama witnessed by a few dozen people in an insignificant Judean village, no one there should doubt the power of the Lord after Lazarus comes from the tomb alive.

What Do You Think?
How do we evaluate the claims of those who say they have seen or experienced the glory of God?
Talking Points for Your Discussion
- Exodus 33:18-23
- Psalm 19:1
- Acts 7:55
- Romans 3:23
- Other

41a. So they took away the stone.

In some unstated way, perhaps by a nod or gesture, Martha grants permission to remove the stone that blocks the tomb's entrance. This may require several strong men using levers. We can only imagine what sort of persuasion this requires, so Martha must be held in very high esteem in the village. Although some translations portray the stone as being "rolled," the text implies that the stone is lifted. We may wonder if a powerful odor does indeed emanate from the tomb when this happens, but the text doesn't say one way or the other.

II. Lazarus Emerges
(JOHN 11:41b-44)
A. Preparing with Prayer (vv. 41b, 42)

41b. Then Jesus looked up and said, "Father, I thank you that you have heard me.

Before proceeding, Jesus pauses to pray. We may not understand the relationship between the Father and the Son in every detail, but we do know that Jesus "can do nothing by himself; he can do only what he sees his Father doing, because whatever the Father does the Son also does" (John 5:19).

Jesus' prayer is thankful and confident. He is confident that what he is about to attempt is actually going to happen. He thanks his Father for having heard him, indicating that Jesus has already bathed this situation in prayer as he was traveling to Bethany.

Perhaps the two-day delay of John 11:6 was for such prayer. What those gathered are about to see will not be a spur of the moment, impetuous action. Rather, everything that is happening is part of a confident plan of one who has prayed to and been heard by God the Father.

What Do You Think?
Under what circumstances does it seem that God is most willing to hear your prayers? Why?
Talking Points for Your Discussion
- Lamentations 3:44
- James 1:6; 4:3
- 1 Peter 3:7
- 1 John 5:14
- Other

---

42. "I knew that you always hear me, but I said this for the benefit of the people standing here, that they may believe that you sent me."

Jesus' prayer has a purpose other than communication with the Father. Jesus wants the villagers who are present to understand the significance of what is about to happen: it is to give them cause to believe in Jesus as having been sent by the Father.

Jesus teaches that believing in him is the same as believing in the Father (see John 12:44). Faith in Jesus is valid only if one accepts that he comes from God and reveals God (see 1:18). "The work of God is this: to believe in the one he has sent" (6:29).

❧ *A Boy Named Dennis* ❧

Dennis, a boy in my third-grade class, had cancer. This small child never complained and seemed to face each day with silent strength. It was the next year, during fourth grade, that his long struggle with cancer ended.

His funeral, held at the school where he had attended, was unforgettable. Space for parking extended onto the main highway out front. Teachers, administrators, and Dennis's classmates formed a standing-room-only crowd of mourners, while seating was filled by family and members of their church.

The aged minister, whose demeanor always exuded a sense of comfort and fatherliness, delivered a poignant message as he reminisced about Dennis's life and struggles, his fun times and his moments of misery. He described the eternal joys and blessings that surrounded this precious child. Hardly a face was dry as each person envisioned this little boy in his new home. There were tears of sadness for losing his presence among us, but grateful tears of joy for his release from pain into a perfect place.

There was something more to that occasion —the celebration in the praises and songs that poured from Dennis's parents. They, of all people, knew what their child had suffered and the mercy that had released him. They realized that this was not the last chapter in their son's life, for he was being called from the earth to life eternal. The resurrection that awaits Dennis when Jesus bids him to come forth from the grave will be ours as well. "Whoever lives by believing in me will never die. Do you believe this?" (John 11:26). —C. M. W.

B. Commanding to Come Forth (vv. 43, 44)

43. When he had said this, Jesus called in a loud voice, "Lazarus, come out!"

The prayer is over and all is ready. We can imagine the crowd is hushed with every eye glued on Jesus. It is not an overstatement to say that this is the most important moment of Jesus' public ministry up to this point. His request to have the tomb opened is undoubtedly seen as the act of a lunatic by some in this crowd (compare John 10:20). Why is he doing this? Shouldn't the dead be allowed to rest in peace? Why is he torturing the two sisters, beloved and upstanding members of their village? Something very good needs to happen or the ministry of Jesus will be ruined just as it is poised to enter its final phase.

Although the drama is high, Jesus' act is simple. There are no incantations, no magic potions, no sacred smoke or fire. Jesus merely speaks *in a loud voice,* a voice of authority, and utters three words: *Lazarus, come out.* Jesus is acting like God himself, the one who speaks creation and living things into existence in Genesis 1. There is no more powerful sign that Jesus has indeed been sent by God, for Jews believe that only God can give life to the dead (see John 5:21; Romans 4:17).

44. The dead man came out, his hands and feet wrapped with strips of linen, and a cloth around his face.

Jesus said to them, "Take off the grave clothes and let him go."

The result of Jesus' command surely leaves the crowd breathless and astounded. The man who was dead comes out of the tomb! Despite artists' depictions, he is probably crawling not walking, because *his hands and feet* are *wrapped with strips of linen*. It is likely that he cannot see clearly, if at all, because *a cloth* is *around his face*. The first order of business, therefore, is to remove these so that Lazarus can walk and see without restriction. We can imagine a short, stunned pause before Lazarus is quickly freed by the willing hands of his grateful friends and relatives.

If we read on in John, we find that many do indeed believe in Jesus because of this mighty miracle (John 11:45). The group that is present may form the core of the crowd that acclaims Jesus on Palm Sunday as the Son of David (see 12:9, 12, 13).

John also relays the incredible detail that the plot of the Jewish leaders to kill Jesus is expanded to include killing Lazarus also, because his presence causes many people to follow Jesus (12:10, 11). For some, the raising of Lazarus does not result in faith but only fear and evil intent. And so Jesus' path to the cross becomes firmer still.

What Do You Think?

What are some ways you can be Jesus' hands in helping release or rescue people from negative situations?

Talking Points for Your Discussion

- Physical bondage (chemical addictions, etc.)
- Spiritual bondage (sin)
- Emotional bondage (dysfunctional patterns of living, etc.)

Conclusion

A. The Hope of Resurrection

The raising to life of a man who had been dead four days was among the greatest of Jesus' miracles. Jesus was working out God's plan to bring faith to his followers, but this faith did not come without personal pain. For the raising of Lazarus to happen, he first had to die, resulting in grief to loved ones.

As marvelous as the raising of Lazarus was, we should remember that it was different from the resurrection of Jesus. On that day outside Bethany, Jesus broke the power of death over Lazarus temporarily since it's fair to assume that he rose only to die again. Jesus' own resurrection, however, broke the power of death permanently.

Traditions claim that Lazarus eventually became a bishop on Cyprus and that his remains are still in the Church of St. Lazarus in the city of Larnaca on that island. This is referred to as the "second tomb" of Lazarus, the final resting place for his body after his second death. Wherever his final resting place, the account of his raising in John 11 points to the hope of his permanent resurrection on the final day; it points to ours as well. Martha held on to this hope even after the untimely death of her brother (John 11:24); we must hold on to it when losing a loved one or facing death ourselves.

The key to having such faith is the resurrection of Jesus himself. His resurrection is "the firstfruits of those who have fallen asleep" (1 Corinthians 15:20). He was the first to be raised permanently. As such, Jesus opens the way to life eternal for all who believe in him. He is the "resurrection and the life," and those who place their faith in him, even though they die, will live again (John 11:25, 26).

Our lesson today is therefore not the final chapter in the story of Lazarus. He, like you and me, will be raised when the resurrection trumpet sounds (1 Thessalonians 4:16). In prefiguring the final resurrection, Lazarus played a key role on that dramatic day in Bethany centuries ago. On the final day, Lazarus, Mary, and Martha will be joined again to feast at the banquet table of the Lord. And we will be there too, if we maintain our faith in the Lord of the resurrection. This is our eternal hope.

B. Prayer

Father, we believe there will be a day when death will no longer hold people captive in their graves. May we be comforted throughout this life by the certainty of this hope. The miseries and pains of today will not last forever. The true forever is with you. We pray in the name of the Son, who has made all this possible. Amen.

C. Thought to Remember

Jesus conquered death.

INVOLVEMENT LEARNING

Enhance your lesson with NIV® Bible Student (from your curriculum supplier) and the reproducible activity page (at www.standardlesson.com or in the back of the NIV® Standard Lesson Commentary Deluxe Edition).

Into the Lesson

Ask learners to name funeral and burial customs of their own culture. Jot responses on the board and discuss the purposes of these customs. Using the Lesson Background, compare and contrast these with such customs of the time of Jesus. *Option:* Ask learners what they know of funeral and burial customs of other cultures today; compare and contrast these with the previous observations.

Make a transition by saying, "Everyone eventually feels the pain of losing a loved one. Today's lesson will show us how Jesus used such an instance as an opportunity to reveal the glory of God."

Into the Word

Summarize John 11:1-37 (see also the Lesson Background) or divide this task among three small groups, which will address text segments as follows: Group 1–verses 1-16; Group 2–verses 17-27; Group 3–verses 28-37. Instruct groups to pay particular attention to the interactions Jesus had with his followers and how each segment addresses the issue of belief. Have groups share their findings in a whole-class discussion.

Ask a learner to read aloud John 11:37-44. Then distribute handouts of these questions for whole-class discussion: 1. How does Martha's statement in verse 39 compare or contrast with her earlier statement of belief in verse 27? 2. How does Jesus' question about seeing "the glory of God" in verse 40 relate to that concept in, for example, Exodus 16:6-10; 24:16, 17; 40:34, 35? 3. How was Jesus' prayer intended to benefit those hearing it? (Use the commentary to supplement responses.)

Option. Form learners into groups of three and give each a handout that features today's text alongside John 19:38–20:10. Challenge learners to examine the two texts to discover similarities and differences between the resurrections of Lazarus and Jesus. After a whole-class discussion of groups' results, wrap up by asking what both of these res-

urrection accounts teach about what awaits those who maintain faith in Jesus.

Option. Distribute copies of the "Belief and Doubt" activity from the reproducible page, which you can download. Allow two minutes for learners to work on this individually, then ask for volunteers to share results in a whole-class discussion.

Make a transition by saying, "Our reactions during times of pain and sorrow, specifically during times of loss of a loved one, can speak volumes to unbelievers around us about our faith in Christ and our hope that extends beyond this world."

Into Life

Distribute blank pieces of paper on which learners are to write the names of one or more relatives and/or close friends who have passed away most recently, individuals for whom they continue to grieve. (If that task is too personal for the nature of your group, have learners do only the next step.) Then ask learners to write the titles and expressions of hymns, songs, and/or poetry that reflect the Christian hope of eternal life. Ask volunteers to share the titles and expressions that are most meaningful to them.

Alternative 1. Give each learner a copy of a poem, hymn, or song that features expressions of the Christian's hope in eternal life. Have learners circle words or phrases that reflect that hope most strongly. Discuss how the themes from these compositions are similar to those found in John 11. Conclude by reading aloud John 11:25, 26a.

Alternative 2. Distribute copies of the "Hope of Eternal Life" activity from the reproducible page for learners to complete as indicated. Allow a couple of minutes, then ask if anyone desires to share his or her composition with the class. Encourage learners to share their compositions with those who need the encouragement and comfort Jesus can provide. Conclude by reading aloud John 11:25, 26a.

PASSOVER

DEVOTIONAL READING: Matthew 26:20-30
BACKGROUND SCRIPTURE: Exodus 12:1-14; Numbers 28:16-25; Mark 14:12-26

EXODUS 12:1-14

[1] The LORD said to Moses and Aaron in Egypt, [2] "This month is to be for you the first month, the first month of your year. [3] Tell the whole community of Israel that on the tenth day of this month each man is to take a lamb for his family, one for each household. [4] If any household is too small for a whole lamb, they must share one with their nearest neighbor, having taken into account the number of people there are. You are to determine the amount of lamb needed in accordance with what each person will eat. [5] The animals you choose must be year-old males without defect, and you may take them from the sheep or the goats. [6] Take care of them until the fourteenth day of the month, when all the members of the community of Israel must slaughter them at twilight. [7] Then they are to take some of the blood and put it on the sides and tops of the doorframes of the houses where they eat the lambs. [8] That same night they are to eat

the meat roasted over the fire, along with bitter herbs, and bread made without yeast. [9] Do not eat the meat raw or boiled in water, but roast it over a fire—with the head, legs and internal organs. [10] Do not leave any of it till morning; if some is left till morning, you must burn it. [11] This is how you are to eat it: with your cloak tucked into your belt, your sandals on your feet and your staff in your hand. Eat it in haste; it is the LORD's Passover.

[12] "On that same night I will pass through Egypt and strike down every firstborn of both people and animals, and I will bring judgment on all the gods of Egypt. I am the LORD. [13] The blood will be a sign for you on the houses where you are, and when I see the blood, I will pass over you. No destructive plague will touch you when I strike Egypt.

[14] "This is a day you are to commemorate; for the generations to come you shall celebrate it as a festival to the LORD—a lasting ordinance."

KEY VERSE

This is a day you are to commemorate; for the generations to come you shall celebrate it as a festival to the LORD—a lasting ordinance. —**Exodus 12:14**

SACRED GIFTS AND
HOLY GATHERINGS

Unit 3: Holy Days
LESSONS 10–13

LESSON AIMS

After participating in this lesson, each learner will be able to:

1. Restate the Lord's instructions for the Passover.

2. Compare and contrast the observance of Passover with that of the Lord's Supper.

3. Write a communion meditation that reflects Passover themes.

LESSON OUTLINE

Introduction
  A. A Night to Remember
  B. Lesson Background
 I. The Lord Speaks (EXODUS 12:1, 2)
  A. Brothers Addressed (v. 1)
  B. Month Designated (v. 2)
 II. Moses and Aaron to Speak (EXODUS 12: 3-14)
  A. Passover Preparations Described (vv. 3-9)
    Remembering the Bitter
  B. Cautions Determined (vv. 10-13)
  C. Continual Observance Demanded (v. 14)
    Fitting
Conclusion
  A. Christ Our Passover
  B. Prayer
  C. Thought to Remember

Introduction

A. A Night to Remember

A Night to Remember was published in 1955 as an account of the sinking of the *RMS Titanic* in 1912. Walter Lord, the author, had interviewed survivors, and he wrote about the tragedy from their points of view. Movies, articles, and other books have been produced that also tell this story, but Walter Lord's work seems to be the one against which all other accounts are measured.

It has been over 100 years since the "unsinkable" ship sank, but each new generation is fascinated by Lord's presentation. It departs from a chronological presentation in order to focus on the emotions of those who lived through that "night to remember."

Nations, families, and individuals have experienced events at night, making each instance "a night to remember." On the national level, the midnight ride of Paul Revere has inspired future generations of Americans. The death of President Abraham Lincoln was also a night to remember. Personal experiences may involve the birth of a child, the death of a family member, and seemingly ordinary events that developed into something quite out of the ordinary.

Many sermons have been preached with "night to remember" motifs concerning the numerous memorable nights found in the Bible (examples: Genesis 28:12; Exodus 14:21-29; Judges 7:19; Daniel 5:30; Matthew 14:25-33; Luke 2:6-20; John 3:1, 2; Acts 12:6-17; 16:25-34). Today's lesson is about an event in Egypt that fits—even defines—this category. It was a night when God proved his superiority over the fictitious gods of Egypt.

B. Lesson Background

In about 2092 BC, God instructed Abraham (at the time known as Abram) to leave his home country and go to the land he would be shown —Canaan (Genesis 12:1-5). Obeying God, Abraham continued on to Egypt because of a famine (12:10). There Pharaoh and his household experienced the first plagues from the Lord on the Egyptians; this time it was to convince Pharaoh that he must return Abraham's wife to him (12:14-20). Later, God informed Abraham that his descendants would be oppressed 400 years "in a country not their own" (15:13).

That land was Egypt, for grandson Jacob and his extended family went there in about 1877 BC —again to escape famine (Genesis 43:1; 45:6; 46:5-7). After 430 years, the Lord was ready to act to free his people from slavery. That was the beginning of many mighty acts to fulfill the promises made to the patriarchs—to Abraham, Isaac, and Jacob. The year was 1447 BC. The occasion was Passover.

I. The Lord Speaks
(EXODUS 12:1, 2)

A. Brothers Addressed (v. 1)

1. The LORD said to Moses and Aaron in Egypt,

The book of Exodus notes the Lord's speaking to Moses dozens of times. By contrast, for the Lord to speak *to Moses and Aaron* simultaneously is rare (only here and in Exodus 6:13; 7:8; 9:8; 12:43). What is about to be said is so important that Aaron—Moses' brother and Israel's future first high priest (28:1-4, 41; 29:9; etc.)—must hear it firsthand. All the other regulations for sacrifices and rituals will be given at Sinai, but the revelation about the observance of Passover is given while the nation of Israel is still *in Egypt*.

B. Month Designated (v. 2)

2. "This month is to be for you the first month, the first month of your year."

The name of the month in question is given as "Aviv" in Exodus 13:4. This month corresponds with late March and early April. The name of this *first month of [their] year* becomes known as "Nisan" during the Babylonian exile (Esther 3:7), for that was the Babylonian name for it.

Aviv/Nisan is used in determining the beginning of the religious year, while Israel's civil year eventually comes to begin with the seventh month (compare 1 Kings 8:2). The first day of any month is heralded by the appearance of a new moon (compare Psalm 81:3; Isaiah 66:23).

II. Moses and Aaron to Speak
(EXODUS 12:3-14)

A. Passover Preparations Described (vv. 3-9)

3. "Tell the whole community of Israel that on the tenth day of this month each man is to take a lamb for his family, one for each household.

The directives continue to both Moses and Aaron, who must pass these on to *the whole community of Israel*. The verb *tell* is a plural imperative, so both men are to provide specific instructions on what the people are to do in preparation for the first Passover observance.

The ceremonial actions are to begin *on the tenth day* of the first month. The selection of the animal on this specific day is never cited again, so some conclude that this feature is intended only for this initial occasion. Forty years later, the Israelites will cross the Jordan River "on the tenth day of the first month" (Joshua 4:19) and will keep the Passover four days later (5:10). But there is no mention of selecting the animals on the exciting day when they cross the Jordan. It is possible that they do, but this more likely takes place later.

The word translated *lamb* is not the usual word for a young sheep. It is a generic term that may refer either to a young sheep or goat (kid). That is made clear in verse 5. The use of either goats or sheep will be a recognized part of the ceremony some 800 years later when King Josiah's workmen find the law in the temple, in about 621 BC. At that time the king renews the practice of keeping the Passover (2 Chronicles 35:7).

HOW TO SAY IT

Aaron	*Air*-un.
Abraham	*Ay*-bruh-ham.
Abram	*Ay*-brum.
Aviv	*A*-viv.
Babylonian	Bab-ih-*low*-nee-un.
Hezekiah	Hez-ih-*kye*-uh.
Josiah	Jo-*sigh*-uh.
Moses	*Mo*-zes or *Mo*-zez.
Nisan	*Nye*-san.
Pharaoh	*Fair*-o or *Fay*-roe.

4. "If any household is too small for a whole lamb, they must share one with their nearest neighbor, having taken into account the number of people there are. You are to determine the amount of lamb needed in accordance with what each person will eat.

The meaning of the verse is clear, but interpretive traditions have risen from it. In the late first century AD, the Jewish historian Josephus wrote that "a company not less than ten belong to every [Passover] sacrifice, for it is not lawful for them to feast singly by themselves, and [that there were often] as many as twenty."

5. "The animals you choose must be year-old males without defect, and you may take them from the sheep or the goats.

The importance of the forthcoming Passover observance is magnified by the requirements that are given for the sacrificial animals. Animals of highest value, those *without defect,* are prescribed. This prerequisite will later be stressed repeatedly for other offerings as well (Leviticus 1:3, 10; Numbers 28:3, 9, 11; etc.). If it is for God, it should be the best. The unblemished animals will be considered as substitutes for the firstborn of people and animals to be spared when the Lord passes through the land (Exodus 12:12). Most Christians are aware of the comparison with Jesus as the perfect, sinless sacrifice (1 Peter 1:19).

6. "Take care of them until the fourteenth day of the month, when all the members of the community of Israel must slaughter them at twilight.

The interval between the tenth day and *the fourteenth day of the month* is more than just for ordinary care of animals. The phrase *take care of them* stresses that special attention is to be given to the selected sacrificial animals. The unblemished animals of the tenth day must not be allowed to become the blemished animals of the fourteenth day! The priesthood of Aaron and his descendants (Leviticus 8–10) has not yet been established; at this time there is no altar, no tabernacle, no central place for worship. As such, the leader of each household is to act as something of a priest to prepare and slay the animal. The special guidelines make this a memorable experience for each family.

The fourteenth day of the month has another implication: since the month begins with a new moon, there will be a full moon by the fourteenth. This will provide light during the hasty departure from Egypt by night.

The phrase *at twilight* is literally "between the two evenings." This awkward (to us) expression has drawn various interpretations. Some think it refers to the time between sunset and when stars become visible. But it probably refers to a two-hour period just prior to full sunset. Josephus wrote that the time is between the ninth and eleventh hours, or from about 3:00 p.m. to 5:00 p.m. The regular evening sacrifice for Israel, when instituted, will usually occur about 3:00 p.m., but it may be earlier on this special day.

7. "Then they are to take some of the blood and put it on the sides and tops of the doorframes of the houses where they eat the lambs.

Exodus 12:22 provides a bit more detail on how the blood of the Passover lamb is to be used. The blood is first caught in a basin. Then "a bunch of hyssop" is used to apply the blood to *the sides and tops of the doorframes* of each Israelite house where people are gathered to eat. A sermon from decades ago had these words in it: "The blood gurgling into the basin proclaimed that something innocent had to die so that others could live." This parallels the doctrine of a substitutionary atoning sacrifice: Christ the innocent died so that we the guilty might live.

8a. "That same night they are to eat the meat roasted over the fire,

Roasting over an open fire is the only method to be used to prepare the Passover lamb. Verse 9, below, further stresses this requirement.

8b. "along with bitter herbs,

Bitter herbs are associated with the life that the Israelites have endured for many years, especially in the year after Moses makes his first approach to Pharaoh. The bitter herbs of Egypt probably include wild lettuce and endive (compare Numbers 9:11).

8c. "and bread made without yeast.

Bread made without yeast (leaven) will end up being thin and flat. Not having to wait until the dough rises points to the haste demanded later. The New Testament usually associates yeast with impurity (example: 1 Corinthians 5:6, 7; note Christ's designation as "our Passover lamb"), and removal of yeast as removal of sin is stressed.

What Do You Think?

Under what circumstances, if any, would a Christian's participation in a modern Passover celebration be appropriate? Why?

Talking Points for Your Discussion
- Positive and negative impact on non-Christians
- Positive and negative impact on fellow believers
- Romans 14; 1 Corinthians 5:7; Galatians 4:10, 11; Colossians 2:16
- Other

❧ REMEMBERING THE BITTER ❧

My community is blessed to have a Christian ministry to homeless women and their children. The ministry offers both short-term emergency shelter and a longer-term "life recovery" option for women to receive training and assistance in breaking free from unhealthy patterns. The longer-term option requires participation in work therapy, counseling, self-evaluation, and coursework designed to help them heal, be accountable to others, and set boundaries for themselves.

Many women who enter the program have been exposed to abuse, rejection, abandonment, addiction, and court involvement. Although the shelter offers the women a way out of dire circumstances, many ladies leave the program before they complete all that is offered. The struggles that come with change are challenging. At times it seems that memories of "life before" grow more attrac-

tive, especially when the inevitable trials of what should be the "new normal" kick in.

The rituals and symbols of Passover were meant to remind participants of the Lord's protection. They also contain an element to bring to mind the bitterness of the past. Then as now, we humans tend to romanticize or minimize trauma of the past as a reaction to the trials of the moment (compare Numbers 11:4-6). Perhaps an honest reflection on yesterday's trials (and sins!) will prevent us from embracing them anew.   —V. E.

9. "Do not eat the meat raw or boiled in water, but roast it over a fire—with the head, legs and internal organs.

The cooking directives are specific in prohibiting the eating of meat that is either *raw or boiled in water*. It must be roasted!

The restriction "do not break any of the bones" in Exodus 12:46 is also a factor, and this is easily avoided by roasting the animal over a spit. Not having a bone broken is cited in John 19:36 as being a fulfillment of prophecy when Jesus is crucified (compare Numbers 9:12; Psalm 34:20; John 19:32, 33).

B. Cautions Determined (vv. 10-13)

10. "Do not leave any of it till morning; if some is left till morning, you must burn it.

A regular future custom for most sacrifices will be to incinerate what cannot be eaten on the first day after making an offering to God (Leviticus 7:15). An exception will be made for freewill offerings or offerings with a vow; such can delay the burning one more day (7:16-18).

11. "This is how you are to eat it: with your cloak tucked into your belt, your sandals on your feet and your staff in your hand. Eat it in haste; it is the LORD's Passover.

The Israelites are to be ready to leave on a journey, and the procedures listed here are regarded as being only for the first Passover. A walking staff is to be readily available when the actual departure from Egypt begins. The word *Passover* is from a verb that primarily means "to spare," so "to pass over" is a valid way to express the idea in view. This is seen especially in Isaiah 31:5, where

God says, "Like birds hovering overhead, the Lord Almighty will shield Jerusalem; he will shield it and deliver it, he will 'pass over' it and will rescue it."

What Do You Think?
What errors involving *haste* do Christians commit? How do we correct these?
Talking Points for Your Discussion
- Areas where more haste is called for
- Areas where less haste is called for

12. "On that same night I will pass through Egypt and strike down every firstborn of both people and animals, and I will bring judgment on all the gods of Egypt. I am the LORD.

The words *pass through* translate a different word from the one translated "Passover" in verse 11, above. The Lord will move *through Egypt* so as to bring about an extraordinary event in that country: the death of *every firstborn of both people and animals*. Egypt has sacred goats, rams, etc., so a greater impact will be made if the firstborn of many types of animals are slain, especially those of the sacred animals in the various temples. Pharaoh will finally understand, at least temporarily, that *all the gods of Egypt* are powerless against the God of Israel!

Regarding the forthcoming human deaths, the guarded palaces of Pharaoh will not be a sanctuary—the deaths of firstborn will happen there as well. This is a judgment on the entire nation of Egypt, top to bottom. The Lord has seen the misery and heard the cries of his people in Egypt (Exodus 3:7), and the time for judgment has come.

What Do You Think?
Which "gods" of modern culture most tempt the wrath of the one true God? What will you do with your conclusions in that regard?
Talking Points for Your Discussion
- Considering 2 Corinthians 4:4
- Considering Galatians 4:8, 9
- Considering Philippians 3:19
- Other

13. "The blood will be a sign for you on the houses where you are, and when I see the blood, I will pass over you. No destructive plague will touch you when I strike Egypt.

The word *blood* occurs more than 400 times in the Bible. From Genesis 4:10 to Revelation 19:13, there is something special about blood. In the verse before us, blood serves as protection for those who are in homes that have had the blood of the lamb or goat applied as instructed. Many gospel songs have used this verse to make application to salvation in Christ.

The message that Moses and Aaron pass along involves much more than "doing something religious." The purpose is to provide protection from the final plague. A study of the plagues reveals that the first three affect both Egyptians and Israelites. Beginning with the fourth, God makes a distinction, sparing Israel. This time, however, it is up to each Israelite household to obey the instructions or suffer the consequences of disobedience.

What Do You Think?
How should the reality that the blood of Jesus, our Passover Lamb, has been applied to our sins affect how we live?
Talking Points for Your Discussion
- Regarding attitudes
- Regarding actions
- Regarding priorities

C. Continual Observance Demanded (v. 14)

14a. "This is a day you are to commemorate; for the generations to come you shall celebrate it as a festival to the LORD

The Israelites are instructed that future generations are to have a similar observance. It will provide reminders about the birth of their nation as it changed from being an enslaved group to being a free and covenant people. It is to prompt a continued faithfulness to the Lord, who covenants with them.

❧ *FITTING* ❧

I recently traveled for a weekend ladies event. My fellow sojourners and I decided to break up the 11-hour drive home, and Kansas City was a logical stopping point. We took advantage of that to visit the International House of Prayer. I had never been there before, but I had watched the ministry's feed on the Internet. I had seen the worship area, a fairly simple setup where young interns perform worship music in two-hour segments continually. That's right—*continually.*

We signed the guest book, entered, found seats, and joined in the acknowledgment of the King of kings. After about an hour, we quietly left and resumed our journey home.

While this experience was not very different from that of Sunday morning worship, one thought dominated my mind: *fitting.* Since 1999, that little room had not seen an interruption of praise and prayer. It has taken a concerted effort of coordination, administration, and willing hearts to keep it going. Yet what could possibly be a more appropriate response to our amazing God than an unending flow of praise, prayer, and worship? May we too be faithful in ceaseless thankfulness and worship of him!   —V. E.

14b. "—a lasting ordinance."

This final phrase seems at first glance to indicate that the Passover is to be kept in perpetuity. But the word *lasting* actually means "into a hidden period of time" or "no end in sight," whether in the future or in the past. A covenant may be ended by either party. If either fails to keep its part, then the covenant is broken. A covenant also terminates when the reasons for its existence—what it is intended to accomplish—are fulfilled.

Very few Passover celebrations are recorded in the Old Testament. The feast is celebrated a year later while the Israelites are at Sinai (Numbers 9:2-14). The next mention is immediately after the Israelites cross the Jordan River, 40 years after the first observance. Prior to the exile of 586 BC, only two other observances are recorded: one in about 715 BC, in the days of Hezekiah (2 Chronicles 30) and another in about 621 BC, during the reign of Josiah (2 Chronicles 35). The text indicates prior neglect of the feast in both instances (30:5; 35:18). After the exile, a Passover celebration is noted in Ezra 6:19, in 515 BC.

Visual for Lesson 10. *Keep this chart posted for all lessons this month to give your learners a bird's-eye perspective on special days of Old Testament Israel.*

Conclusion

A. Christ Our Passover

There are parallels between the salvation of Christians and the deliverance of the Israelites on that special night in Egypt. These are voiced in many sermons and devotional presentations. Listed below are several such comparisons.

1. Israel's deliverance was from impending doom, and so is ours.
2. Israel's deliverance was of God's devising, and so is ours.
3. Israel's deliverance was made possible by obedient faith, and so is ours.
4. Israel's deliverance required continued faithfulness, and so does ours.
5. Israel's deliverance demanded a sacrifice without blemish, and so did ours.
6. Israel's deliverance was accomplished by a sacrifice that was a substitute, and so did ours.

So—what value is there in studying the ancient event of the first Passover?

B. Prayer

Thank you, God, for demonstrating your power and your love for your people! You have fulfilled your promises, and now we look forward to our final deliverance when your Son returns in glory! In his name we pray. Amen.

C. Thought to Remember

God still liberates.

INVOLVEMENT LEARNING

Enhance your lesson with NIV® Bible Student (from your curriculum supplier) and the reproducible activity page (at www.standardlesson.com or in the back of the NIV® Standard Lesson Commentary Deluxe Edition).

Into the Lesson

Ask two learners to share a family story that has been passed down through the generations. After each, ask why that story has been passed down. Make a transition by saying, "Today's lesson investigates a pivotal event in the history of ancient Israel. This event also served to foreshadow an even greater event: Jesus' sacrificial death."

Alternative. With their Bibles closed, ask learners to (1) name the 10 plagues God inflicted on Egypt and (2) put them in chronological order. Jot responses on the board. Check results per Exodus 7–11. Say, "The most important thing about the right order is knowing which plague came last and why. That's the subject of today's lesson."

Option. Place in chairs copies of the "Passover Scramble" activity from the reproducible page, which you can download. Learners can begin working on this as they arrive.

Into the Word

Form learners into three pairs or small groups to receive the following assignments on handouts: *Elements Group*–Identify from Exodus 12:1-14 the Lord's instructions regarding the edible and nonedible elements of the Passover meal. *Timing Group*–Identify from Exodus 12:1-14 the Lord's instructions regarding the chronological factors of the Passover observance. *Lord's Supper Group*–List the elements of the Lord's Supper per Matthew 26:26-29; Acts 20:7; and 1 Corinthians 11:26. Then compare the elements of the Passover with those of the Lord's Supper.

Draw two columns on the board while groups work. Label the left column *Passover* and the right column *Lord's Supper.* As groups share their conclusions, record them in the corresponding column, matching items on the left column with those on the right where possible. The Elements Group should identify instructions regarding the lamb (or goat), the bread, and the blood; these should include directives regarding preparation and sharing, plus disposal of leftovers. The Timing Group should identify instructions regarding month of the year, day of the month, time of day, and frequency of observance.

The Lord's Supper Group should identify (1) bread, connecting it (as Jesus' body) with lamb, and (2) fruit of the vine (the cup), connecting it (as Jesus' blood) with the protective blood on the doorposts. After you draw solid lines to indicate those connections, ask, "Should I draw dotted lines instead of a solid lines to make clear that the connections are figurative rather than literal?" This can lead to a discussion about viewpoints that see the elements of the Lord's Supper as literally the body and blood of Christ vs. viewpoints that do not.

The Lord's Supper Group may be hesitant about chronological connections. Ask learners what they understand the phrases "On the first day of the week we came together to break bread" (Acts 20:7) and "Whenever you eat this bread and drink this cup" (1 Corinthians 11:26) to imply.

Into Life

Write on the board *"Christ, our Passover lamb, has been sacrificed"* (1 Corinthians 5:7). Then say, "Let's use the information we've discovered to write a meditation that could be used for the Lord's Supper." This can be a small-group or whole-class exercise. Challenge learners to include in the meditation(s) the connections recorded on the board.

Have learners brainstorm ways to use their completed meditation(s). (*Possibilities:* when taking the Lord's Supper to shut-ins, for posting on the church's website, and for PowerPoint® display at the appropriate point in Sunday worship.) Make a plan for implementing one or more of these ideas.

Option. Distribute from the reproducible page copies of the "Self-Examination" activity to be completed as indicated.

FESTIVAL OF WEEKS

DEVOTIONAL READING: Romans 7:14-25

BACKGROUND SCRIPTURE: Numbers 28:26-31; Leviticus 23:15-22; Acts 2:1-36

LEVITICUS 23:15-22

15 "'From the day after the Sabbath, the day you brought the sheaf of the wave offering, count off seven full weeks. 16 Count off fifty days up to the day after the seventh Sabbath, and then present an offering of new grain to the LORD. 17 From wherever you live, bring two loaves made of two-tenths of an ephah of the finest flour, baked with yeast, as a wave offer-

ing of firstfruits to the LORD. 18 Present with this bread seven male lambs, each a year old and without defect, one young bull and two rams. They will be a burnt offering to the LORD, together with their grain offerings and drink offerings—a food offering, an aroma pleasing to the LORD. 19 Then sacrifice one male goat for a sin offering and two lambs, each a year old, for a fellowship offering. 20 The priest is to wave the two lambs before the LORD as a wave offering, together with the bread of the firstfruits. They are a sacred offering to the LORD for the priest. 21 On that same day you are to proclaim a sacred assembly and do no regular work. This is to be a lasting ordinance for the generations to come, wherever you live.

22 "'When you reap the harvest of your land, do not reap to the very edges of your field or gather the gleanings of your harvest. Leave them for the poor and for the foreigner residing among you. I am the LORD your God.'"

KEY VERSE

Count off fifty days up to the day after the seventh Sabbath, and then present an offering of new grain to the LORD. —**Leviticus 23:16**

SACRED GIFTS AND HOLY GATHERINGS

Unit 3: Holy Days
LESSONS 10–13

LESSON AIMS

After participating in this lesson, each learner will be able to:

1. Describe the Festival of Weeks and list its key elements.

2. Explain the significance of making provision for the poor in the midst of participating in worship traditions.

3. Suggest one way to better provide for the poor by using the principle in Leviticus 23:22.

LESSON OUTLINE

Introduction
  A. Family Gatherings
  B. Lesson Background
I. Day Determination (LEVITICUS 23:15, 16a)
  A. Seven Sabbaths (v. 15)
  B. Fifty Days (v. 16a)
II. Sacrifice Directives (LEVITICUS 23:16b-20)
  A. Wave Offerings (vv. 16b, 17)
  B. Burnt Offerings (v. 18)
  C. Sin Offerings (v. 19a)
  D. Fellowship (Peace) Offerings (v. 19b)
    Blessing the Blessers
  E. Priest Actions (v. 20)
III. Other Rules (LEVITICUS 23:21, 22)
  A. No Work (v. 21)
  B. No Stinginess (v. 22)
    What Does the Lord Desire?
Conclusion
  A. Pentecost and the Church
  B. Prayer
  C. Thought to Remember

Introduction

A. Family Gatherings

The family reunion for my father's side was always held the first Sunday of September. It was interesting to watch the interactions, especially among the different age groups. The older members of the family could immediately enter into conversations that usually turned to reminiscing. The children would gradually assess each other and then develop their games. The patriarch or matriarch of the family would be introduced to the new members of the clan. The sumptuous meals came from baskets and boxes, full of foods prepared at home.

At the end of the day, the good-byes were said, and comments such as, "See you next year!" were exchanged. Whether the drive home was short or long, it had been a good day.

Cultural changes of the last few decades have ended these customs for many people. Reunion-type events seem rarer, for family members are likely to live anywhere on the globe. Some children enter adulthood having never seen or known certain cousins or other relatives.

Today's lesson demonstrates how God provided an occasion for his people to meet together as a family of Israelites for the giving of thanks, fellowship, forgiveness, and spiritual dedication. This study is about the Festival of Weeks, which is an unusual term for a one-day celebration. Some of its features made it the preferred event for those who lived at great distances from Jerusalem.

B. Lesson Background

The first Passover in Egypt (last week's lesson) demonstrated to the Israelites that God was on their side. This made it easier to leave all that was familiar when it was time to make the exodus from Egypt (Exodus 12). The Israelites did not know what the future held, but they had confidence—at least temporarily—in the one who held the future.

The GPS (God's Positioning System) used by Moses led the Israelites in an unusual direction—not by the way of the Mediterranean seacoast to the land of Canaan, but into the wilderness of the

Red Sea area (Exodus 13:17, 18). The Lord used a pillar of cloud by day and a pillar of fire by night to guide, protect, and assure the people that they were going where he wanted them to be (13:21, 22).

The Israelites experienced at the Red Sea yet another mighty deliverance after Pharaoh changed his mind about the departure of his labor force. He sent hundreds of chariots to bring them back (Exodus 14:5-9), but God had different plans. The dividing of sea waters so as to have a wall of water on each side is an impossibility for humans, but not for God (14:21, 22). The God who created the universe can easily divide a small sea on this tiny planet!

As the journey continued, God met the needs of his people. These needs included provisions of water (Exodus 15:22-27; 17:1-7), food (chap. 16), and a victory over the Amalekites (17:8-16). The interim destination was Sinai, and this new nation arrived in the third month (19:1).

The Israelites knew that the Lord was God, but what did he expect from them? God was ready to tell them, and that was the purpose of their stay at Mount Sinai, which lasted almost a year (Numbers 10:11, 12). When God gave the people manna on the way to Sinai, they learned that God expected them to rest on the seventh day (Exodus 16:23-30), and that expectation was reinforced as part of the Ten Commandments (chap. 20).

This was followed by his giving laws (chaps. 21–23) that collectively are called "the Book of the Covenant" (24:7). It contained upwards of 70 rules that the people needed immediately for the governing of social relationships. It could be called their *bill of rights*, but perhaps *bill of responsibilities for producing a just society* is better.

HOW TO SAY IT

Canaan	*Kay*-nun.
ephah	*ee*-fah.
Mediterranean	*Med*-uh-tuh-**ray**-nee-un.
Pentecost	*Pent*-ih-kost.
Pharaoh	*Fair*-o or *Fay*-roe.
Pharisees	*Fair*-ih-seez.
Sadducees	*Sad*-you-seez.
Sinai	*Sigh*-nye or *Sigh*-nay-eye.

These laws introduced for the first time the fact that the Israelites were to have three festivals during the year (Exodus 23:14-17). Last week's study was about the first one, the Passover Festival. Exodus 12:1-20 adds that this one-day observance was to be followed by seven days during which the only bread that could be eaten was to be unleavened. These seven days constituted the Festival of Unleavened Bread, and the two feasts were functionally considered the same event since they were right next to each other on the calendar.

Today's lesson is about the second of the three annual feasts: the Festival of Weeks. This festival is different from the first (lesson 10) and the third (lesson 13) in that it is not associated with a historical event. There is a tradition that the Festival of Weeks commemorates the giving of the Ten Commandments to Moses at Sinai, but the first mention of that idea is postbiblical.

The Festival of Weeks received its name because it was to be celebrated seven weeks after Passover. Therefore the Festival of Weeks was to take place in late May or early June. It is not given a name in today's text, but it has other names attached to it elsewhere: Festival of Weeks (Exodus 34:22a; Numbers 28:26b), Festival of Harvest (Exodus 23:16a), and sometimes the day of firstfruits (Numbers 28:26a). In the New Testament it is called Pentecost (Acts 2:1; 20:16; 1 Corinthians 16:8), a Greek word that means "fiftieth."

I. Day Determination
(LEVITICUS 23:15, 16a)
A. Seven Sabbaths (v. 15)

15. "'From the day after the Sabbath, the day you brought the sheaf of the wave offering, count off seven full weeks.

This verse refers back to the Festival of Unleavened Bread and the bringing of *the sheaf of the wave offering* in Leviticus 23:10, which was seven weeks before. The counting is to begin *after the Sabbath*. The problem is this: Which Sabbath?

The word *Sabbath*, which means "ceasing," may refer to any day on which labor is prohibited. The Festival of Unleavened Bread has two such days, the first and last days of the festival (Leviticus

23:7, 8). In addition, the regular Sabbath of the week is to be observed. Unless a special Sabbath falls on a regular Sabbath, there can be as many as three Sabbaths in a seven-day period.

When the New Testament era dawns, the Pharisees and the Sadducees have different interpretations about the matter of calculating when the Festival of Weeks (Pentecost) is to occur. The Pharisees prefer the view that the counting is to begin on the sixteenth day of the first month, the day after the first special Sabbath. The Sadducees, however, control the agenda in the temple at the time, and they interpret the word *Sabbath* to refer to the regular weekly Sabbath.

This is very significant, for it means that Pentecost always falls on the first day of the week—50 days after the regular Sabbath in the Festival of Unleavened Bread. This is the day the church was birthed, the first day of the week (Acts 2).

<table>
<tr><td>

What Do You Think?

How can we be more conscientious regarding the things the Lord expects us to count and the things he does not?

Talking Points for Your Discussion
- 1 Chronicles 21:1-7
- Matthew 18:21, 22
- Luke 14:31-33
- Other

</td></tr>
</table>

B. Fifty Days (v. 16a)

16a. "'Count off fifty days up to the day after the seventh Sabbath,"

This half of verse 16 demonstrates a definite connection between the Festival of Unleavened Bread and the Festival of Weeks. God's instructions show that an event within one festival is used to determine the timing of the festival that is to follow.

It is important to note that two of the regular harvests are connected with these festivals (v. 16b, next, will show us why). Passover and the Festival of Unleavened Bread occur in early spring at the beginning of barley harvest (last week's lesson). The Festival of Weeks, for its part, is associated with wheat harvest in late May or early June (Exo-

dus 34:22). The time period from one harvest to the other is on the order of *fifty days*.

II. Sacrifice Directives
(LEVITICUS 23:16b-20)
A. Wave Offerings (vv. 16b, 17)

16b. "'and then present an offering of new grain to the LORD.

Also specifying *an offering of new grain* during this festival is Numbers 28:26.

17. "'From wherever you live, bring two loaves made of two-tenths of an ephah of the finest flour, baked with yeast, as a wave offering of firstfruits to the LORD.

The offering is to be in the form of *two loaves* of bread, the amount of flour used in these being *two-tenths of an ephah*. The dry measure of an ephah is about $3/5$ of a bushel. Therefore, $2/10$ of an ephah computes to about $1/8$ of a bushel (18.6 cups) of flour to be used.

Most biblical scholars conclude that the two loaves are representative gifts for the nation; they are ultimately given to the priest (Leviticus 23:20, below). Another view follows a tradition that Hebrew farmers use a stalk of grain to bind the first shocks of ripe grain. These special bundles are then taken to the priests and presented *to the Lord*.

Leviticus 2:11 is very specific that yeast is not to be burned "in a food offering presented to the Lord." Since yeast is mandated in the *two loaves . . . as a wave offering*, this indicates that these are not to be burned; they are intended for the priest. It is interesting that yeast is forbidden for the eight days of Passover and Unleavened Bread, but is required in the loaves of firstfruits for the Festival of Weeks.

The careful student will notice that a firstfruits offering is connected with the Festival of Unleavened Bread in Leviticus 2:14. Now we see one associated with the Festival of Weeks. How can there be two firstfruit offerings, 50 days apart? The answer is that the first one is an offering at the start of barley harvest in March/April, and the second one is for the day when the firstfruits of the wheat harvest are given as loaves (see comments on v. 16a, above).

B. Burnt Offerings (v. 18)

18. "'Present with this bread seven male lambs, each a year old and without defect, one young bull and two rams. They will be a burnt offering to the LORD, together with their grain offerings and drink offerings—a food offering, an aroma pleasing to the LORD.

A total of 10 animals are to *be a burnt offering to the Lord*. These are to be accompanied by *grain offerings and drink offerings* as described in Numbers 15:4-9. Burnt offerings carry the idea of consecration or dedication.

C. Sin Offerings (v. 19a)

19a. "'Then sacrifice one male goat for a sin offering

Atonement is the dominant factor in *a sin offering*. Such an offering presupposes that the covenant relationship has been broken and needs to be renewed. A sin offering is primarily offered on holidays or when an action is deemed to have broken the relationship with God (Leviticus 4:1–5:13).

D. Fellowship (Peace) Offerings (v. 19b)

19b. "'and two lambs, each a year old, for a fellowship offering.

Some versions of the Bible refer to fellowship offerings as peace offerings. The ideas are the same: restoration of fellowship with God is restoration of peace with him.

The *two lambs* noted here are to be given to the priests (see v. 20, next). For an ordinary fellowship offering, the priests keep for their own consumption the breast and right thigh of animals sacrificed (Leviticus 7:31-36). The rest is eaten by the one offering the sacrifice and others (7:15, 16).

The Festival of Weeks is the only time when fellowship offerings are prescribed for public offerings. Numbers 10:10 notes that trumpets are to be blown over such public offerings, and fellowship offerings are mentioned.

❧ BLESSING THE BLESSERS ❧

I love hearing how church families choose to bless their ministers with various expressions of gratitude! Such expressions include gifts of golf lessons, poems, baked goods, video tributes, new shoes, home remodeling, brunch, plaques, cake, pizza celebrations—the list goes on.

I know of one church that sent its worship minister on a cruise with his wife in gratitude for his 25 years of service. My parents' home church in central Missouri is blessing its minister with a trip to Israel. While this may seem extreme to some, this man has worked a full-time job and been active with the youth and charitable groups in his small community while serving this congregation's needs.

Many ministers find themselves "on call" most of the time. Their congregants' awareness of this may be evident in the creative blessings they offer back. It's interesting that the Lord's directions for the Festival of Weeks include some offerings that were to be burnt to please him, while others were for his servants, the priests. That was commanded by God. We should not need a command today to bless in return those who have been a blessing to us as they serve the church.   —V. E.

E. Priest Actions (v. 20)

20. "'The priest is to wave the two lambs before the LORD as a wave offering, together with the bread of the firstfruits. They are a sacred offering to the LORD for the priest.

We imagine that it is an easy matter to wave *the bread of the firstfruits*. The priest need only lift them upward and swing them back and forth to symbolize their being given to the Lord. It becomes a custom that one of the two loaves (Leviticus 23:17, above) is given to the high priest and the other to the priest who officiates at the service.

The waving of *the two lambs* is more problematic! It is sometimes suggested that the priest lifts and waves each animal while it is still alive; after they are sacrificed, the breast, thigh, and at least one loaf is waved—toward the east and back, and then up and down. Another suggestion is that live animals are led back and forth in front of the tabernacle.

III. Other Rules
(LEVITICUS 23:21, 22)
A. No Work (v. 21)

21. "'On that same day you are to proclaim a sacred assembly and do no regular work. This is to be a lasting ordinance for the generations to come, wherever you live.

The description of how the Festival of Weeks is to be observed bears much similarity to the other festivals of the Lord in Leviticus 23. The characteristic of being *a sacred assembly* is noted for the other observances in Leviticus 23:3, 7, 8, 24, 27, 35, 36. The prohibition against *work* is also seen in Leviticus 23:3, 7, 8, 25, 28, 30, 31, 35, 36. The enduring nature of these statutes is noted in Leviticus 23:14, 31, 41.

The rule against work may be designed to provide protection for servants so that they may participate in the day. See also Numbers 28:26.

B. No Stinginess (v. 22)

22. "'When you reap the harvest of your land, do not reap to the very edges of your field or gather the gleanings of your harvest. Leave them for the poor and for the foreigner residing among you. I am the LORD your God.'"

At first glance, this verse may seem out of place. Its stipulations were given earlier (Leviticus 19:9, 10), so why is it repeated in conjunction with the Festival of Weeks? The answer may be that since this is a harvest celebration, it is appropriate to mention one of the laws of the harvest: God is concerned for the welfare of those in need. The harvesters are to reap so that there will be something left for them.

It is noteworthy that the verse before us does not say that harvested grain is simply to be provided *for the poor and for the foreigner*. Rather, those in need are to go to the fields and do the work of harvesting themselves. An outstanding example of this practice is found in the book of Ruth, specifically chapter 2.

❧ WHAT DOES THE LORD DESIRE? ❧

"It's a scam . . . he probably makes more money than I do." "Don't give her money! She'll just use it to buy drugs!" "They should get jobs." I hear the warnings in my head as I drive past the people with sad eyes and cardboard signs. What should I do? I don't know who is genuinely needy and who is deceitful. I don't know what they will do with a gift I may choose to give them.

I have served on a benevolence committee, and I have given attention to the various ways that limited resources are shared. Some churches open their doors on a certain day of the week (or month), and whoever shows up with needs that day gets help. Some require that those requesting help be known to someone in their church family in order to receive help. Others give without restriction until the benevolence well runs dry. Some churches operate food pantries, provide clothes closets, or focus on specific needs, such as utility or medical bills.

Our passage does not speak of those in need having to go through an application process. What about discernment regarding who should be helped? That question is not addressed here. In fact, there is no human interaction prescribed at all; there is simply a leaving behind of some of the blessings of the land to allow those blessings to be accessible to the needy. How does this relate to passages such as 2 Thessalonians 3:10 and 1 Timothy 5:3-16? —V. E.

Visual for Lesson 11. *Point to this visual as you ask, "When, if ever, is it a good idea to give money rather than food, etc., to someone in need?*

What Do You Think?
Under what circumstance, if any, should the church expect those in need to work for "the harvest" that is made available to them? Why?
Talking Points for Your Discussion
- Regarding food
- Regarding clothing
- Regarding housing
- Other

The Lord is in the process of providing for his people by giving them a land that flows with milk and honey, a land where they can flourish (Deuteronomy 31:20). The Lord also is providing ways for his people to remember the source of their blessings: they are to have festivals that enable them to join with others in celebrations in the giving of thanks. Passover, Unleavened Bread, Weeks, and Tabernacles—they are reminders of the blessings of harvest and/or famous events in the nation's history. God is good, all the time!

Conclusion

A. Pentecost and the Church

The Day of Pentecost—the later designation for the Festival of Weeks—is the birthday of the church (Acts 2). The Bible does not say why God chose this occasion for the church to begin. But the way that it was celebrated made it the perfect tool to fulfill God's plan to spread the gospel from Jerusalem into Judea, Samaria, and "to the ends of

the earth" (Acts 1:8). Pentecost drew many Jews from distant parts of the Roman Empire (compare Acts 2:5-11). The rainy season was over, and the weather was warm and delightful for travel. Some who made a once-in-a-lifetime trip to Jerusalem for Passover perhaps remained "on vacation" through Pentecost.

In any case, it is fascinating that the death and resurrection of Jesus occurred during the time of Passover and Unleavened Bread and that seven weeks later the church began on Pentecost. The people who were in Jerusalem at these times had the privilege of being among the first to be introduced to the gospel, which they could take with them on their return home. About 3,000 people were convinced, and they responded to Peter's instructions to repent and to be baptized for the remission of sins and to receive the gift of the Holy Spirit (Acts 2:38, 41). As they returned to all parts of the Roman Empire and elsewhere, they became the vanguard for the spreading message of redemption.

B. Prayer

Father, may the attitude of gratitude that was to characterize the Festival of Weeks become our own on a daily basis! In Jesus' name. Amen.

C. Thought to Remember

God still expects our expressions of gratitude to include provisions for the poor.

INVOLVEMENT LEARNING

Enhance your lesson with NIV® Bible Student (from your curriculum supplier) and the reproducible activity page (at www.standardlesson.com or in the back of the NIV® Standard Lesson Commentary Deluxe Edition).

Into the Lesson

Ask learners to share family or church traditions that have created fond memories. Expect responses to include family reunions, church homecoming dinners, Christmas caroling, family vacations, etc. After each sharing, ask why the tradition is special enough to continue to be observed.

After three or four rounds of sharing and responding (don't let this drag out), say, "Today's lesson describes what might be called *a mandatory tradition*, wherein God provided instructions for the Israelites to remember and celebrate yearly his provisions for them as witnessed by the wheat harvest that was underway at the time of the observance. The celebration to which we refer is the Festival of Weeks."

Option. As a pretest, place in chairs copies of the "Number Match" exercise from the reproducible page, which you can download, for learners to work on as they begin arriving. Say, "Don't open your Bibles until you are finished!" Have learners score their own results.

Into the Word

Draw three columns on the board and head them *Festival Description / Key Festival Elements / Other Requirements*. Off to the side, affix 14 strips of poster board that feature the phrases below, one per strip, prepared in advance. (These are arranged here in verse order, but you should mix them up before affixing them to the board.)

seven Sabbaths / fifty days after Passover / new grain offering / wave loaves of fine flour / baked with yeast / firstfruits to the Lord / burnt offerings with grain and drink offerings / sin offering and fellowship (peace) offering / offering waved before God / sacred assembly / no work / ordinance for the generations to come / don't harvest corners of field / don't glean fields

Have volunteers take turns reading the lesson text aloud, stopping at the end of each verse. Each time a reader stops, ask the class to identify (1) which strip or strips correspond with the verse just read and (2) under which column heading the strip or strips should be placed. After working through the eight verses of the lesson text, the strips should be arranged as follows.

Festival Description: seven Sabbaths / fifty days after Passover / sacred assembly / ordinance for the generations to come

Key Festival Elements: new grain offering / wave loaves of fine flour / baked with yeast / firstfruits to the Lord / burnt offerings with grain and drink offerings / sin offering and peace offering / offering waved before God

Other Requirements: no work / don't harvest corners of field / don't glean fields

When the columns are complete, review their contents and discuss the significance of the listings. Differences of opinion will provide opportunities for deeper discussion.

Into Life

Referring again to the three columns and their contents, say, "Colossians 2:14-16 tells us that we are not under obligation to observe Old Testament festivals, Sabbaths, etc., since Christ nailed the old law to the cross. Even so, what takeaway principles do you see for Christians living in the twenty-first century?" (*Possible responses:* it is important to celebrate what God is doing for us; we should be intentional about such celebrations; we should give God our best; normal work should not be allowed to distract us in times of celebrating God; we need to make provisions for those in need.)

Brainstorm ways to put these principles into practice in specific ways.

Option. Distribute copies of the "Provide for the Poor" activity from the reproducible page. Have learners work in pairs or groups of three to complete as indicated. Discuss concrete ways to implement one or two ideas as a class.

DAY OF
ATONEMENT

DEVOTIONAL READING: Hebrews 3:1-6
BACKGROUND SCRIPTURE: Numbers 29:7-11; Leviticus 16:1-34; 23:26-32;
Hebrews 7:26-28; 9:24; 10:4-18

LEVITICUS 16:11-19

[11] "Aaron shall bring the bull for his own sin offering to make atonement for himself and his household, and he is to slaughter the bull for his own sin offering. [12] He is to take a censer full of burning coals from the altar before the LORD and two handfuls of finely ground fragrant incense and take them behind the curtain. [13] He is to put the incense on the fire before the LORD, and the smoke of the incense will conceal the atonement cover above the tablets of the covenant law, so that he will not die. [14] He is to take some of the bull's blood and with his finger sprinkle it on the front of the atonement cover; then he shall sprinkle some of it with his finger seven times before the atonement cover.

[15] "He shall then slaughter the goat for the sin offering for the people and take its blood behind the curtain and do with it as he did with the bull's blood: He shall sprinkle it on

the atonement cover and in front of it. [16] In this way he will make atonement for the Most Holy Place because of the uncleanness and rebellion of the Israelites, whatever their sins have been. He is to do the same for the tent of meeting, which is among them in the midst of their uncleanness. [17] No one is to be in the tent of meeting from the time Aaron goes in to make atonement in the Most Holy Place until he comes out, having made atonement for himself, his household and the whole community of Israel.

[18] "Then he shall come out to the altar that is before the LORD and make atonement for it. He shall take some of the bull's blood and some of the goat's blood and put it on all the horns of the altar. [19] He shall sprinkle some of the blood on it with his finger seven times to cleanse it and to consecrate it from the uncleanness of the Israelites."

KEY VERSE

In this way he will make atonement for the Most Holy Place because of the uncleanness and rebellion of the Israelites, whatever their sins have been. He is to do the same for the tent of meeting, which is among them in the midst of their uncleanness. —**Leviticus 16:16**

Graphic: james steidl / iStock / Thinkstock

SACRED GIFTS AND
HOLY GATHERINGS

Unit 3: Holy Days

LESSONS 10–13

LESSON AIMS

After participating in this lesson, each learner will be able to:

1. List the procedures that God ordained for Israel's annual Day of Atonement.

2. Explain the concept of atonement, noting the allusions to Leviticus 16:14, 15 in New Testament texts such as Hebrews 9:7; 10:4.

3. Write a prayer of praise for the atonement for sins available only through Jesus.

LESSON OUTLINE

Introduction
  A. Forgiveness
  B. Lesson Background
I. Atonement for Priests (LEVITICUS 16:11-14)
  A. Bull as Sin Offering (v. 11)
  B. Incense for a Cloud (vv. 12, 13)
  C. Blood for Sprinkling (v. 14)
II. Atonement for People, Places (LEVITICUS 16:15-17)
  A. Goat as Sin Offering (v. 15a)
  B. Blood for Sprinkling (v. 15b)
  C. Places (v. 16)
  D. Duty (v. 17)
    No Exemption
III. Atonement for the Altar (LEVITICUS 16:18, 19)
  A. Blood Applied to the Horns (v. 18)
  B. Blood Sprinkled Seven Times (v. 19)
    We, the Unclean
Conclusion
  A. The Final Day of Atonement
  B. Prayer
  C. Thought to Remember

Introduction

A. Forgiveness

Forgiveness became national news (again) in late 2006 when five Amish schoolgirls were murdered in their one-room schoolhouse in Pennsylvania. A distraught gunman left suicide notes for his family and then went to the school where he shot hostages and then killed himself. The Amish leaders did not respond with anger, but with forgiveness.

To forgive means to give up resentment for an offense committed; to forgive involves cessation of anger toward another. Atonement, however, is more than forgiveness. Atonement includes reparation for the wrong committed. Forgiveness between people is possible without atonement; forgiveness by God requires atonement.

Atonement is often defined as "at-one-ment" with God. That's clever but superficial because it describes the *result* of atonement but not the *basis* for it. That basis is the payment of sin's penalty by Jesus on the cross. This is often referred to as *the substitutionary atonement* because God substitutes the payment paid by his Son so that we do not have to pay the price ourselves—the price of eternity in Hell.

Blood atonement is a key concept in both the books of Leviticus and Hebrews. Without the shedding of blood as atonement, there is no forgiveness by God (Hebrews 9:22).

B. Lesson Background

The Lord prescribed three annual festivals that the people of Israel were to observe at the central sanctuary (Exodus 23:14-17). The first two festivals were subjects of study in the two previous lessons; the third will be considered in the lesson following this one. Just before the third festival was the Day of Atonement, arguably the most important religious event on the Hebrew calendar. This took place on the tenth day of the seventh month (Leviticus 16:29; 23:27), that month being late September and early October. The tenth day was five days before the Festival of Tabernacles (lesson 13).

By the time of the New Testament era, the sacred nature of the high priest's duties compelled him to rehearse what he had to do on the Day of Atonement to avoid mistakes. So seven days ahead of time, he moved into one of the chamber rooms that were on three sides of the temple. There he could ensure that he remained ceremonially clean (by avoiding contact with a dead body, etc.). Just in case, another priest was designated to serve if the high priest became defiled in any way.

During the seven days, the high priest rehearsed his duties of lighting the lamps in the temple, carrying the incense and live coals with a censer, sprinkling and applying blood, and accomplishing the essential features surrounding the burnt offering sacrifices. Others were with him to make certain that he knew each part of the day's events and how they were to be performed.

The high priest ate a light meal on the evening before the Day of Atonement. He had Scripture explained during the night, and he was kept awake in order to avoid any defilement that might occur during sleep (Deuteronomy 23:10).

He wore ordinary clothing as the day began, then bathed and changed into his colorful high-priestly garments to perform the burnt offering that was done each morning (Exodus 29:38-42). As he went through the day, he bathed and changed clothing five times. His hands and feet were washed twice that much.

The high priest did something else unusual on this special day: he actually pronounced the sacred name of God, often seen as *Yahweh*. Devout Jews of the time did not pronounce it for fear of profaning it, so the word *Lord* was the substitute word when Scripture was read.

HOW TO SAY IT

Abihu	Uh-*bye*-hew.
Babylonian	Bab-ih-*low*-nee-unz.
Eleazar	El-ih-*a*-zar or E-lih-*a*-zar.
ephod	*ee*-fod.
Ithamar	*Ith*-uh-mar.
Levites	*Lee*-vites.
Moses	*Mo*-zes or *Mo*-zez.
Nadab	*Nay*-dab.
Talmud	*Tahl*-mood or *Tal*-mud.
Yahweh *(Hebrew)*	*Yah*-weh.

Two other factors should be mentioned. First, the Day of Atonement was a day of fasting for each Israelite, being the only such fast that the Law of Moses prescribed (the meaning of "deny yourselves" in Leviticus 16:29, 31; 23:27). Second, the Day of Atonement was the day that the year of jubilee was to be announced once every 50 years (25:8, 9).

The Day of Atonement was the day when God stated that atonement would be made for "all the members of the community . . . for all the sins of the Israelites" (Leviticus 16:33, 34; compare Hebrews 9:7). Every Christian is aware that permanent atonement for sins didn't happen until the death of Christ. This is developed in Hebrews 9:11–10:14.

I. Atonement for Priests
(LEVITICUS 16:11-14)
A. Bull as Sin Offering (v. 11)

11. "Aaron shall bring the bull for his own sin offering to make atonement for himself and his household, and he is to slaughter the bull for his own sin offering.

The instructions are for Aaron, who is Moses' brother and Israel's first high priest. The high priests who succeed him are to follow these procedures as well (Leviticus 16:32, 33). Aaron will be wearing his majestic high-priestly apparel for the normal sacrifice of the morning. On the Day of Atonement (or Yom Kippur), the regular sacrifices and duties are performed by the high priest only.

Aaron is to bathe and don the four linen garments (Leviticus 16:4; compare Exodus 28) for the special offerings on the Day of Atonement. He is responsible to provide *the bull for his own sin offering*, which is not only *for himself* but also for his family.

Leviticus 16:1 mentions that these instructions are given after the deaths of Aaron's two older sons, Nadab and Abihu. Those two had "offered unauthorized fire before the Lord"; as a result, "fire came out from the presence of the Lord and consumed them, and they died before the Lord" (Leviticus 10:1, 2). That experience brings with it the compelling necessity to know and to do exactly what God says! A casual carelessness about holy things may have disastrous consequences.

In later times there will be many priests available to assist when the high priest sacrifices animals for sin offerings. This time that task is limited to Aaron's two surviving sons, Eleazar and Ithamar (Leviticus 10:12). It is possible that some Levites assist them.

What Do You Think?

What can or should Christians bring to the Lord in light of sins forgiven?

Talking Points for Your Discussion

- Regarding tangibles similar and dissimilar to what the ancient Israelites were to bring
- Regarding intangibles similar and dissimilar to what the ancient Israelites were to bring

---

B. Incense for a Cloud (vv. 12, 13)

12. "He is to take a censer full of burning coals from the altar before the LORD and two handfuls of finely ground fragrant incense and take them behind the curtain.

Aaron's task as high priest is to carry *burning coals* and *incense* through the Holy Place and on into the Most Holy Place, the latter being located *behind the curtain* of the tabernacle (compare Exodus 26:33; Hebrews 6:19; 9:2-5). The burning coals are from the altar of burnt offering, which is near the front of the court of the tabernacle (Exodus 27:1-8); these are to be carried in a censer or fire pan (compare Numbers 16:6, 7, 17, 36-38). Aaron is painfully aware that coals from any other source may risk the consequences of disobedience (again, Leviticus 10:1). The formula for the *fragrant incense* is found in Exodus 30:34-38.

13. "He is to put the incense on the fire before the LORD, and the smoke of the incense will conceal the atonement cover above the tablets of the covenant law, so that he will not die.

After entering the Most Holy Place, Aaron is to set the censer down and place the incense on the burning coals. This will cause a cloud of smoke to rise from the coals, and the smoke will provide a protective screen between Aaron and the symbolic presence of the Lord above the covering of the ark of the covenant, often called the

atonement cover (see Exodus 25:17-22; 26:34). It is sometimes said that the cloud is to keep the priest from viewing the ark, but another thought is that the cloud protects a sinner from the judgment of God. *The tablets of the covenant law* are the Ten Commandments (Exodus 25:16; 31:18; 2 Chronicles 6:11).

Aaron is to leave the censer with the burning incense so that the smoke continues throughout the rituals in the Most Holy Place. He returns through the Holy Place to the courtyard to prepare to make his second entry into the Most Holy Place (sometimes called the Holy of Holies). Entrance into the Most Holy Place, where the ark of the covenant is located, is highly restricted (Leviticus 16:2).

One issue not discussed in any biblical text is when the censer with the incense and coals is removed from behind the veil of the Most Holy Place at the conclusion of the day's ceremonies. A Hebrew document called the Babylonian Talmud provides a solution: it says that the high priest enters the Most Holy Place an additional time for this purpose. It would be precarious to carry both the censer and containers of blood in one trip, so retrieval of the censer may be a separate task.

C. Blood for Sprinkling (v. 14)

14. "He is to take some of the bull's blood and with his finger sprinkle it on the front of the atonement cover; then he shall sprinkle some of it with his finger seven times before the atonement cover."

This part of the ritual is similar to what is done for other sin offerings (see Leviticus 4:6, 7, 17, 18). But in those cases the blood is applied to the altar of incense, which is located immediately in front of the curtain that shields the Most Holy Place. This time the blood is first sprinkled on *the atonement cover*.

Then the high priest uses *his finger seven times* to sprinkle blood on the ground or floor in front of the atonement cover. Hebrews 9:7, 8 explains the significance of this: "But only the high priest entered the inner room, and that only once a year, and never without blood, which he offered for himself and for the sins the people had committed in ignorance. The Holy Spirit was showing by this that the way into the Most Holy Place had not yet been disclosed as long as the first tabernacle was still functioning."

What Do You Think?
What do the meticulous instructions regarding the work of the priest on the Day of Atonement have to say about providing ministry today, if anything?
Talking Points for Your Discussion
- Concerning spiritual preparation
- Concerning mental preparation
- Concerning physical preparation
- Other

II. Atonement for People, Places
(LEVITICUS 16:15-17)

A. Goat as Sin Offering (v. 15a)

15a. "He shall then slaughter the goat for the sin offering for the people

Earlier in the day, two male goats are brought to the door of the tabernacle (Leviticus 16:5, 7). One is selected as *the sin offering* to the Lord, and the other becomes the scapegoat that will be led into the desert to an inaccessible place (16:8-10). The latter represents the removal of sin (16:22). A Jewish legend states that on one occasion the scapegoat returned to the camp. That problem was solved in future years by pushing it backwards off a cliff to guarantee that the goat would not return! Aaron is to be the one to kill the goat that represents the sin offering for the people. The blood is caught in the special container that Aaron will take into the Most Holy Place (next verse).

B. Blood for Sprinkling (v. 15b)

15b. "and take its blood behind the curtain and do with it as he did with the bull's blood: He shall sprinkle it on the atonement cover and in front of it.

Next, Aaron is to reenter the Most Holy Place. His actions with the blood of the goat for the sins of the people are the same as with the blood of the bull that was applied for the sins of the priest (v. 11, above).

What Do You Think?
How does the merciful atonement extended to you by Christ affect your extension of mercy to others? How should it?
Talking Points for Your Discussion
- At the office
- In traffic
- At home
- Other

C. Places (v. 16)

16a. "In this way he will make atonement for the Most Holy Place because of the uncleanness and rebellion of the Israelites, whatever their sins have been.

This is a summary. By doing what is prescribed, the high priest makes atonement for himself, the sins of the people, and *for the Most Holy Place.*

16b. "He is to do the same for the tent of meeting, which is among them in the midst of their uncleanness.

The procedure is not given, but this is probably the occasion when the high priest fulfills what is commanded in Exodus 30:10—that atonement is to be made once each year for the altar of incense that stands just in front of the curtain. The instructions in Exodus say that Aaron is to use the blood of the sin offering. It is assumed that he applies or sprinkles blood on each of the altar's four horns, and then sprinkles blood on this altar seven times. This is done with the blood of both the bull and the goat.

What Do You Think?
What sinful uncleanliness do Christians grapple with most? How do we help them?
Talking Points for Your Discussion
- Regarding spiritually mature Christians
- Regarding backsliding Christians
- Regarding new Christians

D. Duty (v. 17)

17. "No one is to be in the tent of meeting from the time Aaron goes in to make atonement in the Most Holy Place until he comes

out, having made atonement for himself, his household and the whole community of Israel."

No one, not even another priest, is to be with Aaron in the tabernacle when he is making atonement. A gospel song from the past asked the question "Must Jesus Bear the Cross Alone?" The answer is *yes* in the sense that only Jesus can fulfill his high priestly duties in the heavenly tabernacle (Hebrews 9:11, 12).

❧ NO EXEMPTION ❧

It is significant that the instructions for the high priest include making atonement even for himself. This probably does not strike most of us as unusual, for we realize that all have sinned (Romans 3:23). Therefore even the high priest, symbolically the most holy man of all Israel, needed atonement for sin.

Yet this most basic of all principles of religious need has been known to be rationalized away. When I was in Bible college many years ago, a fellow student claimed that he did not need to give financial offerings to the Lord because his entire life was an offering. He found it convenient to overlook the fact that even the priests and Levites were expected to give a tithe of their income (Numbers 18:26). He chose to believe that his life of ministry put him above God's expectations of normal, regular churchgoers.

Similarly, I know of a minister who was involved in multiple affairs with various women of his congregation. One woman later admitted that he had convinced her it was all right because he was in full-time ministry and therefore he was extended privileges that did not apply to regular folk. The temptation to rationalize is so enticing, isn't it?   —J. B. N.

III. Atonement for the Altar
(LEVITICUS 16:18, 19)

A. Blood Applied to the Horns (v. 18)

18. "Then he shall come out to the altar that is before the LORD and make atonement for it. He shall take some of the bull's blood and some of the goat's blood and put it on all the horns of the altar.

When Aaron's work in the sanctuary—which consists of the Holy Place, the Most Holy Place, and their furnishings—is completed, he is to walk outside to the courtyard while carrying the containers of blood of the two animals sacrificed. There he will apply the blood to the four *horns of the altar* of burnt offerings, which stands near the entrance of the tabernacle (Exodus 27:1-8).

This is the same as is done with the blood of other sin offerings when the priest applies the blood (Leviticus 4:25, 30, 34), so this part is not unusual. The practice of later priests is to mix the blood of the two animals before applying it.

B. Blood Sprinkled Seven Times (v. 19)

19. "He shall sprinkle some of the blood on it with his finger seven times to cleanse it and to consecrate it from the uncleanness of the Israelites."

The cleansing needed is not due to the presence of physical dirt. Rather, it is the spiritual *uncleanness of the Israelites* that results in the tabernacle furnishings' being defiled. Many commentators have noted that *seven* serves as a complete number in the Bible. The number *seven* appears more than 40 times in Leviticus alone.

After this cleansing, Aaron is to exit the Most Holy Place to perform the scapegoat ritual of Leviticus 16:20-22.

❧ WE, THE UNCLEAN ❧

Twice our text refers to the "uncleanness" of the Israelites (vv. 16, 19). These are God's chosen people. Yet they were unclean. A leprous person was to shout "Unclean! Unclean!" to warn others (Leviticus 13:45). Spiritually, the Israelites were little better than lepers. A colleague of mine who teaches Old Testament commented that the ancient Israelites were basically a multi-god people. Their unfaithfulness to God was not finally removed until the Babylonian captivity; even then their obedience was often ritualistic, not of the heart.

Paul observed that "Abraham believed God, and it was credited to him as righteousness" (Romans 4:3). Was Abraham, in fact, a righteous man? Not in an absolute sense. He lied to Pharaoh about his wife (Genesis 12:10-13); he did the same thing to the king of Gerar (20:2). Abraham was a sinner, but his faith allowed him to be counted as righteous in the eyes of God.

We too are unclean (Matthew 15:19, 20). We may be regular churchgoers; we may support the church heavily with our finances; we may hold high office or ministry in the church. But our lapses mark us as unclean. It is our acceptance of Jesus' payment of the penalty for our sins that enables us to stand in God's presence and be counted as righteous. That is God's grace.
—J. B. N.

Visual for Lesson 12. *Point to this visual as you ask, "What are some ways that our thoughts and actions can honor Jesus for the clean slate he provides?"*

> **What Do You Think?**
> How can the corporate aspects of the Day of Atonement be applied to the church, if at all?
> *Talking Points for Your Discussion*
> - Nehemiah 9
> - Acts 19:18-20
> - Other

We should not close our lesson without evaluating a legend that has been around for centuries. It is the legend that the high priest had a rope tied to his ankle when he was in the Most Holy Place. This was so that if he sinned and died, others would not have to enter to bring out his body; they could just pull it out by the rope.

As engaging as this legend is, there is no evidence that this procedure was ever practiced. One part of the legend is obviously false—that the priest wore bells, and if the bells were not heard as he walked, then it was time to act. Bells were on "the robe of the ephod" of the high priest (Exodus 28:31-35), but not on what he wore when in the Most Holy Place. (Other garments mentioned in Leviticus 16:4 are "tunic," "sash," and "turban," none of which equates to the "robe" or "ephod," all five being mentioned as separate articles of clothing in Exodus 28:4.) It is a great story, but it is not true.

Conclusion
A. The Final Day of Atonement

The basic thrust of the Day of Atonement concerns the nature of sin, which required that innocent animals give their lives so that human sins could be forgiven. God planned for this to be a temporary arrangement. Eventually, there was to come a perfect sacrifice that need never be repeated.

The writer of the book of Hebrews uses imagery from the Day of Atonement, especially in chapter 9, to make comparisons with the salvation that Christ has accomplished. Hebrews 10:4 declares that "it is impossible for the blood of bulls and goats to take away sins." Hebrews 7:27 affirms that Jesus did not need "to offer sacrifices day after day, first for his own sins, and then for the sins of the people. He sacrificed for their sins once for all when he offered himself."

"Without the shedding of blood there is no forgiveness" (Hebrews 9:22). Christ had to die in order for our sins to be forgiven! The new covenant in his blood is available to all who respond to the great invitation: "Come to me, all you who are weary and burdened, and I will give you rest" (Matthew 11:28).

B. Prayer

Father in Heaven, we marvel at the atonement you have provided! May it compel us to follow the Christ wherever he leads. May we draw others to him as well. In Jesus' name we pray. Amen.

C. Thought to Remember

The atonement by Jesus' death is the only basis for our forgiveness.

INVOLVEMENT LEARNING

Enhance your lesson with NIV® *Bible Student (from your curriculum supplier) and the reproducible activity page (at www.standardlesson.com or in the back of the* NIV® *Standard Lesson Commentary Deluxe Edition).*

Into the Lesson

Give each learner a blank index card. Say, "I'm going to write a word on the board, and your task is to write a definition on your card. After one minute, I will collect the cards and read them to the class. Don't put your name on the card, and no fair looking up a definition in your Bible or on your smartphone! Ready?" Proceed to write *Atonement* in large letters on the board.

Collect the cards and read them, inviting reactions in the process. Conclude by writing this definition on the board: "forgiveness based on reparation for an offense or injury." Say, "Atonement is a vital concept in the New Testament, and for best understanding we should examine how God implemented atonement in the Old Testament."

Into the Word

Have two learners read today's text aloud, alternating with each verse. Then say, "We're going to play a game we'll call *Ultimate Bible Match*. First I need to give you the list of answers to the questions I will reveal." Display the following list in a vertical format. Leave off the superscript enumerations, as those serve as part of the answer key.

bull[1] / censer[2] / fragrant incense[3] / fire before the Lord[4] / smoke[5] / atonement cover[6] / finger[7] / goat[8] / atonement[9] / horns[10]

Form groups of five if your class is larger, groups of two or three if your class is smaller. Continue: "I am going to ask a question about the Day of Atonement. Group One will have three seconds to give the correct answer from the list and score a point. If incorrect, Group Two gets three seconds to answer correctly, etc. No matter which group scores, we move to Group Two for the second question, etc." (*Option:* To make this more difficult, include additional answers that will not be used.)

Pause for a minute to allow each group to establish a rotation procedure for who is to answer for the group. The procedure should ensure that everyone who wants to voice an answer has an opportunity to do so.

Next, proceed through the questions below, which you reveal on strips of poster board. The questions are listed here in the order of the answers in the previous list; therefore mix them up first. Also, do not include the verse numbers and superscripted numerals that are in italics, as those serve as the answer key for you, the teacher.

What was Aaron to bring as sin offering for himself? *(v. 11)*[1] / What was to be full of burning coals? *(v. 12)*[2] / What were Aaron's hands to be filled with? *(v. 12)*[3] / Aaron was to put incense upon the what ? *(v. 13)*[4] / The purpose of the incense was to create what? *(v. 13)*[5] / What was positioned above the tablets of the covenant law? *(v. 13)*[6] / What was to be used to sprinkle blood? *(v. 14)*[7] / What was to be a sin offering for the people? *(v. 15)*[8] / Because of the sins of the people, the Most Holy Place and tabernacle needed what? *(v. 16)*[9] / Aaron was to put blood on what feature of the altar? *(v. 18)*[10]

At the end of the game, allow time to discuss the significance of the procedures that God instituted in observance of the Day of Atonement. *Option:* Reinforce awareness of the procedures by having learners complete the "Proper Order" activity from the reproducible page, which you can download. Have them check their own work.

Into Life

Draw two columns on the board and label them *Bulls and Goats* and *Christ*. Ask a volunteer to read Hebrews 9:1-7; ask another to read 9:11, 12. Have learners identify elements in those texts that relate to the column headings; jot responses on the board in the proper columns. Compare and contrast entries in the columns.

Alternative. Distribute copies of the "Prayer of Praise" activity from the reproducible page for learners to complete as indicated. After either alternative, allow time for expressions of gratitude for the atonement available through Christ's blood.

FESTIVAL OF TABERNACLES

DEVOTIONAL READING: Deuteronomy 8:1-11
BACKGROUND SCRIPTURE: Numbers 29:12-40; Leviticus 23:33-43;
Deuteronomy 16:13-17; Revelation 14:1-5; 1 Corinthians 15:20-29

LEVITICUS 23:33-43

33 The LORD said to Moses, 34 "Say to the Israelites: 'On the fifteenth day of the seventh month the LORD's Festival of Tabernacles begins, and it lasts for seven days. 35 The first day is a sacred assembly; do no regular work. 36 For seven days present food offerings to the LORD, and on the eighth day hold a sacred assembly and present a food offering to the LORD. It is the closing special assembly; do no regular work.

37 ("These are the LORD's appointed festivals, which you are to proclaim as sacred assemblies for bringing food offerings to the LORD—the burnt offerings and grain offerings, sacrifices and drink offerings required for each day. 38 These offerings are in addition to those for the LORD's Sabbaths and in addition to your gifts and whatever you have vowed and all the freewill offerings you give to the LORD.)

39 "So beginning with the fifteenth day of the seventh month, after you have gathered the crops of the land, celebrate the festival to the LORD for seven days; the first day is a day of sabbath rest, and the eighth day also is a day of sabbath rest. 40 On the first day you are to take branches from luxuriant trees—from palms, willows and other leafy trees—and rejoice before the LORD your God for seven days. 41 Celebrate this as a festival to the LORD for seven days each year. This is to be a lasting ordinance for the generations to come; celebrate it in the seventh month. 42 Live in temporary shelters for seven days: All native-born Israelites are to live in such shelters 43 so your descendants will know that I had the Israelites live in temporary shelters when I brought them out of Egypt. I am the LORD your God.'"

KEY VERSES

Live in temporary shelters for seven days: All native-born Israelites are to live in such shelters so your descendants will know that I had the Israelites live in temporary shelters when I brought them out of Egypt. I am the LORD your God. —Leviticus 23:42, 43

SACRED GIFTS AND HOLY GATHERINGS

Unit 3: Holy Days

LESSONS 10–13

LESSON AIMS

After participating in this lesson, each learner will be able to:

1. Describe the historical background for the Festival of Tabernacles and the ways that the celebration helped the people to remember it.

2. Tell why commemorating significant milestones in one's heritage is helpful in passing one's faith to the next generation.

3. Help plan a special service of remembrance for God's historical blessings of his or her church.

LESSON OUTLINE

Introduction
    A. A Good Feeling
    B. Lesson Background
  I. Observance Established (LEVITICUS 23: 33-36)
    A. Month and Days (vv. 33, 34)
    B. Rest and Sacrifices (vv. 35, 36)
  II. Special Days Reviewed (LEVITICUS 23: 37, 38)
    A. Observances and Offerings (v. 37)
    B. Sabbaths, Vows, and Offerings (v. 38)
      The Privilege of "Over and Above"
  III. Observance Explained (LEVITICUS 23:39-43)
    A. Basic Facts Stated (v. 39)
      Lengthy Celebrations
    B. Tree Branches Collected (v. 40)
    C. Yearly Observance Mandated (v. 41)
    D. Booth-living Required (vv. 42, 43)
Conclusion
    A. The Blessing of Memory
    B. Prayer
    C. Thought to Remember

Introduction

A. A Good Feeling

The farmer is able to track his progress visually as he plants fields. He can see at a glance how many acres are yet to be sown, and he may experience a sense of accomplishment as each section is completed. After God gives the increase, the harvest is next. An abundant harvest may result in a good feeling in knowing that the work for the year has been done properly.

Farm families of the past prepared for winter by accumulating and storing foods and fuel (usually wood) for the months ahead. The preparations could include storing hay and grain for livestock; preserving vegetables and fruits by canning, drying, or freezing; and curing hams. As the winds of winter began, the family could have a good, secure feeling of having prepared properly.

Today's lesson is about the third of the three major annual festivals for Israel: the Festival of Tabernacles. This festival has parallels with the situation of the farmer who has come to the end of the harvest season, just before winter begins. That good feeling of a finished harvest was a positive emotion for the ancient Israelites in the fall of the year. It was a time to celebrate with others. But there was more to it than celebration of "harvest home."

B. Lesson Background

The first day of every month on the Hebrew calendar was to be observed by the blowing of trumpets and offering of special sacrifices (Numbers 10:10; 28:11-15). The seventh month—known as *Tishri*, which is late September and early October—was different, however. Its first day was designated for blowing of trumpets (Leviticus 23:23-25; Numbers 29:1-6), and regular labor was forbidden on that day. That was the first of several special events in this special month.

The Day of Atonement (see lesson 12) occurred on the tenth day—the most sacred day of the year—and again normal labor was prohibited. The Festival of Tabernacles added two or three more days of rest to the list (see discussion on Leviticus 23:35, 36 in today's lesson). Beginning five days after the Day of Atonement, this festival replaced the Day of Atonement's solemnity with a joyful atmosphere of thanksgiving. The Festival of Tabernacles, like Passover (lesson 10), had a distinct historical connection. For Tabernacles, that connection was the 40 years that the Israelites lived in tents during the wilderness sojourn.

The three major pilgrimage festivals are mentioned together, in highly condensed form, in Exodus 23:14-17 (compare Deuteronomy 16:16). The Festival of Tabernacles is also known as the Festival of Booths (in older versions of the Bible) or the Festival of Ingathering. The latter designation recognizes a harvest motif (not the harvest of barley or wheat, but of olives, dates, etc.)

I. Observance Established
(LEVITICUS 23:33-36)
A. Month and Days (vv. 33, 34)

33. The LORD said to Moses,

The Bible in its entirety is the Word of God, but in a specific sense the book of Leviticus contains more direct words of the Lord than any other book of the Bible. Dozens of sections begin with the phrase *the Lord said.*

34. "Say to the Israelites: 'On the fifteenth day of the seventh month the LORD's Festival of Tabernacles begins, and it lasts for seven days.

The *Festival of Tabernacles* is similar to the Festival of Unleavened Bread in that both begin on *the fifteenth day* of a month and both last *for seven days,* through the twenty-first day of the month. A new moon determines when a month begins, so a festival that starts on the fifteenth day is accompanied by the brightness of a full moon. This was not only helpful to the Israelites as they left Egypt after the first Passover, it is also a blessing to subsequent celebrants of the Festival of Unleavened Bread and the Festival of Tabernacles. The full moon provides illumination throughout the night.

A contrast in diet characterizes these two seven-day festivals. The restriction on yeast in the spring festival is a way to recall the haste in the departure from Egypt. For the Festival of Tabernacles, there is on hand an abundance of grain for the breads that are a daily staple, with no restriction on yeast.

B. Rest and Sacrifices (vv. 35, 36)

35, 36. "'The first day is a sacred assembly; do no regular work. For seven days present food offerings to the LORD, and on the eighth day hold a sacred assembly and present a food offering to the LORD. It is the closing special assembly; do no regular work.'"

A new thought here is that there is an *eighth day* that is added to the *seven days.* The eighth day is given a special name that is translated as *closing special assembly.* (The word being translated is different from those translated *sacred assembly* twice.) It is interesting that the observance in the spring features the one-day Passover followed by the seven-day Festival of Unleavened Bread, while the fall observance has the reverse: the seven-day Festival of Tabernacles is followed by the one-day closing special assembly.

The first day and *the eighth day* are periods in which no normal work is to be done. These two days of rest are in addition to the regular Sabbath of the week, unless it coincides with one of them (see further in v. 39, below).

> *What Do You Think?*
> What improvements can you make regarding your time-off days? Why is it important to do so?
> *Talking Points for Your Discussion*
> ▪ Regarding increased focus on God
> ▪ Regarding the need for rest itself
> ▪ Regarding reexamination of priorities
> ▪ Other

Most Christians are aware that Jesus' death and resurrection occurred at the time of Passover and the Festival of Unleavened Bread, the first of the three annual pilgrimage festivals. Most also know that the church began seven weeks later on the Day of Pentecost (the Festival of Weeks), the second annual pilgrimage festival. Many may not be aware, however, that an entire chapter of the Gospel of John, chapter 7, is devoted to describing Jesus attending and teaching at a Festival of Tabernacles.

John 7:37, 38 notes his declaration, "Let anyone who is thirsty come to me and drink. Whoever believes in me, as Scripture has said, rivers of living water will flow from within them." Jesus made this statement on "the last and greatest day of the festival" (7:37), and this raises the question of which day is meant. The seventh day is the last day of the festival proper, while the eighth day can be thought of as closing ceremonies. Opinion is divided, but the eighth day is more likely.

II. Special Days Reviewed
(LEVITICUS 23:37, 38)

A. Observances and Offerings (v. 37)

37. ("'These are the LORD's appointed festivals, which you are to proclaim as sacred assemblies for bringing food offerings to the LORD—the burnt offerings and grain offerings, sacrifices and drink offerings required for each day.

Aaron (the high priest) and his sons have much to learn about the regular and special sacrifices, as the Lord keeps adding to the information that was initially given. This verse and the next constitute a brief digression to emphasize that the festival days are mandated by God. These observances are not to be carried out thoughtlessly or insincerely (compare Isaiah 1:11-15). Each has its purposes and procedures. They teach about God's provisions in past and present and expectations for the future.

What Do You Think?
  Besides Christmas and Easter, what significant regular celebrations or observances does your church maintain? Why are these important?
Talking Points for Your Discussion
  ▪ For new Christians
  ▪ For seekers
  ▪ For spiritually mature Christians

The required sacrifices for the Festival of Tabernacles involve more animals than any other festival. The details are given in Numbers 29:12-38. Each day, for seven days, there are 2 rams and 14 lambs sacrificed. The bulls total 70 for the week, but they are offered in a different way, and no reason is given why: 13 the first day, decreasing by 1 each subsequent day so that 7 are offered on the seventh day. These are burnt offerings to be totally consumed on the altar, in addition to the regular

burnt offerings. Eight male goats are to be sacrificed as sin offerings, one each day. The total for these special offerings is 199. That's impressive!

B. Sabbaths, Vows, and Offerings (v. 38)

38. "'These offerings are in addition to those for the LORD's Sabbaths and in addition to your gifts and whatever you have vowed and all the freewill offerings you give to the LORD.'")

This verse sets up a comparison with general references to relatively routine items. God provides instructions concerning gifts, vows, and freewill offerings after the Israelites arrive at Sinai. The Sinai encampment lasts almost one year, so by now the people have been practicing these instructions on a regular basis. It is not necessary to provide specifics about these again.

What Do You Think?
  What is significant about keeping vows that have been made to and before God?
Talking Points for Your Discussion
  ▪ Concerning marriage vows
  ▪ Concerning oaths of office
  ▪ Concerning financial promises
  ▪ Concerning courtroom oaths or affirmations
  ▪ Other

❧ *THE PRIVILEGE OF "OVER AND ABOVE"* ❧

All of us have things we do regularly, and then there are things we do "over and above." The regular is what is expected in the normal course of events. I am expected to mow the grass, trim the bushes, wash the car, and clean out the garage. If my wife is tired or ill, I may also run the vacuum cleaner, wash the dishes, or even cook a meal. Such things are over and above the call of normal duty for me, but they need to be done.

The same is true in church. I give regularly, but sometimes there is a special need, so I give over and above what I regularly give. This raises the question of *attitude*. God established what was to be the regular giving pattern of the Israelites. But he also established the "over and above" obligation, as noted by the two occurrences of the phrase *in addition* in verse 38. When an "over and above" need presents itself to us today, how do we react? With an "Oh no, not again!" grumbling? Or with a spirit of gratitude toward God, who makes it possible for us to meet the need?   —J. B. N.

III. Observance Explained
(LEVITICUS 23:39-43)
A. Basic Facts Stated (v. 39)

39. "'So beginning with the fifteenth day of the seventh month, after you have gathered the crops of the land, celebrate the festival to the LORD for seven days; the first day is a day of sabbath rest, and the eighth day also is a day of sabbath rest.

The Lord is now ready to provide new information on how to observe the Festival of Tabernacles. He prefaces this with a review of the basic data about when the festival is to begin, its length, and the essential factor that it has two days *of sabbath rest*. Those two are in addition to the regular Sabbath of the week if that Sabbath doesn't fall on the first or eighth days. The word translated *sabbath* (twice) is not the regular word for Sabbath, because it has an extra syllable at the end. This creates an abstract reference to *rest* that is to characterize the days in question.

As Moses receives this legislation, it is evident that he is privileged to anticipate the time when the goals of the new nation are realized and the people actually occupy and harvest the land that the Lord has promised. Harvesting involves much physical labor, and it is a slow process. Harvesting

HOW TO SAY IT

Apocrypha	Uh-*paw*-kruh-fuh.
Babylon	*Bab*-uh-lun.
Judas Maccabaeus	*Joo*-dus *Mah*-kuh-**bee**-us.
Maccabees	*Mack*-uh-bees.
Nehemiah	*Nee*-huh-**my**-uh.
Persia	*Per*-zhuh.
Solomon	*Sol*-o-mun.
Syrians	*Sear*-ee-unz.
Tabernacles	**Tab**-burr-*nah*-kulz.
Tishri	*Tish*-ree.
Zechariah	*Zek*-uh-**rye**-uh.

in ancient times is entirely different from what is seen today as large combines harvest more in a few minutes than several ancient people can in an entire day. The successful completion of such arduous labor is to be celebrated by taking time to remember the Lord, who makes it possible.

❧ *LENGTHY CELEBRATIONS* ❧

Question: What do America's 10 annual federal holidays all have in common? Answer: each is of only a single day's duration! The same is true of all statutory holidays in Canada. At least officially, that is.

Whether by ingenuity or necessity, we seem to have unofficial ways of turning holidays into celebrations of more than just a single day. Some years ago, one of our daughters traveled 2,000 miles to come home for Christmas. Because of schedule complications, she arrived about December 15 and stayed for a week. Then our other daughter arrived on Christmas Day from 600 miles' distance. We didn't complain. The result was that we celebrated Christmas twice over a three-week period.

Other cultures have national holidays of more than one day's duration. Golden Week, for example, is a weeklong celebration in the People's Republic of China. God gave the ancient Israelites two weeklong observances (Unleavened Bread and Tabernacles), and that may make us wonder if longer celebrations should be a model for us. Are the seven or more consecutive days that many Christians take off around Christmas and New Year's Day a good idea, or is that often just "too much time on our hands"?   —J. B. N.

B. Tree Branches Collected (v. 40)

40. "'On the first day you are to take branches from luxuriant trees—from palms, willows and other leafy trees—and rejoice before the LORD your God for seven days.

The people are to use *the first day* of the festival for gathering boughs and branches of trees that have broader leaves. Other guidelines develop over time—the exact types of trees, in which hand each branch is to be carried, and prohibitions regarding trees from places where idols are worshiped. A natural response while carrying the branches is to enjoy waving them. This joy should characterize the attitude of the people for all *seven days*.

C. Yearly Observance Mandated (v. 41)

41. "'Celebrate this as a festival to the LORD for seven days each year. This is to be a lasting ordinance for the generations to come; celebrate it in the seventh month.

This verse repeats previous information, with a new element added: *This is to be a lasting ordinance for the generations to come.* Do the people of Israel indeed keep this mandate from the Lord? There are several biblical references to indicate that it is kept at times, but not in a faithfully consistent way. The next reference to it is when Solomon dedicates the temple in 959 BC (1 Kings 8:2), and that is almost 500 years after the legislation is given to Moses.

The nation of Israel divides after the death of Solomon in 930 BC—Israel to the north and Judah in the south. Judah has the temple, so the first king of the northern nation institutes "a festival on the fifteenth day of the eighth month, like the festival held in Judah. . . . On the fifteenth day of the eighth month, a month of his own choosing, he offered sacrifices on the altar he had built at Bethel. So he instituted the festival for the Israelites and went up to the altar to make offerings" (1 Kings 12:32, 33). It is rather evident that his purpose is to provide an alternative to the popular Festival of Tabernacles, held in Jerusalem in the seventh month.

When the first group of exiles returns to Jerusalem from captivity in Babylon in about 538 BC, one of the first things they do is construct the altar of burnt offerings so that sacrifices can resume (Ezra 3:1-3). Then they celebrate the Festival of Tabernacles, the first of the three major festivals that this group is able to keep after their return (3:4). The exile teaches them how serious God is about obedience. The *lasting ordinance for the generations to come* stipulation still applies after 900 years!

Even so, people in all circumstances have a way of drifting away from God and his requirements. Nehemiah comes from Persia to Jerusalem in 444 BC to provide a wall for the city. As Ezra reads Scripture at the dedication of the wall, information about the Festival of Tabernacles is discovered anew, and the festival is celebrated (Nehemiah 8:14-17). We can only wonder why the festival falls into oblivion in the 94 years since being observed in 538 BC, especially since those returning from Babylon had suffered their own wilderness experience!

> **What Do You Think?**
> What causes churches in general and Christians in particular to stop observing special days or milestones they once did?
> *Talking Points for Your Discussion*
> - Good reasons
> - Poor reasons
> - Concerning Romans 14:5, 6
> - Concerning Colossians 2:16

Moses writes that the law is to be read every seven years at this festival (Deuteronomy 31:10-13). The account in Nehemiah is interesting in that the two are reversed: it is in the process of the law being read that the people discover they are to celebrate the Festival of Tabernacles. The prophet Zechariah, a contemporary of Ezra (see Ezra 5:1; 6:14), predicts a time when those who had attacked Jerusalem would go there not to attack but to worship the Lord of hosts and to celebrate the Festival of Tabernacles (Zechariah 14:16).

During the period between the Old and New Testaments, Jews under Judas Maccabaeus recapture Jerusalem from the Syrians on December 14, 164 BC. The rededication of the temple becomes an eight-day ceremony, and 2 Maccabees 10:6 (in the nonbiblical Apocrypha) says that this occurs "as in the feast of the tabernacles."

D. Booth-living Required (vv. 42, 43)

42. "'Live in temporary shelters for seven days: All native-born Israelites are to live in such shelters

The branches that are collected are not just to wave; they are to be used to make small huts in which families live for a period of *seven days* (compare Nehemiah 8:15, 16).

Along the way, traditions develop about these shelters or booths. Each one is to have three walls made of the branches. The top is to provide shade, but some sunlight should also shine through. Those able to do so are to sleep, eat, and generally live in the shelters for the seven days. Exceptions are made for unusual circumstances such as hard rains—the proximity of the rainy season making that a distinct possibility.

43. "'so your descendants will know that I had the Israelites live in temporary shelters when I brought them out of Egypt. I am the LORD your God.'"

Each generation has the responsibility to teach the next generation concerning the history of and reasons for this annual, joyous event (Deuteronomy 31:13). The example above reveals a period of time when those who came back from Babylon failed to do so. We have all heard the dire warning that Christianity is always only one generation away from extinction. We prevent that warning from becoming reality by teaching children everything that Jesus commanded.

Conclusion

A. The Blessing of Memory

Memory is a special gift from God. The word *remember* has been used in slogans to make sure that events and the lessons they impart remain in a nation's memory. Sometimes the word *remember* is used to stimulate people for a determined effort in a war. Two rallying cries that were popular in that regard in years past are *Remember the Alamo!* and *Remember Pearl Harbor!* Sometimes *remember* is substituted by *never forget*, as in *Never forget 9/11!*

Two famous "remember passages" in the Bible are "Remember the Sabbath day by keeping it holy"

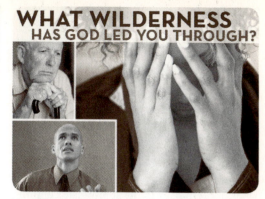

Visual for Lesson 13. *Pose the caption question to start a discussion on the personal "wilderness experiences" of your learners.*

(Exodus 20:8) and "Remember Lot's wife!" (Luke 17:32; compare Genesis 19:26). Combining both *remember* and *never forget* is Deuteronomy 9:7: "Remember this and never forget how you aroused the anger of the Lord your God in the wilderness." God designed the Festival of Tabernacles precisely so that the Israelites would keep in their hearts that 40-year period in their nation's history.

It is helpful to have a way to remember significant events of the past. For Israel, the holidays that were scattered through the year helped to achieve this, but the evidence is that the flow of events pushed the past out of their minds. The same temptations and tendencies are still with us. It is easy to allow the tyranny of the urgent to overwhelm what is really important: remembering God's redemptive act through Jesus Christ.

If we become too busy to remember what God has done, then we are too busy. A reordering of priorities is in order! What examples in this regard are we setting for the next generation?

B. Prayer

O Lord, thank you for the gift of memory that I may ever remember the price of my salvation and then give thanks for the people who taught me about it. Those are precious memories indeed! In Jesus' name. Amen.

C. Thought to Remember

Remember to remember the things of God.

INVOLVEMENT LEARNING

Enhance your lesson with NIV® Bible Student (from your curriculum supplier) and the reproducible activity page (at www.standardlesson.com or in the back of the NIV® Standard Lesson Commentary Deluxe Edition).

Into the Lesson

Before learners arrive, make four columns on the board with these headings, one each: *Passover / Festival of Weeks / Day of Atonement / Festival of Tabernacles.* Begin by asking learners to recall from previous lessons some facts about the first three; jot responses in the appropriate columns. Remind learners that an overarching purpose of these special times was for the Israelites to remember their status before God and what he had done for them. Then say, "Today, we will study the last of these special times that God instituted for Israel: the Festival of Tabernacles."

Into the Word

Have a learner read today's text aloud, stopping after each verse. Whenever your reader pauses, ask learners to call out features of the Festival of Tabernacles they see. As learners respond, jot their observations in that column on the board.

When finished, the Tabernacles column should contain the following facts: held on fifteenth day of seventh month for seven days (v. 34); no work allowed on first day (v. 35); no work allowed on the special assembly of the eighth day (v. 36); burnt offerings all seven days (v. 36); grain, sacrifice, and drink offerings daily (v. 37); coincided with a harvest (v. 39; but not a grain harvest, per the Lesson Background); gathering of tree branches (v. 40); ordinance for every generation (v. 41); dwelling in shelters for seven days (v. 42). After your reader reads verse 43, say, "This verse tells us why God instituted this festival."

Review the list and ask learners to speculate on God's reasons for various elements of the festival. (Examples: Why did God say no work on the first and eighth days? Why did God require so many offerings? Why branches of particular kinds of trees?) Use the lesson commentary to add insights and correct misconceptions. Then discuss how the elements of the festival were designed to help the people and succeeding generations reflect on the time when Israelites lived in temporary shelters in the wilderness after God brought them out of bondage in Egypt.

Option. For a unit review, give each learner a copy of the "Days to Remember" activity from the reproducible page, which you can download. Assure learners that they will score their own work; you will not collect them. Work through correct answers as a class.

Into Life

Say, "The lessons over these last four weeks have shown us ways that God designed the heritage of his faithfulness to be passed to future generations of Israelites. As they did so, they ideally were passing along the heritage of their faithful response of obedience as well." Then pose these questions for discussion, jotting responses on the board: Why is it important to pass on a heritage of faithfulness? What are some "heritage milestones" of our church's history that need to be passed to future generations? What are some ways our church has commemorated these milestones so far? (Be prepared with responses of your own to each.)

After a time of open discussion on the above, ask, "If we were to plan a special service of remembrance for God's historical blessings on our church, what would that service include?" This can be a whole-class discussion for smaller classes; larger classes can use small groups. Tell your learners that you will pass along their ideas to your church's leadership.

Option. To challenge learners to reflect on and commemorate their personal milestones of faith, distribute copies of the "Milestones of Life" activity from the reproducible page. Ask, "Generally speaking, what are some personal milestones that Christians can commemorate?" Responses can serve as a stimulus for personalized responses on the activity handout.

THE GIFT
OF FAITH

Special Features

		Page
Quarterly Quiz		226
Quarter at a Glance	Tom Thatcher	227
Get the Setting	Jon Weatherly	228
This Quarter in the Word (Daily Bible Readings)		229
Ministry Sites of Jesus (Map Feature)		231
Important Tools (Teacher Tips)	Richard Koffarnus	232
Student Activity Reproducible Pages (annual Deluxe Edition only)		481
Student Activity Reproducible Pages (free download)	www.standardlesson.com	
In the World (weekly online feature)	www.standardlesson.com/category/in-the-world	

Lessons
Unit 1: Tests of Faith

March 6	Powerful Faith	Mark 9:14-29	233
March 13	Simple Faith	Mark 10:17-31	241
March 20	Struggling Faith	Mark 14:26-31, 66-72	249
March 27	Resurrection Faith	Mark 16:1-8	257

Unit 2: Restorative Faith

April 3	Amazing Faith	Luke 7:1-10	265
April 10	Shameless Faith	Luke 7:36-50	273
April 17	Recovered Faith	Luke 8:26-36	281
April 24	Tested Faith	Luke 15:11-24	289

Unit 3: Fullness of Faith

May 1	Increased Faith	Luke 17:1-10	297
May 8	Grateful Faith	Luke 17:11-19	305
May 15	Humble Faith	Luke 18:9-14	313
May 22	Childlike Faith	Luke 18:15-17; Mark 10:16	321
May 29	Joyous Faith	Luke 19:1-10	329

QUARTERLY QUIZ

Use these questions as a pretest or as a review. The answers are on page iv of This Quarter in the Word.

Lesson 1

1. The father of the demonized son said, "I do believe; help me overcome my _____!" *Mark 9:24*

2. After being freed from the impure spirit, the man's son seemed to be what? (dead, in his right mind, speaking in tongues?) *Mark 9:26*

Lesson 2

1. Jesus referred to the eye of a _____ in an illustration. *Mark 10:25*

2. Jesus said that some things are impossible even for God. T/F. *Mark 10:27*

Lesson 3

1. After the last supper, Jesus and the disciples went to the Mount of _____. *Mark 14:26*

2. Jesus prophesied that Peter would deny him _____ times. *Mark 14:30*

Lesson 4

1. The women brought tools to move the stone that covered Jesus' tomb. T/F. *Mark 16:3*

2. At the tomb, the women were told that Jesus was headed to Galilee. T/F. *Mark 16:7*

Lesson 5

1. The centurion had built what for the Jews of Capernaum? (temple, synagogue, dock?) *Luke 7:5*

2. In Capernaum, Jesus healed the what of a Roman centurion? (ear, wife, servant?) *Luke 7:10*

Lesson 6

1. The sinful woman wet Jesus' feet with her tears. T/F. *Luke 7:37, 38*

2. Simon the Pharisee washed Jesus' feet better than the sinful woman did. T/F. *Luke 7:44*

Lesson 7

1. Where did the Gerasene man who was possessed by demons live? (on the beach, in tombs, in a tree?) *Luke 8:27*

2. Jesus sent the Gerasene man's demons into a herd of what? (pigs, goats, sheep?) *Luke 8:33*

Lesson 8

1. The prodigal son encountered what in the far country? (a flood, a famine, a plague?) *Luke 15:14*

2. The prodigal son became so hungry that he was willing to eat pig food. T/F. *Luke 15:16*

Lesson 9

1. Jesus taught that we should forgive a person only once for any particular sin. T/F. *Luke 17:4*

2. Jesus discussed faith in terms of a grain of _____ seed. *Luke 17:6*

Lesson 10

1. The healed leper who returned to thank Jesus was what? (Samaritan, Greek, Jewish?) *Luke 17:16*

2. Jesus told the healed leper that he had been made well by his faith. T/F. *Luke 17:19*

Lesson 11

1. Jesus told a parable about a _____ and a tax collector who prayed at the temple. *Luke 18:10*

2. The tax collector claimed to fast twice a week. T/F. *Luke 18:11, 12*

Lesson 12

1. Who didn't want infants brought for Jesus to touch them? (the Pharisees, the infants' parents, Jesus' disciples?) *Luke 18:15*

2. Regarding little children, Jesus said God's kingdom "belongs to such as these." T/F. *Luke 18:16*

3. Jesus touched the children, but he did not bless them. T/F. *Mark 10:16*

Lesson 13

1. Jesus encountered Zacchaeus in what city? (Jericho, Jerusalem, Joppa?) *Luke 19:1, 2*

2. Jesus declared Zacchaeus to be a son of whom? (Abraham, the devil, a Samaritan?) *Luke 19:9*

QUARTER AT A GLANCE

by Tom Thatcher

WHAT IS faith? The author of Hebrews famously tells us that faith "is confidence in what we hope for and assurance about what we do not see" (Hebrews 11:1). This verse highlights a certain paradox, or perhaps risk, of the Christian life: on the one hand, faith gives us power to rest on the promises of God in the most challenging circumstances; on the other hand, faith can be challenged by the common circumstances of everyday life, because it requires us to trust in something we cannot see or touch. How many of us have doubted, in the face of a trial or temptation, the reality of what we believe or our own ability to live up to it?

Like us, Jesus' first followers faced many challenges in their attempts to understand the way that God was working in the world. This quarter's lessons will demonstrate that faith, although it may be tested, can empower us to act far beyond ourselves.

Faith That Endures

Most of us can relate to the cry, "I do believe; help me overcome my unbelief!" (Mark 9:24). In Jesus' time as ours, people struggled to understand how an all-powerful God could stand silent in the face of evil (lesson 1) or seemingly leave us vulnerable to our enemies (lesson 3). Other tests come in the form of challenges to our obedience when our intuitive sense of what we should do runs counter to what we know to be God's calling (lesson 2). When we don't understand God's plan and feel lost with no sense of direction, faith keeps us moving toward what we know to be true.

Faith That Empowers

Although faith can be tried and tested, it can also empower us to live beyond our human inclinations. In these cases, faith acts as a beacon that leads us through the fog of life, even at times when our own unfaithfulness has led us far from God.

Such faith can lead the most hopeless sinner to seek forgiveness, even in (or especially in) the face of his or her own weakness. Such faith brings healing and hope to those who walk in the valley of the shadow of death. We see all this in the accounts of the Roman centurion whose servant was healed (lesson 5), the sinful woman who received forgiveness when she threw herself at Jesus' feet (lesson 6), the man who was freed from demonic oppression (lesson 7), and the parable of the prodigal son (lesson 8).

One result of such faith is gratitude when the depth of God's grace and mercy is revealed (lesson 10). When we experience that grace, we cannot help but to forgive those who have hurt us

> When we . . . feel lost with no sense of direction, faith keeps us moving toward what we know to be true.

deeply (lesson 9); indeed, faith gives us the power to do so.

All this requires that we let go of our pride and view the world differently (lessons 11 and 12). As we do, we are enabled to overcome our own sinfulness and produce fruit in keeping with true repentance (lesson 13). Faith serves as the fuel for the change that is necessary to push through our own limitations.

Faith That Conquers

Just before his death, Jesus reminded his disciples that sufferings would come. Even so, they could enjoy peace in the face of trials because "I have overcome the world" (John 16:33). The apostle John, who recorded these famous words, was perhaps reflecting on them when he reminded his readers of "the victory that has overcome the world, even our faith" (1 John 5:4). We are indeed "more than conquerors through him who loved us" (Romans 8:37).

GET THE SETTING

by Jon Weatherly

EW WORDS are as common in the church as *faith*. To modern ears, "having a faith" means adhering to a particular set of beliefs, affirming a particular understanding of who God is, and observing a particular tradition of worship.

That way of understanding *faith* has just enough in common with the word's use in the Bible to be confusing. We can make better sense of what we read in the Bible, then, if we set aside our way of using the word and listen to the way the Bible's ancient audience used it.

Faith as Basis

In the cultures of the Bible, faith was the basis of a relationship between persons. It was the trust and trustworthiness that bonded people together. In families, communities, and businesses, faith meant putting confidence in the others and in turn being the kind of person who deserved such confidence. Such faith was the social glue that held people together.

As ancient people thought about their relationship with the divine, faith was a natural concept to use. Pagan peoples struggled with their understanding of the gods, who were seldom of a character to inspire confidence in their followers. But many who worshipped such gods still believed that proper faith in them was the foundation of society. Such belief affirmed that the gods existed, but it carried something more. If a person believed, then that person must act on that belief. To believe in the gods meant to honor the gods.

Faith as God's Commitment

In the Bible, this concept of faith is hardly different, though the object of faith is very different. The biblical God is unlike the fictitious gods of the pagans: powerful in every way, but also utterly good, just, and holy.

This God is also gracious, merciful, loving, and forgiving. He has made a commitment to bring the entire world back under his beneficent rule. He expressed his commitment throughout the pages of the Old Testament. Though his people, like all of humanity, proved unfaithful, he pursued them with persistent faithfulness, inviting them back into relationship with him by his grace.

That contrast between humans' failure of faith and God's persistent faithfulness comes to its climax in the New Testament in the person of Jesus Christ. Jesus was the one person who proved faithful to God. Jesus lived in utter submission to God the Father, trusting completely in him. That trust took Jesus to the cross, where he expressed the full measure of God's own faithfulness to wayward humanity.

In turn, God the Father was utterly faithful to his faithful Son, raising him from the dead and seating him at the right hand of power. God the Father and God the Son then faithfully poured out God's own Spirit on God's people, those who belong to him through Christ. Through the Spirit, God faithfully empowers and directs his people today, committed to remain with them always until the Son returns to gather them to himself.

Faith as Our Commitment

What does it mean to have faith in this faithful God? Well, certainly it is more than a *yes* answer to the survey question, "Do you believe in God or a higher power of some kind?" Faith in the faithful, triune God is a lifetime commitment of trust that produces faithful obedience.

The faithful have no worries about their future, confident that God supplies and protects. The faithful have no doubt as to how to live their lives, shaping them trustfully in submission to God's Word and Christ's own example. Like servants whose master has left but has promised to return, they daily pursue the mission with which their faithful Lord has entrusted them.

THIS QUARTER IN THE WORD

Mon, Feb. 29	Faithful God	Genesis 15:1-6
Tue, Mar. 1	Saving God	Genesis 50:15-21
Wed, Mar. 2	Eternal God	Isaiah 43:5-13
Thu, Mar. 3	Healing God	Matthew 9:27-33
Fri, Mar. 4	Forgiving God	John 5:19-24
Sat, Mar. 5	Fulfilling God	John 6:35-40
Sun, Mar. 6	Powerful God	Mark 9:14-29
Mon, Mar. 7	Faith in Riches?	Psalm 49:1-6, 16-19
Tue, Mar. 8	Practical Faith	Proverbs 22:1-4; 23:3-5
Wed, Mar. 9	Abundant Faith	Isaiah 55:1-6a
Thu, Mar. 10	Authoritative Faith	Matthew 7:24-29
Fri, Mar. 11	Faith and Freedom	Galatians 5:1-13
Sat, Mar. 12	Priorities of Faith	Luke 16:10-14
Sun, Mar. 13	Complete Faith	Mark 10:17-31
Mon, Mar. 14	Uniting Faith	Jeremiah 3:12-18
Tue, Mar. 15	Enlightening Faith	Isaiah 2:1-6
Wed, Mar. 16	Suffering Faith	1 Peter 4:10-19
Thu, Mar. 17	Faith Restored	Psalm 85:4-13
Fri, Mar. 18	Faith That Overcomes	Romans 12:14-21
Sat, Mar. 19	Marks of Faith	Galatians 5:22-26
Sun, Mar. 20	Failure and Remorse	Mark 14:26-31, 66-72

Mon, May 16	Peaceful Faith	Isaiah 11:1-9
Tue, May 17	Children of Light	1 Thessalonians 5:1-11
Wed, May 18	Children of Freedom	Galatians 3:23-29
Thu, May 19	Children of God	Romans 8:12-17
Fri, May 20	Innocent Faith	Matthew 18:1-5
Sat, May 21	Certain Faith	Luke 1:46-56
Sun, May 22	Like a Child	Luke 18:15-17; Mark 10:16
Mon, May 23	Singing Faith	Isaiah 44:23-26
Tue, May 24	Dancing Faith	Jeremiah 31:11-14
Wed, May 25	Proclaimed Faith	Psalm 19:1-4, 14
Thu, May 26	Fruitful Faith	Galatians 5:19-26
Fri, May 27	Sending Faith	3 John 2-8
Sat, May 28	Connected Faith	John 15:1-11
Sun, May 29	Saving Faith	Luke 19:1-10

Answers to the Quarterly Quiz on page 226

Lesson 1—1. unbelief. 2. dead. Lesson 2—1. needle. 2. false. Lesson 3—1. Olives. 2. three. Lesson 4—1. false. 2. true. Lesson 5—1. synagogue. 2. servant. Lesson 6—1. true. 2. false. Lesson 7—1. in tombs. 2. pigs. Lesson 8—1. famine. 2. true. Lesson 9—1. false. 2. mustard. Lesson 10—1. Samaritan. 2. true. Lesson 11—1. Pharisee. 2. false. Lesson 12—1. Jesus' disciples. 2. true. 3. false. Lesson 13—1. Jericho. 2. Abraham.

Mon, Mar. 21	**Commandment Living**	Deuteronomy 6:1-9
Tue, Mar. 22	**Fear and Serve the Lord**	1 Samuel 12:19-24
Wed, Mar. 23	**Faithful and Fearless**	Psalm 23
Thu, Mar. 24	**Grace-filled Living**	Romans 1:1-7
Fri, Mar. 25	**Living Again**	1 Peter 1:21-25
Sat, Mar. 26	**Resurrection Living**	1 Peter 3:14b-22
Sun, Mar. 27	**Basis for Faith**	Mark 16:1-8
Mon, Mar. 28	**Rebuilding Health**	Isaiah 58:6-12
Tue, Mar. 29	**Healing Wings**	Malachi 3:16-4:2
Wed, Mar. 30	**Words of Healing**	Proverbs 12:1, 2; 13:16, 17; 16:22-24
Thu, Mar. 31	**Total Health**	Matthew 4:23-25; 5:3-11
Fri, Apr. 1	**Emotional Health**	Matthew 6:16-27
Sat, Apr. 2	**Eternal Health**	John 5:24-30
Sun, Apr. 3	**Renewed Health**	Luke 7:1-10
Mon, Apr. 4	**Israel's Salvation**	Exodus 14:30-15:3
Tue, Apr. 5	**David's Deliverance**	2 Samuel 22:2-7, 17-20
Wed, Apr. 6	**Prevailing Trust**	Psalm 13
Thu, Apr. 7	**Fulfilled Trust**	2 Samuel 7:8-12
Fri, Apr. 8	**Triumphant Trust**	Psalm 54
Sat, Apr. 9	**Trust Without Shame**	2 Timothy 1:8-14
Sun, Apr. 10	**A Fresh Start**	Luke 7:36-50
Mon, Apr. 11	**Completeness in God**	Isaiah 61:1-7
Tue, Apr. 12	**Renewed Relationship**	Jeremiah 31:21, 31-35
Wed, Apr. 13	**Steadfast Love**	Psalm 119:41-48
Thu, Apr. 14	**Disciplined Freedom**	1 Corinthians 9:19-27
Fri, Apr. 15	**Freedom in the Spirit**	Romans 8:1-11
Sat, Apr. 16	**Christian Freedom**	Philippians 2:1-11
Sun, Apr. 17	**Thinking Clearly**	Luke 8:26-36
Mon, Apr. 18	**The Father's Gift**	Matthew 7:7-12
Tue, Apr. 19	**Called into Family**	2 Timothy 1:3-10
Wed, Apr. 20	**The Generosity of God**	2 Corinthians 9:6-11
Thu, Apr. 21	**Eternal Family**	Romans 5:12-21
Fri, Apr. 22	**The Lost Brought Home**	Luke 15:1-10
Sat, Apr. 23	**The One Who Was Dead Is Alive**	Luke 15:25-32
Sun, Apr. 24	**A Family Reunion**	Luke 15:11-24
Mon, Apr. 25	**Kept by God's Faithfulness**	Genesis 28:13-17
Tue, Apr. 26	**Fed by God's Faithfulness**	Deuteronomy 2:4-8
Wed, Apr. 27	**Helped by God's Faithfulness**	Psalm 121
Thu, Apr. 28	**Saved by God's Faithfulness**	Jeremiah 23:33-24:6
Fri, Apr. 29	**Living with Integrity**	Psalm 101:1-4, 6, 7
Sat, Apr. 30	**Strength for Faithful Living**	Luke 21:33-38
Sun, May 1	**Lord, Increase Our Faith**	Luke 17:1-10
Mon, May 2	**God Cares for All**	Deuteronomy 11:12-21
Tue, May 3	**A Psalm of Thanksgiving**	Jonah 2:2-9
Wed, May 4	**Powerful God**	Psalm 9:1-4, 7-10
Thu, May 5	**Thankful Reverence for God**	Hebrews 12:25-28
Fri, May 6	**Living Gratefully**	Colossians 2:6-12
Sat, May 7	**Giving Thanks**	Luke 22:14-20
Sun, May 8	**Saying Thank You**	Luke 17:11-19
Mon, May 9	**Faith in a Merciful God**	Deuteronomy 4:32-40
Tue, May 10	**Faith in a Trustworthy God**	Daniel 9:15-19
Wed, May 11	**Living Humbly**	Micah 6:6-8; 7:18, 19
Thu, May 12	**Living a Blessed Life**	Matthew 5:1-10
Fri, May 13	**Living a Peaceful Life**	1 Peter 2:9-16
Sat, May 14	**Living a Fulfilled Life**	Luke 1:68-80
Sun, May 15	**Valuing Humility**	Luke 18:9-14

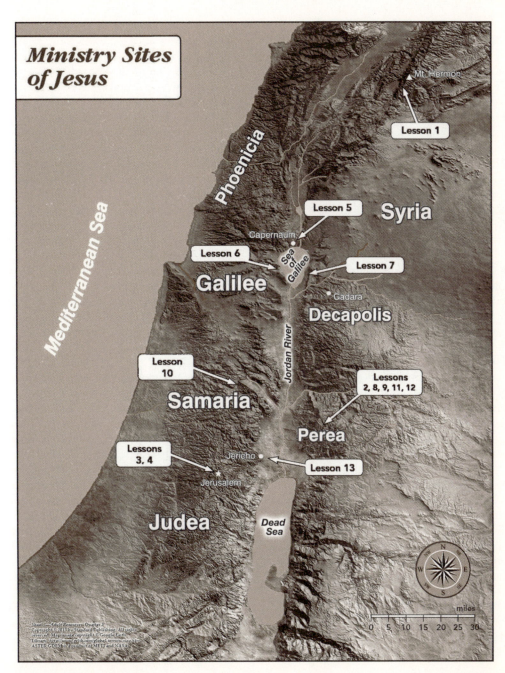

Ministry Sites of Jesus

Mt. Hermon

Lesson 1

Phoenicia

Mediterranean Sea

Lesson 5

Syria

Capernaum

Lesson 6

Sea of Galilee

Lesson 7

Galilee

Gadara

Decapolis

Jordan River

Lesson 10

Lessons 2, 8, 9, 11, 12

Samaria

Perea

Lessons 3, 4

Jericho

Lesson 13

Jerusalem

Judea

Dead Sea

miles
0 5 10 15 20 25 30

IMPORTANT TOOLS

Teacher Tips by Richard Koffarnus

MY FATHER was a very good amateur carpenter, and my father-in-law was a union carpenter for over 40 years. That means I've spent a lot of time around woodworkers! One thing I noticed very early on: wherever there is a carpenter, there is the ever-present tool belt.

When I was a boy, tool belts were simple affairs. They were intended to carry just the essential tools of the trade. They had places for a hammer, a tape measure or folding ruler, a pencil, a pair of pliers, a razor knife, and a screwdriver or two. With these few tools at hand, the carpenter was ready to tackle most common tasks.

When Bible teachers stand before their classes, they must be prepared to communicate the lesson and deal with challenges to the learning process. Like carpenters, teachers need certain essential tools to complete the job. Here are three important tools I use when I teach.

The Bible+

Of course, the Bible is always the primary tool of the Bible teacher. When I speak of "the Bible+," I mean the Bible plus references, notes, a concordance, maps, and introductions to each Bible book. These tools are essential to doing background preparation for teaching.

You can find all these tools in a study Bible (such as the *Standard Lesson Study Bible*) or in Bible software programs and apps for computers, tablets, and smartphones. Such software gives the user the ability to do rapid searches for Bible words, topics, etc. Like a Swiss army knife, study Bibles and Bible software offer a collection of essential tools for teachers of the Bible.

Visual Aids

There was a time when almost every church classroom had a set of Bible-era visuals that included maps, diagrams, pictures, time lines, etc.

These aids depicted the exodus, the 12 tribes of Israel, the layout of Jerusalem in the time of Jesus, Paul's missionary journeys, and Herod's temple. Such aids were essential to helping students visualize the world of the Bible.

They still are. According to one university study, 60 percent of learners can recall content three days after hearing a presentation that was supported by visual aids. On the other hand, only 10 percent can recall content three days after presentations made without such support. Even the best lesson is a failure if it is quickly forgotten.

The advent of computerized presentation programs, such as PowerPoint® and Prezi, makes the use of visual aids as easy as connecting a laptop to a video projector or a flat-screen television. Bible software programs and the Internet offer thousands of quality images and maps that can be downloaded and displayed for your class. Let learners see what you are discussing!

Handouts

If your congregation is like mine, you may have noticed that young children rarely leave Bible school without some reminder of the day's lesson. This reminder may be in the form of a picture, a puzzle, a cut-out character, a memory verse, etc. The purpose of that handout is simply to reinforce and continue the lesson after the class is over. Why shouldn't adults benefit from the same technique?

I offer learners a printed handout with every week's lesson. The handout may be of background material on the Bible book we are studying, an outline of the day's lesson, a series of discussion questions, or a printout of the PowerPoint® slides I am displaying for the class. Not every learner keeps the material, but many do. One of my learners has used our class handouts for his own Bible study with inmates at our local men's prison.

The Bible teacher's tool belt—don't teach class without it!

POWERFUL
FAITH

DEVOTIONAL READING: Genesis 50:15-21
BACKGROUND SCRIPTURE: Mark 9:14-29

MARK 9:14-29

¹⁴ When they came to the other disciples, they saw a large crowd around them and the teachers of the law arguing with them. ¹⁵ As soon as all the people saw Jesus, they were overwhelmed with wonder and ran to greet him.

¹⁶ "What are you arguing with them about?" he asked.

¹⁷ A man in the crowd answered, "Teacher, I brought you my son, who is possessed by a spirit that has robbed him of speech. ¹⁸ Whenever it seizes him, it throws him to the ground. He foams at the mouth, gnashes his teeth and becomes rigid. I asked your disciples to drive out the spirit, but they could not."

¹⁹ "You unbelieving generation," Jesus replied, "how long shall I stay with you? How long shall I put up with you? Bring the boy to me."

²⁰ So they brought him. When the spirit saw Jesus, it immediately threw the boy into a convulsion. He fell to the ground and rolled around, foaming at the mouth.

²¹ Jesus asked the boy's father, "How long has he been like this?"

"From childhood," he answered. ²² "It has often thrown him into fire or water to kill him. But if you can do anything, take pity on us and help us."

²³ "'If you can'?" said Jesus. "Everything is possible for one who believes."

²⁴ Immediately the boy's father exclaimed, "I do believe; help me overcome my unbelief!"

²⁵ When Jesus saw that a crowd was running to the scene, he rebuked the impure spirit. "You deaf and mute spirit," he said, "I command you, come out of him and never enter him again."

²⁶ The spirit shrieked, convulsed him violently and came out. The boy looked so much like a corpse that many said, "He's dead." ²⁷ But Jesus took him by the hand and lifted him to his feet, and he stood up.

²⁸ After Jesus had gone indoors, his disciples asked him privately, "Why couldn't we drive it out?"

²⁹ He replied, "This kind can come out only by prayer."

KEY VERSE

Immediately the boy's father exclaimed, "I do believe; help me overcome my unbelief!" —**Mark 9:24**

THE GIFT OF FAITH

Unit 1: Tests of Faith

LESSONS 1–4

LESSON AIMS

After participating in this lesson, each learner will be able to:

1. Describe the plight of the boy, the desperate faith of his father, and Jesus' response.

2. Compare and contrast the father's mixture of faith and unbelief with his or her own status in that regard.

3. Plan a ministry project that will stretch the faith of those who participate.

LESSON OUTLINE

Introduction
  A. The Best Water You Ever Drank
  B. Lesson Background
 I. Prelude (MARK 9:14-16)
  A. Scene Interrupted (vv. 14, 15)
  B. Question Asked (v. 16)
 II. Problem Analyzed (MARK 9:17-22)
  A. Demon's Domination (vv. 17, 18)
  B. Jesus' Exasperation (v. 19)
  C. Boy's Presentation (v. 20)
  D. Father's Explanation (vv. 21, 22)
 III. Problem Solved (MARK 9:23-27)
  A. Faith's Power (v. 23)
  B. Father's Quandary (v. 24)
    Belief and Unbelief
  C. Jesus' Command (vv. 25-27)
 IV. Problem Explained (MARK 9:28, 29)
  A. Disciples' Failure (v. 28)
  B. Jesus' Response (v. 29)
    Exorcisms, Then and Now
Conclusion
  A. The Enemy of Faith
  B. Prayer
  C. Thought to Remember

Introduction

A. The Best Water You Ever Drank

What was the best water you ever drank? That may seem like an odd question. After all, most of the water we drink daily varies little in taste.

But most of us can name a time when we truly savored a drink of water. We were thirsty, maybe hot. Perhaps we were working hard in the heat or playing a vigorous sport. Perhaps we were traveling where water was not readily available. We were desperate. When we finally received the water we needed, it tasted wonderful! Our experience of relief was intense because our need was intense.

The Bible says something similar about faith in God. There is never a time when we do not need God. But we can easily spend most of our time unconscious of that need, living as if we needed no one but ourselves. But into every life come situations that strip us of our sense of self-sufficiency. These are times when we realize that we have nothing or no one else on which to rely except God. So we cry out for his help. In those moments, we discover what real faith is.

Today's text presents a man who had just such an experience. His son was in desperate need, and the father knew that he was powerless to help. What this man said in his anxious weakness will show us much about our own situation.

B. Lesson Background

Our text brings together several themes that interweave and build throughout the Gospel of Mark. One of these themes is Jesus' authority over impure spirits. The first recorded miracle of Jesus in this Gospel is the casting out of such a spirit from a tormented man (Mark 1:23-27); Jesus went on to exercise this power on other occasions (3:11; 5:1-20; 7:24-30).

Another interwoven theme is the failure of Jesus' disciples. Their failure to rely on his strength in difficult circumstances led him to challenge their lack of faith and hardness of heart (Mark 4:35-41; 6:45-52; 8:14-21). When Jesus questioned the disciples regarding their conclusion of his identity, Peter replied, "You are the Messiah" (8:29). But the next recorded interaction between the two shows Peter attempting to "correct" Jesus' prediction of his own death and resurrection. This earned Peter a sharp rebuke from Jesus: "Get behind me, Satan!" (8:33).

Later, two disciples presumed to request places of authority (Mark 10:35-45), having already been taught that "Anyone who wants to be first must be the very last, and the servant of all" (9:35). Another disciple went on to betray him, one to deny him, and all to abandon him (14:17-21, 43-51, 66-72).

A third interwoven theme is the faith of the needy and outcast. Although the 12 disciples failed to trust in Jesus as they should have, those who were at the end of their rope in one way or another expressed a deep faith born of their deep need. Marginalized "tax collectors and sinners" wanted to be close to Jesus (Mark 2:13-17). A woman whose medical condition made her an "unclean" social outcast believed she could be healed merely by touching Jesus' garment (5:24-34). A Syro-Phoenician (non-Israelite) woman replied to Jesus' hard saying with persistent faith (7:24-30). These individuals had a deep realization of their need to rely on Jesus—a realization that the 12 disciples often didn't seem to have.

Today's text comes at an intersection of these themes. Following hard on Jesus' transfiguration (Mark 9:2-13), the mountaintop experience of encounter with divine glory became a valley encounter with the demonic. (Parallel accounts are in Matthew 17:14-21 and Luke 9:37-43a.)

I. Prelude
(MARK 9:14-16)

A. Scene Interrupted (vv. 14, 15)

14. When they came to the other disciples, they saw a large crowd around them and the teachers of the law arguing with them.

Jesus arrives on the scene, having just come from a high mountain where he had been transfigured before Peter, James, and John (see the Lesson Background). Those whom Jesus encounters at this point fall into three distinct groups: (1) *the other disciples*, referring to the 9 of the 12 who had not accompanied him to the mountain, (2) *a large crowd*, which tries to follow him everywhere (see Mark 3:7-10, 20, 32; 4:1; 6:30-44), and (3) *the teachers of the law*, who may be here to collect evidence against Jesus to take back to the Sanhedrin in Jerusalem (compare 3:22; 7:1).

The experts in the Law of Moses often dog Jesus with their confrontational questions. Lacking Jesus to pick on at this point, they seem to be settling for the next best thing: challenging his disciples.

> *What Do You Think?*
> What can we do to ensure that our discussions with skeptics end up shedding "light" and not "heat"?
> *Talking Points for Your Discussion*
> - In private conversations
> - When others are listening
> - Proverbs 15:1, 18; 20:3
> - 1 Peter 3:15

15. As soon as all the people saw Jesus, they were overwhelmed with wonder and ran to greet him.

The crowd of people has been watching the conflict between the teachers of the law and the disciples. The word translated *overwhelmed with wonder* occurs only four times in the New Testament, and only in this Gospel (here and in Mark 14:33; 16:5, 6). It is not the arguing of the teachers and disciples that provokes the people's reaction, but the arrival of Jesus himself. So they rush toward him.

B. Question Asked (v. 16)

16. "What are you arguing with them about?" he asked.

Jesus inserts himself into whatever controversy is taking place between the disciples and the teachers of the law, whom other versions of the Bible refer to as "scribes." They, however, are not the ones who respond to Jesus (next verse).

HOW TO SAY IT

Moses	*Mo*-zes or *Mo*-zez.
Sanhedrin	*San*-huh-drun or San-*heed*-run.
Syro-Phoenician	*Sigh*-roe-Fih-**nish**-un.

II. Problem Analyzed

(MARK 9:17-22)

A. Demon's Domination (vv. 17, 18)

17. A man in the crowd answered, "Teacher, I brought you my son, who is possessed by a spirit that has robbed him of speech.

Mark draws our attention away from the teachers of the law and the multitude to focus on a particular *man in the crowd*. The first word of his address to Jesus indicates respect for Jesus' authority. The man clearly hopes that his son can be delivered from *a spirit that has robbed him of speech*, which Matthew 17:18 and Luke 9:42 call a "demon." Verse 20, below, refers to the man's son as a *boy*, although the son's age is not given.

In the parallel text of Matthew 17:15, the father says the boy "has seizures," using a word in the original language that literally means "moon-struck." Matthew 4:24 uses the same word to describe a condition, usually considered to be epilepsy, that Jesus alleviated in many sufferers earlier in his ministry.

We note that the more abbreviated version of Matthew 17:15 records only the father's description of his son's symptoms, not their cause. Today's text as well as Matthew 17:18 and Luke 9:39, 42 leave no doubt regarding a demonic basis.

18a. "Whenever it seizes him, it throws him to the ground. He foams at the mouth, gnashes his teeth and becomes rigid.

The boy's condition involves more than just loss of speech. He often (see v. 22a) is overcome suddenly by the spirit, with the results we read here. The phrase *throws him to the ground* is a rather loose translation of a verb that means "to break." This same verb is translated "tear" in Matthew 7:6 and "burst" in Mark 2:22, indicating some kind of self-destructive behavior. Three observable symptoms accompany this: foaming at the mouth, grinding of teeth, and rigidity (the original word behind *becomes rigid* is translated *shriveled* in Mark 3:1 and *withered* in Mark 4:6; 11:20, 21).

18b. "I asked your disciples to drive out the spirit, but they could not."

Not finding Jesus, the man had asked Jesus' disciples *to drive out the spirit*. Jesus has granted them the authority to do so (Mark 6:13), but for some reason they have failed in this instance. This is probably the point of discussion between the disciples and the teachers of the law in Mark 9:14, above. The desperate situation now seems more desperate still.

B. Jesus' Exasperation (v. 19)

19. "You unbelieving generation," Jesus replied, "how long shall I stay with you? How long shall I put up with you? Bring the boy to me."

Jesus' initial reaction may surprise us. Instead of expressing compassion for the plight of the afflicted person and his father, he voices impatience with the faithlessness of those who should know better. This includes the disciples who have failed to drive out this demon. The phrase *unbelieving generation* connects them with the Israelites who had experienced the exodus from Egypt but failed to trust God when challenged to do so (Numbers 14).

That phrase also serves to warn Jesus' wider audience of failure to respond to what God is doing in Jesus. Moses had come down from the mountain where he had received God's law only to be confronted with unbelief (Exodus 32). Now Jesus has come down from the mountain of his transfiguration only to be confronted by the unbelief of those who should have more faith (compare Mark 3:5; 4:40; 6:50, 52; 8:12, 17-21).

Jesus warns that the time is short and his patience is not boundless. Only after he issues this warning does Jesus command that the afflicted boy be brought to him.

C. Boy's Presentation (v. 20)

20. So they brought him. When the spirit saw Jesus, it immediately threw the boy into a convulsion. He fell to the ground and rolled around, foaming at the mouth.

Demonic spirits are able to recognize Jesus' authority and power (see Mark 1:23, 24; 5:7), and this one is no exception. The boy's terrible condition is immediately revealed as a result. Clearly, the boy has not been helped at all by the disciples. If anyone is to deliver him, it must be Jesus.

D. Father's Explanation (vv. 21, 22)

21, 22a. Jesus asked the boy's father, "How long has he been like this?"

"From childhood," he answered. "It has often thrown him into fire or water to kill him.

As Jesus inquires further, we learn that essentially the boy's entire life has been dominated by the demon. The father's elaboration allows us to see more of the danger that the lad faces constantly: as demonic seizures come upon him, he is in mortal danger of falling into a fire to be burned to death or into water to drown. The boy is utterly helpless in both cases and requires constant monitoring. Talk about family stress!

22b. "But if you can do anything, take pity on us and help us."

Expressing his desperation, the father now speaks in a way that implies the failure of others to provide relief. No one, not even Jesus' disciples, has been able to help. Can Jesus now do what others cannot? The man's *if you can* expresses the natural doubt that arises from repeated disappointment. Yet in that doubt he still asks.

III. Problem Solved
(MARK 9:23-27)

A. Faith's Power (v. 23)

23. "'If you can'?" said Jesus. "Everything is possible for one who believes."

Jesus' reply picks up on the doubt in the man's plea. By repeating *if you can* back to him, Jesus poses the challenge as to whether the man is just another member of the "unbelieving generation" that sees God's mighty works in Jesus yet fails to

Visual for Lesson 1

Keep this map posted throughout the quarter to give your learners a geographical perspective.

believe (Mark 9:19, above). Such a failure of faith ultimately becomes the obstacle to God's action (Matthew 13:58). Yet for those who do believe, *everything is possible* because God will act on behalf of those who trust in him (Matthew 21:21; Mark 11:23-24; Luke 17:6).

So, is the man expressing faith or doubt? Is his faith the kind to which God responds, or is it too weak? Does Jesus take action only for those whose faith is faultless? The answer comes next.

> **What Do You Think?**
> When have you seen someone's level of faith play a key role in a Christ-honoring outcome to a negative situation? What did you learn from this?
> *Talking Points for Your Discussion*
> - Regarding a spiritual issue
> - Regarding a medical matter
> - Regarding a relationship problem
> - Other

B. Father's Quandary (v. 24)

24. Immediately the boy's father exclaimed, "I do believe; help me overcome my unbelief!"

The father's response may change the way we look at Jesus' challenge and the very nature of true faith. The man first insists that he does indeed *believe,* but with spontaneous sincerity he also confesses frankly his *unbelief.* In expressing this paradoxical condition, the man speaks for all of us at one time or another. Our faith is not always an unwavering confidence that is characterized by no shred of doubt. Rather, our faith is often the cry that arises from a desperate, longing need that has been battered and bruised by harsh experience.

Yes, my faith is weak, confesses the man. But he begs for help anyway—help for his weak faith so that Jesus can help his suffering son. No matter what prayer requests we lift to God, our first need is always for stronger faith.

> **What Do You Think?**
> When was a time your prayer was similar to what the father expressed? How did things turn out?
>
> *Talking Points for Your Discussion*
> - During a spiritual crisis
> - During a financial crisis
> - During a health crisis
> - During a relationship crisis
> - Other

❧ *BELIEF AND UNBELIEF* ❧

I've often thought the apostle Thomas got bad press. Because of his disbelief about the resurrection of Jesus (John 20:24, 25), we call him Doubting Thomas. Yet this same Thomas earlier had said that if Jesus was going to put himself in mortal danger by returning to Judea, then "Let us also go, that we may die with him" (John 11:16). This is not doubt; this is faith unto death.

Marking the line between belief and unbelief is often difficult. We believe that God can cure a person's cancer; but when we pray for healing, we really don't expect it. We agree that God "is able to do immeasurably more than all we ask or imagine" (Ephesians 3:20), but we don't pray for something because we don't think God will do it.

Years ago, I was talking with a Bible college student whose Pentecostal background taught him to pray for a thing and then act as if it were going to happen. He was taught that if you don't believe it will happen, then your lack of faith will guarantee it won't. It is easy for us to criticize the father for asking, "If you can." Yet his hesitancy is a mirror of us all. We believe, and God is able to build our faith by overriding our unbelief. —J. B. N.

C. Jesus' Command (vv. 25-27)

25. When Jesus saw that a crowd was running to the scene, he rebuked the impure spirit. "You deaf and mute spirit," he said, "I command you, come out of him and never enter him again."

Before the burgeoning crowd and in response to the father's expression of desperate faith, Jesus now acts. His authoritative command is longer than any other directive to demons in an exorcism in this Gospel (16 words in the Greek compared with 5 words in Mark 1:25 and 8 words in 5:8). If we wonder whether the father's imperfect faith will receive a half-hearted response, the length, authority, and specificity of Jesus' rebuke to *the impure spirit* shows us the opposite. We also note in passing that in speaking of the spirit as *deaf and mute,* Jesus is referring to two of the ill effects it has had on the boy.

26. The spirit shrieked, convulsed him violently and came out. The boy looked so much like a corpse that many said, "He's dead."

In response to Jesus' command, the spirit can only cry out and cause a final, dramatic shaking before departing. The boy lies motionless in the immediate aftermath. Many in the crowd, still lacking faith, conclude that the boy is dead, implying that Jesus has failed.

27. But Jesus took him by the hand and lifted him to his feet, and he stood up.

Jesus' action in taking the boy *by the hand* is like the action by which he had raised a dead girl to life in Mark 5:41 (compare Matthew 9:25; Mark 1:31; Luke 8:54; Acts 3:7). The power of Satan is being broken, as it will be most dramatically in Jesus' death and resurrection.

IV. Problem Explained
(MARK 9:28, 29)

A. Disciples' Failure (v. 28)

28. After Jesus had gone indoors, his disciples asked him privately, "Why couldn't we drive it out?"

This is not the first time that the disciples have waited for privacy to pose a question to Jesus for clarification (see Mark 4:10; 7:17), nor will it be the last (see 10:10). With the crowd out of ear-shot, the disciples bring to the fore the question that has loomed in the background throughout the story: *Why couldn't we drive it out?* Jesus has already given the disciples authority to cast out demons (Mark 3:13-15; 6:7), and they have done so (6:13). So why in this instance were the disciples unable to do the same? Was this a failure of God's power?

B. Jesus' Response (v. 29)

29. He replied, "This kind can come out only by prayer."

Jesus' response implies that the disciples had attempted to cast out the impure spirit by their own authority and power. They have become reliant not on God and his divine authority but on themselves. The faith that believes (Mark 9:23, above) is also the faith that prays. Unlike the boy's father, who openly admits his weakness and asks for help, the disciples seem somehow to have arrived at the point of believing that their own power is sufficient for the need.

A footnote in the NIV states that some manuscripts have "prayer and fasting." The Bible relates prayer with fasting in the lives of several people of great faith (see Ezra 8:23; Nehemiah 1:4; Daniel 9:3; Luke 2:37; Acts 13:3; 14:23).

What Do You Think?

In what ways do a Christian's prayers reveal his or her spiritual maturity? Why?

Talking Points for Your Discussion

- Regarding what is prayed for (Luke 6:28; 1 John 5:16)
- Regarding motive (Matthew 6:5; James 4:3)
- Regarding form (Matthew 6:7)
- Regarding priority and frequency of prayer (Luke 18:1; 1 Timothy 2:1)
- Other

❧ EXORCISMS, THEN AND NOW ❧

When I was in Bulgaria several years ago, I saw a priest attempting to exorcise evil spirits from an automobile. We may chuckle at this, but some attempts at exorcism are no laughing matter. For instance, two women in Germantown, Maryland, ended up being charged with murder and attempted murder in 2014 in the stabbing deaths of two children and the wounding of two others as the result of attempted exorcisms. One of the women was the mother of all four victims.

Exorcism as a religious ritual is a fascinating subject. There are numerous references to exorcisms in the Scriptures. The Roman Catholic Church has practiced a rite of exorcism for centuries, last revising the ritual in 1999.

In the early 1970s, the book *The Exorcist* and the movie based on it contributed greatly to the modern fixation on this topic. While the book and movie certainly contain objectional elements, the question they pose is still fascinating. That question is this: *How does a society that tries to explain away the supernatural react when confronting real, supernatural evil?* But this question is not confined to our era, as today's text shows (also see Acts 19:13-16). This is an enduring caution! —J. B. N.

Conclusion

A. The Enemy of Faith

Belief and unbelief, faith and failure characterize today's lesson. What we saw in the father we also see in the disciples and in ourselves. The father's plea "help me overcome my unbelief" was refreshingly honest. May that man's honesty be ours as well!

B. Prayer

O Lord, we do believe! But help our unbelief. When we begin to rely on ourselves, teach us again to rely on you. We pray in Jesus' name. Amen.

C. Thought to Remember

The enemy of faith is self-reliance.

VISUALS FOR THESE LESSONS

The visual pictured in each lesson (example: page 237) is a small reproduction of a large, full-color poster included in the *Adult Resources* packet for the Spring Quarter. That packet also contains the very useful *Presentation Tools* CD for teacher use. Order No. 020039216 from your supplier.

INVOLVEMENT LEARNING

Enhance your lesson with NIV® Bible Student (from your curriculum supplier) and the reproducible activity page (at www.standardlesson.com or in the back of the NIV® Standard Lesson Commentary Deluxe Edition).

Into the Lesson

Display this affirmation as your class assembles: *Faith always affects behavior!* Ask class members to cite biblical examples of this truth. If they need help getting a list started, suggest they skim Hebrews 11.

After several biblical examples are noted, ask, "Whom do you know personally who has made life choices based on a high level of faith?" Your learners may note Christians who have chosen to live and work in other cultures to spread the gospel.

Make a transition by saying, "Mark 9 gives us another example of one who acted on a belief; he saw what needed to be done, and he did it."

Into the Word

Describe the intersection of themes, according to the Lesson Background, that serves as the contextual backdrop for today's lesson. Have five learners read aloud the 16 verses of the lesson text, assigning them the parts of the narrator, Jesus, the father of the demonized boy, "many" (last two words of v. 26 only), and the disciples (last line of v. 28 only).

Inform learners that you are going to do some "reporter on the scene" interviews, as if class members were in the crowd that was awaiting Jesus' arrival. (Having a microphone in hand will add to the imagery; perhaps wear a "WMARK" identification badge as well.) Say, "As I roam the class and ask questions randomly, feel free to speculate on answers based on what seems reasonable or use the facts from Mark's record. If you don't wish to be interviewed, simply say, 'Sorry, I just got here and didn't see anything.'" (*Option:* Work with several class members in advance so they can preplan their responses.) Move about the group and ask questions such as these:

- What were the teachers of the law asking the nine disciples before Jesus arrived with the other three?
- How did the nine respond to them?
- Where was Jesus during that argument?
- What excuses did you hear from the disciples when it become evident that they themselves were unable to heal the boy?
- What happened when Jesus arrived?
- What was Jesus' attitude toward the unsuccessful disciples?
- From what the father said, how bad was his son's affliction?
- When Jesus said, "Everything is possible for one who believes," what did you expect?
- How was the son behaving before Jesus healed him?
- How did people react when the father replied, "I do believe; help me overcome my unbelief"?
- Would you say that many people changed their minds today about who Jesus is?

Option 1. To examine further people's tendency to hold belief alongside unbelief, distribute copies of the "Belief and Unbelief" activity from the reproducible page, which you can download. You can divide the six assignments among small groups for faster completion.

Option 2. Distribute copies of the "Desperation!" activity from the reproducible page. Complete the top half as a whole-class exercise, and use it as a transition to the Into Life segment as learners complete the bottom half individually. After one minute of private reflection, ask for volunteers to share what they have written.

Into Life

Give each learner a wide rubber band that is of a size suitable for wearing around one's wrist. Have learners write *Stretch my faith, Lord!* on these. Suggest that learners wear their bands daily in the week ahead as reminders of today's lesson. (*Option:* Ask learners to wear these to class next Sunday and be prepared to explain how the bands relate to the text for that lesson.)

SIMPLE FAITH

DEVOTIONAL READING: Galatians 5:1-13
BACKGROUND SCRIPTURE: Mark 10:17-31

MARK 10:17-31

17 As Jesus started on his way, a man ran up to him and fell on his knees before him. "Good teacher," he asked, "what must I do to inherit eternal life?"

18 "Why do you call me good?" Jesus answered. "No one is good—except God alone. 19 You know the commandments: 'You shall not murder, you shall not commit adultery, you shall not steal, you shall not give false testimony, you shall not defraud, honor your father and mother.'"

20 "Teacher," he declared, "all these I have kept since I was a boy."

21 Jesus looked at him and loved him. "One thing you lack," he said. "Go, sell everything you have and give to the poor, and you will have treasure in heaven. Then come, follow me."

22 At this the man's face fell. He went away sad, because he had great wealth.

23 Jesus looked around and said to his disciples, "How hard it is for the rich to enter the kingdom of God!"

24 The disciples were amazed at his words. But Jesus said again, "Children, how hard it is to enter the kingdom of God! 25 It is easier for a camel to go through the eye of a needle than for someone who is rich to enter the kingdom of God."

26 The disciples were even more amazed, and said to each other, "Who then can be saved?"

27 Jesus looked at them and said, "With man this is impossible, but not with God; all things are possible with God."

28 Then Peter spoke up, "We have left everything to follow you!"

29 "Truly I tell you," Jesus replied, "no one who has left home or brothers or sisters or mother or father or children or fields for me and the gospel 30 will fail to receive a hundred times as much in this present age: homes, brothers, sisters, mothers, children and fields —along with persecutions—and in the age to come eternal life. 31 But many who are first will be last, and the last first."

KEY VERSE

Jesus looked at him and loved him. "One thing you lack," he said. "Go, sell everything you have and give to the poor, and you will have treasure in heaven. Then come, follow me." —**Mark 10:21**

THE GIFT OF FAITH

Unit 1: Tests of Faith

LESSONS 1–4

LESSON AIMS

After participating in this lesson, each learner will be able to:

1. Describe key elements in the interaction between Jesus, the rich man, and Jesus' disciples.

2. Explain to what extent Jesus' command to the rich man applies to disciples today.

3. Identify one area of overreliance on self and write a prayer of confession.

LESSON OUTLINE

Introduction
  A. Longing to Do It Yourself
  B. Lesson Background
I. Jesus and the Rich Man (MARK 10:17-22)
  A. Question (v. 17)
  B. Reply (vv. 18, 19)
  C. Assertion (v. 20)
  D. Rejoinder (v. 21)
  E. Reaction (v. 22)
II. Jesus and the Disciples (MARK 10:23-31)
  A. Where the Rich Stand (vv. 23-25)
    The Camel and the Needle
  B. What God Can Do (vv. 26, 27)
  C. What the Disciples Have Done (v. 28)
  D. What Will Result (vv. 29-31)
    Hundreds of Relatives
Conclusion
  A. Camels or Children?
  B. Prayer
  C. Thought to Remember

Introduction

A. Longing to Do It Yourself

Do you remember as a child longing to do things for yourself? When we were very young, we depended on adults to do almost everything for us. Adults dressed us, washed us, fed us, transported us—they took care of us in every way. But children are intent on doing things themselves. They want to learn to tie their own shoes, drive the car, and live life independently in every way. After we have established our independence as adults, we take pride in having done something on our own. We value our independence, and we like to express it.

But none of us is truly independent. We depend on others all the time. Most of what we have, what we use, and what we do depends on what others have done to make those things and actions possible in the first place. As we approach the end of life, we often struggle against becoming more and more dependent on others.

We desire to be independent not only of other people but of God as well. At the core of what the Bible calls *sin* is the human desire to become like God by becoming king of our own lives (Genesis 3:5). Sin is more than breaking God's rules; it is declaring our independence from God.

Today's text deals with this universal human desire. As the story develops, it lays bare our most stubborn illusion: the false belief that we can live life on our own. It draws us back to depend on God's ever-sufficient grace and mercy.

B. Lesson Background

Today's text comes at a point where at least two key themes in the story of Jesus come together in Mark's Gospel. One such theme is the attention that Jesus gave to the weak and marginalized of his culture.

From his first public actions in Mark, Jesus deliberately acted on behalf of those who did not belong to the upper levels of society. He acted on behalf of "all the sick and demon-possessed" (Mark 1:32). He had fellowship with despised "tax collectors and sinners" (2:15). He criticized and warned those in power (7:6-8; etc.). In doing all this, Jesus turned upside down the cultural mores of his day, putting the lowly in the highest place and reducing those at the top to be at the very bottom.

A second theme in today's passage is the implication that Jesus intends his followers to be like children as he addresses them that way (Mark 10:24). In the section of text immediately preceding the one for this lesson, Jesus rebuked his disciples for forbidding children to come to him for blessing. Instead, he said that anyone who wanted to belong to God's kingdom had to become "like a little child" (Mark 10:15; see also lesson 12).

Taken together, these two themes speak against the idea of self-reliance when it comes to being part of the kingdom of God. Today's text adds to our understanding in this regard. (Matthew 19:16-30 and Luke 18:18-30 are parallels.)

I. Jesus and the Rich Man
(MARK 10:17-22)
A. Question (v. 17)

17. As Jesus started on his way, a man ran up to him and fell on his knees before him. "Good teacher," he asked, "what must I do to inherit eternal life?"

Jesus is on his final trip to Jerusalem (Mark 10:32). As he starts *on his way*, he is met by someone who shows him exceptional respect. Verse 22 tells us that this man is wealthy. When this information is combined with the words *young* in Matthew 19:20 and *ruler* in Luke 18:18, we end up with a picture of a man who is commonly known to Bible students as "the rich young ruler."

The man's approach by running indicates urgency. Reaching Jesus, he kneels in a position of submission, like a servant before a master or a subject before a king. His address of Jesus as *Good teacher* indicates that he respects Jesus' moral uprightness and wisdom. Jesus is now in the third

HOW TO SAY IT

Deuteronomy	Due-ter-*ahn*-uh-me.
Isaiah	Eye-*zay*-uh.
Sinai	*Sigh*-nye or *Sigh*-nay-eye.

year of his public ministry, and his reputation has spread widely.

The man has a specific question that is of profound significance: *what must I do to inherit eternal life?* To our ears, the last two words may sound like the man is asking a question about life after death. While that is certainly a crucial part of the man's question, he is asking about more. Eternal life is the life that belongs to the new age of blessing that God is establishing. It means a life that experiences all the goodness that God intends for his people. Jesus has come to declare that God is now bringing his promises to fulfillment, so that the old era is about to be eclipsed by the new one of God's blessing. This man wants to be part of that.

Despite the importance of the man's question, it is flawed. When he asks *what must I do?* he wrongly presumes that the life of God's age of fulfillment is something that he can obtain by his own actions.

B. Reply (vv. 18, 19)

18. "Why do you call me good?" Jesus answered. "No one is good—except God alone.

Jesus' response draws attention to the implications of the man's words. As a thoughtful, observant Jew (see vv. 19, 20, below), the man understands that being truly *good* is a characteristic only of God. Furthermore, asking Jesus how to obtain eternal life means that the man is asking a question that only God himself can truly answer. Is the man ready to confess plainly what he is implying about Jesus' divine nature?

19. "You know the commandments: 'You shall not murder, you shall not commit adultery, you shall not steal, you shall not give false testimony, you shall not defraud, honor your father and mother.'"

Without waiting for a response to his question of verse 18, Jesus continues his challenge. What God has told his people to do is very clear, being spelled out in the Law of Moses. The particular commandments Jesus quotes are representative of all of them (Exodus 20:12-16; Deuteronomy 5:16-20; 24:14). What is a person to do in light of God's goodness? Keep God's commandments!

But in listing some commandments, Jesus is also reminding the man of their context. The man knows these commandments are from the books of Exodus and Deuteronomy, books that not only detail God's law but also narrate how God's people failed to keep them.

That failure began even as the law was being given: while Moses received the law on Mount Sinai, the Israelites worshipped a golden calf below (Exodus 32). If the man knows the commandments, he also knows the history of his people's failure to keep them. Consequently, he should also know of his own failure in that regard. These laws reveal that the law-giving God alone is good; the recipients themselves are not. Again, the implied lesson is that if eternal life is to be had, it must come through God, not through human effort.

C. Assertion (v. 20)

20. "Teacher," he declared, "all these I have kept since I was a boy."

Jesus' appeal to the man's conscience is not yet successful. Rather than acknowledging God's unique goodness and his own sinfulness, the man asserts that he has kept the law faithfully since he was young. What the man is claiming is not absolute moral perfection but sincere, consistent observance as compared with other people. Measured against the lives of others, this man sees himself as good.

That comparison, however, is his failing: he compares himself with other people instead of with God. The man's self-perceived goodness is what drives him. Yet the man seems to lack assurance that eternal life is really in his possession, given his question in verse 17, above.

What Do You Think?
How do you respond to someone who voices a do-it-yourself approach to eternal life?
Talking Points for Your Discussion
- When the person accepts biblical truth
- When the person does not accept biblical truth

D. Rejoinder (v. 21)

21. Jesus looked at him and loved him. "One thing you lack," he said. "Go, sell everything you have and give to the poor, and you will have treasure in heaven. Then come, follow me."

Mark tells us first that love is the basis of Jesus' rejoinder. To point out what the man lacks is not uncaring—quite the opposite!

Jesus first tells the man to *sell everything you have and give to the poor.* For any person, rich or otherwise, this action would be extraordinary (compare Mark 10:28, below; 12:44). Indeed, the Gospels do not record Jesus' telling any other person to do something like this so specifically. So why this man?

From the opening of this conversation, we conclude that Jesus sees the man's primary problem to be that he thinks he "has it all together." This is the problem of self-reliance. Having possessions in abundance gives one the illusion that self-reliance is possible (see Luke 12:15-21). But having nothing tells us that we cannot rely on ourselves. Before and after God gave Israel his law, he led them into and through places where they had no means to sustain themselves. They needed to learn to trust God to provide food and water (Exodus 15:22–17:7).

Selling all and giving to the poor would put this man in the same situation. He would have no means to provide for himself, no illusion of his own self-sufficiency, and so nowhere to turn but to God.

This is the sense of the next statement, about having *treasure in heaven.* This refers not simply to what the man will receive after death. Rather, the word *heaven* reminds us of the dwelling place of God, as the place of God's presence. So *treasure in heaven* is the assured, abundant blessing that the God who dwells in Heaven provides for his people when they admit their need.

The instructions do not end there. Jesus further says *come, follow me.* How does one obtain eternal life? Only through Jesus. He is the one who can rightly accept the title *Good teacher* and can therefore require that those who seek eternal life must follow him to receive it.

E. Reaction (v. 22)

22. At this the man's face fell. He went away sad, because he had great wealth.

Whatever response the man is expecting from Jesus, what he hears is not it! He is unwilling to trade his self-sufficiency for reliance on Jesus. The man prefers to remain under the powerfully false perception that his *great wealth* provides security.

We note that the man's rejection of Jesus is not that of scoffing dismissal (contrast Luke 16:14; Acts 17:32; 2 Peter 3:3). Rather, he departs with the sadness of a person who has sought something he knows to be of great value—eternal life—but has failed to attain it. He has counted the cost, and he has concluded that that cost is too high (compare Luke 14:25-33). Such is "the deceitfulness of wealth" (Mark 4:19).

> *What Do You Think?*
> What luxury items can or should a Christian allow himself or herself to own, if any? Why?
> *Talking Points for Your Discussion*
> ▪ Definition of "luxury item"
> ▪ Mark 14:3-9
> ▪ "The more stuff you own, the more it owns you"
> ▪ Other

II. Jesus and the Disciples
(MARK 10:23-31)
A. Where the Rich Stand (vv. 23-25)

23. Jesus looked around and said to his disciples, "How hard it is for the rich to enter the kingdom of God!"

To enter the kingdom of God is to receive the blessings of God's promised rule that Jesus is bringing. Many in his day believe that having wealth is a sign of God's favor (compare Job 1:10; 42:10; Isaiah 3:10). Wealth is also seen to confer the advantage of being able to spend more time and money in careful observance of the law. But Jesus overturns this line of thinking.

24. The disciples were amazed at his words. But Jesus said again, "Children, how hard it is to enter the kingdom of God!

Reflecting the common outlook, *the disciples* are deeply surprised that Jesus views wealth as a hindrance to entering God's kingdom. Their

astonishment prompts Jesus to restate his warning. There must be no misunderstanding here.

But Jesus also begins to hint at the solution to the problem as he addresses the disciples as *children*. Earlier, he had said that one must receive God's kingdom as a child would (Mark 10:14, 15). The contrast between the rich man in his seeming strength and the child in weakness is vital.

25. "It is easier for a camel to go through the eye of a needle than for someone who is rich to enter the kingdom of God."

Jesus now repeats his warning in sharp, vivid terms. Camels are the largest animals commonly seen in Jesus' culture, and *the eye of a needle* is among the smallest of familiar openings. Jesus' comparison paints a picture of impossibility.

> *What Do You Think?*
> What self-tests can we perform to determine if we are serving God or money?
> *Talking Points for Your Discussion*
> ▪ When money is relatively scarce
> ▪ When money is relatively plentiful

❧ THE CAMEL AND THE NEEDLE ❧

A common teaching when I was a youngster was that at the time of Jesus there was a small gate in the Jerusalem wall that was known as the Needle's Eye. To pass through this gate, a camel would have to be unloaded, get down on its knees, and crawl. Therefore the meaning of what Jesus said was that we have to abandon our possessions and assume a prayerful lifestyle ("get down on our knees") before we can enter the kingdom of Heaven.

That makes for a nice illustration, and it was popularized in E. W. Bullinger's *The Companion Bible,* published in the early twentieth century. Apparently, the first person to debunk the application was J. W. McGarvey (1829–1911), longtime professor of sacred literature at The College of the Bible in Lexington, Kentucky. McGarvey noted that there is no evidence that there ever was such a gate at Jerusalem.

Jesus is known to have used extreme language in his teachings (examples: Matthew 7:3-5; Luke

With God
ALL THINGS
are possible

Visual for Lesson 2. *Start a discussion by pointing to this visual as you ask, "How do the two images you see here relate to Jesus' statement of verse 27?"*

14:26). With all good intentions, various interpreters have attempted to soften those extremes to make the teachings more palatable. We should exercise great caution in this regard lest we end up robbing the teaching of what Jesus really intended!

—J. B. N.

B. What God Can Do (vv. 26, 27)

26. The disciples were even more amazed, and said to each other, "Who then can be saved?"

The disciples' astonishment only increases. In wondering *Who then can be saved?* they reveal again that they hold to the conventional wisdom noted in verse 23, above. Thus Jesus' words are as startling to the disciples as his instructions were saddening to the rich man a minute earlier. If it is impossible for the rich to enter God's kingdom, how can there be hope for anyone?

27. Jesus looked at them and said, "With man this is impossible, but not with God; all things are possible with God."

Now the point becomes clearer. The problem is not simply wealth. Wealth promotes the problem, but it is not the problem itself.

God's blessing comes to those who recognize their own inadequacy and therefore reach out in their deep need to receive his unmerited gift. A person who relies on self can never enter God's kingdom. But by God's grace and mercy, anyone can receive the gift that he freely gives. Those who

rely on themselves, like the rich man, miss out on God's blessing. Those who approach God as children, relying utterly on him as heavenly Father, receive the fullness of his blessing.

C. What the Disciples Have Done (v. 28)

28. Then Peter spoke up, "We have left everything to follow you!"

The exchange with the rich man and Jesus' declarations lead Peter to wonder about himself and the other disciples. They have, in fact, done what Jesus said: they left their livelihoods behind when they accepted his invitation to follow him (Mark 1:16-20). Does this mean that they have done what the rich man was unwilling to do?

What Do You Think?
What has your discipleship cost you? What should it cost you?
Talking Points for Your Discussion
- Concerning relationships
- Concerning standard of living
- Concerning job opportunities
- Other

D. What Will Result (vv. 29-31)

29. "Truly I tell you," Jesus replied, "no one who has left home or brothers or sisters or mother or father or children or fields for me and the gospel

In reply, Jesus first lists some of the many things that the Twelve and others have left and will leave behind as they follow him. These things include home and relationships, which give a sense of security and belonging. If God is indeed fulfilling his promises, then nothing is too great to give up in order to receive the blessings of that fulfillment.

What Do You Think?
How can we keep devotion to family members from interfering with our devotion to God?
Talking Points for Your Discussion
- Before a problem occurs
- After a problem has occurred

30. "will fail to receive a hundred times as much in this present age: homes, brothers, sisters, mothers, children and fields—along with persecutions—and in the age to come eternal life.

There is no loss in sacrifice for the person who relies on God in following Jesus. God amply meets all real needs, and he does so in far greater measure than what one gives up. What God supplies, both in the present and in the eternal future, is far greater than what anyone leaves behind in this life in service to him.

❧ *Hundreds of Relatives* ❧

Back when I was in Bible college, a fellow student named Frank (name changed) had a deep desire to become a foreign missionary. His family was not in favor. They supported his desire to be a minister, but not to a foreign country. Frank, however, was undeterred. When he graduated from college, he married his girlfriend, raised support, and went abroad as a missionary.

Things were very difficult at first. Frank had to learn the language, the culture, and different customs in adjusting to a completely different way of life. This was made even more difficult by the fact that his family had all but rejected him. They wrote to him only on rare occasions, and then usually to berate him for leaving.

Finally, however, things began to open up for Frank in his ministry. He was instrumental in bringing numerous individuals to Christ, and he started a couple of churches. Frank became known in the area for his integrity, and even nonbelievers often came to him for advice and arbitration. More churches were started, and eventually there were hundreds of Christians. After three decades of ministry, the mission was well planted. Men he had trained for ministry were taking greater responsibility for local evangelism as more of Frank's time was spent in administration of the expanding work.

Frank once remarked to me that as he looked back over his ministry, he could see that God had given him a larger family than he had back in the States. The new family loved him deeply. Parents, brothers, sisters, and children had been multiplied to him, just as Jesus had said. And so it can be for each of us as well.

—J. B. N.

31. "But many who are first will be last, and the last first."

In God's view, human status and power count for nothing, but need counts for everything. Those who see themselves as self-sufficient will be brought low, as God shows them the reality of their situation. Those who recognize their deep need for what only God can give will be exalted by his unmerited blessing. God's kingdom is populated not with the self-sufficient but with children.

Conclusion
A. Camels or Children?

So, how do we evaluate ourselves? Do we see ourselves as accomplished, capable, resourceful, and righteous? Or do we see ourselves as weak, vulnerable, needy, and guilty?

Do our possessions—either those we have or those we aspire to have—form the basis of our security and status? Or are they a stewardship from God to be used to serve him in generosity that reflects his own?

One evaluation puts us on the path of attempting to enter God's kingdom as camels trying to pass through eyes of needles, an impossibility. The other evaluation has us approaching God's kingdom and eternal life as children who rely solely on God's grace. The choice is ours.

B. Prayer

Heavenly Father, those of us who live in prosperous Western democracies are especially at risk of seeing ourselves as self-sufficient. May our possessions, status, and cultural security structures not blind us to our weakness and need! Teach us to live as children, always relying on you to provide, both now and forevermore. We pray in Jesus' name. Amen.

C. Thought to Remember

Be children,
not camels!

INVOLVEMENT LEARNING

Enhance your lesson with NIV® Bible Student (from your curriculum supplier) and the reproducible activity page (at www.standardlesson.com or in the back of the NIV® Standard Lesson Commentary Deluxe Edition).

Into the Lesson

Prepare three large flash cards, with the letters *D, I, Y,* one each. Show the letters briefly one at a time in the order *Y, I, D.* Say, "Quite often these three letters are used as an acronym for a simple imperative. What is the correct order, and what does it stand for?" After the expected response of *DIY, Do It Yourself,* ask, "What are the potential advantages and disadvantages of taking this route for home repairs and remodeling?"

After several responses, say, "Today's study is of a man who wanted to use a DIY approach to spiritual matters. Let's see how things turned out for him."

Alternative. Place in chairs copies of the "I Want to Do It Myself" activity from the reproducible page, which you can download, for learners to begin working on as they arrive. Ask for volunteers to share results. Make a transition by saying, "Let's see how your experiences compare and contrast with those of a certain do-it-myself man who sought out Jesus."

Into the Word

Have the lesson text read aloud by calling for four volunteers to read the parts of Jesus, the rich man, the narrator, and Peter. The rest of the class will read in unison the part of "the disciples" (last five words of verse 26 only).

Next, give each learner a copy of the following word-find puzzle, face down. Say, "This will be a race to see who can finish first. When I say go, your first task will be to flip over your paper and find within the puzzle the 13 words listed at the bottom, words that we might use to characterize the man who approached Jesus in today's text. The words can be forwards, backwards, vertical, horizontal, and/or diagonal. After you find all 13, your second task is to skim through the puzzle left to right and top to bottom to see the 6-word phrase that the unused letters spell as an additional characterization. When you think you have the right

phrase, flip your paper face down, raise your hand, but don't say anything. Ready, set, go!" Call time after three learners have raised their hands.

```
T A U G H T D I H D S
L U F T C E P S E R U
E A P W I S E G A P N
P A O I R N N T R E W
Y D G H I E M O T H I
S D E E L L U F B S L
A N E L R D D D R I L
I S A E L B A V O L I
A H P P N O I N K O N
C A R E F U L T E O G
I N G T O J E S N F US
```

Include all the spoken directions with the puzzle in writing. Words to be found are *careful, challenged, eager, foolish, heartbroken, lovable, needy, proud, respectful, rich, taught, unwilling, wise.* The unused letters will reveal this phrase: *disappointed himself and disappointing to Jesus.*

After congratulating your speediest learners, discuss how the lesson text reveals that the man can be characterized by the 13 words and the 6-word phrase. Wrap up by noting that the 2-letter *US* in the final position is intentional. Ask, "And what of *us?* How can we keep from being disappointed and disappointing?"

Into Life

Give each learner a piece of paper that features only the letter *I* (very large). Say, "Place this letter *I* where you will see it frequently for a few days, perhaps in the Bible you use for daily readings. Let it remind you of the temptation of over-dependence on self. After a few days, write across it a prayer of confession for the sin in failure to trust God rather than self. Use your prayer as a commitment to depend more and more on God and less and less on self."

Option. Distribute copies of the "Handling Disappointment" activity from the reproducible page. Have learners pair off to complete and discuss.

STRUGGLING FAITH

DEVOTIONAL READING: Jeremiah 3:12-18
BACKGROUND SCRIPTURE: Mark 14:26-31, 66-72

MARK 14:26-31, 66-72

26 When they had sung a hymn, they went out to the Mount of Olives.

27 "You will all fall away," Jesus told them, "for it is written:

> "'I will strike the shepherd,
>   and the sheep will be scattered.'

28 But after I have risen, I will go ahead of you into Galilee."

29 Peter declared, "Even if all fall away, I will not."

30 "Truly I tell you," Jesus answered, "today—yes, tonight—before the rooster crows twice you yourself will disown me three times."

31 But Peter insisted emphatically, "Even if I have to die with you, I will never disown you." And all the others said the same.

· ·

66 While Peter was below in the courtyard, one of the servant girls of the high priest came by. 67 When she saw Peter warming himself, she looked closely at him.

"You also were with that Nazarene, Jesus," she said.

68 But he denied it. "I don't know or understand what you're talking about," he said, and went out into the entryway.

69 When the servant girl saw him there, she said again to those standing around, "This fellow is one of them." 70 Again he denied it.

After a little while, those standing near said to Peter, "Surely you are one of them, for you are a Galilean."

71 He began to call down curses, and he swore to them, "I don't know this man you're talking about."

72 Immediately the rooster crowed the second time. Then Peter remembered the word Jesus had spoken to him: "Before the rooster crows twice you will disown me three times." And he broke down and wept.

KEY VERSE

"Truly I tell you," Jesus answered, "today—yes, tonight—before the rooster crows twice you yourself will disown me three times." —**Mark 14:30**

Graphic: Dynamic Graphics / liquidlibrary / Thinkstock

THE GIFT OF FAITH

Unit 1: Tests of Faith

LESSONS 1–4

LESSON AIMS

After participating in this lesson, each learner will be able to:

1. Summarize Jesus' prediction of Peter's denial and its fulfillment.

2. Suggest reasons why a disciple today can sink from great confidence of faith to denial in the space of a few hours.

3. Create a small group to encourage one another's faith and perseverance.

LESSON OUTLINE

Introduction
  A. When Reality Doesn't Match the Plan
  B. Lesson Background
I. To the Mount of Olives (MARK 14:26-31)
  A. Supper Ends (v. 26)
  B. Jesus Predicts (vv. 27, 28)
    Scattered Flocks
  C. Peter Counters (v. 29)
  D. Jesus Specifies (v. 30)
  E. Peter Vows (v. 31)
    No Hubris
II. At the Place of Trial (MARK 14:66-72)
  A. First Confrontation (vv. 66-68)
  B. Second Confrontation (vv. 69, 70a)
  C. Third Confrontation (vv. 70b-72)
Conclusion
  A. Gospels' Variations
  B. Hubris and Redemption
  C. Prayer
  D. Thought to Remember

Introduction

A. When Reality Doesn't Match the Plan

"Be Prepared" is the motto made famous by Robert Baden-Powell, the founder of the Boy Scouts, in his 1908 book *Scouting for Boys*. Baden-Powell explained this broad statement to mean that "you are always in a state of readiness in mind and body to do your duty."

When I joined the scouts nearly eight decades later, I was bound and determined to exemplify this motto. In particular, I set a goal for myself to master every type of first-aid training available. In the case of an emergency, I would be prepared. I would save a life.

My test came in my late 20s when a customer began choking while I was waiting tables in a Cincinnati diner. Remembering my training, I began to perform the Heimlich maneuver. It didn't work. The patron was unable to get the food dislodged, even with all my training and best intentions. I was indeed prepared and acted as best I knew how, but the reality did not match my plan.

The apostle Peter was one whose plan did not end up matching reality. His best intentions of exhibiting faithfulness to Jesus fell apart when the moment of crisis came. His struggle remains an enduring caution.

B. Lesson Background

After Jerusalem fell in 586 BC, the people of the southern kingdom of Judah found themselves in dire straits. Even after their return from Babylonian exile, the Jews were subjected to the whims of evil rulers and foreign powers who sought to impose conformity to their own pagan outlook.

Numerous biblical and nonbiblical accounts reveal how the people of God reacted to such trying circumstances. One biblical account is that of Daniel, who survived in a lion's den when he refused to pray to Darius, the king of Persia (Daniel 6). One nonbiblical example is that of eight devout Jews—seven brothers and their mother—choosing to undergo torture and death rather than capitulate to pagan demands (2 Maccabees 7).

Persecutions for faith continued into the first century AD. In Mark's Gospel, two such trials of faith stand out—one official and the other unofficial. The official one was that of the trials and crucifixion of Jesus. The unofficial one was that of the bystanders' confrontation of Peter while proceedings against Jesus were underway. Peter's failure is the subject of today's lesson.

I. To the Mount of Olives
(MARK 14:26-31)

Today's study takes us to "the first day of the Festival of Unleavened Bread, when it was customary to sacrifice the Passover lamb" (Mark 14:12; compare Exodus 12:1-20). It is Thursday night of Jesus' final week, and crucifixion looms. Parallel accounts of this section of our lesson are Matthew 26:30-35; Luke 22:31-34, 39; and John 13:36-38; 16:32; 18:1.

A. Supper Ends (v. 26)

26. When they had sung a hymn, they went out to the Mount of Olives.

The singing of *a hymn* marks the conclusion of the last supper, held in the upper room (Mark 14:12-25). Traditionally, the last four of the Hallel Psalms (that is, chapters 115–118 of Psalms 113–118) are sung to conclude a Passover meal. (The word *Hallel*, the first half of the word *Hallelujah*, means "praise.") Whether those particular psalms are sung here is uncertain, however, since the first record of a Jewish tradition in this regard dates back only to the second century AD.

The night walk *to the Mount of Olives* involves an eastward trek of no more than a mile, out of Jerusalem and across the Kidron Valley. The destination is a familiar one, frequently visited by

HOW TO SAY IT

Babylonian	Bab-ih-*low*-nee-un.
Darius	Duh-*rye*-us.
Galilean	Gal-uh-*lee*-un.
Gethsemane	Geth-*sem*-uh-nee (G as in *get*).
Kidron	*Kid*-ron.
Maccabees	*Mack*-uh-bees.
Persia	*Per*-zhuh.
Zechariah	Zek-uh-*rye*-uh.

Jesus (Luke 21:37; 22:39; John 18:1, 2). More specifically, Jesus is headed to "a place called Gethsemane" (Mark 14:32; compare Matthew 26:36). Passover occurs at the time of a full moon, so illumination for the short walk is adequate.

B. Jesus Predicts (vv. 27, 28)

27. "You will all fall away," Jesus told them, "for it is written:
"'I will strike the shepherd,
and the sheep will be scattered.'

Jesus begins his post-supper discourse with the sad prediction that they *will all fall away*. Jesus underlines his prediction by citing Zechariah 13:7. In the original context of that prophecy, God unleashes his own fury against his anointed shepherd and follows that action with a time of testing for the sheep (people). The testing will involve being put "into the fire," for God "will refine them like silver" (13:9).

The testing that is to come upon the disciples in general and Peter in particular will reveal their weaknesses. The ultimate result, however, will be men of unwavering faithfulness (Acts 4:18-20; 5:27-32; etc.). But the testing has to come first.

❧ SCATTERED FLOCKS ❧

A young minister and his wife decided to start a church in their home by inviting neighbors to a Bible study. Within three years, the church had grown to over 500 people; the congregation had a beautiful building and became a powerful force for the gospel. For the next 36 years, this minister and his wife faithfully served the members of their congregation through the trials and joys of life.

Then one fateful evening the minister was killed by a drunk driver. The congregation was stunned. The elders didn't know what to do. There was no succession plan in place. Over the next year, the church's leaders tried calling a new minister, but no one seemed capable of filling the shoes of the deceased. The congregation all but disappeared within three years, and the leadership was forced to sell the building and the land. When the man whom the people saw as the shepherd of their church was no longer among them, the flock he was leading scattered.

Perhaps the problem was that everyone was focused on a human shepherd rather than on the great shepherd Jesus. If we keep our focus on Jesus, any scatterings we endure will ultimately turn out for the good (compare Acts 8:1b-8). Decide now what you will do when the going gets rough—look to Jesus, stick to your post, and don't even think about desertion. But be sure to make all such plans without hubris (see below).　　　　—D. C. S.

> **What Do You Think?**
> What is most likely to cause "the sheep" to be scattered today? How can we prevent this?
> *Talking Points for Your Discussion*
> ▪ Regarding situations within the church
> ▪ Regarding situations outside the church

28. "But after I have risen, I will go ahead of you into Galilee."

To Zechariah's prophecy Jesus adds two of his own. *After I have risen* is the fourth time that Jesus has predicted his resurrection in this Gospel, following those in Mark 8:31; 9:31; and 10:34. (Mark 9:9 might be counted as an additional such prediction.) Attached to it is a promise of a journey to Galilee that is to follow (compare Mark 16:7). Luke 24:36-43 and John 20:19-29 establish that the risen Jesus interacts with the disciples in Jerusalem before that time, so Galilee is another meeting place after the resurrection (Matthew 28:16; John 21:1).

The importance of this verse should not be overlooked. Its positive message serves to offset the negative message of the verse before it. Yes, God "will strike the shepherd," but that shepherd will rise again. Yes, "the sheep will be scattered," but the disciples will be reunited with their risen Lord in Galilee. What Peter has to say in the next verse seems to indicate that he misses the positive counterbalance here.

C. Peter Counters (v. 29)

29. Peter declared, "Even if all fall away, I will not."

Peter's knee-jerk response to Jesus' prediction "you will all fall away" in verse 27 is consistent with his outspokenness elsewhere in the Gospels

(example: Matthew 16:22). In the case at hand, Peter offers his own counterprediction by declaring that he has what it takes to stand firm, regardless of the actions of others.

D. Jesus Specifies (v. 30)

30. "Truly I tell you," Jesus answered, "today —yes, tonight—before the rooster crows twice you yourself will disown me three times."

Roosters have a natural predisposition to crow during the early hours of the morning. This reference to a rooster crowing also sheds light on the illegality of Jesus' trial. According to prevailing Jewish legal tradition, a trial for a capital offense cannot be conducted at night; such clandestine judicial meetings are often perversions of justice.

Mark's account is unique in that it notes Jesus' predicting of a double crowing in conjunction with a threefold denial. This mention of a double crowing will be repeated when the prediction is fulfilled (Mark 14:72).

The verb *disown* has the sense of "renounce." The same Greek root is translated "deny" in Mark 8:34, where Jesus says, "Whoever wants to be my disciple must deny themselves and take up their cross and follow me." Considered alongside the verse at hand, the two choices are either (1) deny self and affirm Christ or (2) affirm self and deny Christ. One cannot affirm both self and Christ. We either choose him to be our master or we do not. Therefore, the seriousness of Jesus' prediction cannot be overestimated. Peter's forthcoming denial—not once, not twice, but three times!—will not be insignificant. It will constitute a major moral failing.

E. Peter Vows (v. 31)

31a. But Peter insisted emphatically, "Even if I have to die with you, I will never disown you."

Peter's self-confidence knows no bounds at this juncture. Mark's note of Peter's replying *emphatically* is the strongest expression of its fervency among the four Gospels. Indeed, the Greek word behind this translation appears only here in the entire New Testament.

Peter sees himself as no exception to the expectation that faithful, loyal servants are to be prepared to die defending their masters. This is in keeping with the teaching Jesus gave earlier in the evening that the greatest act of love is "to lay down one's life for one's friends" (John 15:13).

The fact that Peter is carrying a sword may give him a sense of bravado in this regard; he plans to use the weapon at the first sign of trouble, and he ends up doing so (Matthew 26:51; Mark 14:47; Luke 22:38, 50; John 18:10). If Peter has any expectation of death, in all likelihood it is that of armed confrontation, not trial and execution (compare Matthew 16:22).

31b. And all the others said the same.

Peter's declaration emboldens the rest of the disciples. Their intentions are noble, but the imminent fire of adversity will prove their resolve to be lacking.

> **What Do You Think?**
> Under what circumstances should we make strong affirmations as did the disciples? Why?
> *Talking Points for Your Discussion*
> ▪ Proverbs 15:23; 23:9
> ▪ Ecclesiastes 5:2
> ▪ Amos 5:13
> ▪ Matthew 7:6
> ▪ Acts 5:42
> ▪ 1 Peter 3:15
> ▪ Other

❧ *No Hubris* ❧

Hubris is a type of pride that ultimately results in a person's downfall. It is sometimes characterized by a sense of invincibility. Quite often, those suffering from this condition are in positions of power that only perpetuate their detachment from reality. They often view reasonable boundaries with contempt. They violate moral codes like it is no big deal—as if those sorts of restrictions just don't apply to them.

A prime example is the gangster Al Capone (1899–1947). His "success" at criminal activities only served to reinforce his sense of being above accountability. Through the use of bribes, threats, and other notorious means, he always managed to stay a step ahead of the law. Even when he was

finally brought to trial for tax evasion, he was confident that his organization's efforts at bribing the jurors would allow him to skate free. But the presiding judge, having been made aware of the bribery, negated the problem simply by trading juries with another magistrate. Capone was convicted.

Peter was certainly no Al Capone! But it's possible that Peter and the other disciples were also infected by a form of hubris on the night of Jesus' arrest. Let us be ever on guard against this attitude taking root in our own hearts. "'Not by might nor by power, but by my Spirit,' says the Lord Almighty" (Zechariah 4:6).   —D. C. S.

II. At the Place of Trial
(MARK 14:66-72)

Mark 14:32-65 (not in today's text) describes Jesus' agony in Gethsemane and subsequent arrest and trial. Our next section of text shifts the focus back to Peter. After losing courage in Gethsemane (v. 50), Peter follows Jesus and his captors "at a distance, right into the courtyard of the high priest" (v. 54). There he places himself in the company of the high priest's servants around a fire for warmth. That which follows is also described in Matthew 26:69-75; Luke 22:56-62; and John 18:25-27.

A. First Confrontation (vv. 66-68)

66. While Peter was below in the courtyard, one of the servant girls of the high priest came by.

Scholars think the location of *the courtyard . . . of the high priest* to be in Jerusalem's affluent west side, also known as "the upper city." Mark appears to offer an intentional parallel in that a servant of Jesus, namely Peter, is confronted by a servant of the high priest at the same time that Jesus is being charged by the high priest himself.

67. When she saw Peter warming himself, she looked closely at him.

"You also were with that Nazarene, Jesus," she said.

It is difficult to ascertain exactly how a young servant of the high priest is able to identify Peter by sight, especially in the less than ideal illuminations of a full moon and a courtyard fire. Since females are not customarily involved in the sort of police action that has led to Jesus' arrest, the best explanation is that she has seen Peter sometime during the previous week in Jerusalem, while Jesus was teaching openly with his disciples.

The association of Jesus' name with Nazareth occurs frequently in the Gospels. This may be due at least partly to the fact that the name *Jesus* (equivalent to the Hebrew name *Joshua*, meaning "Yahweh is salvation") is a common Jewish name at the time. But the designation is also a fulfillment of prophecy (Matthew 2:23), with *Nazarene* as a term of scorn (John 1:46). The designation "Jesus of Nazareth" continues to be used after the resurrection (Acts 2:22; 3:6; 4:10; 6:14; 10:38; 26:9), even by Jesus himself (22:8).

68. But he denied it. "I don't know or understand what you're talking about," he said, and went out into the entryway.

Peter's response is to feign ignorance. He pretends to be caught off guard by the servant's accusation, in effect declaring that he has neither a personal relationship with Jesus nor knowledge of anything about him. Attempting to escape further scrutiny, Peter exits the area and heads for *the entryway* (probably a colonnaded vestibule).

What Do You Think?
Where can and should we seek help when our faith is tested? Why?
Talking Points for Your Discussion
- In cases of overt faith-challenges from unbelievers
- In cases of subtle faith-challenges from culture
- In cases of moral failures of church leaders
- Other

B. Second Confrontation (vv. 69, 70a)

69, 70a. When the servant girl saw him there, she said again to those standing around, "This fellow is one of them." Again he denied it.

A second accusation now comes, this time apparently intended to draw in the bystanders. The accusation is essentially the same; it implies that Peter has something to answer for.

Mark's account of Peter's second denial is more condensed than Matthew's. The latter includes an oath of denial (Matthew 26:72), which ignores Jesus' teaching concerning oaths (Matthew 5:33-37; compare James 5:12). It perhaps even breaks the commandment prohibiting taking the Lord's name in vain (Exodus 20:7) as oaths are often made in the name of the Lord (Numbers 30:2).

C. Third Confrontation (vv. 70b-72)

70b. After a little while, those standing near said to Peter, "Surely you are one of them, for you are a Galilean."

Something about Peter has betrayed him—apparently his Galilean accent, whatever the nature of that accent may be (Matthew 26:73; compare Judges 12:5, 6). The accent must be distinctive since it seems to show through even when the apostles speak miraculously in foreign tongues on the Day of Pentecost (Acts 2:7).

71. He began to call down curses, and he swore to them, "I don't know this man you're talking about."

To call down curses does not mean that Peter is using profanity, as we normally think the word *curse* to indicate. The idea, rather, involves calling down curses on one who perpetuates falsehood (compare Genesis 27:12) and the swearing of an oath. In saying *I don't know this man you're talking about,* Peter is ashamed even to mention the name *Jesus* (see Mark 8:38). Peter is also bearing false witness, in violation of Exodus 20:16. It is a sad downward spiral that has played itself out many times: sin usually requires additional sin in order to perpetuate itself. Peter is in too deep, and his failure is now complete.

What Do You Think?
How can a Christian use an experience of failure of faith to warn and teach others?
Talking Points for Your Discussion
- In formal teaching settings (Sunday school, etc.)
- In informal teaching settings (one on one)
- In family settings

---

72. Immediately the rooster crowed the second time. Then Peter remembered the word

Jesus had spoken to him: "Before the rooster crows twice you will disown me three times." And he broke down and wept.

Peter thus fulfills the prophecy that Jesus uttered so recently. Luke 22:61 adds that Peter has a direct line of sight with Jesus, and their eyes meet for a moment after *the rooster crows*. Anguish and remorse come crashing onto Peter, and there is nothing to do at this point but weep.

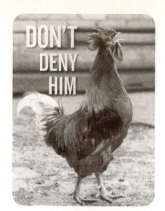

Visual for
Lesson 3

Point to this visual as you pose to the class the discussion question associated with verse 68.

What Do You Think?
Which Bible characters most inspire you to claim Christ when it is particularly difficult—even dangerous—to do so? Why?
Talking Points for Your Discussion
▪ Old Testament personalities
▪ New Testament personalities

Conclusion

A. Gospels' Variations

Today's text is one of four Gospel accounts that witness to Jesus' accurate prediction of Peter's denial. This has led numerous commentators to question why these four accounts are not identical in their reporting.

As we read these parallel texts, we must keep in mind that the truth of the testimony of multiple witnesses is gauged not by how their stories match word for word but rather by the agreement of the meaning of their testimonies.

The latter is what we see in the Gospel accounts of Peter's denial: (1) Jesus accurately predicted the denial (Matthew 26:34; Mark 14:30; Luke 22:34; John 13:38); (2) Peter's denial happened while Jesus' own trial was underway (Matthew 26:69; Mark 14:66; Luke 22:55; John 18:15); (3) Peter did not use a single chance to affirm his allegiance to Jesus, regardless of who did the accusing; and (4) Peter's failure was marked by the predicted crowing of a rooster (Matthew 26:75; Mark 14:72; Luke 22:60, 61; John 18:27).

The Gospels offer slightly divergent testimonies in these areas, depending on what the individual writer wished to emphasize. But all four affirm the same truth: Jesus correctly predicted Peter's denial.

B. Hubris and Redemption

Eager to prove his faithfulness, Peter made bold claims. How often do we similarly overestimate our own spiritual fortitude? The human tendency in this regard may be why Paul advocates fleeing from certain sins (1 Corinthians 6:18; 10:14) rather than hanging around to try to fight them. Spiritual arrogance can lead to ruin. Truly, we can do all things through Christ who gives us strength (Philippians 4:13), but "pride goes before destruction, a haughty spirit before a fall" (Proverbs 16:18).

Yet we must not forget that Peter's failure was not the end of the story. After his reinstatement per John 21:15-19, his track record as a primary witness to the resurrection of Jesus was nearly flawless after he received the gift of the Holy Spirit. (We say "nearly" because of Peter's error noted in Galatians 2:11-21.) Today's lesson of failure must always be tempered with hope. Yes, there are serious repercussions for denying Christ, but such failure does not create an impossible situation.

C. Prayer

Father, grant us victory over both pride and fear through the strength of your Holy Spirit. We pray in Jesus' name. Amen.

D. Thought to Remember

Find strength in the power of the Holy Spirit.

INVOLVEMENT LEARNING

Enhance your lesson with NIV® Bible Student (from your curriculum supplier) and the reproducible activity page (at www.standardlesson.com or in the back of the NIV® Standard Lesson Commentary Deluxe Edition).

Into the Lesson

To half your class distribute envelopes (one per learner) in which you have placed the following six phrases on separate slips of paper: A life of / faithfulness to Christ / will involve / setbacks and failures, / in spite of / our best intentions. Have these envelopes labeled *Sentence A*.

Do the same for the other half of your class, using these six phrases: Yet even in this / crucible of disappointment, / the promises of forgiveness and / reinstatement to discipleship / are ever before / the faithful believer. Have these envelopes labeled *Sentence B*. Each learner should end up with one envelope containing six slips of paper, either the six slips of sentence A or the six slips of sentence B. Mix up the slips so they are in random order within the envelopes.

Say, "Open your envelope and assemble the phrases into a significant truth related to today's study." After a minute or two, ask for *Sentence A* to be read aloud, then *Sentence B*. Say, "That first sentence is an important but regrettable reality we will see in today's lesson. Its truth makes us grateful for the additional truth of *Sentence B*."

Alternative. Place in chairs copies of the "Peter and Jesus" activity from the reproducible page, which you can download. This exercise will help set a broader framework for Peter's relationship with Jesus and how various aspects of this are seen yet today. Learners can begin working on this as they arrive. Save discussion of entries in the rightmost column for the Into Life segment.

Into the Word

Give each learner a handout that you have titled *Peter's Senses*. Below the title have listed the following column headings: His Eyes / His Ears / His Nose / His Skin. Say, "In today's text, we will see Peter being flooded, even overwhelmed, with a number of significant stimuli. As we read through the text, jot verse numbers and notes regarding what stimuli come his way according to the column headings. You need not restrict your entries to what is explicitly stated in the text; you can use your 'sanctified imaginations' to make reasonable assumptions as well."

Read audibly the 13 verses of the lesson text. Do this at a leisurely pace, but without unnatural pauses. After the reading, form learners into pairs or groups of three to work through the text again to complete the lists. During the whole-class discussion that follows, expect the following observations: *eye*—the sadness on Jesus' face (v. 30), the resolute expressions of Peter's fellow disciples (v. 31), the suspicious glances of those around the fire (v. 67) and entryway (vv. 68b-70); *ears*—the sadness in Jesus' voice (v. 30), the resolute tone of his fellow disciples' declarations (v. 31), three accusations (vv. 67, 69, 70), the crowing of the cock (v. 68, 72); *nose*—the smoke of the fire (v. 67); *skin*—the chill of the night air and the warmth of the fire (v. 67), the tears running down his face (v. 72).

Discuss how sensory overload could have contributed to Peter's failure and can contribute to ours at times. Note that other texts establish many other sensory stimuli at work that night. (*Option:* Compare and contrast Peter's failure in today's text with his failure noted in Galatians 2:11-14.)

Into Life

Announce that you are forming a small group for mutual encouragement and perseverance. Pass around a sign-up sheet to that effect for those willing to talk on occasion with other class members who are struggling with faith and doubt. Distribute copies of the list next week. Stress that everyone is subject to times of spiritual crisis, and your learners can share burdens in that regard.

Alternative. Distribute copies of the "Memory Associations" activity from the reproducible page to be completed as indicated. This can be a small-group or whole-class brainstorming exercise.

RESURRECTION
FAITH

DEVOTIONAL READING: Psalm 23
BACKGROUND SCRIPTURE: Mark 16

MARK 16:1-8

¹ When the Sabbath was over, Mary Magdalene, Mary the mother of James, and Salome bought spices so that they might go to anoint Jesus' body. ² Very early on the first day of the week, just after sunrise, they were on their way to the tomb ³ and they asked each other, "Who will roll the stone away from the entrance of the tomb?"

⁴ But when they looked up, they saw that the stone, which was very large, had been rolled away. ⁵ As they entered the tomb, they saw a young man dressed in a white robe sitting on the right side, and they were alarmed.

⁶ "Don't be alarmed," he said. "You are looking for Jesus the Nazarene, who was crucified. He has risen! He is not here. See the place where they laid him. ⁷ But go, tell his disciples and Peter, 'He is going ahead of you into Galilee. There you will see him, just as he told you.'"

⁸ Trembling and bewildered, the women went out and fled from the tomb. They said nothing to anyone, because they were afraid.

KEY VERSE

"Don't be alarmed," [the angel] said. "You are looking for Jesus the Nazarene, who was crucified. He has risen! He is not here. See the place where they laid him." —**Mark 16:6**

THE GIFT OF FAITH

Unit 1: Tests of Faith

LESSONS 1–4

LESSON AIMS

After participating in this lesson, each learner will be able to:

1. Describe the women's experience at the tomb.

2. Evaluate the level of faith demonstrated by the women.

3. Share the good news of Jesus' resurrection with one person in the week ahead.

LESSON OUTLINE

Introduction
  A. Surprised by Life
  B. Lesson Background: Gospels' Witness
  C. Lesson Background: Joseph's Actions
I. Expecting a Corpse (MARK 16:1-3)
  A. Spices of Sorrow (v. 1)
  B. Path of Mourning (v. 2)
  C. Stone of Defeat (v. 3)
II. Encountering a Man (MARK 16:4-6)
  A. Stone Out of Place (v. 4)
  B. Messenger in White (v. 5)
  C. Victor over Death (v. 6)
    Where Is Jesus?
III. Receiving a Message (MARK 16:7, 8)
  A. Instruction (v. 7)
    It's Personal
  B. Reaction (v. 8)
Conclusion
  A. Singular Event
  B. Vital Reality
  C. Prayer
  D. Thought to Remember

Introduction

A. Surprised by Life

In C. S. Lewis's classic *The Lion, the Witch, and the Wardrobe,* the White Witch demands, by law, the life of a traitor. In response, the great lion Aslan (whose figure represents Jesus) takes the place of the traitor and is put to death on a great stone table by the witch. The witch thereby believes she has conquered all of Narnia.

But Aslan overcomes death by means of a greater law, a law that existed from before the dawn of time. The witch did not know about this law since her knowledge went back only to the dawn of time. Otherwise she would have known that when an innocent individual voluntarily allowed himself to be killed in a traitor's stead, the stone table would crack and death itself would start working backward.

Satan knows lots of things. He knows what people do (Job 1:6, 7), he knows the Scriptures (Matthew 4:3-6), and he knows how to persuade (1 Chronicles 21:1). But the ability to know everything (that is, being *omniscient*) is an attribute of God, not of Satan (or of any other created being for that matter). Satan was able to persuade Judas to betray Jesus (Luke 22:3, 4; John 13:2, 27), which resulted in Jesus' crucifixion and apparent defeat. But would Satan have gone ahead with his plan if he could have foreseen Jesus' subsequent victory over death? Common sense tells us *no.*

Satan was not the only one unable to foresee Jesus' victory through resurrection, although Jesus had predicted it (compare Luke 18:31-34; John 20:9). The women who went to the tomb were not expecting him to be alive, given their intentions to prepare his body properly. They had witnessed the last moments of his life, had seen Joseph of Arimathea place the body in his own tomb (Matthew 27:55-61; Mark 15:40-47; Luke 23:49-55; John 19:25-42). They went to do what should be done for the dead; they ended up being surprised by life.

B. Lesson Background: Gospels' Witness

The four Gospels share divine inspiration and a common purpose. Yet each Gospel was written in a distinctive way for the needs of a particular original audience. In that regard, the four Gospel accounts of the resurrection of Jesus complement one another in the aspects and details they provide, but each is a condensed account. For example, Mark's especially brief account does not mention the guards posted by Pilate (compare Matthew 27:62-66) and notes only one of the two men (angels) who were present at the tomb (compare Luke 24:4).

The Gospel of Mark constitutes only about 18 percent of the four Gospels taken together, and this brevity is a basis for Mark's being called *the Gospel of action*. In rapidly shifting scenes, we see Jesus encounter the world's sinfulness time after time, overcome its adversity, and alter the course of events profoundly as a result. Mark's fast-paced biography comes to its climax at the empty tomb —where death itself is overcome by the power of the one able to grant eternal life.

C. Lesson Background: Joseph's Actions

The closing verses of Mark 15 recount Joseph of Arimathea's reverential kindness and courage in requesting from Pilate the body of Jesus. Having received permission, Joseph placed it in his own new tomb, which was "cut out of a rock" (Mark 15:46; compare Matthew 27:60). The fact that Joseph was "a rich man" (Matthew 27:57) fulfilled the prophecy about Jesus in Isaiah 53:9: "He was assigned a grave . . . with the rich in his death." But Jesus' body was not to remain there.

I. Expecting a Corpse
(MARK 16:1-3)
A. Spices of Sorrow (v. 1)

1. When the Sabbath was over, Mary Magdalene, Mary the mother of James, and Salome bought spices so that they might go to anoint Jesus' body.

The women mentioned here had watched Jesus die on Friday, and at least two of them had seen Joseph of Arimathea place the body in his own tomb (Mark 15:40, 47). Joseph had been assisted by Nicodemus, who had brought along a large amount of myrrh and aloes for the interment

(John 19:39). The two men had followed Jewish burial customs as best they could (Mark 15:46; John 19:40), but they had acted in necessary haste since they had to finish before the Sabbath began at sundown (Mark 15:42; John 19:31).

<hr>

What Do You Think?
How can various grief traditions help us realize God's presence? How can we use those traditions to point unbelievers to Christ?
Talking Points for Your Discussion
- Regarding funerals/memorial services
- Regarding graveside services
- Regarding visitations/wakes
- Regarding funeral dinners
- Other

<hr>

The grief-stricken women apparently do not believe that the burial preparations have been adequate. So after resting on the Sabbath (Luke 23:56), they return with *spices so that they might go to anoint Jesus' body.*

The designation *Mary Magdalene* is not a first-name/last-name format that is familiar to us. Rather, the designation *Magdalene* likely indicates that she is from the town of Magdala. Jesus had delivered this devout woman from great spiritual oppression (Mark 16:9; Luke 8:2), hence her dedication to him.

Mary the mother of James (and Joseph; see Mark 15:40) is otherwise unknown to us. *Salome* is probably the mother of the James and John who are sons of Zebedee (so identified by combining Matthew 4:21; 27:56; and Mark 15:40).

B. Path of Mourning (v. 2)

2. Very early on the first day of the week, just after sunrise, they were on their way to the tomb

The women had set out "while it was still dark" (John 20:1), intending to complete their task before the hours of another day furthered the decomposition of Jesus' body. Their desired ministry is an acknowledgment that death has had its way. They expect the body to have no warmth of its own, the precious life of the teacher now gone from it. To them, the fact that this is *the first day of the week* has no special significance—not yet, anyway. The women are merely resolved to do their work in spite of their grief, which acknowledges the triumph of death. And so they arrive at the tomb *just after sunrise.*

C. Stone of Defeat (v. 3)

3. and they asked each other, "Who will roll the stone away from the entrance of the tomb?"

At some point along the way, before they come within sight of the tomb, the women realize that they have forgotten about a major obstacle that lies between them and the fulfillment of their purpose. So they belatedly ask *each other, "Who will roll the stone away from the entrance of the tomb?"*

They had watched while the stone was rolled into place to close the tomb's entrance (Mark 15:46, 47). Thus they already know that the stone that seals the tomb will be much too heavy for them to move. This is especially so if the groove in which it rests is sloped upward from the stone's resting place over the opening. Such a design discourages entry by grave robbers, who would steal costly spices, etc.

The women's anxiety likely mounts as they consider that this obstacle may defeat the fulfillment of their purpose. They had been unable to prevent the death of Jesus; now they may be unable even to complete the proper burial of his body.

HOW TO SAY IT

Arimathea	*Air*-uh-muh-***thee***-uh (*th* as in *thin*).
Galilee	*Gal*-uh-lee.
Jairus	*Jye*-rus or *Jay*-ih-rus.
Lazarus	*Laz*-uh-rus.
Magdala	*Mag*-duh-luh.
Magdalene	*Mag*-duh-leen or Mag-duh-*lee*-nee.
Nazarene	*Naz*-uh-reen.
Nicodemus	*Nick*-uh-***dee***-mus.
omniscient	ahm-*nish*-unt.
Pilate	*Pie*-lut.
Salome	Suh-*lo*-me.
Shunammite	*Shoo*-nam-ite.
Zebedee	*Zeb*-eh-dee.

Yet their love for Jesus and commitment to their purpose are undeterred by this prospect; they do not turn back in despair. And because they do not turn back, they are soon amazed by life where they expected the dead.

II. Encountering a Man
(Mark 16:4-6)
A. Stone Out of Place (v. 4)

4. But when they looked up, they saw that the stone, which was very large, had been rolled away.

This verse reveals that the conversation in verse 3 occurs before the women come within sight of the tomb. Perhaps to this point the women have been entirely focused on the path just ahead of them so as not to stumble in the dim light. But lifting their gaze rather suddenly, they realize they have arrived at the tomb.

To see the stone *rolled away* is perplexing! There is more than one possible reason for this. But it is likely that the women do not know which explanation to favor over any other in this moment of surprise. The explanation that the women undoubtedly consider least likely—if they consider it at all—is that Jesus is risen from the dead (compare John 20:11-15). What John observes concerning himself and Peter, that "they still did not understand from Scripture that Jesus had to rise from the dead" (John 20:9), is true of the women as well.

> *What Do You Think?*
> In what ways have you experienced God's power and presence through the uncertainties that accompanied the loss of a loved one?
> *Talking Points for Your Discussion*
> - When surrounded by the support of others
> - When alone

B. Messenger in White (v. 5)

5. As they entered the tomb, they saw a young man dressed in a white robe sitting on the right side, and they were alarmed.

The women's devotion impels them to venture into *the tomb.* They seek a dead body, but instead they find themselves face to face with *a young man* who seems to be waiting for them. Matthew 28:2-5 tells us specifically that he is an angel. This fact is strongly implied in the text before us by Mark's description of his attire (compare Luke 24:4) and the women's reaction. Fear is the common reaction by a human when seeing an angel (compare Matthew 28:4; Luke 1:11, 12; 2:9; Acts 10:4).

What Do You Think?

What are some experiences you have had while visiting a cemetery that were startling at first but ended up strengthening your faith?

Talking Points for Your Discussion

- Regarding comments at a graveside service
- Regarding inscriptions on headstones
- Other

C. Victor over Death (v. 6)

6. "Don't be alarmed," he said. "You are looking for Jesus the Nazarene, who was crucified. He has risen! He is not here. See the place where they laid him."

The angel's words of comfort are typical in angelic encounters with humans (compare Luke 1:13, 30; 2:10). He knows why the women have come (*You are looking for Jesus the Nazarene*), but he negates their intention to anoint Jesus' body by declaring, *He has risen! He is not here.* This tomb, which had been an abode of the dead, is now the epicenter of resurrection life!

What Do You Think?

When was a time that belief in resurrection was especially helpful? How did things turn out?

Talking Points for Your Discussion

- Regarding a serious illness
- Regarding the unexpected loss of a loved one
- Other

The invitation to *see the place where they laid him* stands against various attempts through the centuries to dismiss the witness of the women as being faulty because of their inability to return to the correct tomb. This is the very tomb in which

they had seen the body of Jesus laid. They have indeed come to the place in which the lifeless body of the teacher had been resting. But that body is no longer lifeless; it has no further need of a cold, dark tomb.

❧ *WHERE IS JESUS?* ❧

I'll never forget my first experience teaching Vacation Bible School. I found myself in a class with a precocious 4-year-old who had many questions. One question was, "God could die if he wanted to, right?" Just when I began to think I knew something, God brought a child into my life to prove otherwise. (By the way, that little guy grew up to become a lawyer!)

I felt safer with school-age children who seemed to have been socialized to the point where they knew not to ask things that were too hard for their teachers to answer. Even so, I was caught off guard when a young lady in a grade-school Sunday school class asked this: "Why do we bow our heads to pray if Jesus is in Heaven? Shouldn't we look up?" After taking a moment to regain my composure, I told her, "Good question!" I replied that we bowed our heads as a sign of reverence and respect.

And yet, her bold query made me think. How many times do I try to do things in my own cleverness and power rather than looking up to the one who promises to give me wisdom, if I'll just ask? Why do I feel alone when he is alive and the Holy Spirit is advocating for me? Two thousand years later, Christians still have moments of feeling defeated—times when we forget that he is not in a cold tomb, but seated on the throne in Heaven. At those times, shouldn't we look up?

—V. E.

III. Receiving a Message
(MARK 16:7, 8)

A. Instruction (v. 7)

7. "But go, tell his disciples and Peter, 'He is going ahead of you into Galilee. There you will see him, just as he told you.'"

The women had seen Jesus crucified (Mark 15:40) and his body interred (15:46, 47), and now they see the empty tomb. In something of a precursor to the Great Commission of Matthew 28:19, 20, the women are to *go* and *tell* of what they now experience. The message is not yet for the unbelieving world at large, however, but for the sheep of the flock that has been scattered (Mark 14:27), namely the disciples.

Of those disciples, *Peter* is specifically mentioned. This may be because he, having forsaken and three times denied that he even knew Jesus, is especially devastated. Peter in particular needs to know that Jesus wants to see him again (compare John 21:15-19).

Jesus had stated to the disciples prior to his crucifixion that "after I have risen, I will go ahead of you into Galilee" (Mark 14:28). Thus the message the women are to convey is not a new piece of information. The disciples had heard it three days previous (*just as he told you*), but they need to hear it again. Jesus may have chosen Galilee as a rendezvous point so the disciples can recover from the toxic atmosphere of Jerusalem (compare John 20:19). What happens subsequently in Galilee is recorded in Matthew 28:16-20; John 21.

❧ It's Personal ❧

I was age 6 when I first understood what God had offered me, what Jesus had done for me. Before then I had the idea that good people went to Heaven and bad people did not. But on that Sunday morning, our minister said that we don't go to Heaven because of being good.

I asked my mom what that meant. Sitting on the sofa in our living room, she explained to me that God's grace saves us. She explained that Jesus took our punishment, and since we are not able to be good enough, he suffered for us.

That was for me! I connected the idea with the pictures in our church building of Jesus leaving the flock of sheep to search for the one lost sheep that needed him. *And I was the one!* Jesus' substitutionary death on the cross is available to anyone and everyone who is willing to accept it. God doesn't want to lose one single person. God loves the world—the whole world—but we don't come into his kingdom in bulk or via group tickets. We come in one at a time.

Jesus knows how to rescue each of us from our lives of sin and, later, from our backsliding, Christ-denying ways. Is there a "backslidden Peter" you know who needs a reminder of Christ's message of victory? God's invitation to that individual is just as personal now as ever—and you may be the one through whom God wants to voice it personally.

—V. E.

B. Reaction (v. 8)

8. Trembling and bewildered, the women went out and fled from the tomb. They said nothing to anyone, because they were afraid.

An avalanche of emotions overwhelms the women and prompts their hasty departure *from the tomb*. The result at this point is not understanding but continuing fear—fear that results in their saying *nothing to anyone*. Fear is a typical reaction in the Gospel of Mark on the part of those confronted with the true nature of Jesus (see Mark 4:41; 5:15, 33; 6:50; 9:6). The women speak freely after they calm down a bit (see Matthew 28:8; Luke 24:9).

> *What Do You Think?*
> What part have you seen fear play in a Christian's witness for Christ?
> *Talking Points for Your Discussion*
> ▪ Positive experiences when fear was overcome
> ▪ Negative experiences when fear was not overcome

Conclusion
A. Singular Event

The resurrection of Jesus is a singular event in history. It is in a category that consists of just that one item. It is distinct from other resurrections in the Bible, such as the raisings of the Shunammite woman's son (2 Kings 4:32-37), the son of the widow of Nain (Luke 7:11-15), the daughter of Jairus (Luke 8:49-56), and Lazarus (John 11:38-44). Those resuscitations were instances of temporary restoration of physical life by the reunion of soul and body—temporary because all those people died again later. The resurrection of Jesus, by contrast, is *permanent*.

That permanence is attested by Jesus himself: "I am the Living One; I was dead, and now look, I am alive for ever and ever!" (Revelation 1:18a). That permanence has vital implications. Death is God's penalty for sin (Genesis 2:16, 17; Romans 5:12), but now the risen Jesus holds "the keys of death and Hades" (Revelation 1:18b).

Another characteristic that sets Jesus' resurrection apart from the others noted above is that his body was *transformed*, not merely resuscitated. After his resurrection, he appeared and disappeared in ways he had not done previously (Luke 24:31, 36, 51; John 20:19, 26), although he still had a physical body that could be touched (Luke 24:37-43; John 20:27).

The transformation of Jesus' body prefigures the transformation to come of those who belong to him when we are raised on the last day (1 Corinthians 15:42-57; compare Philippians 3:21, below). The lost also will undergo a transformation, though theirs will be in preparation for eternal death rather than eternal life (Daniel 12:2).

B. Vital Reality

From our vantage point some 2,000 years later, the open, empty tomb is the universal image of Christ's victory over death. The women who found the tomb to be open on that first Lord's Day morning had prepared themselves to be confronted with death. Instead, they were confronted with the announcement of life.

The reality of death confronts all, and we make preparations for it. We help friends and family members in funeral planning. We purchase cemetery plots. We acknowledge our own forthcoming deaths by writing wills. But the best preparation is to let our thoughts dwell on the life that is to follow: resurrection life.

Jesus has promised that what was accomplished in him on that third day will also be accomplished in us when he returns. The power of life over death that he demonstrated for himself is the same power that will instantly and forever transform us. As Paul joyfully proclaimed, Christ "who, by the power that enables him to bring everything under his control, will transform our lowly bodies so that they will be like his glorious body" (Philip-

Talk about it!

Visual for Lesson 4

Point to this visual as you ask, "Why does this imperative differ from the 'don't tell' of Mark 1:44?"

pians 3:21). Jesus is Lord over death, having conquered it. That makes him Lord over eternal life —our eternal life.

Therefore as we prepare for death, we keep in mind that "the last enemy to be destroyed is death" (1 Corinthians 15:26). Death is our enemy, but it is ultimately a defeated enemy. When Jesus Christ returns (and every day brings us closer), we all will be changed. In a moment, in the twinkling of an eye, death will be no more. Then we will walk where death can never again rip us asunder, neither soul from body nor one from another.

The women on that first Lord's Day ran in fear from the empty tomb; our task today is to run in joy with the message of the empty tomb. May we ever proclaim Christ's victory over his death; may we never lose sight of the fact that his victory is ours as well—for eternity.

C. Prayer

Father, thank you for purchasing for us resurrection life, eternal life! Although we live in a fallen world that lies under the sentence of death, may we ever remember that Christ has conquered death for us to live forever with him. Empower us daily to walk joyfully in the light and power of his victory. We pray in his name. Amen.

D. Thought to Remember

The resurrection of Jesus
guarantees our own.

Involvement Learning

Enhance your lesson with NIV® Bible Student (from your curriculum supplier) and the reproducible activity page (at www.standardlesson.com or in the back of the NIV® Standard Lesson Commentary Deluxe Edition).

Into the Lesson

Before learners arrive, remove several things that are typically and conspicuously present in your learning area. If no one has commented on the changes by the time class begins, ask, "What's missing from our classroom that is usually here?"

After several missing items are noted, say, "We come into situations and settings with expectations that are based on previous experiences. That makes us wonder what happened when our expectations are not met. That's the case in today's text: something that people expected to find was missing! Let's see what and why."

Alternative. Distribute copies of the "Honoring the Dead" activity from the reproducible page, which you can download. Have learners work in pairs or groups of three to complete as indicated. Discuss the final passage on the exercise (Mark 16:1) as a transition to Into the Word.

Into the Word

Distribute on separate slips of paper the questions below, randomly arranged, to learners. (Do not include the italicized information, which serves as your answer key.) Instruct: "Do not look for answers to the questions, but rather look for the verse in today's text that has the answer."

For verse 1: What did the women take to the tomb? Why did the women go to there?

For verse 2: On which day of the week did the events occur? What time of day did the women arrive at the tomb?

For verse 3: What barrier to the women's work came to their minds?

For verse 4: What did the women unexpectedly see when they came within sight of the tomb?

For tomb 5: What sight caught the women's eyes as they entered the tomb? What reaction did the women have to the one in the tomb?

For verse 6: What's the first thing the young man said to the women? What startling news did

the young man give the women regarding the object of their visit?

For verse 7: What directions did the young man give the women? Where did the young man indicate that the disciples would see Jesus?

For verse 8: To how many people did the women give the news on their way back?

Direct your learners' attention to the text. After you read verse 1, ask, "Who has a question that can be answered with this verse?" Repeat the procedure for the remaining seven verses.

Alternative. Give each learner a handout of all the questions, in random order and without verse numbers. Say, "Look at Mark 16:1-8 and identify verses that can answer the questions." Allow learners no more than 90 seconds to work independently. Then discuss results as a class.

Say, "All lessons of this quarter deal with *faith*. Where do you see indicators of faith and lack of it in the women's thoughts and actions?" (*Potential responses:* they did not expect a resurrection, even though the Lord had prophesied it; they stayed to hear the young man out despite their fear; they seemed to believe the young man, since they obeyed his instruction to "go.")

Into Life

Give each learner a peel-and-stick label (fabric friendly) on which is printed *E/R*. Say, "Wear this sometime in the week ahead. When someone asks what it means, say, 'It stands for *Empty, Resurrected* in honor of my risen Lord.' This will allow you an opportunity 'to give an answer to everyone who asks you to give the reason for the hope that you have' according to 1 Peter 3:15."

Option. Distribute copies of the "Honoring the Living One" activity from the reproducible page. After allowing a few minutes for individual completion, ask, "Did you remember to include the commands of the Great Commission in Matthew 28:19, 20?" Discuss.

AMAZING
FAITH

DEVOTIONAL READING: Malachi 3:16–4:2
BACKGROUND SCRIPTURE: Luke 7:1-10

LUKE 7:1-10

¹ When Jesus had finished saying all this to the people who were listening, he entered Capernaum. ² There a centurion's servant, whom his master valued highly, was sick and about to die. ³ The centurion heard of Jesus and sent some elders of the Jews to him, asking him to come and heal his servant. ⁴ When they came to Jesus, they pleaded earnestly with him, "This man deserves to have you do this, ⁵ because he loves our nation and has built our synagogue." ⁶ So Jesus went with them.

He was not far from the house when the centurion sent friends to say to him: "Lord, don't trouble yourself, for I do not deserve to have you come under my roof. ⁷ That is why I did not even consider myself worthy to come to you. But say the word, and my servant will be healed. ⁸ For I myself am a man under authority, with soldiers under me. I

tell this one, 'Go,' and he goes; and that one, 'Come,' and he comes. I say to my servant, 'Do this,' and he does it."

⁹ When Jesus heard this, he was amazed at him, and turning to the crowd following him, he said, "I tell you, I have not found such great faith even in Israel." ¹⁰ Then the men who had been sent returned to the house and found the servant well.

KEY VERSE

When Jesus heard this, he was amazed at him, and turning to the crowd following him, he said, "I tell you, I have not found such great faith even in Israel." —**Luke 7:9**

THE GIFT OF FAITH

Unit 2: Restorative Faith
LESSONS 5–8

LESSON AIMS

After participating in this lesson, each learner will be able to:

1. Retell the story of the faith of the centurion.

2. Compare and contrast what impressed Jesus about the centurion with what impressed those who spoke on the centurion's behalf.

3. Describe one way he or she will exercise "centurion faith" in the week ahead.

LESSON OUTLINE

Introduction
  A. What Is Faith?
  B. Lesson Background
I. Faith That Asks (LUKE 7:1-8)
  A. Centurion's Request (vv. 1-3)
    Going to Jesus First
  B. Centurion's Character (vv. 4, 5)
  C. Centurion's Confidence (vv. 6-8)
II. Faith That Receives (LUKE 7:9, 10)
  A. Jesus' Astonishment (v. 9)
    Surprising People
  B. Servant's Healing (v. 10)
Conclusion
  A. Understanding Genuine Faith
  B. Accepting God's *No*
  C. Prayer
  D. Thought to Remember

Introduction

A. What Is Faith?

Have you ever wished that God would simply prove himself to you—prove that he exists, that he loves you, that he has power over your problems—by doing some great thing that would undeniably reveal his presence? We've all felt that way, particularly in times when we realize that we don't have much or any control over negative circumstances. Perhaps this is why serious illness, either our own or that of a loved one, often brings out both the greatest faith in God and the greatest frustration with him.

Experiences of this kind test not only our faith in God but also our very understanding of faith itself. While we may think that some personalized, visible sign of God's existence and power would make our faith stronger, the author of Hebrews defines faith as "confidence in what we hope for and assurance about what we do not see" (11:1). If faith is indeed belief in something we have not yet achieved or experienced, would some visible "proof" of God's existence actually make our faith stronger, or would it simply turn faith into a form of scientific knowledge? And if we wonder why God has not answered our prayers for healing, does our disappointment mean that we really don't believe in him?

Today's lesson tells of an encounter between Jesus and a man who was very much like many of us. The man was a Roman soldier, a person who doubtless had faced death on many occasions. But one day he found himself standing helplessly by the bedside of a beloved household member whose life was ebbing away. Circumstances of this kind can be the truest test of one's heart and convictions.

B. Lesson Background

The Bible records many stories in which Jesus heals someone, and two aspects of today's passage are unusual in that regard. One relates to the nature of the healing itself. Luke 7:1-10 is one of only three instances recorded where Jesus healed someone from a distance—that is, the person who was healed was not in the presence of Jesus when the healing occurred. (The other two distance-healings are recorded in Matthew 15:21-28 and John 4:46-54; some students think the account in John and that in today's text are one and the same, but that is doubtful.)

The second unusual aspect relates to the nature of the individual who requested the healing in today's lesson: he was a Gentile, and a Roman centurion at that. The Gospels very rarely show Jesus interacting with Gentiles, and in fact record him stating that his mission was focused on Israel (Matthew 10:5, 6; 15:24-26).

A centurion was a Roman officer in command of a company of 100 soldiers (compare the English word *century,* a span of 100 years). The Romans began to rule over the land of Israel in 63 BC, and in Jesus' day the Roman army was an occupation force that maintained law and order. Units of soldiers, commanded by centurions and stationed in local neighborhoods, were the backbone of Rome's program to control the Jewish population.

I. Faith That Asks
(LUKE 7:1-8)

A. Centurion's Request (vv. 1-3)

1. When Jesus had finished saying all this to the people who were listening, he entered Capernaum.

The fact that Jesus has *finished saying all this to the people* indicates a transition from the events of Luke 6:17-49, which records his famous Sermon on the Plain. This may suggest that what now follows will illustrate some of the key principles from that sermon (see the Conclusion).

The large village of *Capernaum* (population of about 1,500) is located on the northern shore of

HOW TO SAY IT

Capernaum	Kuh-*per*-nay-um.
centurion	sen-*ture*-ee-un.
Cornelius	Cor-*neel*-yus.
Gentiles	*Jen*-tiles.
Israelites	*Iz*-ray-el-ites.
Nebuzaradan	*Neb*-you-zar-*a*-dun.
synagogue	*sin*-uh-gog.

the Sea of Galilee. Its importance is seen in the fact that it is mentioned 16 times in the Gospels. Capernaum serves as something of a headquarters for Jesus during his Galilean ministry (Matthew 4:13; Mark 2:1).

2. There a centurion's servant, whom his master valued highly, was sick and about to die.

This verse provides three key pieces of information that set the stage for the remainder of the story. First, the person who is about to ask Jesus for help is a centurion, a Gentile in the service of the Roman Empire, assigned to help keep the Jews in line (see the Lesson Background).

Second, this Gentile has a servant who is very ill. The precise nature of the affliction is not stated in Luke's account, but Matthew 8:6 notes that the servant "lies at home paralyzed, suffering terribly." Luke stresses the severity of the situation: the servant is on the verge of death, so time is short.

That urgency is enhanced by a third piece of information: the centurion holds this particular servant in very high esteem. Servants in the Roman world are considered members of their master's household, living and working closely with the family. In verse 7, below, Luke uses a Greek word for *servant* that is often translated "child" elsewhere (the same term is used throughout Matthew's version of the story; see Matthew 8:6, 8, 13). The servant in question, then, may be a child born into the centurion's household and reared with his own children, as is typical in that culture. The stakes are therefore very personal for this centurion!

What Do You Think?
  How can you contribute to your church's ministry to those who are on the verge of death?
Talking Points for Your Discussion
  ▪ Regarding ministry to unbelievers
  ▪ Regarding ministry to fellow Christians

---

3. The centurion heard of Jesus and sent some elders of the Jews to him, asking him to come and heal his servant.

Jesus has already performed numerous miracles in Capernaum by this time (Luke 4:23, 31-41). Therefore it is likely that the centurion, a resident of the village, is already aware of, or has even seen, Jesus' displays of power. In that case, *heard of* means something like, "he heard that Jesus was back in town." On the other hand, the language of this verse may mean that the man has merely "heard reports about" Jesus. In that case, the centurion's faith is even more impressive, being based entirely on the testimony of others.

Either way, the centurion's actions here very much reflect the culture and customs of the Roman empire. Following the rules of Rome's complex system of patronage, a Gentile would not presume to approach an influential Jewish rabbi and holy man like Jesus with a direct request. Instead, the centurion directs his appeal through *some elders of the Jews* (that is, the leaders of the Jewish community in Capernaum) with whom he regularly interacts, asking them to serve as intermediaries between himself and Jesus.

What Do You Think?

Under what circumstances should you agree to a request to intercede on another's behalf? Why?

Talking Points for Your Discussion

- Considering the motive of the one asking
- Considering the possible consequences in not doing so
- Other

❧ *GOING TO JESUS FIRST* ❧

A mother walks the floor with a feverish toddler. A caregiver keeps vigil at the bedside of a confused elderly woman. A neighbor has just been diagnosed with a rare form of cancer. People everywhere, every day, experience these and other distressing circumstances of health. And, naturally, they look for solutions.

When difficulties seem to multiply around us, we may begin to wonder when our turn is coming. And when it does come, how will we deal with it? Will our first thought be of a famous medical center that handles the kind of problem we have? After we've first considered, and perhaps availed ourselves of, our sources of earthly help, do we then say something like, "I don't know anything else to do, so now I'll pray"?

Putting prayer somewhere other than at the very top of our list of priorities means we don't take our problems to Jesus first. That can be more of a temptation today than in the first century AD because we have available to us many more medical interventions than did the centurion of our story. Even so, we don't know whether Jesus was a first resort for him or a last resort; the text doesn't say (compare Mark 5:25-29). Although we don't have that information, the centurion still stands as a model of faith; Jesus himself said as much (Luke 7:9, below). The centurion knew who had the answer to his problem. Do we?   —C. M. W.

B. Centurion's Character (vv. 4, 5)

4, 5. When they came to Jesus, they pleaded earnestly with him, "This man deserves to have you do this, because he loves our nation and has built our synagogue."

It is important that these two verses not be misunderstood, lest they give a false impression to modern readers about the relationship between the centurion's character and the requested healing. The text is not suggesting here that the centurion's servant should be healed because the centurion is a particularly righteous man. Nor is it suggesting that God does not answer our prayers for healing because we are not good enough.

The point here is quite different. The Jewish leaders realize that Jesus is by now a famous rabbi; perhaps they also know that he does not typically include Gentiles in the scope of his ministry (see the Lesson Background). Therefore they may assume that he will reject their request out of hand simply because it comes from a Gentile.

Anticipating such an objection, the elders of the Jews immediately stress that the centurion is indeed a worthy person. Unfortunately, the NIV and other versions obscure this assertion with the translation *deserves* instead of *worthy*. In the culture of the day, the word being translated does not refer so much to a person's innate goodness or moral excellence as it does to the quality of one's actions.

The centurion doubtless has many flaws, but he has shown himself to be a friend of the Jews. This is a rare trait in a commander of an occupation force, and the elders thereby believe that this makes him eligible for a hearing with Jesus. To establish this point, the elders note that the man *has built our synagogue*, apparently providing financial resources and/or labor for its construction.

Overall, then, these verses do not portray the centurion as an especially spiritual man to be granted a miracle because he is unusually righteous. A centurion is, on the surface, someone far outside the realm of God's favor—a Gentile oppressor of God's people. This centurion's actions, however, reveal a faith that transcends his background. That, to these Jewish leaders, should make all the difference in a desperate situation.

> **What Do You Think?**
> How does your church respond to the needs of non-members, if at all? What can you do to assist in this area?
> **Talking Points for Your Discussion**
> - Regarding church policy
> - Regarding church procedure

C. Centurion's Confidence (vv. 6-8)

6, 7. So Jesus went with them.

He was not far from the house when the centurion sent friends to say to him: "Lord, don't trouble yourself, for I do not deserve to have you come under my roof. That is why I did not even consider myself worthy to come to you. But say the word, and my servant will be healed.

Having received a favorable response to his request, the centurion remarkably proceeds to challenge the very point that the Jewish elders have just made in his favor! In fact, he seems concerned that the elders have misrepresented him: the centurion never asked Jesus to come to his house, because he knows that he is, as he now says twice, unworthy to have a man like Jesus in his home. Having lived as a Gentile among Jews for some time, the centurion realizes by now that a proper Jewish rabbi regards him and his home to be unclean—certainly, Jesus would not make himself unclean to help a lowly Gentile!

We know from reading the Gospels that the centurion is misguided on this point. Jesus does

Visual for Lesson 5. *Point to this visual as you pose the discussion question that is associated with verse 9.*

indeed associate with sinful and unclean people—and is criticized for doing so (Luke 5:30; etc.). The centurion's further remarks, however, reveal his understanding of Jesus to be deeper than that of the Jews of the time. He knows that Jesus does not need to come to the house to heal the servant; Jesus can heal simply by speaking *the word* from a distance. The significance of this unusual request is highlighted when one considers how seldom Jesus performs healings of this kind (see the Lesson Background).

8. "For I myself am a man under authority, with soldiers under me. I tell this one, 'Go,' and he goes; and that one, 'Come,' and he comes. I say to my servant, 'Do this,' and he does it."

The centurion now proceeds to compare Jesus' spiritual authority with his own earthly authority. As an officer, the centurion need not be personally present at every place a job needs to be done; instead, he commands his subordinates. In a similar way, he knows Jesus is able to command the spiritual powers over which he has authority to come to the man's house and heal his servant.

While this line of thinking may seem a bit odd to modern readers, it is consistent with pagan understandings of the supernatural world, where gods and goddesses are presumed regularly to command deities lower on the totem pole to accomplish things in the human realm. Perhaps the centurion, having lived long among the Jews and having developed a faith in their God, has come to understand that God can command an army of angelic beings to carry out his plans.

Similarly, the man's plea may reflect his awareness of Jesus' power over demons. This could be evident from the exorcisms that Jesus has already performed, especially in Capernaum (see Luke 4:31-37). Whatever the nature of the servant's illness, Jesus can command an angel to attend to the need (compare Matthew 26:53). The centurion's analogy reveals a remarkable faith not only in God but also in Jesus himself—specifically, a faith that Christ has power over sickness and death.

> **What Do You Think?**
> When was a time that someone else's confident faith during a difficult situation helped you face a similar circumstance later?
>
> **Talking Points for Your Discussion**
> - Regarding a health crisis
> - Regarding a financial crisis
> - Regarding a relationship crisis
> - Other

II. Faith That Receives
(LUKE 7:9, 10)
A. Jesus' Astonishment (v. 9)

9. When Jesus heard this, he was amazed at him, and turning to the crowd following him, he said, "I tell you, I have not found such great faith even in Israel."

This verse reveals, in a poignant way, the human side of Christ—the part of him that is fully vested not only with a physical body but also with human emotions. Jesus is both surprised and frustrated. His surprise comes from the centurion's faith in God's power to heal and, more significantly, from the man's perception of Jesus' identity and power. The surprise is magnified by the fact that the man is a Gentile—a person who has not grown up with an understanding of God or expecting a "Christ" to come.

Of the three cases where Jesus heals from a distance (see the Lesson Background), this is the only one where someone asks him to do so. The startling nature of the request is highlighted by the fact that the centurion himself does not actually meet Jesus to make the request. All this time, he has remained at home and communicated through Jewish elders and friends (vv. 3, 6, above).

Jesus' pleasant surprise, however, is accompanied by an unfavorable comparison that reflects his ongoing frustration: Why won't his own people, the Jews, believe in him? On earlier occasions, Jesus was almost killed by a mob in his hometown of Nazareth (Luke 4:16-30), has been confronted by Pharisees and other experts on the Law of Moses for claiming to forgive sins and for breaking the Sabbath (5:17-26; 6:1-11), and was criticized for fraternizing with tax collectors and sinners (5:27-32). In the eyes of his own people, Jesus apparently can do nothing right. Yet here is a Gentile who understands the implications of Jesus' actions!

❧ SURPRISING PEOPLE ❧

The Bible is full of surprises, things we don't expect given our day-to-day experiences. One category of surprises is that of foreign soldiers who seem to be more in tune with the things of God than are God's own covenant people.

Consider the case of Nebuzaradan, commander of the imperial guard of the Babylonian army. The prophet Jeremiah had warned the people of Jerusalem time and again of coming disaster. But his warnings fell on deaf ears, and he was imprisoned for daring to make such predictions. Nebuzaradan was the one to release him, revealing in the process an understanding of God's will (Jeremiah 40:1-3).

Another case is that of the centurion named Cornelius, about whom an angel declared, "Your prayers and gifts to the poor have come up as a memorial offering before God" (Acts 10:4). Cornelius became privileged to be the starting point for expansion of the gospel to the Gentiles after Jesus' ascension. Earlier, some Roman soldiers had come in repentance to John the Baptist (Luke 3:14). An unnamed centurion exclaimed at Jesus' death, "Surely this man was the Son of God!" (Mark 15:39). That declaration may have been more from fear than from faith, but even so it showed a respect for Jesus that the Jewish leaders certainly did not exhibit on that day.

Just as the Bible surprises us in this way, so may life today. We can find ourselves startled by the faith we find in some people. Our task is to be ready to affirm that faith and help it grow.

—R. L. N.

B. Servant's Healing (v. 10)

10. Then the men who had been sent returned to the house and found the servant well.

One can only imagine the centurion's reaction when he realizes that his request has been granted! The healing actually occurs before the friends he had sent to Jesus return *to the house* and therefore presumably before the centurion has learned of Jesus' verbal response to his plea.

Conclusion

A. Understanding Genuine Faith

Several themes from Jesus' Sermon on the Plain (Luke 6:17-49) are reflected in today's lesson. In that sermon, Jesus pronounced blessings on those who grieve (as the centurion was doing; compare v. 21b) and are hated (as the centurion would have been hated by many Jews; compare v. 22a). Jesus also taught people to love their enemies and do good for them, because this is how God himself treats all people (note the love of the centurion for Israel as described by the Jewish elders; compare vv. 27-36).

Further, Jesus' Sermon on the Plain noted that people, like trees, define themselves by the "fruit" (behavior) they produce (as the centurion revealed his true nature through his actions; compare Luke 6:43-45). Jesus went on to instruct that the wise person builds life on his teaching, just as a wise builder lays the foundation of his house on rock rather than sand (and as the centurion placed trust in Jesus; compare vv. 46-49).

Such connections would have been quite unexpected in Jesus' day in view of the fact that the centurion was a Gentile and a servant of the Roman Empire—someone whom devout Jews would not normally view as a candidate either for God's love or their own. All these thematic connections sharpen the point of our story: you can't judge a book by its cover. As Jesus himself declared, "I have not found such great faith even in Israel." May our faith match that of the centurion's!

B. Accepting God's *No*

Fortunately for the centurion and his servant, our story has a happy ending: healing was needed, healing was granted, and the servant was saved from death. As we all know from experience, however, the outcome isn't always so positive. All the faith in the world has never kept, nor can ever keep, a person alive indefinitely. Sometime after the events of Luke 7, the centurion's servant did indeed die as all humans eventually do. At that time, no amount of prayer could have saved him, as we know from the simple fact that that individual is not alive today. Sometimes God says *no*, and when it comes to health issues, he always says *no* in the end.

Rather than being a source of discouragement, the fact that faithful people can't always pray someone out of the hospital should help us better understand the point of stories like today's. While faith can be powerful to effect healing, the main issue for God isn't the healing; it's the faith. The real victory for the centurion in today's passage did not come when Jesus healed his servant, but before the healing: the centurion had already proven his faith by believing before Jesus answered his request.

C. Prayer

Father, give us the strength to trust you even in the most difficult times and a faith that remains hopeful in the face of every obstacle. We pray in Jesus' name. Amen.

D. Thought to Remember

"Faith is not belief without proof, but trust without reservation." —Elton Trueblood (1900–1994)

INVOLVEMENT LEARNING

Enhance your lesson with NIV® Bible Student *(from your curriculum supplier) and the reproducible activity page (at www.standardlesson.com or in the back of the* NIV® Standard Lesson Commentary Deluxe Edition*).*

Into the Lesson

Invite someone who has recovered from a serious illness or injury to share a two-minute testimony in that regard. Request that the focus be on the strengthening of his or her faith prior to and during recovery. Then ask another who suffers currently from a chronic ailment to offer a two-minute testimony. Request that the focus be on the strengthening of his or her faith when prayers do not result in the desired outcome.

Next, form small groups of three or four to discuss the similarities and differences between the testimonies. This should naturally result in learners sharing how God has strengthened their own faith during difficult times. Make a transition by saying, "Today we will consider an individual whose unexpected faith serves as a model for faith being 'confidence in what we hope for and assurance about what we do not see,' as Hebrew 11:1 puts it."

Into the Word

Say, "The setting of our lesson is Capernaum, a village where Jesus had previously performed miracles." Summarize those per Luke 4:23, 31-41. Continue: "The people there were familiar with Jesus' healing power, but we don't know whether the Gentile in today's story had witnessed that power himself or had only heard about it. Either way, his faith was remarkable, given that he was a Roman centurion." Explain the status of a centurion and the relationship between the Roman Empire and Israel in the first century AD (see Lesson Background).

Recruit learners in advance to dramatize the parts of Jesus, an elder (or elders) of the Jews, and a friend (or friends) of the centurion. An additional learner, remaining seated, will take the part of the narrator. The assigned text segments from Luke 7 are verses 1-4a, 6a, 9a, 10 for the narrator; verses 4b, 5 for elder(s) of the Jews; verses 6b-8 for friend(s) of the centurion; and verse 9b for Jesus. If you recruit learners to represent more than one

elder and/or friend of the centurion, those "extra" participants will remain silent while nodding in agreement at appropriate times. Encourage participants to add dramatic elements as appropriate.

Next, pose these questions for discussion: 1. Why did the centurion send the elders of the Jews to Jesus rather than come himself? 2. Why did the centurion believe he was not worthy to have Jesus come to his home? 3. Why did the centurion believe that Jesus could heal the servant? When discussing question 1, be prepared for someone to mention Matthew 8:5, 6, which has the centurion making the request without intermediaries. (When someone used intermediaries to deliver a message in that era, it had the same force as doing so personally.)

Following that discussion, lead the class in comparing and contrasting the reason the elders of the Jews were impressed by the centurion with the reason Jesus was impressed by that man. Note that the centurion demonstrated a faith that transcended his background as a Gentile.

Option. Form learners into pairs to complete the "Jesus Heals at a Distance" activity from the reproducible page, which you can download. Following completion, discuss as a class how faith characterizes each story.

Into Life

Have learners return to the small groups of the Into the Lesson segment. Encourage learners to discuss areas in their lives where healing is needed (spiritual, physical, or emotional) or situations where faith in God is a struggle (job security, relationships, etc.). Groups can further discuss (1) how to have faith in God's power even though he cannot be seen and (2) how to have strength when his response is other than what is desired.

Option. Distribute copies of the "My Prayer, from a Distance" activity from the reproducible page to be completed as indicated.

SHAMELESS FAITH

DEVOTIONAL READING: Psalm 13
BACKGROUND SCRIPTURE: Luke 7:36-50

LUKE 7:36-50

³⁶ When one of the Pharisees invited Jesus to have dinner with him, he went to the Pharisee's house and reclined at the table. ³⁷ A woman in that town who lived a sinful life learned that Jesus was eating at the Pharisee's house, so she came there with an alabaster jar of perfume. ³⁸ As she stood behind him at his feet weeping, she began to wet his feet with her tears. Then she wiped them with her hair, kissed them and poured perfume on them.

³⁹ When the Pharisee who had invited him saw this, he said to himself, "If this man were a prophet, he would know who is touching him and what kind of woman she is—that she is a sinner."

⁴⁰ Jesus answered him, "Simon, I have something to tell you."

"Tell me, teacher," he said.

⁴¹ "Two people owed money to a certain moneylender. One owed him five hundred denarii, and the other fifty. ⁴² Neither of them had the money to pay him back, so he forgave the debts of both. Now which of them will love him more?"

⁴³ Simon replied, "I suppose the one who had the bigger debt forgiven."

"You have judged correctly," Jesus said.

⁴⁴ Then he turned toward the woman and said to Simon, "Do you see this woman? I came into your house. You did not give me any water for my feet, but she wet my feet with her tears and wiped them with her hair. ⁴⁵ You did not give me a kiss, but this woman, from the time I entered, has not stopped kissing my feet. ⁴⁶ You did not put oil on my head, but she has poured perfume on my feet. ⁴⁷ Therefore, I tell you, her many sins have been forgiven—as her great love has shown. But whoever has been forgiven little loves little."

⁴⁸ Then Jesus said to her, "Your sins are forgiven."

⁴⁹ The other guests began to say among themselves, "Who is this who even forgives sins?"

⁵⁰ Jesus said to the woman, "Your faith has saved you; go in peace."

KEY VERSE

"I tell you, her many sins have been forgiven—as her great love has shown. But whoever has been forgiven little loves little." —**Luke 7:47**

The Gift of Faith

Unit 2: Restorative Faith

Lessons 5–8

Lesson Aims

After participating in this lesson, each learner will be able to:

1. Summarize the account of Jesus' anointing by a sinful woman.

2. Compare what the woman did for Jesus and what Jesus said Simon failed to do with modern expressions of devotion to Christ.

3. Role-play the scenario of today's text in a modern setting.

Lesson Outline

Introduction
  A. Shameful Behavior, Shameless Faith
  B. Lesson Background
 I. The Saint and the Sinner (LUKE 7:36-39)
  A. Pharisee's House (v. 36)
  B. Woman's Actions (vv. 37, 38)
    Grateful Response
  C. Pharisee's Thoughts (v. 39)
 II. The Two Debtors (LUKE 7:40-43)
  A. Probing Question (vv. 40-42)
  B. Correct Answer (v. 43)
 III. Faith That Saves (LUKE 7:44-50)
  A. Proof of Change (vv. 44-47)
  B. Declarations by Jesus (vv. 48-50)
    Modeling Grace
Conclusion
  A. What Would You Do?
  B. Prayer
  C. Thought to Remember

Introduction

A. Shameful Behavior, Shameless Faith

If we were to create a "top 10" list of shameful behaviors that have occurred throughout history, the buying and selling of slaves would undoubtedly be on it. One name that is indelibly linked to that practice is John Newton (1725–1807).

Newton's father, a sea captain, took John to sea at the early age of 11—he literally grew up on ships, among sailors, and in ports of call. When he became a sea captain himself, Newton was actively involved in the slave trade from 1748 to 1754. He struggled to find peace with himself and with God throughout that period. Things changed, however, when he suffered a stroke.

Following that brush with death, Newton left that business and began serving as a lay minister, eventually becoming a highly respected Anglican preacher. In 1788, having served the church for some 30 years, Newton published an influential exposé of the horrors of the slave trade. This served as a public confession of his shame and sorrow at his former involvement in that sordid business.

Newton's vibrant preaching, emphasis on pastoral care, and focus on God's mercy made him one of the most prominent churchmen of his day. His life stands as a fitting example of how shameful behavior can give way to shameless faith. The lyrics to the hymn "Amazing Grace," which Newton authored, are part of his enduring legacy. It is a legacy that testifies to God's acceptance of the vilest sinner, as today's lesson does.

B. Lesson Background

Today's text sets forth one of many stories in the Gospels that play on the contrast between two types of people: *the saint* and *the sinner*. We use those two categories somewhat loosely since they are not mutually exclusive (example: Christians are both saints [the word used in other translations of Romans 1:7; 16:15; etc.] and sinners [3:23; 5:12]). Jesus regularly associated with both types, and—much to the surprise of his contemporaries, even his disciples—he praised and encouraged penitent sinners while blasting those whom most devout Jews admired as models of saintly faithfulness.

Jesus' parables often contrast a stereotypically "righteous" person with someone whom most would view as an unlikely candidate for salvation. Examples include the parables of the good Samaritan (Luke 10:30-37), the prodigal son (15:11-32), and the Pharisee and the tax collector (18:9-14). In context, Jesus used such stories to make two critical points: (1) God forgives those who trust in his grace, regardless of how sinful they have been, and (2) since God himself forgives sinners who repent, Jesus expects his followers to do the same.

The text of today's lesson stands out for the extreme nature of its contrast between a person thought to be one of the most righteous and another viewed as being one of the most sinful. (Some propose that this incident is the same as that recorded in Matthew 26:6, 7 and its parallels in Mark 14:3 and John 12:1-3, but that is unlikely.)

I. The Saint and the Sinner
(LUKE 7:36-39)
A. Pharisee's House (v. 36)

36. When one of the Pharisees invited Jesus to have dinner with him, he went to the Pharisee's house and reclined at the table.

This verse sets the stage by introducing the "saint" in the story. *The Pharisees* constitute a Jewish sect that is widely respected for strict commitment to the Law of Moses and personal purity. Whatever might compromise a Pharisee's ritual or moral integrity—any thing, activity, or person that might make him "unclean" in God's sight—is carefully avoided.

As a result, the masses widely regard the Pharisees as spiritual leaders, and Pharisees often hold prominent positions as teachers and leaders in synagogues across the Roman world. This is particularly so in the environs of Judea and Galilee, Jesus' home turf. Although Jesus has very negative things to say about Pharisees at times (Matthew 23; etc.), it is important to stress that today's text does not assume that this particular Pharisee is a closet sinner. Simon, his name per Luke 7:40, is presumably a respected figure in his community, with his life being very much in keeping with the Scriptures and Jewish traditions.

Simon's motive for inviting Jesus to dinner is unclear. On the surface, one can readily understand why a local religious leader would invite a traveling celebrity to a meal. It seems likely, however, that Simon's agenda is not entirely one of hospitality, since Pharisees have attempted to discredit Jesus on other occasions up to this point in his ministry (see Luke 6:7; etc.).

B. Woman's Actions (vv. 37, 38)

37. A woman in that town who lived a sinful life learned that Jesus was eating at the Pharisee's house, so she came there with an alabaster jar of perfume.

Luke now introduces the sinner in a dramatic way. In Jesus' time, meals are normally eaten in a reclining position: diners lie on low couches or mats with their heads facing the table and feet generally pointing away. As Jesus and Simon converse in this posture, a woman enters *the Pharisee's house*. Luke's description of her as someone *who lived a sinful life* and Simon's immediate recognition of her as a notorious figure in his community (v. 39, below) strongly suggest that she is a prostitute.

Apparently, this woman has heard of Jesus and knows of his reputation as a rabbi who associates with all classes of people (Luke 5:27-32; etc.). The fact that she brings *an alabaster jar of perfume* indicates a considerable investment of money on her part regarding what she intends to do (next verse).

> *What Do You Think?*
> How does the cost and nature of the woman's gift speak, if at all, to what our own giving should be like?
> *Talking Points for Your Discussion*
> - Regarding the motive (Matthew 5:14-16; 6:1-4; John 12:3-8; Acts 5:1-11; etc.)
> - Regarding the amount (Matthew 2:11; Mark 12:41-44; 1 Corinthians 16:2; etc.)
> - Other

38. As she stood behind him at his feet weeping, she began to wet his feet with her tears. Then she wiped them with her hair, kissed them and poured perfume on them.

The remainder of the scene reflects the awkwardness of the encounter. The woman has not come to engage in doctrinal discussion with prominent religious leaders over dinner. Rather, she is here to express contrition to Jesus in the best way she knows how. We easily imagine the room falling silent except for the sound of the woman's weeping as Simon and others who may be present look on with various mixtures of embarrassment, disbelief, annoyance, pity, disdain, etc.

The woman's lack of propriety and willingness to humiliate herself publicly underline her sincerity. We may wonder what, if anything, Jesus has already done for this woman to draw such a reaction from her. Has he cured her of some disease or freed her from demon possession? The text doesn't say. But that's not really important to the point of the story, as we shall see.

❧ GRATEFUL RESPONSE ❧

After the fall of the Soviet Union, churches in Ukraine grew exponentially. They began meeting in theaters and public buildings. One group of believers learned about a school building that they could purchase as a permanent worship facility. They did not have enough money to do so, but they knew they had to act quickly.

Missionaries sent an envoy back home to raise funds from supporters. Even so, the Ukrainian believers did not wait for churches from afar to provide the money. They forged ahead by contributing as much as they could from their salaries. When that did not suffice, they began to sell their possessions. They sold living-room rugs. They pawned wedding rings. Some even removed gold and silver teeth to sell the metal!

These people knew about God's grace. Many had grown up hearing that God did not exist. Some had worked actively against Christians during the Communist era. But having experienced God's love, they responded extravagantly like the woman in today's story. Their sacrifices spurred brothers and sisters across the ocean into giving as well. Before long, the congregation had purchased the building, which now stands as a testimony of gratefulness for God's grace. What does your giving say about your level of gratitude? —L. L. W.

C. Pharisee's Thoughts (v. 39)

39. When the Pharisee who had invited him saw this, he said to himself, "If this man were a prophet, he would know who is touching him and what kind of woman she is—that she is a sinner."

Simon says nothing. But as he watches the scene unfold, he immediately comes to the only conclusion he can, given his religious outlook and frame of mind. No true prophet would voluntarily allow himself to become unclean by letting a notoriously sinful person touch him. Since Jesus is in fact allowing physical contact by this *kind of woman*, then Jesus must not be a prophet, despite all popular claims to the contrary (see Luke 7:16). Or so Simon thinks.

> **What Do You Think?**
> What can we do to ensure that physical contact with another is appropriate to the context?
> *Talking Points for Your Discussion*
> ▪ When others are present
> ▪ When others are not present

Luke has already highlighted the stark contrast between *the Pharisee* (Simon) and the woman—one a model of spirituality, the other a desperate sinner. Now, however, Luke sets the stage for Simon to be contrasted with Jesus on the basis of the way that each reacts to the woman.

II. The Two Debtors
(LUKE 7:40-43)

A. Probing Question (vv. 40-42)

40, 41. Jesus answered him, "Simon, I have something to tell you."

"Tell me, teacher," he said.

"Two people owed money to a certain moneylender. One owed him five hundred denarii, and the other fifty.

Jesus, having divine insight into what Simon is thinking, begins to correct the man's attitude toward both "sinners" and Jesus himself. But rather than merely say something like, "Simon, you're wrong and here's why," Jesus introduces a parable to lead Simon to arrive at the correct conclusion on his own. As Simon listens to the story about three hypothetical people—*a certain money-lender* and two debtors, one of whom owes the creditor 10 times as much as the other—he will find himself challenged to match up their identities with people in reality.

42. "Neither of them had the money to pay him back, so he forgave the debts of both. Now which of them will love him more?"

Much to the surprise of the debtors (not stated but easy to imagine), the creditor simply forgives their debts! This is most unusual, as anyone with a mortgage or car loan can attest. Although the parable itself seems to focus on the unusual action of the creditor, Jesus' question directs Simon's attention to the anticipated reactions of the debtors.

B. Correct Answer (v. 43)

43. Simon replied, "I suppose the one who had the bigger debt forgiven."

"You have judged correctly," Jesus said.

The point of the analogy relates to the position of the debtors: lenders have the upper hand, and borrowers are at creditors' mercy (see Proverbs 22:7). Similarly, sin puts the sinner in God's debt, a position where we can only acknowledge that we owe him something.

Following this logic, the relevance of the parable is clear: the woman is very deeply in debt to God. The Pharisee, by contrast, has generally done what the law calls him to do. He has tried to live a life pleasing to God. The issue, however, is not whether God can or will forgive either of them—in the parable, both are forgiven—but rather the way that each responds when he does.

Simon undoubtedly thinks he is playing into a trap. But the answer to Jesus' question is so obvious that he is compelled to voice it, grudgingly we imagine. While anyone would be happy to have a debt forgiven, the person who owes more will feel

HOW TO SAY IT

denarii	dih-*nair*-ee or dih-*nair*-eye.
denarius	dih-*nair*-ee-us.
Pharisees	*Fair*-ih-seez.

Visual for
Lessons 6 & 11

Point to this visual to introduce your discussion of verse 47.

greater relief and appreciation. The word translated "denarii" in verse 41 refers to a typical day's wages for a laborer. To owe 500 days' wages represents a crushing, impossible debt for most people in Jesus' time. The removal of such a burden would bring greater relief and thankfulness than removal of a debt-burden of 50 days' wages.

III. Faith That Saves
(LUKE 7:44-50)
A. Proof of Change (vv. 44-47)

44. Then he turned toward the woman and said to Simon, "Do you see this woman? I came into your house. You did not give me any water for my feet, but she wet my feet with her tears and wiped them with her hair.

Many of Jesus' teachings and accounts of his ministry involve a contrast between a saint and a sinner that reverses common understanding—the sinner is the one who is really the saint in the end (example: Luke 18:9-14, lesson 11). The remainder of our passage depicts this reversal in dramatic form as a judgment against the saint that the parable represents: Simon the Pharisee.

If righteousness is measured on a scale of grateful humility, then Simon has little to show for himself. While earlier it was mentioned that Simon has invited Jesus to dinner, we now learn that the host's hospitality is in fact very restrained. People in his culture typically wash their feet upon entering someone's home simply because the dusty streets and open sandals make for dirty feet. Yet Simon has not given Jesus water for his feet, let alone having washed them himself. This is in stark contrast with the woman's lavish gestures of appreciation. She not only washes Jesus' feet, she provides her own water in the form of her tears and provides her own towel in the form of her hair!

> **What Do You Think?**
> What are some ways to ensure that we welcome Jesus into our homes in the best way possible?
> *Talking Points for Your Discussion*
> - Regarding what is heard in our homes
> - Regarding what is seen in our homes

45. "You did not give me a kiss, but this woman, from the time I entered, has not stopped kissing my feet.

In the culture of Jesus' day (and in some modern cultures), it is common for friends to greet one another by embracing and kissing on the cheek. This practice carries into the first-century church in the form of the "holy kiss" that Paul mentions in his letters (see Romans 16:16; 1 Corinthians 16:20; 2 Corinthians 13:12; 1 Thessalonians 5:26). Simon had not offered Jesus this welcome, apparently snubbing him while at the same time hosting him as a dinner guest! The woman, by contrast, has kissed Jesus' feet, an ultimate gesture of humility.

46. "You did not put oil on my head, but she has poured perfume on my feet.

Perfumed oils in antiquity are luxuries that might be exchanged between close friends. Since Simon does not know Jesus well, we perhaps are not surprised that Simon has not offered such a luxury to Jesus. This fact, however, serves to make the woman's willingness to use her ointment on Jesus' feet all the more striking. Viewed through the lens of love, the woman, who seems to realize the seriousness of her sin as it corresponds with the depth of Christ's mercy, shows greater awareness than the Pharisee.

47. "Therefore, I tell you, her many sins have been forgiven—as her great love has shown. But whoever has been forgiven little loves little."

Jesus now pronounces a judgment, which implicitly encourages Simon to repent. The woman, like the person who owed 500 days' wages, loves much because she has been forgiven much—she senses Jesus' ability to remove her huge load of sin-debt, and she is deeply appreciative.

The last line of the verse before us says less about the state of Simon's salvation than it does regarding the state of his heart. He exhibits little love. Thinking of oneself as having little if anything of which to be forgiven leads to a sense of self-righteousness. In chain reaction, this results in viewing others condescendingly (see v. 39, above). The best scenario clearly would be to love much and be forgiven little because one has sinned little. This would mean avoiding sin while being grateful for God's mercy for the few sins not avoided. Simon fails in this regard.

B. Declarations by Jesus (vv. 48-50)

48, 49. Then Jesus said to her, "Your sins are forgiven." The other guests began to say among themselves, "Who is this who even forgives sins?"

Jesus normally faces a surprised response, as here, on occasions when he forgives sin (example: Luke 5:17-26). His detractors believe that only God can forgive sins, and they are correct in that belief. But they are blind to the fact that Jesus, being God in the flesh, has the authority to do so. The woman is indeed forgiven, and she can be confident of this fact even though she does not live up to the standards of the Pharisees. Her love for Jesus, shown through her humble service to him, stands in sharp contrast with the skepticism of the others present.

❧ MODELING GRACE ❧

There she stood in front of the congregation confessing her sin. She couldn't have been older than 15 because she did not yet have a driver's license. "I want to raise my baby," she said. "I know I'll need your help; I hope you can forgive me."

Silence reigned as she stood there in her father's embrace. I glanced at the faces of people I knew so well. I saw the woman who had been divorced twice. I saw the young man whose girlfriend had aborted their baby. Many had endured bumpy, sinful roads themselves—roads of their own creation. How would they react to this confession? I feared that they would overlook their own sins and shun her for hers.

Instead, people rose and went to the front of the auditorium. They surrounded her, hugged her, cried with her. Unlike Jesus, I did not have the ability to perceive if anyone had condemning thoughts similar to those of Simon the Pharisee. But I knew what I saw: Christians remembering God's forgiveness of their own sins and modeling that same grace to the scared girl.

That emotional night showed me the nature of grace better than a score of sermons could have. We mess up. Sometimes our sin hurts only ourselves; sometimes there is lots of collateral damage. But when we see sin and repentance in others, we can rise to the occasion and display the grace that God has shown us. May we do so until the Son returns in his glory!   —L. L. W.

What Do You Think?
What can churches do to ensure a proper balance in communicating God's willingness to forgive as well as his disapproval of sin?

Talking Points for Your Discussion
- In worship services
- In what the church leaders model
- In curriculum selection
- Other

---

50. Jesus said to the woman, "Your faith has saved you; go in peace."

The story ends with the most radical statement of all—even the woman must be surprised to hear it! Despite her many faults, she has shown true faith by casting herself at Jesus' feet. She has shown trust and love in a shameless, public way.

What Do You Think?
What difference does having the peace of God's forgiveness make in your life?

Talking Points for Your Discussion
- When you look at your past
- As you look to the future

Conclusion
A. What Would You Do?

Since 1982, many of us have seen the quirky series of TV ads that ask, "What would you do for a Klondike® Bar?" After leading with that question, the ads show individuals doing ridiculous, embarrassing things to earn one of the chocolate-covered ice cream treats. Copying the theme, Internet videos show people attempting embarrassing, even dangerous, stunts in order to get things such as Super Bowl tickets.

In one case, a pregnant woman offered to paint her stomach with a company logo for the tickets. Another person agreed to allow a ticket donor to destroy his beloved car. One couple offered that anyone who gave them tickets to the game could name their newborn baby. One man offered a kidney in exchange for tickets. What would you be willing to do for something you really wanted but couldn't get?

The wording of the question must be rearranged when it comes to forgiveness of sins and eternal life. In this case, the question is *What would God be willing to do for something we really need but couldn't get on our own?* What he was willing to do —and did do—was send his Son to die and pay the penalty of the sin-debt that we owe. On that basis, God offers forgiveness for even the worst sins. He clears our debts because the debts have been paid. Our response is to humble ourselves in realizing that we have thereby escaped having to pay that debt ourselves by eternal punishment. May our gratitude for this match that of the sinful woman in today's story!

B. Prayer

Father, show us the way to true humility in expressions of gratitude for what your Son has done. May we never try to construct an edifice of self-righteousness! We have sinned much; now may we love much. We pray in Jesus' name. Amen.

C. Thought to Remember
"He that cannot forgive others breaks the bridge over which he must pass himself."
—Thomas Fuller (1608–1661)

INVOLVEMENT LEARNING

Enhance your lesson with NIV® Bible Student (from your curriculum supplier) and the reproducible activity page (at www.standardlesson.com or in the back of the NIV® Standard Lesson Commentary Deluxe Edition).

Into the Lesson

Write the words *Saints* and *Sinners* on the board as column headings. Ask, "How does secular culture use these terms today?" Jot learners' responses under the appropriate word; be prepared to offer examples you have researched in advance. Follow this discussion by asking for examples of how the Bible uses those two terms. Be prepared to offer some examples if learners do not. (The word *saint[s]* occurs about a hundred times in the *King James Version*—Romans 12:13; 15:26; etc., but not at all in the *New International Version*; the word *sinner[s]* is a very common in both—Romans 3:7; 5:8; etc.)

Make a transition by saying, "Though we might be more apt to invite saints instead of sinners to our homes for dinner, today's lesson reveals Jesus' preference for dining with those labeled *sinners*. The reason was because he had 'not come to call the righteous, but sinners to repentance' (Luke 5:32). In fact, Jesus often regarded such people as entering the kingdom of God ahead of those thought to be saints (see Matthew 21:31)."

Into the Word

Ask a volunteer to read Luke 7:36-38. Say, "According to local awareness of this woman's lifestyle, she was known as 'a sinner.'" Have learners call out the actions of and information about the woman from the text. Jot responses on the board under the *Sinners* heading. Use the commentary to clarify the woman's lifestyle and actions. *Option:* for deeper study, compare and contrast the anointing in Luke 7:38 with the different one in Matthew 26:6, 7 and parallels in Mark 14:3; John 12:1-3.

Next, have a volunteer read Luke 7:39-43. After noting that a denarius was equivalent to a day's wages for a laborer, ask learners to identify who and what the nouns in the parable stand for in reality. (*Expected responses*: the creditor is God, the debtor owing 50 denarii is Simon, the debtor owing 500 denarii is the woman, and the

debt itself is what is owed to God because of sin.) *Option:* For deeper study, compare and contrast with Matthew 18:23-35.

Ask a volunteer to read Luke 7:44-50. Say, "As we note what the woman did, what did Simon fail to provide or do for Jesus?" Jot responses on the board under the appropriate heading. Say, "Today, we would find it odd for someone to wash another's feet at a dinner party. Even so, there are actions that demonstrate our thankfulness for forgiveness and our devotion to Christ. What are some of those?" Jot on the board actions of modern-day devotion to Christ as learners mention them. After each suggestion, ask, "How is that one equivalent in some way to what the woman did for Jesus?" *Option:* For deeper study, compare and contrast with John 13:5-17.

Option. Distribute copies of the "Jesus and the Pharisees" activity from the reproducible page, which you can download. Have learners complete it in pairs as indicated. Discuss.

Into Life

Call for volunteers to form two small groups to role-play today's lesson in a twenty-first century setting. (Some class members may wish to be spectators only.) Have the first group role-play today's lesson in such a way that the "sinner" is treated as the Pharisee thought she should be treated. Then have the second group role-play the lesson as Jesus actually treated her.

Discuss these questions: What was the difference between the two role-plays? How did it feel to see the "sinner" be treated as the Pharisee thought she should? How did it feel to see the "sinner" be treated with grace and forgiveness? What impact will these role-plays have on the way you relate to others?

Option. Distribute copies of the "Grace!" activity from the reproducible page. Allow learners time to complete as indicated.

RECOVERED FAITH

DEVOTIONAL READING: Philippians 2:1-11
BACKGROUND SCRIPTURE: Luke 8:26-39

LUKE 8:26-36

26 They sailed to the region of the Gerasenes, which is across the lake from Galilee. 27 When Jesus stepped ashore, he was met by a demon-possessed man from the town. For a long time this man had not worn clothes or lived in a house, but had lived in the tombs. 28 When he saw Jesus, he cried out and fell at his feet, shouting at the top of his voice, "What do you want with me, Jesus, Son of the Most High God? I beg you, don't torture me!" 29 For Jesus had commanded the impure spirit to come out of the man. Many times it had seized him, and though he was chained hand and foot and kept under guard, he had broken his chains and had been driven by the demon into solitary places.

30 Jesus asked him, "What is your name?"

"Legion," he replied, because many demons had gone into him. 31 And they begged Jesus repeatedly not to order them to go into the Abyss.

32 A large herd of pigs was feeding there on the hillside. The demons begged Jesus to let them go into the pigs, and he gave them permission. 33 When the demons came out of the man, they went into the pigs, and the herd rushed down the steep bank into the lake and was drowned.

34 When those tending the pigs saw what had happened, they ran off and reported this in the town and countryside, 35 and the people went out to see what had happened. When they came to Jesus, they found the man from whom the demons had gone out, sitting at Jesus' feet, dressed and in his right mind; and they were afraid. 36 Those who had seen it told the people how the demon-possessed man had been cured.

KEY VERSE

The people went out to see what had happened. When they came to Jesus, they found the man from whom the demons had gone out, sitting at Jesus' feet, dressed and in his right mind. —**Luke 8:35**

THE GIFT OF FAITH

Unit 2: Restorative Faith

LESSONS 5–8

LESSON AIMS

After participating in this lesson, each learner will be able to:

1. Outline the sequence of events concerning Jesus' interaction with the Gadarene demoniac.

2. Explain how the text contributes to his or her larger understanding of Jesus' identity and mission.

3. Write a prayer thanking God for the figurative demons that he has driven from his or her life.

LESSON OUTLINE

Introduction
    A. So, Where's My Joy?
    B. Lesson Background
  I. Conquering a Legion (LUKE 8:26-33)
    A. Trip by Boat (v. 26)
    B. Encounter While Ashore (v. 27)
    C. Reaction by Demoniac (vv. 28, 29)
    D. Superiority of Jesus (vv. 30-33)
      Remember Who Wins
  II. Restoring a Life (LUKE 8:34-36)
    A. Reactions by the Herdsmen (v. 34)
    B. Fear of the Situation (vv. 35, 36)
      Atheist Bumper Stickers
Conclusion
    A. On the Other Side of the Tunnel
    B. Prayer
    C. Thought to Remember

Introduction

A. So, Where's My Joy?

As a child and into her high-school years, Karen had been a happy and relatively carefree person. Following college, she started a career with a company that placed high priority on speed and success. She managed well through her 20s and early 30s, but hit a roadblock after marrying and having her first child.

She became depressed and conflicted after the baby came. Karen returned to work, but felt overwhelmed by the responsibilities of job and family. By the time she turned 40, Karen was experiencing bouts of depression on a regular basis. An underlying sense of guilt magnified these feelings. "I'm a Christian," she would tell her friends. "I'm supposed to be joyful in Christ. I don't know why I can't trust God and stop feeling so anxious." Sometimes when she felt particularly discouraged or helpless, she would challenge God in her prayers: "So, where's my joy?"

About 18 percent of the U.S. adult population suffers from some form of anxiety-related disorder, according to the Anxiety and Depression Association of America. For Christians, it seems that there should be an inverse correlation between these afflictions and one's level of faith, but often there is not. Today's lesson can help us get on the right track in that regard.

B. Lesson Background

Most modern readers of the Bible are aware that the land of Israel was controlled by the Roman Empire during Jesus' life. Israel was, however, on the extreme eastern edge of that empire, literally on the frontier of Rome's influence. Not far east of the Jordan River, one entered the Nabatean kingdom; this was where Paul fled for safety after becoming a Christian (see Galatians 1:17, where he refers to the region as "Arabia"). The Romans did not finally seize control of Nabatean-held areas until AD 106.

A bit farther north, an area known as the Decapolis (literally, "ten cities") was situated between the southeastern shore of the Sea of Galilee and a Nabatean-controlled area (compare

Mark 5:20; 7:31). The Decapolis was an independent but unofficial league of city-states. These municipalities were not under Rome's control but were allies of the empire. This area is where today's lesson is situated.

The heritage of the population of the Decapolis was very mixed: some inhabitants came from native Arabic people-groups; some were Greek and Roman colonists and business people; some had migrated from lands farther east (the old Persian and Babylonian empires); some were Jews who had moved to the eastern side of the lake. Despite the presence of the latter, Jesus had entered Gentile territory as we come to Luke 8:26. (Parallel accounts of today's encounter are found in Matthew 8:28-34 and Mark 5:1-16.)

I. Conquering a Legion
(LUKE 8:26-33)
A. Trip by Boat (v. 26)

26. They sailed to the region of the Gerasenes, which is across the lake from Galilee.

The word *they* refers to Jesus and the 12 disciples, the latter by now also designated as "apostles" (see Luke 6:13). The verses just prior to the one before us and the word *sailed* here make clear that their mode of travel is by boat.

The precise location of today's lesson has long been a point of debate, due to some variations in the naming of the area among the Gospels of Matthew, Mark, and Luke. The text before us says that the group arrives at *the country of the Gerasenes,* which matches Mark 5:1. But Matthew 8:28 refers to the area as being "the country of the Gadarenes." Actually, these refer to the same area, with the towns of Gerasa and Gadara (from which come the designations *Gerasenes* and *Gadarenes,* respectively) both located in the region.

The footnotes to Matthew 8:28; Mark 5:1; and Luke 8:26 in the NIV reveal certain manuscript variations in the spelling of these designations. But more significant than the exact designation of the area is its location on the map: being east of the Sea of Galilee, it lies outside the boundary of the Roman Empire and (mostly) outside the traditional borders of Israelite habitation (see the Lesson

Background). This is one of Jesus' rare trips into Gentile territory (compare Matthew 10:5; 15:24).

B. Encounter While Ashore (v. 27)

27. When Jesus stepped ashore, he was met by a demon-possessed man from the town. For a long time this man had not worn clothes or lived in a house, but had lived in the tombs.

Disembarking from the boat, Jesus experiences a strange welcome as he is confronted by a demonized man. Only Luke's account notes that this man's condition has existed for *a long time.* Apparently, there had been a time when the man was in control of himself, a time when he was not yet afflicted by demons. We presume we had lived a normal life in that earlier period, just like anyone else, with his family in the nearby village.

But things changed somewhere along the line, although none of the Gospel accounts tells us how the man came to be in the sad state we see him in here. Had he opened himself up to being demonized by participating in occult practices? We simply do not know. Rather than addressing any of that, Luke moves us right to his current status: the man now subsists—somehow—without the basics of clothes and housing.

We can imagine that at some point in his torment he stripped himself naked and ran from the town, only to end up milling about in a nearby cemetery. We do not know if he is Jewish, but the Law of Moses establishes that contact with a dead body makes one unclean (compare Leviticus 21:11; Numbers 5:2; 19:11; Matthew 23:27). This makes *the tombs* where the man dwells the most unclean place imaginable.

The social and psychological consequences of the man's bizarre behavior and lifestyle almost go without saying: the man clearly has no job, no social connections, etc. To be demonized does not always mean that one is driven to the fringes of society or becomes an outcast altogether (compare Luke 4:33, 34; 9:38, 39). But it does mean just that in this particular case. Everyone who knows or encounters the man fears him. He seems to be more animal than human, apparently incurable. He has fallen as low as anyone can. Of course, Jesus specializes in cases of this kind!

C. Reaction by Demonic (vv. 28, 29)

28. When he saw Jesus, he cried out and fell at his feet, shouting at the top of his voice, "What do you want with me, Jesus, Son of the Most High God? I beg you, don't torture me!"

What the disciples think as they observe the crazed man is not recorded. But whatever their level of anxiety, it certainly does not match the level of distress exhibited by the demons that indwell the man!

Here as elsewhere, the cause of their distress is quite interesting: the demons are well aware of Jesus' power; consequently, they fear what he may do to them. Jesus received a similar reaction in the exorcism of Luke 4:34. It is fascinating that the spiritual forces of darkness readily acknowledge Jesus' true identity as *Son of the Most High God* while the experts in the Law of Moses are unable or unwilling to do so (Luke 5:21; etc.).

29. For Jesus had commanded the impure spirit to come out of the man. Many times it had seized him, and though he was chained hand and foot and kept under guard, he had broken his chains and had been driven by the demon into solitary places.

Exorcisms both ancient and modern often involve elaborate, lengthy rituals that include the voicing of incantations, use of sacred objects and symbols, and applications of herbs and potions. Jesus, however, casts out demons simply by commanding them to leave. Of course, Jesus' power to heal would be no less miraculous if this man were mentally ill rather than demon-possessed. But a significant aspect of our story relates to the reality that Jesus can resolve even the most difficult problems—including problems that are not of a medical nature.

The verse before us offers details similar to those in Mark 5:4. The attempts to bind the demonized man with chains should not be seen as acts of cruelty. People apparently have tried to keep him from harming himself and others in the only way they know how. The man's symptoms of uncontrollable outbursts and a range of antisocial and self-destructive behaviors might be associated today with severe mental illness. Luke is clear, however, that this individual's problem is supernatural in nature: the man is controlled *by the demon.* The people of the first century know the difference between mental, physical, and spiritual afflictions (see Matthew 4:24).

D. Superiority of Jesus (vv. 30-33)

30. Jesus asked him, "What is your name?"
"Legion," he replied, because many demons had gone into him.

Names are viewed as symbols of identity and power in the ancient world. To know the true name of a supernatural being is thought to have power over that entity. For this reason, ancient exorcisms typically invoke names as a way to gain command over supernatural beings (compare Acts 19:13-16). Jesus, of course, doesn't really have to ask *What is your name?* because he already knows everything about the *many demons* that beset the man.

Jesus' question forces the demons to disclose that there are in fact many spirits indwelling the troubled man. *Legion* is the designation of a Roman military unit of up to 5,400 men. As the Roman legions had taken control of the land of Israel and oppressed its inhabitants, so also the demons have assumed total control over this helpless individual. Whether there are literally 5,400 demons or figuratively just lots and lots of them indwelling the man ultimately doesn't matter because they now meet their match.

31. And they begged Jesus repeatedly not to order them to go into the Abyss.

The word *Abyss* is a transliteration, meaning that the letters of the Greek word have merely been converted to their English-sounding equivalents. We also see this word in Revelation 9:1, 2, 11; 11:7; 17:8; 20:1, 3, but it is translated "the deep" in Romans 10:7. In the Revelation passages, *the Abyss* is a place where certain enemies of God are temporarily imprisoned. Following release from there, these enemies are defeated and thrown into "the lake of burning sulfur" (see Revelation 19:19–20:10; compare Matthew 25:41). The evil spirits who inhabit the man seem to be well aware of the fate that awaits them!

32. A large herd of pigs was feeding there on the hillside. The demons begged Jesus to let them go into the pigs, and he gave them permission.

The presence of *a large herd of pigs* is a further indication that Jesus and the disciples are in Gentile territory (see the Lesson Background) since pigs are unclean animals to Jews (Leviticus 11:7; Deuteronomy 14:8; see also Luke 15:15 in next week's lesson). When the demons beg him to send them *into the pigs,* Jesus grants their request. They realize that they cannot challenge Jesus' authority and power, so they bargain for the best possible outcome.

Doubtless the demons prefer to seek out one or more new human victims, but Jesus does not allow it. Their pitiful request to enter the unclean

animals—to become a legion of lowly pigs—shows how utterly powerless they are in Jesus' presence. Despite the impressive level of control over the man that the demons have exhibited, the showdown ends quickly. The fact that Jesus does not here or elsewhere send demons directly to "the Abyss" is consistent with his current mission not of meting out judgment (John 12:47) but of calling people to repent and warning of what will happen if they do not (see Matthew 13:24-30; Luke 13:1-8).

> *What Do You Think?*
> How do you draw strength from the fact that Jesus is greater than the one who is in the world (1 John 4:4)?
> *Talking Points for Your Discussion*
> - When facing challenges at work or school
> - When facing family challenges
> - When facing temptation
> - Considering Ephesians 6:12
> - Other

33. When the demons came out of the man, they went into the pigs, and the herd rushed down the steep bank into the lake and was drowned.

The dramatic conclusion to the one-sided battle underscores Christ's ability to defeat the forces of evil. The new home of the demons turns out to be quite temporary. They seem unable to control their new hosts: the herd immediately stampedes *down the steep bank into the lake* and drowns, forcing the demons to flee to unknown quarters. Mark 5:13 sets the number of pigs at "about two thousand," so that may indicate that at least that many demons are present if we assume at least one demon inhabits each pig.

❧ REMEMBER WHO WINS ❧

Cutting is self-injurious behavior that primarily affects young people who are trying to cope with problems. The preadolescent and teen years see 90 percent of this practice. Nearly half of those who engage in this behavior have been sexually abused, and females make up 60 percent of self-harmers. Self-injurious behavior may also present

HOW TO SAY IT

abyss	uh-*bis*.
demoniac	duh-*moe*-nee-ak.
Gadara	*Gad*-uh-ruh.
Gadarenes	*Gad*-uh-reens.
Galilee	*Gal*-uh-lee.
Gerasa	*Gur*-uh-suh.
Gerasenes	*Gur*-uh-seenz.
Nabatean	*Nab*-uh-*tee*-un.

itself in a young person (or anyone, for that matter) who engages in reckless driving, substance abuse, promiscuity, etc. Regardless of the form that self-injury takes, the problem is often evidence of intense emotional pain, a poor sense of self-worth, and frustration with seemingly unresolvable life situations.

The demonized man of today's lesson also engaged in self-destructive behavior. In this regard, Mark's account includes a detail that Luke's does not: "Night and day among the tombs and in the hills he would cry out and cut himself with stones" (Mark 5:5). Was he cutting himself voluntarily out of frustration with his inability to overcome the demons? Was this something the demons forced him to do? We don't know; the text does not say.

What we do know is that Jesus' healing of the man proved that God has power over all forces that may align against us, whether natural or supernatural. Jesus is still the one who can save us both from ourselves and from all other forces. "The seventy-two returned with joy and said, 'Lord, even the demons submit to us in your name.' He replied, 'I saw Satan fall like lightning from heaven'" (Luke 10:17, 18).

Whenever we find ourselves seemingly without hope, the first step back to wholeness is to remember that Jesus wins, not Satan. —C. R. B.

What Do You Think?

When was a time you saw God's power at work in a way you did not expect? How do you apply that lesson?

Talking Points for Your Discussion

- God's work in the life of an unbeliever
- God's work in the life of a Christian

II. Restoring a Life
(LUKE 8:34-36)

A. Reactions by the Herdsmen (v. 34)

34. When those tending the pigs saw what had happened, they ran off and reported this in the town and countryside,

Those tending the pigs are the herdsmen. What they witness makes a profound impression!

Whether or not they know the reason for the suicidal stampede is unclear. Mark 5:2 and Luke 8:27 seem to indicate that the exorcism takes place on the shoreline, while Mark 5:11 and Luke 8:32, 33 establish the location of the herd to be on an elevated area that Matthew 8:30 says is "some distance from them." So the two locations may be out of earshot from one another.

Even if the herdsmen have not been able to hear the conversation between Jesus and the demonized man, they certainly can see the result! So they depart quickly to report the incident to anyone *in the town and countryside* who will listen.

B. Fear of the Situation (vv. 35, 36)

35, 36. and the people went out to see what had happened. When they came to Jesus, they found the man from whom the demons had gone out, sitting at Jesus' feet, dressed and in his right mind; and they were afraid. Those who had seen it told the people how the demon-possessed man had been cured.

Those who come *to see what had happened* undoubtedly include the owners of the pigs. Those owners (who probably are not the herdsmen; compare John 10:12, 13) have just suffered a substantial loss financially, so it's natural to expect them to be among those who come to investigate.

In due course, they and others find Jesus talking with a familiar figure. The man who is now *sitting at Jesus' feet, dressed and in his right mind* is the very one who "had often been chained hand and foot" (Mark 5:4)! The witnesses at the scene, which include the disciples, relate the full story. The man's new condition, contrasting so markedly from what it was before, testifies to the totality of his cure.

Even so, the reaction of the crowd is troubling. Jesus has just offered a remarkable display of God's power, and at the very least the result solves a problem for those living nearby. The locals, however, are *afraid.* This is not fear in the positive sense of "reverential awe" of God (see Psalms 22:23; 33:8; 119:120; 130:4; Luke 5:26; 7:16), but rather fear in the negative sense of "apprehensiveness," of being alarmed to the point of wanting to have nothing to do with something.

The result is that "all the people of the region of the Gerasenes asked Jesus to leave them" (Luke 8:37, not in today's text). If most of the crowd is Gentile, they would tend to view Jesus as a powerful shaman or some kind of sorcerer—able to do great good but also great harm. They see both good and harm side by side in the case at hand: the cure of a man and the loss of a herd. In asking Jesus to leave, they reveal what concerns them more.

Visual for Lesson 7. *Start a discussion by pointing to this visual as you ask, "Why do people resist submitting their lives to Jesus today?"*

> **What Do You Think?**
> Under what circumstances should we investigate personally reports of what God is claimed to be doing somewhere? Why?
> *Talking Points for Your Discussion*
> - Regarding reports involving claims of miracles
> - Regarding reports not involving claims of miracles
> - Considering Romans 1:8-11; Acts 8:14
> - Other

❧ ATHEIST BUMPER STICKERS ❧

Have you seen any atheist bumper stickers lately? Here are just two:

Religion: You can't start a war without it!

Science flies you to the moon.
Religion flies you into buildings.

The latter connects religious belief with the tragedy of 9/11, of course. Neither of these two bumper stickers reveals any awareness of the distinction between proper and improper application of Christian principles, let alone acknowledging a distinction between Christianity and other religions.

We might be tempted to dismiss such sloganeering as mere whimsy. However, such expressions witness to a growing stridency on the part of atheists to overthrow Western culture's once-strong belief in the divine. An increasing number of people seem to find society's avowed trust in God to be a nuisance at best and a tyrannical excuse for evil at worst.

A similar attitude may have infected those who saw the aftermath of the healing of the demonized man. A great financial loss had been suffered in the drowning of 2,000 pigs. As the people

looked at the floating carcasses, the healed man, and Jesus, they seemed to realize that a force they could not control—a force that could inflict further financial ruin—was present. They found themselves face to face with God in the flesh, and they found the situation intolerable. Fear won out. Could that same sentiment be what's behind the strident atheism of today?   —C. R. B.

Conclusion
A. On the Other Side of the Tunnel

With Christ all things are possible! The demoniac in today's lesson had lived in a dark tunnel for a long time; through Christ, he finally came out into the light. Yet his calling was not to forget his past. Instead, Jesus sent him back to testify to the people who had seen his struggles, proclaiming God's power and mercy in rescuing him (Luke 8:39). Jesus calls us to do the same.

B. Prayer

Father, continue to grant us deliverance from the evil that would torment us! Help us also to bear the burdens of others so that they too may be shining examples of your Son's deliverance. We pray in Jesus' name. Amen.

C. Thought to Remember

Nothing can come against us
that God cannot defeat.

INVOLVEMENT LEARNING

Enhance your lesson with NIV® *Bible Student (from your curriculum supplier) and the reproducible activity page (at www.standardlesson.com or in the back of the* NIV® *Standard Lesson Commentary Deluxe Edition).*

Into the Lesson

Ask, "How do we know that the people of the first century AD knew the difference between *mental illness* and *demon possession*?" Challenge learners to back up their responses with Scripture. If no learner does so, mention Matthew 4:23, 24, which lists "demon-possessed" as distinct from other maladies. Note that mental illness (without demon possession) is mentioned also in 1 Samuel 21:13, 14; Daniel 4:31-36; and Acts 26:24, 25.

Make a transition by saying, "Today's story centers on a man who was not in his right mind; he was in desperate need of Christ's healing. The symptoms of his problem might sound similar to those of mental illness, but the problem was that he was possessed by demons. We should not confuse what the Bible describes as demon possession with mental illness. Even so, those who suffer from mental illness, or who have cared for those who do, will be able to empathize with the man in today's story and find hope in the outcome."

Into the Word

Say, "In Luke 9:1, 2, Jesus was about to send his disciples on a mission to preach and heal." Read that passage, then say, "Prior to that sending, Jesus demonstrated his power and authority over nature, disease, and death." Summarize quickly the events of Luke 8:22-25 (calming the storm) and 8:40-56 (raising a dead girl and healing a woman). Continue: "Between these accounts, Jesus demonstrated his lordship over the spirit world." Point out the location of the events of today's text on a map.

Have two learners read Luke 8:26-39 aloud, alternating verses. Review the text as a class by outlining on the board the events as recorded in Luke. Explain that this story is also recorded in Matthew and Mark, but each record has different details.

Divide the class in half. Assign Matthew 8:26-34 to one group and Mark 5:1-16 to the other. Ask each group to compare and contrast its assigned passage with Luke's account as outlined. After a few minutes, call for conclusions to be shared with the class as a whole. Use the information in the Lesson Background to add clarity.

Conclude the discussion by noting how the demon-possessed man identified Jesus (Luke 8:28; Matthew 8:29; Mark 5:7). Discuss why demons acknowledged Jesus' identity when so many Jews of the day seemed unable or unwilling to do so (John 10:20; etc.). Dig deeper by discussing how these accounts contribute to our own understanding of Jesus' identity and mission.

Option. Distribute copies of the "Traveling with Jesus" activity from the reproducible page, which you can download. After no more than one minute of individual work, have learners call out their conclusions. Compare and contrast results.

Into Life

State, "Demon possession seems to have been much more widespread in Jesus' culture than it is in our own, and Luke 10:18 may give the reason why. In any case, Jesus is in charge, not Satan. Jesus can handle seemingly impossible problems, including problems that do not originate in this world. Let's take a minute to write a two- or three-sentence prayer thanking God for the real and figurative demons (fear, anxiety, temptations, etc.) that he has driven from our lives." After learners do so, ask for volunteers to read theirs, but don't put anyone on the spot.

Option 1. Distribute copies of the "The Differences Christ Makes" activity from the reproducible page to be completed and discussed in groups of three.

Option 2. Invite a Christian mental health professional to suggest ways the church can assist in adding a spiritual component to the healing process of those being treated for mental illness. Discuss also how the church can assist primary caregivers of those suffering from Alzheimer's, etc.

TESTED
FAITH

DEVOTIONAL READING: Luke 15:1-7
BACKGROUND SCRIPTURE: Luke 15:11-32

LUKE 15:11-24

11 Jesus continued: "There was a man who had two sons. 12 The younger one said to his father, 'Father, give me my share of the estate.' So he divided his property between them.

13 "Not long after that, the younger son got together all he had, set off for a distant country and there squandered his wealth in wild living. 14 After he had spent everything, there was a severe famine in that whole country, and he began to be in need. 15 So he went and hired himself out to a citizen of that country, who sent him to his fields to feed pigs. 16 He longed to fill his stomach with the pods that the pigs were eating, but no one gave him anything.

17 "When he came to his senses, he said, 'How many of my father's hired servants have food to spare, and here I am starving to death! 18 I will set out and go back to my father and say to him: Father, I have sinned against heaven and against you. 19 I am no longer worthy to be called your son; make me like one of your hired servants.' 20 So he got up and went to his father.

"But while he was still a long way off, his father saw him and was filled with compassion for him; he ran to his son, threw his arms around him and kissed him.

21 "The son said to him, 'Father, I have sinned against heaven and against you. I am no longer worthy to be called your son.'

22 "But the father said to his servants, 'Quick! Bring the best robe and put it on him. Put a ring on his finger and sandals on his feet. 23 Bring the fattened calf and kill it. Let's have a feast and celebrate. 24 For this son of mine was dead and is alive again; he was lost and is found.' So they began to celebrate."

KEY VERSE

"This son of mine was dead and is alive again; he was lost and is found." So they began to celebrate.

—Luke 15:24

THE GIFT OF FAITH

Unit 2: Restorative Faith

LESSONS 5–8

LESSON AIMS

After participating in this lesson, each learner will be able to:

1. Summarize the parable of the prodigal son.
2. Identify elements of the parable that emphasize the depth of God's grace.
3. Commit to showing grace to a modern prodigal.

LESSON OUTLINE

Introduction
  A. The Prodigal Returns
  B. Lesson Background
 I. The Fall (LUKE 15:11-16)
  A. Receiving a Share (vv. 11, 12)
  B. Spending It All (vv. 13, 14)
    The Worst Thing to Waste
  C. Suffering from Hunger (vv. 15, 16)
 II. The Breaking Point (LUKE 15:17-20a)
  A. Clear Thinking (v. 17)
  B. Resolute Planning (vv. 18-20a)
    The Enabling Problem
III. The Homecoming (LUKE 15:20b-24)
  A. Father's Compassion (v. 20b)
  B. Son's Repentance (v. 21)
  C. Father's Joy (vv. 22-24)
Conclusion
  A. To Know Better Than God
  B. Prayer
  C. Thought to Remember

Introduction

A. The Prodigal Returns

Alan was the son of loving parents who were deeply committed Christians. Through their influence, he accepted Christ at an early age. But a family move proved to be a difficult transition for Alan, and he found himself drawn to peers whose lifestyles were at odds with his parents' faith and example. By his early 20s, Alan had become not only a drug user but also a dealer. This proved to be so profitable that he decided to move to a major coastal city to expand the operation.

One evening soon after the move, a police officer confronted Alan and his cronies, asking to search their car. A panicked flight ensued, but they didn't get far. Alan did not call his parents, who had been distressed for years by his decline into sin. From jail he instead called a friend; the friend contacted Alan's cousin; the cousin informed his own father; and that man broke the news to Alan's parents.

Alan's father immediately drove more than three hours in the middle of the night to post bond. Through his parents' efforts, Alan was restored not only to sobriety but also to Christ and family. He is certain that he would have taken his own life if his parents had not demonstrated such love.

For families that have experienced the return of a prodigal child, the parable of today's lesson can have a special poignancy. But that use of the parable should be recognized as an extended application since Jesus crafted the story for a different purpose—a purpose we dare not overlook.

B. Lesson Background

Everywhere he went, Jesus told people to prepare for the kingdom of God. But that is a complex concept, with many doctrinal and ethical implications. So Jesus used parables as illustrations. For example, the parable of the good Samaritan was more effective at communicating the ideal of neighbor-love than a philosophical discussion would have been.

Reflecting the idea that such stories served to illustrate Jesus' deeper teachings, parables often are oversimplified as being "earthly stories with heavenly meanings." But Jesus did not use parables simply to make difficult concepts comprehensible to his audiences of common people. In fact, when multitudes gathered during the height of his popularity, Jesus used parables for exactly the opposite reason! To those crowds, he told stories that were not easily understood. Later, those truly interested would question him in a more private setting, allowing for complete explanation (see Matthew 13:10-17; Mark 4:33, 34).

At other times, Jesus used parables to address Jewish leaders. These stories were often meant to be "in your face" tweaks aimed at their hypocrisy. In the parable told at his house, Simon the Pharisee was to understand that he was the debtor who "loves little" (Luke 7:47, lesson 6). "The chief priests, the teachers of the law, and the elders" were to know that the parable of the tenants was directed at them (Mark 12:1-12). The three parables in Luke 15 are similar: they were meant to be clear rebukes of pious leaders who disdained Jesus because he "welcomes sinners" (v. 2).

I. The Fall
(LUKE 15:11-16)
A. Receiving a Share (vv. 11, 12)

11. Jesus continued: "There was a man who had two sons.

Parables begin with images from common experience. This one, addressed to a hostile audience of "the Pharisees and the teachers of the law" (Luke 15:2), is quite typical in that regard.

12a. "The younger one said to his father, 'Father, give me my share of the estate.'

While many parables save their twists for later, this one introduces an unexpected element at the outset. The request *give me my share of the estate* expresses the younger son's desire to receive that part of the inheritance he should expect after his father dies. But the father is still living!

Jesus' audience knows that the oldest son in a family has privileges and responsibilities that other sons do not (Genesis 25:31). One privilege is to receive a double share of the estate (Deuteronomy 21:15-17). Since the father in the story has

only two sons, this means that *the younger one* is requesting one-third of the father's estate right now—this son wants to "cash out."

12b. "So he divided his property between them.

Those listening doubtless are struck by the disrespectful nature of the son's request, although perhaps they, like we, are aware of similar situations. Family problems are not a modern invention. The most surprising element, however, is the father's response: he agrees to give the son what he asks, with no strings attached!

Viewed from any cultural perspective, this is startling indeed. The younger son does not seem to be well grounded in life, since the rest of the story implies that he's not married and has no children. Is the father being simply naïve in granting the request (Proverbs 20:21)?

What Do You Think?

What should a parent consider when deciding between saying *no* to a child or saying *yes* in order to let the child learn a life lesson?

Talking Points for Your Discussion
- Regarding relationship choices
- Regarding recreational choices
- Regarding financial decisions
- Other

B. Spending It All (vv. 13, 14)

13. "Not long after that, the younger son got together all he had, set off for a distant country and there squandered his wealth in wild living.

The story changes scenes as *the younger son* hits the road. If the father's actions seem surprising, the outcome does not: lacking a clear sense of direction and foresight, the son burns through his money quickly.

The language of this verse leaves little room for sympathy. But it also clarifies that a motive of the younger son is that he wants to be free of his father's oversight. This is evident by the fact that the son moves to *a distant country*, thereby cutting family ties completely. There is no indication that the son's original request was motivated by any good or responsible purpose—quite the opposite! (See Proverbs 29:3.)

A man decided to visit his newlywed son and wife. While there, the father turned on lights and left them on as he walked throughout the house. When the son asked his father about this odd behavior, the father replied, "Remember all those years when I begged you to turn off the lights and not waste the electricity? I've just been waiting for the chance to see how you like it, now that you're paying the electricity bill!"

By one count, there are 2,350 verses in the Bible that address the proper and improper use of money. But money management is not what this parable is about. Neither is it intended to give hope to parents who are estranged from their children. Rather, Jesus wants the characters and their actions in the story to point to a different reality: how the wasting of one's spiritual inheritance is recognized and properly addressed.

The "wild living" that the son embraced in exchange for "his wealth"—the inheritance he cashed out—undoubtedly includes more than one of the evil activities listed in 1 Corinthians 6:9, 10. To adopt the mind-set behind these behaviors is to forfeit one's inheritance in the kingdom of God. Some who have entangled themselves in sin's snare will come to their senses (see 1 Peter 2:25), but some will not. How is your prayer life regarding the prodigals of God's kingdom?   —C. R. B.

This verse also gives the story its familiar name: the parable of the prodigal son. While the word *prodigal* is often associated with the son's decision to rebel against parental oversight and leave home prematurely, the word actually means "recklessly wasteful of one's property or means." This definition therefore points to the son's poor stewardship more than his desire to cut ties with his family, although the two concepts are related here.

HOW TO SAY IT

Deuteronomy	Due-ter-*ahn*-uh-me.
Isaiah	Eye-*zay*-uh.
Leviticus	Leh-*vit*-ih-kus.
Pharisees	*Fair*-ih-seez.
prodigal	*praw*-dih-gull.

14. "After he had spent everything, there was a severe famine in that whole country, and he began to be in need.

Famine, generally resulting from drought, is a common occurrence in the ancient world; the word itself occurs about a hundred times in the Bible. Rapid refrigerated transportation methods, which could move food expeditiously from an area of plenty to an area of need, do not exist. Therefore, virtually no one in a famine-stricken area escapes its effects, with the poorest always being hit hardest.

What Do You Think?
What lessons about money did you learn as a young(er) person that still influence you today? How do you pass these lessons along?
Talking Points for Your Discussion
▪ Lessons learned from the teaching or examples of others
▪ Lessons learned by experience ("the hard way")

C. Suffering from Hunger (vv. 15, 16)

15. "So he went and hired himself out to a citizen of that country, who sent him to his fields to feed pigs.

As food prices rise and his money evaporates, the wasteful son is forced to take whatever work he can find. He is reduced to the hand-to-mouth existence of a day laborer.

To underscore the prodigal's plight, Jesus introduces an element that is particularly troubling to Jewish people: the destitute man is hired *to feed pigs*—unclean animals (Leviticus 11:7; Deuteronomy 14:8; see also last week's lesson on Luke 8:32). This is a serious problem for Jews, because it would be nearly impossible to honor the Law of Moses in such a context. A Gentile employer would have no concern for Jewish purity laws and certainly would have no sympathy for keeping the Sabbath.

16. "He longed to fill his stomach with the pods that the pigs were eating, but no one gave him anything."

As the famine lingers, prices continue to climb beyond a point where the meager wages of a day laborer can provide even basic sustenance. Probably never having known such severity of need in his entire life, the man now finds himself fantasizing about eating *the pods* he is feeding *the pigs*. This son from an affluent family (note the mention of "hired servants" in the next verse) simply cannot sink any lower.

II. The Breaking Point
(Luke 15:17-20a)

A. Clear Thinking (v. 17)

17. "When he came to his senses, he said, 'How many of my father's hired servants have food to spare, and here I am starving to death!

Eventually, the son hits rock bottom as he longs to eat food fit for the pigs. Abandoned by fair-weather friends and living as a stranger in a foreign land, his thoughts turn to home. Whatever he previously had found to be objectionable about that earlier lifestyle suddenly doesn't seem so bad!

B. Resolute Planning (vv. 18-20a)

18, 19. "I will set out and go back to my father and say to him: Father, I have sinned against heaven and against you. I am no longer worthy to be called your son; make me like one of your hired servants.'

The *father*, for his part, seems to have done nothing to cut ties. This is seen in the fact that the son does not expect that his return will be resisted. With the door seemingly left open, the prodigal assumes he can return, but with no expectation other than that of becoming one of the *hired servants*.

What Do You Think?

How do we know when it's better to go and seek out a wayward one rather than waiting for him or her to return by personal decision?

Talking Points for Your Discussion
- Considering the cause of the estrangement
- Considering personality traits
- Considering track record
- Considering the danger of enabling
- Other

The son realizes the magnitude of what he has done, and also that he has no good way to account for what has happened to the money. The son therefore prepares a confession that he hopes will at least save his life.

His self-assessment to be *no longer worthy* as a son is quite true in a legal sense: in accepting an early cash settlement on the estate, the son has removed himself from any obligation on his father's part to support him. He therefore cannot appeal to any rights he formerly enjoyed as an heir to his father's estate. At best, he can appeal to his father's love and ask for a job as a laborer. This will at least keep him alive. The man's assessment of his situation is realistic, and his remorse seems genuine. He has no one to blame but himself, and he knows it.

20a. "So he got up and went to his father."

We wonder how long the self-assessment process takes before the man hits the bricks for home —the text doesn't say. Unlike both the story of Alan in our introduction and the parable of the lost sheep in Luke 15:1-7, the *father* does not take the initiative to come looking for the son; rather, it is the other way around.

❧ *The Enabling Problem* ❧

As a young man, William Griffith Wilson (1895–1971) studied law and economics in college, but failed to graduate because he was drunk at the time of the final exam. Even so, he began working on Wall Street and soon distinguished himself with his advice to brokerage houses. But his considerable success was overcome by his heavy drinking.

While in the pit of depression, Wilson was visited in 1934 by a friend whom he knew to be severely alcoholic. The friend refused the drink Wilson offered, saying that he had overcome his own drinking problem through association with a certain fellowship. One thing led to another, and Wilson founded the organization that is his legacy: Alcoholics Anonymous. He took his last drink at the age of 40 and lived sober for another 35 years.

Various addiction-recovery programs recognize the problem of *enabling*, which involves protecting an erring person from the consequences of his or her behavior. Wilson's friend offered help without being an enabler. Neither was the father in today's parable an enabler. He did nothing to protect his son from the consequences of his wrong thinking and actions, allowing him to hit rock bottom and realize his need in the process.

Jesus intended this parable to be understood in the context of his response to Pharisees and teachers of the law who were saying, "This man welcomes sinners and eats with them" (Luke 15:2). Those sinners, whom God had allowed to experience the earthly consequences of their sin, were ready to come home—ready to return to the household of the heavenly Father.

For us to be ready to welcome wayward sinners back while not enabling their error at the same time can be a tricky thing. But prayer and godly counsel can help us do so.   —C. R. B.

III. The Homecoming
(Luke 15:20b-24)

A. Father's Compassion (v. 20b)

20b. "But while he was still a long way off, his father saw him and was filled with compassion for him; he ran to his son, threw his arms around him and kissed him.

What better reception can the son hope for? The father's welcome is unconditional! This is another point of surprise for those listening to the story. They know that the emotions of family conflicts can take years to dissipate. Perhaps they expect the parent to reject the son outright. Perhaps they imagine the father asking for an accounting of the money and demanding restitution for the shame the son has brought to his family. None of this happens, however.

> *What Do You Think?*
> How do we recognize when the return of a prodigal is genuine rather than just an attempt to manipulate?
> *Talking Points for Your Discussion*
> - Regarding spiritual estrangements
> - Regarding family estrangements
> - Other

B. Son's Repentance (v. 21)

21. "The son said to him, 'Father, I have sinned against heaven and against you. I am no longer worthy to be called your son.'

The son's words match his plan of verses 18, 19 (compare Psalm 51:4). At this point in our analysis of the parable, it's important to stress what should be obvious: Jesus is not merely telling a heartwarming story about family reconciliation, but rather the story of every person who has ever turned away from God and squandered the blessings of his love and grace.

This observation explains the father's startling behavior at the outset: God might not stop a person from turning to a sinful lifestyle. But he is always ready to take back the repentant. He watches in silence as we go away, but he leaves the door open for our return.

> *What Do You Think?*
> What circumstances of repentance and return call for public confession of sin? Why?
> *Talking Points for Your Discussion*
> - Regarding sins of commission
> - Regarding sins of omission
> - Considering the extent of collateral damage caused by the sin
> - Other

C. Father's Joy (vv. 22-24)

22. "But the father said to his servants, 'Quick! Bring the best robe and put it on him. Put a ring on his finger and sandals on his feet.

Jesus now shifts full attention to the father's response. Here, the principle of the unexpected reaches its apex. Jesus emphasizes the depth of God's love and grace for the lost by highlighting the lavish nature of the father's reception of his lost son. As the son doubtless comes home dressed in rags, the father immediately offers *the best robe* to cover his son's shame (compare Isaiah 61:10).

The *ring* the father offers is widely understood to be the family's signet ring. People in antiquity use such rings to impress the family crest into hot wax for "signing" written contracts. By giving the returning prodigal such a ring, the father implies that he is receiving him back not as a servant but as a fully vested son. The request for *sandals* implies that the returning son has been reduced to walking barefoot.

23. 'Bring the fattened calf and kill it. Let's have a feast and celebrate.

To celebrate his son's homecoming, the father immediately proceeds to organize a feast where he can reintroduce the returning one to family and friends. Those listening to the parable as Jesus tells it probably think the father is going too far. Isn't the father setting himself up to be deceived yet again?

24. 'For this son of mine was dead and is alive again; he was lost and is found.' So they began to celebrate."

The father's words about his son being *dead* and *lost* are true in a legal sense: the son had separated himself from the family by requesting and receiving the early inheritance. That plus his absence means that for all family purposes the prodigal had been as good as dead.

The focus of the verse before us lies in the fact that the father chooses to view his son as being *alive again*. In a relational sense, the prodigal has been reborn.

Conclusion

A. To Know Better Than God

While the parable of the prodigal son is powerful in its own right, its application is magnified when we reconsider its context. Luke 15:1, 2 says that Jesus offered this parable in response to complaints from the Pharisees and the teachers of the law—religious leaders of the day and experts on the Bible. Those folks "muttered, 'This man welcomes sinners and eats with them.'" The self-righteous religious leaders were looking for a Messiah who would embrace fellowship with the righteous while rejecting the unrighteous. But here was this fellow Jesus doing the opposite!

The fact that Jesus was willing to receive sinners —going so far as even to eat with them!—served as proof to the Pharisees and teachers of the law that he didn't appreciate the importance of remaining "clean." What the religious leaders seemed to

Visual for Lesson 8. *Point to this visual as you introduce the discussion question that is associated with verses 18, 19.*

have overlooked was the possibility of *repentance*. Jesus came not "to call the righteous, but sinners to repentance" (Luke 5:32).

While the parable can be viewed on a personal level in illustrating God's acceptance of repentant individuals, many students see a larger theme here: the prodigal son as representing the Gentiles. Surely the religious experts of Jesus' day had read Isaiah 49:6, where God promised that his servant would not only "restore the tribes of Jacob and bring back those of Israel," but also was to be "a light for the Gentiles, that my salvation may reach to the ends of the earth" (quoted in Acts 13:47).

This speaks to how we are to view people-groups today. As Jesus welcomed them, so must we. It is our Great Commission to do so (Matthew 28:19, 20). By not doing so, are we pretending to know better than God?

B. Prayer

Heavenly Father, people have done things that have made us angry and resentful. Help us to follow Jesus' example of forgiving acceptance where repentance is real. We pray in the name of the Son who forgives us of so much. Amen.

C. Thought to Remember

"To forgive is to set a prisoner free and discover that the prisoner was you."
—Lewis B. Smedes (1921–2002)

INVOLVEMENT LEARNING

Enhance your lesson with NIV® Bible Student (from your curriculum supplier) and the reproducible activity page (at www.standardlesson.com or in the back of the NIV® Standard Lesson Commentary Deluxe Edition).

Into the Lesson

Give each learner a copy of the following parable (or another of your choosing) that is attributed to Aesop, along with the questions that follow.

The Bull and the Calf

A bull was striving with all his might to squeeze himself through a narrow passage that led to his stall. A young calf came up and offered to go before and show him the way by which he could manage to pass. "Save yourself the trouble," said the bull. "I knew that way long before you were born."

1. Who or what does the bull represent? 2. Who or what does the calf represent? 3. What does the bull's too-large size represent? 4. What does the bull's attitude represent? 5. What is the moral to the story?

Say, "Take 90 seconds to read the story silently and jot first-impression responses to the questions quickly. No talking, please!"

After calling time, have learners voice their responses to the questions. Use the differing responses to illustrate that the challenge of parables and figurative language is to match their elements with people, places, things, etc., in real life as the author intends. Make a transition by summarizing from the Lesson Background the nature of Jesus' parables, how he used them, and why.

Into the Word

Write the words *Father* and *Son*, widely separated horizontally, at the top of the board. Create two columns under the word *Father*, labeling them "Actions and Statements" and "Motives." Do the same under the word *Son*.

Say, "In order to better understand today's parable, we will compare the actions and statements of the two main characters, but also consider what might be the motive behind each of those." Ask someone to read Luke 15:11-16. Then have learners call out the actions and statements of the father and the son and suggest possible motives for each.

Jot responses on the board. Repeat this procedure for verses 17-20 and then for verses 21-24.

Next, divide learners into groups of three or four. Give each group the following questions to answer: 1. Whom do the father and the son represent in the context of the parable as being Jesus' response to his critics per Luke 15:1, 2? 2. In the same context, how do we interpret the fact that the father *does not* go out searching for the son, while the shepherd of 15:3-7 *does* go out searching for a lost sheep and the woman of 15:8-10 *does* search for her lost coin? 3. How have you seen the parable of the prodigal son misapplied? 4. How is this parable a picture of grace, as described in Ephesians 2:8, 9?

Into Life

Say, "Unfortunately, everyone probably knows someone who has wandered away from God and is currently like the lost son when he was far from home. We need to prepare to be welcoming like the father." Discuss the phrase "when he came to his senses" found in Luke 15:17, noting how this was a turning point for the son. Then use the following discussion questions to brainstorm ideas: 1. How do we recognize when a spiritual prodigal has reached the point of being willing to return to God? 2. What "welcome back" preparations can the church make to celebrate a prodigal's return? 3. What are ways that we as individuals can show grace to spiritual prodigals in the week ahead?

Option 1. Distribute copies of the "Poem or Prayer of Grace" activity from the reproducible page, which you can download. To keep preparation time short, encourage no more than five words per line. Allow volunteers to read theirs.

Option 2. Distribute copies of "Song of the Prodigal" from the reproducible page. Lead the class in singing the three stanzas and/or encourage learners to keep these in their Bibles for daily devotions in the week ahead.

INCREASED FAITH

DEVOTIONAL READING: Jeremiah 23:33–24:6
BACKGROUND SCRIPTURE: Luke 17:1-10

LUKE 17:1-10

¹ Jesus said to his disciples: "Things that cause people to stumble are bound to come, but woe to anyone through whom they come. ² It would be better for them to be thrown into the sea with a millstone tied around their neck than to cause one of these little ones to stumble. ³ So watch yourselves.

"If your brother or sister sins against you, rebuke them; and if they repent, forgive them. ⁴ Even if they sin against you seven times in a day and seven times come back to you saying 'I repent,' you must forgive them."

⁵ The apostles said to the Lord, "Increase our faith!"

⁶ He replied, "If you have faith as small as a mustard seed, you can say to this mulberry tree, 'Be uprooted and planted in the sea,' and it will obey you.

⁷ "Suppose one of you has a servant plowing or looking after the sheep. Will he say to the servant when he comes in from the field, 'Come along now and sit down to eat'? ⁸ Won't he rather say, 'Prepare my supper, get yourself ready and wait on me while I eat and drink; after that you may eat and drink'? ⁹ Will he thank the servant because he did what he was told to do? ¹⁰ So you also, when you have done everything you were told to do, should say, 'We are unworthy servants; we have only done our duty.'"

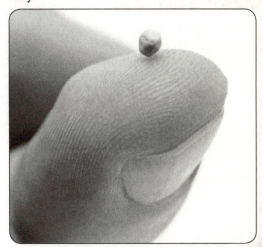

KEY VERSE

Watch yourselves. If your brother or sister sins against you, rebuke them; and if they repent, forgive them.
—**Luke 17:3**

THE GIFT OF FAITH

Unit 3: Fullness of Faith

LESSONS 9–13

LESSON AIMS

After participating in this lesson, each learner will be able to:

1. List some duties of a Christian as set forth by Jesus.

2. Explain the relationship between growing faith and forgiveness.

3. Identify one way to practice forgiveness on a daily basis.

LESSON OUTLINE

Introduction
    A. Keeping Score
    B. Lesson Background
  I. Protecting and Forgiving (LUKE 17:1-4)
    A. Little Ones (vv. 1, 2)
    B. Offending Ones (vv. 3, 4)
       Card Counting
  II. Growing and Serving (LUKE 17:5-10)
    A. Bigger Faith (vv. 5, 6)
    B. Enduring Faith (vv. 7-9)
    C. Obedient Faith (v. 10)
       A Sense of Entitlement
Conclusion
    A. Mustard Seeds or Scorecards?
    B. Prayer
    C. Thought to Remember

Introduction

A. Keeping Score

Have you ever wanted to "get even" with someone? If we are offended or mistreated, we may believe we have a right to retaliate, thus evening the score. There is a sense of entitlement here, a belief that bad behavior toward us gives us a right to pay back. Of course, if we *really* want to stand up for ourselves, our response will be a little greater, thereby "teaching a lesson" to our tormentor. We don't just get even; we must win.

Lest we think the above is simply the schoolyard attitude of childhood, we should look at what happens in many workplaces. Petty grudges are held for years. Certain coworkers are feared or loathed because they will let no offense, no matter how tiny or unintentional, go by without a negative reaction. Such behavior can be found all the more in the online world of social media, where face-to-face behavioral etiquette doesn't seem to apply.

At the core of all this is the belief that life should be fair and that we are both (1) the judges of what is fair treatment and (2) enforcers of punishment on those who step over the lines—our lines. We think ourselves to be justified in keeping behavioral scorecards in our relationships. Such score keeping can be found in extended families, marriages, and churches. It should not be.

In this lesson, Jesus addresses the dynamics of relationship offenses. His solid, practical principles that applied to his disciples in the first century AD are vital yet today. These begin with an understanding of our place in the arena of relationships. This helps us see ourselves as people of faith whose service to God is far more important than keeping score with other people.

B. Lesson Background

In Luke 17, Jesus was on his final journey to Jerusalem and the cross that awaited him there. The trip narrative begins in Luke 9:51 and ends with the triumphal entry in chapter 19. Many teaching opportunities are recorded in this section of 10-plus chapters. Sometimes Jesus was teaching the crowds, sometimes just his 12 disciples. Today's lesson falls in the second category.

This lesson focuses on the topics of forgiveness and faith. Forgiveness in particular was a much studied and discussed issue for the Jewish people of Jesus' day. Their Scriptures (our Old Testament) taught them about the necessity of asking and receiving God's forgiveness (see Psalms 32:1, 2; 79:9). The Scriptures also spoke to forgiveness between people, seen as both necessary and wise (see Proverbs 17:9).

The Day of Atonement (Yom Kippur) was a national holy day that addressed the forgiveness of the people for another year as the high priest offered the specified sacrifices (Leviticus 16). Yet just as the relationship of the people to the Lord had been complicated by many rituals and regulations, so too had the process of forgiving others. Rather than letting forgiveness occur naturally as a loving act between people, some wanted to define its terms and limit its frequency. Thus, the act of grace that forgiveness was to represent had become something much less gracious: a response to certain criteria (conditions) that had to be met. In short, forgiveness for the Jews of Jesus' day had to be earned.

Jesus taught that a world without forgiveness was a cruel and cold place. By the time of today's lesson, he had taught his disciples to pray for forgiveness from God as they forgave others (Matthew 6:12, 14, 15). But there was more yet for them to learn on this topic.

I. Protecting and Forgiving
(LUKE 17:1-4)
A. Little Ones (vv. 1, 2)

1. Jesus said to his disciples: "Things that cause people to stumble are bound to come, but woe to anyone through whom they come.

Jesus begins his teaching by saying what everyone knows: *things that cause people to stumble are bound to come*. Even the best of relationships have problems from time to time. Even the strongest marriages have to work through issues. Even the best of friends are sometimes at odds.

The word *stumble* translates a Greek word from which we derive our word *scandal*. It can refer to a stumbling block, something one trips over, as

it is translated in Romans 11:9. This word is also used to refer to a trap, a snare set for animals in order to catch them. In the realm of relationships, the word refers to something that breaks fellowship. As depicted here, these *things that cause people to stumble* are therefore bad, sinful obstacles (compare Matthew 13:41). To this we may contrast Romans 9:33, which describes the reverse; although Jesus is certainly not a sinful obstacle, he is nevertheless "a stone that causes people to stumble and a rock that makes them fall [scandal]"—the one who is tripped over by those pursuing righteousness by works.

Jesus pronounces a dire warning, a *woe*, regarding the sources of such sinful obstacles. It is bad enough to fail to resist a temptation and thereby commit sin. It is even more grievous to be the cause of the sin of others. This is sin compounded: (1) guilt for setting a trap that should not have been set in the first place, and (2) some responsibility for the other person who falls.

2. "It would be better for them to be thrown into the sea with a millstone tied around their neck than to cause one of these little ones to stumble.

Millstones are essential for grinding wheat or barley into flour. This is a normal task of village life. Although grain can be roasted and eaten whole, flour is required for the much preferred bread (compare Matthew 24:41). Millstones for this purpose range in size from those used in the hand mills of a household (weighing perhaps 30 to 50 pounds) to large village versions that might be powered by a donkey. Every millstone has a hole carved in the center so it can be rotated on a stationary stone underneath. This allows grain between the stones to be crushed and ground.

The millstone imagery immediately resonates with the life experiences of Jesus' disciples. What is new to the disciples, however, is the imagery of a deadly millstone necklace. If a millstone's center hole were to be threaded with a strong rope and then secured around a person's neck, drowning would quickly result should that person be *thrown into the sea*. It would be better for a person to die such a death than to be the cause of sin for *one of these little ones*.

More than anything, I want...

Visual for Lesson 9. *Start a discussion by asking, "What percentage of people would finish the statement in this picture with the words 'more faith'?"*

We traditionally understand *little ones* to refer to children (see Matthew 18:2-6), but the application is broader here: they are the naïve ones in our world, whether children or adults, who should be protected from sin rather than enticed into it. People who are wise to the sin traps of the world have a responsibility not to encourage others to fall into those traps—traps that those wiser folks may have yielded themselves to at one time or another. Instead, we are to be rescuers and protectors, snatching others from the fire (Jude 23).

B. Offending Ones (vv. 3, 4)

3, 4. "So watch yourselves.

"If your brother or sister sins against you, rebuke them; and if they repent, forgive them. Even if they sin against you seven times in a day and seven times come back to you saying 'I repent,' you must forgive them."

Jesus shifts his focus from causing others to sin to situations when we ourselves have been wronged. We sometimes think that sin only involves offenses against God, forgetting that most sinful behavior is also tied to behavior between people. So what should we do when others sin against us?

Verses 3 and 4 should be considered together. Verse 3 gives a simple formula: recognize sin, rebuke the one committing it, expect repentance, and then forgive when repentance is forthcoming. By itself, this verse tells us *how* but not *how much*,

thereby allowing us to keep a scorecard on forgiveness frequency. By including verse 4, though, we can understand Jesus' main point: don't keep score on forgiveness. Keep forgiving. Be quick, ready, and willing to forgive (compare Matthew 18:21, 22). This is not weakness, but strength.

> **What Do You Think?**
> In your experience, what makes corrective rebukes effective?
> *Talking Points for Your Discussion*
> - Regarding the rebuke's content ("what you say")
> - Regarding the rebuke's form ("how you say it")
> - Regarding the medium used (in person, by e-mail, by phone, etc.)
> - Considering the spiritual maturity and personality types of those involved
> - Other

"But," we might object, "we will be taken advantage of if we always forgive like this! Shouldn't we be a little bit stingy when it comes to forgiveness, a little bit selfish?" Jesus answers this question with a firm *no*. We are to be consistent leaders when it comes to forgiving. We must give up our score keeping and our desire to get even. Let us be people of forgiveness.

> **What Do You Think?**
> How can we apply Jesus' words without enabling bad behavior?
> *Talking Points for Your Discussion*
> - Considering the difference between *forgiveness* and *consequences*
> - Considering criminal vs. noncriminal behavior
> - Other

But what about those who don't repent? Should we withhold our forgiveness? That's a tricky question, not addressed here. Some will point out that as Jesus dies on the cross he says, "Father, forgive them, for they do not know what they are doing" (Luke 23:34) even though the ones who put him there had not repented of that sin. Others will point out in response that Jesus does not say "I forgive you" in that situation, but requests the Father's forgiveness of them—forgiveness that the Father will grant only if they repent. We can at least conclude that Jesus wants us to have a ready and willing attitude of forgiveness. His disciples are to be extravagant forgivers.

❧ CARD COUNTING ❧

Card counting is a method that casino gamblers use to improve their odds of winning at blackjack. This technique assigns a point-value to each card as it is dealt, with players keeping track of the changing point total with each hand. Most casinos take various countermeasures to this practice.

The above should not be taken as approval of casino gambling, whether to count cards or not. Instead, it is merely to illustrate that keeping a "forgiveness record" can be a bit like card counting—it tells us when it's time to say, "No more cards. I call." But when it comes to forgiving those who wrong us, the Lord doesn't want us to be "forgiveness counters." To do so is to invite God to do the same to us.

Forgiveness is not a game of moral blackjack. Forgiveness is not a game at all! Forgiveness is a requirement from Jesus, the one against whom we have all sinned, the one who has paid the sin-debt that was ours to pay. Those who "count cards" in limiting their forgiveness can expect to hear these words on Judgment Day: "You wicked servant. . . . I canceled all that debt of yours because you begged me to. Shouldn't you have had mercy on your fellow servant just as I had on you?" (Matthew 18:32, 33).   —C. R. B.

II. Growing and Serving
(LUKE 17:5-10)
A. Bigger Faith (vv. 5, 6)

5. The apostles said to the Lord, "Increase our faith!"

The topic moves from forgiveness to faith. The disciples (called *apostles* since Luke 6:13) ask Jesus to *increase* their *faith*. Our understanding of this request will be influenced by what we understand faith to be.

One view of faith is that of a logical process of coming to belief based on acceptance of evidence. Others see faith as entirely a gift of God. These,

then, are the extremes: (1) faith as a human reaction to circumstances or (2) faith as a supernatural endowment from God. The Bible presents both views as having some validity. In the final analysis, lack of faith is our choice, and being faithless is our responsibility (see Luke 9:41). On the other hand, faith is also a spiritual gift that is bestowed by God (see Romans 12:3; 1 Corinthians 12:9).

For what, then, are the disciples asking? It doesn't quite make sense for them to be asking for faith in the sense of the first type, above. How can Jesus increase faith if it is a human choice that concerns the disciples' evaluation of circumstances? Neither is the second type of faith in view since the disciples are not faithless fools asking for something they do not already have. They are already men of faith, people who have chosen to follow Jesus.

What they are asking is that Jesus help them have a stronger faith. These men know their weaknesses and doubts. They are laying themselves before Jesus in all their inadequacy and repeating the request of the father of the demon-afflicted boy, "I do believe; help me overcome my unbelief!" (Mark 9:24, lesson 1).

> **What Do You Think?**
> How do you know if and when your faith is growing?
> *Talking Points for Your Discussion*
> - Evidence from your prayers
> - Evidence from level of contentment or worry
> - Evidence from your worship
> - Evidence from your Christian service
> - Other

6. He replied, "If you have faith as small as a mustard seed, you can say to this mulberry tree, 'Be uprooted and planted in the sea,' and it will obey you.

Jesus answers their request by giving an illustration of what powerful faith is capable of doing. He uses two extremes to make his point.

The *mustard seed* is well known for its tiny size (see the picture on page 297). One mustard seed of a certain variety weighs about 2 milligrams, so it would take over 225,000 such seeds to make a pound. This is serious smallness! The *mulberry tree* is mentioned not because of its huge size but because it is known for having very deep roots. Jesus' word picture is that of commanding a deeply anchored tree to pull itself out of the ground, roots and all (not merely cut itself off above the ground), and replant itself *in the sea*.

Jesus' declaration has this impact: the one having even a tiny amount of faith that is unblemished by doubt can do very mighty things. This pronouncement does not immediately increase the faith of Jesus' disciples, but it does indicate his approval of their request. More faith means more things done for the kingdom of God (compare Matthew 17:20; 21:21; Mark 11:23).

> **What Do You Think?**
> When was a time you saw "mustard-seed faith" result in an unanticipated outcome? How did your faith change as a result?
> *Talking Points for Your Discussion*
> - Involving your church as a whole
> - Involving someone's ministry gifts in particular
> - Involving a direction-of-life decision
> - Other

B. Enduring Faith (vv. 7-9)

7. "Suppose one of you has a servant plowing or looking after the sheep. Will he say to the servant when he comes in from the field, 'Come along now and sit down to eat'?

Jesus offers another illustration concerning the nature of faith. Imagine a farm servant who completes his tasks of *plowing or looking after the sheep*, then returns to the house at the end of the workday. Does the one in charge say, "*Come along now and sit down to eat*"? Jesus' disciples know the answer: no head of household in this era would say this. Servants are subject to be on duty whenever required, and something else has to happen before the servant has dinner.

8. "Won't he rather say, 'Prepare my supper, get yourself ready and wait on me while I eat and drink; after that you may eat and drink'?

Jesus answers his own question, and his answer is what any of the disciples would give. The ser-

vant may have worked long hours in the field, but before he dines, the head of the household expects his own evening meal first. Servants eat and rest only after that.

9. "Will he thank the servant because he did what he was told to do?

Jesus pushes this illustration a step further. Does *the servant* deserve any special thanks for doing his duty? In the harsh world of heads of households and servants, there is no recognition or praise for obedience, so the answer is *no*. The obedience of the servant is simply expected. Servants of Jesus' day do not get participation trophies.

C. Obedient Faith (v. 10)

10. "So you also, when you have done everything you were told to do, should say, 'We are unworthy servants; we have only done our duty.'"

This verse serves as the answer to the request of the disciples in verse 5, the appeal for more faith. Jesus tells them to continue to act faithfully, to do *everything you were told to do*. Faith in this sense is not so much something you possess as it is something you do. Faith must be worked out in humility, with a self-deprecating sense that *we are unworthy servants*. The right kind of faith is not characterized by congratulatory high-fives or expectations of praise. Faith is to be steady and reliable. The consistent practice of obedient faith makes it stronger and more mature.

> **What Do You Think?**
> What does this verse have to say about a Christian's being able to "exceed expectations" in various areas of life?
> *Talking Points for Your Discussion*
> - In the business arena
> - In home life
> - In volunteer work
> - Other

❧ A SENSE OF ENTITLEMENT ❧

A grandmother asked her 5-year-old grandson what he wanted for Christmas. She showed him a toy store's Christmas catalog and asked him to pick out a few things he might like to receive. Looking through the catalog, the boy ended up pointing to each item on every page, saying, "I want this and this and this and . . ." Even at his early age, the child had developed a sense of entitlement.

An entitlement epidemic seems to infect our culture. It knows no age boundaries. Some propose that the roots of the Great Recession of 2008–2011 can be traced to a cultural mind-set that in effect told us that we were entitled to own homes. As a result, people ended up with variable-rate mortgages that stretched them beyond their abilities to repay when interest rates rose. When unemployment began to rise and the housing bubble burst, a massive number of overextended homeowners saw their houses go into foreclosure.

Jesus' illustration warns against having a sense of entitlement when it comes to the things of God. The only thing we are entitled to in God's economy "is death, but the gift of God is eternal life in Christ Jesus our Lord" (Romans 6:23). A sense of spiritual entitlement was a big problem in Jesus' day (see Luke 3:7-9; etc.). May it not be so in ours as we exercise obedient faith in gratitude for Christ's work. —C. R. B.

Conclusion

A. Mustard Seeds or Scorecards?

In today's lesson, Jesus confronted the issue of forgiveness in a way that cannot be ignored. He knew that the community of his disciples (the future church) had to be a place of forgiveness and grace. Otherwise, it would be no different from the hard-edged communities of "earned forgiveness" of his day. In that light, Jesus taught his disciples how to forgive and implored them to not place limits on their forgiveness.

The model situation is for us to recognize when we are wronged, confront the wrongdoer, receive

HOW TO SAY IT

Corinthians	Ko-*rin*-thee-unz (*th* as in *thin*).
Jerusalem	Juh-*roo*-suh-lem.
Leviticus	Leh-*vit*-ih-kus.

an apology, and release any grudge or ill feelings. But we know that the process doesn't always work so smoothly!

The process breaks down when the one who has wronged us refuses to accept correction and does not repent. The expectation of an apology can make things worse. This holds true on a daily basis, whether at work or at home, whether in a supermarket or in a restaurant.

But before we are tempted to set aside Jesus' model as unrealistic for our day, we should flip it around and ask ourselves some questions: How do *we* react to a deserved rebuke? How do *we* respond to a fellow Christian who comes to us to register a complaint about our behavior? Is our first impulse one of self-justification (example: 1 Samuel 15:19, 20) or one of self-examination (example: 2 Samuel 12:11-13a)? Do we facilitate the process of forgiveness or do we (stumbling)block it?

These questions relate closely to Jesus' teaching on faith in this lesson. Do we expect praise or congratulations for doing the right thing? Must our acts of faithful obedience be rewarded in order for us to continue to do the right thing? Receiving correction in a humble spirit is an act of faith, maybe as difficult an act of faith as there is for a Christian. Humility is not easy, because we do not live in a world that prizes or encourages the humble heart. The worldly model is one of "getting even" for offenses against us.

Let's put the scorecards away! Let's have faith much bigger than a tiny mustard seed and allow God to transform our world for him. Mustard seeds and scorecards don't mix.

B. Prayer

O God, you are always faithful. May we be faithful like you. You are always forgiving. May we be forgiving like you. Give us faith to trust what you say. May you transform us into servants in the model of your Son. As he does not keep a scorecard against us, may we not do so either against others. In Jesus' name we pray. Amen.

C. Thought to Remember

Exercise the kind of faith that
forgives extravagantly.

INVOLVEMENT LEARNING

Enhance your lesson with NIV® Bible Student (from your curriculum supplier) and the reproducible activity page (at www.standardlesson.com or in the back of the NIV® Standard Lesson Commentary Deluxe Edition).

Into the Lesson

Ask who is familiar with the series of *Death Wish* movies, starring Charles Bronson. If someone is, have him or her give a very brief synopsis of the series. If no one can do so, say, "Bronson plays the part of a vigilante who seeks revenge against those who killed his wife. In the process, he kills various evildoers." Then ask, "What is it about these types of movies that some people find so satisfying?" Briefly lead a discussion on the human desire for revenge and getting even.

Then say, "These movies usually neglect to show the harmful effects of harboring bitterness. Today we will look at what Jesus has to say about the place of forgiveness in the life of faith."

Into the Word

Distribute the following four assignments to four groups of three or four, one per group. (Create duplicate assignments for larger classes.)

Millstone Necklace Group—Provide the group with a square of poster board, scissors, and a long string. Tasks: read Luke 17:1, 2, then use the materials to make a "millstone necklace." Discuss these questions: 1. In what ways might a person cause a child or other naïve person to sin? 2. In what way does the image of a millstone necklace illustrate how serious the consequences will be for those who do so?

Forgiveness Unlimited Group—Provide the group with one blank sheet of paper along with four index cards on which are written the words *forgive, sin, repent, rebuke*, one word per card. Tasks: read Luke 17:3, 4, then put the words in the correct sequence. Use the blank sheet to create a sign to represent Jesus' teaching. Discuss these questions: 1. Why does Jesus say we should rebuke those who sin against us—can't we just forgive silently and move on? 2. By telling us to forgive "seven times in a day," what is Jesus implying about forgiveness?

Mustard-Seed Faith Group—Provide the group with a mustard seed (or picture of one, see page 297) and a picture of a tree with deep root systems, along with the information from the commentary on these verses. Tasks: read Luke 17:5, 6 and the commentary thereto. Discuss these questions: 1. What is it about a mustard seed that makes it so useful for Jesus' illustration? 2. How does the tree illustrate the types of things that are possible for those who have even a tiny amount of unblemished faith?

Obedient Servants Group—Provide the group with a plate, cutlery, and cup. Tasks: read Luke 17:7-10; then use what you've been given to make a place setting. Discuss these questions: 1. When servant and head of the household have been working all day, why does the latter get to eat first? 2. What does the head of the household's treatment of the servant teach us about our duty to God?

Have groups present conclusions in whole-class discussion, using their visual aids as appropriate.

Option. Distribute copies of the "Bad Advice/ Good Advice" activity from the reproducible page, which you can download. Have learners work in pairs to complete as indicated.

Into Life

Distribute handouts of the following scenario:

> *You spoke in confidence to a youth minister about concerns you have regarding your son using drugs. Although the youth minister promised to keep it confidential, he did talk to his wife, who has experience counseling drug addicts. She mentioned it as a prayer request in her small group, and some of those people have been telling you that they are praying for you. According to Jesus' instructions on forgiveness, how should you handle this situation?*

Discuss either as a class or in small groups.

Option. Distribute copies of the "Forgiveness Formula" activity from the reproducible page. Encourage learners to use as indicated.

GRATEFUL FAITH

DEVOTIONAL READING: Colossians 3:12-17
BACKGROUND SCRIPTURE: Luke 17:11-19

LUKE 17:11-19

¹¹ Now on his way to Jerusalem, Jesus traveled along the border between Samaria and Galilee. ¹² As he was going into a village, ten men who had leprosy met him. They stood at a distance ¹³ and called out in a loud voice, "Jesus, Master, have pity on us!"

¹⁴ When he saw them, he said, "Go, show yourselves to the priests." And as they went, they were cleansed.

¹⁵ One of them, when he saw he was healed, came back, praising God in a loud voice. ¹⁶ He threw himself at Jesus' feet and thanked him—and he was a Samaritan.

¹⁷ Jesus asked, "Were not all ten cleansed? Where are the other nine? ¹⁸ Has no one returned to give praise to God except this foreigner?" ¹⁹ Then he said to him, "Rise and go; your faith has made you well."

KEY VERSE

One of them, when he saw he was healed, came back, praising God in a loud voice. —**Luke 17:15**

The Gift of Faith

Unit 3: Fullness of Faith

LESSONS 9–13

LESSON AIMS

After participating in this lesson, each learner will be able to:

1. Tell the story of the grateful Samaritan leper.
2. Explain how gratitude can be a barometer of one's faith.
3. Write a prayer expressing gratitude.

LESSON OUTLINE

Introduction
  A. Unending Ungratefulness
  B. Lesson Background: Leprosy
  C. Lesson Background: Samaritans
I. Ten Desperate Men (LUKE 17:11-14)
  A. Jerusalem Calls (v. 11)
  B. Lepers Beg (vv. 12, 13)
  C. Jesus Commands (v. 14)
II. One Grateful Man (LUKE 17:15-19)
  A. Samaritan's Return (vv. 15, 16)
  B. Jesus' Concern (vv. 17, 18)
    Attitude of Ingratitude?
  C. Jesus' Declaration (v. 19)
    Faith Healers
Conclusion
  A. Healing Faith
  B. Prayer
  C. Thought to Remember

Introduction

A. Unending Ungratefulness

Those who live in Western democracies enjoy standards of living that people of centuries past would scarcely comprehend. By one estimate, those in the very bottom 10 percent of income in America are in the top 30 percent of income in the world as a whole. Relatively few in such a culture lack basic necessities, yet many are dissatisfied. Why is that? Shouldn't people who have so much be happy and content?

Author Steve Maraboli observes that, "The more I understand the mind and the human experience, the more I begin to suspect there is no such thing as unhappiness; there is only ungratefulness." Is he right? Are the happiest people those who are most grateful?

The religious heritage of ancient Israel linked gladness with thanksgiving. Joy, praise, and gratitude are interconnected (see Psalms 35:18; 69:30; 95:2; 100:4). Key elements of worship included both rejoicing and giving thanks. An oft-repeated worship refrain centers on thankfulness: "Give thanks to the Lord, for he is good; his love endures forever" (Psalm 118:1; compare Jeremiah 33:11). There is a fuzzy distinction at best between praising God and thanking God, both being at the very heart of worship.

Even so, the Bible depicts many ungrateful people. The history of the exodus could have been that of a celebration and quick victory march into the promised land. But grumbling, griping, and murmuring made it otherwise (see Deuteronomy 1:27). The dissatisfied heart always wants more, and greediness nullifies gratefulness. Even so, God "is kind to the ungrateful and wicked" (Luke 6:35). This week's lesson looks at a mighty act of kindness bestowed on 10 desperate men, of whom only one exhibited gratefulness. As we consider this account, may we search our own hearts to see if greed or gratefulness is our ensign.

B. Lesson Background: Leprosy

My father was a practicing physician for over 40 years. He once returned from a medical meeting in California where an acquaintance had taken him to a local hospital to see a special case: a patient who had been diagnosed with leprosy, now known as Hansen's disease The friend claimed that his was the only known case in the state. It was also the only time in my father's long medical career that he had any contact with this ancient disease.

Relatively few people today are afflicted with this loathsome, legendary ailment. There are perhaps no more than 300 new cases annually in the U.S. But leprosy was well known in the ancient world, being described in the records of many cultures. Left unchecked, the disease results in visible lesions and deformations. Traditionally, those so afflicted have been forced to live under quarantine conditions, even into modern times. Leprosy was incurable until the advent of antibiotic drug therapies in the twentieth century.

Leprosy as described in the Old Testament probably included a wide range of afflictions of the skin, not just Hansen's disease as we know it today. Laws concerning lepers are found especially in Leviticus 13:1-46; 14:1-32. To be a leper was to be "unclean," often permanently. Those so afflicted had to warn others with cries of "Unclean! Unclean!" (13:45) and were required to live apart (13:46). Therefore, lepers suffered not only from the illness itself but also from being ostracized socially. That was the condition of the 10 men of this lesson.

C. Lesson Background: Samaritans

At least one of the lepers in today's lesson was a Samaritan. Samaritans, who lived in central Palestine, were distant relatives of first-century Jews.

HOW TO SAY IT

Bartimaeus	*Bar*-tih-*me*-us.
Galilean	Gal-uh-*lee*-un.
Galilee	*Gal*-uh-lee.
Gerizim	*Gair*-ih-zeem or Guh-*rye*-zim.
kyrie eleison (Latin)	*keer*-ee-ey eh-*lay*-uh-sawn.
Leviticus	Leh-*vit*-ih-kus.
Moses	*Mo*-zes or *Mo*-zez.
Samaria	Suh-*mare*-ee-uh.
Samaritans	Suh-*mare*-uh-tunz.
Shechem	*Shee*-kem or *Shek*-em.

There was great animosity between the two groups in Jesus' day (see Luke 9:51-53; John 4:9; 8:48), a type of bitter tribalism that had been fueled by centuries of negative incidents. The Old Testament traces the time line of these from 2 Kings 17 through Ezra 4 and Nehemiah 4. The period of time between the Old and New Testaments saw further antagonism develop.

Concerning lepers, the Samaritans followed the regulations found in Leviticus. This included exclusion from regular village life of those so afflicted. The 10 diseased outcasts of this week's lesson seem to have consisted of both Jews and Samaritans. We can liken this to a homeless camp made up of folks from divergent backgrounds, having been thrown together by desperate circumstances.

I. Ten Desperate Men
(LUKE 17:11-14)
A. Jerusalem Calls (v. 11)

11. Now on his way to Jerusalem, Jesus traveled along the border between Samaria and Galilee.

Jesus and his followers are still on the *way to Jerusalem* for Passover—Jesus' final Passover. This Gospel marks this final trip as beginning in Luke 9:51. At that time, Jesus had sent messengers ahead "into a Samaritan village to get things ready for him; but the people there did not welcome him, because he was heading for Jerusalem" (Luke 9:52, 53; see the Lesson Background regarding this animosity).

Jesus prefers to minister in places that are open to his message, so he bypassed that particular Samaritan village (Luke 9:53; compare 9:5; 10:10, 11). He does not avoid Samaria as a whole, however, since the verse before us says he is passing *along the border between Samaria and Galilee* (compare John 4:4). No geographical features separate the two areas in an obvious way. The distinction is determined by the makeup of the villages, with the Jewish villages of Galilee lying to the north of the Samaritan region. The Samaritans, for their part, are centered in the Shechem valley near Mount Gerizim and the surrounding area, roughly 25 miles due north of Jerusalem.

B. Lepers Beg (vv. 12, 13)

12. As he was going into a village, ten men who had leprosy met him. They stood at a distance

We are not told if this particular village is Galilean (Jewish) or Samaritan. Both Jews and Samaritans isolate lepers (see the Lesson Background), so it may be either.

The fact that the 10 noted to have leprosy stand *at a distance* is in compliance with the Law of Moses (see Leviticus 13:46; Number 5:2). They stay near the village, where some of them may have family members who provide food and clothing. But the men do not venture close. Lepers who ignore the expectation of maintaining proper distance might be driven away by having rocks thrown at them from fear and loathing.

13. and called out in a loud voice, "Jesus, Master, have pity on us!"

The physical distance between Jesus and the lepers—perhaps a hundred yards or more—is highlighted by the need for the men to call *out in a loud voice* to be heard. The author gives the impression that they shout in unison, indicating a plan formulated before Jesus' visit.

These 10 men therefore seem to have access to the community grapevine of information, despite their isolation. Friends or relatives who provide for them likely have shared stories they have heard about Jesus as a healer. The preparedness of this band of desperate men indicates that Jesus' arrival at this particular village is expected and eagerly anticipated.

Their cry is a simple request for Jesus to *have pity*. The Greek behind this expression is usually translated "have mercy" (examples: Luke 18:38, 39), and that is the sense here. This is not a plea for a specific action, but a general appeal for favorable attention. This reveals awareness that Jesus is a compassionate Master. If he notices the men's plight, then he may extend his healing power to relieve their suffering.

Requests for God's mercy occur frequently in the Psalms (examples: Psalms 30:10; 51:1; 57:1). In choral music, the phrase *kyrie eleison,* meaning "Lord, have mercy," is familiar (in particular, the first movement of Mozart's Coronation Mass in C major).

There is sad irony in this request from these 10 men. They have experienced precious little mercy in the recent past. They have been excluded from their homes. They likely are targets of jests and taunts by the young boys of the village (compare 2 Kings 2:23). And most of all, they probably believe that God is punishing them in a merciless fashion (compare John 9:2).

Many things can cause a person to become unclean temporarily (example: Numbers 19:11). But since there is no effective cure for leprosy in this day, to be afflicted by this ailment is usually to remain permanently in an unclean status—a life sentence. This is why leprosy is so feared. Its appearance is a life-altering event that usually ends only with death.

C. Jesus Commands (v. 14)

14. When he saw them, he said, "Go, show yourselves to the priests." And as they went, they were cleansed.

The simple command *Go, show yourselves to the priests* is for the purpose of verifying that the men no longer have the signs of leprosy. This task is a responsibility entrusted to priests under the Law of Moses (see Leviticus 14:2, 3; compare Luke 5:14). A positive certification will mean that the 10 men will be able to resume their roles in family and village life.

There is a bit of drama to this miraculous healing that we will overlook if we do not read carefully. The text does not indicate that the 10 are healed immediately (contrast Luke 5:12, 13). Instead, the impression we are given is that healing comes only as the 10 with leprosy obey Jesus by beginning to walk away from him to seek out the priests. It is at that point in time the symptoms of leprosy vanish.

We assume this means deformed fingers are made whole, and skin lesions disappear. Hair that had become unnaturally white (Leviticus 13:2, 3) returns to its natural color. And certainly those healed just feel better! They realize their trip to the priests is not a fool's errand, but rather is the first step in reclaiming their normal lives.

A simple lesson here is that faith that results in obedience leads to healing (compare 2 Kings 5).

For the 10 individuals of our text, this is physical healing. For us, it may be spiritual healing, a cleansing of our leprous, unclean hearts when we obediently follow Jesus (Acts 2:38-41).

> **What Do You Think?**
> When have you had a need met in such a way that God's involvement was clear? How did you grow spiritually from this experience?
> *Talking Points for Your Discussion*
> - Regarding a family situation
> - Regarding a medical need
> - Regarding a housing need
> - Other

II. One Grateful Man
(Luke 17:15-19)

A. Samaritan's Return (vv. 15, 16)

15. One of them, when he saw he was healed, came back, praising God in a loud voice.

One of the healed men postpones his trip to the priests. Seeing all symptoms of his leprosy disappear, he makes a U-turn back to Jesus. And he doesn't come quietly! His previous cry of "Unclean! Unclean!" (Leviticus 13:45) is now replaced with praise *in a loud voice*. Perhaps the man is *praising God* for the first time in many years. He recognizes the miracle of healing and knows its source.

> **What Do You Think?**
> What experiences have helped you be more grateful for God's blessings?
> *Talking Points for Your Discussion*
> - Regarding blessings via other Christians
> - Regarding blessings via unbelievers
> - Regarding blessings directly from God himself

16a. He threw himself at Jesus' feet and thanked him

For the man to throw *himself at Jesus' feet* is the posture of worship, appropriate only for worshipping God (see Revelation 19:10). This is the man's instinctive reaction. He may not understand everything that has just happened, but one thing he does know: this man, Jesus, is God's instrument in causing him to be healed, to be cleansed. The man has been shown mercy!

In the midst of this startling turn of events, the man cleansed of leprosy does the right thing. This man, who has suffered more than most of us can imagine, has not lost his humanity. His suffering may have caused doubts, but he still believes that God is in control—he knows that God is worthy of worship, praise, and thanksgiving.

16b. —and he was a Samaritan.

Here is the surprise twist to the story. The Jews consider the Samaritans to be something like inferior cousins (see the Lesson Background). How can it be that a Samaritan is the only one who understands that God should be praised and Jesus be thanked for the healing? The irony of this is similar to that of Jesus' parable of the good Samaritan (Luke 10:30-35), where a Samaritan is the only one who understands what love for one's neighbor truly is.

> **What Do You Think?**
> What was an occasion you were surprised by someone's expression of gratitude? What did this teach you?
> *Talking Points for Your Discussion*
> - Regarding a short-term need
> - Regarding a long-term need

B. Jesus' Concern (vv. 17, 18)

17, 18. Jesus asked, "Were not all ten cleansed? Where are the other nine? Has no one returned to give praise to God except this foreigner?"

In posing the questions we see here, Jesus transforms this miracle event into a teaching opportunity. The questions are almost like a mathematical story-problem: If 10 individuals are healed from leprosy, how many should give thanks and praise to God? What—only 1 came back to do so? What has happened to the other 9? Has God's miraculous power failed and the 9 are still unclean lepers who have run away in bitter disappointment? No, that is not the case, because everyone present knows that all 10 have been *cleansed*. The 9 neglect to give thanks.

19. Then he said to him, "Rise and go; your faith has made you well."

After addressing the onlookers, Jesus turns to the Samaritan himself with the declarations we see here. The man's new life has begun, and he can get up and go about his business, which first entails getting the blessing of the priests. The man is right to give the credit for the healing to God, but Jesus teaches him a lesson as well: it is through his faith that he has been healed.

This does not mean that the man has had the power to heal himself all along. It does not mean that the power of his personal faith in and of itself has brought about the healing. It means, rather, that his trust in God (as demonstrated by his initial act of obedience to seek out the priests) is pleasing to God, by whose power the leprosy has been vanquished.

> **What Do You Think?**
> How does an "attitude of gratitude" contribute to a growing faith?
> *Talking Points for Your Discussion*
> - Regarding the Christian's outlook on so-called entitlements
> - Romans 6:17, 23; 7:25
> - 1 Corinthians 15:57
> - Ephesians 2:8, 9
> - Other

> **What Do You Think?**
> How can we do better at expressing gratitude?
> *Talking Points for Your Discussion*
> - Concerning methods for doing so
> - Concerning increasing our awareness of a need to do so
> - Other

Another curiosity is that the one who did come back is, of all people, a non-Jew, a *foreigner*! This is a subtle rebuke to the Jews within earshot who assume that they are superior to Samaritans. In the end, relationship with God is demonstrated by one's actions, not by ancestral connections or lack thereof (see Luke 3:8).

❧ ATTITUDE OF INGRATITUDE? ❧

A few years ago, a Florida TV station reported on a mother of 15 children who was complaining about a lack of help from social services. She had indeed been receiving assistance, and the father of 10 of her children also had provided some support. But after he was arrested, she was evicted from her apartment and ended up in a hotel room with 12 of the children. She lashed out: "Somebody needs to pay for all my children. . . . Somebody needs to be held accountable, and they need to pay."

The video went viral on the Internet, chalking up over 180,000 viewings. As you might expect, the woman's attitude resulted in a firestorm of criticism. On the other hand, she also received sympathetic responses from people who offered various reasons for why she was justified in feeling unfairly treated. Overall, however, many felt that her statements indicated a lack of gratitude for the support that others had provided.

Attitudes of ingratitude have a long history! Had the nine who didn't return to Jesus simply never learned to express gratitude? Were they so overjoyed at being healed that, as they ran to share the news, they forgot to thank Jesus in the process? Did they feel that they were entitled to their healings, given their lengthy suffering? Let us remember: "Give thanks in all circumstances; for this is God's will for you in Christ Jesus" (1 Thessalonians 5:18).
—C. R. B.

❧ FAITH HEALERS ❧

Medical charlatans have a long and colorful history. Purveyance of "snake oil" is not limited to centuries past, as hucksters even now promote products as miracle cures for a myriad of ailments. Christians are targets, and some practitioners of fraudulent "faith healing" are occasionally exposed in the process.

The Committee for Skeptical Inquiry is an organization that specializes in examining claims that involve the paranormal; a bias against anything supernatural seems to be foundational to their work. Faith healers provide fodder for the skepticism of committee members. In at least one notable case, a well-known healer was proven to be receiving information via radio transmissions from backstage, messages that the healer claimed to be a "word from God" regarding an affliction to be cured. He frequently "cured" nonexistent ailments.

Unfortunately, charlatans parading as faith healers create doubt even among Christians as to whether God will heal. Indeed, he can and does! But for reasons of his own, God does not always choose to do so (compare 2 Corinthians 12:7-9). We keep in mind that the healing of one's spirit is more important than the healing of one's body, which eventually perishes anyway.   —C. R. B.

Conclusion
A. Healing Faith

This week's story is not a lesson that any Christian can be healed if he or she simply has enough faith. The darker side of such an idea is to believe that any Christian who suffers from illness or ailment is lacking in faith. Certainly, the lesson is about the importance of faith, but it is much more a lesson about the need for gratefulness whenever God blesses us.

Several times in the Gospels, Jesus heals people and pronounces that their faith has healed them. Examples include the woman with the issue of blood (Luke 8:43-48) and blind Bartimaeus (Mark 10:46-52). There is a double meaning for one of the words in these texts, for a term in Greek that is translated "has healed" is the same word that is translated "saved" in verses like John 3:17: "For God did not send his Son into the world to condemn the world, but to save the world through him." Healing and salvation are both signs of being made well or whole.

While we might be skeptical of some claims of healing in the church today, there is no need to dismiss them all. Our God is a God of healing, a lesson that Jesus taught repeatedly in his ministry. Miraculous healing is a gift of God; it is not something to be controlled by a human. Certain individuals might be instruments of God's healing power, but God is the one from whom healing comes.

Although we may never have witnessed it, a miraculous healing of a physical ailment would be

Of the 9 or 1?

Visual for Lesson 10. *Point to this visual as you pose the discussion question that is associated with verses 17, 18.*

easy for us to understand. If a person had visible symptoms of leprosy that suddenly disappeared, then we would conclude that God had acted. But the Bible accounts of such miracles should push our thoughts beyond that of physical healing. They should push us to understand how our hearts need to be healed. Our hearts have been diseased by sin, hardened by selfishness, and broken by loss. Can they ever be made whole?

Here is the lesson: the grateful man who had leprosy was healed in more than body; *his heart was made whole as well.* That's what the other nine missed—how sad! Healing begins with faith, with trusting God. We begin to heal when we yield our independence and throw ourselves into the arms of our Father. Healing is nurtured when we follow this faith with gratefulness as expressed through praise and thanksgiving. If a physician saves my life through skillful heart surgery, it would be natural to want to thank him or her. How much more should we turn and thank God, who heals our hearts and makes us whole for eternity!

B. Prayer

O God, heal our hearts! Teach us to praise you gratefully even in the midst of trouble. We pray this in the name of the one who healed the lepers: Jesus our Lord. Amen.

C. Thought to Remember

Healing begins with faith.

INVOLVEMENT LEARNING

Enhance your lesson with NIV® *Bible Student (from your curriculum supplier) and the reproducible activity page (at www.standardlesson.com or in the back of the* NIV® *Standard Lesson Commentary Deluxe Edition).*

Into the Lesson

Give each learner a blank index card. Say, "Take 60 seconds to jot down five things you are grateful for that you have used or enjoyed so far today." After calling time, offer learners a chance to share their lists. Then say, "Most of you probably named some everyday things that you normally don't even think about as stuff to be thankful for. One observer has said, 'The more I understand the mind and the human experience, the more I begin to suspect there is no such thing as unhappiness; there is only ungratefulness.' Is he right?"

After a few minutes of discussion, make a transition by saying, "Today we will see 10 men who had an excellent reason for being happy, but only 1 of them took the time to express gratitude."

Option. Before class begins, place in chairs copies of the "What Do You Know About Leprosy?" quiz from the reproducible page, which you can download. Learners can begin working on this as they arrive.

Into the Word

Enlist several learners to read the lesson text aloud: one as narrator, one as Jesus, and three or four to read in unison the request of the lepers. (The reading will go more smoothly if you give the readers handouts with their parts highlighted.)

Give the following lists of questions to three groups, one list each, to prepare interviews of Jesus, of one of the nine healed men who did not return, and of the one healed man who did return. Also give each group relevant information from the commentary.

Instruct: "Work within your groups to come up with responses to the questions. For some questions you will need to use your 'sanctified imagination,' as not all responses can be derived from either today's text in particular or the Bible as a whole. Select two people to play the parts of the interviewer and the interviewee. Remember that a

critical part of an interview is the follow-up question, so see if you can develop a few of those."

Interview 1: Jesus. What was the context in which you encountered the men who had leprosy? Why did you instruct them as you did? Why were you surprised that only one of the healed men came back to express gratitude? What did you mean by "Your faith has made you well"?

Interview 2: One of the nine who did not return. Since it's unusual for Jews and Samaritans to associate, why were you doing so? What did you and your fellow sufferers know about Jesus before calling out to him? Why did you stand so far away that you had to shout to be heard? What did you really expect when you implored Jesus to show pity? After you had turned to go to the priests, how did you know you were healed? Why didn't you return to thank Jesus for healing you?

Interview 3: The one who did return. What was the worst part about having leprosy? What did you really expect when you implored Jesus to have pity on you? Why do you suppose he gave you the instructions that he did? What was your first reaction when you realized you were healed? Why didn't the others return with you? What part did your faith play in your healing?

Allow groups time to present their interviews.

Into Life

Write the word *ACTS* vertically on the board. Explain that this represents the four-part prayer pattern of *adoration, confession, thanksgiving, supplication.* Focus on the third element by asking, "In relation to the other three elements, how much of a typical Christian's prayer life consists of thanking God?" Use the ensuing discussion to challenge learners to improve the quality and quantity of their prayers in this regard.

Option. Distribute copies of the "How Grateful Are You?" activity from the reproducible page. Have learners complete it as indicated.

HUMBLE
FAITH

DEVOTIONAL READING: Micah 6:6-8; 7:18, 19
BACKGROUND SCRIPTURE: Luke 18:9-14

LUKE 18:9-14

9 To some who were confident of their own righteousness and looked down on everyone else, Jesus told this parable: 10 "Two men went up to the temple to pray, one a Pharisee and the other a tax collector. 11 The Pharisee stood by himself and prayed: 'God, I thank you that I am not like other people—robbers, evildoers, adulterers—or even like this tax collector. 12 I fast twice a week and give a tenth of all I get.'

13 "But the tax collector stood at a distance. He would not even look up to heaven, but beat his breast and said, 'God, have mercy on me, a sinner.'

14 "I tell you that this man, rather than the other, went home justified before God. For all those who exalt themselves will be humbled, and those who humble themselves will be exalted."

KEY VERSE

"The tax collector stood at a distance. He would not even look up to heaven, but beat his breast and said, 'God, have mercy on me, a sinner.'" —**Luke 18:13**

The Gift of Faith

Unit 3: Fullness of Faith

Lessons 9–13

Lesson Aims

After participating in this lesson, each learner will be able to:

1. List the attitudes and actions of the tax collector and the Pharisee.

2. Explain the inverse relationship between humiliation and exaltation.

3. Examine his or her own approach to humility and make a plan for corrective action.

Lesson Outline

Introduction
  A. Society's Extremes
  B. Lesson Background: Pharisees
  C. Lesson Background: Tax Collectors
I. Parable's Target (Luke 18:9)
  A. View of Self (v. 9a)
  B. View of Others (v. 9b)
    15,000 Articles?
II. Tale of Two Men (Luke 18:10-13)
  A. Trips to the Temple (v. 10)
  B. Story of Self-Praise (vv. 11, 12)
  C. Story of Self-Humiliation (v. 13)
III. Lesson in Exaltation (Luke 18:14)
  A. Different Outcomes (v. 14a)
  B. Different Life Patterns (v. 14b)
    At What? Compared with Whom?
Conclusion
  A. The Source of Humility
  B. Prayer
  C. Thought to Remember

Introduction

A. Society's Extremes

I was recently visiting a church in a medium-sized city and chatting with a friend before the worship service began. A man and his wife walked by; I was introduced, and we shook hands. As the couple went to their seats, my friend whispered, "That's our chief of police." My immediate reaction was likely what yours might have been: impressed. I did not know him, but assumed the chief was a person deserving respect.

Contrast this with another encounter I had in a coffee shop in Los Angeles a few years ago. As I sat working on my computer, a 30-something man came in with two young women who were dressed in a suggestive, immodest fashion. His hands were all over those women. I don't know what their business was, but my mind assumed the worst. My opinion of this stranger was one of disgust and contempt. I figured that he was using or abusing those young women in ways that I would disapprove of strongly.

One-time encounters. Two people I didn't know. Why the difference in my reactions? Why did I consider one a respectable citizen and the other a contemptible lowlife? We sometimes form opinions of people based on scant information, strong opinions that may be resistant to change. Should we trust the neat and clean man who is dressed in a smart business suit or the young man wearing baggy gang-style apparel and sporting many tattoos? We form quick opinions, but the reality might be that the businessman is a crook while the other man is a youth minister.

Today's lesson is the story of two men from Jesus' world who were on opposite ends of society's respect gauge. The lesson that Jesus gives shows us that God judges us by what is in our hearts, not by our perceived reputation or social status.

B. Lesson Background: Pharisees

The Pharisees were an elite group of Jewish men in the first century AD. They played a prominent role as frequent opponents of Jesus in the four Gospels. We wish we knew more about this group, because some information about the Pharisees from sources outside the New Testament is inconsistent and even conflicting. Although the majority of Pharisees lived in the cities and villages of Israel (see Luke 5:17), they were also located in the Jewish quarters of the cities of the Roman Empire. For example, Paul was a Pharisee (as was his father, per Acts 23:6), although he grew up in Tarsus, a city in the Roman province of Cilicia, about 355 miles north of Jerusalem.

The Pharisees were zealous for keeping the Law of Moses with exacting detail. In addition, Pharisees were concerned with a body of unwritten regulations, sometimes called "the tradition of the elders" (Mark 7:5). This was understood as oral tradition that was delivered to Israel by Moses at the time the written law was received, and the Pharisees believed it was equally authoritative.

A great concern of the Pharisees was to be "faultless" when it came to the law (Philippians 3:6). Even so, the Pharisees of Jesus' day were targets of his teaching regarding hypocrisy (Luke 12:1). Jesus knew that while the Pharisees went to great pains to appear to be righteous keepers of the law, the hearts of some were far from righteous (Matthew 23:27). Luke portrays them as covetous (Luke 16:14).

C. Lesson Background: Tax Collectors

Compared with Pharisees, tax collectors were at the opposite end of the approval spectrum. They had entered into the employment of the hated Roman overlords to collect various taxes and tolls from fellow Jews. While the Pharisees were held in high esteem by the common people, tax collectors were universally reviled and hated. They were not seen as civil servants but as collaborators with the enemy—traitors.

Their reputation was further sullied by the way they went about their task, for they were known to use their positions of authority to extort, keeping the extra for themselves (compare Luke 19:1-8, lesson 13). The Romans overlooked this corruption as long as sufficient tax money flowed into their coffers. As a result, tax collectors operated without fear of prosecution or punishment.

Like some of the Pharisees, tax collectors tended to be wealthy (example: Luke 19:2). But unlike Pharisees, tax collectors had no incentive to give even the appearance of righteousness. Some lived a riotous lifestyle of heavy drinking and keeping company with prostitutes, for tax collectors had little to lose in the court of public opinion. Jesus received condemnation from Pharisees for consorting with tax collectors (Luke 5:30; 15:1, 2). Jesus even chose a tax collector to be an apostle (Matthew 9:9; 10:3; Luke 5:27, 28).

I. Parable's Target
(LUKE 18:9)
A. View of Self (v. 9a)

9a. To some who were confident of their own righteousness

A parable invites comparison; this is seen clearly here in the story that follows. The immediate context for this parable is Jesus' rhetorical question, "When the Son of Man comes, will he find faith on the earth?" (Luke 18:8). The parable at hand answers this question.

A preeminent Old Testament text that condemns the idea of trusting in oneself for attaining righteousness, what we call "being self-righteous," is Isaiah 64:6: "All of us have become like one who is unclean, and all our righteous acts are like filthy rags" (see also Psalms 14:2, 3; 53:2, 3 [quoted in Romans 3:10, 11]). The Old Testament speaks of what we might call being righteous in a relative sense (2 Samuel 22:21-25; etc.). But we cannot make ourselves wholly righteous, for we are all flawed and stained by sin.

This means our righteousness must come from an external source (compare Isaiah 61:10). The great truth of the gospel is that we become righteous through faith in Jesus (Romans 1:17; 3:21-26; Philippians 3:9; etc.). We cannot accomplish this by or for ourselves.

HOW TO SAY IT

Cilicia	Sih-*lish*-i-uh.
Moses	*Mo*-zes or *Mo*-zez.
Pharisees	*Fair*-ih-seez.
phylacteries	fih-*lak*-ter-eez.
Tarsus	*Tar*-sus.

B. View of Others (v. 9b)

9b. and looked down on everyone else, Jesus told this parable:

A mind-set of self-righteousness leads to the equally pernicious practice of judging other people to be unrighteous. Our personal smugness concerning our own sterling behavior causes us to despise them. We begin to say, "Well, I have my faults, but I am not as bad as others I know."

Again, the false underlying assumption is that we are adequate judges of righteousness, whether it be of ourselves or the lives of others. We must leave such judging to God (Luke 6:37). We are to trust that he will find us righteous through faith in Christ, not holding our sins against us.

> **What Do You Think?**
> How do we know when we've crossed the line from having a holy *God-confidence* to having an unholy *self-confidence*?
> *Talking Points for Your Discussion*
> ▪ In thoughts
> ▪ In behavior
> ▪ Considering 2 Corinthians 11:16-30
> ▪ Other

❧ *15,000 Articles?* ❧

An editorial cartoon a few years back showed two sloppily dressed high-school students looking at a newspaper. Its headline read, "Asian Students Exceed American Students in Science and Math." The caption of the cartoon had one of the fellows saying to the other, "Yeah, but I'll hold our self-esteem up to them any day!"

The beginning of the so-called Self-Esteem Movement has been traced to the influential paper "The Psychology of Self-Esteem," published by Nathaniel Brandon in 1969. The movement gained momentum in 1986 when the state of California passed legislation creating "The State Task Force to Promote Self-Esteem and Personal and Social Responsibility" to implement self-esteem principles. The foundation of such principles is that feelings of self-worth are a key to success in life.

By 2009, more than 15,000 scholarly articles had been written on the subject. Their conclusions, according to Kay Hymowitz, are that high self-esteem "doesn't improve grades, reduce anti-social behavior, deter alcohol drinking or do much of anything good for kids. In fact, telling kids how smart they are can be counterproductive."

Jesus noted a similar outcome among many religious leaders of his time: those who had been taught to have the greatest self-esteem with regard to their own righteousness did not, in fact, demonstrate superior spirituality—quite the opposite! The challenge of the apostle Paul still applies: "By the grace given me I say to every one of you: Do not think of yourself more highly than you ought, but rather think of yourself with sober judgment" (Romans 12:3).   —C. R. B.

II. Tale of Two Men
(Luke 18:10-13)
A. Trips to the Temple (v. 10)

10. "Two men went up to the temple to pray, one a Pharisee and the other a tax collector.

The temple in Jerusalem has many functions for the Jews of Jesus' day. It is a place of sacrifices, a place of worship, a place to give offerings, and a place *to pray* (see Acts 3:1). Jesus' parable in regard to the latter features *two men*, and the contrast between them can hardly be greater for his audience!

One of the men is *a Pharisee,* a man who automatically is respected by fellow Jews (see the Lesson Background). He is a paragon of virtue, a model citizen. He loves the law so much that he makes keeping it his life's pursuit and obsession.

The crowds notice visits by Pharisees to the temple, for Pharisees wear clothing that indicates their status. Such attire includes phylacteries (leather headpieces containing Scriptures) and cloaks with especially showy fringes or tassels (see Matthew 23:5; compare Numbers 15:38; Deuteronomy 6:8).

The crowds also notice any visit by *a tax collector.* They too are well dressed. Yet their attire is not designed to show piety, but to flaunt wealth. They might be accompanied by servants to attend to their every whim and act as bodyguards. On seeing a tax collector in the temple, the people might mutter, "What is that snake doing here? He cheated me and got away with it! His very presence makes a mockery of our temple!"

Yet the two men are bound together by the need to pray. The wording *went up to the temple* could indicate that both men are from out of town, having come some distance to the city of Jerusalem, which is at a higher elevation than the surrounding area (compare Luke 2:42; 10:30; etc.). The farther they have come, the greater their yearnings to speak with God and have him speak to them. But their motives are different, as we shall see.

B. Story of Self-Praise (vv. 11, 12)

11. "The Pharisee stood by himself and prayed: 'God, I thank you that I am not like other people—robbers, evildoers, adulterers—or even like this tax collector.

If *the Pharisee* is visiting from a village many miles distant, the opportunity to pray in the temple is very special for him, since he is not able to come to the temple daily. But whether living locally or farther away, this is an opportunity to parade his righteousness before crowds of admirers.

The prayer of the Pharisee is proud and public. He undoubtedly chooses a place to stand and offer his prayer that will give him maximum exposure to the crowd. We are given the impression that his words are more for public consumption than for sincere dialogue with God (compare Matthew 6:5, recorded by a former tax collector).

The Pharisee uses words of thanksgiving, but they are hardly thanks to God. They are self-congratulatory praises for what he has done with his life. He lists three categories of sin that he sees himself as having risen above: (1) he is not one of the *robbers*, which can include those who use legal maneuvers to steal from others; (2) he is not one of the *evildoers*, reminding his audience that he keeps the law perfectly; and (3) he is not one of the many *adulterers*, meaning his sexual conduct is above reproach.

But most of all, our Pharisee prides himself in not being like the nearby *tax collector*, a man whom the crowd may assume to be guilty of all three of the aforementioned sinful qualities. Those listening to the parable as Jesus tells it can imagine easily the disgust in the fictional Pharisee's voice.

What Do You Think?

Under what circumstances, if any, is it appropriate to compare ourselves with others? Why?

Talking Points for Your Discussion
- At work or school
- At home
- Considering Judges 8:1-3; 2 Corinthians 10:12-18; and Galatians 6:4
- Other

12a. "'I fast twice a week

Having listed the things he does not do, the Pharisee now trumpets the righteous things he does do on a regular basis. He fasts not once, but *twice a week* (compare Luke 5:33). An observant Jew is expected to keep the annual fast on the Day of Atonement (Leviticus 16:29-31; 23:26-32), but fasting twice a week is far beyond Old Testament requirements.

Ancient sources indicate that Pharisees fast on Mondays and Thursdays regularly. This practice surely began for godly reasons, but had devolved into a way of demonstrating piety (compare Zechariah 7:2-5). Times of fasting are accompanied by public displays to ensure the fasting is noticed by others (see Matthew 6:16).

12b. "'and give a tenth of all I get.'

The Pharisee is also proud to announce his rigorous tithing practices, something the onlookers assume of him. Elsewhere, Jesus condemns the

Visual for
Lessons 6 & 11

Point to this visual as you ask, "What is the relationship between humility and love?"

Pharisees' practice of scrupulous tithing as hypocritical because of their neglect of "the more important matters of the law—justice, mercy and faithfulness" (Matthew 23:23). Tithing is never taught in the New Testament as a way to gain favor with God. We are to give cheerfully as an act of worship (2 Corinthians 9:7), not as a way to receive praise from others (compare Matthew 6:1-4).

What Do You Think?
How might differences between *humility* and *self-righteousness* be evident as people participate in various worship activities today?
Talking Points for Your Discussion
- Regarding singing
- Regarding observance of the Lord's Supper
- Regarding the receiving of offerings
- Other

C. Story of Self-Humiliation (v. 13)

13. "But the tax collector stood at a distance. He would not even look up to heaven, but beat his breast and said, 'God, have mercy on me, a sinner.'"

The visual image above is of a crowd attending to the loud and showy prayer of the Pharisee. By contrast, *the tax collector* stands *at a distance* from that spectacle as he prays. He is not depicted as unnoticed, though, for Jesus paints a picture of the Pharisee's drawing attention to him in his own prayer (v. 11, above).

Unlike the Pharisee, the tax collector does not have a sense of self-righteousness. He has sold out to the Romans, but his resulting wealth gives no comfort for his soul. He is without hope, and all the money in the world cannot make up for a life without hope.

As such, he does not assume a posture of confident expectation for his praying. No raised arms, no head lifted toward God in Heaven. Instead, he acts with humility bordering on shame. It is almost as if he is afraid to make eye contact with God. He is like the ashamed child who droops his head to look at his shoes when confronted with wrongdoing by a parent. Jesus even pictures the tax collector pounding his chest, an act of self-humiliation (compare Luke 23:48).

The wealthy tax collector does nothing to justify himself and the sinful lifestyle we are to assume he has been leading. We are told nothing specific about this man. But the condemnation against him in the Pharisee's prayer is surely the way we should understand him. This is a man who has profited from his nation's misery under brutal Roman rule, filling his personal coffers with silver and gold extorted from fellow Jews.

Even so, he is no hypocrite, and he seeks to hide nothing despite his shame. He prays for one thing: God's mercy. His only hope for a restored relationship is based on the nature of God himself, the Lord who is merciful to his children even when they sin. If God withholds his mercy, all is lost.

What Do You Think?
Which of Jesus' personal actions helps you most to emulate his humility?
Talking Points for Your Discussion
- Considering Jesus' service
- Considering Jesus' sacrifice
- Considering Jesus' prayers
- Other

III. Lesson in Exaltation
(LUKE 18:14)

A. Different Outcomes (v. 14a)

14a. "I tell you that this man, rather than the other, went home justified before God.

Jesus ends the parable with a conclusion that undoubtedly surprises his hearers. Those listening expect positive recognition of the Pharisee, for he is the one the crowd looks to as a model of righteousness. They also expect a condemnation of the tax collector, for he is seen to be about as far from being righteous as any Jew they can imagine.

But that is not the outcome Jesus gives: the tax collector is the one who departs *justified*. This term is the verb form of the noun *righteousness*. The despised tax collector is the example Jesus wants to lift up—not for his lifestyle, but for the sincere humility of his prayer. Jesus is teaching that God is merciful. He attends to the prayer of the tax collector, while the self-serving prayer of the Pharisee results in nothing as far as God is concerned.

B. Different Life Patterns (v. 14b)

14b. "For all those who exalt themselves will be humbled, and those who humble themselves will be exalted."

Jesus ends this teaching story with a lesson that seems counterintuitive to his hearers and may be equally confusing to many today. Those who seek to exalt self will ultimately find this to be a losing effort. Self-exaltation is the same as self-justification as seen in the self-congratulatory prayer of the Pharisee. Although there may be no fault in that man's behavior, true exaltation, true justification, can come only from the Lord.

God still looks for the humble heart as the tax collector demonstrated (compare Psalm 51:17). No matter how right our actions might be, if our hearts are wrong, then we are not in God's favor. "[God] mocks proud mockers but shows favor to the humble" (Proverbs 3:34; quoted in James 4:6; 1 Peter 5:5). Even someone with the cleanest, holiest life can be proud and arrogant. Even the worst sinner can find a spirit of humility and recognition of shame.

❧ AT WHAT? COMPARED WITH WHOM? ❧

"I am the greatest," pronounced boxer Muhammad Ali in 1964. Boastful athletes and other high-profile individuals before and after him have made similar claims. We see it in the Old Testament (Ezekiel 35:13; etc.). We see it in today's headlines. In response, such claims can make us wonder *Greatest at what? Greatest compared with whom?*

The Pharisee put himself in the same company as Ali and other boasters both ancient and modern. On the *at what?* question, he fancied himself to be greatest at avoiding all the negative things listed in verse 11 and in performing the positive things listed in verse 12. On the *compared with whom?* question, the object of his derision was a despised tax collector. An interesting thought to entertain is how the Pharisee would have seen himself in comparison with the high priest!

That's the problem of comparing ourselves with others—our conclusions change depending on the standard of comparison that is used. When we compare ourselves with God's unchanging standards, however, our conclusions should always be the same: we have fallen short, and we need God's grace. "For it is by grace you have been saved, through faith—and that is not from yourselves, it is the gift of God—not by works, so that no one can boast" (Ephesians 2:8, 9). —C. R. B.

Conclusion

A. The Source of Humility

While Jesus used polar-opposite characters in the parable to make his point, there is nothing that precludes a person who lives in a righteous manner from being humble. Likewise, there is nothing about a grossly sinful lifestyle that automatically engenders humility. Humility is a matter of the heart and of understanding our relationship with the Lord. We should never presume his mercy, just as we must realize we can never earn it.

Any attempt to justify ourselves by pointing out our many good deeds will fall short. Paul reminds us that no one is righteous through personal effort (Romans 3:11, 12). What should we do then? What hope do we have? Our only hope is found in humbly trusting God and his mercy. This is the essence of Christian faith: the recognition that we cannot save ourselves. The best efforts of dedicated people like the Pharisees, people obsessed with keeping the law, fall short. May God be merciful to us, for we too are sinners.

B. Prayer

Merciful Father, remove from us the impulses to exalt ourselves. May our hearts be humble, trusting, and compliant to your will. We pray in the name of Jesus. Amen.

C. Thought to Remember

Be humble in all things.

INVOLVEMENT LEARNING

Enhance your lesson with NIV® Bible Student (from your curriculum supplier) and the reproducible activity page (at www.standardlesson.com or in the back of the NIV® Standard Lesson Commentary Deluxe Edition).

Into the Lesson

Display a picture of a man with tattoos and gang-type clothing alongside a picture of a respectable looking businessman. Ask learners to voice their first impressions of the possible employment and character of the two men.

Then say, "It's easy to form opinions about people based only on their appearance. Would it surprise you if the first picture were that of a former gang member who now serves as a youth minister? What if the second picture were that of someone who is cheating on his wife and embezzling money from his company? In today's lesson, Jesus uses a parable to make the point that things aren't always what they seem regarding the kingdom of God."

Into the Word

Using the Lesson Background, summarize the characteristics, roles, and reputations of Pharisees and tax collectors (or have two learners do so). Then give each learner a handout titled "Actions Reveal Attitudes" that features three columns headed *Pray-ers / Actions / Attitudes*. Have the words *Pharisee* and *Tax Collector* listed under the first heading as captions of two rows that extend across the other two columns.

Form learners into groups of four or five to complete the chart according to the lesson text. In whole-class discussion, compare and contrast groups' discoveries. Differing conclusions will be opportunities for deeper study. Use the commentary to resolve misconceptions.

Alternative. Distribute copies of the "Character Analysis" activity from the reproducible page, which you can download. Have learners work in pairs to complete it as indicated. In the ensuing whole-class discussion, read each word aloud and ask pairs to give reasons for their choices. Encourage challenges from those whose answers differ; this will create opportunities for deeper discussion. Wrap up by asking, "With all those negative

traits and actions ascribed to the tax collector, why was he the one who 'went home justified' and not the Pharisee?"

Follow either activity by reading verse 14b aloud. Then lead a discussion on that statement by posing these questions: 1. What was wrong with the Pharisee's idea about how to present himself as righteous to God? 2. How does an attempt to exalt oneself contradict the idea of grace?

As learners respond to question 1, work in Paul's declaration that "all have sinned and fall short of the glory of God" (Romans 3:23), a conclusion he held even given his background "in regard to the law, a Pharisee; . . . as for righteousness based on the law, faultless" (Philippians 3:5, 6). As learners respond to question 2, be sure to point out that "by grace you have been saved, through faith—and this is not from yourselves, it is the gift of God—not by works, so that no one can boast" (Ephesians 2:8, 9).

Into Life

Give each learner a handout that reproduces these two situations: *Scenario 1*–A wealthy woman in the congregation frequently offers to host Bible studies in her home. *Scenario 2*–A recovering alcoholic leads an Alcoholics Anonymous group in a church classroom each week.

Say, "The main character in each scenario could have the attitude of either the Pharisee or the tax collector. Identify words or actions that would reveal which would be present." Have learners work in pairs or groups of three. Allow time for pairs/groups to share their results in whole-class discussion. Mention the possibility that a humble heart can be found in the well-to-do, and a self-righteous attitude can be seen in a reformed sinner.

Option. Distribute copies of the "Humble at Heart?" activity from the reproducible page. Due to the highly personal nature of this exercise, it should be a take-home activity.

CHILDLIKE
FAITH

DEVOTIONAL READING: Isaiah 11:1-9
BACKGROUND SCRIPTURE: Luke 18:15-17; Mark 10:13-16

LUKE 18:15-17

 [15] People were also bringing babies to Jesus for him to place his hands on them. When the disciples saw this, they rebuked them. [16] But Jesus called the children to him and said, "Let the little children come to me, and do not hinder them, for the kingdom of God belongs to such as these. [17] Truly I tell you, anyone who will not receive the kingdom of God like a little child will never enter it."

MARK 10:16

[16] And he took the children in his arms, placed his hands on them and blessed them.

KEY VERSE

"Truly I tell you, anyone who will not receive the kingdom of God like a little child will never enter it."
—Luke 18:17

The Gift of Faith

Unit 3: Fullness of Faith

LESSONS 9–13

Lesson Aims

After participating in this lesson, each learner will be able to:

1. Retell the story of Jesus' blessing the children.

2. Explain why Jesus used children as an example of the ideal candidate for the kingdom of God.

3. Examine himself or herself for the absence of childlike faith and make a plan for change.

Lesson Outline

Introduction
  A. The Gift and the Burden of Children
  B. Lesson Background
I. Jesus' Correction (LUKE 18:15-17)
  A. Disciples Forbid (v. 15)
    The Ultimate Rejection of Babies
  B. Children Welcomed (v. 16a)
    Bringing Children to Jesus
  C. Kingdom Illustrated (vv. 16b, 17)
II. Jesus' Action (MARK 10:16)
  A. Holding Children (v. 16a)
  B. Blessing Children (v. 16b)
Conclusion
  A. Jesus Loves the Children
  B. Jesus Loves the Childlike
  C. Prayer
  D. Thought to Remember

Introduction

A. The Gift and the Burden of Children

The headline of August 14, 2013, read "Average cost to raise a kid: $241,080." That figure summarized the U.S. Department of Agriculture's report that estimated the 18-year cost of raising a child born in the U.S. in that year; another projection has costs in Canada to be similar.

The USDA's estimate includes just about every expense one can think of except for college. Adjusted regionally, the costs in some parts of the U.S. can reach nearly $450,000, while dipping to less than $150,000 in other parts. Even assuming the lower figure, a family with three children can find itself being pushed toward half a million dollars in child-rearing expenditures, before even considering the cost of college!

As a minister, I have experienced many occasions when a young couple told me they were expecting a baby. I first say, "Congratulations!" Later, however, I will tell them, "Your life has changed forever," and I'm not speaking just about the financial aspect. The differences between a family with children and a family without children are significant. Parents agree that children can bring some of the greatest joy available on this earth; at other times, they can bring some of the deepest heartaches. Rearing a child is not a part-time commitment. It is a serious, long-term responsibility.

These and other factors are behind a growing movement among women to choose voluntarily not to have children. Critics see the so-called childfreedom movement as driven by selfishness. Yet there are serious arguments that childless adults are able to contribute more to society because of their lack of family obligations.

The idea of remaining voluntarily childless within marriage would have seemed strange to the people whom Jesus walked among in the first century AD. To them, having children was not only the norm but also required (Genesis 1:27, 28). Children were therefore present and prevalent in all aspects of daily life in the Israel of Jesus' day. He drew on this fact to illustrate what it means to be a child of God in the best possible way.

B. Lesson Background

Children were valued differently among Jews and Gentiles in the ancient world. Many Gentile households saw children as a necessary nuisance. This is illustrated by the idea that slaves and children had the same status in a Gentile household (compare Galatians 4:1). This is not because slaves were valued, but because children were not.

The main value of a child in the Greco-Roman world was that he or she would eventually grow up and become a productive adult. In that light, children could be treated like assets that would mature at a later date. This was the reason for educating and privileging them in special ways. In particular, male children were valued for their potential to provide for parents in their old age. These cultural assumptions regarding children were "a given" for many of the earliest readers of the Gospel of Luke, which the author seems to have directed toward Christians who came from a Gentile background. Indeed, that probably was Luke's own status.

The Jewish people, on the other hand, viewed children differently. Children were seen as gifts from God to be cared for and nurtured. The future of the nation and the retention of its heritage depended on children. They were to be brought up to appreciate their responsibilities and to be faithful to the covenant they had been given. Children were to be taught Scripture and have its precepts embedded deeply in their hearts (Deuteronomy 6:7; compare 2 Timothy 3:14, 15). Large families were prized (see Psalm 127:3-5), and childless women were disappointed (see Luke 1:24, 25).

Children were not coddled in extreme ways in Jewish households, however. Early on, they were given work tasks around the home and in a family's business. We assume that Jesus learned the trade of his earthly father's carpentry business from a very early age, by both observing and doing (Mark 6:3). Although Jesus himself was unmarried and without children, the fact that he was the Son of God meant that his teaching on the subject of children was and is authoritative.

I. Jesus' Correction
(LUKE 18:15-17)

The parable of the Pharisee and the tax collector (Luke 18:9-14, last week's lesson) is followed by the first segment of today's lesson text. These stories are connected by the theme of *humility*, a character trait Jesus finds in little children. (Matthew 19:13-15 and Mark 10:13-16 are parallel.)

A. Disciples Forbid (v. 15)

15a. People were also bringing babies to Jesus for him to place his hands on them.

The fact that the children under consideration are *babies* means that they probably are not yet a year old. The word in the original language being translated is also used for the newborn baby Jesus (Luke 2:12, 16) and even for John the Baptist while he was still in his mother's womb (1:41, 44). The babes-in-arms of the verse before us are innocent treasures of humanity, as are all other infants.

Some have interpreted the parents' desire that Jesus touch their babies to mean that these infants are ill, in need of healing. But that does not seem to be what is going on here. A touch by Jesus would be an act of blessing, accompanied by prayer. Jesus' reputation has preceded him!

15b. When the disciples saw this, they rebuked them.

The parents' plans are temporarily derailed by Jesus' overprotective *disciples*. Their rebuke means that they harshly forbid access to their Master. We are not told why they do this, but their motives are likely positive. It is not that they devalue children, but probably because they want to shield Jesus from another demand on his time and energy.

❧ *The Ultimate Rejection of Babies* ❧

Roe v. Wade has been a part of the American vocabulary since 1973. That was the case by which the U.S. Supreme Court overturned various

HOW TO SAY IT

Deuteronomy	Due-ter-*ahn*-uh-me.
Galatians	Guh-*lay*-shunz.
Gentile	*Jen*-tile.
Pharisee	*Fair*-ih-see.

federal and state laws restricting abortion. This landmark decision served to polarize a debate that continues to this day.

At one end of the spectrum are those who see the issue purely in terms of a woman's "right to choose"; those in this group use euphemisms such as "product of conception" and "fetal tissue" to deny that a baby is involved. At the other end of the spectrum are those who would prohibit all abortions, period.

Most people seem to be somewhere in the conflicted middle on this issue. Many in this block are in favor of the increasing number of restrictions being enacted on abortion processes and procedures. By one count, 70 restrictions on abortion services were adopted in 22 states in 2013. Such regulations address, among other things, parental involvement for their underage daughters to have abortions, limitations on insurance coverage, and bans on late-term abortions.

Abortion seems to be the ultimate rejection of babies. Jesus' disciples were not guilty of anything so draconian in their rebuke of the parents. But those disciples were nonetheless misguided, despite good intentions. It's easy to point out both the wrong actions and wrong motives of others on various issues, abortion or otherwise. It's not so easy to recognize our own wrong actions when they are impelled by our good motives. May the Lord give us wisdom to be aware of both!   —C. R. B.

What Do You Think?

What are some ways a church may unintentionally restrict access to Jesus today? How do we prevent this from happening?

Talking Points for Your Discussion

- Regarding the Elders Generation (those born before 1946)
- Regarding Baby Boomers (those born between 1946 and 1964)
- Regarding Generation X (those born between 1965 and 1983)
- Regarding the Millennials Generation (those born between 1984 and 2002)
- Regarding Generation Z (those born after 2002)

B. Children Welcomed (v. 16a)

16a. But Jesus called the children to him and said, "Let the little children come to me, and do not hinder them,

The first line of this half-verse seems to indicate that there is some physical distance between Jesus and the mini-drama involving the disciples and the parents. Jesus is aware of what is happening despite this distance, and he countermands the disciples' rebuke of the previous verse. The disciples are not to forbid access to Jesus. (The parallel of Mark 10:14 adds that Jesus "was indignant.")

The word translated *little children* here is different from the word translated "babies" in verse 15. *Little children* is a broader term, including both infants and youngsters who are beyond the infancy stage (compare Matthew 11:16; 18:2-5; 19:13; Mark 10:13; Luke 1:59, 66). Jesus is saying that he welcomes all children—whether infants, toddlers, or otherwise.

This moment has often been portrayed artistically as Jesus being seated with small children in his lap and at his knees. This is likely very close to what happens as parents stand nearby. Jesus had several younger siblings (Matthew 13:55, 56), so we should not be surprised either at his gentle ease in holding these children or their comfort level with him.

❧ *BRINGING CHILDREN TO JESUS* ❧

The origins of the Sunday school movement are traced to the initiative of Robert Raikes in Great Britain in the 1780s. Sunday schools soon caught on in America, and most children were attending Sunday school by the mid-1800s. The curriculum included religious teaching as well as the "3 Rs" (reading, writing, and arithmetic), with literacy taught through the reading of the Bible. Prayer and hymn-singing were also a part of the educational process.

With the advent of universal, compulsory state-sponsored education in the 1870s, the role of Sunday schools began to change. Even so, a large number of children continued to attend Sunday school regularly. Cultural changes in recent decades have made Sunday school a less significant part of childhood experience, even among Christian families.

The secular forces that are at work in modern culture may not go so far as actually forbidding children from coming to Jesus, but they certainly make it more difficult. Participation in organized youth sports on Sunday and parental disregard for their children's spiritual needs can both contribute to the lessening of the impact Sunday school can have in the lives of youngsters. What solutions can you propose for this problem?

—C. R. B.

C. Kingdom Illustrated (vv. 16b, 17)

16b. "for the kingdom of God belongs to such as these.

Ever the teacher, Jesus not only receives the children but also uses them to give a surprising lesson. The previous narrative used a tax collector as an unlikely example of humility, and now children are presented in somewhat similar fashion as ideal members of *the kingdom of God*.

This is not what Jesus' audience expects. According to Jewish heritage, an ideal member of the kingdom of God is a great leader like Moses, a mighty king like David, or a powerful prophet like Isaiah. The noble Pharisee of the parable of last week's lesson might be the embodiment of the kingdom of God in the eyes of the common people. But children? What is there about a small child that has anything to do with citizenship in the kingdom of God? Jesus answers this question in the next verse.

17. "Truly I tell you, anyone who will not receive the kingdom of God like a little child will never enter it."

Jesus' brief answer draws us to think of several ways in which children might be presented as examples for adults to follow. First, young children are highly dependent. Without the care and protection of a parent or guardian, a young child will not survive. Kingdom members should depend on the Lord, not on themselves. This is hard, because adults are expected to be independent. But any attempt to deny our need for the Lord will fail.

Second, children are receptive to new things and fresh teaching. They are naturally inquisitive and want to learn. They might say *No!* a lot, but they are not set in their ways and impervious to change. They do not have hard hearts. Kingdom members should be open to God's leading, even if it is down paths of service that require new ways of thinking. God wants people with compliant hearts, people who will change in response to the teaching of his Word.

Third, children are naturally creatures of faith. It is not without good reason that we speak of "childlike faith." Trust is a natural condition for children. It is "unfaith" that is learned through disappointing experiences. Kingdom members must be people of the deep kind of faith that a child has in his or her parents. Just as children may not always understand when they are called to obey, people of faith obey God's Word because of their deep trust in the Lord.

Fourth, the youngest children (babies) are models of humility. They make no boasts; they have no claim to fame; they live without arrogance. They may cry a lot, but there is nothing evil in this. Babies have no merits or accomplishments to commend them. It would be unthinkable for a baby to act in such a way as to attempt to earn God's favor.

Humility is a companion of innocence, and there is no more innocent human being than a sweet, newborn baby. It is admittedly difficult for an adult voluntarily to become as humble and trusting as a baby, yet this is what Jesus requires. When we hold on to our stubbornness and demand to be in control of every aspect of our lives, we are rejecting Jesus' gracious invitation to be part of *the kingdom of God*. By faith we receive the power "to become children of God" (John 1:12), and this is not merely figurative. Faith is coming to God as a child.

What Do You Think?
How do we keep the little-child aspect that Jesus desires of us while not remaining spiritual infants in the process?
Talking Points for Your Discussion
- Matthew 21:16
- Luke 10:21
- 1 Corinthians 3:1-3; 14:20
- Ephesians 4:12-15
- Hebrews 5:11–6:3
- 1 Peter 1:14
- Other

II. Jesus' Action
(MARK 10:16)

Our lesson ends by looking at a verse from the parallel account of this incident in the Gospel of Mark. (Matthew 19:15 is also parallel.)

A. Holding Children (v. 16a)

16a. And he took the children in his arms, placed his hands on them

Here we see the physical aspect of Jesus' interaction with the gathering children. One by one, he takes the little ones *in his arms.* The man who has no children adopts the posture of a loving parent holding the precious joy of the family. We can imagine Jesus looking deeply into the eyes of each child, just as a loving, wondering mother or father might do. He is smiling at them, and perhaps they smile back.

What Do You Think?
What role should physical contact play in ministry to children today? Why?
Talking Points for Your Discussion
- Considering parental desires
- Considering church policy
- Considering cultural expectations
- Considering federal, state, and local law
- Other

B. Blessing Children (v. 16b)
16b. and blessed them.

To be *blessed* is to have divine approval. The children will retain this state of blessedness as they grow in learning to love God with all their hearts, souls, and minds. Jesus' blessing on the gathered children likely includes a peace prayer for their health and future prosperity.

These are moments to remember for the families involved. Surely, at least some of these children grow up to be followers of Jesus after his resurrection. They will grow up with the story told and retold to them (if they were too young to remember it personally) of the day they were blessed by Jesus of Nazareth, the man who proved himself to be the Son of God, the chosen Messiah sent by the heavenly Father. They will have a story to tell and a witness to share that very few experience personally.

What Do You Think?
What are some ways the church can bestow Christ's blessings on children today?
Talking Points for Your Discussion
- In educational ministries
- In relationship structures
- In service projects
- Other

Conclusion
A. Jesus Loves the Children

One of the first songs I learned in church told me that "Jesus loves the little children, all the children of the world." This was often paired with another favorite song that proclaimed "Jesus loves me, this I know, for the Bible tells me so."

My simple thinking of those formative years connected all this. I figured that if Jesus loves all the children of the world, then I was one of them. And when I was told to sing that Jesus loves me, I couldn't help but love him back.

What a great truth to teach our children: *Jesus loves you! The Son of God loves you!* Today's lesson reveals that Jesus was disturbed when his disciples tried to keep children away from him. He wanted to be with the children, to hold them, to bless them. This truth has not grown old for me; I have never forgotten it. The Jesus who held and blessed the children so many centuries ago is the risen Christ who held me spiritually throughout my childhood.

The love that Jesus exhibited for children is one of the things that endears the human Jesus to us so much. He did not see them as a bother or a nuisance; he saw them as a treasure. The ministries in some churches are tilted overly toward adults because, after all, little children cannot give much in the way of offerings or serve on committees. But those who teach and minister to children are the guardians of one of the church's greatest treasures.

The people of Israel knew they needed to train their children so they could be future leaders. So also Christians need to care for the souls of their children so that the work of the church will continue into the next generation without faltering. Neglecting or shortchanging ministry to children may seem prudent in the short term, but in the long run it is the most unwise plan that any church can possibly follow!

We have children in our churches who are the future of the church, but too often we let them slip away. They are not nurtured in ways that result in a smooth transition from the childlike faith of "Jesus loves the little children" to "Jesus loves me forever." When picking up their children from Sunday school, the parents' first question should not be "Did you have fun today?" but rather "What did you learn about God today?" May we never neglect the spiritual development of our children!

B. Jesus Loves the Childlike

In addition to the tender picture of Jesus holding, loving, and blessing children, our lesson has

VISUALS FOR THESE LESSONS

The visual pictured in each lesson (see example above) is a small reproduction of a large, full-color poster included in the *Adult Resources* packet for the Spring Quarter. That packet also contains the very useful *Presentation Tools* CD for teacher use. Order No. 020039216 from your supplier.

Visual for Lesson 12. *Start a discussion by pointing to this visual as you ask, "What are some characteristics of being childish vs. being childlike?"*

a second focus: we are reminded that we must be like children to be proper members of the kingdom of God.

God wants our trust. God wants us to be humble. God wants a childlike faith. On some of my darkest days as an adult, I have sung those songs "Jesus loves the little children" and "Jesus loves me, this I know" from my childhood to remind myself that I am still loved by the Savior of the world. I am still a child in his kingdom.

If children ruled the world, the result would be chaos. If children led the church, things would be a mess. But if the world and the church were led by responsible, spiritually mature adults who had childlike faith and humble spirits, what a difference we would see! What will you do in the week ahead to make that difference a reality?

C. Prayer

Heavenly Father, thank you for loving us when we were innocent children and for not withholding your love when we became adults. Thank you for showing us how important children are to you and teaching us how important they must be for us. Make us more like children who trust you without reserve. May we rest in your arms and receive your blessings in Jesus' name. Amen.

D. Thought to Remember

Childlike faith makes us fit
for the kingdom of God.

INVOLVEMENT LEARNING

Enhance your lesson with NIV® Bible Student (from your curriculum supplier) and the reproducible activity page (at www.standardlesson.com or in the back of the NIV® Standard Lesson Commentary Deluxe Edition).

Into the Lesson

Ask learners in advance to bring pictures of children as babies or toddlers. Place the photos on display or pass them around. Bring the naturally occurring discussion to a conclusion by saying, "It's easy to see why people are fond of talking about their little ones. If Jesus were here, I'm sure we would want him to hold them close and bless them. Let's read about a time when he did just that." (If you have learners who have suffered the loss of a child or are unable to have a baby, you may wish to use the alternative activity.)

Alternative. Before class begins, place in chairs copies of the "Childlike or Childish?" activity from the reproducible page, which you can download, for learners to begin working on as they arrive. List results on the board under the headings *Childlike* and *Childish*. Then say, "When Jesus told the disciples in today's lesson that they should be more like children, he had the positive qualities in mind. Let's see why."

Into the Word

Use the Lesson Background to summarize the different views toward children by the Gentiles and Jews in Jesus' day (or ask two learners to do so). Then have four volunteers read aloud the four verses of the lesson text, one verse each.

After the reading, pose the following questions for discussion. These will challenge your learners to push beyond the obvious "what happened" to ponder "why it happened," which will not be so evident. Pose only one question at a time and discuss it before revealing the next.

1. Why did the parents want Jesus to touch their infants?

2. Since Jewish culture valued children highly, why would the disciples try to keep the children away from Jesus?

3. Since various passages in the New Testament condemn the idea of remaining infants spiritu-

ally, what did Jesus mean by his pronouncement in Luke 18:17?

After learners offer their ideas, mention also the following if no one has done so: 1–Because of Jesus' reputation, the parents may have been hoping for a spiritual blessing (see commentary on Luke 18:15a). 2–The disciples may have been trying to protect Jesus from too many demands on his time and energy (see commentary on Luke 18:15b). 3–The reasons may be that young children are models of dependence, are receptive, are naturally creatures of faith, and in their youngest years are models of humility (see commentary on Luke 18:17). These observations will serve as a natural lead in to the Into Life segment. (*Option:* Time permitting, the "various passages" you may wish to discuss for contrast with spiritual infancy are 1 Corinthians 3:1-3; 14:20; Ephesians 4:12-15; and Hebrews 5:11–6:3.)

Option. Put the three questions on handouts to be discussed in small groups.

Into Life

Form the class into four pairs or small groups. Give each pair/group a strip of paper that has one of the following four statements: 1–Young children are highly dependent, unable to survive without adult care. 2–Young children are receptive to new things and are eager to learn. 3–Young children are naturally creatures of faith, very trusting. 4–The youngest children are models of humility.

Say, "First discuss the truth of the statement on your strip. Then discuss its level of importance as an attitude necessary for entry into the kingdom of God." Have pairs/groups present conclusions in whole-class discussion.

Option. Distribute copies of the "As a Little Child" from the reproducible page. Allow time for learners to complete this individually. Encourage them to ponder it daily during private devotional time in the week ahead.

JOYOUS
FAITH

DEVOTIONAL READING: Isaiah 44:23-26
BACKGROUND SCRIPTURE: Luke 19:1-10

LUKE 19:1-10

[1] Jesus entered Jericho and was passing through. [2] A man was there by the name of Zacchaeus; he was a chief tax collector and was wealthy. [3] He wanted to see who Jesus was, but because he was short he could not see over the crowd. [4] So he ran ahead and climbed a sycamore-fig tree to see him, since Jesus was coming that way.

[5] When Jesus reached the spot, he looked up and said to him, "Zacchaeus, come down immediately. I must stay at your house today." [6] So he came down at once and welcomed him gladly.

[7] All the people saw this and began to mutter, "He has gone to be the guest of a sinner."

[8] But Zacchaeus stood up and said to the Lord, "Look, Lord! Here and now I give half of my possessions to the poor, and if I have cheated anybody out of anything, I will pay back four times the amount."

[9] Jesus said to him, "Today salvation has come to this house, because this man, too, is a son of Abraham. [10] For the Son of Man came to seek and to save the lost."

KEY VERSE

"The Son of Man came to seek and to save the lost." —**Luke 19:10**

THE GIFT OF FAITH

Unit 3: Fullness of Faith
LESSONS 9–13

LESSON AIMS

After participating in this lesson, each learner will be able to:

1. Tell how Zacchaeus came to be declared "a son of Abraham."

2. Suggest how to demonstrate the faith of Zacchaeus.

3. Commit to an extravagant act of faith to benefit another.

LESSON OUTLINE

Introduction
   A. The Bullied Get Revenge
   B. Lesson Background
I. Two Desires (LUKE 19:1-6)
   A. Place and Person (vv. 1, 2)
   B. Problem and Solution (vv. 3, 4)
   C. Statement and Reaction (vv. 5, 6)
      Always a Joyful Response?
II. Three Attitudes (LUKE 19:7-10)
   A. Crowd Complains (v. 7)
   B. Zacchaeus Promises (v. 8)
      Restitution
   C. Jesus Blesses (vv. 9, 10)
Conclusion
   A. Seeking the Lost
   B. Prayer
   C. Thought to Remember

Introduction

A. The Bullied Get Revenge

The past few years have seen a great deal of attention on the problem of bullying. We all remember bullies from our growing-up years: girls and boys who picked on those seen as weak or shy. Bullies sometimes did this to extort money or possessions, sometimes to gain status among peers, sometimes simply for the perverse enjoyment of tormenting others. A new twist on this in the twenty-first century is the extension of bullying via social media. One tragic result is highly publicized suicides of vulnerable adolescents.

The other side of bullying has been the payback factor, with instances of mass shootings in schools attributed to boys seeking revenge for having been bullied. But revenge for bullying can come in other, less violent ways. Sometimes an adult who was bullied as a child will use a position of influence in the business world to exact delayed revenge in various ways. For example, those who were always favored in school because of good looks or athletic ability may become the unfavored ones for career advancement and work assignments.

Perhaps that was the situation of Zacchaeus in today's lesson. Luke 19:3 tells us that "he was short." Using our "sanctified imagination," we might speculate that this resulted in his being teased as a child and becoming a target of bullies. So in his adult occupation as a tax collector for the hated Roman overlords, he was in a position to enforce his will on his fellow Jews. It's easy to speculate that this little man exacted revenge over and over for his childhood traumas. The bullied boy (again, speculation) had become the oppressive tax man. But an encounter with Jesus changed that situation.

B. Lesson Background

The site of today's lesson is Jericho, a city mentioned dozens of times in the Bible. Indeed, this locale had held a prominent place in the history of Israel back to around 1400 BC (Numbers 22:1; Joshua 2:1; etc.). At that time, Jericho was the first city to be conquered by the Israelites after crossing the Jordan River to enter the promised land of Canaan. Jericho's downfall came about in dramatic fashion when God caused the protecting walls to collapse (Joshua 6:20). Centuries later, King Zedekiah, the last king of Judah, was captured by the Babylonians "in the plains of Jericho," to which he had fled after the fall of Jerusalem in 586 BC (Jeremiah 39:5).

Jericho was located less than 10 miles north-northwest of the Dead Sea, in a western fringe of the Jordan River valley. The city was an oasis settlement, having been built around a spring of fresh water in an arid region. This resulted in the settlement being known as "the City of Palms" (Deuteronomy 34:3). Since the city had its own water supply, it did not need to be located near the Jordan River, which was four or five miles away. Archaeologists estimate that Jericho is one of the oldest sites for human settlement in the world, with remains dating back thousands of years.

At the time of Jesus, Jericho was both an agricultural hub and a resort city, features that still characterize the area today. Ancient farmers cultivated date palms and profited from the prized dates, a sweet fruit that could be dried and easily transported. Modern Jericho, sited only a mile and a half southeast of the ruins of ancient Jericho, still features date groves. Some wealthy priests of Jerusalem in Jesus' day maintained homes in Jericho; they could make the 15-mile trip in a day or two when they were off duty from temple service.

Jericho was also the last major stop for Jews traveling from Galilee to Jerusalem for Passover and other observances. Indeed, Jesus was headed to Jerusalem for his final celebration of Passover when he encountered Zacchaeus, a tax collector in Jericho. (See the Lesson Background for lesson 11 regarding tax collectors.)

I. Two Desires
(Luke 19:1-6)
A. Place and Person (vv. 1, 2)

1. Jesus entered Jericho and was passing through.

The city of *Jericho* figures prominently in the pages of the Bible (see the Lesson Background). In a sense, Jesus is *passing through* an ancestral home, since a person in his lineage—namely Rahab—had lived there centuries before (see Joshua 2; Matthew 1:5; Hebrews 11:31).

Arrival in Jericho marks the beginning of the final leg of Jesus' journey to Jerusalem and the cross that awaits him there, a journey that began in Luke 9:51. The route he is taking is the common one for Jews traveling to Jerusalem from Galilee, except for the fact that Jesus does not avoid Samaritan territory along the way as Jews normally would (Luke 9:52-56).

What Do You Think?

What reactions can we expect when Jesus "comes to town" today through a newly planted church? Why?

Talking Points for Your Discussion
- From unbelievers
- From Christians
- From ministers in the area
- From local government
- Others

---

2. A man was there by the name of Zacchaeus; he was a chief tax collector and was wealthy.

In Jericho we encounter *a man . . . by the name of Zacchaeus.* We conclude that he is a Jew because, among other things, he has a Hebrew name. That name means "innocent one" or "pure," which is ironic for the fact that he is anything but!

Being *a chief tax collector* means that Zacchaeus is an achiever. Over the years, he has managed to get himself promoted to an administrative level in the tax collection function so that now he supervises several field employees. At this point in his career, Zacchaeus is likely insulated from the unpleasantness of exacting tax payments personally from the citizens of Jericho and from merchants who must pay tolls to travel through the city with commercial goods. A man in the position of Zacchaeus can let his minions do the actual collecting.

The fact that Zacchaeus is wealthy is no surprise, for this is the usual situation for such tax collectors. He retains a portion of the taxes collected by his underlings, passing along the necessary amount to the Roman governing officials. If Zacchaeus has set up this operation to run smoothly, it likely produces a steady personal income with little effort on his part. He may be among the richest men in the city.

B. Problem and Solution (vv. 3, 4)

3. He wanted to see who Jesus was, but because he was short he could not see over the crowd.

The arrival of *Jesus* in Jericho is a major event, for by this time his reputation as a teacher and miracle worker has preceded him. A *crowd* follows him as a result (compare Luke 18:36). People have just witnessed a miraculous healing (18:43), and the excitement is palpable.

Zacchaeus is well connected with the news of his city, for his control of the tax situation requires information. He has heard of Jesus and knows that he is in town. Zacchaeus's desire *to see* Jesus is more than a mere desire to gaze upon someone who is famous. Zacchaeus wants to know more about the man, perhaps even meet him.

But Zacchaeus finds that his wealth does not yield him a choice viewing position. The presence of so many people—who likely stand shoulder to shoulder, several layers deep—serves to block his view. The fact that Zacchaeus is short means that he is so small that he cannot get even a peek at the famous Jesus. Zacchaeus, despised as he is (see v. 7, below), has no friends here, and no one steps aside to give him a front-row view.

4. So he ran ahead and climbed a sycamore-fig tree to see him, since Jesus was coming that way.

Zacchaeus is nothing if not a survivor (see the Lesson Background). One does not get to the position of being "a chief tax collector" (v. 2, above) without being able to solve problems! Zacchaeus quickly realizes that fighting the crowd will be futile, so he runs ahead to a place where he assumes Jesus will pass within the next few moments. Zacchaeus undoubtedly is quite familiar with the layout of Jericho, so he knows of a tree suitable for climbing that borders the route.

The *sycamore-fig tree* of Palestine (binomial name *Ficus sycomorus*) is not the same as the syc-amore tree of North America (binomial name *Platanus occidentalis*), so we take care not to confuse them with one another. The tree familiar to Zacchaeus has branches that spread horizontally before growing vertically. Such trees are valuable for the figs that they bear (see also 1 Kings 10:27; Amos 7:14).

For Zacchaeus to be short does not mean he is disabled. So he is able to reach the lower limbs of the tree to have an adequate field of view. For this wealthy man to climb a tree is undignified, so we sense how eager he is to see Jesus.

C. Statement and Reaction (vv. 5, 6)

5a. When Jesus reached the spot, he looked up

We can imagine Jesus walking slowly, greeting and blessing those in the admiring crowd as he goes. He is making eye contact at street level, so what causes him to look up and notice Zacchaeus? Is the man waving his hands to get Jesus' attention? The text doesn't say, but Jesus nonetheless stops, looks up, and sees the little man in the tree. It must be a bit comical, and we can almost imagine a slight smile on Jesus' face.

5b. and said to him, "Zacchaeus, come down immediately. I must stay at your house today."

Luke intends us to be surprised by what comes next. First, Jesus calls Zacchaeus by name! This is a display of Jesus' supernatural knowledge, for the text gives us no reason to think that the two have met previously.

Second, Jesus tells Zacchaeus to *come down immediately* from the tree, which is an invitation for him to meet Jesus personally. Jesus eliminates

HOW TO SAY IT

Abraham	*Ay*-bruh-ham.
Canaan	*Kay*-nun.
Israelites	*Iz*-ray-el-ites.
Jericho	*Jair*-ih-co.
Judah	*Joo*-duh.
Pharisees	*Fair*-ih-seez.
Rahab	*Ray*-hab.
Samaritan	Suh-*mare*-uh-tun.
Zacchaeus	Zack-*key*-us.
Zedekiah	Zed-uh-*kye*-uh.

the barrier of the crowd with just a few words, for the people are expected to part and let the little man through.

Third, Jesus announces that he will spend some time at Zacchaeus's home. Jesus has already been criticized for eating with tax collectors (Luke 5:27-30; 15:1, 2). Sharing a meal is a strong symbol of acceptance and fellowship, and the scrupulously religious Pharisees and teachers of the law disdain any interaction with people like Zacchaeus. And this man is not just any tax collector; he is the boss of the tax collectors, the chief of all sinners of his ilk in this city! His home is more suitable for prostitutes and drunkards, not respectable Jewish teachers.

6. So he came down at once and welcomed him gladly.

Zacchaeus quickly realizes what a great opportunity is being presented to him. He surely has entertained no expectation that Jesus might linger in Jericho at Zacchaeus's own home! So he quickly does as Jesus bids, welcoming *him gladly* in the process. This probably indicates a physical act such as an embrace. The effect is to say, "Yes, please come to my home. You are most welcome!"

What Do You Think?
What are some practical ways the church as a body can demonstrate the joy of knowing Christ? Why is it important to do so?
Talking Points for Your Discussion
▪ To its members individually
▪ To members of other churches
▪ To unbelievers
▪ Other

❧ *ALWAYS A JOYFUL RESPONSE?* ❧

Paying college tuition doesn't seem like a "jump for joy" proposition, especially since the cost keeps rising year after year. Educational loans only postpone the day of reckoning when one has to start paying off, with interest, the cost of the college experience. Joy is further eroded if a tight labor market prevents one from getting a job that pays well enough to allow the borrower to make the payments on the loans.

One Christian university has developed a program it calls "Joyful Response" to encourage its students to make regular payments while still in college. The idea seems to be to foster the right attitude in fulfilling tuition payment obligations. At least one church also names its giving program "Joyful Response" as it enables church members to fulfill their donation commitments automatically via electronic transfers from congregants' bank accounts. This is promoted as being "just like most utility bill pay programs." Many would question whether giving to the Lord's work should be compared with paying for water and sewer services!

Further, some may react with cynicism to the "Joyful Response" naming of the two programs above. But shouldn't we always react with joy when offered an opportunity to support the Lord's work? Issues of financial support aside, the Lord invites us weekly to a time of fellowship with him in worship. Do we always respond to that invitation with "Zacchaeus joy"? If not, why?

—C. R. B.

II. Three Attitudes
(LUKE 19:7-10)
A. Crowd Complains (v. 7)

7. All the people saw this and began to mutter, "He has gone to be the guest of a sinner."

Jesus' fellowship with people like Zacchaeus has been the source of criticism from the Pharisees and teachers of the law (again, Luke 5:27-30; 15:1, 2). Now it is the common folk who express concern. Zacchaeus has a reputation in Jericho, and it is not a good one. He is labeled *a sinner*, probably a well-deserved moniker for the city's chief tax collector. His home is not a shrine to righteousness, and Zacchaeus is not one to be obsessed with keeping the Law of Moses.

Jesus knows all of this. He also knows that the angels of God rejoice over a sinner who repents (Luke 15:10). Jesus can see that the seeds of faith and repentance are in Zacchaeus's heart. The attitude of the crowd therefore has no effect on Jesus' decision to go to the home of this man, no matter how many "sinners" he might find there.

B. Zacchaeus Promises (v. 8)

8a. But Zacchaeus stood up and said to the Lord, "Look, Lord! Here and now I give half of my possessions to the poor,

We have a scene change to the home of Zacchaeus, probably after a quickly arranged banquet is over. It is the time for speeches and words of blessing. Zacchaeus, as the master of the house, begins. His heart has been convicted by Jesus in ways we are not told. From his upbringing as a Jewish lad, he recalls the law's demand to care for *the poor* (Deuteronomy 15:11; etc.). He well knows that tax collecting for the Romans is a shady business at best, with the line between extortion and legitimate taxation often crossed. So Zacchaeus announces a new direction for his life.

That new direction includes renouncing greed. He will put his repentance into action by giving half of his possessions for poverty relief. This undoubtedly involves an enormous sum of wealth! When carried through, the distribution will have a significant impact on Jericho's poor.

8b. "and if I have cheated anybody out of anything, I will pay back four times the amount."

Zacchaeus takes his repentance further by pledging restitution of *four times the amount* to those whom he has cheated (compare Luke 3:12, 13). Perhaps he is recalling the law's demand for this level of restitution: "Whoever steals an ox or a sheep and slaughters it or sells it must pay back five head of cattle for the ox and four sheep for the sheep" (Exodus 22:1).

This does not seem to be an idle promise. Zacchaeus knows there are witnesses in the room who will observe whether or not he keeps his word. His two promises will significantly reduce his net worth! Tax collectors like Zacchaeus and Levi (Luke 5:27) are assured a comfortable living if they follow the rules and collect only the taxes that are due. Yet their positions allow for broad interpretations of tax rates, and such positions are easily and commonly abused because tax collectors have the authority of Rome behind them.

Greed has a tendency to be insatiable. For some people, being *wealthy* is never as good as being *wealthier*. This fact makes the vows of Zacchaeus truly remarkable! His desire to make amends for cheating people is at complete odds with what everyone has come to expect from him.

❧ RESTITUTION ❧

Child sexual abuse is a horrific problem that is made worse when criminals distribute pornographic images of the assaults. A 1994 U.S. federal law provides that victims of child pornography may sue for restitution from those convicted of producing, distributing, or possessing such images.

A case involving this statute came before the U.S. Supreme Court in 2014. The assault that resulted in the pornographic images took place some 20 years earlier, and the now-grown woman was suing for restitution in the amount of $3.4 million to pay for years of therapy, lost wages, and legal fees. The justices agreed on the principle that offenders should make restitution for their crimes. But they struggled with how to make the law work so that the victim was properly compensated. Upwards of 70,000 people were said to have viewed the images; should they all be made to pay? If so, how could this be accomplished?

In the case of Zacchaeus, no court of law was involved to enforce restitution. Instead, it was the presence of Jesus that resulted in that man's vow to repay. Jesus was not interested in "playing the judge" during his time on earth (compare Luke 12:13, 14), and he did not do so in the case of Zacchaeus. That man's decision was of his own volition. The Spirit of God working on the heart is a far more powerful force than that of any human effort at law enforcement. In which do you place the most trust?   —C. R. B.

C. Jesus Blesses (vv. 9, 10)

9. Jesus said to him, "Today salvation has come to this house, because this man, too, is a son of Abraham.

Those gathered must be reeling from the surprising speech of Zacchaeus. But the surprises are not over yet! Jesus sends out his own shock wave by acknowledging the tax man's change of heart. He pronounces a type of blessing on Zacchaeus's house, saying that it is being visited by *salvation* right then and there. This is a roundabout way of saying that Zacchaeus's change of heart is accepted by God, and this wayward son has been welcomed back into God's family. This is a gripping real-life story of a prodigal who realizes his spiritual poverty. The son who had been considered as good as dead is now alive (Luke 15:24; see lesson 8).

Jesus reinforces this by reminding those gathered, especially his critics, that whatever they may think of Zacchaeus, he *is a son of Abraham,* an heir of the covenant (compare Luke 13:16). We are not told the reactions of those gathered. But we can expect that some, like the elder brother of the prodigal son, are furious (Luke 15:28-30).

10. "For the Son of Man came to seek and to save the lost."

Our lesson ends with one of the most important verses in all the New Testament. In just a few words, Jesus reveals his purpose, his mission: it is *to seek and to save the lost* (compare Luke 15:4-10). Jesus is not satisfied to leave people like the despised Zacchaeus on the outside, lost in sin and without hope of salvation. Jesus' mission is to restore even the vilest of sinners to his Father. Jesus doesn't care that Zacchaeus is rich, short, or hated. He loves him and is unwilling to let him perish (see 2 Peter 3:9).

Visual for Lesson 13. *Start a discussion by pointing to a word other than* faith *and asking, "How does this word relate to faith?"*

Conclusion

A. Seeking the Lost

If we truly seek the lost in our communities, what will we find? What sort of sinners would we be willing to bring into the fellowship of our church? Prostitutes? Drug dealers? Addicts and drunks? Unscrupulous millionaires? All these folks need salvation, whether they live in mansions or on the street.

Jesus is no longer among us physically to seek and save the lost. He has given that task to us (Matthew 28:19, 20). We, like Simon Peter, are to fish for people (Luke 5:10), and the fisherman's net does not discriminate. When cast broadly, the net brings in all manner of fish. We must not withhold the message of salvation from anyone. We must not block anyone's view of Jesus. Instead, we are to see the unsaved in the unlikeliest of places and invite ourselves, as ambassadors for Jesus, into their lives. And when they respond with joyous faith, we too experience joy as do the angels in Heaven.

B. Prayer

Father, we are humbled at your Son's acceptance of a man such as Zacchaeus! We praise you for accepting us as you did him. We pray in the name of the Son who makes this possible. Amen.

C. Thought to Remember

Don't overlook the Zacchaeuses of the world.

INVOLVEMENT LEARNING

Enhance your lesson with NIV® Bible Student (from your curriculum supplier) and the reproducible activity page (at www.standardlesson.com or in the back of the NIV® Standard Lesson Commentary Deluxe Edition).

Into the Lesson

Write these names on the board: *Danny DeVito, Dudley Moore, Gary Coleman, Martin Scorsese, Mickey Rooney.* Ask, "What physical characteristic do these five have in common?" (*Answer*: all are/were short, being under 5'6" tall.)

Then say, "We can add Zacchaeus to that list of names. Since (1) Luke 19:3 says he "was short" and (2) the average height back then was a few inches shorter than the 5'9½" height of the average male in modern Israel, then (3) he was probably well under 5'6" tall. But he didn't let that keep him from seeing Jesus in a crowd!"

Into the Word

Have four learners read the lesson text aloud, taking the parts of narrator, Jesus, Zacchaeus, and the crowd. Then form learners into three groups and give each group one of the assignments below, on handouts. Say, "You will conduct interviews with people from today's text. Each group is to select someone to conduct the interview and someone to be interviewed." As you distribute the handouts, encourage groups to adapt them as they see fit. They may need to use their "sanctified imaginations" to answer some questions.

Zacchaeus Group. Why were you so eager to see and meet Jesus? What did you have to do to make that happen? How did you react when Jesus stopped and spoke to you directly? Why was your interaction with Jesus during dinner so different from that between him and the rich man in Luke 18:18-23? How will your life change because of meeting Jesus?

Person-in-the-Crowd Group. Since Zacchaeus is such a wealthy person, what level of respect does he have among the residents of Jericho? What surprised you about what Jesus said to Zacchaeus? What was your reaction when Jesus said he intended to visit the house of Zacchaeus rather than *your* house?

Jesus Group. With such a large crowd milling around, what was there about Zacchaeus that caused you to stop and talk to him in particular? Why did you invite yourself to his house rather than merely say, "Go and sin no more"? Since Zacchaeus, being Jewish, was already a "son of Abraham," why did you make your pronouncement in that regard?

Allow time for each group to prepare and present its interview.

Option. Distribute facedown copies of the "The Truth About Zacchaeus" activity from the reproducible page, which you can download, for learners to work on individually. Say, "This is a closed-Bible checkup. When I give the signal, flip your copy over and correct a single word in each of the 10 sentences. See how fast you can finish." Have learners check their own answers afterward. To the one who finishes first with all correct answers, give a gag prize inscribed *The winner, who didn't come up short.* (Expect groans!)

Into Life

Review the reasons why Zacchaeus was despised by most of the people in Jericho. Speculate about the type of people he probably hung out with. Then ask, "If we had to describe someone similar today—someone who would be rejected by 'decent' people—what line of unethical work would be comparable to that of Zacchaeus?" Jot responses on the board.

Then ask, "If you encountered any such individual who seemed open to the gospel, would you bring him or her to church?" After some discussion, inquire, "How can we ensure that we have the same 'to seek and to save' attitude that Jesus had toward everyone?" Encourage open discussion.

Option. Distribute copies of the "Grand Gestures" activity from the reproducible page. Since this exercise asks for responses of a highly personal nature, it may best be used as a take-home.

TOWARD A NEW CREATION

Special Features

Page

Quarterly Quiz 338
Quarter at a Glance. . . . . Douglas Redford 339
Get the Setting . . . . Mark S. Krause 340
This Quarter in the Word (Daily Bible Readings) 341
The Magnificent Book of Romans (Chart Feature) 343
Give It an Hour (Teacher Tips). . . . . Richard Koffarnus 344
Student Activity Reproducible Pages (annual Deluxe Edition only). 497
Student Activity Reproducible Pages (free download). . . . . www.standardlesson.com
In the World (weekly online feature). . . . . www.standardlesson.com/category/in-the-world

Lessons

Unit 1: Judgment and Salvation

June 5   The Day of the Lord . . . . *Zephaniah 1:4-6, 14-16; 2:3* 345
June 12   That Day Is Coming . . . .*Zephaniah 3:1-8* 353
June 19   A Day of Joy for the Remnant . . . . *Zephaniah 3:9-14, 20* 361

Unit 2: A World Gone Wrong

June 26   Ignoring God's Plain Truth . . . . *Romans 1:18-32* 369
July 3   Needing More Than Law . . . . *Romans 2:17-29* 377
July 10   Struggling Under Sin's Power . . . . *Romans 3:9-20* 385
July 17   God Set Things Right . . . . *Romans 3:21-31* 393

Unit 3: Life on God's Terms

July 24   Unwavering Hope . . . . *Romans 5:1-11* 401
July 31   From Death to Life . . . . *Romans 6:1-4, 12-14, 17-23* 409
August 7 More Than Conquerors. . . . . *Romans 8:28-39* 417
August 14 Living Under God's Mercy . . . . *Romans 9:6-18* 425
August 21 Grafted In . . . . *Romans 11:11-24* 433
August 28 Love Fulfills the Law . . . . *Romans 12:1, 2; 13:8-10* 441

QUARTERLY QUIZ

Use these questions as a pretest or as a review. The answers are on page iv of This Quarter in the Word.

Lesson 1
1. Zephaniah proclaimed that the "great day of the Lord" was near. T/F. *Zephaniah 1:14*
2. Zephaniah prophesied that the "day of the Lord" would be a day of God's what? (wrath, mercy, blessings?) *Zephaniah 1:14, 15*

Lesson 2
1. What leadership group of ancient Jerusalem was called "evening wolves" by Zephaniah? (Pharisees, treasurers, rulers?) *Zephaniah 3:3*
2. God's devouring fire is connected with his jealousy. T/F. *Zephaniah 3:8*

Lesson 3
1. What was needed to call upon the Lord properly? (purified lips, a righteous priesthood, paid-up tithes?) *Zephaniah 3:9*
2. The remnant of God's people would no longer tell _____. *Zephaniah 3:12, 13*

Lesson 4
1. Some of the invisible qualities of God are clearly seen in the natural world. T/F. *Romans 1:20*
2. A foolish error is to worship _____ things rather than the _____. *Romans 1:25*

Lesson 5
1. God's name had been blasphemed among the Gentiles because of Jewish law-breaking. T/F. *Romans 2:17, 23, 24*
2. Paul says the circumcision that really matters is circumcision of the _____. *Romans 2:29*

Lesson 6
1. Paul believed Jews to be more righteous than Gentiles. T/F. *Romans 3:9, 10*
2. Paul said "the poison of vipers" was on people's _____. *Romans 3:13*
3. The law makes us conscious of what? (peace, love, sin?) *Romans 3:20*

Lesson 7
1. Because all have sinned, all come short of the _____ of God. *Romans 3:23*
2. The opposite of the law of works is the law that requires what? (faith, hope, love?) *Romans 3:27*

Lesson 8
1. What does suffering produce in a believer? (gullibility, bitterness, perseverance?) *Romans 5:3*
2. Paul says that few people would be willing to _____ for another person. *Romans 5:7*

Lesson 9
1. When we are baptized, we are buried with Christ into his _____. *Romans 6:3*
2. The wages of sin is _____, but the gift of God is eternal _____. *Romans 6:23*

Lesson 10
1. In all things God works for the good of those who _____ him. *Romans 8:28*
2. There are only a few things that can separate us from the love of God. T/F. *Romans 8:39*

Lesson 11
1. Paul notes that God hated Jacob but loved Esau. T/F. *Romans 9:13*
2. God used Pharaoh to show God's what? (mercy, power, patience?) *Romans 9:17*

Lesson 12
1. The unbelief (transgression) of the Jews was beneficial to the Gentiles. T/F. *Romans 11:11, 12*
2. Paul used what kind of tree in his grafting illustration? (apple, olive, palm?) *Romans 11:17*

Lesson 13
1. We are to present our bodies to God as a _____ sacrifice. *Romans 12:1*
2. Acting in love is a denial of the law. T/F. *Romans 13:10*

QUARTER AT A GLANCE

by Douglas Redford

FOLLOWING A SERIES of parables, the master teacher made this comparison: "Therefore every teacher of the law who has become a disciple in the kingdom of heaven is like the owner of a house who brings out of his storeroom new treasures as well as old" (Matthew 13:52). The lessons for this quarter draw from both the Old and New Testaments to highlight truths that form a crucial part of the Bible's message.

At first glance, the books of Zephaniah and Romans, the two sources for this quarter's lessons, would seem to have little in common. A closer look, however, will reveal a number of important similarities. These similarities highlight humanity's sinful condition and its desperate need for the "new creation" that Jesus came to bring about.

The Human Condition

Neither the prophet Zephaniah nor the apostle Paul minces words about the reality of God's wrath. Zephaniah predicted a coming "day of the Lord," described as a "day of wrath" against God's people (Zephaniah 1:14, 15, lesson 1). That day arrived when the Babylonians carried out God's judgment in 586 BC. Judgment was also promised on *all* nations (3:8, lesson 2).

In the book of Romans, Paul established humanity's need for the good news of the gospel by first pronouncing the bad news of human sinfulness. "The wrath of God is being revealed from heaven against all the godlessness and wickedness of people" (Romans 1:18). His inventory of humanity's rebellion against its Creator in the remainder of this chapter (lesson 4) will cause a reader to think the apostle is describing the twenty-first century rather than the first!

The imagery used by each man to characterize the depravity of his time is quite striking. The prophet depicts the leaders of God's people as "roaring lions" and "evening wolves" (Zephaniah 3:3, lesson 2). The apostle, for his part, uses the language of the Old Testament to paint a disgusting picture of humanity without God (lesson 6). Both prophet and apostle agree that those without God are devoid of any sense of shame or remorse for their actions (lessons 2 and 4).

The Divine Solution

However, judgment does not have the last word with either Zephaniah or Paul. The two lessons from Zephaniah that present the reason for God's coming judgment (lessons 1 and 2) are followed by a promise of joy for the remnant, as God promises "I will bring you home" from captivity (Zephaniah 3:20, lesson 3). In the big picture of God's redemptive plan, this promise could well be predicting what Jesus does to free people from humanity's ultimate captivity: bondage to sin.

That bondage is what Paul so masterfully outlines in his sobering assessment of the human condition at the beginning of Romans (lessons 4–6). But following that harsh appraisal, Paul offers the remedy: "But now apart from the law the righteousness of God has been made known. . . . This righteousness is given through faith in Jesus Christ to all who believe" (Romans 3:21, 22; lesson 7). Lessons 8–13 then present studies from the

> *Judgment does not have the last word with either Zephaniah or Paul.*

remainder of Romans to highlight "Life on God's Terms," the title of the third unit.

Both Old Testament prophet and New Testament apostle thus address issues that are timeless. Humanity's most oppressive bondage remains the bondage to sin. The solution is the "new life" that God provides to those who offer themselves as willing "slaves of God" (Romans 6:4, 22; lesson 9) through Jesus Christ. This is an old treasure that is ever new!

Get the Setting

by Mark S. Krause

THIS QUARTER features lessons from the rather obscure Old Testament book of Zephaniah and from what some consider to be the most important book in the New Testament: Romans. Despite the almost 20 centuries that separate us from the setting of Romans and the 650 or so years that intervene between Romans and Zephaniah, both are set in contexts that resonate with the human condition in the year 2016.

Zephaniah's Time

Zephaniah prophesied during the reign of Judah's godly King Josiah in the seventh century BC. It was a time of danger from foreign powers, with the deliverance from Assyria in 701 BC (see Isaiah 37:36, 37) having provided only temporary respite. Jerusalem and its surrounding territory remained vulnerable.

But returning to prominence on the national stage would have to involve much more than the flexing of economic and military might. The spiritual foundations of the nation were crumbling, and the Lord was no longer willing to overlook rampant sin. The evil excesses of King Manasseh had sealed the fate of Jerusalem (2 Kings 24:2-4) despite the efforts of godly Josiah (23:25-27), Manasseh's grandson. When Josiah lost his life in an ill-conceived military action (23:29), Judah's downward spiral into idolatry resumed. Judgment was coming.

God's judgment, however, was not merely for the purpose of destroying the unrighteous. He had a bigger plan in mind: he intended to re-create Judah by means of a holy remnant. A bird's-eye view of the Bible as a whole reveals that the purpose of that remnant was to usher in the Messiah. He would be the one to offer to everyone the possibility of becoming a new creation.

Paul's Time

Our other Bible author for the quarter is Paul, the great apostle to the Gentiles. As Zephaniah's time was steeped in idolatry and other sin, so was the Greco-Roman world of Paul (Acts 17:16). His background and training meant that no one understood the judgment message of prophets such as Zephaniah better than he. God's coming judgment was just as certain in Paul's day as it was in Zephaniah's (Romans 1:18; 2:5).

The system Paul was raised within taught him that the only way to please God was to know his law exhaustively and keep it in every detail. But Paul came to realize that every person fails to keep the law perfectly in its entirety. Even the great patriarch Abraham was justified by his faith, not by his keeping of the law. Jews knew the law but failed to keep it. Gentiles knew of God through creation but chose to ignore that knowledge.

Whereas Zephaniah saw the coming judgment of God brightly but his subsequent mercy only dimly, Paul saw both with absolute clarity. He knew that salvation could never come from our own efforts. God's heart of mercy is seen in his offer of grace. The combination of grace and faith that had transformed Paul was for everyone.

Our Time

Without the uncompromising message of prophets such as Zephaniah, we would not understand the danger we are in. Without the forceful message of Paul, we might still think the solution to avoiding God's wrath is to be found in keeping rules. Without Paul, we might place confidence in our merits as "good people," as our culture tempts us to compare ourselves with those whom it defines as "bad people." We need both Zephaniah and Paul, because it is biblical writers such as they who point us to our need—everyone's need—for Jesus.

THIS QUARTER IN THE WORD

Mon, May 30	A Day of Celebration	Exodus 23:14-19
Tue, May 31	A Day of Rest	Exodus 16:25-30
Wed, June 1	A Day of Agreement	Deuteronomy 26:14b-19
Thu, June 2	A Day Without Tears	Isaiah 65:13-19
Fri, June 3	A Day to Finish	2 Timothy 4:1-8
Sat, June 4	A Day for Faithfulness	Matthew 24:42-47
Sun, June 5	A Day of Reckoning	Zephaniah 1:4-6, 14-16; 2:3
Mon, June 6	Remember the Commandments	Deuteronomy 4:9-14
Tue, June 7	Godly Planning	Proverbs 16:1-9
Wed, June 8	Ungodly Planning	Ezekiel 33:27-33
Thu, June 9	Promised Rest	Matthew 11:25-30
Fri, June 10	Humble Planning	1 Peter 5:1-6
Sat, June 11	Faithful Planning	1 Peter 5:7-11
Sun, June 12	Consequences of Disobedience	Zephaniah 3:1-8
Mon, June 13	Encouraging Others	Hebrews 10:19-25
Tue, June 14	Pleasing God	Hebrews 11:1-6
Wed, June 15	Obeying God	Hebrews 11:7-12
Thu, June 16	Trusting God	Hebrews 11:13-22
Fri, June 17	Serving God	Hebrews 11:23-28
Sat, June 18	Commendable Faith	Hebrews 11:29-39
Sun, June 19	The Joy of Restoration	Zephaniah 3:9-14, 20

Mon, Aug. 15	Restoration After Repentance	Isaiah 49:8-13
Tue, Aug. 16	Repent and Return	Hosea 14:1-7
Wed, Aug. 17	Repent and Repair	Ezra 9:5-9
Thu, Aug. 18	Repent and Live	Zechariah 8:9-17
Fri, Aug. 19	Repent and Grow Strong	Zechariah 9:16, 17; 10:6-12
Sat, Aug. 20	Repent and Bear Fruit	John 15:1-8
Sun, Aug. 21	Finding Common Ground	Romans 11:11-24
Mon, Aug. 22	Diligence and Law	1 Timothy 4:11-16
Tue, Aug. 23	Obedience and Law	Deuteronomy 11:1-9
Wed, Aug. 24	Choose the Law and Life	Deuteronomy 11:13-21
Thu, Aug. 25	Take Care and Live	Joshua 22:1-6
Fri, Aug. 26	Love and the Law	1 John 3:4-11
Sat, Aug. 27	Prayer and Love	Ephesians 3:14-21
Sun, Aug. 28	Love for Others	Romans 12:1, 2; 13:8-10

Answers to the Quarterly Quiz on page 338

Lesson 1—1. true. 2. wrath. **Lesson 2**—1. rulers. 2. true. **Lesson 3**—1. purified lips. 2. lies. **Lesson 4**—1. true. 2. created, Creator. **Lesson 5**—1. true. 2. heart. **Lesson 6**—1. false. 2. lips. 3. sin. **Lesson 7**—1. glory. 2. faith. **Lesson 8**—1. perseverance. 2. die. **Lesson 9**—1. death. 2. death, life. **Lesson 10**—1. die. **Lesson 11**—1. false. 2. power. **Lesson 12**—1. love. 2. false. **Lesson 13**—1. living. 2. false.

Mon, June 20	A Man of God	1 Kings 17:17-24
Tue, June 21	Judging Deceit	Psalm 52
Wed, June 22	Liars and Truth Speakers	Psalm 63:1-5, 11
Thu, June 23	God Hates Injustice	Isaiah 59:12-16
Fri, June 24	Utter Contempt for Truth	Jeremiah 5:1-5
Sat, June 25	Seek Good and Truth	Amos 5:10-15
Sun, June 26	Willful Ignorance Leads to Disaster	Romans 1:18-32
Mon, June 27	Dark vs. Light	John 1:1-9
Tue, June 28	Hate vs. Love	John 15:18-27
Wed, June 29	Doubt vs. Faith	2 Corinthians 4:1-6
Thu, June 30	Grace vs. Law	Galatians 2:11-21
Fri, July 1	Lies vs. Truth	Ephesians 4:25-32
Sat, July 2	Wicked vs. Righteous	Isaiah 26:1-12
Sun, July 3	Inadequacy of the Law	Romans 2:17-29
Mon, July 4	No One Without Sin	John 8:2-11
Tue, July 5	Forgiveness of Sin	Acts 13:36-41
Wed, July 6	Confess Our Sins	Psalm 38:17-22
Thu, July 7	Open Their Eyes	Acts 26:12-18
Fri, July 8	Enduring Temptation	James 1:12-18
Sat, July 9	Walk Free of Sin	1 John 2:1-6
Sun, July 10	None Righteous . . . Not One	Romans 3:9-20
Mon, July 11	Free in Christ	Galatians 4:28-5:1
Tue, July 12	One in Christ	1 Corinthians 1:10-17
Wed, July 13	Rich in Christ	Romans 11:30-36
Thu, July 14	United in Christ	1 Corinthians 12:12-20
Fri, July 15	Dwelling in Christ	Ephesians 2:15-22
Sat, July 16	Believing in Christ	John 12:40-50
Sun, July 17	Both Just and Justifier	Romans 3:21-31

Mon, July 18	Hope in God	Isaiah 40:27-31
Tue, July 19	Redeemed in God	Isaiah 52:7-12
Wed, July 20	Safe in God	Isaiah 54:9-14
Thu, July 21	Restored in God	Jeremiah 29:10-14
Fri, July 22	Help in God	Psalm 42
Sat, July 23	Fulfilled in God	Matthew 12:15-21
Sun, July 24	Not Without Hope	Romans 5:1-11
Mon, July 25	Kept in Christ	John 17:1-6, 12-15
Tue, July 26	Raised in Christ	1 Corinthians 15:12-19
Wed, July 27	Alive in Christ	1 Corinthians 15:51-57
Thu, July 28	Ambassadors in Christ	2 Corinthians 5:17-21
Fri, July 29	In Christ for Others	Philippians 1:20-26
Sat, July 30	Pressing On in Christ	Philippians 3:7-14
Sun, July 31	Choose Life	Romans 6:1-4, 12-14, 17-23
Mon, Aug. 1	Safe in Evil Times	Psalm 12
Tue, Aug. 2	God's Safety and Care	Ezekiel 39:25-29
Wed, Aug. 3	Living Safely	Proverbs 28:18-20, 26, 27
Thu, Aug. 4	Living Steadfastly	2 Thessalonians 3:1-5
Fri, Aug. 5	God Is Truth	1 John 5:13, 18-21
Sat, Aug. 6	God Is Love	1 John 4:7-16
Sun, Aug. 7	Safe in God's Love	Romans 8:28-39
Mon, Aug. 8	Reproach and Mercy	Deuteronomy 3:22-29
Tue, Aug. 9	Sovereign Mercy	2 Samuel 7:20b-29
Wed, Aug. 10	Awesome Mercy	Psalm 68:20, 24-26, 32-35
Thu, Aug. 11	Hopeful Mercy	1 Peter 1:3-9
Fri, Aug. 12	Wise Mercy	James 3:13-18
Sat, Aug. 13	Patient Mercy	James 5:7-12
Sun, Aug. 14	Children of Promise	Romans 9:6-18

The Magnificent BOOK of ROMANS

I. Opening Thoughts
(1:1–17)

II. Heart of the Gospel:
Justification by Faith
(1:18–4:25)

Lesson 4, "Ignoring God's Plain Truth"
Lesson 5, "Needing More than Law"
Lesson 6, "Struggling Under Sin's Power"
Lesson 7, "God Set Things Right"

III. Assurance from the
Gospel: Hope of Salvation
(5:1–8:39)

Lesson 8, "Unwavering Hope"
Lesson 9, "From Death to Life"
Lesson 10, "More than Conquerors"

IV. Defense of the Gospel:
Problem of Israel
(9:1–11:36)

Lesson 11, "Living Under God's Mercy"
Lesson 12, "Grafted In"

V. Power of the Gospel:
Conduct of Christians
(12:1–15:13)

Lesson 13, "Love Fulfills the Law"

VI. Closing Thoughts
(15:14–16:27)

GIVE IT AN HOUR

Teacher Tips by Richard Koffarnus

I**T HAPPENS.** I woke up one recent Sunday morning fully intending to worship with my local congregation and teach my adult Sunday school class. But I had a stabbing pain in my lower back that sent me back to bed and, eventually, to the doctor. Now I had two problems. The first was my physical condition. The second was getting someone to teach my class that morning.

Over the years, I've been on both sides of that second problem. Sometimes I've been in need of a last-minute substitute teacher, and a few times I've been asked to be the substitute. If you are a teacher, the odds are good that sooner or later you will be asked to teach a class on short notice. The good news is that the *Standard Lesson Commentary* gives you the tools to answer that call. You can prepare to teach an SLC lesson in 60 minutes if you follow the simple formula below.

Pray, Read, Pray (5 Minutes)

First, pray! Ask for God's guidance in your preparation and teaching. Nothing is more important than this. Then read the Scripture text for the lesson, both the background passage and the text for the lesson itself. Even if you are familiar with the Scriptures at hand, reread them anyway to refresh your memory of the details. As you read, ask yourself, *What is the biblical author saying? How does it reflect the title of the lesson?* Then pray again.

Review the Aims and Outline (5 Minutes)

Next, read the Lesson Aims and survey the Lesson Outline. These will tell you where the lesson writer is trying to lead your students and how the lesson will take them there. There are always three aims for each lesson, one each for content (knowledge), concept (comprehension), and conduct (application). Each aim begins with an action verb that suggests how the aims will be achieved. If you're tempted to skip this step—don't!

Review the Commentary (30 minutes)

Next, carefully read the lesson commentary, including the background. Highlight important statements and concepts you want to emphasize in class. Each lesson in the SLC is six pages long (not counting the Scripture page at the beginning and the Involvement Learning page at the end), so you have an average of five minutes per page to complete this step of preparation.

Decide the Teaching Mix (20 minutes)

Your lesson will involve some mixture of straight lecture, discussion via questions, and learning activities. The relative amounts of class time you apportion among these three will be based on your personality, the nature of the class to be taught, the physical characteristics of your learning area, and the nature of the lesson text to be studied.

As you ponder the above, recognize that there are distinct advantages to using discussion questions (via the "What Do You Think?" boxes in the commentary) and/or learning activities (via the Involvement Learning and student activity reproducible pages). First, they encourage learners to participate actively in the lesson, which promotes retention.

Second, discussion and activities "shorten" the teaching time. That is, the more your learners say and do, the less you have to. A common mistake by teachers is to talk too much. Asking questions and allowing learners to respond will make the class time seem to fly by. So will learning activities. Your job will be much easier as a result.

Facing the Class, Not the Music

With one last prayer, you are ready to face the class! Keep in mind that your learners aren't enemies or critics. They are on your side. They want you to succeed, and they will help you do so. Be upbeat and confident that you are prepared, and you will do well.

THE DAY OF THE LORD

DEVOTIONAL READING: Isaiah 25:6-10
BACKGROUND SCRIPTURE: Zephaniah 1:2–2:4

ZEPHANIAH 1:4-6, 14-16

4 "I will stretch out my hand against Judah
and against all who live in Jerusalem.
I will destroy every remnant of Baal worship in this place,
the very names of the idolatrous
priests—
5 those who bow down on the roofs
to worship the starry host,
those who bow down and swear by the
LORD
and who also swear by Molek,
6 those who turn back from following the
LORD
and neither seek the LORD nor inquire
of him."

. . . .

14 The great day of the LORD is near—
near and coming quickly.
The cry on the day of the LORD is bitter;
the Mighty Warrior shouts his battle
cry.
15 That day will be a day of wrath—
a day of distress and anguish,
a day of trouble and ruin,
a day of darkness and gloom,
a day of clouds and blackness—
16 a day of trumpet and battle cry
against the fortified cities
and against the corner towers.

ZEPHANIAH 2:3

3 Seek the LORD, all you humble of the land,
you who do what he commands.
Seek righteousness, seek humility;
perhaps you will be sheltered
on the day of the LORD's anger.

KEY VERSE

*Seek the LORD, all you humble of the land, you who do what he commands. Seek righteousness, seek humil-
ity; perhaps you will be sheltered on the day of the LORD's anger.* —**Zephaniah 2:3**

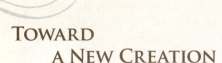

TOWARD A NEW CREATION

Unit 1: Judgment and Salvation

LESSONS 1–3

LESSON AIMS

After participating in this lesson, each learner will be able to:

1. List characteristics of "the day of the Lord."

2. Compare and contrast what Zephaniah says about the coming "day of the Lord" with what the New Testament says about "the day of the Lord," when Christ returns.

3. Identify one hindrance in his or her life to seeking righteousness and make a plan to remove it.

LESSON OUTLINE

Introduction
  A. Creator and Re-creator
  B. Lesson Background
 I. God's Intentions (ZEPHANIAH 1:4-6)
  A. Against the Idolaters (vv. 4, 5)
  B. Against the Indifferent (v. 6)
    From Utopia to Dystopia and Back
 II. Great Day's Anguish (ZEPHANIAH 1:14-16)
  A. Coming Soon (v. 14)
  B. Coming with Sorrow (vv. 15, 16)
 III. People's Attitude (ZEPHANIAH 2:3)
  A. Call to Repent (v. 3a)
  B. Consequences of Humility (v. 3b)
    Avoiding Divine Correction
Conclusion
  A. Ready or Not, Here It Comes
  B. Prayer
  C. Thought to Remember

Introduction

A. Creator and Re-creator

When we pronounce the word *recreation,* we usually say the first syllable with a short *e* (so that it comes out sounding like the *e* in *wreck*). As such, the word typically refers to some kind of leisure activity that provides a break from daily routine.

Literally, the word *recreation* consists of the prefix *re-* (meaning "again") attached to the word *creation.* So *recreation* describes being created anew. This is the thought expressed in the title "Creator and Re-creator" above. Not only does God create (as in Genesis 1 and 2), he also re-creates, thereby providing the opportunity for each person to become a new creation in Jesus (2 Corinthians 5:17). That promise is part of the title of the lessons for this quarter of studies: "Toward a New Creation."

Someone has observed that the grand theme or big picture of the Bible can be stated as follows: God is out to get back what is rightfully his. His original creation was ruined by sin, but God declared his intention to reverse the curse of sin by means of the seed of the woman (Genesis 3:15). This is the first promise in the Old Testament regarding Jesus, and it highlights the purpose of his coming: to crush the head of the serpent—Satan (Romans 16:20; Revelation 12:9).

B. Lesson Background

As the history of God's people unfolded, he raised up prophets. Their messages included not only challenges to the people of their day but also glimpses into the future time of the Messiah, what we might call "the era of re-creation."

One such prophet was Zephaniah, whose writings are part of the Old Testament grouping of 12 books known as the Minor Prophets. We keep in mind that these are called "minor" not because they are of lesser significance, but because they are not as lengthy as the books grouped under the heading of Major Prophets. (The book of Lamentations is an exception; it is shorter than three books in the Minor Prophets, but it is included in the Major Prophets grouping because Jeremiah is thought to be the author.) Like the other Old Testament prophets, Zephaniah was guided by the Spirit of God as he spoke (2 Peter 1:21).

Zephaniah 1:1 establishes this prophet to have been the great-great-grandson of King Hezekiah, who reigned about 727–698 BC. Zephaniah carried out his ministry during the seventh century BC. A contemporary of prophets Nahum and Jeremiah, he delivered the Lord's message to the southern kingdom of Judah during the reign of King Josiah, who ruled from 640 to 609 BC.

To put all this in the larger context of history, Josiah's reign began about 300 years after the nation of Israel split into northern and southern kingdoms and almost 40 years before the Babylonian ruler Nebuchadnezzar began a series of incursions into Judah that climaxed in the fall of Jerusalem in 586 BC.

Josiah was one of Judah's best kings, spiritually speaking. His efforts to restore the nation to a position of favor with God were sparked by the discovery of "the Book of the Law" while the temple was being renovated (2 Kings 22:3-10). Perhaps we can think of Zephaniah's efforts as working in tandem with those of the godly king. Their attempts to turn the nation back to God became the last ray of hope before Judah plunged into a spiritual free fall. The result of that continued decline was divine judgment.

I. God's Intentions

(ZEPHANIAH 1:4-6)

The book of Zephaniah begins with a broad-brush warning of judgment: "'I will sweep away everything from the face of the earth,' declares the Lord" (Zephaniah 1:2). This perspective, shared by other Old Testament prophets, looks beyond the prophet's own time to the distant future. But Zephaniah also addresses the spiritual crisis of his day: the sad state of Judah and its capital, Jerusalem.

A. Against the Idolaters (vv. 4, 5)

4a. "I will stretch out my hand against Judah and against all who live in Jerusalem.

At times, God's intention to *stretch out* his hand and/or arm is to demonstrate his power to bless his people (examples: Exodus 6:6; Deuteronomy 4:34;

5:15) or to strike their enemies (examples: Exodus 3:20; 7:5). Here, however, the Lord intends not to work for his people but against them. Indeed, they have become his enemies because of their sinful conduct.

4b. "I will destroy every remnant of Baal worship in this place, the very names of the idolatrous priests—

The message of judgment is further emphasized by the word *destroy*; the underlying Hebrew is also translated "cut off" in the Old Testament to express divine judgment (examples: Genesis 17:14; Leviticus 7:20, 21; 22:3). It is unclear in some cases whether the term predicts death or simply some kind of excommunication.

Those to be destroyed are specified. *Every remnant of Baal worship* refers to those who continue to pay homage to that pagan deity. Baal is believed to be the god who controls issues related to fertility—the giving of life and productivity to humans, animals, and crops. To worship him is totally incompatible with the recognition of the Lord as the one who creates and sustains all.

Baal worship has been a problem among God's people going back to the time of the judges, more than seven centuries previous (Judges 2:10-13). Following the division of the nation of Israel in 930 BC, such worship was promoted in the northern kingdom through the efforts of King Ahab and his wife, Jezebel (1 Kings 16:29-33). The Lord

HOW TO SAY IT

Ahab	*Ay*-hab.
Ammonites	*Am*-un-ites.
Baal	*Bay*-ul.
Babylonian	Bab-ih-*low*-nee-un.
Hezekiah	Hez-ih-*kye*-uh.
Jezebel	*Jez*-uh-bel.
Josiah	Jo-*sigh*-uh.
Judah	*Joo*-duh.
Malachi	*Mal*-uh-kye.
Molek	*Mo*-lek.
Nahum	*Nay*-hum.
Nebuchadnezzar	*Neb*-yuh-kud-**nez**-er.
Obadiah	O-buh-*dye*-uh.
Zephaniah	Zef-uh-*nye*-uh.

raised up the prophets Elijah and Elisha some 200 years before Zephaniah's time to thwart this influence. Apparently, Judah has failed to learn a lesson from the judgment that God brought upon the northern kingdom in 722 BC because of its idolatrous behavior (2 Kings 17:7-20).

The Hebrew root behind the phrase *the idolatrous priests* suggests prostrating oneself in an act of worship and reverence. The word used by Zephaniah is quite rare in the Old Testament. One other occurrence is 2 Kings 23:5, where godly King Josiah is said to have removed from office "the idolatrous priests" who were sacrificing to Baal.

To destroy or cut off *the very names* of these priests is an especially humiliating act. To cause someone to be nameless in ancient times is to bring great shame upon that individual.

> ### What Do You Think?
> How do we overcome the various false gods that threaten our relationship with the true God?
> *Talking Points for Your Discussion*
> - Regarding the god of "me first"
> - Regarding the god of success and achievement
> - Regarding the god of pleasure-seeking
> - Other

5a. "those who bow down on the roofs to worship the starry host,

Those who *worship the starry host*, which refers to the heavenly array (Deuteronomy 4:19; 17:3; 2 Kings 23:5), will also be destroyed in judgment. In his description of those who have turned from God to embrace sinful practices, Paul mentions people who "worshiped and served created things rather than the Creator" (Romans 1:25 [see lesson 4]; compare 2 Kings 17:16; 21:4, 5). That certainly applies to those indicted by Zephaniah!

That the worshippers engage in this activity *on the roofs* reflects how deeply this practice has permeated the people's conduct. It is not enough for them to worship at a pagan shrine or altar (2 Kings 21:5); they go so far as to do homage at their own homes, where their children, sadly, will be further influenced by their parents' bad example (compare Jeremiah 19:13).

5b. "those who bow down and swear by the LORD and who also swear by Molek,

Molek is the false god described in 1 Kings 11:5 as "the detestable god of the Ammonites" (compare 1 Kings 11:33; 2 Kings 23:13). Zephaniah declares the Lord's judgment upon those who desire to worship both the Lord and this fictitious deity. Such people want "the best of both worlds" and do not give their total allegiance to the Lord. This violates the First Commandment (Exodus 20:3).

God requires complete devotion simply because he is the only God there really is. He does not want us to live our lives worshipping a fraud, which is what Molek and all other so-called gods are.

> ### What Do You Think?
> What are some ways to resist temptations to compromise our sole allegiance to the Lord?
> *Talking Points for Your Discussion*
> - Before temptation occurs
> - While in the midst of being tempted

B. Against the Indifferent (v. 6)

6. "those who turn back from following the LORD and neither seek the LORD nor inquire of him."

While the previous verse describes those who blend their devotion to the Lord with pagan practices, this verse pictures a group that seems to have lost all interest in serving the Lord. The description *those who turn back from following the Lord* seems to imply a former commitment to him. For whatever reason, that passion is gone. Any interest in pursuing spiritual matters in truth is nonexistent. One may think of Jesus' parable of the sower and the seed, where some of the seed failed to mature fully due either to persecution or worldly influences (Matthew 13:20-22). Those are conditions that have always posed a threat to genuine discipleship.

❧ FROM UTOPIA TO DYSTOPIA AND BACK ❧

Humans enjoyed a utopian existence in the Garden of Eden. Then sin entered the picture, and utopia was no more. History ever since has witnessed humanity's attempts to find (or recreate) utopia.

The result of every such attempt has been mere failure at best and increasing dystopia at worst. Dystopia—an environment where people are unhappy and afraid—serves as fodder for literature and movies. The popularity of fictional superheroes who fight society's evils speaks to people's hunger for a better world. In September 2014, TV offered the "reality" show *Utopia*, where 15 people went to an isolated location to create a perfect society.

The prophet Zephaniah tells us that God, the ultimate hero, is the only one who can and will bring back utopia (Revelation 22:1-5). But as he looks down on the dystopia that sinful, idolatrous humans create, he knows he has to take corrective action first. What is God calling you to do as he brings his plans to fruition? —C. R. B.

What Do You Think?
What techniques, resources, etc., do you use to maintain your spiritual passion so that you continue to seek the Lord?
Talking Points for Your Discussion
- When alone
- In the context of the gathered church
- In the home
- At work or school
- Other

II. Great Day's Anguish
(ZEPHANIAH 1:14-16)

Verses 7-13, not in today's text, introduce the "day of the Lord" concept in this book. Such a day is emphasized by several Old Testament prophets. Isaiah 13:6; Joel 2:1, 31; Amos 5:18-20; Obadiah 15; and Malachi 4:5 provide just a few examples.

Some believe that the idea of such a day has its roots in ancient near-eastern terminology. Kings would boast of having won a battle or conquered a city or nation in a single day. In the passages noted above (as in Zephaniah), the day is associated with the Lord's judgment.

A. Coming Soon (v. 14)

14. The great day of the LORD is near— near and coming quickly. The cry on the day of the LORD is bitter; the Mighty Warrior shouts his battle cry.

Many of God's covenant people assume that *the great day of the Lord* will be a day in which his judgment is to be poured out on other nations. God's people anticipate that they will triumph over their enemies and bring them into complete submission at that time.

Those who hold this view seldom pause to consider whether they themselves are in fact the ones who are the enemies of the Lord! They become his enemies because of inconsistency between what they claim to believe and how they actually live. The prophet Amos declared, "Woe to you who long for the day of the Lord!" and noted that that day will be one of darkness, not light, for God's people. This will be so because of their insincere worship and their failure to live the righteous lives expected of the covenant people (Amos 5:18-24).

Thus *the cry* to be heard on that great day will not be one of delight and gladness. The translation *the Mighty Warrior shouts his battle cry*, referring to God, is a change from "the shouting of the warrior there" in the 1984 edition of the NIV, based on the latest scholarly research.

B. Coming with Sorrow (vv. 15, 16)

15. That day will be a day of wrath— a day of distress and anguish, a day of trouble and ruin, a day of darkness and gloom, a day of clouds and blackness—

Zephaniah uses repetition to hammer home the tragic nature of the coming day of the Lord. It certainly will not be the day of joy and deliverance that many anticipate! First and foremost, it *will be a day of wrath*—the righteous anger of the Lord against his sinful people. We are reminded of the description in Revelation of those who will cry in vain to the mountains and rocks for shelter: "Fall on us and hide us from the face of him who sits on the throne and from the wrath of the Lamb! For the great day of their wrath has come, and who can withstand it?" (Revelation 6:16, 17).

16. a day of trumpet and battle cry against the fortified cities and against the corner towers.

The ominous description continues. In a time before electronic communication, trumpets are used to sound alarms so people can prepare to defend themselves against an invader. But such will prove futile in this case. Even those in *the fortified cities*—where one expects to be most prepared to withstand an assault—will find themselves powerless to resist the attacker. For in truth they will not be fighting against a human enemy; they will be fighting against the Lord himself, who is carrying out his sentence of judgment. Doom is certain.

Corner towers are the key defensive positions along city walls. Inhabitants of the city of Jerusalem, which has such defenses (2 Chronicles 26:9, 15), will find them to be worthless since the Lord's holy purpose is being carried out (compare Zephaniah 3:6-8).

III. People's Attitude

(ZEPHANIAH 2:3)

Zephaniah 1:17, 18 (not in today's text) describes further the dire consequences of pending judgment. But chapter 2 opens with a glimmer of hope.

A. Call to Repent (v. 3a)

3a. Seek the LORD, all you humble of the land, you who do what he commands. Seek righteousness, seek humility;

Zephaniah offers an invitation to the people to change course—simply put, to repent. He uses the word *seek* three times, again employing repe-

tition to highlight his appeal. Other prophets use this same terminology to challenge God's people to take the steps necessary to escape the kind of doom pictured by Zephaniah (compare Jeremiah 29:13; Amos 5:4, 14).

The quality of being *humble* or having *humility* is highlighted twice in the half verse before us. A humble heart recognizes its utter dependence on the Lord for help and salvation. It desires to follow his standards of righteousness—to seek him on his terms and his terms alone.

B. Consequences of Humility (v. 3b)

3b. perhaps you will be sheltered on the day of the LORD's anger.

Escaping the terror associated with *the day of the Lord's anger* can happen only if the people humble themselves before the Lord and flee to him for shelter. Zephaniah himself does not know when the day of the Lord's anger will occur; all he can do is warn his people to prepare themselves for it.

The same principle applies to the Christian's preparation for the coming "day of the Lord," when Jesus returns. That day will come like a thief (Matthew 24:42-44; 2 Peter 3:10). We must live daily in a spirit of preparation, knowing that as each day passes we draw ever closer to "the day." The people of Zephaniah's time cannot escape God's wrath by fleeing *from* him, but by fleeing *to* him. The same is true for us.

❧ AVOIDING DIVINE CORRECTION ❧

Adam and Eve set the tone for us all when they decided they knew better than God. Many millennia later, humanity still has not discovered the virtue of humility in this regard.

The Great Recession of 2007–2011 should remind us of the danger of hubris. The economy we enjoyed prior to that downturn had generated a prideful belief that humanity was too smart and sophisticated to suffer ever again an economic situation like the Great Depression of the 1930s.

Zephaniah's admonition runs contrary to our nature: he tells us the cure for our situation is to seek righteousness and humility. The source of any "good life" we have is the Lord. To congratulate ourselves vainly on what we have accomplished is to risk a divine correction like that experienced by King Nebuchadnezzar, either individually or as a nation. See Daniel 4:28-37.   —C. R. B.

ANY day could be THAT day!

Visual for Lessons 1 & 2. *Point to this visual as you pose the discussion question that is associated with verse 15.*

Conclusion

A. Ready or Not, Here It Comes

During my time in Bible college a little over 40 years ago, I was preaching in a church in rural Kentucky. One of the songs that the congregation would often sing during Sunday morning worship included the following words, penned by Will L. Thompson (1847–1909):

There's a great day coming, a great day coming;
There's a great day coming by and by,
When the saints and the sinners shall be parted right and left,
Are you ready for that day to come?

The refrain repeats the question of that last line:

Are you ready? Are you ready? Are you ready for the judgment day? Are you ready? Are you ready? For the judgment day?

We do not know whether the prophet Zephaniah was a singer. (He does describe the Lord as "singing" in Zephaniah 3:17.) But he clearly warned God's people that there's a great day coming (1:14). The New Testament echoes that thought as it foresees the day of Jesus' return.

This is a crucial question: Who shall be able to stand on the great day of the Lord? The answer: those who treat each day as the day of the Lord in order to be ready when that day actually arrives. This means seeing each day as a gift from God and as a day to trust that Jesus will keep his promise to return, in spite of scoffers (2 Peter 3:3, 4).

Psalm 90:12 provides an appropriate prayer for each day: "Teach us to number our days, that we may gain a heart of wisdom." Many are familiar with the words of Psalm 118:24: "Let us rejoice today and be glad." We often refer to Sunday as "the Lord's Day," but in truth each day is his—a gift to be used in his service to his glory. Thus if we are living each day as faithful servants of the Lord, then the great day coming will be a day of joy. If we are like the people described in Zephaniah 1:6, who "neither seek the Lord nor inquire of him," then we will be among those who cry bitterly.

Most in that congregation in Kentucky where I preached years ago have gone on to be with the Lord. But the question they sang cannot be silenced: Are you ready for the judgment day?

B. Prayer

Father, help us live with an eternal perspective in mind, preparing ourselves for the place prepared by Jesus himself for his faithful servants of righteousness. We pray in Jesus' name. Amen.

C. Thought to Remember

Be ready, always.

VISUALS FOR THESE LESSONS

The visual pictured in each lesson (see example above) is a small reproduction of a large, full-color poster included in the *Adult Resources* packet for the Summer Quarter. That packet also contains the very useful *Presentation Tools* CD for teacher use. Order No. 020049216 from your supplier.

INVOLVEMENT LEARNING

Enhance your lesson with NIV® Bible Student (from your curriculum supplier) and the reproducible activity page (at www.standardlesson.com or in the back of the NIV® Standard Lesson Commentary Deluxe Edition).

Into the Lesson

Have the phrase *Recreation Time!* displayed as learners arrive. Ask, "How would you say this?" Your goal is to have someone say *RE-creation* (with a long *e* in the prefix) as a lead-in to discussing both the quarter's theme and the lesson's Introduction.

To set a context for today's study, have a learner stand and read 2 Kings 22:1, 2, 8-11, 18-20; 23:2, 3, 19-21, 25, 26 regarding King Josiah and his reforms. Note that Zephaniah was undoubtedly aware of all this, since he prophesied in Josiah's day (see the Lesson Background).

Alternative 1. Deliver the following dramatic monologue (or have a learner do so) in the role of King Josiah:

> Though I was young when I became king, I had been taught well by my mother and others; I wanted to do what was right in God's sight. After a copy of God's law was found in the temple as it was being cleaned, I was stunned as it was read to me—stunned by the utter sinfulness of my people. God made it clear that our sinfulness would be punished. So I proclaimed in a public assembly that we would walk after the Lord, that we would keep his commandments. Elements of Baal worship were torn down; idolatrous priests were done away with. Wizards and false teachers? Destroyed! As I reinstituted the Passover observance, my nation of Judah began to look new . . . and right!

Alternative 2. Set the wider context of "the day of the Lord" concept by distributing copies of the "The Day of the Lord" exercise from the reproducible page, which you can download. Have learners complete as indicated, individually or in pairs.

Into the Word

Have Zephaniah 1:4-6, 14-16; 2:3 read aloud. Then give each learner a face-down copy of the word-find puzzle below. Give these directions verbally, also including them printed at the top of the puzzle: "Find the 11 words listed, all being from Zephaniah 1:4-6, 14-16. When you finish, the unused letters will form an important phrase when read left to right, top to bottom. When you discover the phrase, raise your hand." Before saying *go*, announce that this is a contest to see who can finish first. *(Words to find: Baal, clouds, darkness, distress, great, host, Jerusalem, Judah, remnant, trumpet, wrath.)*

```
T M E L A S U R E J
R S H H E D G A Y D
E D O T F T R H E I
M U A A L O E R D S
N O T R H E A D A T
A L Y W K O T F T R
N C H T E N L L O E
T R S D Z X E A Z S
Q O H A D U J S A S
H T R U M P E T S B
```

Call time after three learners have raised their hands. The phrase to be found is *the day of the Lord.* After congratulating the winner, say, "What a sad and dreary list! Which word or words seem like they shouldn't be on this list, and why?" Various responses are possible, one being "Jerusalem, because it was supposed to be the holy city."

Option. Distribute copies of the "God's Clear Intentions" exercise from the reproducible page. The second part of this activity can serve as a segue into the Into Life segment.

Into Life

Give each learner a 3" x 5" index card, a pen, and a pencil. Say, "Fold your card across the middle to end up with two panels of 3" x 2½" each. Then write the word *Righteousness* in ink on the inside of the left half, and one hindrance to righteousness in pencil on the inside of the right half. Take this card and stand it on a desk or counter in such a way that you can see both words daily in the week ahead. Every time you glance at it, remind yourself that the hindrance can be erased!"

THAT DAY
IS COMING

DEVOTIONAL READING: Deuteronomy 8:11-18
BACKGROUND SCRIPTURE: Zephaniah 3:1-8

ZEPHANIAH 3:1-8

¹ Woe to the city of oppressors,
  rebellious and defiled!
² She obeys no one,
  she accepts no correction.
She does not trust in the LORD,
  she does not draw near to her God.
³ Her officials within her
  are roaring lions;
her rulers are evening wolves,
  who leave nothing for the morning.
⁴ Her prophets are unprincipled;
  they are treacherous people.
Her priests profane the sanctuary
  and do violence to the law.
⁵ The LORD within her is righteous;
  he does no wrong.
Morning by morning he dispenses his
    justice,
  and every new day he does not fail,
  yet the unrighteous know no shame.
⁶ "I have destroyed nations;
  their strongholds are demolished.
I have left their streets deserted,
  with no one passing through.
Their cities are laid waste;
  they are deserted and empty.

⁷ Of Jerusalem I thought,
  'Surely you will fear me
  and accept correction!'
Then her place of refuge would not be
    destroyed,
  nor all my punishments come upon her.
But they were still eager
  to act corruptly in all they did.
⁸ Therefore wait for me,"
  declares the LORD,
  "for the day I will stand up to testify.
I have decided to assemble the nations,
  to gather the kingdoms
and to pour out my wrath on them—
  all my fierce anger.
The whole world will be consumed
  by the fire of my jealous anger."

KEY VERSE

"Therefore wait for me," declares the LORD, "for the day I will stand up to testify." —**Zephaniah 3:8**

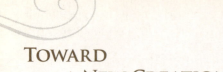

TOWARD A NEW CREATION

Unit 1: Judgment and Salvation
LESSONS 1–3

LESSON AIMS

After participating in this lesson, each learner will be able to:

1. Identify the objects of the Lord's condemnation and the reasons for it.

2. Explain why the topic of God's judgment is as relevant today as it was to Zephaniah's audience.

3. Tell specifically how the theme of God's judgment will influence his or her daily living and message to an unsaved world.

LESSON OUTLINE

Introduction
  A. A Special Date
  B. Lesson Background
 I. Rebellious City (ZEPHANIAH 3:1, 2)
  A. Defiled (v. 1)
    What Happens in Vegas . . .
  B. Defiant (v. 2)
II. Ruthless Leaders (ZEPHANIAH 3:3, 4)
  A. Civic (v. 3)
    No Moral Compass
  B. Spiritual (v. 4)
III. Righteous God (ZEPHANIAH 3:5-8)
  A. Every Day (v. 5)
  B. Every Nation (v. 6)
  C. Evil City (v. 7)
  D. Extensive Judgment (v. 8)
Conclusion
  A. Preparing for Finals
  B. Prayer
  C. Thought to Remember

Introduction

A. A Special Date

June 12, 2016, the day on which this lesson is to be taught, is a special one for my wife and me—it's our 40th wedding anniversary! Now, the reader should keep in mind that when I began work on this lesson it was early 2014, more than two years before the date's arrival. As I was writing, I had no specific plans for celebrating the day. And of course there is no guarantee that either of us will still be living when the time comes. But there is no question as to when the date of our 40th wedding anniversary should be observed.

Getting ready for the day of the Lord is quite different, mainly because we do not know when that specific day will be. The prophet Zephaniah warned of a day of judgment in his own time, but he also prophesied a sweeping, global administration of divine judgment. Jesus provided an unmistakable warning regarding that final day: "About that day or hour no one knows, not even the angels in heaven, nor the Son, but only the Father" (Matthew 24:36). This is not a date that one can circle on a calendar as we would "save the date" for an upcoming wedding. A better word of advice comes from Peter on the Day of Pentecost: "Save yourselves from this corrupt generation" (Acts 2:40).

In truth, the only way one can prepare for the coming day of the Lord is to be a devoted, day-by-day servant of Jesus. To be faithful to him, even in the little things, is to be making big plans for that special day.

B. Lesson Background

Last week's lesson introduced us to the man and message of Zephaniah. The focus of that study was on his opening warning of judgment on the sinful people of Judah. The prophet followed with a series of similar announcements of judgment on peoples and nations beyond Judah's borders, including the Philistines (Zephaniah 2:4-7), Moab and Ammon (2:8-11), the Cushites or Ethiopians (2:12), and Assyria (2:13-15).

Today's lesson text refocuses the theme of judgment back on Judah, specifically the capital city of Jerusalem.

I. Rebellious City

(ZEPHANIAH 3:1, 2)

A. Defiled (v. 1)

1. Woe to the city of oppressors, rebellious and defiled!

Woe is a word in Scripture that often introduces oracles of judgment against individuals or nations. Several decades earlier, Isaiah declared a series of woes against God's people (Isaiah 5:8-23); several centuries later, Jesus will utter a series of woes against the teachers of the law and Pharisees (Matthew 23). Here the woe is directed against *the city of oppressors, rebellious and defiled*. But which city?

We initially may think the reference is to the city of Nineveh, which is mentioned by name just three verses earlier. But the content and context of what follows indicate that the reference is to Jerusalem. The idealized "holy city" of Isaiah 52:1 is anything but!

🦎 *"WHAT HAPPENS IN VEGAS . . ."* 🦎

Many fine Christians live in Las Vegas, Nevada, but the rest of the world doesn't seem to be aware of that fact. Most people have been taught to think of Vegas as "Sin City."

That reputation was promoted by the "What Happens in Vegas Stays in Vegas" marketing campaign that began in 2003, as commissioned by the Las Vegas Convention and Visitors Authority. One of the first video ads featured a sultry woman in a slinky dress inside a limousine as it departed from downtown Las Vegas. She ended

up wearing a business suit and having her hair in a bun as she exited the limo at the airport on her way back home.

In other words, the message is that you can "let your hair down" in Vegas and become someone else for a while. But as you depart, you can leave your alter ego behind, no harm done! No one back home will know what wild things you did while in Sin City. When shown the ads, women in certain focus groups said they found them to be "empowering"—whatever that means!

In Zephaniah's time, Jerusalem was a morally polluted city that oppressed its inhabitants in various ways. That was the cause for the wrath of God that destroyed the city in 586 BC. That should make us wonder: How much patience does God have left when he sees all the moral pollution and oppression that exist today?   —C. R. B.

What Do You Think?

What are some ways to address the tragic spiritual condition of modern cities? What will be your part in this?

Talking Points for Your Discussion

▪ Regarding involvement with existing ministries
▪ Regarding creation of new ministries
▪ Other

B. Defiant (v. 2)

2a. She obeys no one,

Zephaniah proceeds with a litany of charges against the city. (In the Hebrew Old Testament, the feminine pronoun *she* is used of cities because they are considered to be "mothers" of those who live within them; see 2 Samuel 20:19.) The *one* not obeyed is the Lord, the only one to whom his people should be giving their attention. As one of the Lord's prophets, Zephaniah speaks for him. But it appears that his words fall on deaf ears.

2b. she accepts no correction.

The fact that Jerusalem *accepts no correction* highlights the people's arrogance toward God. They are unwilling to be disciplined by the Lord's standards. The Hebrew word translated *correction* occurs 30 times in the book of Proverbs, often translated there as "instruction" (examples: Proverbs 1:8; 4:1). In its sense of "discipline" (as used

HOW TO SAY IT

Ammon	*Am*-mun.
Assyria	Uh-*sear*-ee-uh.
Blagojevich	Blah-*goi*-yuh-vich.
Ethiopians	E-thee-*o*-pee-unz (*th* as in *thin*).
Judah	*Joo*-duh.
Lamentations	Lam-en-*tay*-shunz.
Nineveh	*Nin*-uh-vuh.
Pentecost	*Pent*-ih-kost.
Philistines	Fuh-*liss*-teenz or *Fill*-us-teenz.
Reuben	*Roo*-ben.
Zephaniah	Zef-uh-*nye*-uh.

here), it describes a result of living by the principles of wisdom (compare Proverbs 1:2, 3; 3:11, 12).

**2c. She does not trust in the LORD,
she does not draw near to her God.**

To refuse to *trust in the Lord* is to ignore the admonishment to do so that appears throughout Scripture (examples: Psalm 20:7; Proverbs 3:5, 6; Isaiah 26:3, 4; Hebrews 2:13). To fail to *draw near* to God is to spurn one of his most gracious invitations (Isaiah 55:1-7; Hebrews 7:19). Zephaniah's list of charges reveals the rejection of some of the most essential and foundational attitudes that are to characterize God's covenant people. The city's spiritual condition is tragic indeed.

II. Ruthless Leaders
(ZEPHANIAH 3:3, 4)
A. Civic (v. 3)

**3. Her officials within her
are roaring lions;
her rulers are evening wolves,
who leave nothing for the morning.**

Zephaniah cites a major contributor to Jerusalem's sad spiritual state: the leadership is corrupt. The phrase *her officials* likely refers to kings of Judah and their royal sons. After the death of godly King Josiah (see last week's Lesson Background), none of the four kings who rule Judah until its fall in 586 BC—three of whom are sons of Josiah—are considered righteous (see 2 Kings 23:30–24:20). Here they are portrayed as lions on the prowl, roaring as they seek their prey.

Corruption extends to the city's *rulers*, or judges. These men are supposed to be just and fair. Instead they are ruthless, like wolves that stalk their prey

under cover of darkness. Such judges consider themselves to be above the law.

The phrase *who leave nothing for the morning* describes the thoroughness of these judges' heartless efforts. Nothing remains when they finish devouring their victims. Jesus will use similar language of the religious leaders of his day, of men who "devour widows' houses" (Luke 20:47).

❧ NO MORAL COMPASS ❧

For several years, the state of Illinois suffered the infamy of being the only state in America with two former governors serving prison terms at the same time. They were George Ryan and Rod Blagojevich. Ryan, governor from 1999 to 2003, was convicted of racketeering; Blagojevich, governor from 2003 to 2009, was convicted on various corruption charges, including trying to sell President Obama's former seat in the U.S. Senate.

Two other Illinois governors sent to prison were Dan Walker, governor from 1973 to 1977, and Otto Kerner Jr., governor from 1961 to 1968. This isn't meant to pick on Illinois, however. All states and nations have had leaders who disgraced themselves by misusing the power of their offices.

The problem seems to have been even worse in ancient Jerusalem, the city that was supposed to be ruled by the laws of God. Zephaniah's description of her corrupt leaders boggles the mind. Of all the people who should have known better! With elections approaching, how high do morals and ethics count on your list of criteria regarding which candidates will receive your vote? —C. R. B.

B. Spiritual (v. 4)

**4a. Her prophets are unprincipled;
they are treacherous people.**

While the previous verse focuses on those who might be termed the civic leaders of Jerusalem, here Zephaniah indicts the spiritual leaders. *Prophets* should speak God's truth, but these men do not. The Hebrew verb translated *unprincipled* is rare. It occurs in Judges 9:4, where it describes certain people who lack moral compunction as "reckless scoundrels," and in Genesis 49:4, where it characterizes the man Reuben as "turbulent." A closely related word is used in Jeremiah 23:32 to describe the recklessness of "those who prophesy false dreams." It means nothing to these *treacherous people* to trivialize God's Word.

4b. Her priests profane the sanctuary and do violence to the law.

The sanctuary cannot remain holy when unholy priests officiate there. The prophet Ezekiel will later describe some of the hideous, disgusting practices that are taking place in the temple (Ezekiel 8). Such activities will eventually result in the Lord's glory departing from there (8:6; 10:15-19).

Using the same two Hebrew words that Zephaniah uses, Ezekiel will also have his say regarding how "her priests do violence to my law" (Ezekiel 22:26). And as Ezekiel will go on to note in that same passage, it is not just the law that suffers from such shameful actions by the priests; the Lord himself is "profaned among them."

The words of Jeremiah, a contemporary of Zephaniah, offer a fitting summation of Judah's plight: "A horrible and shocking thing has happened in the land: the prophets prophesy lies, the priests rule by their own authority, and my people love it this way. But what will you do in the end?" (Jeremiah 5:30, 31). With such leaders guiding God's people, can his judgment be far behind?

What Do You Think?
In addition to praying, what can we do when leaders fail to carry out their responsibilities?
Talking Points for Your Discussion
- Regarding the local church
- Regarding church leaders on the national stage
- Within the home

III. Righteous God
(ZEPHANIAH 3:5-8)
A. Every Day (v. 5)

5. The LORD within her is righteous;
he does no wrong.
Morning by morning he dispenses his justice,
and every new day he does not fail,
yet the unrighteous know no shame.

In contrast with how far God's people have strayed from him, God himself has never moved one inch from his own holy standards. The fact that he is *within her* implies that he sees everything that goes on among his people and their leaders. It is similar to how Jesus describes himself as walking "among the seven golden lampstands" (Revelation 2:1), which represent the seven churches (1:20). He knows their works and says so at the beginning of each of his seven messages (2:2, 9, 13, 19; 3:1, 8, 15).

Zephaniah's statement *morning by morning he dispenses his justice* is similar to that of Lamentations 3:22, 23, which proclaims that the Lord's "compassions . . . are new every morning." God works among his people on a daily basis, though admittedly we as finite human beings may not be able to recognize every such instance of justice or compassion. The final Day of Judgment will be the consummation of what God the righteous judge has been doing all along.

Everything about *the Lord* who *is righteous* stands in sharp contrast with *the unrighteous* who *know no shame*. In their minds, they have outgrown the need for God's straitjacket of right and wrong standards. Like many today, they do not sin secretly, but rather they gloat and boast over actions of which they should be ashamed. As Jeremiah astutely puts it, "Are they ashamed of their detestable conduct? No, they have no shame at all; they do not even know how to blush" (Jeremiah 6:15).

What Do You Think?
How can shame be used to honor God today?
Talking Points for Your Discussion
- In witnessing
- In disciplining children
- In preaching and teaching
- In holding a fellow believer accountable
- In standing up for a specific moral issue
- Other

B. Every Nation (v. 6)

6. "I have destroyed nations;
their strongholds are demolished.
I have left their streets deserted,
with no one passing through.
Their cities are laid waste;
they are deserted and empty.

Thus far this chapter has focused on the judgment that awaits God's covenant people. But by no means is it limited to them. Though the nations have built *strongholds*, such efforts are useless in withstanding divine judgment (1:16, 17).

A complete desolation is pictured here: *their cities are laid waste,* and no inhabitants remain. Consider, for example, what the prophet Isaiah declared concerning mighty Babylon, which arose after his day: "Babylon, the jewel of kingdoms, the pride and glory of the Babylonians, will be overthrown by God like Sodom and Gomorrah. She will never be inhabited or lived in through all generations" (Isaiah 13:19, 20). Isaiah's prophecy comes to pass, as does Zephaniah's.

C. Evil City (v. 7)

7. "Of Jerusalem I thought,
'Surely you will fear me
and accept correction!'
**Then her place of refuge would not be
destroyed,
nor all my punishments come upon her.
But they were still eager
to act corruptly in all they did.**

Here the Lord's words are redirected to Jerusalem. God expects more from the city of David, the holy city, the home of the temple. Surely its inhabitants will not reach the point where they will have to *be destroyed* in judgment! Surely they will be willing to *accept correction* from the Lord!

ANY day could be THAT day!

ZEPHANIAH 1:14
SAVE the DATE
Day of the Lord

Visual for Lessons 1 & 2. *As you discuss the lesson's Introduction, point to this visual and ask, "In what senses can we and can we not 'save the date'?"*

But no—if anything, they are as determined as ever to refuse to listen. Their eagerness to pursue wrongdoing seems to know no bounds. Of course, this will not escape the attention of the Lord, who "morning by morning" implements his justice (v. 5, above).

What Do You Think?
What place should fear of God have in our daily walk with him? Why?
Talking Points for Your Discussion
- Regarding times when we seek his will
- Regarding times when we carry out his will
- Considering "do fear" passages (1 Peter 2:17; Philippians 2:12; Revelation 14:7; etc.) in relation to "no fear" passages (Luke 12:32; 1 John 4:18; Revelation 1:17; etc.)

D. Extensive Judgment (v. 8)

8. "Therefore wait for me,"
declares the LORD,
"for the day I will stand up to testify.
I have decided to assemble the nations,
to gather the kingdoms
and to pour out my wrath on them—
all my fierce anger.
**The whole world will be consumed
by the fire of my jealous anger.**"

Sometimes in Scripture the command to wait for the Lord is meant to offer comfort and encouragement to those who are enduring an especially trying experience. Two notable examples of this are found in Psalm 27:14; 37:7. Here, however, the command to *wait for me* is associated with God's intention to *stand up to testify* and *pour out* his *wrath,* that is, to carry out his judgment. Thus individuals such as the leaders of God's people who have treated people as prey (Zephaniah 3:3, above) will end up finding themselves to be the Lord's prey in turn.

But God's judgment, as he has earlier stated in verse 6, will also encompass *the nations* and *the kingdoms.* The language of pouring out judgment is similar to that found in Revelation 16 concerning the bowls of God's wrath that are to be poured out upon the earth.

God also speaks in this verse of *the fire of my jealous anger*. God's jealousy should not be viewed in the same way we think of jealousy as being wrong for people, which implies covetousness. Just as God's wrath is his holy anger against sin, his jealousy reflects his holy zeal for what is right and his passionate hatred of what is wrong. He is jealous in a positive sense for his people, desiring only what is good for them and despising anything that threatens their relationship with him.

God earnestly desires that his people choose what is right and remain faithful, and he is deeply grieved when they do not. But at the same time, he allows people to choose whether or not they will obey. Judgment awaits those who turn from God and spurn his mercy, but rich blessings are promised to those who remain faithful. We will consider some of those blessings in next week's third and final study from Zephaniah.

Conclusion

A. Preparing for Finals

The late comedian George Carlin is quoted as saying, "I was thinking about how people seem to read the Bible a whole lot more as they get older; then it dawned on me—they're cramming for their final exam." In the process of receiving certain degrees as part of my education, I learned what it's like to have to prepare for a major exam.

Prior to receiving my Master of Divinity degree, I had to prepare for an oral examination, during which I was to be questioned about various subjects that were part of my field of study. Some years later, I had to prepare for a series of written examinations as I neared the completion of a doctoral program. Believe me, there were plenty of "butterflies," especially the night before these exams were administered!

Even so, things were made easier by the fact that every exam was scheduled for a certain day or a series of days. I knew exactly when each was to occur and could plan my preparation accordingly. I shudder to think what my frame of mind would have been if a test could have happened at any time and I had to live "on pins and needles" knowing that any night I could receive a phone call saying, "Tomorrow's the day of the test. Be here at 8:00 a.m.!"

However, we don't know the day or the hour when we will take God's "final exam." Such a day is indeed coming—a Day of Judgment—and no one will be exempt (2 Corinthians 5:10; Romans 14:12). But even though we do not know when that day will be, we do not have to live in a constant state of dread regarding whether or not we will "pass our final." We know that we can stand before the Lord, the righteous judge, on that day, because Jesus took the penalty for our sins upon himself at the cross (1 Peter 2:24).

As 1 John 2:1 tells us, we have an "advocate" to speak up on our behalf, "Jesus Christ, the Righteous One," so that we will have nothing to fear when we face the ultimate judge. We can rest assured knowing that the "wages of sin" (Romans 6:23) have been paid in full. As Elvina M. Hall (1822–1899) put it in these oft-sung words:

> Jesus paid it all,
> All to Him I owe;
> Sin had left a crimson stain,
> He washed it white as snow.

Even so, we are cautioned by the fact that Judah, the nation of God's covenant people, is the first nation mentioned by name in Zephaniah's judgment list (Zephaniah 1:4). This calls to mind the truth in 1 Peter 4:17: "For it is time for judgment to begin with God's household."

The promise of a coming *day of the Lord* should never produce a sense of smugness among Christians that all the sinners will get their just deserts in the end. The promise of that day should instead move us to remain continually humble before the Lord and to be more committed than ever to helping others prepare for the day of the Lord.

B. Prayer

Father, we recognize that your wrath against sin is real and that our sin is real. But just as real is your grace demonstrated in Jesus' payment for our sins on the cross. We praise you for being not only just but also merciful. We pray in Jesus' name. Amen.

C. Thought to Remember

Prepare for the final day every day.

INVOLVEMENT LEARNING

Enhance your lesson with NIV® Bible Student (from your curriculum supplier) and the reproducible activity page (at www.standardlesson.com or in the back of the NIV® Standard Lesson Commentary Deluxe Edition).

Into the Lesson

Give each learner a blank calendar sheet (template) for a month. Have the year *2016* prominent at the top; have listed column headings for the seven days of the week. Do not include the name of a month or numerals for days.

Give this direction: "Pick a month—past, present, or future—in the year 2016 that has a day that is special to you in some way and fill in the numerals for all the days of that month." (Have a 2016 calendar handy to help learners know the correct numbering for any particular month.)

After learners finish, say, "Draw a star on any day that either did or will require special planning on your part." After a minute or two, ask for volunteers to tell about the dates they chose, the reasons, and the planning required.

Following that time of sharing, say, "Now write this on your calendar on any day of your choosing, with a question mark: *The Day of the Lord?*" Ask, "What preparations can one make for that day?" Allow a few brief responses, then comment, "Today's text pictures a people of God who are not expecting such a day, or at least they don't expect such a day to be wielded against them. Consequently, they do not prepare for it. Let's see how all this relates to us."

Alternative. Place in chairs copies of the "Big Little Words" activity from the reproducible page, which you can download, for learners to begin working on as they arrive. This will introduce the importance of the coming day of the Lord.

Into the Word

Say, "About 40 years before it was destroyed, God said of Jerusalem [read Zephaniah 3:1, 2]. He explained why things are so bad this way: [read verses 3 and 4]."

Assign each learner one of these four designations to research: *official, ruler (judge), prophet, priest.* Say, "Look at verses 3 and 4 to develop quickly a list of adjectives and behaviors that are expressed or implied for the type of individual you have been assigned. You have 90 seconds. Go!"

After calling time, encourage free discussion. Ask for explanations where appropriate. Sample responses that are possible and/or expected: *official*—loud, threatening, ready to kill; *ruler (judge)*—cruel, voracious, unjust, deceitful; *prophet*—treacherous, reckless, careless with truth; *priest*—profane, lawless, impure. Jot responses on the board. Wrap up by asking rhetorically, "Is it any wonder that God characterized Jerusalem as filthy, polluted, and oppressive?"

Direct learners' attention to verses 5-8. After someone reads them aloud, ask, "What contrasts do you see between God and his corrupt people?" As learners respond, refer as appropriate to the list you made regarding officials, rulers (judges), prophets, and priests. *Possible responses:* God is just, his justice is sure and constant, he speaks truth, he is completely dependable, he hates sin.

Be ready to point out responses that are not contrasts. Example: "God expects obedience" is a true statement, but it is not a contrast with the corrupt leaders, since they too expect obedience. Paint a vivid word picture of how ungodly the Jerusalem leadership had become.

Into Life

Give each learner a 2" x 3½" card (size of a business card) featuring *THAT DAY Is Coming!* on the front and *How does That Day affect THIS DAY for me?* on the back. Have learners read in unison first the front, then the back. Comment: "The fact that God intends a day of universal judgment and justice should influence our behavior every day. Carry your card as a daily reminder."

Option. Distribute copies of the "That Day Is Coming" activity from the reproducible page. Form learners into pairs to complete and discuss as indicated.

A Day of Joy for the Remnant

DEVOTIONAL READING: Hebrews 11:29-39
BACKGROUND SCRIPTURE: Zephaniah 3:9-20

ZEPHANIAH 3:9-14, 20

9 "Then I will purify the lips of the peoples,
  that all of them may call on the name of
  the LORD
  and serve him shoulder to shoulder.
10 From beyond the rivers of Cush
  my worshipers, my scattered people,
  will bring me offerings.
11 On that day you, Jerusalem, will not be
    put to shame
  for all the wrongs you have done to me,
because I will remove from you
  your arrogant boasters.
Never again will you be haughty
  on my holy hill.
12 But I will leave within you
  the meek and humble.
The remnant of Israel
  will trust in the name of the LORD.
13 They will do no wrong;
  they will tell no lies.
A deceitful tongue
  will not be found in their mouths.
They will eat and lie down
  and no one will make them afraid."

14 Sing, Daughter Zion;
  shout aloud, Israel!
Be glad and rejoice with all your heart,
  Daughter Jerusalem!"

. . . .

20 "At that time I will gather you;
  at that time I will bring you home.
I will give you honor and praise
  among all the peoples of the earth
when I restore your fortunes
  before your very eyes,"

                    says the LORD.

KEY VERSE

Sing, Daughter Zion; shout aloud, Israel! Be glad and rejoice with all your heart, Daughter Jerusalem!
—Zephaniah 3:14

TOWARD A NEW CREATION

Unit 1: Judgment and Salvation
LESSONS 1–3

LESSON AIMS

After participating in this lesson, each learner will be able to:

1. List characteristics of "the remnant of Israel."

2. Describe specific qualities that people who are part of the remnant should demonstrate daily.

3. Suggest a specific way that he or she will demonstrate at least one quality from that list in the coming week.

LESSON OUTLINE

Introduction
A. Saving the Remnant
B. Lesson Background
I. Purified People (ZEPHANIAH 3:9-14)
A. Unified (vv. 9, 10)
B. Trusting (vv. 11, 12)
"Have You No Shame?"
C. Unafraid (v. 13)
Looking for an Honest Man
D. Glad (v. 14)
II. Precious Promises (ZEPHANIAH 3:20)
A. Gathered by God (v. 20a)
B. Praised by People (v. 20b)
Conclusion
A. "When Are We Going Home?"
B. Prayer
C. Thought to Remember

Introduction

A. Saving the Remnant

Pieces of leftover fabric on bolts of cloth are often called *remnants*. When I checked the dictionary definition of that word, I found the following: small, fragment, scrap, unsold, unused, trace, and vestige. Some of these words have rather negative connotations or imply that a remnant is something that few people would care to have. Yet those who are skilled in sewing can find such pieces of cloth very useful. My wife used to make puppets with them; the youth in our church then used those puppets to present Bible-themed plays.

The existence of a remnant is a very important concept in God's redemptive plan. The remnant is made up of those who remain to carry out his plan after his judgment has been administered.

B. Lesson Background

The prophet Isaiah states the crucial nature of the remnant of God's people: "Once more a remnant of the kingdom of Judah will take root below and bear fruit above. For out of Jerusalem will come a remnant, and out of Mount Zion a band of survivors. The zeal of the Lord Almighty will accomplish this" (Isaiah 37:31, 32). At the heart of the concept of a remnant lies the grace and mercy of God. He is the one who takes the "leftovers" or "scraps," people who might be considered of little or no value in the eyes of the world, and uses them to fulfill his grand design.

I. Purified People
(ZEPHANIAH 3:9-14)

Today's lesson begins immediately after the final verse of last week's lesson. That study concluded on a note of judgment not only on God's people but also on all nations. Even so, God promised his favor on "the remnant of the people of Judah" (Zephaniah 2:7). With today's lesson, the focus shifts to a promise of hope.

A. Unified (vv. 9, 10)
9a. "Then I will purify the lips of the peoples,

Isaiah, when confronted in a vision with the holiness of the Lord, confessed himself to be "a man of unclean lips" and that he was living "among a people of unclean lips" (Isaiah 6:5). One may consider the unpleasant words James uses in describing the untamable tongue: "It is a restless evil, full of deadly poison" (James 3:8). How different is the scene presented by Zephaniah: he pictures a people whose lips have been purified. The reference is not to proper grammar and syntax, but to holiness in what one says.

9b. "that all of them may call on the name of the Lord
and serve him shoulder to shoulder.

To *call on the name of the Lord* suggests turning to him for the help that he alone can provide. Numerous passages of Scripture encourage this (compare Psalms 86:5; 145:18; Jeremiah 29:12; 33:3; 1 Peter 1:17; contrast Psalms 14:4; 53:4; 79:6). The prophet Joel links calling on the Lord's name with deliverance or salvation (Joel 2:32). To call on a deity other than the one true God is idolatry (1 Kings 18:25).

By using the word *peoples* in verse 9a, Zephaniah pictures individuals from many nations calling on the Lord's name in order to *serve him shoulder to shoulder.* The prediction conveys unity —those representing a variety of nations and languages engaged in a single purpose of serving the one God.

We may reflect on how this is a reversal of what transpired at the Tower of Babel. Until that arrogant effort, "the whole world had one language and a common speech." But God decided to "confuse their language" so they could "not understand each other" (Genesis 11:1, 7), because those building the tower were united against his purpose.

What Zephaniah pictures here may be compared with the scene that John witnesses in Revelation 7:9: "a great multitude that no one could count, from every nation, tribe, people and language" gathered before the heavenly throne. It may be viewed as a prophetic glimpse of the "new Jerusalem" witnessed by John as "coming down out of heaven from God" (Revelation 21:2). Such a diverse gathering calls to mind God's intent that

his church reach and teach all nations with the gospel of his Son (Matthew 28:18-20).

10. "From beyond the rivers of Cush
my worshipers, my scattered people,
will bring me offerings.

Zephaniah's prophetic vision includes pure-language people *from beyond the rivers of Cush.* This location is also known as *Ethiopia,* as in the *King James Version* of this passage. It refers to the territory of African Sudan on a modern map, not the area that is modern Ethiopia. Any lands beyond this territory are likely unknown to the ancient Israelites. This is therefore another way of saying that even from the most distant and unfamiliar realms, people who have been dispersed will take part in the worship of the Lord by bringing offerings to him.

The reference to those who are *scattered* brings to mind again what occurred at the Tower of Babel. The Lord "scattered" the people from that place after they had determined not to scatter (Genesis 11:4, 8, 9). In the chapter immediately following that account, God called Abraham and made a covenant with him that included this promise: "All peoples on earth will be blessed through you" (12:3). With that statement, notes Paul in Galatians 3:8, God "announced the gospel in advance to Abraham," declaring his plan to bless "all nations" as he draws the scattered peoples of the earth back to him.

The second line in the verse before us is more literally translated "my worshipers, daughter of my scattered people." It is unfortunate that the NIV does not include the word *daughter,* since it communicates the fatherly relationship the Lord desires. Compare "Daughter Zion" and "Daughter Jerusalem" in Zephaniah 3:14 (below).

B. Trusting (vv. 11, 12)

11a. "On that day you, Jerusalem, will not be put to shame for all the wrongs you have done to me,

The word *Jerusalem* does not appear in the Hebrew text of this verse, but the translators have inserted it appropriately since the Hebrew word behind *put to shame* is feminine singular. (See comments in last week's lesson on Zephaniah 3:2 concerning the use of the feminine gender to refer to cities.) That city has been the prophet's primary concern in this chapter since verse 1. Previously he had called attention to those in Jerusalem who knew no shame for their sinful actions (3:5). But when one experiences a sense of shame or guilt for one's actions, such a person is then in a position to receive the good news of God's forgiveness. In Christ the shame can be replaced by the joy that accompanies the awareness of that forgiveness.

❧ *"HAVE YOU NO SHAME?"* ❧

A generation ago, the question above, when voiced, was often successful in changing bad behavior. The same question today would largely fall on deaf ears, as evidenced by all the shameful pictures and videos that people post of themselves on the Internet. Truly "the unrighteous know no shame" (Zephaniah 3:5; last week's lesson).

But there is another extreme to this issue of shame, as seen in certain countries and communities where an honor/shame culture predominates. From these we hear reports of "honor killings" in which family members murder one of their own for having brought shame on the family in some way. The murdered family member is often a woman, perhaps killed because she dated or married outside her religion or embraced Western values in some way. Even more shocking, she may be a rape victim who is victimized again (by being killed) to restore "family honor." How tragic!

The United Nations reports some 5,000 honor killings in the world each year. These occur mostly in Islamic countries, but a small percentage also take place in Western democracies. We have sound biblical reasons for opposing strongly such an extreme view of honor/shame. But when we point fingers, we risk having more fingers—even

our own fingers—point right back at our own culture's seeming inability to feel any shame whatsoever for various behaviors.

The inhabitants of Jerusalem in Zephaniah's day should have been ashamed of their unfaithfulness, but they were not. They mistakenly assumed God would not judge them in that regard. Western culture should take heed! —C. R. B.

11b. "because I will remove from you your arrogant boasters.

A separation is to take place, similar to that which will occur on Judgment Day as the sheep, separated from the goats, are welcomed to share in the kingdom prepared for them "since the creation of the world" (Matthew 25:31-34). One may look back to Zephaniah's earlier description of those within Jerusalem who stubbornly refuse to obey or trust in the Lord and accept discipline from him (Zephaniah 3:2). Arrogance is at the root of such behavior. Lack of humility and misplaced priorities always seem to go hand in hand.

11c. "Never again will you be haughty on my holy hill.

My holy hill is another way of referring to Jerusalem (compare Isaiah 66:20; Daniel 9:16; Joel 3:17; Zechariah 8:3). Those who have taken pride in residing where the temple is situated and who see its presence as a guarantee against any kind of divine judgment (Jeremiah 7:1-15) are in for quite a shock. Haughtiness and holiness do not mix. This is why the prophet has already pleaded with the people to "seek humility" (Zephaniah 2:3).

What Do You Think?
Where are Christians most in danger of becoming haughty? How do we address this problem?
Talking Points for Your Discussion
- Concerning church affiliation or membership
- Concerning an area of service to the Lord
- Concerning personal accomplishments
- Other

---

12. "But I will leave within you the meek and humble. The remnant of Israel will trust in the name of the Lord.

After the haughty are removed, the ones left are *the meek and humble.* Those whom society considers as scraps or rejects will be part of God's remnant, because they *will trust in the name of the Lord.* Such individuals are highlighted by Jesus in the first of the Beatitudes: "Blessed are the poor in spirit, for theirs is the kingdom of heaven" (Matthew 5:3).

James has the cure for pride: "Grieve, mourn and wail. Change your laughter to mourning and your joy to gloom" (James 4:9). Such an attitude is counter to what modern culture promotes as the path to "fulfillment" or "self-actualization." Indeed, those who live by the principles of the Scriptures may be despised by the world and considered fools according to its standards. But to humble oneself before the Lord is to possess a wealth that the world cannot take away since the world is not its source.

C. Unafraid (v. 13)

13. "They will do no wrong;
they will tell no lies.
A deceitful tongue
will not be found in their mouths.
They will eat and lie down
and no one will make them afraid."

The first half of this verse is echoed in Revelation 14:5: "No lie was found in their mouths; they are blameless." God has great plans for his remnant! In the place where they will reside, there will be plenty to eat and absolute safety. This means that the oppression that existed before (Zephaniah 3:1) will be no more.

How can such a perfect, ideal state exist? It cannot exist in this broken, sin-cursed world; it can come only by God's initiative in creating "a

HOW TO SAY IT

Babylon	*Bab*-uh-lun.
Deuteronomy	Due-ter-*ahn*-uh-me.
Diogenes	Die-*ah*-jin-eez.
Ezra	*Ez*-ruh.
Isaiah	Eye-*zay*-uh.
Jeremiah	Jair-uh-*my*-uh.
Sinope	Suh-*nawp*.
Zephaniah	Zef-uh-*nye*-uh.

new heaven and a new earth, where righteousness dwells" (2 Peter 3:13). Nothing impure or corrupt will be present in that place, for God will have eliminated the very source of evil: Satan and his cohorts. God will confine them for eternity in "the lake of burning sulfur" (Revelation 20:10).

No threat of any kind will disrupt the harmony of God's new creation. The scene calls to mind the picture of God as the shepherd of his people, caring for their every need and protecting them from danger. Perhaps Psalm 23:2 provides the best description: "He makes me lie down in green pastures, he leads me beside quiet waters."

Christians possess this assurance because Jesus is "the good shepherd" (John 10:11). For now, his presence sustains us through the brokenness that we experience in this world. But someday we will be in his home where the brokenness will be gone "for the old order of things has passed away" (Revelation 21:4).

> *What Do You Think?*
> How can we keep from letting fear of the world control our attitudes and actions?
> *Talking Points for Your Discussion*
> - Regarding ungodly influences on family members
> - Regarding national trends
> - Regarding financial security
> - Other

❧ *LOOKING FOR AN HONEST MAN* ❧

Diogenes of Sinope (died 323 BC) was one of the founders of the Cynic school of Greek philosophy. He believed it was more important to live by one's principles than to proclaim them. His ideas made his hometown citizens uncomfortable, so he migrated to Athens.

Diogenes challenged established customs and values with his questioning attitude. He argued that most people accepted established values unthinkingly when they should be questioning the true nature of the various evils in Greek life and culture. Perhaps the most famous anecdote about Diogenes's life concerns his walking through the streets of Athens at midday carrying a lighted lantern. His explanation was that he was looking for an honest man!

Although not a person of the Bible, had Diogenes lived in Jerusalem in the days of Zephaniah, he might well have sided with that prophet! As Zephaniah walked the streets of that city, he saw only a remnant that was true to God. Only a remnant lived by the law that God had ordained. In both Old and New Testaments, the biblical writers challenge us to do more than give lip service to truth. Our Lord still looks for honest people whose godly lives confront the evils of a culture that ignores him. Are you such a one? —C. R. B.

D. Glad (v. 14)

14. "Sing, Daughter Zion;
 shout aloud, Israel!
Be glad and rejoice with all your heart,
 Daughter Jerusalem!"

What is the appropriate response to the promises described thus far? Consider the imperatives in the verse before us: *sing, shout, be glad,* and *rejoice.* Such reactions result from a situation that stands in stark contrast with the pictures of judgment found at the beginning of this book. There only the sounds of wailing and bitter cries are predicted (Zephaniah 1:10, 11, 14).

What Do You Think?
Who is an example of the kind of joy of which the Scriptures often speak? How does this individual's example help you discover joy?
Talking Points for Your Discussion
- Biblical examples
- Personal acquaintances
- Christians about whom you've read or heard
- Other

II. Precious Promises
(Zephaniah 3:20)

Verses 15-19 (not in today's text) offer additional encouraging words to the remnant. Verse 17 describes the Lord as singing, a beautiful way to picture the joy the Lord himself experiences as he blesses the faithful remnant. The coming day of the Lord will be a day of joy, not only for the remnant but for the Lord as well! The Father will take great delight in blessing his beloved daughter, his faithful people.

A. Gathered by God (v. 20a)
20a. "At that time I will gather you;
 at that time I will bring you home.

Once more we note a contrast between the conclusion and the beginning of this book. The prophet's opening words relay God's promise to "sweep away everything from the face of the earth" in judgment (the verb phrase *sweep away* appears three times in Zephaniah 1:2, 3). The prophet now closes his book with God's promise to gather his faithful people. The "woe" with which chapter 3 begins is gone.

Certainly the return from captivity in Babylon, described in the early chapters of the book of Ezra, will fulfill this promise in part. God had previously given his people such "homecoming" promises (Deuteronomy 30:4; Micah 4:6, 7), but there is a wider, global impact in this chapter, as we have already seen. This impact is further highlighted in the second half of verse 20, next.

B. Praised by People (v. 20b)
20b. "I will give you honor and praise
 among all the peoples of the earth
when I restore your fortunes
 before your very eyes,"

 says the LORD.

Zephaniah's prophetic ministry takes place about 40 years before Jerusalem is destroyed in 586 BC, resulting in the people's being exiled to Babylon. That captivity will end when Cyrus the Great of Persia decrees that any of God's people who desire to return from captivity may do so (Ezra 1:1-4). But being released from Babylonian captivity will not mean the Jews are free of foreign domination, as history shows (compare Daniel 2:31-45; 7:1–8:25).

Zephaniah's words may thus point to a deliverance more significant than one that is only political or national in nature. Just as the prophet speaks of a global day of judgment to come, so also here he may be viewing the future recognition of God's people on a global scale at the final gathering to take place when Jesus returns. The release from the ultimate captivity of sin will be complete at that time, and God's people will truly be home—not in an earthly sense, but home with the Father forever.

This promise forms another noteworthy contrast with the somber picture of the "day of the Lord" that is found back in Zephaniah 1:14-16, which was part of the text for lesson 1. There that day is characterized by gloom and doom. God also states, "I will bring such distress on all people that they will grope about like those who are blind, because they have sinned against the Lord" (1:17).

Now, however, God declares his intention to fulfill his promises of blessing *before your very eyes.* It will be a sight to behold indeed! Jesus' first coming was also a sight to behold, but not everyone had eyes to see (Matthew 13:13-15; 23:16-19, 24, 26). His second coming, however, will be seen by everyone, even by those who do not want to see it (Revelation 1:7).

Visual for Lesson 3. *As you discuss the lesson's Conclusion, point to this visual and ask, "What do you anticipate most about Heaven?"*

> **What Do You Think?**
> What are some ways to improve your church's witness among all people(s) of the earth?
> *Talking Points for Your Discussion*
> - Steps individuals can take
> - Steps families can take
> - Steps the congregation as a whole can take
> - Other

The phrase *says the Lord* is a most encouraging way to conclude Zephaniah's picture of the joyful future awaiting God's remnant. We are assured that the prophet's words are not the product of his own creativity. They do not reflect his personal hopes and wishes for things to turn out right in the end. His words are nothing less than the very words of Almighty God. Zephaniah's hearers both then and now can rest assured that the Lord will bring his promises to pass in his time.

Conclusion

A. "When Are We Going Home?"

When I was 4 years old, my family moved to a house in the country that has remained "home" to this day. Although I was too young to remember it, my mother tells me that when she began to tuck me in bed on the first night in the new house, I suddenly sat up and asked, "Hey, when are we going home?" Mom assured me that I *was* home, that the house we were in was where we would be living. I had to adjust my thinking to that new reality.

When a person becomes a Christian, he or she "comes home" to God in a very real sense. Even so, we are not yet fully home with the Lord until Jesus returns. In the meantime, we take care not to get too attached to the present world, which is destined to pass away (2 Peter 3:10-13). If we have not yet adjusted our thinking to this future reality, we must do so! A greater homecoming awaits us, a homecoming that Zephaniah's concluding words foreshadow.

B. Prayer

Father, it is at times so frustrating to live in a world in such constant turmoil from the curse of sin. We become impatient to be home with you and free from the brokenness of sin, dwelling in a place where all things are made new. We thank you that through Jesus there is a promise of such a place. Help us, we pray, to live patiently and faithfully until the time for our "homecoming." We pray in Jesus' name. Amen.

C. Thought to Remember

Homecoming day is not yet, but will be.

INVOLVEMENT LEARNING

Enhance your lesson with NIV® Bible Student (from your curriculum supplier) and the reproducible activity page (at www.standardlesson.com or in the back of the NIV® Standard Lesson Commentary Deluxe Edition).

Into the Lesson

Give each learner a small scrap of fabric and have the letters *AEMNNRT* displayed. Ask learners to unscramble the letters to reveal a word that describes their scraps of fabric. When someone responds *remnant*, make a transition with this statement: "Remnants may look like mere scraps, good for little more than cleaning one's eyeglasses. But in the hands of a skilled seamstress, such scraps can become something beautiful and functional." (*Option:* Demonstrate this by displaying a patchwork item created from cloth or leather.)

Continue: "Likewise, God can take a remnant and make something marvelous. Out of the remnant of Old Testament Israel came Christ and his church. Therein lies the importance of the biblical concept of *remnant*, which is a focus of our study."

Into the Word

Have the lesson text read aloud. Then say, "I'm going to show you some attributes of God's remnant. Your task will be to see how each characterizes God's remnant in today's text." Reveal the following words on very large flash cards, one at a time: *Confident / Pure / Honest / Humble / Glad / Obedient / Trusting / Truthful / United.*

Encourage class members to respond as each is revealed. After responses have been offered and recorded on the board for all nine words, ask, "How do you see these characteristics 'alive and well' in the church?" (*Alternative*: instead of asking this question once, ask it after each card is revealed following responses that relate the card's characterization of Old Testament Israel.) Again, jot responses on the board.

Draw learners' attention back to the text by distributing handouts on which it is reproduced. Give these directions: "In each verse, circle one or two groups of three words that you consider to be striking. For example, I might circle *shoulder to shoulder* in verse 9 because that phrase depicts the unity that will characterize the redeemed remnant. Work quickly—you have 90 seconds. Go!"

After you call time, go verse by verse as you ask what learners circled and why. Learner choices should be easily relatable to the list of attributes introduced earlier; request clarification for those that are not. Example: from verse 13, *tell no lies* matches the characteristic *truthful*. (*Option:* For larger classes, form learners into pairs or groups of three for discussing this part of the exercise.)

Draw learners' attention again to verse 20 and ask how many promises they see there. This can lead to in-depth discussion as learners grapple with conflicting answers. (Example: Do the two phrases "At that time I will gather you" and "at that time I will bring you home" constitute two promises or just one promise repeated in different words?) Wrap up by asking learners to summarize the promises in two statements. (Examples: *loved by God* and *praised among people*.)

Option. Time permitting, discuss 1 Kings 19:9-18 as referred to in Romans 11:1-5.

Into Life

Distribute handouts listing the nine attributes introduced in the Into the Word segment. Include a line at the top on which learners are to write their names. Say, "Thinking of these as God's list of characteristics for his remnant, circle one that seems to be a particular challenge for you. Then make a concerted effort this week to demonstrate that attribute daily." Offer a personal example.

Options. Distribute copies of the "Remnant Characteristics" and/or "Feel Like a Remnant?" activities from the reproducible page, which you can download, for learners to complete as indicated. You may also contrast God's intentions for his remnant with his intentions for the wicked per the "God's Clear Intentions" exercise of lesson 1.

As learners depart, say to each, "Remember: homecoming day is not yet, but will be."

IGNORING GOD'S PLAIN TRUTH

DEVOTIONAL READING: Psalm 52
BACKGROUND SCRIPTURE: Romans 1:18-32

ROMANS 1:18-32

18 The wrath of God is being revealed from heaven against all the godlessness and wickedness of people, who suppress the truth by their wickedness, 19 since what may be known about God is plain to them, because God has made it plain to them. 20 For since the creation of the world God's invisible qualities—his eternal power and divine nature—have been clearly seen, being understood from what has been made, so that people are without excuse.

21 For although they knew God, they neither glorified him as God nor gave thanks to him, but their thinking became futile and their foolish hearts were darkened. 22 Although they claimed to be wise, they became fools 23 and exchanged the glory of the immortal God for images made to look like a mortal human being and birds and animals and reptiles.

24 Therefore God gave them over in the sinful desires of their hearts to sexual impurity for the degrading of their bodies with one another. 25 They exchanged the truth about God for a lie, and worshiped and served created things rather than the Creator—who is forever praised. Amen.

26 Because of this, God gave them over to shameful lusts. Even their women exchanged natural sexual relations for unnatural ones. 27 In the same way the men also abandoned natural relations with women and were inflamed with lust for one another. Men committed shameful acts with other men, and received in themselves the due penalty for their error.

28 Furthermore, just as they did not think it worthwhile to retain the knowledge of God, so God gave them over to a depraved mind, so that they do what ought not to be done. 29 They have become filled with every kind of wickedness, evil, greed and depravity. They are full of envy, murder, strife, deceit and malice. They are gossips, 30 slanderers, God-haters, insolent, arrogant and boastful; they invent ways of doing evil; they disobey their parents; 31 they have no understanding, no fidelity, no love, no mercy. 32 Although they know God's righteous decree that those who do such things deserve death, they not only continue to do these very things but also approve of those who practice them.

KEY VERSE

Since the creation of the world God's invisible qualities—his eternal power and divine nature—have been clearly seen, being understood from what has been made, so that people are without excuse. —**Romans 1:20**

TOWARD A NEW CREATION

Unit 2: A World Gone Wrong

LESSONS 4–7

LESSON AIMS

After participating in this lesson, each learner will be able to:

1. List some ways that people change the truth of God into lies.

2. Explain how God's general revelation makes humans morally responsible to him.

3. Identify in his or her life one besetting sin and the worldly lie behind it and make a plan for change.

LESSON OUTLINE

Introduction
  A. Accept No Substitutes
  B. Lesson Background
 I. Willfully Ignorant (ROMANS 1:18-20)
  A. Revealed Wrath (v. 18)
  B. Revealed Glory (vv. 19, 20)
   In a Kansas Wheat Field
 II. Displacing God (ROMANS 1:21-23)
  A. Darkened Hearts (vv. 21, 22)
  B. Graven Images (v. 23)
   The Rise of the Nones
 III. Receiving Penalty (ROMANS 1:24-32)
  A. Unnatural Relations (vv. 24-27)
  B. Corrupt Minds (vv. 28-32)
Conclusion
  A. Pointing Fingers
  B. Prayer
  C. Thought to Remember

Introduction

A. Accept No Substitutes

The title above is a classic slogan in advertising. Many businesses try to persuade us that their products are original, genuine, the best. Of course, in some cases we cannot tell the difference between the so-called genuine item and a substitute. We occasionally may conclude that the substitute offers better value. But in many instances, we avoid substitutes and insist on "the real thing."

Today's text is about life's most important choice regarding the genuine and substitutes. Our text insists that the one, true God is clearly revealed to all people. None can rightly say that they have no knowledge of the true God.

Tragically, however, we see how people ignore the true God and accept substitutes. That choice is tragic because it leads to the degradation and disharmony that ruin lives. More seriously, it also leads to eternal punishment.

B. Lesson Background

Our lesson text comes from Paul's letter to the Romans, probably written from the city of Corinth during his third missionary journey, in about AD 58. The church in Rome had been planted by others many years before, and Paul sought the Roman Christians' support as he planned to travel to Spain (Romans 15:23-28).

The nature of the church in Rome was influenced by an edict, issued by Emperor Claudius in about AD 49, that had forced Jews living in the city to leave (Acts 18:2). The Roman historian Suetonius tells us that Claudius "banished from Rome all the Jews, who were continually making disturbances at the instigation of one Chrestus," the word *Chrestus* likely referring to *Christ*. This experience probably fostered a certain division within the Roman church between Gentile and Jewish believers, with each group contending that it had better claim on salvation in Christ than did the other (compare Romans 11:13-24, lesson 12).

The expulsion of Jews from Rome resulted in Gentile Christians being in the majority in the church there, if they had not been the majority already (Romans 1:5, 6, 13). Their majority status seems to have continued even after the death of Claudius in AD 54 allowed Jews to return to the imperial city (compare Acts 18:2 with Romans 16:3-5a). Much of Paul's letter is therefore directed specifically to the Gentile believers there (11:13).

I. Willfully Ignorant
(ROMANS 1:18-20)
A. Revealed Wrath (v. 18)

18a. The wrath of God is being revealed from heaven against all the godlessness and wickedness of people,

Paul addresses the division noted in the Lesson Background by noting that all people, Gentile and Jew alike, are guilty of sin (compare Romans 3:23). The apostle's broad statement in the verse before us allows no exceptions. There is no division between Gentile and Jew in this regard!

Unlike the inconsistent anger that humans exhibit, *the wrath of God* is utterly consistent. The righteous God is angry only with what violates his purpose. His wrath ultimately destroys completely, but it destroys only that which destroys the good. So, Paul says, God's wrath is set against *all the godlessness and wickedness of people.*

The word *godlessness* is commonly used to refer to inappropriate, dishonorable behavior toward the deity. The word *wickedness* is used to refer to behavior that violates standards of justice and goodness. The first suggests rebellion against God; the second, disregard for other people. God's wrath stands against people in general because people generally have actively destroyed God's good purpose (compare Colossians 3:5, 6).

18b. who suppress the truth by their wickedness,

Are people even aware of what they have done? The word *suppress* indicates that the answer is *yes.* In their pursuit of things that violate justice

HOW TO SAY IT

Claudius	*Claw*-dee-us.
Corinth	*Kor*-inth.
Suetonius	Soo-*toe*-nee-us.

and goodness, people censor the truth that God reveals. Ignorance of God's truth is willful ignorance. Humans live not in ignorance but in denial.

B. Revealed Glory (vv. 19, 20)

19. since what may be known about God is plain to them, because God has made it plain to them.

God has made truth about himself clear to all people. It exists in or among us, well within the reach of all. God has revealed it; clever people did not discover it in their cleverness or good people in their goodness (compare Acts 14:17).

20. For since the creation of the world God's invisible qualities—his eternal power and divine nature—have been clearly seen, being understood from what has been made, so that people are without excuse.

The revealed truth concerns God himself, the one who cannot be seen. He reveals himself in what can be seen: the world that he created (compare Psalm 19:1). His creation demonstrates *his eternal power*: only one who exists without beginning could cause the beginning of the universe. His creation demonstrates his *divine nature,* or his very essence as God. Only a God greater than all things can be the Creator of all things.

Paul's argument is simple and devastating: the very fact that the world exists tells us that we owe ourselves to the God who made us. To live as if we were in charge instead of God is to deny and suppress the most essential of truths.

❧ IN A KANSAS WHEAT FIELD ❧

I was no more than 10 years old. It was the dark of night, and Mother was driving our old station wagon on the Kansas turnpike, to visit relatives in Topeka, when the car began making a strange noise. Spying a farmhouse on the other side of the highway, she pulled over and set out for it on foot to get help. (No cell phones in the 1960s!)

In her absence, restlessness impelled me toward the adjacent wheat field. It was a time of year when no crop was growing; the field was barren of everything except dirt clods. Scaling the token fence, I walked about five yards into the field, where I proceeded to lie on my back and look up.

What I saw absolutely stunned me: it was the majestic Milky Way, clearly visible from horizon to horizon. There was nothing to block or dim the view—no trees, no clouds, no "light pollution" of a city, no moon. I had seen stars before, of course, but never like this! That's when I knew that there had to be a Creator. There just had to be.

When I think of those who live as if there is no Creator, I wonder if they have ever bothered to look up. "The heavens declare the glory of God; the skies proclaim the work of his hands" (Psalm 19:1).
—R. L. N.

> *What Do You Think?*
> In what specific ways do you see creation revealing God's nature?
> *Talking Points for Your Discussion*
> - Regarding his power
> - Regarding his goodness
> - Regarding his wisdom
> - Other

II. Displacing God
(Romans 1:21-23)

A. Darkened Hearts (vv. 21, 22)

21. For although they knew God, they neither glorified him as God nor gave thanks to him, but their thinking became futile and their foolish hearts were darkened.

Though people know God—that is, know that he must exist—they do not respond as that truth requires. God the Creator should be glorified and submitted to as the all-powerful king. He should be thanked as the one who sustains and blesses.

Failure to glorify and thank God comes through a process of self-delusion. Humans use their capacity for thought to ignore and explain away God's glory. *Their thinking,* the complex workings of the mind, end up being *futile,* empty, and without purpose or meaning. The power to reason becomes pointless when God is ignored. The human heart, our capacity to make decisions and commitments, ends up being *darkened,* filled with ignorance and falsehood (compare Ephesians 4:17, 18).

Those who reject God build their lives on a lie, and thereby ruin themselves with the rebellious self-destruction that results. As he makes this point, Paul is addressing the pride that many people have in human accomplishments in discovery. That is indeed a great capacity, created by God as a blessing. But without knowledge of God, it becomes the seedbed of a curse.

22. Although they claimed to be wise, they became fools

The accomplishments of the human mind are considerable, as amazing in Paul's time as in ours. But in ignoring God, human wisdom becomes a disguise for foolishness. Psalms 14:1; 53:1 declare that the one who says there is no God is a fool, and Paul draws on that idea here. To deny the existence of the Creator God is to commit the most fundamental and destructive foolishness (compare Jeremiah 10:14; 1 Corinthians 1:20).

B. Graven Images (v. 23)

23. and exchanged the glory of the immortal God for images made to look like a mortal human being and birds and animals and reptiles.

The fundamental misunderstanding of God makes itself known in the creation of idols. Paul's world is full of physical images created to represent mistaken notions of the spirit world (compare Acts 17:16). Idols typically are images of humans, but they also mimic other creatures; Paul lists here a range of such creatures that are depicted in idols.

The absurdity of exchanging the true God for such things is obvious. Paul underlines this point with one contrast: humans and animals, unlike God, are *mortal.* Their vulnerabilities are constantly apparent. How can anyone be so foolish as to trade the eternal, all-powerful God for a creature that lives briefly and dies unnoticed?

> *What Do You Think?*
> How do we guard against subconsciously attaching more importance to temporary things than to the eternal God?
> *Talking Points for Your Discussion*
> - Regarding relationships
> - Regarding social causes
> - Other

Perhaps you have heard someone say, "I'm a spiritual person, but I'm not religious." The Pew Research Center calls these people *the Nones*. They are the fastest growing group in terms of spiritual orientation, comprising one-fifth of the U.S. public and one-third of adults under 30. They are distinct from agnostics and atheists. The Nones may consider themselves to be spiritual, but they want nothing to do with organized religion. As one self-identified None put it, "I like the ambiguity of going without a label. I prefer to stress the importance of acting with compassion rather than choosing a predetermined system of beliefs."

The logic problems here are easy to see: the "rather than" declaration implies that one must make an *either/or* choice instead of adopting a *both/and* stance; to want to be known as one who acts with compassion is itself to embrace a label; etc. But those problems ultimately are secondary to this one: unless one acknowledges the existence of the Creator God, then how one thinks and acts will have no firm anchor point.

Such was the problem of the idol worshippers of Paul's day, and such is the road that the Nones of today are on. How do we reach them? —C. R. B.

III. Receiving Penalty
(ROMANS 1:24-32)
A. Unnatural Relations (vv. 24-27)

24. Therefore God gave them over in the sinful desires of their hearts to sexual impurity for the degrading of their bodies with one another.

Paul now begins a series of three statements that show how the denial of God correlates with destructive, debasing behaviors. Each statement begins with the phrase *God gave them over*. In response to human rejection of God, he allows people to have in full the things that they choose in place of him. In effect, God says, "If that is what you want, I will let you have that in abundance."

The word *therefore* indicates that the first *gave them over* statement links the idolatry of verse 23 with *sexual impurity*, two seemingly unrelated behaviors. Paul speaks of human sexual desire

operating without boundaries, which causes people to pursue things that are wrong by nature. Sexual activity that does not acknowledge God's purpose for human sexuality—its expression only in the context of faithful, exclusive marriage to one person of the opposite sex—becomes something by which people bring degradation to *their bodies*. Having lost sight of God, people live in a way that loses sight even of themselves.

25. They exchanged the truth about God for a lie, and worshiped and served created things rather than the Creator—who is forever praised. Amen.

Paul repeats his point about humans having traded the true, eternal God for false gods that are represented by images of created things. This repetition further ties idolatry to sexual immorality, both being expressions of rejecting God. In Paul's world, the worship of idols often involves sexual misdeeds, sometimes with prostitutes of both sexes who work from pagan temples.

What Do You Think?
In what ways do people today exchange the truth of God for delusions and untruth? Why is that?
Talking Points for Your Discussion
▪ In goals they pursue
▪ In how they spend money
▪ In what they admire
▪ In what they worry about
▪ Other

---

26. Because of this, God gave them over to shameful lusts. Even their women exchanged natural sexual relations for unnatural ones.

The second statement in which Paul says *God gave them over* focuses on the further degradation of humanity in sexual sin. *Shameful lusts* are desires for things that bring dishonor. Where sexual sin is concerned, the person who is degraded by such behavior is ultimately oneself. In sexual sin, one sins against one's own body (1 Corinthians 6:18).

As the rest of the Bible does, Paul takes for granted that sexuality is intended for expression with the opposite sex. So he speaks of women exchanging *natural sexual relations for unnatural ones* as a way of referring to sexual activity between members of the same sex. Everyone can know the true nature of human sexuality. But when humans reject the true God, they come to reject even the obvious.

27. In the same way the men also abandoned natural relations with women and were inflamed with lust for one another. Men committed shameful acts with other men, and received in themselves the due penalty for their error.

Paul underlines his point by reminding readers of men who pursue sexual activity with other men. Again, his assumption is that same-sex activity represents rejection of the obvious design of sexuality (compare Leviticus 18:22; 20:13; 1 Corinthians 6:9, 10). In the pursuit of what is not the Creator's intention, people experience payback (*the due penalty*); that is, the sinful act itself is a fitting punishment for the rebellion that allows it.

The issue of homosexual relations ("gay rights") is much debated today. Many argue that same-sex relations are "natural," because some people are persistently attracted to members of the same sex. As we consider this question, we should realize that all of us are fallen sexually from a biblical perspective. That is, we all at one time or another desire to satisfy strong sexual urges with acts outside the Creator's design of faithfulness in opposite-sex marriage (compare Matthew 5:28). Our purpose as sexual beings is fulfilled not when we do whatever we want but when we learn to submit our desires to the will of the one who made us.

What Do You Think?
How might Paul respond to various "gay rights" arguments today?
Talking Points for Your Discussion
- Responses similar to those in today's text
- Responses in addition to those in the text

B. Corrupt Minds (vv. 28-32)

28. Furthermore, just as they did not think it worthwhile to retain the knowledge of God, so God gave them over to a depraved mind, so that they do what ought not to be done.

This third *God gave them over* reemphasizes the correlation between rejection of God and the punishment that results from the life that the rebellious choose. *Depraved* translates a word meaning "tested and found inadequate." The phrase *ought not to be done* translates an expression meaning "not fit or suitable." If we find God as failing the fitting-and-suitable test, then God lets us discover the resulting life that is itself unfitting and unsuitable.

29a. They have become filled with every kind of wickedness, evil, greed and depravity.

Paul now begins a list of evils that characterize a life that rejects God. Such attitudes and behaviors move life far from the justice that the Creator intends and humans should long for.

There are several such "vice lists" in the New Testament, and this one is the longest. *Every kind of wickedness* leads the list, signifying the absence of justice. *Evil* is an umbrella term that addresses all kinds of wrongdoing. Paul equates *greed* with idolatry in Colossians 3:5. The word translated *depravity* is also translated *malice* in 1 Corinthians 5:8.

29b. They are full of envy, murder, strife, deceit and malice. They are gossips,

The focus here is more specifically on ways that humans refuse to live well with each other. *Envy* is hostility toward others for what they have or are (compare 1 Peter 2:1). *Murder* is, of course, the outright destruction of others. *Strife* points to dividing up into mutually hostile groups; the same word in the original language can be translated "dissension" (as it is in Romans 13:13), "quarrels/quarreling" (1 Corinthians 1:11; 3:3), and "rivalry" (Philippians 1:15). *Deceit* is willful dishonesty (also translated "trickery/trying to trick" in 2 Corinthians 12:16; 1 Thessalonians 2:3). *Malice* desires bad things to happen to others. The inclusion of *gossips* (those who engage in rumormongering) puts that sin in its true light. Ultimately, this can be no less destructive than other sins listed here (compare 2 Corinthians 12:20).

30. slanderers, God-haters, insolent, arrogant and boastful; they invent ways of doing evil; they disobey their parents;

The catalog of social sins continues. *Slanderers* are those who speak ill of others (again, compare 2 Corinthians 12:20); the Bible also calls such folks "malicious talkers" (see 1 Timothy 3:11, although a different word is being translated there). Those who hate their fellow humans, who bear God's image, thereby also are *God-haters* (1 John 4:20).

Such behaviors reflect an inflated view of oneself, the desire to rule one's own life as supreme monarch. So Paul includes the *insolent* (having contempt for others because of a high view of self), the *arrogant*, and the *boastful* in the list. Such people use their divinely given creative capacity to find new *ways of doing evil*. They reject all authority outside themselves, even to the point that *they disobey their parents* (compare 2 Timothy 3:2).

31. they have no understanding, no fidelity, no love, no mercy.

In the original language, all the terms in this verse begin with the *a* sound. Each term expresses a negative, the lack of something that true justice and goodness demand. Without acknowledgement of the Creator, *understanding* of what is most important is lost. This leads people to have *no fidelity* (faithfulness). Such hardened people also have *no love*. *Mercy* is thwarted when God, the source of mercy, is rejected.

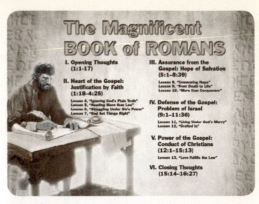

Visual for Lesson 4. *Keep this visual posted for the remainder of the quarter to give your learners a bird's-eye view of the book of Romans.*

that he indeed judges all people. Those who are guilty of the attitudes and actions listed *deserve death* because they know better. And how much worse it is when we deliberately and by example lead others to do the same! See Luke 17:1, 2.

Conclusion

A. Pointing Fingers

Paul described the worst of pagan society as his fellow Jews were accustomed to seeing it. But Paul's description is also very close to the way Israel's prophets had condemned Israel for similar denial of God. As noted in last week's lesson, one finger that points at others leaves the rest of the fingers pointing back at ourselves.

In the end, none can condemn others without condemning oneself. Realizing that, we can do nothing except to receive and rely on the mercy of God, who invites us back to him by his grace.

B. Prayer

God our Creator, when we look at creation, may we always see your hand behind it. When we look at Jesus Christ, may we ever see in him the new creation you have revealed. We pray in Jesus' name. Amen.

C. Thought to Remember

Right attitudes and actions begin with acknowledging the Creator.

> *What Do You Think?*
>
> What can we include in a list of characteristics of a life in submission to God, in contrast with what Paul lists for the life in rebellion against God?
>
> *Talking Points for Your Discussion*
> - Regarding attitudes
> - Regarding actions
> - Regarding values
> - Regarding goals
> - Other

32. Although they know God's righteous decree that those who do such things deserve death, they not only continue to do these very things but also approve of those who practice them.

To conclude, Paul reasserts that knowledge of God is available to all. To know that there is a Creator is to know that we are responsible to him,

INVOLVEMENT LEARNING

Enhance your lesson with NIV® Bible Student (from your curriculum supplier) and the reproducible activity page (at www.standardlesson.com or in the back of the NIV® Standard Lesson Commentary Deluxe Edition).

Into the Lesson

Display pictures of beautiful nature scenery (mountains, oceans, flowers, etc.) and play a recording of nature (singing birds, babbling brook, etc.). Ask learners to offer thoughts about the nature of God from these, pretending they do not know anything about him except what they see in the pictures and hear in the recording. Jot responses on the board. Discuss how creation provides evidence for the existence of a Creator.

Say, "In today's text, Paul states that although God cannot be seen, he has revealed himself to all people through creation. This is called 'general revelation,' as compared with the 'special revelation' of the Bible. Let's see what general revelation should result in and how it is resisted."

Into the Word

Say, "In today's text, Paul constructs an argument that will form a basis for the lessons to follow this one. Therefore, we should take great care in understanding Romans 1:18-32."

Read Romans 1:18-20 aloud, then pose the questions below. The bracketed statements serve as your response key. *Option:* Reproduce the questions on handouts for learners to consider in small groups; do not include the bracketed statements.

1. If the words *godlessness* and *wickedness* in verse 18 were flipped to their positive counterparts *godliness* and *righteousness*, which three other words would need to change as well? What would they change to? [The words *wrath*, *against*, and *suppress* would need to change to *love*, *toward*, and *speak*, respectively, or something similar.]

2. Why are *godlessness* (rebellion against God) and *wickedness* (disregard for others) the opposite of the two commandments in Matthew 22:36-40? [Since those two establish love for God and love for others to be primary, then rebelling against God and disregarding people would be their violations.]

3. Why can no one use a defense of "I never had a Bible, so I didn't know God's will"? [Creation itself provides enough information so that no one can rightfully claim ignorance of him; see also Romans 2:14, 15.]

Read Romans 1:21-23 aloud. Form groups to discuss these questions (on handouts): 1. How do people engage in "futile" thinking and end up with "darkened" hearts? 2. How does the answer to question 1 relate to the world's tendency to glorify almost anyone/anything instead of God?

Use the commentary to correct misconceptions when groups present their conclusions in the ensuing whole-class discussion. Then say, "Paul next sketches consequences of failure to glorify God." Read these three sections: 1:24, 25 / 1:26, 27 / 1:28-32. Pause for reactions after each is read. Draw attention to the phrase *God gave them over* in each case. Lead the class in seeing how that phrase relates to the rest of the segment.

Summarize: "Paul's argument is simple and devastating: the very fact that the world exists means that we owe ourselves to the Creator. When we accept a substitute, the result is all the bad things we see in our text and in the world today."

Option. Enhance discussion of Romans 1:28 with the "The Lies People Tell Themselves" activity from the reproducible page, which you can download. This can be a whole-class exercise.

Into Life

Brainstorm ways to reject the lies that lead to the sinful behaviors of Romans 1:24-32. Then ask, "Which way does it work: Do we help someone see the futility of such behaviors so he or she might turn to God, or do we help someone turn to God so he or she will see the futility of such behaviors?"

Option. Distribute copies of the "Glorify God" activity from the reproducible page. This can be a take-home exercise, but it is better to allow a few minutes for in-class completion.

NEEDING MORE THAN LAW

DEVOTIONAL READING: 1 Peter 1:13-23
BACKGROUND SCRIPTURE: Romans 2

ROMANS 2:17-29

¹⁷ Now you, if you call yourself a Jew; if you rely on the law and boast in God; ¹⁸ if you know his will and approve of what is superior because you are instructed by the law; ¹⁹ if you are convinced that you are a guide for the blind, a light for those who are in the dark, ²⁰ an instructor of the foolish, a teacher of little children, because you have in the law the embodiment of knowledge and truth—²¹ you, then, who teach others, do you not teach yourself? You who preach against stealing, do you steal? ²² You who say that people should not commit adultery, do you commit adultery? You who abhor idols, do you rob temples? ²³ You who boast in the law, do you dishonor God by breaking the law? ²⁴ As it is written: "God's name is blasphemed among the Gentiles because of you."

²⁵ Circumcision has value if you observe the law, but if you break the law, you have become as though you had not been circumcised. ²⁶ So then, if those who are not circumcised keep the law's requirements, will they not be regarded as though they were circumcised? ²⁷ The one who is not circumcised physically and yet obeys the law will condemn you who, even though you have the written code and circumcision, are a lawbreaker.

²⁸ A person is not a Jew who is one only outwardly, nor is circumcision merely outward and physical. ²⁹ No, a person is a Jew who is one inwardly; and circumcision is circumcision of the heart, by the Spirit, not by the written code. Such a person's praise is not from other people, but from God.

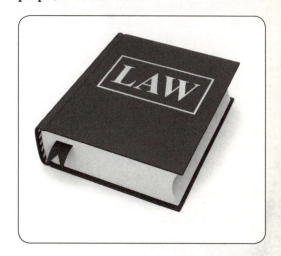

KEY VERSE

It is not those who hear the law who are righteous in God's sight, but it is those who obey the law who will be declared righteous. —**Romans 2:13**

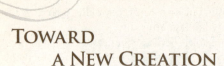

TOWARD A NEW CREATION

Unit 2: A World Gone Wrong

LESSONS 4–7

LESSON AIMS

After participating in this lesson, each learner will be able to:

1. State the difference between knowing God's law and obeying God's law.

2. Contrast the person who knows more of God's law but does not obey with the person who knows less yet does obey.

3. Repent of failure to act on what he or she knows of God's law.

LESSON OUTLINE

Introduction
    A. With Privilege Comes Responsibility
    B. Lesson Background
I. High Calling (ROMANS 2:17-20)
    A. Boastful Knowledge (vv. 17, 18)
    B. Self-Assured Ability (vv. 19, 20)
II. Betrayed Calling (ROMANS 2:21-23)
    A. Preaching but Not Practicing (vv. 21, 22)
    B. Boasting but Not Honoring (v. 23)
III. Sad Results (ROMANS 2:24, 25)
    A. Blasphemy (v. 24)
        Corrupting the Calling
    B. Uncircumcision (v. 25)
IV. True Sign (ROMANS 2:26-29)
    A. Not Lineage but Obedience (vv. 26, 27)
    B. Not Outward but Inward (vv. 28, 29)
        What's on the Inside?
Conclusion
    A. Claiming Privilege
    B. Prayer
    C. Thought to Remember

Introduction

A. With Privilege Comes Responsibility

The story is told that when Queen Elizabeth II of England was a young girl, her father, King George VI, told her to do something.

"I am a princess," she is said to have replied, "and I will do as I please."

"Yes, you are a princess," said her father. "And that is why, for the rest of your life, you will never simply do as you please."

Privilege brings not just honor or power but responsibility. The greater the privilege, the greater the responsibility. Our lesson text is a solemn restatement of this principle. Paul reminded his Christian readers of Jewish background that their high calling as guardians of God's law carried the responsibility of obedience. This is a responsibility that they, along with all people, had failed.

B. Lesson Background

Among Paul's aims in his letter to the church at Rome is to demonstrate that the gospel is God's power for salvation for both Jew and Gentile (Romans 1:16). Both had failed to submit to the God who created them and revealed himself to them, despite any claim of advantage one group might press over the other.

Although Gentiles had not received the special revelation of God's law that had been given to Israel through Moses, Gentiles were nonetheless fully responsible for their rebellion against God. This is because God had sufficiently revealed himself and his will to them in creation itself (Romans 1:18-20; last week's lesson).

In Romans 2, Paul turned to Jews to show them the problem of their own situation. Israel's law and history stood together in Israel's sacred Scriptures. That history showed repeatedly the failure of those who received God's law to keep it. Any advantage that Israel had in receiving God's law at Sinai had been squandered through disobedience.

This realization could come to Jews through more than just reading their people's history in the Scriptures. Observing the world around them could demonstrate the same. Many Jews of the period regarded the priestly leadership of the temple as corrupt and illegitimate. Pressure to conform to social norms meant that many Jews lived more like their Gentile neighbors than as people devoted to God's law. There were few reasons for religiously sensitive Jews to think that their generation was better at keeping God's law than their ancestors had been. For those who thought otherwise, Paul had some sobering—and stern—reminders.

I. High Calling
(ROMANS 2:17-20)
A. Boastful Knowledge (vv. 17, 18)

17. Now you, if you call yourself a Jew; if you rely on the law and boast in God;

Paul addresses a portion of his audience very directly here, with emphasis on *you* as if to speak to each Jewish Christian individually. Does a person call himself or herself *a Jew* as a way of claiming status as one of God's people? Does that person rely on the Law of Moses to establish that standing? Does that person express pride in being a member of God's people and not part of the pagan rabble who know nothing of the true God?

Paul is beginning to show that such confidence is misplaced. Since the dawn of Israel's history, true membership in God's people has depended on more than just belonging to the nation or receiving God's law. Israel's prophets decried confidence that was placed in outward markers of identity (Jeremiah 7:4; 8:8). Paul's words are in line with theirs (compare Luke 3:8).

18. if you know his will and approve of what is superior because you are instructed by the law;

The description of the person who claims privilege of membership in God's people contin-

HOW TO SAY IT

centurion	sen-*ture*-ee-un.
Cornelius	Cor-*neel*-yus.
Gentiles	*Jen*-tiles.
Isaiah	Eye-*zay*-uh.
Jeremiah	Jair-uh-*my*-uh.
Malachi	*Mal*-uh-kye.
Sinai	*Sigh*-nye or *Sigh*-nay-eye.

ues. This person has not simply received the Law of Moses but also knows it well, having been instructed in it continually.

As a result, such a person can clearly describe how God's law provides a better way of living than do the ways of the pagan world. This is the individual who loudly endorses the teaching of God's Word, pointing out how far others have strayed from it. Being part of the "in-group," knowing and approving of what the in-group believes, is for such a person the basis for believing that one is right with God.

B. Self-Assured Ability (vv. 19, 20)

19. if you are convinced that you are a guide for the blind, a light for those who are in the dark,

Now the description begins to look outward. A Jew can fairly claim that God has called the people of Israel to make him known to the pagan nations around them. Surrounded by peoples who are ignorant of God and filled with moral corruption, it is easy to characterize others as *blind* and *in the dark*. It is easy to see one's own knowledge of God's law as the solution.

But notice how easily such a perception can turn to arrogance. When forgetting that God had to rescue Israel time and again from consequences of disobedience, the Jew can begin to imagine that God's "chosen" people are simply better than others. This line of self-delusion leads one to become not *a guide for the blind* but one of the hypocritical "blind guides" that Jesus condemned (Matthew 23:16, 24).

What Do You Think?
What will be your role in improving your church's efforts in being a "guide" and a "light" to those in spiritual darkness?
Talking Points for Your Discussion
- In sharing the gospel
- In improving your own discipleship
- Other

---

20. an instructor of the foolish, a teacher of little children, because you have in the law the embodiment of knowledge and truth—

As the argument continues, it becomes more obvious that Paul is describing one who takes a condescending position. The term translated *instructor* is used especially of those who teach youngsters, and that implication is strengthened in the phrase *a teacher of little children*.

What Do You Think?

In what ways do Christians sometimes project a "holier than thou" attitude because of their knowledge of God's Word? How do we deal with this problem?

Talking Points for Your Discussion

- Language we use
- Attitudes we exhibit
- Actions we take
- Assumptions we make
- Other

II. Betrayed Calling
(ROMANS 2:21-23)

A. Preaching but Not Practicing (vv. 21, 22)

21. you, then, who teach others, do you not teach yourself? You who preach against stealing, do you steal?

Paul turns from describing the individual who claims privilege as God's person to pointing out that person's hypocritical failure. Claiming to be a guide, a light, a teacher is one thing, but heeding one's own teaching is another. Are Paul's readers practicing what they preach?

As Paul asks about *stealing*, we can imagine a person responding, "No, I have never stolen anything." But we must keep in mind that being innocent of theft outwardly is not all there is to this issue. Jesus stressed that true righteousness exists on the inside as well as the outside (compare Matthew 23:25-28). The Law of Moses made the same point with the last of the Ten Commandments prohibiting coveting, which is an inward disposition (Exodus 20:17). Withholding of tithes to the temple (Malachi 3:8-10) or failing to give support to the poor (Isaiah 10:1, 2) were forms of theft in the view of Israel's prophets. Selfishness constitutes theft from the standpoint of the God who examines the human heart.

22. You who say that people should not commit adultery, do you commit adultery? You who abhor idols, do you rob temples?

The description of hypocrisy continues. Those who condemn the pagan world's sexual immorality need to consider whether their own hearts harbor lust (Matthew 5:27, 28). Those who condemn idolatry need to consider whether their behavior is more in line with worship of an idol than devotion to the true God.

Israel's prophets had condemned hypocritical worship in the temple as being more directed to false gods than the true God (Jeremiah 7:9-11; etc.). Those who claim to know God's Word must be at least as mindful of such things as they are of others' failures.

B. Boasting but Not Honoring (v. 23)

23. You who boast in the law, do you dishonor God by breaking the law?

Paul states the dangerous problem directly. The person who boasts *in the law* is the one who claims special identity and privilege because he or she knows God's law. But if knowing does not lead to obeying, it is hardly of value. God is not at all honored by the person who knows his Word but does not follow it. To boast in such a thing is to invite condemnation, not to receive blessing.

The right response is to make our identity not in what we know but in what God has done for us. God's people have always been God's people because of his grace, not because of their knowledge or any accomplishment. To make our stand on God's grace leads to obedience that reflects our gratitude to and dependency on the one who has saved us.

What Do You Think?

In what areas do Christians seem to need most to improve in making their practice of God's Word match their knowledge of it? Why?

Talking Points for Your Discussion

- Regarding what can be seen by everyone
- Regarding what can be seen only by family members and close friends
- Regarding what can be seen only by God

III. Sad Results
(ROMANS 2:24-25)

A. Blasphemy (v. 24)

24. As it is written: "God's name is blasphemed among the Gentiles because of you."

The place where this *is written* is the old Greek version of Isaiah 52:5. Thus the issue of bringing disgrace to *God's name* is hardly new. Hypocrisy among God's people brings his reputation into disrepute among those who do not know him. Israel's calling is to bring light to the nations (Isaiah 49:6). But Israel's failure to obey God creates an excuse for *the Gentiles* to continue to reject Israel's God.

❧ CORRUPTING THE CALLING ❧

Before the scandals of evangelists Jim Bakker in 1987, Jimmy Swaggart in 1988 and 1991, and Ted Haggard in 2006, there was that of Aimee Semple McPherson (1890–1944). Her notoriety was such that it resulted in a Broadway musical titled *Scandalous: The Life and Trials of Aimee Semple McPherson*. One synopsis of the play states that she "was the world's first media superstar evangelist whose passion for saving souls equaled her passion for making headlines."

And make headlines she did! She was divorced more than once (quite a scandalous thing in the first half of the twentieth century). She was accused of lying. She built a 5,000-seat megachurch in Los Angeles. In 1926, she was thought to have drowned in the Pacific Ocean, then rumored to have been kidnapped for $500,000 ransom, then strangely appeared walking alone out of a Mexican desert into Douglas, Arizona. She knew how to use the media, and they loved her for it. Her followers idolized her, but many other Christians saw her as an embarrassment.

The world enjoys finding cracks in the façade of Christianity. As the publicity circus around McPherson's life demonstrates, this is especially true with regard to Christian leaders. Paul's challenge to us, whether leaders or not, is to live with such integrity that the cause of Christ is never subject to reproach (compare 1 Timothy 3:2-7; 1 Peter 2:12). Do we?   —C. R. B.

B. Uncircumcision (v. 25)

25. Circumcision has value if you observe the law, but if you break the law, you have become as though you had not been circumcised.

Circumcision was the sign that God gave to Abraham to show that God had given that man a covenant promise (Genesis 17:1-14). Circumcision identified the male members of the people of that covenant, bound to obey God's commands and anticipating fulfillment of his promises. In that respect, circumcision was a valuable, important act for the people of Israel.

But to receive circumcision without keeping God's law was to make this covenant marker meaningless. The prophet Jeremiah stressed that genuine circumcision is focused on the inner person (Jeremiah 4:4). To claim to belong to God on the basis of physical circumcision alone is to reduce God to one who cares only for appearances.

The issue of circumcision is important for Paul's readers. Some first-century Jewish Christians insist that Gentile Christians must be circumcised to belong to God's people. Paul, along with the other apostles and church leaders, insists that the fulfillment of God's promises in Christ means that anyone can belong to God's people without that indicator (Acts 15:1-29; Galatians 2:1-16).

What Do You Think?

What are some "externals" that may become sources of false confidence for today's Christians? Why?

Talking Points for Your Discussion

- Regarding ceremonies undergone
- Regarding organizational affiliations
- Regarding personal accomplishments
- Other

IV. True Sign
(ROMANS 2:26-29)

A. Not Lineage but Obedience (vv. 26, 27)

26. So then, if those who are not circumcised keep the law's requirements, will they not be regarded as though they were circumcised?

To this point, Paul has described the person who claims membership in God's people but

Visual for Lesson 5. *Use this visual to start a discussion regarding how believers and unbelievers react to God's truth.*

does not follow God's will as expressed in his law. Now Paul describes the opposite: the person who has no claim to membership in God's historic people but follows God's law nonetheless, knowing it as something written on the heart (Romans 2:15).

A key example is Cornelius, a Roman centurion described as "devout and God-fearing; he gave generously to those in need and prayed to God regularly" (Acts 10:2). His generosity to the needy contrasts with supposedly devout Jews of his day who use tradition to sidestep the Law of Moses (example: Mark 7:6-13).

So if an uncircumcised person does what the law requires, that person demonstrates true identity with God's people, true circumcision. The inward reality is what gives rise to obedience.

27. The one who is not circumcised physically and yet obeys the law will condemn you who, even though you have the written code and circumcision, are a lawbreaker.

When Gentiles exhibit obedience to God, they provide a sharp contrast with the lack of obedience on the part of many in Israel. When Gentiles follow God's law even though they do not know him, they bring shame on Jews who claim to know him but fail to obey.

So simply being circumcised, simply belonging to the right group, brings no advantage. In fact, it brings the threat of judgment for those who claim the identity but do not live by it.

B. Not Outward but Inward (vv. 28, 29)

28. A person is not a Jew who is one only outwardly, nor is circumcision merely outward and physical.

Paul sums up. Some (many? most?) of the Christians in Rome who claim special standing because of their Jewish identity and longstanding knowledge of God's law have reduced his concerns to the outward only. But the God who made the world knows the inner world of everyone. The God who reclaims his world through Christ seeks to rule over all people both outwardly and inwardly. Those who appear to belong to God's people outwardly but have no inner reality in that regard make a mockery of his authority.

The inward reality is where the problem exists for the seemingly righteous person. We may imagine ourselves "good enough" to belong to God if we consider only outward appearance and behavior in contrast with that of others. Yet the inward reality is what shows us our need despite our seeming status (Matthew 23:27). Likewise when our outward failures seem to condemn us, the inward reality of our readiness to receive God's merciful forgiveness is what makes us able truly to be part of his people (Luke 18:9-14).

29. No, a person is a Jew who is one inwardly; and circumcision is circumcision of the heart, by the Spirit, not by the written code. Such a person's praise is not from other people, but from God.

In the final statement of this section, Paul ties together many of the earlier biblical strands that make the same point. The inner life—that *of the heart, by the Spirit, not by the written code*—is what truly controls a person (compare 2 Corinthians 3:6). From the account of Cain's sin against Abel, in which anger provided the sinful impulse the power to act (Genesis 4:5-8), to Jesus' denunciation of hypocrisy among the religious leaders (Matthew 23:1-36), the Bible shows that our pride in ourselves masks the persistent evil that lurks inside.

God's focus has always been first on the inward life. He spoke to Cain about that inward reality before Cain committed his terrible deed. He reminded Samuel, who was seeking the king whom God had chosen, that "people look at the outward appearance, but the Lord looks at the heart" (1 Samuel 16:7). God's aim has always been to write his Word on the hearts of his people (Jeremiah 31:33). Simply knowing *the written code* offers no benefit if it is unaccompanied by the inner life. To live otherwise is to care more about what people think than about God's evaluation. For him to do his redemptive work in us, we must recognize our inner selves for what they are and allow God to create in us new attitudes of obedient submission.

❧ *What's on the Inside?* ❧

In 1925, acclaimed poet T. S. Eliot wrote a 98-line poem titled "The Hollow Men" that envisioned the decline of Western civilization. The poem likened Western (Christian) culture to scarecrows stuffed with straw, which have the outward appearance of being alive but have no life inside.

Eliot's words have proven amazingly predictive. Some 90 years later, we see the evidence in a post-Christian Europe, where many of the great cathedrals are now mere museums. We can also see the evidence in historically Christian Canada and the U.S., nations that are increasingly secularized in philosophy and lifestyle. Eliot saw the world as he knew it coming to an end "Not with a bang but a whimper," as the spiritual forces that once gave life would simply give up and give in.

Jesus criticized religious leaders for appearing outwardly "as righteous" while being "full of hypocrisy and wickedness" on the inside (Matthew 23:28). Some Christians in Rome apparently placed their faith in the externals of religious observance instead of the internal virtues of a living faith. The danger of becoming "hollow Christians" is ever with us. Beware!   —C. R. B.

What Do You Think?
  What are some good steps Christians can take to become better circumcised-in-heart?
Talking Points for Your Discussion
  - Regarding awareness of one's situation
  - Regarding "blind spots"
  - Regarding interactions with the world
  - Regarding prayer life
  - Other

Conclusion
A. Claiming Privilege

The Israelites' failure to keep God's law affected not just themselves. God's promise was that all nations would be blessed through Abraham's offspring (Genesis 22:18), that Israel would become "a light for the Gentiles" (Isaiah 42:6; 49:6). So it seemed that Israel's unfaithfulness could prove to be the undoing of God's plans for the world.

But the gospel reveals something vital. Though Israel proved unfaithful, God brought his plan to fulfillment through one in Israel who *did* prove faithful, namely Jesus. His faithfulness, seen in submitting to death on the cross to take the punishment of the guilty, fulfilled God's purpose and solved the problem of human failure for both Jews and Gentiles. How great is our failure? The cross shows us. How powerful is God's solution to our failure? The cross shows us.

For the vast majority of us today, claiming spiritual privilege because of Jewish identity or circumcision seems very foreign. But we know how easy it is to claim such privilege on similar grounds. Looking at the chaotic world around us, we are tempted to congratulate ourselves that we know God and his Word. It is easy to observe the ignorance of the world and contrast that ignorance with what we know of God. Then it is all too easy to take the next step and think the difference has to do with something special about ourselves.

We would be better off contemplating the contrast between the good that other people see in us outwardly and the evil that we know still lives in our hearts. That reflection will lead us to think how God has welcomed us by his grace despite our failures. That in turn will remind us of how much we have in common with the world and of how much we have to share with it.

B. Prayer

O God, we surrender our innermost selves to you! May we be yours, inside and out. We pray in the name of Jesus, who helps us make it so. Amen.

C. Thought to Remember
Let the inward match the outward.

INVOLVEMENT LEARNING

Enhance your lesson with NIV® Bible Student (from your curriculum supplier) and the reproducible activity page (at www.standardlesson.com or in the back of the NIV® Standard Lesson Commentary Deluxe Edition).

Into the Lesson

Distribute handouts of an abstract outline of a human in the top half and lines for writing in the bottom half. Say, "Taking no more than a minute, list at the bottom some characteristics of a person who follows Christ truly." After calling time, ask learners to draw lines to connect those characteristics with the relevant parts of the human outline. (*Expected connections:* behaviors connect to hands and feet, spoken words to mouth, Bible knowledge to brain, and feelings to heart.)

Ask for volunteers to share their lists with the class as a whole. Working your way through the four areas of *behaviors, spoken words, knowledge,* and *feelings*, ask, "What would happen to the other three areas if this one were not in tune with God?" Make a transition by saying, "Following Christ involves the whole person. Outward obedience must demonstrate an inward reality. Let's see how Paul helps us understand this further."

Into the Word

Ask someone with dramatic skills to read aloud Romans 2:17-29. Each phrase of verses 17-20 should be read as if it were an accolade being conferred; verses 21-25 should be read with an accusatory tone; verses 26-29 should be read with a matter-of-fact tone.

Working through verses 17-23, ask learners to identify words or phrases that deal with "the inward" as distinct from those that deal with "the outward." Jot observations on the board in two columns with those labels. Discuss how the inward and outward interrelate (or should interrelate). Use the commentary to explain words and phrases as necessary. At appropriate points, ask learners how they might react if they were first-century Jewish Christians reading these words of a fellow Jew.

When you reach verse 24, say, "Paul concludes his rebuke by quoting the prophet Isaiah to remind his readers of Jewish background that their wrong attitudes and actions were nothing new." Read verse 24, then ask, "In what ways would a first-century Jewish Christian find Paul's statement here easy to agree with?" After responses, ask, "How about difficult to agree with, and why?" Follow up: "In what ways is the name of God blasphemed today because of the actions of Christians?"

Introduce discussion of verses 25-29 by summarizing the background of circumcision as a covenant sign per Genesis 17:1-14. Then form learners into groups and ask each to create a three- or four-sentence summary of Paul's argument in Romans 2:25-29, focusing on the distinction between *knowing* the law and *obeying* it. As groups share summaries in the ensuing whole-class discussion, ask for New Testament examples of those who did not have the law, yet obeyed it anyway.

Make a transition by asking, "In what ways are Christians in danger of—or actually guilty of—elevating the outward over the inward, the letter of the law over its spirit?" Encourage free discussion.

Option. Distribute copies of the "The Laws of God" activity from the reproducible page, which you can download. Work through the exercise as a class, comparing results with today's text.

Into Life

Give each learner a handout on which you have reproduced the two great commandments of Matthew 22:37-39. Ask for two minutes of silence for learners to reflect on and write down their thoughts, words, and actions that failed to live up to the spirit of these two commandments in the past week.

Alternative. Distribute copies of the "Circumcision of the Heart" activity from the reproducible page. Read aloud the passages indicated, discussing as appropriate. Allow time for learners to complete the three steps individually. Encourage learners to use the completed exercise or the above reflection activity for daily review this week.

STRUGGLING UNDER SIN'S POWER

DEVOTIONAL READING: 1 John 1:5-10

BACKGROUND SCRIPTURE: Romans 3:1-20

ROMANS 3:9-20

⁹ What shall we conclude then? Do we have any advantage? Not at all! For we have already made the charge that Jews and Gentiles alike are all under the power of sin. ¹⁰ As it is written:

"There is no one righteous, not even one;
¹¹   there is no one who understands;
      there is no one who seeks God.
¹² All have turned away,
      they have together become worthless;
there is no one who does good,
      not even one."
¹³ "Their throats are open graves;
      their tongues practice deceit."
"The poison of vipers is on their lips."
¹⁴   "Their mouths are full of cursing and
      bitterness."

¹⁵ "Their feet are swift to shed blood;
¹⁶   ruin and misery mark their ways,
¹⁷ and the way of peace they do not know."
¹⁸   "There is no fear of God before their
      eyes."

¹⁹ Now we know that whatever the law says, it says to those who are under the law, so that every mouth may be silenced and the whole world held accountable to God. ²⁰ Therefore no one will be declared righteous in God's sight by the works of the law; rather, through the law we become conscious of our sin.

KEY VERSE

No one will be declared righteous in God's sight by the works of the law; rather, through the law we become conscious of our sin. —**Romans 3:20**

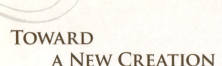

TOWARD A NEW CREATION

Unit 2: A World Gone Wrong

LESSONS 4–7

LESSON AIMS

After participating in this lesson, each learner will be able to:

1. Summarize humanity's situation in relation to God's law.

2. Rebut the argument that, since everyone sins, it's not a problem; God will save us anyway.

3. Write a prayer of confession and repentance for one area of sin that besets him or her.

LESSON OUTLINE

Introduction
    A. An Honest Look at Ourselves
    B. Lesson Background
  I. Humanity's Problem (ROMANS 3:9)
 II. Scripture's Declarations (ROMANS 3:10-18)
    A. Lostness (vv. 10-12)
    B. Death (vv. 13, 14)
    C. Violence (vv. 15-17)
      Our Violent Century
    D. Godlessness (v. 18)
III. Law's Result (ROMANS 3:19, 20)
    A. Blameworthy Before God (v. 19)
      Our Guilt
    B. Awareness of Sin (v. 20)
Conclusion
    A. Saved from Sin's Power
    B. Prayer
    C. Thought to Remember

Introduction

A. An Honest Look at Ourselves

Do you believe what you see in the mirror? Certainly we all know that the images we see there are those of ourselves, not someone else. But do we really recognize the significance of what we see in the mirror? Do we notice that we no longer look as we once did? Or do we still mostly see the person in the mirror from years back? Do we see the way we have become different, or do we imagine we look and can act as we once did?

The reality of changing appearance is hard to admit as years pass. Harder still are the intangible realities regarding who we truly are as people. Some have an unrealistically negative view of themselves: I'm a failure; no one can love me; surely God is very unhappy with me. Others may have the opposite: an unrealistically positive view of themselves. In either case, we may arrive at our unrealistic view because we compare ourselves with others, concluding that we are markedly better or worse than the people we know.

The gospel is a reality check, like an honest look in a mirror, on our estimate of ourselves. Today's text summarizes a key aspect of that reality check.

B. Lesson Background

In his letter to the Romans, Paul addressed Christians of Jewish and Gentile backgrounds who struggled to receive and respect each other as members of Christ's body. Paul mounts an argument in the first three chapters to show that neither has an advantage over the other. Gentiles might claim that they are not responsible for their sin because they did not have God's law. But Paul notes that they have violated the will of God that is demonstrated in creation, visible to every person (Romans 1:18-32; lesson 4).

As for his fellow Jews, Paul points out that *having* God's law and *obeying* it are very different things. Jews who have the law are put to shame by those who never had the law but still manage to obey it. History reveals that Israelites with God's law were no better at obeying him than were Gentiles without the law (Romans 2:1-29; lesson 5).

Paul's argument was not to deny the importance either of God's call to Israel or the law that was given to that nation. The Jews held an advantageous position historically since they "have been entrusted with the very words of God" (Romans 3:1, 2). The law performed a vital function even when disobeyed, showing Israel and all humanity how deeply everyone needs God's gracious salvation. Even if every person is shown to be unfaithful, God is still faithful (3:3, 4).

Our text today brings to a climax the arguments from these early chapters of Romans, addressing the issue of *advantage* further still.

I. Humanity's Problem
(Romans 3:9)

9. What shall we conclude then? Do we have any advantage? Not at all! For we have already made the charge that Jews and Gentiles alike are all under the power of sin.

This verse summarizes much of what Paul has said in the early chapters of Romans. His question *What shall we conclude then?* introduces the implication of his line of reasoning to this point.

As he continues, Paul uses *we* to include himself among the Jewish-Christian readers, and *they* to refer to Christians of Gentile background. But even if the pronouns were reversed, the meaning would be the same. All people, *Jews and Gentiles alike*, have demonstrated rebellion against God. "Whatever historical privilege the Jews may have, these do not place Jews in a superior position in God's judgment" (Douglas Moo).

Here for the first time in Romans, Paul uses the Greek noun for *sin* (the word translated *sinner* in Romans 3:7 is an adjective in Greek). He does so with a special emphasis. By speaking of all people as being *under the power of sin*, the apostle explains that everyone has lived under its reign. Sin is a power at work. It is not that we have simply made a few mistakes. Neither is it that no one has ever done anything godly or virtuous. It is, rather, that all of human experience has been tainted by evil.

No group or individual can claim to be exempt. Nowhere can we point to someone who is free of evil's influence. Sin's mark is found in every human

endeavor. The created order itself "has been groaning," reflecting this tragic reality (Romans 8:22, 23). There is no advantage for anyone in this situation, and no opportunity for escape through one's own power.

What Do You Think?
What misconceptions do people hold regarding sin? How do we correct these?
Talking Points for Your Discussion
- Concerning its definition
- Concerning its cause
- Concerning its effects
- Concerning its prevalence
- Other

II. Scripture's Declarations
(Romans 3:10-18)
A. Lostness (vv. 10-12)

10. As it is written:
"There is no one righteous, not even one;

Here Paul begins to recite a collection of quotations from the Old Testament, each undoubtedly familiar to readers who share his Jewish heritage. The first quotation is from Psalms 14:1-3; 53:1-3. These two psalms are remarkable in that they are essentially identical. It is as if the message is so important that it needs to be said twice. We can also detect part of Ecclesiastes 7:20. The message is one found repeatedly in Israel's Scriptures.

Beginning with the declaration, "The fool says in his heart, 'There is no God,'" Psalms 14 and 53 go on to state that all humans essentially deserve the label *fool* for their failure to be righteous (compare Romans 1:22, lesson 4). Righteousness—God's own standard of justice and goodness—is at odds with what we see in all of human life. The repetition in the verse before us drives home the universality of sin. It has tainted everyone.

11. "there is no one who understands;
there is no one who seeks God.

Paul continues the quotation from Psalms 14 and 53 as those speak of God's looking down from Heaven to inspect human life; he desires to see whether any goodness can be found. We are reminded of God's finding only evil among the people of Noah's day (Genesis 6:5) and in Sodom and Gomorrah in Abraham's time (18:16-33). Those episodes are not isolated. They are typical.

The words quoted here are especially potent for Paul's audience. Regardless of whether one is a recipient of God's law or not, no one can claim genuine understanding. Though many might claim to seek God, the consistent sincerity of their quest is betrayed by their desire to follow their own will. That was the story of Adam and Eve, the parents of all humanity. Placed in a paradise by God, they sought to become independent of him by disobeying his one restriction on their lives (Genesis 3:1-7).

12. "All have turned away,
 they have together become worthless;
there is no one who does good,
 not even one."

The quotation of Psalms 14 and 53 continues, further describing universal human rebellion. *All have turned away* describes people's departing from God's path to choose their own. In so doing, humans *become worthless,* that is, useless to God, to one another, and to themselves. Only by submitting to his rule and following his way can a person live out the true purpose God has for humanity.

The final statement in the verse before us is quite powerful—distressingly so. Not a single person can be found who has expressed God's goodness. That is, not a single person has done so except for Christ. As Paul offers these quotations, he prepares readers to understand what God has accomplished with the cross of Christ (next week's lesson). Human sinfulness is such a huge problem, so much bigger than we typically recognize, that it required a huge solution in Christ and the cross.

What Do You Think?

How does the cross of Christ help you grasp the depth of the human problem of sin?

Talking Points for Your Discussion

- In terms of Christ's innocence
- In terms of Christ's suffering
- In terms of Christ's abandonment
- In terms of Christ's obedience
- Other

B. Death (vv. 13, 14)

13a. "Their throats are open graves; their tongues practice deceit."

Having presented humanity's lost state in general, Paul turns to quotations that focus on the dishonest, malicious way that people speak and act toward one another. Quoted now is Psalm 5:9. This psalm is a lament in which the psalmist cries out to God for deliverance from oppressive enemies. Such people have *throats* like *open graves,* speaking words filled with death.

13b. "The poison of vipers is on their lips."

This part of the verse is from Psalm 140:3, a psalm that also includes a lament that cries out for deliverance from enemies. The portion before us compares the speech of such people to *the poison of* venomous snakes (*vipers*). It was not just Eve and Adam who listened to the voice of the serpent, and not just the serpent who spoke with that deadly voice. Though many have been victims of humanity's evil, all have also been participants in it.

14. "Their mouths are full of cursing and bitterness."

The series of quotations now shifts to Psalm 10:7. This psalm also calls out to God for help against oppressive enemies. Their violent intentions are expressed by speech that calls down evil things on others (*cursing*) and expresses angry hostility (*bitterness*; your English translation of Psalm 10:7 doesn't look the same because Paul is quoting from the Septuagint, which is the old Greek version of the Old Testament). Were such experiences uncommon, we might question whether Paul understands things rightly. But we must sadly admit that we have all experienced such things, and we all have done them ourselves.

C. Violence (vv. 15-17)

15. "Their feet are swift to shed blood;

Thoughts and words now become deeds in Paul's quoted description of human sinfulness. The source at this point is Isaiah 59:7, with Proverbs 1:16 being similar. Both texts depict the person who is so inclined to evil that he or she is ready to run to commit violence.

This particular quotation is especially pointed for Paul's Jewish-Christian readers. In Isaiah 59, the prophet specifically addressed Judah's sin that ultimately led to the nation's exile in pagan Babylon. As the Jewish-Christian audience of Paul's day hears these familiar words, they have to respond, "Yes, that refers to me as well."

16. "ruin and misery mark their ways,

The quotation of Isaiah 59:7 continues. Where do feet dedicated to violence tread? The answer is here: on the path characterized by *ruin* and human *misery*. Far from being the agents of God's goodness in the world, human beings—even those who have received God's Word—are agents of death.

17. "and the way of peace they do not know."

The quotation continues to the opening phrase of Isaiah 59:8. The violent hatred that characterizes human sinfulness excludes any possibility of *peace*. We should remember that in its biblical usage, peace is more than just a cease-fire in the relentless pattern of hostility. God's true peace is a positive condition that means fellowship, love, and well-being among people.

This peace is the assurance God gives as he promises to solve the problem of human rebellion (Isaiah 9:1-7; chap. 11). To recognize the absence of peace in the present is to reckon with one's own rebellion.

❧ OUR VIOLENT CENTURY ❧

If there is any one word that can be said to characterize these opening years of the twenty-first century, it is *violent*. The century had hardly begun when the terrorist attacks of 9/11 killed nearly 3,000 innocent people. Then came an extended war in Afghanistan, which saw a multinational force arrayed against the fanatical Taliban.

Concurrent with the war in Afghanistan was the invasion of Iraq. That effort overthrew a

HOW TO SAY IT

Abraham	*Ay*-bruh-ham.
Ecclesiastes	Ik-*leez*-ee-*as*-teez.
Gomorrah	Guh-*more*-uh.
Septuagint	Sep-*too*-ih-jent.
Sinai	*Sigh*-nye or *Sigh*-nay-eye.
Sodom	*Sod*-um.

tyrant, but also spawned the years of tribal and sectarian violence that followed. The so-called Arab Spring of 2011 and the ensuing years saw revolutions topple autocratic governments in Egypt and Libya, a lengthy civil war in Syria (in which the number of deaths approaches 200,000 at the time of this writing), and violent demonstrations in many nations throughout the Middle East and northern Africa. And, of course, sporadic warfare continued between Israel and the Hamas faction in Palestine. The tragic list seems to be unending.

Paul characterizes the problems of the ancient world as swiftness in shedding blood, walking in the ways of destruction, and knowing nothing about the ways of peace. Paul's words are as true now as they were when he wrote them! Human nature has not changed. We know the cure for the violence: it's the gospel of Jesus Christ. But the question is, how do we get the message out?

—C. R. B.

D. Godlessness (v. 18)

18. "There is no fear of God before their eyes."

The quotations come to their conclusion with Psalm 36:1. This psalm begins with a description of human sinfulness, contrasting it in the second part of the psalm with God's faithfulness and goodness. As Paul uses the statement we see here, he creates a fitting climax to the litany. The despair, hostility, and violence that arise from human sinfulness all reflect the absence of *fear of God*.

That expression needs careful attention. Used often in the Bible, *fear of God* indicates the profound, awe-filled respect that the creature must have for its Creator. Recognizing and submitting to God's utter superiority in power, wisdom, and goodness is what *fear of God* represents.

Such fear does not imply living in constant dread that God's displeasure and judgment will come upon us. But it does mean having a deeply felt acknowledgement that God will indeed overcome his enemies, that he will judge the wicked. The person who fears God in this way seeks to obey God. Ironically, the one who fears God's authority has the least to fear of God's displeasure.

What Do You Think?

How should an appropriate "fear of God" be demonstrated?

Talking Points for Your Discussion

- Regarding thought processes
- Regarding attitudes toward others
- Regarding behavior
- Regarding manner of speech
- Other

III. Law's Result
(ROMANS 3:19, 20)
A. Blameworthy Before God (v. 19)

19. Now we know that whatever the law says, it says to those who are under the law, so that every mouth may be silenced and the whole world held accountable to God.

To bring the collection of quotations into perspective, Paul speaks of the nature of the books from which they are drawn. The Law of Moses was God's gift to ancient Israel, intended to speak especially to them. The advantage that the law gives is in seeing one's own sinfulness. Israel is no better off than the pagan Gentiles. If Israel listens to its deposit from God, then Israel realizes its guilt before God.

By implication, this applies to the rest of Israel's Scriptures as well. This includes the books of prophets such as Isaiah, who by God's Spirit applied the law's principles to the issues of his own time. Also included are the Psalms and Proverbs, which express those principles of law poetically. The litany of quotations has laid out the point that Paul now sums up.

As the law makes Israel's guilt clear, creation itself makes clear the guilt of the rest of the world. Gentiles and Jews, pagans and God-worshippers —all are *held accountable to God*.

❧ OUR GUILT ❧

Sally (name changed) grew up in a fine Christian family. But as she reached her teen years, she began to think church people were too old-fashioned. She sometimes remarked, "The church doesn't want you to have any fun." Soon enough, it became apparent what Sally meant by *fun*: she was dating a married man. When she became pregnant with his child, it wasn't so much "fun" anymore.

To her credit, Sally carried the baby to full term. Some tongues wagged during the months of her pregnancy, but there were changes taking place in her heart. After the baby was born, Sally came before the church with a repentant heart and publicly confessed her sin. Her Christian brothers and sisters acknowledged her repentance and welcomed her back.

From that point on, Sally's life was exemplary. Not every story of this nature has such a happy ending, but Sally's experience reminds us of an important truth: we are all Sally. Our guilt may not be exactly the same as hers, but we are all guilty of sin nonetheless. When we fail, the world is ready and willing to point out hypocrisy; but that's nothing compared with standing condemned in the sight of God! But the one who has the right to condemn us the most is also the one in whom forgiveness is found.   —C. R. B.

B. Awareness of Sin (v. 20)

20. Therefore no one will be declared righteous in God's sight by the works of the law; rather, through the law we become conscious of our sin.

With the word *therefore* Paul brings to a close the first part of the letter to the Romans. As he says in the discussion immediately preceding today's text, the law is a great boon despite Israel's unfaithfulness (Romans 3:1-8). But how can the law be such a boon if it is disobeyed? It brings to light the very sinfulness of humanity, including especially the sinfulness of those who have received the law. The law tells us how far humanity has fallen. It makes impossible any attempt to excuse oneself for rebellion against the Creator. When one understands the law, it is impossible to believe that one can *be declared righteous.*

The books of the law themselves demonstrate this point. Those five Old Testament books, Genesis through Deuteronomy, contain not just laws but also narratives of Israel's history. Those narratives show the consistent failure to keep the law on the part of those who received it. Indeed, as God gave Moses the tablets of the law on Mount Sinai, the Israelites were openly engaged in idolatrous worship at the bottom of the mountain (Exodus 32).

Reading the law gives us little hope that we can do better than they. Paul has made this point in various ways to his readers, and he now sums up that point: the law makes us *conscious of our sin.* Even those who are identified as God's people are rebels unworthy of his blessing. To see others' sin —of Israel in the past, of pagans around us in the present—is to be drawn to confess our own sin if we read God's Word rightly.

Visual for Lesson 6. *Start a discussion by pointing to this visual as you ask, "How do we keep from fooling ourselves in this regard?"*

problem is to be solved, then God must be the one to solve it.

We modern-day Christians can easily fail to hear how this message addresses us. Certainly we see Israel's failure as we read the Old Testament. But, we think, that is them, not us. We have no problem affirming the power of sin in our own world. We see it all around us in others' degraded, chaotic, ruined lives. But, we think, that is them, not us.

Forgetting what our lives would be without God's work in Christ, ignoring how sin's power still reveals itself in us, we can imagine that the universal power of sin is not a factor in our lives. If we succumb to such thinking, we become the kind of people Paul corrected in Romans: those who imagine that their position as God's people gives them a superior status over others.

May our study of this text remind us that we, like they, are victims of sin's power, to be saved from it only by God's grace.

What Do You Think?

How has Scripture helped you understand your position as one who has rebelled against God?

Talking Points for Your Discussion

- In terms of attitudes revealed
- In terms of actions interpreted
- In terms of stories hitting home
- In terms of excuses swept away
- Other

Conclusion

A. Saved from Sin's Power

The words of today's text are quite discouraging if read by themselves. But thanks be to God, they bring to a close what is only the beginning of the message of Romans! The problem of human sin is deep and wide. It goes back to the very beginning of the human family and extends to every member in every place in the world. This problem cannot be solved by human endeavor; we know only how to create and perpetuate the problem. If the

B. Prayer

Gracious God, grant that we can see ourselves as we really are, as you see us. Purge from our hearts the power of sin. We rely utterly on your forgiveness in Jesus. We pray in his name. Amen.

C. Thought to Remember

We can seek God's grace
when we recognize our sin.

INVOLVEMENT LEARNING

Enhance your lesson with NIV® Bible Student (from your curriculum supplier) and the reproducible activity page (at www.standardlesson.com or in the back of the NIV® Standard Lesson Commentary Deluxe Edition).

Into the Lesson

Form learners into groups of three to five. Provide each group with magazines, newspapers, markers, glue sticks, scissors, and a half sheet of poster board. Instruct each group to create a picture and word collage in response to this question: *What is wrong in the world today?* After five minutes, ask each group to display its collage. Discuss the commonalities and differences among them.

Say, "When asked the same question in about 1910, Christian author and theologian G. K. Chesterton purportedly responded, 'I am.'" Discuss that response and compare it with the collages. Then say, "Let's see how Chesterton's response serves as an introduction to today's text."

Into the Word

Read Romans 3:9 aloud. Say, "Last week, Paul rebuked the Jews for focusing on physical circumcision rather than the circumcision of the heart. Here in verse 9, he now addresses the common sinful state of Jews and Gentiles."

Pose these questions for whole-class discussion: 1. Why was it important for Paul to remind both Jews and Gentiles they were all under sin? 2. How should the reality of everyone's sinfulness inform our relationships with others?

Next, say, "Paul begins to recite a series of Old Testament Scriptures to continue to support his argument that all are under sin."

Divide the class into three groups and provide instructions as follows. *Lostness Group*—Read Romans 3:10-12, then describe the journey of biblical characters who failed in their attempts to follow God. In what ways are people still lost? *Death Group*—Read Romans 3:13, 14, then discuss how the spoken word can be deadly and deceitful; compare with James 3:2-12. *Violence and Godlessness Group*—Read Romans 3:15-18, then discuss where people are experiencing violence (physical force, unjust power) in the world. Compare

verse 18 with the beginning of Paul's argument in Romans 1:18-20.

Have groups share conclusions in whole-class discussion. Ask how Christ is the exception to all of the verses read. Then read Romans 3:19, 20 before posing this question: "How would you respond to someone who says that since everyone sins, it's not a problem because God will save us anyway?"

Alternative. Instead of considering Romans 3:10-18 in the manner above, distribute copies of the "Old Testament References" activity from the reproducible page, which you can download. If your class has eight or fewer learners, this exercise can be accomplished with greater speed by assigning only one or two references per learner. For nine or more learners, form them into pairs or small groups to complete an appropriate number each. Have individuals, pairs, or groups report their findings in the ensuing whole-class discussion.

Make a transition by asking, "When we ponder what's wrong with the world today, how does our lesson text indicate that should we join with G. K. Chesterton in saying, 'I am'?"

Into Life

Ask each learner to compose a prayer as follows: *Part 1*—Write a confession of personal sins (especially besetting sins) that are highlighted in Romans 3:10-18. *Part 2*—Write a repentance statement that describes how he or she will turn away from those sins and turn toward God. *Part 3*—Write a statement that thanks God for his forgiveness and grace. (*Option:* Provide handouts that list the above instructions along with adequate blank space for writing.) Before learners begin, stress that you will ask them to share part 3 with the class as a whole, but not parts 1 and 2.

Option. Following the above, shift the focus from sins against God to the impact of sin on others by having learners complete the "The Impact of Sin" activity from the reproducible page.

GOD SET THINGS RIGHT

DEVOTIONAL READING: Ephesians 2:1-7
BACKGROUND SCRIPTURE: Romans 3

ROMANS 3:21-31

²¹ But now apart from the law the righteousness of God has been made known, to which the Law and the Prophets testify. ²² This righteousness is given through faith in Jesus Christ to all who believe. There is no difference between Jew and Gentile, ²³ for all have sinned and fall short of the glory of God, ²⁴ and all are justified freely by his grace through the redemption that came by Christ Jesus. ²⁵ God presented Christ as a sacrifice of atonement, through the shedding of his blood—to be received by faith. He did this to demonstrate his righteousness, because in his forbearance he had left the sins committed beforehand unpunished—²⁶ he did it to demonstrate his righteousness at the present time, so as to be just and the one who justifies those who have faith in Jesus.

²⁷ Where, then, is boasting? It is excluded. Because of what law? The law that requires works? No, because of the law that requires faith. ²⁸ For we maintain that a person is justified by faith apart from the works of the law. ²⁹ Or is God the God of Jews only? Is he not the God of Gentiles too? Yes, of Gentiles too, ³⁰ since there is only one God, who will justify the circumcised by faith and the uncircumcised through that same faith. ³¹ Do we, then, nullify the law by this faith? Not at all! Rather, we uphold the law.

KEY VERSES

There is no difference between Jew and Gentile, for all have sinned and fall short of the glory of God, and all are justified freely by his grace through the redemption that came by Christ Jesus. —**Romans 3:22-24**

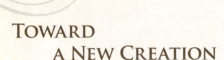

Toward a New Creation

Unit 2: A World Gone Wrong

LESSONS 4–7

LESSON AIMS

After participating in this lesson, each learner will be able to:

1. Identify the only means that can make people right.

2. Describe how Christ's death and resurrection enable God to be both just and justifier of those who believe.

3. Express gracious acceptance to others as a result of having received God's grace.

LESSON OUTLINE

Introduction
  A. The Mystery Revealed
  B. Lesson Background
I. Righteousness Through Faith (ROMANS 3:21, 22)
  A. Role of the Law (v. 21)
  B. Role of the Christ (v. 22)
II. Justified by Grace (ROMANS 3:23, 24)
  A. Short of the Glory (v. 23)
    Self-Esteem Run Amok
  B. Redemption in Christ (v. 24)
III. Planned by God (ROMANS 3:25, 26)
  A. Patient Judge (v. 25)
  B. Just Justifier (v. 26)
IV. Result of Faith (ROMANS 3:27-31)
  A. Boasting Excluded (vv. 27, 28)
  B. Gentiles Included (vv. 29, 30)
    Healing Divisions
  C. Law Upheld (v. 31)
Conclusion
  A. The Mystery Solved
  B. Prayer
  C. Thought to Remember

Introduction

A. The Mystery Revealed

The mystery is a popular kind of story. The puzzle at the story's beginning is solved by the detective who discovers all the clues and figures out "whodunit." The story moves to a climax when the mystery is revealed.

The problem of evil in the world is arguably the greatest mystery. Why does the world contain so much suffering? Why do human beings seem so persistently wicked? Skeptics wonder if there is a God, one who is good and powerful, then why does he allow such things to go on?

Yet if God were to end evil in the world, would he not have to destroy evil humanity (compare Genesis 6:5-7)? And in the end, has not every human who knows right from wrong proven to be a participant in the pervasive evil? How could anyone survive God's just judgment? How can he be merciful and still bring judgment on evil?

Today's text makes the bold assertion that through Jesus Christ, God has revealed the solution to that great mystery. In Christ, God has brought his righteous judgment on evil. In Christ, God has made mercy freely available to everyone. In Christ, God has solved the mystery of the ages.

B. Lesson Background

Bringing the opening section of Romans to a climax, our lesson text draws on the important Old Testament theme regarding what it means to belong to God's people. One key concept in this regard is the distinct calling of ancient Israel as God's people. The Old Testament asserts that Israel's God is the only true God, the Creator of all that exists and the world's true sovereign. Why then was he worshipped by only one tiny, insignificant nation? That situation was to be temporary, as explained by God's dealing with Abraham: God promised that through that man all nations would be blessed (Genesis 12:1-3; 22:15-18).

Closely related to this promise was the role of God's law in the life of Israel. The Law of Moses was God's gift to Israel distinctly (Exodus 20). While much of the law expressed God's justice and purpose for all peoples, many parts of it expressed specific commands that God gave Israel to express that nation's distinct identity in the world. All peoples—both Gentiles and Jews—were held accountable to laws such as those prohibiting murder and stealing. But only ancient Israel was bound to certain others.

This raised a difficult question: When God fulfilled his promise to bless all nations, did that mean that all nations were to become part of Israel and keep Israel's distinct laws, such as circumcision? Or would God receive Gentiles without those markers of Israel's identity?

Paul worked to answer this question at the famous Jerusalem Council (Acts 15:5). In the early part of Romans, he labored further to answer it. Today's lesson text picks up where last week's ended.

I. Righteousness Through Faith
(Romans 3:21, 22)
A. Role of the Law (v. 21)

21. But now apart from the law the righteousness of God has been made known, to which the Law and the Prophets testify.

From Romans 1:17 to 3:20, Paul establishes that sin makes everyone—Gentile and Jew alike—unworthy of God's blessing. With the phrase *but now,* the apostle begins to explain how God resolves this problem. He does so in a way that shows utter faithfulness to his promises and to his nature. As God's wrath has been revealed (1:18), so now his way of righteousness also is being *made known.*

This way of righteousness is *apart from the law.* For Israel, the Law of Moses had demonstrated people's sinfulness, but it did not provide the means of overcoming that sin permanently. For Gentiles, that law marked a dividing line between them and God's covenant people. These were not failures of the law, however. Rather, these were the

HOW TO SAY IT

Abraham	*Ay*-bruh-ham.
Gentiles	*Jen*-tiles.
Mosaic	Mo-*zay*-ik.
propitiation	pro-*pih*-she-*ay*-shun.

very purposes for which God gave the law. And neither is the way of righteousness, now revealed, a contradiction of *the Law and the Prophets.* This way of righteousness fulfills the law by bringing about what God's Word to Israel had always promised. Through this righteousness that is *apart from the law,* Jews (who have failed the law) and Gentiles (who have been excluded by the law) come to God on equal footing.

B. Role of the Christ (v. 22)

22. This righteousness is given through faith in Jesus Christ to all who believe. There is no difference between Jew and Gentile,

What is this way to righteousness? Paul answers that God makes this way not through the law but *through faith in Jesus Christ.* To have faith is to affirm that something is true and to demonstrate trust in the reality of that truth. So faith in Jesus is belief that he is indeed God's divine Son and that he lived, died, and rose again. True faith—assent plus trust—inevitably yields faithfulness: living according to what one believes.

In the original language, the phrase *faith in Jesus Christ* has also been translated "faith of Jesus Christ" to describe the faithfulness that Jesus demonstrated rather than our response of faith in him. Some biblical scholars advocate such a reading, which suggests that Paul emphasizes first that Christ's faithfulness makes God's way of righteousness possible.

Certainly in Romans and elsewhere, Paul both assumes Christ's faithfulness and asserts that all people must approach God through genuine faith in Christ. But many scholars observe that the construction in the original language most often points not to Christ's own faithfulness but to Christ as the one in whom people are to have faith. We are probably wise to take it that way as well here. (Technically speaking, this question of interpretation is that of "subjective genitive" vs. "objective genitive.")

This way of righteousness through faith in Christ has many significant implications. But the first that Paul emphasizes is that there can be no distinctions among people. Jews with the law and Gentiles without it—all come to God through faith in what God did in Christ.

II. Justified by Grace

(ROMANS 3:23, 24)

A. Short of the Glory (v. 23)

23. for all have sinned and fall short of the glory of God,

This verse reminds us of Paul's argument in the prior sections of Romans. Except for Christ himself, no human can claim superiority to any other due to the fact that all have rebelled against God.

That sinful rebellion stands in sharp contrast with *the glory of God*. In this context, *glory* refers to the overwhelming greatness and goodness of God, the very characteristics that require worship from all his creatures. Having been created in God's image (Genesis 1:26, 27), we might be said to share in God's glory if we reflect his goodness. But sin alienates us from any claim to such glory.

❧ SELF-ESTEEM RUN AMOK ❧

The 1960s saw culture begin to turn away from traditional morality. The "hippie" rebellion, Woodstock, and the free-sex movement arrived, urging one and all to "do your own thing." Various books fueled this line of thought as they taught people to give up "inauthentic" ways. Self-acceptance was seen as the key to a fulfilling, authentic life. Thus, the self-esteem movement was born.

Today, we hear the humanistic concepts of the self-esteem movement couched in phrases such as, "We each have our own truth, and all truths are equally valid." Paul's statement that "all have sinned" is rejected. How quaint that sounds in a supposedly "enlightened" era!

History teaches us, however, that the most destructive wars of the twentieth century were fought between the most highly educated, "enlightened" countries. Regardless of how out-of-touch the biblical idea of sin might seem to modern culture, it remains a sad fact of life. The ills of society demonstrate that evil and sin still abound. No amount of rationalizing can change the fact that we live in a sin-sick world. Jesus, not self-esteem, is the cure for that.   —C. R. B.

Visual for Lesson 7. *Use this visual to discuss how the concept of grace relates to the other three concepts depicted.*

> *What Do You Think?*
> How does a person's coming "short of the glory of God" reveal itself today?
> *Talking Points for Your Discussion*
> - Regarding wisdom
> - Regarding commitment
> - Regarding love
> - Other

B. Redemption in Christ (v. 24)

24. and all are justified freely by his grace through the redemption that came by Christ Jesus.

The answer to human sinfulness is God's gift in Christ. It is a gift that no one can earn but that all may receive freely. The gift is to be *justified*. This word means "to make or count as righteous."

In receiving the sinner who has faith in Christ, God pronounces that sinner to be righteous despite the guilt of sin. This comes about *through the redemption* that Christ effects. That concept suggests a payment that brings freedom to a captive; compare the word *ransom* in Mark 10:45 and 1 Timothy 2:6. God had liberated Israel from bondage in Egypt in the exodus, and now Christ liberates sinners from bondage to sin.

The means by which this happens is the subject of verse 25, next. But before moving on, Paul wants to make sure we realize this comes freely (unearned by us) because it is the gift of God's *grace*, the favor that he bestows despite the fact that we do not deserve it. Indeed, to be deserving of grace would be a contradiction in terms (see Romans 11:6).

Without God's grace, the situation for the sinner would be hopeless. Without Christ's redemptive death, God's grace would be an unrealized intention. But with these, otherwise hopeless sinners have solid assurance that they have an unshakably right standing as God's people, now and forever.

> **What Do You Think?**
> How does knowing that you are justified by grace, not your own goodness, make a difference in your life? How should it?
>
> *Talking Points for Your Discussion*
> - Regarding hope versus discouragement
> - Regarding confidence versus fear
> - Regarding life purpose versus meaninglessness
> - Other

III. Planned by God
(ROMANS 3:25, 26)
A. Patient Judge (v. 25)

25. God presented Christ as a sacrifice of atonement, through the shedding of his blood —to be received by faith. He did this to demonstrate his righteousness, because in his forbearance he had left the sins committed beforehand unpunished—

But is not God's justice violated when he receives sinners? Paul now begins to answer this important question. The question does not arise for the first time with the preaching of the gospel of Jesus. It has existed as long as God has withheld his judgment on the guilty.

God's *forbearance,* his delay in bringing on sinners the punishment of their sin, is as old as the story of humanity itself. Having warned Adam that he would die if he ate of the tree of knowledge of good and evil (Genesis 2:16, 17), God did not in fact inflict that punishment instantly for disobedience. The same is true for every sinner: God holds back his punishment, allowing time for repentance and restoration. But how can he withhold judgment and still remain the righteous judge?

Paul's answer is that Christ's death provides *a sacrifice of atonement* (see also 1 John 2:2; 4:10). Other Bible versions translate this as *propitiation,* a rare word that describes a concept more common in Paul's day than in ours. It means "an offering that satisfies the wrath of a deity." Regarding pagan sacrifices, this might strike us as rather like bribery. Pagans believe in fickle gods who become angry unpredictably. An angry god may bring disaster at any moment. So the pagan makes offerings to them—sacrifices of animals, etc.—hoping to please them and turn aside their wrath.

For the true God, the concept is different. First, God's wrath, unlike that of pagan gods, is entirely consistent in being his righteous response to evil. God's wrath reveals his determination to bring judgment in order to eradicate evil from his world. Of course, since all are sinners, then all are objects of God's wrath. How can any escape?

The answer is that God in his mercy provides the very offering that turns aside his own wrath. This offering is not like a bribe, since it does not come from anyone but God himself. The offering is that of a sinless divine being, Jesus, who willingly suffers in the sinner's place.

For ancient Israel, the sacrifice of animals in the temple was propitiatory, established by God to satisfy his righteous response to sin. The animal took the place of the sinner. But such an arrangement was not a permanent solution. An animal is not equal in status or value to a human, and it certainly cannot be a willing substitute (compare Hebrews 10:1-4).

Christ provided the true sacrifice, the offering that satisfied God's righteous wrath for all people who receive the gift by faith. Ancient Israel's sacrifices pointed forward to this. Christ provides the fitting substitute: a human, not an animal; one who died not for his own sin (for he had none), but for the sins of others. As the divine Son of God, Christ is truly the offering that God the Father provided to satisfy his own righteous wrath. As the divine Son of God, infinite in his being, Christ provided a substitute sufficient not just for one person but for all people.

God has not been unrighteous in delaying punishment for sin. Rather, he has exercised mercy in anticipating the fulfillment of his plan to take the punishment for sin on himself. Can there be a more satisfactory or more surprising solution to the problem of evil?

What Do You Think?

In what ways does Christ's death on your behalf help you better understand God's character?

Talking Points for Your Discussion
- In terms of his commitment
- In terms of his goodness
- In terms of his mercy
- In terms of his wisdom
- Other

B. Just Justifier (v. 26)

26. he did it to demonstrate his righteousness at the present time, so as to be just and the one who justifies those who have faith in Jesus.

Paul reminds us that God had the arrival of Christ as the climax of the divine plan, the full demonstration of *his righteousness*. This plan shows that God is truly *just*—morally upright and fair in all his dealings. At the same time, God is the true *justifier*—the one who counts his people as righteous even though they are sinners.

But how can God be both holy (responding to evil with righteous anger that brings punishment) and merciful (responding to sin with forgiveness)? The answer, again, is found in Christ's atoning (propitiatory) sacrifice, where God takes the punishment of sin on himself. Thereby his holiness is satisfied and his mercy is made possible.

Even so, mercy offered must become mercy received to be effective. God's offer of justification is available to all. But only those who respond to that offer with *faith in Jesus* actually receive it.

IV. Result of Faith
(ROMANS 3:27-31)

A. Boasting Excluded (vv. 27, 28)

27. Where, then, is boasting? It is excluded. Because of what law? The law that requires works? No, because of the law that requires faith.

The focus of God's plan is on his action, not ours. If Jews claim that their status as God's chosen people gives them priority, they forget that God's plan for Israel has been to bring his salvation to humanity by means of one in Israel, namely Jesus. He is the one who fulfilled Israel's promises

and destiny despite Israel's sin. If Gentiles claim the higher status because of Israel's failure, they must likewise reckon with the fact that they stand within God's people only by his grace through Christ.

So Israel's law, which showed Israel its sin and thereby showed sin to be the condition of all humanity, did not bring God's salvation. Rather, the law points to God's salvation accomplished in Christ. The law reveals God's plan not by showing us the works we can do to earn salvation; we know that our actions cannot satisfy a holy God. Rather, the law points to the need for faith in Christ. That *law that requires faith* is now fulfilled as Christ has done what God promised. We lay hold of those fulfilled promises as we put our faith in what God has done in Christ.

28. For we maintain that a person is justified by faith apart from the works of the law.

The works of the law, or following the Law of Moses, constitute the very program at which Israel has failed and from which Gentiles have been excluded. But to be *justified by faith* is an avenue open to all, Jew and Gentile alike, no matter how often or deeply we fall short of God's glory. In passing, we can note the numerous parallels that exist between Romans 3:27, 28 and chapter 4.

What Do You Think?

How does (or should) the truth of verse 28 affect a Christian's life?

Talking Points for Your Discussion
- Attitudes to have toward God
- Attitudes to have toward others
- Attitudes regarding oneself

B. Gentiles Included (vv. 29, 30)

29. Or is God the God of Jews only? Is he not the God of Gentiles too? Yes, of Gentiles too,

Paul continues to lay out the implications of the atoning sacrifice of Christ's death. If membership in God's people comes through keeping the Mosaic law, then only Jews can be members. Gentiles would then have to become Jews (by circumcision, etc.) in order for God to become their God. But a Gentile who becomes a Jew is no longer a Gentile! Through Christ, God receives people as they are in their differences.

The world continues to struggle with issues of race, ethnicity, tribalism, class distinctions, etc. The negative results of such struggles vary widely. Sometimes the result is subtle forms of discrimination. At the other extreme is the horror of genocide.

Within the church, we see divisive struggles over various doctrinal issues. The Jew-and-Gentile issue that Paul addressed in Romans still resonates in other ways two millennia after that letter was written.

How should we respond when tensions threaten to destroy the church from within? Every attempt at a solution should have this as its starting point: a look upward in prayer to the one who is the God of everyone. He can heal divisions by changing hearts and minds. And we may be surprised to discover that the first heart he changes is our own!

—C. R. B.

30. since there is only one God, who will justify the circumcised by faith and the uncircumcised through that same faith.

Circumcision, ordained by God himself (Genesis 17), had an exalted place in the life of ancient Israel. To be God's covenant people meant being *the circumcised*. Conversely, to be *the uncircumcised* meant exclusion from the covenant people. But under the new covenant, it is faith in Christ, not circumcision, that is the true mark of God's people.

What Do You Think?
How does God's grace help you experience unity and fellowship with other Christians?
Talking Points for Your Discussion
- Concerning those of different race or ethnicity
- Concerning those of different economic status
- Concerning those whose family structures differ markedly from your own
- Other

C. Law Upheld (v. 31)

31. Do we, then, nullify the law by this faith? Not at all! Rather, we uphold the law.

Paul's declarations undoubtedly cause some to wonder whether he is saying that God's law is therefore pointless. His answer is a resounding *Not at all!* As the apostle explains the human predicament and God's remedy for it, the Law of Moses has a distinct and vital place. It simply is not the place that many imagine it to be. God's plan was not that all the world's peoples would keep that law. Rather, the plan was that through the nation defined by that law, namely Israel, God would bring the one who would reconcile to himself people of every nation. This was the law's purpose all along.

Therefore, the gospel makes the law of great importance because the gospel accomplishes the law's very purpose. Jesus, "born under the law" (Galatians 4:4), brings that purpose and Israel's mission to the fulfillment that God intends: reconciling repentant sinners from all the nations to him.

Conclusion

A. The Mystery Solved

In the best mystery stories, the audience is uncertain as to how the mystery will be solved until the very end. All the clues are clear, but how they fit together is obscure. When the solution is revealed, a good mystery prompts the audience to express satisfaction with the outcome. "Yes, that makes sense. It had to be that way."

The gospel is just such a solution to the mystery discussed in the Introduction. If there is any meaning in the world, there must be a God who demands justice. But if God is just, then we are subject to his judgment because of our sins. We need a God who is merciful.

In Christ, God is both just and justifier, both righteous and merciful. The cross solves the mystery and answers our deepest need.

B. Prayer

Father, we thank you that through Christ's blood we sinners are counted as your righteous people. By your mercy, lead us to accept one another in our differences as graciously as you have accepted us. We pray in Jesus' name. Amen.

C. Thought to Remember

God always sets things right—always.

INVOLVEMENT LEARNING

Enhance your lesson with NIV® Bible Student (from your curriculum supplier) and the reproducible activity page (at www.standardlesson.com or in the back of the NIV® Standard Lesson Commentary Deluxe Edition).

Into the Lesson

Form learners into groups of three or four. Provide each group with a half sheet of poster board and felt-tip markers in a variety of colors. Ask each group to create a storyboard of the life of Jesus, from birth to ascension. (Possible formats include a timeline, a Roman-numeral outline, and picture sketches.) Display completed storyboards and discuss.

Then say, "For the past three weeks, we have studied the words of Paul to the church in Rome by considering parts of Romans 1:18–3:20. Today we conclude this unit by considering Paul's introduction of good news. The story of Jesus is good news for both Jew and Gentile—everyone!"

Option. Place in chairs copies of the "The Sobering Reminder" activity from the reproducible page, which you can download, for learners to begin working on as they arrive.

Into the Word

Say, "Throughout the first three chapters of Romans, Paul repeatedly states that sin has made all people unworthy of God's blessings. With the phrase 'but now' to open today's text, he begins his explanation of how God has solved the problem of sin and demonstrated his faithfulness to his promises. Although God's wrath has been revealed (Romans 1:18), now his way of righteousness is made known."

Read Romans 3:21, 22 aloud, then compare these verses with 1:16, 17. Ask learners to identify phrases that describe the righteousness of God in these four verses. Discuss how 3:21, 22 frames Paul's argument for the need of the righteousness that comes from God.

Read Romans 3:23, 24 aloud, then pose these questions: 1. How does our sin contrast with God's glory? 2. How do the concepts *justified, grace,* and *redemption* relate with one another? (Use the commentary to correct misconceptions.)

Read Romans 3:25, 26 aloud, then ask for learners' reactions to the phrase *atoning sacrifice.* Discuss what it means for God to be both *just* and *justifier* because of Christ's atoning sacrifice. If no one does so, be sure to stress that God must punish sin in order to be *just,* but his love compels him to find a way to release us from the punishment we deserve. Use the commentary to explain how both happen through the sacrifice of Jesus Christ.

Next, say, "Paul moves his argument forward by asking and answering a series of questions that indicate the focus to be on God's action, not ours." Ask a learner to read Romans 3:27-31. In two columns on the board, record the questions asked and the responses given. Ask learners to add to this list the questions they have, or have heard from others, about Christ's sacrifice, God's grace, and our faith. Using Paul's own words whenever possible, suggest responses.

Option. At the beginning of the Into the Word segment, distribute copies of the "Paul's Argument and Good News" activity from the reproducible page. This exercise will recap the book of Romans up to the point of today's lesson. Form learners into four pairs or small groups and assign to each one of the four categories indicated. Discuss findings as a class.

Into Life

Assign the two scenarios below to two groups, one each. If your class is larger, form more groups and give duplicate assignments. Have groups present their responses in whole-class discussion.

Scenario 1: A friend says to you, "Since I am justified by faith and not by works, my works don't matter; I can do as I please!" How do you respond?

Scenario 2: A friend continually points out the faults and sins of others, but never acknowledges his or her own personal sin. How do you respond?

Conclude by rereading Romans 3:23, 24. Close with a prayer of thanksgiving for God's grace.

UNWAVERING HOPE

DEVOTIONAL READING: Psalm 42
BACKGROUND SCRIPTURE: Romans 5:1-11

ROMANS 5:1-11

¹ Therefore, since we have been justified through faith, we have peace with God through our Lord Jesus Christ, ² through whom we have gained access by faith into this grace in which we now stand. And we boast in the hope of the glory of God. ³ Not only so, but we also glory in our sufferings, because we know that suffering produces perseverance; ⁴ perseverance, character; and character, hope. ⁵ And hope does not put us to shame, because God's love has been poured out into our hearts through the Holy Spirit, who has been given to us.

⁶ You see, at just the right time, when we were still powerless, Christ died for the ungodly. ⁷ Very rarely will anyone die for a righteous person, though for a good person someone might possibly dare to die. ⁸ But God demonstrates his own love for us in this: While we were still sinners, Christ died for us.

⁹ Since we have now been justified by his blood, how much more shall we be saved from God's wrath through him! ¹⁰ For if, while we were God's enemies, we were reconciled to him through the death of his Son, how much more, having been reconciled, shall we be saved through his life! ¹¹ Not only is this so, but we also boast in God through our Lord Jesus Christ, through whom we have now received reconciliation.

KEY VERSE

Hope does not put us to shame, because God's love has been poured out into our hearts through the Holy Spirit, who has been given to us. —**Romans 5:5**

TOWARD A NEW CREATION

Unit 3: Life on God's Terms

LESSONS 8–13

LESSON AIMS

After participating in this lesson, each learner will be able to:

1. Give reasons why Christians have unapologetic, unashamed hope.

2. Explain the relationship between justification and the believer's expressions of faith, peace, and love.

3. Write a poem, song, or other expression of joy to celebrate the receiving of reconciliation through our Lord Jesus Christ.

LESSON OUTLINE

Introduction
A. Stuck in the Snow
B. Lesson Background
I. Unashamed Hope (ROMANS 5:1-5)
A. Result: Peace with God (vv. 1, 2)
   Access, Granted and Denied
B. Result: Gift of the Spirit (vv. 3-5)
II. Unearned Salvation (ROMANS 5:6-11)
A. Basis: Christ's Death (vv. 6, 7)
B. Basis: God's Love (vv. 8, 9)
C. Basis: Christ's Resurrection (vv. 10, 11)
   Reconciled, Saved
Conclusion
A. Proven Love
B. Prayer
C. Thought to Remember

Introduction

A. Stuck in the Snow

One December while I was in college, a friend and I were driving together to our hometown in Idaho for Christmas vacation. To get there, we had to navigate several tricky roads (one of which is known as "Deadman Pass") in the Blue Mountains of eastern Oregon. It was snowing, and my little sports car ultimately spun out and went off the roadway into a snow bank. We were not hurt, but the car was stuck, traffic was very light, and we were alarmed. Providentially it was only a few minutes until a large SUV pulled over to check on us. The driver offered us a lift to the next town, which would save us from freezing to death.

Then something remarkable happened. This kind man, who was in a hurry to make an appointment, noticed a pillow in the back of my car that had the insignia of my college fraternity. He said, "My two boys were members of that house." And he spent the next 90 minutes digging us out of the snow bank, freeing my car. He then followed us to the next town, where he filled my gas tank before he went his way. A dangerous situation became a gracious rescue, more than we expected or deserved (given our foolhardy travel during dangerous winter conditions in an ill-equipped car).

Today's lesson tells the much bigger story of God's loving us so much that he acted to save us from an eternal death that we deserve. This is a core teaching in the book of Romans.

B. Lesson Background

The apostle Paul was involved in several great travel adventures, the last of which was his trip to Rome for a hearing before the emperor. The book of Acts ends with Paul awaiting this trial (Acts 28:30, 31). Rome was a destination he had desired for many years (Romans 1:13).

Prior to that visit, Paul had spent several months in Greece toward the end of his third missionary journey (Acts 20:2, 3). There, probably while in the city of Corinth, he wrote to the church in Rome in AD 57 or 58. Included in the letter are the apostle's understanding of the Old Testament background for the Christian message, the nature of Christian salvation based on the atoning death of Christ, the centrality of faith as the only path for human salvation, the relationship between Jewish and Gentile Christians in the plan of God, and several other matters.

All this makes Romans both the most challenging of Paul's letters to understand and the richest depository of what he calls "my gospel" (Romans 2:16; 16:25). The basis and reality of being justified by faith is the subject of Romans 1–4 in general and 3:24, 28 in particular (last week's lesson). Paul quoted Habakkuk 2:4 in Romans 1:17 to set the tone for the entire book: "the righteous will live by faith." This means that faith—complete trust in God—is the only way that life may be found. It cannot be earned by obedience, although obedience is important. It is not inherited by ancestry, although this is not unimportant (see Romans 3:1, 2; 9:4, 5). True life, eternal life, the life of salvation, is only found in trusting God to save us.

Abraham, the great patriarch of the Jews, was justified by faith (Romans 4:3, quoting Genesis 15:6). Thus the idea of faith in God as the core element of one's life is not a Christian innovation. Such faith is to be the foundation of our relationship with God. This was intended as central in the pre-Israel period (Abraham), in the nation of Israel itself (Habakkuk), and in the church. This fact takes us into today's text.

I. Unashamed Hope
(ROMANS 5:1-5)
A. Result: Peace with God (vv. 1, 2)

1. Therefore, since we have been justified through faith, we have peace with God through our Lord Jesus Christ,

HOW TO SAY IT

Bathsheba	Bath-*she*-buh.
Corinth	*Kor*-inth.
Habakkuk	Huh-*back*-kuk.
Leviticus	Leh-*vit*-ih-kus.
patriarch	*pay*-tree-ark.
Pentecost	*Pent*-ih-kost.
shalom *(Hebrew)*	shah-*lome*.

The result of our justification by faith is *peace with God.* This peace is more than a mere cessation of hostilities, a peace treaty. Rather, it is an Old Testament kind of peace, as exemplified by the Hebrew word *shalom.*

In this sense, *peace* has the meaning of "satisfaction," or "payment for an offense." For example, Leviticus 24:21a states that a person who kills another's animal must replace it. This half-verse uses the verb form of *shalom,* which is central to this process of making peace with another. Making peace with God is not simply saying, "God, I'm not going to fight you any more." According to Paul, some sort of restitution must occur to have peace with God. That restitution happens *through our Lord Jesus Christ* (compare Ephesians 2:14). This is the theme that Paul will unpack in the remainder of our lesson.

> **What Do You Think?**
> In what ways does having peace with God affect the way you live daily? How should it?
> *Talking Points for Your Discussion*
> - At home
> - At work/school
> - When traveling
> - Other

2. through whom we have gained access by faith into this grace in which we now stand. And we boast in the hope of the glory of God.

The word *access* gives a picture of being in the presence of God (compare Ephesians 2:18; 3:12). Access to God was limited under the Law of Moses. Direct access to God's presence in the temple's Holy of Holies was reserved for the high priest, and he could claim this access but once a year (see Leviticus 16; Hebrews 9:7). But the curtain of the temple has been torn open through the death of Christ (Matthew 27:51; Hebrews 10:19, 20), and access is now available to all.

This is not because of our own efforts, but by the grace of God. We are spiritually able to stand in God's presence, to have a living, dynamic relationship with our Creator despite our sin. This is a cause for rejoicing, since it removes the curse of sin that has broken this essential relationship. We can anticipate the future with hope. We need not fear being in God's presence.

❧ Access, Granted and Denied ❧

My dad inherited an old piece of furniture called *a secretary*. Its distinguishing feature was a large panel that was attached to the main body of the unit by horizontal hinges. When swung open, that panel served as a writing surface.

The panel had a lock to keep it secure when in the closed position. Unfortunately the key to the lock had been lost. One day my father removed the lock so he could take it with him to flea markets, where some booths would have large jars of old keys. Dad tried all those keys in the lock, eventually finding a fit. As a result, he could lock the secretary but gain access whenever he desired.

So often it seems that people pay great attention to locking up their physical valuables (house, car, etc.) while living "lock free" lives in an ethical and moral sense. They want the freedom to do and say anything, and they don't mind allowing unholy ideas or persons to gain access to them in return. They believe that moral locks are to be left open or removed altogether, with no need for a key.

But the Bible notes the importance of keys in a spiritual sense (examples: Matthew 16:19; Revelation 1:18; 3:7; 9:1; 20:1). Sin had locked us out of access to God, but Christ became the key that unlocks. May we ever hold that key dear!

—C. R. B.

B. Result: Gift of the Spirit (vv. 3-5)

3, 4. Not only so, but we also glory in our sufferings, because we know that suffering produces perseverance; perseverance, character; and character, hope.

Paul turns from grand expressions of spiritual hope to the realities of our lives. How do we attain the hope of verse 2 in the real world, in the daily grind of life? Paul knows that the Christians in Rome are experiencing *sufferings* for their faith in Christ (compare 1 Peter 1:5-7). This may be true particularly of Jewish Christians if they are constantly threatened with persecution by the more established and powerful non-Christian Jews of the city. This applies to us too, for not everything

about being a follower of Christ is easy and without personal cost. As Jesus predicted, following him requires that we take up our own crosses (Mark 8:34), to die to self and live for him (see Romans 6:6).

Paul reminds his readers of the *perseverance* they learn when they suffer (compare James 1:2, 3). The causes of suffering are not always eliminated quickly. Sometimes these situations must be patiently endured. Enduring hardships serves to give us *character*. This has the sense of seasoning our souls, thereby giving us *hope*, because as we have endured suffering in the past, we will be able to endure it in the future.

Pain is not a sign that God has abandoned us. Our hope can never be taken from us, for it is based on the gracious expression of God's love through the giving of his Son, Jesus our Lord.

> *What Do You Think?*
> What have been some personal costs to you in following Christ? How do you deal with the sense of loss that these costs entail?
> *Talking Points for Your Discussion*
> ▪ Regarding costs in relationships
> ▪ Regarding costs of career opportunities
> ▪ Regarding financial costs
> ▪ Other

5. And hope does not put us to shame, because God's love has been poured out into our hearts through the Holy Spirit, who has been given to us.

We are *not put . . . to shame* by holding this hope in front of us. In addition to a sense of "being unashamed," hope also includes the idea of "not being disappointed." Our hope is not mere wishful thinking. It has a solid basis, for it springs from mighty acts of God that affect our lives. Paul will go on to explain the powerful implications of Christ's death, but at this point he gives another, more immediate confirmation and benefit of our hope: *the Holy Spirit, who has been given to us.*

By using the concept of pouring, Paul creates a vivid word-picture of a spiritual reality: God's pouring the Holy Spirit into the hearts of believers. It is reminiscent of the Day of Pentecost, where the dramatic reception of the Holy Spirit among the gathered disciples was seen as a fulfillment of Joel's prophecy that God would "pour out" his Spirit in the last days (Acts 2:17, 33; compare Titus 3:5, 6).

Paul has not yet experienced the fellowship of the Roman church personally, but he is confident of a spiritual connection with its members. All Christians share in the gift of the Holy Spirit, freely given by God to comfort and guide us. Christianity is not a do-it-yourself faith. It is a living reality shared similarly by all Christians, who are vessels of God's holy presence in their lives. This reality is a confirming factor in our hope, the "deposit" (down payment) of our great future with God (see 2 Corinthians 5:5).

Visual for Lesson 8. *Point to this visual as you ask learners how* hope *relates to the eight other concepts noted.*

What Do You Think?

What connections do you experience between having the Holy Spirit and having love in your heart toward others?

Talking Points for Your Discussion

- When the Holy Spirit seems active in your life
- When the Holy Spirit seems inactive in your life

II. Unearned Salvation
(ROMANS 5:6-11)

A. Basis: Christ's Death (vv. 6, 7)

6. You see, at just the right time, when we were still powerless, Christ died for the ungodly.

Having given context for our great hope, Paul now further explains how our salvation is made possible. First, he quickly sketches the human plight. The word translated *powerless* is often used in the New Testament to refer to physical illnesses, afflictions of those in need of healing (example: Luke 10:9). But the apostle uses it here to refer to spiritual sickness, our weakness when it comes to obeying the will of our Creator.

All of the tragic stories of the Old Testament are summed up in the phrase *when we were still powerless*: Adam and Eve's eating fruit of the forbidden tree, the Israelites' partying around a golden calf, David's committing adultery and murder because of his lust for Bathsheba, etc. In every case, spiritual weakness led to sin. That is

our situation as well. We are on the way to spiritual death, and nothing we do can restore ourselves to health. What is the solution?

The answer is that *at just the right time, . . . Christ died for the ungodly.* Let's be very clear: those who are *powerless* are *the ungodly.* Our spiritual weakness has brought us to a contempt for God, a frightening and dangerous lack of reverence and awe for the king of the universe. Yet despite this heinous disrespect, God has done something for us that only he can do: he sent his Son to die for us.

7. Very rarely will anyone die for a righteous person, though for a good person someone might possibly dare to die.

Paul slows down a bit to explain in more detail. Why is it so extraordinary for Christ to die for sinners? Paul answers with the analogy of everyday life, probing the deep feelings of his readers. It would be unusual for someone to give his or her life for another, even *for a righteous person.* Perhaps, Paul says, it is within the realm of possibility for one to sacrifice his life for an extremely *good person*, but everyone knows that this is a rare and unlikely occurrence.

In the 1960s, former president Dwight D. Eisenhower suffered a series of heart attacks and was near death. At the time, a new medical procedure was making headlines: heart transplants. Many World War II veterans who had served under Eisenhower offered to donate their own healthy hearts for their beloved former army commander, an example of someone daring to die for a good man. None of these well-intended offers was accepted, of course, but the willingness to die for another made headlines nonetheless. Thus Paul's point still stands.

B. Basis: God's Love (vv. 8, 9)

8. But God demonstrates his own love for us in this: While we were still sinners, Christ died for us.

Paul brings us to a great irony, a great mystery of the Christian faith. When Christ died for us, it was not a deserved act for a beloved and relatively good man like Eisenhower. It was a selfless, inexplicable expression of God's love for sinners.

Paul describes this as God's demonstrating *his own love for us*. This has a sense of "proving" or "giving an unquestionable display"—a strong statement! Who can doubt God's love when realizing that he freely gave his Son to be the sacrifice for our sins? The great mystery is why God loves us so much! He chooses to love us even though we deserve exactly the opposite.

9. Since we have now been justified by his blood, how much more shall we be saved from God's wrath through him!

The implications of Christ's death for sinners include past, present, and future aspects. First, the death of Christ is a past, historical event. The great sacrifice for human sin was accomplished during a Passover week in Jerusalem more than a quarter century ago from Paul's perspective. Jesus needed to die only once, for he was the perfect and final sacrifice for sin (see Romans 6:10; compare Hebrews 9:28a).

Second, the blood of Christ and our faith in its saving power have the effect of making us righteous, *justified*. This legal language indicates salvation in the present. We don't have to wait for justification. We are justified by grace right now.

Third, the Bible promises that all will be subject to judgment after death (see Acts 17:31; Hebrews 9:27). Paul promises that Christ will save us from the deserved verdict of our judgment, the *wrath* of God against sin. The righteous, perfect judgment of God is sure. But also

assured is our salvation through the atoning death of God's own Son, for he will come again to save us (see Hebrews 9:28b).

C. Basis: Christ's Resurrection (vv. 10, 11)

10. For if, while we were God's enemies, we were reconciled to him through the death of his Son, how much more, having been reconciled, shall we be saved through his life!

Paul presses further by describing our unsaved state as having been *God's enemies*. This is a warfare analogy, but God was not the aggressor—we were! We were the cause of hostilities! We were the perpetrators! We were found to be fighting against God (compare Acts 5:39; 26:14). And in the midst of this one-sided battle, he brought peace. We are now *reconciled to him*.

Whereas the language of justification in verse 9 is legal in nature, the language of reconciliation here speaks to a personal relationship. Reconciliation is a key concept for Paul (see 2 Corinthians 5:18-20). It is the process by which adversaries become friends. This is central to the gospel message, that we no longer need fear that God hates us and wants to destroy us. Instead, we believe that he loves us and that there is no remaining cause for alienation and no excuse for rejecting his offer of salvation.

Paul drives this home by reminding us of the hope we have for the future. This is especially based on *his life*, referring to Christ's resurrection. We are saved now by his atoning death, and we will be saved in the future by our resurrected and living Savior. He will not forget us when he comes again in power and glory.

❧ RECONCILED, SAVED ❧

Years ago, I had a friend who built his own house. He had a full-time job, but evenings and weekends he spent on this project. He contracted for some of the work, such as wiring and plumbing. But by and large, he did most of the construction himself: he laid floors, put up wallboard, installed windows and cabinets, painted, hung lights, etc.

When construction was finished almost two years later, he and his family moved in. We would think, of course, that that was the natural and reasonable thing to do. That's why he was building the house in the first place. To have abandoned the house upon its completion would be far outside the bounds of expected behavior!

God has gone to great lengths to reconcile us through the Son so the Holy Spirit can "move in." Would God finish construction only to abandon us? Of course not! Collectively, we "are being built into a spiritual house" (1 Peter 2:5). Those he reconciles, he will also save. This we can cling to even in (or especially in) our darkest hours.

—C. R. B.

What Do You Think?

When was a time that your reconciliation with someone bore similarities with how people are reconciled with God? What did you learn from this experience?

Talking Points for Your Discussion

- Regarding who made the first move in reconciling (Matthew 5:24)
- Regarding how the first move was received
- Regarding the permanence of the reconciliation
- Other

---

11. Not only is this so, but we also boast in God through our Lord Jesus Christ, through whom we have now received reconciliation.

These are not grim words of judgment and warning; the apostle is rejoicing as he explains these things. Earlier he noted that people of faith should be people of hope. Now, he concludes this section by saying that people of faith and hope will also be people able to *boast in God*.

The reason why is summed up in the word *reconciliation*. This noun carries forward the thought of the previous verse, where as a verb it is rendered "reconciled" (twice). This word is used in the financial world of Paul's day to refer to paying up an account, making good what is deficient. It is not far removed from today's accounting world, where "reconciling accounts" refers to making records come out evenly. The debt for sin is paid by God's Son. Our personal account, with all its sin debt, is paid off by the sacrificial death of Jesus Christ. No wonder Paul is so thankful!

What Do You Think?

What can we do to put aside the felt need to "even the accounts" with other people?

Talking Points for Your Discussion

- At work
- In marriage
- With a sibling
- On the freeway
- Other

Conclusion

A. Proven Love

How do you "prove" love? How do you prove to someone that you love him or her? In medieval times, a man would bend a silver coin and give it to his sweetheart as a promise of his love and intention to marry. This is similar in some ways to a man giving an expensive engagement ring to his fiancée. In both cases, this is wealth not easily spent. At the core, this is a demonstration of love that is proven by actions, not simply by words.

God's love for us is more than promises or words. He has proven his love by sending his only Son to die for us while we were hostile and disobedient. The fact that the sinless one gave himself for sinners means that we need never doubt his love for us. So when you feel that life is rotten and unfair, remember that God has proven his love for you. When it seems that he has abandoned you, remember that he has proven his love for you. When you feel worthless and insignificant, remember that God has proven his love for you. He does so now and forevermore.

B. Prayer

Loving Father, we do not fully understand why you love us, but we believe it. When we were weak-souled because of sin, you loved us. At the right time, you proved your love by sending your Son to die for us. May we love you more and more each day. We pray this in the name of Jesus. Amen.

C. Thought to Remember

God's proven love is the basis
of the Christian's hope.

INVOLVEMENT LEARNING

Enhance your lesson with NIV® Bible Student (from your curriculum supplier) and the reproducible activity page (at www.standardlesson.com or in the back of the NIV® Standard Lesson Commentary Deluxe Edition).

Into the Lesson

Pass around a container in which you have placed the following six items: a fake lottery ticket; a large index card featuring the words *401(k), IRA, real estate, stocks, bonds*; a picture of a family; a work ID (real or created); a bottle of multivitamins; and a cross. Have learners blindly pick one item each until all are drawn.

Ask for items to be held up one at a time, in the above order, for all to see as you ask, "Why is this one a good or bad basis on which to put hope for the future?" Discussion of the sixth item, the cross, will serve as your transition to the Into the Word segment.

Into the Word

Give each learner a worksheet that you have headed "What Difference Does the Cross Make . . ." Below that heading have these three categories listed:

1. In our relationship with God (Romans 5:1, 2, 9-11)?
2. In our life experiences (Romans 5:1-5)?
3. In our love for Jesus Christ (Romans 5:5-8)?

Have these words listed across the bottom of the handout: *access, boast, character, enemies, faith, hearts, hope, glory, justified, love, peace, perseverance, reconciled, saved, sufferings, wrath.*

Form learners into study pairs as you distribute the handouts. Assign each pair one of the three questions to answer, using the verses indicated. (If you have more than three pairs, assign duplicate questions.) Pairs should try to use words from the list at the bottom of the handout, but encourage learners to go beyond those as they see fit.

After calling time, request pairs to share their conclusions. Possible responses:

1. The cross allows us to be justified by our faith and results in peace with God. We have access to God and will be received into his presence.

Because we are saved and reconciled with God, we don't have to fear his wrath.

2. The cross means we can rejoice in the hope we have because of the grace God extends to us. When we have trials and sufferings, we are assured that God has not abandoned us. God works in us to produce perseverance, which gives us more character and results in hope for the future.

3. The cross causes us to love Jesus more as we realize what he did for us when we were unable to help ourselves. Because he was willing to die for us when we were his enemies, we know we are reconciled to God and saved for eternity.

Alternative. Distribute copies of the "Stacking Up Benefits" activity from the reproducible page, which you can download. Have learners work in pairs to complete as indicated. (*Option:* Make this a contest to see which pair can finish first; give a token prize to the winners.) Ask which concepts learners find most difficult; use the commentary to correct misconceptions.

Into Life

Form learners into groups of three. Give each group a large cross cut from poster board along with markers and/or colored pencils. Instruct groups to write on their crosses some expressions to celebrate the receiving of reconciliation through the Lord Jesus Christ. Encourage the most artistic person in each group to write the words creatively and decorate them expressively. Have each group show the results of its artwork.

Option. Distribute copies of the "Sing a Song of Hope" activity from the reproducible page along with hymnals or other worship songbooks for use as indicated. When learners finish, ask for volunteers to share their song titles with the class. Encourage learners to take their lists home as a stimulus to sing the listed songs during their devotions in the week ahead. Select a familiar song to sing to adjourn class.

FROM DEATH TO LIFE

DEVOTIONAL READING: 2 Corinthians 5:17-21
BACKGROUND SCRIPTURE: Romans 6

ROMANS 6:1-4, 12-14, 17-23

¹ What shall we say, then? Shall we go on sinning so that grace may increase? ² By no means! We are those who have died to sin; how can we live in it any longer? ³ Or don't you know that all of us who were baptized into Christ Jesus were baptized into his death? ⁴ We were therefore buried with him through baptism into death in order that, just as Christ was raised from the dead through the glory of the Father, we too may live a new life.

. . . .

¹² Therefore do not let sin reign in your mortal body so that you obey its evil desires. ¹³ Do not offer any part of yourself to sin as an instrument of wickedness, but rather offer yourselves to God as those who have been brought from death to life; and offer every part of yourself to him as an instrument of righteousness. ¹⁴ For sin shall no longer be your master, because you are not under the law, but under grace.

. . . .

¹⁷ But thanks be to God that, though you used to be slaves to sin, you have come to obey from your heart the pattern of teaching that has now claimed your allegiance. ¹⁸ You have been set free from sin and have become slaves to righteousness.

¹⁹ I am using an example from everyday life because of your human limitations. Just as you used to offer yourselves as slaves to impurity and to ever-increasing wickedness, so now offer yourselves as slaves to righteousness leading to holiness. ²⁰ When you were slaves to sin, you were free from the control of righteousness. ²¹ What benefit did you reap at that time from the things you are now ashamed of? Those things result in death! ²² But now that you have been set free from sin and have become slaves of God, the benefit you reap leads to holiness, and the result is eternal life. ²³ For the wages of sin is death, but the gift of God is eternal life in Christ Jesus our Lord.

KEY VERSE

We were therefore buried with him through baptism into death in order that, just as Christ was raised from the dead through the glory of the Father, we too may live a new life. —**Romans 6:4**

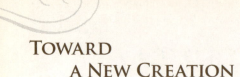

TOWARD A NEW CREATION

Unit 3: Life on God's Terms

LESSONS 8–13

LESSON AIMS

After participating in this lesson, each learner will be able to:

1. Summarize the dramatic change that occurs in the life of one who turns to Christ.

2. Explain the death/life and slave/free metaphors that Paul uses.

3. Identify a part of himself of herself to offer more fully as an instrument of righteousness to God and make a plan to do so.

LESSON OUTLINE

Introduction
  A. "Gotta Serve Somebody"
  B. Lesson Background
I. Death and Life (ROMANS 6:1-4, 12-14)
  A. Faulty Logic (vv. 1, 2)
  B. Correct Thinking (v. 3)
  C. New Life (v. 4)
  D. Godly Imperatives (vv. 12, 13)
  E. Saving Grace (v. 14)
II. Sin and Righteousness (ROMANS 6:17-23)
  A. Different Masters (vv. 17-20)
    Servant to . . . What?
  B. Different Results (vv. 21-23)
    The Good Purpose
Conclusion
  A. Lingering Sin
  B. Prayer
  C. Thought to Remember

Introduction

A. "Gotta Serve Somebody"

In 1979, the iconoclastic folk singer Bob Dylan announced his conversion to Christianity with a new album titled *Slow Train Coming*. It featured the Grammy Award–winning "Gotta Serve Somebody," a song that expressed that new Christian's understanding of how life really works. Dylan sang of the fact that life involves service either to Satan or to the Lord.

Dylan's spiritual journey since then has been the subject of much speculation. But the words of his song ring true today, nearly 40 years later. Many people think they serve only themselves. Their highest good is their own pleasure and satisfaction. They reject God's authority in their lives, often by denying his existence.

Yet as Dylan discovered, we are all servants of another. We delude ourselves if we think we are the masters of our fate and the captains of our souls. That outlook leads us to become slaves to our passions, which in turn leads to horribly messy lives and an eternity without Christ. The apostle Paul stresses that we are either servants to sin or servants to righteousness. There is no middle ground. This is the topic for today's lesson.

B. Lesson Background

Much of Romans 6 uses the metaphor of slavery. This fact brings with it a problem of certain mental associations, since slavery in the ancient world was not always equivalent to the slavery of the U.S. into the nineteenth century.

America's sordid history of slavery involved slave traders "harvesting" people in Africa, transporting them from their homeland, then selling them as commodities. This was often justified on the racist theory that such Africans were inferior, even subhuman. This horrific legacy tends to dominate our understanding of the practice of slavery.

In Paul's day, however, people became slaves for various reasons. Most slaves were the human spoils of war, peoples from nations conquered by the Roman legions. Roman slavery was not based on race, and there was no assumption that slaves were soulless or intellectually inferior.

Some slaves were highly educated, and their masters were known to free them after a period of service. Such people thus attained the status of loyal freedmen (compare "the Synagogue of the Freedmen" in Acts 6:9). But unless such freedom was granted, slaves were considered possessions of their owners, and we should not think that slaves were never abused in that regard. Even so, slavery in the first century AD did not have the across-the-board odious reputation we generally associate with that word now.

We also acknowledge that slavery in the first-century Roman Empire and in nineteenth-century America operated under similar assumptions. There was a master, and slaves were obligated to serve that master. Disobedience could be punished harshly. The will of the master was primary, and the slave had to obey. This is the background for much of what Paul has to say when he refers to people as "slaves to sin."

I. Death and Life
(ROMANS 6:1-4, 12-14)
A. Faulty Logic (vv. 1, 2)

1. What shall we say, then? Shall we go on sinning so that grace may increase?

Paul begins this section with two rhetorical questions. These are questions for which the answers should be obvious. The second question deserves close scrutiny, and we can see in it this flow of logic: (1) Since forgiveness of sin is a sign of God's grace to us and (2) since grace is a good thing, then (3) why not sin all the more so that we may get more grace from God?

Paul is using a technique known as "reduction to the absurd." In this method, an argument is boiled down to a level at which supporting it seems crazy. Anyone who would argue that continuation of sin is a good thing because it results in more opportunities for God to forgive us has missed the

HOW TO SAY IT

Galatians	Guh-*lay*-shunz.
synagogue	*sin*-uh-gog.
Thessalonians	*Thess*-uh-*lo*-nee-unz (*th* as in *thin*).

point entirely! Do we think we are doing God a favor by increasing his grace business?

What Do You Think?
What techniques, tactics, etc., have you found to be helpful in overcoming persistent sin?
Talking Points for Your Discussion
- Before being tempted
- While being tempted

---

2. By no means! We are those who have died to sin; how can we live in it any longer?

Paul answers his own question, using some of the strongest language found in his letters: *By no means!* We can sense impatience and even anger in his tone.

Paul then poses another question that highlights the absurdity of sinning in order to receive more grace: If we have died to sin, why would it still be a living force in our lives? Is sin dead or alive for us? The idea of having *died to sin* is central to what follows.

Lest we think that Paul is merely opposing first-century nuttiness, let us cast this in modern terms: Is it possible for a Christian to engage in ongoing sinful behavior and still feel good about it? Why are so many Christians comfortable doing things the Bible condemns as sin? Does the assurance of forgiveness make sin less serious?

Paul is demanding that we take a sober look at continuing sin. He begins this discussion with a surprising object lesson: our baptism (next verse).

B. Correct Thinking (v. 3)

3. Or don't you know that all of us who were baptized into Christ Jesus were baptized into his death?

Paul appeals to baptism as a shared experience. He asks if his readers understand baptism to be a type of death. While this is a sort of rhetorical question, the answer may not be obvious to all. The expected response may be, "No, I did not understand baptism that way. I'm listening. Tell me more." Remember that unlike his other letters, Romans is written to a congregation where Paul has not taught in person. Some of his teachings may be new to these readers.

Visual for Lesson 9. *Point to this visual as you ask,
"What is your reaction to this illustration?" Encourage free discussion.*

Baptism is an act rich with symbolism, but death is not the obvious way of understanding it. Baptism is biblically depicted as a type of washing that accompanies a spiritual cleansing of sins (see Acts 22:16; compare 1 Peter 3:21). This is why we find baptism tied to repentance, a renouncing of sin (see Luke 3:3). For Paul, we find baptism also connected with a personal identification of the believer with Christ (see Galatians 3:27).

C. New Life (v. 4)

4. We were therefore buried with him through baptism into death in order that, just as Christ was raised from the dead through the glory of the Father, we too may live a new life.

Paul now explains the baptism/death analogy. The key connection is the image of burial. Only dead people are buried. Since baptism is a type of burial, it therefore must involve a death —the death is the sinful life of the believer. Baptized persons put sin to death and bury it when they believe, repent, and are baptized (see Colossians 2:12). Churches have practiced baptism in various ways from early centuries, but it is worth noting that the burial analogy works best if we understand baptism as a full immersion of a person under water.

Paul's lesson does not end under the water, however. Baptized persons come up out of the water, and Paul sees this as parallel with Christ's coming out of the grave in resurrection. Jesus died,

but God brought him back to life. Paul wants his readers to understand that at the point of conversion (symbolized here by baptism), the believer's old life of sin has died and a new life begins.

This analogy has splendid teaching points, and these are worth pointing out when a person is baptized. There is a sense of death when one is completely under the water, for normal sensory perceptions are suspended. You cannot hear. You cannot smell. With eyes probably closed, you cannot see. It is like a momentary death.

What Do You Think?
In what ways do others see newness of life in you? What adjustments in that regard do you need to make?
Talking Points for Your Discussion
▪ Regarding what fellow Christians see
▪ Regarding what unbelievers see

D. Godly Imperatives (vv. 12, 13)

12. Therefore do not let sin reign in your mortal body so that you obey its evil desires.

Here in the first half of Romans, Paul personifies three spiritual realities as being tyrants; each has dominion as it reigns over us. All this is described with language derived from a king's reigning over his subjects or from a master's ruling over his slaves.

The first of these three is *death*, introduced as a reigning tyrant in Romans 5:14. The second is *sin*, explicitly seen as the reigning tyrant in the verse before us. The third is *the law*, spoken of extensively in chapters 2 and 3, but introduced fully as having "authority" in 7:1 (but see 6:14, below). These three oppress us in different ways. We fear death, we suffer because of sin, and we are judged inadequate by the law (see 2:12).

Paul urges his readers not to allow the ominous spiritual tyrant of sin to exercise any sort of authority in their lives. He's not talking about abstract sins of the intellect, but about real-world physical acts that involve our bodies. Such sins come from yielding to *evil desires*. The underlying Greek reflects language Paul uses elsewhere when talking about sexual sins (Romans 1:24; see 1 Thessalonians 4:5).

Sexual passion in and of itself is not a sin, but adultery and fornication definitely are. We do not necessarily sin when we have desires (Matthew 5:28 being an exception), but when we yield to them. It works this way: "after desire has conceived, it gives birth to sin; and sin, when it is full-grown, gives birth to death" (James 1:15). This is letting the tyrant of sin have lordship.

13. Do not offer any part of yourself to sin as an instrument of wickedness, but rather offer yourselves to God as those who have been brought from death to life; and offer every part of yourself to him as an instrument of righteousness.

The phrase *any part of yourself* refers to the parts of the human body, such as hands or ears. Paul urges his readers to reserve each part of their bodies *as an instrument* to be used for God's right purposes.

We cannot live lives of divided loyalties, serving two masters. We must yield fully every aspect of ourselves to the service of God. We are not partly alive and partly dead. We are completely alive from the dead (Ephesians 2:5). In the new life, we serve only God in acts of righteousness.

E. Saving Grace (v. 14)

14. For sin shall no longer be your master, because you are not under the law, but under grace.

Paul returns to his tyrant language, insisting again that sin cannot be our master. The reason for this is found in the controlling rule by which we live. If we allow sin to dominate us, then we position ourselves to be subject to the law. Paul certainly has the Jewish law in mind here, but the application is broader if *under the law* is understood to mean "under the old realm." Paul has already argued that if we are under the law, then we are judged to be guilty (see Romans 3:19, 20). Anyone who attempts to be righteous by rule-keeping will fail (3:23).

Instead, we are to be ruled by *grace*. It is not about which law or set of rules we try to keep, but about which master we serve. Even when we avoid sinful behavior, we are mastered by sin if we are doing this in an attempt to earn favor with God

(the way of law). If our motivation is to serve God, then righteous behavior will follow naturally.

II. Sin and Righteousness
(ROMANS 6:17-23)

A. Different Masters (vv. 17-20)

17. But thanks be to God that, though you used to be slaves to sin, you have come to obey from your heart the pattern of teaching that has now claimed your allegiance.

Paul knows that the repatterning of a life to avoid serving sin is not a simple or easy thing. It does not happen accidentally or by chance. It comes from a solid *pattern of teaching* that is faithfully conveyed.

This is the process of discipling, the instruction of a newly baptized person in the ways of the Christian faith. Such is the core of the famous Great Commission of Jesus (Matthew 28:19, 20). The initial steps of conversion are not enough. Those must be strengthened by intentional instruction of the new believer.

18. You have been set free from sin and have become slaves to righteousness.

Paul sums up with a simple equation: to be *set free from sin* = being *slaves to righteousness*. We are not freed from sin to serve ourselves. If we think this is the case, then we are still slaves to sin. We serve righteousness, which is the polar opposite of sin. Sin is choosing to do the wrong thing, the thing God does not want. Righteousness is doing the right thing, the thing that is pleasing to God. When we serve righteousness, we are serving God.

What Do You Think?
What are some ways you have seen people try (and fail) to be neither a servant of sin nor a servant of righteousness?
Talking Points for Your Discussion
- In the business world
- In family life
- In recreational activities
- Other

19. I am using an example from everyday life because of your human limitations. Just as

you used to offer yourselves as slaves to impurity and to ever-increasing wickedness, so now offer yourselves as slaves to righteousness leading to holiness.

Paul acknowledges that by *using an example from everyday life*, he is speaking in simple, basic terms. This is because of his readers' *human limitations*, meaning the ways in which sin has corrupted them and perverted their perceptions. Paul is not being condescending, but rather is being meticulously clear. The stakes are high, and he wants no misunderstanding. Here is the bottom line: sin and righteousness are not intended to coexist in the life of a believer. *Impurity* and *wickedness* are incompatible with *righteousness* and *holiness*.

❧ SERVANT TO . . . WHAT? ❧

I was on the teaching staff of a small Bible college in the mid-1970s. That was when college students all across the country were demanding more freedoms on campus. In so doing, those students questioned authority, staged protests, occupied deans' offices, etc. Our small Bible college did not experience all those behaviors, but at one point students made demands to the board of trustees for more freedom from the rules and regulations.

A particular student whom I got to know quite well was the president of the student body. In that capacity, he requested a meeting with the board to explain the students' requests (or "demands"). But as the time to meet drew near, he came to realize what the students really desired: more freedom to do their own thing. They were not interested in serving any greater good; they just wanted to be allowed to follow their own personal (selfish) desires. Upon that realization, the student-body president dropped the petition and did not even meet with the board. He had no interest in fueling the student's immature lack of responsibility.

This is roughly what Paul is warning against. Once freed from the bondage of sin, we are not then just "independent contractors" who can do our own thing. We are called to a higher purpose, to serve righteousness. A willingness to accept this service is a mark of spiritual maturity. —C. R. B.

20. When you were slaves to sin, you were free from the control of righteousness.

Sometimes it is worth looking back on our lives. In that regard, the equation of verse 18 applies in the negative as well: to be *free from the control of righteousness* = being *slaves to sin*. When we were in the thrall of sin, we cared little about doing the right thing, about following the will of God. If we are slaves to our passions, we are not seeking to serve God.

B. Different Results (vv. 21-23)

21. What benefit did you reap at that time from the things you are now ashamed of? Those things result in death!

By asking about *benefit*, Paul means "What things of lasting value did you harvest in your previous lives of sin?" The things of which we *are now ashamed* are the acts of sin that are in the past. Paul's pointed question still rings true: Was your life better when it was full of sin? We may think of the Israelites who were freed from slavery in Egypt by the mighty power of God, yet later wanted to return (Numbers 14:1-4). The lure of sin is powerful, especially when sin was at one time a deeply established lifestyle.

Thoughtful analysis of the past reveals that it was not all joyful fun and games. It was pain, disappointment, broken relationships, etc. As Paul puts it, *those things result in death!* This can be true physically and spiritually. Sin kills both body and soul (compare Romans 7:5).

22. But now that you have been set free from sin and have become slaves of God, the benefit you reap leads to holiness, and the result is eternal life.

The contrast is stark. The readers' previous lives as slaves to sin became a highway to death. But freedom from that ill-chosen life results in *the benefit* that *leads to holiness*, a life in concert with God's will. The holy life is the absolute opposite of the life of sin. The holy life is a highway that leads to *eternal life,* not eternal death (compare 1 Peter 1:9).

❧ THE GOOD PURPOSE ❧

Some philosophers have proposed that to understand people we need to understand what purposes drive them. To evaluate the "goodness" or "badness" of a human purpose involves observing how peoples' actions turn out. If the result of a certain action is beneficial, then we are able to say that the purpose that drives it is good; if the result of a certain action is harmful, then we are able to say that the purpose that drives it is bad.

But that's more than a bit simplistic! Because the sale of Joseph into slavery ultimately turned out to be beneficial, should we conclude that the actions of his brothers in that regard reveal a good purpose on their part (Genesis 50:20; etc.)? That added complexity is the result of living in a fallen world.

But God doesn't live in a fallen world. He is the one who establishes both the purpose of everlasting life and the nature of the good actions of producing the benefits of holiness that accompany such a result. So don't be fooled by "hollow and deceptive philosophy, which depends on human tradition and the elemental spiritual forces of this world rather than on Christ" (Colossians 2:8). When others criticize or mock your life of holiness, just remember where they get their wisdom —and where you get yours. —C. R. B.

23. For the wages of sin is death, but the gift of God is eternal life in Christ Jesus our Lord.

Paul sums up with one of the most important and oft-quoted verses in the New Testament. By *wages*, he means "earned and deserved payment." This is not an inheritance or a gift. Our sin earns a specific end-result: *death*. The tyrant of sin becomes the tyrant of death. This is more than physical death, the fate of all men and women. This is eternal death. Those who die as slaves to sin will die forever, separated from God eternally.

Paul does not leave us hanging on this dreary note, because there is an alternative: God's grace can be received as a *gift*. Receiving this gift is an act of faith, and more than anything else this gift is what Paul has been talking about this whole chapter. God's gracious gift is our freedom from sin, release from the bondage of that life-long tyrant. Our future *is eternal life in Christ Jesus our Lord*.

What Do You Think?
In what ways do people still attempt to earn God's favor? How do we convince them of their folly?
Talking Points for Your Discussion
- Regarding behaviors
- Regarding speech
- Regarding thoughts

Conclusion

A. Lingering Sin

Why does sin linger in our lives? Can we ever truly die to sin? It is wise to acknowledge our struggles with ungodly attitudes and behaviors, as Paul himself did in Romans 7:14-23. Denial of sin just makes the situation worse. But here is the lesson of Paul: we must not be dominated by sin. Our focus, our goal, our passion must be for obedience to God's will.

To accomplish this transformation, Paul tells us to remember our baptism, remember how we pledged our lives to the Lord Jesus and chose to live for him! Don't look back on your pre-baptismal life with any fondness. Allow the Holy Spirit to empower you for victory over sins, sins that may be large or small. Don't just die to these sins—renew your determination to live for Christ.

B. Prayer

Holy God, may you help us in our ongoing struggle to leave sinful things behind and live for you. We pray this in the name of our Savior, Jesus Christ. Amen.

C. Thought to Remember

Allow Jesus to break the bondage of sin in every area of your life!

INVOLVEMENT LEARNING

Enhance your lesson with NIV® *Bible Student (from your curriculum supplier) and the reproducible activity page (at www.standardlesson.com or in the back of the* NIV® *Standard Lesson Commentary Deluxe Edition).*

Into the Lesson

Arrange for someone who has been set free from an addiction (smoking, drinking, overeating, etc.) to give a five-minute testimony describing what life was like while enslaved to the addiction and how different life is after being set free. (This will be especially meaningful if a personal relationship with Christ was part of the healing process.)

After thanking your guest, say, "Sin is indeed a tyrant, isn't it? This is humanity's problem in every era. But Paul knows how this tyrant is defeated."

Alternative. Place in chairs copies of the "What Does It Say?" activity from the reproducible page, which you can download, for learners to begin working on as they arrive. After completion, say, "Today we're going to explore exactly what Paul meant when he wrote this important message." (Save discussion of the two visuals for Into Life.)

Into the Word

Form groups of three to five, giving each group one of the following two assignments. If you have more than two groups, assign fewer questions to the groups that have duplicate assignments. Include these instructions: "Read today's lesson text. Then select one person to be the reporter and another person to respond to the questions for the whole-class discussion that will follow. Discuss the best ways for the respondent to answer."

Life and Death Interview Questions. 1. You say God is merciful and forgiving. So, what's the big deal if Christians continue to sin? Doesn't that just give God more opportunities to be merciful and gracious? 2. Why would anyone agree to be dunked in the water at baptism? 3. Since a person is already "alive" before becoming a Christian, how can anything make him or her more alive? 4. What is one good reason why I should become a Christian?

Slave and Free Interview Questions. 1. Some people say that sinners enjoy life more because they are free to do whatever they want. Why is this either true or not true? 2. Isn't a Christian more of a slave than an unbeliever since the Christian has to keep all those rules and laws? 3. Since some unbelievers are rich and successful, doesn't the life of sin sometimes pay off better than being a Christian? 4. What is one good reason why I should become a Christian?

After each group presents its interview, allow time for the other group(s) to add insights.

Next, divide the class in half for a memorization exercise regarding Romans 6:23. Write it on the board in three lines like this:

> *For the wages of sin is death,*
> *but the gift of God is eternal life*
> *in Christ Jesus our Lord.*

Have half the class say the first line in unison, the other half respond the same way with the second line, with everyone saying the third line. After doing this three times, have the two halves of your class switch phrases as you repeat the process three more times. Finally, erase the verse and have everyone say it from memory in unison.

Next, discuss the meaning of Romans 6:23 by posing these questions: 1. Why the word *wages* in the first phrase but *gift* in the second? 2. What's the difference between what sinners receive and what followers of Jesus Christ receive?

Into Life

Say, "Let's think about how the eyes, ears, mouth, hands, etc., are involved in the ongoing struggle against sin. What strategy could one use regarding [name a body part] to set about making that part an instrument of righteousness per verse 13?" Repeat this question for other body parts; jot responses on the board. (*Option:* Ask volunteers to share stories of victory in this regard.)

Option. If you used the reproducible page in Into the Lesson, discuss at this point the application of the two visuals at the bottom.

MORE THAN CONQUERORS

DEVOTIONAL READING: 1 John 4:7-16
BACKGROUND SCRIPTURE: Romans 8:28-39

ROMANS 8:28-39

²⁸ And we know that in all things God works for the good of those who love him, who have been called according to his purpose. ²⁹ For those God foreknew he also predestined to be conformed to the image of his Son, that he might be the firstborn among many brothers and sisters. ³⁰ And those he predestined, he also called; those he called, he also justified; those he justified, he also glorified.

³¹ What, then, shall we say in response to these things? If God is for us, who can be against us? ³² He who did not spare his own

Son, but gave him up for us all—how will he not also, along with him, graciously give us all things? ³³ Who will bring any charge against those whom God has chosen? It is God who justifies. ³⁴ Who then is the one who condemns? No one. Christ Jesus who died—more than that, who was raised to life—is at the right hand of God and is also interceding for us. ³⁵ Who shall separate us from the love of Christ? Shall trouble or hardship or persecution or famine or nakedness or danger or sword? ³⁶ As it is written:

"For your sake we face death all day long;
we are considered as sheep to be
slaughtered."

³⁷ No, in all these things we are more than conquerors through him who loved us. ³⁸ For I am convinced that neither death nor life, neither angels nor demons, neither the present nor the future, nor any powers, ³⁹ neither height nor depth, nor anything else in all creation, will be able to separate us from the love of God that is in Christ Jesus our Lord.

KEY VERSE

What, then, shall we say in response to these things? If God is for us, who can be against us?

—Romans 8:31

TOWARD
A NEW CREATION

Unit 3: Life on God's Terms
LESSONS 8–13

LESSON AIMS

After participating in this lesson, each learner will be able to:

1. Tell how believers are "more than conquerors" through Jesus.

2. Suggest some challenges that seek to separate Christians from the love of Christ, and tell why they cannot succeed.

3. Make a statement of faith in Christ, expressing confidence in Jesus' ability to keep him or her in the love of God.

LESSON OUTLINE

Introduction
    A. Everything Happens for a Reason?
    B. Lesson Background
I. No Chaos of Purpose (ROMANS 8:28-30)
    A. Working for Good (v. 28)
    B. Proceeding to Glorification (vv. 29, 30)
II. No Disconnect from Love (ROMANS 8:31-36)
    A. Nothing Spared (vv. 31, 32)
        When God Is for Us
    B. No One Condemns (vv. 33, 34)
    C. Nothing Separates (vv. 35, 36)
III. No Defeat by Foes (ROMANS 8:37-39)
    A. Our Overwhelming Victory (v. 37)
        Of Pain and Conquest
    B. God's Conquering Love (vv. 38, 39)
Conclusion
    A. Undefeated
    B. Prayer
    C. Thought to Remember

Introduction

A. Everything Happens for a Reason?

When a much-loved person dies, we often hear these sorts of things being said to the grieving: "God knows what he is doing; this is for the best." "It's hard for you to understand now, but God has a plan." "Someday you will understand why God did this." These are variations of the flippant statement, "Everything happens for a reason."

To make such statements is to put us in the untenable position of saying that our loving God is responsible for a horrible tragedy that has ripped hearts open. Yet this is not a Christian idea. It might "work" in Buddhism or possibly in extreme forms of Islam, but it is not a biblical idea. Why?

The Law of Cause and Effect proposes that there are reasons (causes) for all things that happen (effects). At one level, this is true, but there are two angles to consider. First, if we live in an entirely mechanistic world, then everything that happens is preordained because of the physical nature of the things involved. If this is correct, then it means that there is no free will because everything we do is merely the result of chemical processes in our brains; this is the worldview of science without God.

In contrast, those who hold to the cause-and-effect worldview but who also believe in God say that the only exceptions to mechanical processes are God's deliberate manipulations of the forces of nature. In other words, these two choices say that human tragedy is either the result of inevitable mechanical processes or the intentional intervention of God. Everything happens for a reason? Tragedy must then be a product either of impersonal natural processes or the willful actions of a supernatural God.

Yet this is not what most folks have in mind when they say, "Everything happens for a reason." What they usually mean is "Everything happens for a good reason." The implication is that something good always comes out of tragedy, even if we have to wait a long time to experience it.

All of this seems to have a biblical veneer when proof-texted by verses such as Romans 8:28: "We know that in all things God works for the good."

But how does this play out in real life, especially in the time of tragedy? Is there comfort to be found in "everything happens for a reason"? Today's lesson, taken from the marvelous words of Romans 8, will help us see things from a biblical perspective.

B. Lesson Background

One of the most popular Roman deities of Paul's day was the goddess Fortuna, equivalent to the Greek goddess Tyche. Her popularity can be seen in that one of Paul's companions was Tychicus (Ephesians 6:21), a Greek name that means "fortunate one." Roman coinage of the first century often bore an image of Fortuna.

The Romans believed that gods and goddesses like Fortuna were in control of destinies. Much pagan religious activity was based on either determining the will of such deities through divination or influencing them through temple offerings or worship. The Romans believed their gods were capricious and unreliable, and that fortunes or luck could take a turn for the better or worse on a god's whim. In the book of Romans, Paul presents a view of the Christian God that is entirely different.

I. No Chaos of Purpose
(ROMANS 8:28-30)
A. Working for Good (v. 28)

28. And we know that in all things God works for the good of those who love him, who have been called according to his purpose.

The context for this lesson is summarized by Romans 8:18: "I consider that our present sufferings are not worth comparing with the glory that will be revealed in us." Even a time of the darkest night of the soul does not mean we are cut off from our God. Paul has an unshakable faith that all things are under the control of God, *that in all things God works for the good to those who love him.* Faith in the sovereign God means believing that

HOW TO SAY IT

Fortuna (*Latin*)	Fawr-*too*-naw.
Tychicus	*Tick*-ih-kuss.
Tyche (*Greek*)	*Too*-kay.

he is in control of all things. Even the evil in our world that causes the suffering of righteous people is not beyond his control.

Our problem is that of limited perspective. Only God can see how all things work together for good. The question about suffering, then, is not to be *why?* (compare Judges 6:13), but *how long?* The "why" is because of human decision to turn away from God (Genesis 2:16, 17; 3:19; 6:3; Romans 1:21, 28). The question can only be "how long"—how long will the suffering continue until my soul is flooded again by God's love and comfort? (Compare Psalms 6:3; 94:3; Revelation 6:10.)

What Do You Think?
What are appropriate and inappropriate ways to use verse 28 when counseling a fellow Christian who is in distress?
Talking Points for Your Discussion
- Regarding job loss
- Regarding a health crisis
- Regarding a death in the family
- Other

B. Proceeding to Glorification (vv. 29, 30)

29. For those God foreknew he also predestined to be conformed to the image of his Son, that he might be the firstborn among many brothers and sisters.

Paul's confidence in God's control over all things extends beyond present sufferings. The apostle speaks of our future and our past in powerful, dramatic ways. God knows us intimately and has known us even before our birth (Psalm 139:13). God foreknows us, meaning there has been no past time when God was unaware of us.

Furthermore, God has always had a single, deliberate plan for humanity: *to be conformed to the image of his Son.* This is both a new creation and a re-creation, for to be made in the image of Christ is to be restored to our original, unsullied state of having been created in the image of God (Genesis 1:27). It is to be included *among many brothers and sisters* in the true family of God.

Paul's description of Christ as *the firstborn* is a reference to his resurrection (see Colossians 1:18). The promise of our own resurrection is the ultimate hope we have in the midst of our sufferings (compare Acts 23:6; 1 Corinthians 15).

30. And those he predestined, he also called; those he called, he also justified; those he justified, he also glorified.

Paul now explains in more detail this plan of God for our glorification. Although elaborate and troubling doctrines have been offered to explain the concept of predestination, it is a rather simple idea as presented by Paul. The word translated *predestined* means that God has made an earlier decision about our future. God is not making this up as he goes; he is in control of all things, even our destiny.

This predetermined plan has three stages. First, God has *called* us, giving us the opportunity to respond to the gospel by faith. Second, that response leads to being *justified*, declared righteous through our faith in Christ because of his sacrifice on our behalf (Romans 3:24-26, lesson 7). The final stage is our being *glorified* when our own resurrections take place and we join Christ in Heaven for all eternity (compare 1 Corinthians 15:42-58).

II. No Disconnect from Love
(ROMANS 8:31-36)

A. Nothing Spared (vv. 31, 32)

31. What, then, shall we say in response to these things? If God is for us, who can be against us?

As he often does in Romans, Paul teaches by posing rhetorical questions. These are questions for which the answer should be obvious to the reader. But it is important that we answer them if we are to understand his meaning.

First question: *What, then, shall we say in response to these things?* In other words, what should our reaction be to our present sufferings and to our future hope of glorification? The answer is implied in the second question: *If God is for us, who can be against us?* No one who matters, for Almighty God is the one who is in control of all things.

❧ WHEN GOD IS FOR US ❧

Every night, the parents reassured the children that they loved them, that God loved them, and that he would be with them, even if the family could not be together. This family lived in Ukraine during Soviet times. The state had outlawed teaching youth about religion, and those caught doing so could have their children taken from them. The family knew that any night the police could come and do just that.

This threat of separation hung over their heads for years. It had happened to others they knew. Yet the parents taught their children about Jesus despite the danger, and five of the seven siblings ended up in Christian ministry. They led and served vibrant churches that, after the fall of the communist government, reached their communities in ways unimaginable during Soviet times. Grandchildren grew up to form the backbone for many other ministries. Now great grandchildren are following in those same faithful footsteps.

All of this because two parents chose to "obey God rather than human beings" (Acts 5:29). Hardships push us to rely on God's strength to overcome our foes and fears. Truly, if God is for us, then nothing can be against us!   —L. L. W.

What Do You Think?
What was a negative situation in your life where things ultimately turned out God's way despite circumstances and people arrayed against you?
Talking Points for Your Discussion
- Regarding a personal crisis of temptation
- Regarding a family crisis
- Regarding a church issue
- Other

---

32. He who did not spare his own Son, but gave him up for us all—how will he not also, along with him, graciously give us all things?

Third question: Will God refuse to *give us all things?* Paul answers this within the question itself by reminding us that God has already given us his greatest treasure: *his own Son* (compare John 3:16). It stands to reason that if God did not withhold the life of his precious Son, then it is unimaginable that God will withhold anything else.

We are reminded of Jesus' prayer in the garden when he stressed to the Father a desire to be released from the looming crucifixion (Matthew

26:39). God did not grant this desire, for he was willing even to give the life of his Son. This is the ultimate basis of our understanding of God's love for us (Romans 5:8).

B. No One Condemns (vv. 33, 34)

33. Who will bring any charge against those whom God has chosen? It is God who justifies.

Fourth question: Who is capable of accusing us of not being righteous, of not being *those whom God has chosen?* The answer is the same as for the second question: no one that matters. God is the ultimate and final judge, and he has justified us. This means God counts us as innocent of all charges that might be brought to bear. God's judgments are consistent, so we do not need to fear he will change his mind.

The phrase *those whom God has chosen,* by which Paul refers to himself and other believers, connects back to verse 30, above. The call of God that leads to our glorification is not some mysterious, impenetrable process. It is God's working out of his plan to restore us to his image and bring us to glorification through our own resurrection from the dead. These are the comforting promises that give us hope in our present sufferings.

34. Who then is the one who condemns? No one. Christ Jesus who died—more than that, who was raised to life—is at the right hand of God and is also interceding for us.

Fifth question: *Who then is the one who condemns?* In other words, who even has the right to judge us guilty and therefore ineligible for eternal life? One possibility is Christ himself, the man untainted by sin who now sits in a position of judgment *at the right hand of God.* But such a condemnation by Christ is unthinkable, for even though he has the right to condemn us, he died and rose again to do the opposite. He *is also interceding for us* as he pleads our case.

C. Nothing Separates (vv. 35, 36)

35. Who shall separate us from the love of Christ? Shall trouble or hardship or persecution or famine or nakedness or danger or sword?

Sixth and final question: *Who shall separate us from the love of Christ?* That is, who has the power

Visual for Lesson 10. *Start a discussion by pointing to this visual as you pose the question that is associated with verses 38, 39.*

to nullify the love that Christ has demonstrated for us in the past and continues to do so in the present?

The hypothetical yet real-world possibilities are sweeping. Can we be separated from Christ's love by difficult times and the distress that comes with them? No. Can our persecutors cause Christ to withhold his love for us? No. What about lack of food for daily sustenance? No. How about a lack of clothing that is necessary for warmth and self-dignity? No. Can personal danger and threat of death undo Christ's love for us? No.

The final image, the sword, is perhaps the most terrifying, since it is the brutal weapon of soldiers and the instrument of execution for Roman citizens. Paul himself will die by the sword about 10 years after he writes this letter. But we can be sure he never doubts the love of Christ, even as the blade touches his neck.

What Do You Think?
How can the threats of verse 35 actually serve to draw us closer to God?
Talking Points for Your Discussion
- When we are threatened personally
- When fellow Christians are threatened

---

36. As it is written:
"For your sake we face death all day long;
we are considered as sheep to be slaughtered."

I recently had a class of college freshmen write essays on this passage of Scripture, and I was surprised at how much this verse (a quotation of Psalm 44:22) resonated with them. Several wrote, "That's how I feel!" They were responding to their situations of personal persecution for their commitment to Christ in the face of unbelieving and taunting family and/or friends.

Paul reveals how difficult his own path has been by this quotation. In his worst times of trouble, he has felt like a sheep being helplessly led to the place of killing and butchering. This image also helps us identify with Christ himself, for this imagery is applied to him as well (Acts 8:32).

What Do You Think?

How do you deal with opposition for being a Christian?

Talking Points for Your Discussion
- In family relationships
- In work/school situations
- From the political arena
- Other

III. No Defeat by Foes
(Romans 8:37-39)

A. Our Overwhelming Victory (v. 37)

37. No, in all these things we are more than conquerors through him who loved us.

Paul gives an emphatic answer to the multiple conditions of hardship he has set forth in verse 35. We are not defeated by these very real trials, and we are not mere survivors either. Rather, *we are more than conquerors.* Those five words translate just one word in the original language. It is a striking word that conveys the idea of being "hyper-victors." Although the recipients of this letter may feel defeated, they are in fact winners, not losers. They are not helpless sheep lined up for slaughter. They are the ultimate winners, with gold medals draped around their necks.

We must not neglect the last part of this verse, though. Our victory is not one we have earned on our skill or merits, but one that has come *through him who loved us.* External threats cannot separate us from the love of Christ; let us not separate our-

selves by claiming a victory apart from him. We are the champions solely because of Christ and his victory over the tyrants of sin, death, and the law (last week's lesson; also see John 16:33).

❧ *Of Pain and Conquest* ❧

My friend's parents divorced during her teenage years. For most of her young adulthood, she resented her parents for the pain they caused her, for the way their decisions affected her. She eventually married and started a family of her own, forgiving her family of origin in the process.

Years into the marriage, she and her husband hit the inevitable struggles that relationships bring. Financial issues, job loss, health problems, and psychological issues took their toll. But at one point she said to me, "My parents' divorce saved my marriage." She explained that seeing and experiencing the pain of that divorce caused her to realize that dissolution of that marriage had not solved the problems, but had merely changed their expression. This experience gave her the courage to stay in her own marriage and work through the issues that she and her husband had.

Although the pain resulting from her parents' problems seemed insurmountable at the time, my friend came to realize that God had worked through those difficulties to produce in her a determination to keep her commitments to him, her husband, and her children. God can indeed use the trials of life to cause us to be more than conquerors!

—L. L. W.

B. God's Conquering Love (vv. 38, 39)

38, 39. For I am convinced that neither death nor life, neither angels nor demons, neither the present nor the future, nor any powers, neither height nor depth, nor anything else in all creation, will be able to separate us from the love of God that is in Christ Jesus our Lord.

Paul ends with four additional sets of possibilities for being separated from the love of Christ. His list is breathtakingly exhaustive, covering the breadth of his frame of reference. These are not posed as questions but as answers to any possible objections that might be raised by anyone who doubts Christ's love.

The first set, *death . . . life*, addresses our mortality. Whether we are alive or dead, we are still bound to the love of Christ. This is an assurance that there is an existence beyond this current life, and that our loving God will not abandon us to the grave (compare 1 Corinthians 3:22).

The second set, *angels . . . demons*, addresses spiritual realities. Neither good spiritual forces nor evil ones have any capability to sever our connection with Christ's love. Paul understands Christ's victory over death as a defeat of the evil spiritual powers (see Colossians 2:15). They are still able to cause us grief (Ephesians 6:12), but they cannot isolate us from Christ and his love.

Paul's third set addresses the possibilities of separation from a time perspective. There is nothing in the *present* time period and nothing in a *future* time period that can separate us from Christ's love. Nothing now, nothing tomorrow, nothing a year from now, nothing a thousand years from now.

Following a general reference to *powers*, the fourth set, *height . . . depth*, presents a spatial spectrum. There is nothing too high, whether the highest mountain peak or Heaven itself, to cut us off from Christ. There is no place so low, whether the depths of the ocean or the underworld, that can cause us to lose our connection with Christ. The final category of *anything else in all creation* is an inclusive catch-all to refer to any created thing.

God has shown us that he has no inclination or intention to withhold his love for us. God has proven this love through the giving of his precious Son as the necessary sacrifice for our sins. Since we do not have to doubt God's love, we do not need to fear any possible scenario where we can be separated from this mighty, marvelous love. The apostle emphatically highlights this by stating the fullest version of this love. His shorthand has been "the love of Christ" (v. 35). His longhand is *the love of God that is in Christ Jesus our Lord.*

What Do You Think?
  How can you live a more victorious Christian life?
Talking Points for Your Discussion
  ▪ During spiritually "up" times
  ▪ During spiritually "down" times

Conclusion
A. Undefeated

As this lesson is being written in early 2014, a rare thing has happened in college basketball: a team has finished its regular season without any losses, going 31–0. Despite this flawless record, the team is not ranked #1 in the national polls as it heads into the year-end tournaments. Teams that have losses are ranked ahead of this undefeated team. Several reasons are cited, but the main one is that this team does not belong to one of the so-called power conferences, and therefore its competition ("strength of schedule") has been inferior. Its victories therefore don't count as much. This is frustrating for the fans of this team. What more could their team do than win all of its games?

We may feel sometimes that our lives are rather unimportant since we don't belong to a "power conference" of high-visibility Christians. We may feel that our daily struggles to love and obey God are insignificant and even trivial compared with those Christians whose lives seem very influential. Yet that is not the perspective of Romans 8. All of us are important to God. All people are valuable to him. His love is so inclusive that he gave his Son as a sacrifice for the sins of all people, not just the rich or famous.

When Paul shouts, "We are more than conquerors," he does not leave some of us out. When the apostle roars that nothing can separate us from the love of God, he does not follow with a list of exceptions. Let us live each day in the full assurance that God will never pull his love from us and that we have overcome the world through our faith in his Son.

B. Prayer

Loving God, sometimes we feel abandoned. May we take heart in the promises of Paul that we are never separated from you and your love for us, not even for an instant. May you dry the tears of our cold, hard lives with the warmth of your love. We pray this in the name of your Son. Amen.

C. Thought to Remember
Never doubt God's love for you.

INVOLVEMENT LEARNING

Enhance your lesson with NIV® Bible Student (from your curriculum supplier) and the reproducible activity page (at www.standardlesson.com or in the back of the NIV® Standard Lesson Commentary Deluxe Edition).

Into the Lesson

Display a collage of superheroes from comic books or pictures from the Internet. Be sure to include the more famous ones such as Superman, Spiderman, and Wonder Woman. Have this question displayed on the board as learners arrive: *When you were younger, which superhero power or powers did you most wish you had and why?*

After several minutes of discussion, make a transition by saying, "Sometimes when we felt especially helpless and vulnerable when younger, we may have fantasized about having superpowers that would solve our problems. But as Christians, we are in a better position than any fictional superhero. 'We are more than conquerors through him who loved us' (Romans 8:37). Let's see how and why."

Alternative. Distribute copies of the "Know Your Fears" activity from the reproducible page, which you can download. Say, "Take no more than two minutes to complete this. No fair using smartphones to look up answers!" After discussing the answers, say, "It's not surprising that most of you weren't familiar with these rather obscure fears. But there are more common fears we know well: fear of suffering, fear of not being loved, or fear of God's displeasure. In today's text, Paul gives us powerful reasons why we can conquer our fears and feel safe in God's love and protection."

Into the Word

Form learners into pairs. Give each pair one or more of the following questions and accompanying Scripture references, printed on strips of poster board. For classes that can form more than six pairs, distribute duplicate strips.

"I'm really suffering—what is God doing about it?" (Romans 8:28) / "How can I overcome this feeling that my life has no purpose?" (Romans 8:29, 30) / "Why does everyone, including God, seem to be against me?" (Romans 8:31, 32) / "Since

I've messed up so badly, how can Jesus not be upset with me?" (Romans 8:33, 34) / "How can I stop feeling like a total failure?" (Romans 8:35-39).

After pairs develop responses, have one person from each pair read the question and the other give the proposed answer. Possibilities: *Verse 28*: God is aware of our suffering and cares about us. He desires that we trust him to bring good out of our situation. *Verses 29, 30*: Since before we were born, God's purpose has been to conform us into the image of his Son. Everyone can respond to God's call, be justified through Jesus, and look forward to the glory of resurrected life in Heaven. *Verses 31, 32*: No matter how the circumstances of life seem stacked up against us, we can be confident that God is always on our side. He showed how much he cares for us by sending his Son to die on our behalf. *Verses 33, 34*: In sending Jesus to die, God was making it possible for us to escape the penalty we deserve for our sins. Since Jesus does not condemn us, we certainly should not condemn ourselves. *Verses 35-39*: Although life in a fallen world seems to bring defeat after defeat, Christ's ability to win the victory is stronger than anything that may cause us to feel as if we've failed. Paul's own life was a witness to these facts.

Into Life

Write on the board *No, Jesus loves me!* Point to it as you say, "Instead of the familiar chorus 'Yes, Jesus loves me,' respond in unison with this phrase, if you really believe it, each time I ask a question." Voice the following question seven times, using a different word or phrase within the brackets each time: "Will [*suffering, persecution, hardship, danger, death, Satan, anything else in all creation*] separate you from the love of Christ?" Close with a prayer praising Jesus for his great love.

Option. Distribute copies of the "Overcome Your Fears" activity from the reproducible page. Allow time to complete in class as indicated.

LIVING UNDER GOD'S MERCY

DEVOTIONAL READING: James 5:7-12
BACKGROUND SCRIPTURE: Romans 9:6-29

ROMANS 9:6-18

6 It is not as though God's word had failed. For not all who are descended from Israel are Israel. 7 Nor because they are his descendants are they all Abraham's children. On the contrary, "It is through Isaac that your offspring will be reckoned." 8 In other words, it is not the children by physical descent who are God's children, but it is the children of the promise who are regarded as Abraham's offspring. 9 For this was how the promise was stated: "At the appointed time I will return, and Sarah will have a son."

10 Not only that, but Rebekah's children were conceived at the same time by our father Isaac. 11 Yet, before the twins were born or had done anything good or bad—in order that God's purpose in election might stand: 12 not by works but by him who calls—she was told, "The older will serve the younger." 13 Just as it is written: "Jacob I loved, but Esau I hated."

14 What then shall we say? Is God unjust? Not at all! 15 For he says to Moses,

"I will have mercy on whom I have mercy, and I will have compassion on whom I have compassion."

16 It does not, therefore, depend on human desire or effort, but on God's mercy. 17 For Scripture says to Pharaoh: "I raised you up for this very purpose, that I might display my power in you and that my name might be proclaimed in all the earth." 18 Therefore God has mercy on whom he wants to have mercy, and he hardens whom he wants to harden.

KEY VERSE

Therefore God has mercy on whom he wants to have mercy, and he hardens whom he wants to harden.

—**Romans 9:18**

Graphic: domi8nic / iStock / Thinkstock

TOWARD
A NEW CREATION

Unit 3: Life on God's Terms
LESSONS 8–13

LESSON AIMS

After participating in this lesson, each learner will be able to:

1. Identify "the children of the promise."

2. Explain how "the children of the promise" receive their status.

3. Create a plan to be a spiritual mentor to one or two people whom he or she can help lead to Christ or help deepen their discipleship.

LESSON OUTLINE

Introduction
  A. Hard, Hard Hearts
  B. Lesson Background: Promises to Israel
  C. Lesson Background: Readers in Rome
  I. Children of the Promise (ROMANS 9:6-8)
  A. Not All Are of Israel (vv. 6, 7a)
  B. Not All Are of Isaac (vv. 7b, 8)
    On Heritage
  II. Two Sons Times Two (ROMANS 9:9-13)
  A. Sarah and Rebekah (vv. 9, 10)
  B. Esau and Jacob (vv. 11-13)
  III. Mercy and Hardening (ROMANS 9:14-18)
  A. God Is Always Just (vv. 14, 15)
  B. God Is Always Sovereign (vv. 16-18)
    Why We Praise
Conclusion
  A. Living the Life of Mercy
  B. Prayer
  C. Thought to Remember

Introduction

A. Hard, Hard Hearts

What is a hard heart? When we apply this to personalities, we are looking at emotional conditions. In common parlance, hard-hearted persons are emotionally stunted and cold. They act only in self-interest and cannot empathize with others who might need their help. They are the Simon Legrees and Ebenezer Scrooges of literature.

This is not exactly what the Bible authors mean when they use the image of the hard heart. In the pages of the Bible, the heart is more than the emotional center of human personality. More fundamentally, the heart is the center of the will, of the decision-making process. When persons in the Bible are described as having a hard heart, they have a will that is turned against God. They deny his authority in their lives. They refuse to repent of sin. The hard-hearted person does not love God.

Such rebellion reveals itself in daily choices. If I hate God, will I love others? No. The two great commandments to love God and love others (Matthew 22:36-40) will more likely become *I hate God, so why not hate others?* The emotional companions of the hard heart are bitterness, impatience, and arrogance. We see these in abundance in today's world. Today's lesson teaches us about a different, better path.

B. Lesson Background: Promises to Israel

An important backdrop to Romans 9 is the multi-generational saga that began with Abraham. It began in Genesis 12:1-3, where God made certain promises to that patriarch. These promises included assurance that Abraham's descendants would become a great nation and a blessing to "all peoples on earth." *Generation one* featured Abraham, his wife Sarah, and handmaid Hagar.

Generation two featured Isaac (son of Abraham and Sarah) and Ishmael (son of Abraham and Hagar). Abraham later married another wife, Keturah, and had six sons by her (Genesis 25:1, 2), but these do not figure into Paul's discussion in Romans 9.

Generation three spotlighted Isaac's two sons, Jacob and Esau. But God's promises were passed down only through Jacob. His name changed to *Israel* (Genesis 32:28), and the promises eventually extended to his 12 sons (by four women). The descendants of these 12 became the nation of Israel.

C. Lesson Background: Readers in Rome

In his letter to the church in Rome, Paul discussed God's plan for the nation of Israel (Romans 9:1-5). This topic was important to that church, because it was made up of Christians of both Jewish and Gentile backgrounds, with apparent friction between the two groups (compare 11:13-24, lesson 12). One of the issues seems to have revolved around God's promises to the nation of Israel. Perhaps some Jewish Christians touted these promises arrogantly, making the Christians of Gentile background feel inferior and second class. A response from the Gentiles to this might have been that the promises to Israel were irrelevant because of Christ (see lesson 12).

Paul condoned neither position. He wanted the readers to know that things were not so simple. The apostle bared his heart to confess his agony over the unbelief of the majority of his fellow Jews regarding Jesus. Paul said he would be willing even to have God's curse fall upon him if they would come to faith (Romans 9:3). He assured his readers that Jews had many blessings and advantages, including the Law of Moses, worship at the temple, and the promises given to their ancestors (9:4, 5a). Most of all, the nation of Israel was blessed by being the source of the Messiah himself (9:5b).

Paul was convinced that the promises given to Abraham (and therefore to Israel) had not come

HOW TO SAY IT

Abraham	*Ay*-bruh-ham.
Edom	*Ee*-dum.
Esau	*Ee*-saw.
Hagar	*Hay*-gar.
Idumea	Ih-dyuh-***me***-uh.
Ishmael	*Ish*-may-el.
Keturah	Keh-***too***-ruh.
patriarch	*pay*-tree-ark.
Pharaoh	*Fair*-o or *Fay*-roe.
Sinai	*Sigh*-nye or *Sigh*-nay-eye.

to an end. God still had a plan for the salvation of Israel. But before we address that in next week's lesson, Paul had some important preliminaries to establish.

I. Children of the Promise
(ROMANS 9:6-8)
A. Not All Are of Israel (vv. 6, 7a)

6, 7a. It is not as though God's word had failed. For not all who are descended from Israel are Israel. Nor because they are his descendants are they all Abraham's children.

Paul uses the phrases *God's word* and "the word of God" numerous times in his letters to refer to the message of the gospel (examples: Colossians 1:25; Titus 2:5). Here, however, it is more likely that this phrase refers to the promises and privileges of Israel that he has just listed in Romans 9:4, 5. Paul is beginning to reveal that the true community of believers (the church) supersedes and replaces any notion of the people of God as being merely the physical descendants of the man Abraham.

The apostle has already touched on this topic in Romans 2:28, 29; 4:16, 17 (compare Luke 3:8). Here he probes deeper with a declaration that is difficult to understand: *not all who are descended from Israel are Israel.* How can anyone be "not-Israel" and "Israel" at the same time? Verse 7a clarifies: just being one of Abraham's *descendants* does not make a person one of his *children* (a spiritual offspring).

In other words, belonging to Israel in a physical sense is not the same thing as belonging to Israel in a spiritual sense. Having the DNA of Abraham in one's genes does not mean a person is a guaranteed heir to the promises. Having the blood of Abraham coursing through one's veins does not automatically convey to such a person the faith of Abraham and his relationship with God. Further explanation follows.

B. Not All Are of Isaac (vv. 7b, 8)

7b, 8. On the contrary, "It is through Isaac that your offspring will be reckoned." In other words, it is not the children by physical descent who are God's children, but it is the children

of the promise who are regarded as Abraham's offspring.

The fact that not every physical child of Abraham was his promised heir is evident within the pages of the Old Testament itself. Only Isaac was the child of promise, the son of faith (Genesis 21:12). Ishmael was Abraham's son through the slave Hagar by an act of unbelief. Abraham and Sarah did not trust God's promise of many descendants, so they cooked up a way to provide a son through their own actions (Genesis 16:1-4).

> **What Do You Think?**
> When are Christians most tempted to replace God's plan with one of their own? How have you seen such substitutions work out?
> *Talking Points for Your Discussion*
> ▪ Regarding lifestyle choices
> ▪ Regarding stewardship of resources
> ▪ Other

But God did not nullify his promise, despite Abraham and Sarah's unfaithful act. In their old age, they received their promised son, Isaac (Genesis 21:1-3). Ishmael had the DNA of Abraham, but not God's promise to that man. Through only one son did the promise flow, and that son was Isaac. Claiming Abraham as a physical ancestor does not make one his spiritual heir.

❧ ON HERITAGE ❧

Muslims and Jews share something in common: they both believe that they are the chosen people of God. Both acknowledge Abraham as their ancestral father. They have parallel stories involving identical characters, but with the outcomes switched: Muslims believe that Ishmael, not Isaac, was the chosen son. That is a primary point of doctrine where Islam and Judaism diverge.

As important as it is to get that doctrine right, Paul reminds us of something of greater importance: being in right standing with God is not a matter of biological connections or family trees (compare Matthew 3:9). Rather, it is a matter of the condition of one's heart. Those who come to Christ in faith are the true children of Abraham (compare Galatians 3:7).

Let us also not fall into the trap of seeing our spiritual heritage (denominational identity, etc.) as a measure of our maturity in Christ or favor before God. Paul warned against devoting time to "endless genealogies" (1 Timothy 1:4), and the warning applies to spiritual heritage as well as to biological ancestries. We will be held accountable for our own motives and actions, no matter who our physical and spiritual ancestors were. —D. C. S.

> **What Do You Think?**
> What spiritual heritage should Christians leave?
> *Talking Points for Your Discussion*
> ▪ To their own children
> ▪ To their children in the faith (1 Timothy 1:2)

II. Two Sons Times Two
(ROMANS 9:9-13)
A. Sarah and Rebekah (vv. 9, 10)

9. For this was how the promise was stated: "At the appointed time I will return, and Sarah will have a son."

Paul now shifts between persons. First, he reminds us of *how the promise was stated* when given by God (Genesis 18:10, 14). The promised son was Isaac, born in Abraham and Sarah's old age (17:17; 18:13; 21:5). The birth of Isaac was understood by this couple as a fulfillment of God's promise.

10. Not only that, but Rebekah's children were conceived at the same time by our father Isaac.

Paul moves to the next generation, the generation of Isaac and Rebekah. There are two sons at issue in this situation also, the twins Esau and Jacob. There are no competing mothers this time (contrast Genesis 16:4-6), only competing sons. One of these two was to be the heir of the promise to Abraham and to Isaac (26:2-5).

B. Esau and Jacob (vv. 11-13)

11. Yet, before the twins were born or had done anything good or bad—in order that God's purpose in election might stand:

Just as God's primary promise was not extended to both Ishmael and Isaac, such was also the case for brothers Esau and Jacob. Paul does not explain why. Instead, he merely lays out a stark fact: God made a choice between those two before they were even born. God's decision was made before they had proven themselves by doing *anything good or bad*. When it came to sin, neither son was more righteous than the other. Jacob took advantage to cheat Esau out of both his birthright and his father's blessing (Genesis 25:29-34). Esau chose wives that grieved his parents (26:34, 35); he also plotted murder against Jacob (27:41).

What Do You Think?

Which most determines how a child will turn out: *nature* or *nurture*? Why?

Talking Points for Your Discussion

- What you have seen in favor of *nature* or *heredity* (what a person inherits genetically)
- What you have seen in favor of *nurture* or *environment* (how a person is reared)
- Regarding Bible examples of either

12a. not by works but by him who calls—

Paul stresses a vital point: God's choice was not made on the basis of *works* on the part of either Jacob or Esau. This fact is applicable in two ways in the Roman situation that Paul is addressing. First, neither Jews nor Gentiles can earn God's favor. He did not choose the nation of Israel for any reason other than his own purposes. His plan was for a certain nation to be the recipients of his divine law and to be the nation to usher in his promised Messiah. That nation came into being through the call of Jacob, not Esau (Genesis 28:13-15).

12b. she was told, "The older will serve the younger."

Paul quotes a portion of Genesis 25:23. That prophecy went against prevailing cultural norms, which dictated that the older son held the primary position as heir. (Compare God's later declaration in Deuteronomy 21:15-17.) Normally, this also should have been the case with twins Esau and Jacob, even if Esau was *the older* by no more than a few minutes.

This is an epic prophecy about much more than the sibling rivalry we read about in Genesis 25:29-34; 27:1-41. These sons of Isaac became the patriarchal ancestors of two nations or peo-

ples: those of Edom (of son Esau; chap. 36) and Israel (of son Jacob; 49:1-28). Although blood kin, these two peoples ended up being in constant conflict (Numbers 20:14-21; 1 Chronicles 18:12, 13; 2 Chronicles 21:8-10; etc.).

The rift between the people of Israel/Jacob and Edom/Esau never healed (see Psalm 137:7; Isaiah 34:5). The reversal of Esau and Jacob's positions regarding preeminence, astounding at the time, was in the deliberate plan of God.

13. Just as it is written: "Jacob I loved, but Esau I hated."

Paul's discussion to this point has been based on the book of Genesis. Now he fast-forwards more than 1,400 years to quote Malachi 1:2, 3 to show the result of God's promise being directed through Jacob rather than Esau. Malachi prophesied after some Jews had returned from Babylonian captivity to rebuild Jerusalem and its temple. His prophecy pictured Edom as "a wasteland and left . . . to the desert jackals" (1:3) and promised that God would never allow that nation to rebuild (1:4). This justifies Malachi's historical verdict: God had loved Jacob (Israel) but hated Esau (Edom).

Although it took centuries for God's promise to be fulfilled, it proved sure and trustworthy. In Paul's day, Edom is called *Idumea* (Mark 3:8) and is but a shadow of its ancient self—further support for Paul's illustration. God had chosen to favor Israel, even in the midst of Roman occupation, while Edom languished.

III. Mercy and Hardening
(ROMANS 9:14-18)

A. God Is Always Just (vv. 14, 15)

14. What then shall we say? Is God unjust? Not at all!

Paul now pauses his history lesson to ask a difficult question: Does all this mean that God is unjust? This is unthinkable for Paul and is similar to his question in Romans 6:1, "Shall we go on sinning so that grace may increase?" This is the *reduction to the absurd* argument, the answer to which is quite obvious. To charge God with being unjust or unrighteous is preposterous. God is the one who defines justice and righteousness! However difficult it may be for us to understand the history of Isaac and Ishmael, of Jacob and Esau, there can be no question about the integrity of God (compare Deuteronomy 32:4).

15. For he says to Moses,
"I will have mercy on whom I have mercy,
and I will have compassion on whom I
have compassion."

Paul now resumes historical argumentation, but moves from the time of Malachi (just quoted in v. 13, above) to the time of Moses, a jump backward of about 1,000 years. In so doing, Paul quotes a word from the Lord to Moses (Exodus 33:19), which was delivered as the people of Israel were camped at Mt. Sinai.

The dialogue occurred in the context of Moses' personal relationship with God, for Moses had found favor with the Lord (Exodus 33:17). Moses had begged the Lord to accompany Israel as it prepared to depart for the promised land, thereby revealing his presence to the other nations. The divine response reminded Moses that God alone decides which nation(s) he will favor. Israel had done nothing to deserve special treatment from God, for they were a stubborn lot (see Exodus 33:5). It was God's decision.

What Do You Think?
How should we react when God treats (or seems to treat) people differently?
Talking Points for Your Discussion
- Regarding bestowal of blessings on believers
- Regarding bestowal of blessings on unbelievers
- Regarding differing bestowals of spiritual gifts
- Other

B. God Is Always Sovereign (vv. 16-18)

16. It does not, therefore, depend on human desire or effort, but on God's mercy.

Paul now makes a most crucial point. His historical examples show that God's favor is not contingent *on human desire or effort*. We cannot wish for God's graciousness and cause it to happen. We cannot work for God's favor and find it as a reward. It is up to God to show mercy to us (compare Ephesians 2:8, 9). Paul has shown decisively in Romans 1–3 that no human is deserving

of mercy, otherwise it would not be mercy! The only reward we earn for our lives of sin is death (Romans 6:23).

17. For Scripture says to Pharaoh: "I raised you up for this very purpose, that I might display my power in you and that my name might be proclaimed in all the earth."

With reference to Exodus 9:16, Paul continues his lesson on God's graciousness. The point at hand involves Pharaoh, the man who held the people of Israel as his slaves in Egypt. He was reluctant to free his workforce of slaves as Moses demanded. God therefore sent a series of plagues on Egypt.

Despite the great suffering these caused, Pharaoh refused to listen to Moses. It was just before the seventh plague that Moses delivered the words Paul quotes here, declaring that Pharaoh's power had nothing to do with him as a man. Rather, power had been given to him by the Lord. Pharaoh was an instrument in the divine drama that was orchestrated by the God of the universe for the purpose of declaring his name *in all the earth* through the new nation of Israel.

18. Therefore God has mercy on whom he wants to have mercy, and he hardens whom he wants to harden.

Paul ends with a *therefore* conclusion that contains both some of the most comforting and most chilling words in all the Bible. This is an astounding statement of God's graciousness in concert with his purposes. First, Paul reminds the reader that the mercy of God is at his initiative. What comfort in knowing that we serve a merciful God! We can leave behind any attempts to earn his favor and simply serve him out of love and gratitude.

Second, though, we are reminded that the purposes of God required the hardening of people like Pharaoh. This is the chilling part. Why would God use Pharaoh in this way? Doesn't this seem unfair? To come to grips with this, we must read the larger account of the hardening of Pharaoh's heart in the book of Exodus. When we do, we find that it speaks not only of God's hardening Pharaoh's heart (Exodus 4:21; 7:3; 9:12; 14:4), but also of Pharaoh's hardening his own heart earlier (8:15, 32). Pharaoh was a willing, stubborn, arrogant partner in his own hardening.

Likewise, we are entirely capable of maintaining an unrepentant spirit even though we see the evidence of God's mercy in his Word and in our lives. God's use of Pharaoh's evil heart is no excuse for Pharaoh's actions. While we may stand in wonder at the purposes of God in the history of Israel, we must also stand in awe of God's willingness to show mercy to us, rebellious sinners who do not deserve his favor.

> **What Do You Think?**
> How do you guard yourself against becoming hard-hearted?
> **Talking Points for Your Discussion**
> - Toward unbelievers
> - Toward fellow Christians

Visual for Lesson 11

Point to this visual as you ask, "How can we work together to communicate God's mercy to the lost?"

❧ WHY WE PRAISE ❧

In a brawl in the parking lot of a bar, one young man pushed another, who fell and hit his head on a car stop. The result was death. At his sentencing, the convicted man fell at the feet of his victim's mother, pouring out his remorse in tears. The mother raised him up, assured him of her forgiveness, and visited him frequently in prison. One of the most difficult actions to understand is that of a parent who forgives the killer of his or her child. And yet it does happen.

The basis for that is (or should be) the mercy and forgiveness of God that we see throughout history and which we have experienced. The prophet seemed amazed when he wondered, "Who is a God like you, who pardons sin? . . . You do not stay angry forever but delight to show mercy" (Micah 7:18). The Lord longs for sinners to repent so that he can shower them with merciful grace. He is the Father willing to forgive sinful humans who killed his own Son.

Yet there are those who harden their hearts toward God and everything he holds dear. Even on deathbeds, some remain defiant. The way to keep from being one of those is to reflect on the ways that God has poured his abundant mercy and grace on you. When you do, you will be unable to do anything except offer up praise and thanks for his compassion.   —D. C. S.

Conclusion
A. Living the Life of Mercy

The Christian life should not be one of cowering in fear of the wrath of God. Yes, we deserve punishment for our rebellious sin. But we have been given life through our faith in Jesus and his atoning death. We may not be a titan of the world stage like Abraham, but we are important to God.

His mercy is personal, tailored for each of us according to our situation. Some of us are colossal sinners with epic résumés of evil in our past. Others are milquetoast sinners, with relatively bland personal histories. But all of us come to God with sin, and we escape his wrath because of his mercy.

Let us therefore live as joyous freed slaves rather than as gloomy victims. Let us be children of the free woman (Galatians 4:31), not slaves of sin. Let us not have brick-hard hearts, but soft, pliant ones that pump out love for God and others.

B. Prayer

Merciful Father, thank you for saving us from the justice our sins deserve. Protect us from hard hearts so we can share the good news of Jesus with others. We pray in his name. Amen.

C. Thought to Remember

Live as if you have received God's mercy—because you have.

INVOLVEMENT LEARNING

Enhance your lesson with NIV® Bible Student (from your curriculum supplier) and the reproducible activity page (at www.standardlesson.com or in the back of the NIV® *Standard Lesson Commentary Deluxe Edition).*

Into the Lesson

Draw three hearts on the board, labeling them *Physical, Emotional,* and *Spiritual.* Ask learners what would characterize a heart that is hardened in a physical sense. (Possible responses will be along the lines of "hardening of the arteries," etc.). Then ask what characterizes an emotionally hard heart. (Possible responses may include "being unmoved by the hurts and distress of others.") Finally, ask what characterizes a spiritually hard heart. Guide learners to the fact that the heart is the center of the will in biblical usage. A person with a spiritually hard heart is in rebellion against God.

Then ask, "What Bible character was said to have a hard heart that God made even harder?" (Expected response: Pharaoh.) Continue: "Today's lesson will show how God has worked through human sin and shortcomings to bestow his gift of mercy on the world."

Into the Word

Form learners into pairs or groups of three to work on the following three assignments (on handouts you prepare), one per group. If you have more than nine learners, form additional groups and give duplicate assignments.

Isaac Group (Romans 9:6-9). 1. How does the story of Isaac and Ishmael (Genesis 21:1-13) establish the point that "not all who are descended from Israel are Israel"? 2. How is it possible for Gentiles (non-Israelites) to be considered children of Abraham (see Galatians 3:7, 28, 29)?

Jacob Group (Romans 9:10-14). 1. Why was it astonishing for God to proclaim "The older will serve the younger" (Genesis 25:23; compare Deuteronomy 21:15-17)? 2. How did God use what might appear as an "unfair" or "unjust" choice to accomplish his purpose to show mercy to the world?

Moses and Pharaoh Group (Romans 9:15-18). 1. On what basis does God show and not show mercy to people and nations? 2. How do we know Pharaoh wasn't treated unfairly when God hardened his heart to achieve divine purposes (compare Exodus 8:15, 32 with 4:21; 7:3; 9:12; 14:4)?

Have groups present their conclusions in the ensuing whole-class discussion. Use Matthew 3:9 and John 8:39 to challenge learners to deeper thought on physical vs. spiritual offspring.

Option. Begin the Into the Word segment by distributing copies of the "Sons of the Promise—and Not" activity from the reproducible page, which you can download. After a few minutes, ask volunteers to share their answers. This exercise will provide a visual backdrop to the lesson text.

Into Life

Write this question on the board for brainstorming: "If you were to create a plan to be a spiritual mentor to help someone grow in spiritual maturity by using today's lesson text, what would that plan include?" Encourage rapid-fire responses, jotting them quickly on the board. Discuss as deeply as learners desire.

Option. Distribute the following statements on handouts to pairs of learners, giving duplicate assignments as necessary. 1. Ivy says, "When mom remarried after my dad died, she and my stepdad had my little sister. She's always been their favorite! Even as adults, they are still helping her out, while I make my own way. It's just not fair!" How do you respond? 2. James says, "When I became a Christian, my atheist parents disowned me. Now that they have died and left all their money to my brother, I wonder why God has allowed me to be treated so unfairly." How do you respond?

Ask pairs to share their responses in whole-class discussion.

Alternative. Distribute copies of the "Spiritual Family Tree" activity from the reproducible page. Allow only 90 seconds for individual completion, then ask volunteers to share results.

GRAFTED IN

DEVOTIONAL READING: John 15:1-8
BACKGROUND SCRIPTURE: Romans 11:11-36

ROMANS 11:11-24

[11] Again I ask: Did they stumble so as to fall beyond recovery? Not at all! Rather, because of their transgression, salvation has come to the Gentiles to make Israel envious. [12] But if their transgression means riches for the world, and their loss means riches for the Gentiles, how much greater riches will their full inclusion bring!

[13] I am talking to you Gentiles. Inasmuch as I am the apostle to the Gentiles, I take pride in my ministry [14] in the hope that I may somehow arouse my own people to envy and save some of them. [15] For if their rejection brought reconciliation to the world, what will their acceptance be but life from the dead? [16] If the part of the dough offered as firstfruits is holy, then the whole batch is holy; if the root is holy, so are the branches.

[17] If some of the branches have been broken off, and you, though a wild olive shoot, have been grafted in among the others and now share in the nourishing sap from the olive root, [18] do not consider yourself to be superior to those other branches. If you do, consider this: You do not support the root, but the root supports you. [19] You will say then, "Branches were broken off so that I could be grafted in." [20] Granted. But they were broken off because of unbelief, and you stand by faith. Do not be arrogant, but tremble. [21] For if God did not spare the natural branches, he will not spare you either.

[22] Consider therefore the kindness and sternness of God: sternness to those who fell, but kindness to you, provided that you continue in his kindness. Otherwise, you also will be cut off. [23] And if they do not persist in unbelief, they will be grafted in, for God is able to graft them in again. [24] After all, if you were cut out of an olive tree that is wild by nature, and contrary to nature were grafted into a cultivated olive tree, how much more readily will these, the natural branches, be grafted into their own olive tree!

KEY VERSE

Consider therefore the kindness and sternness of God: sternness to those who fell, but kindness to you, provided that you continue in his kindness. Otherwise, you also will be cut off. —**Romans 11:22**

TOWARD A NEW CREATION

Unit 3: Life on God's Terms
LESSONS 8–13

LESSON AIMS

After participating in this lesson, each learner will be able to:

1. Identify the wild and natural branches in Paul's metaphor.

2. Explain the significance of faith in whether one is grafted into the tree or cut off.

3. Tell one way that he or she will continue in the Lord's goodness.

LESSON OUTLINE

Introduction
  A. Grafting Branches
  B. Lesson Background
I. Holy Root, Holy Branches (ROMANS 11:11-16)
  A. Jews and Jealousy (vv. 11, 12)
  B. Rejection and Reconciliation (vv. 13-16)
II. Wild Branches, Cultivated Tree (ROMANS 11:17-24)
  A. Breaking and Boasting (vv. 17-21)
    Honoring God's Treasure
  B. Goodness and Grafting (vv. 22-24)
    Family Plans, Individual Billing
Conclusion
  A. Where to Focus
  B. Prayer
  C. Thought to Remember

Introduction

A. Grafting Branches

Humans have been experimenting with ways to improve cultivated food production for thousands of years. Ancient farmers discovered that trees had the potential of providing many nutritious fruits and nuts, but multiplying trees through seeds was a slow and unpredictable process. Those farmers discovered that better results could be obtained by taking cuttings from a healthy tree and allowing these cuttings to produce roots. These miniature trees could then be planted in soil and would grow quickly.

Around 1000 BC, farmers learned another way to use these cuttings. They discovered that a branch from one tree could be inserted into a cut on another tree, and this foreign branch would become part of the new tree. This allowed for the use of a mature root and trunk system in production of fruit different from the "host" tree.

We can only imagine the wonder this must have produced among ancient farmers, to have a tree with red apples on some branches and golden apples on others! This method, known as *grafting*, is an important part of orchard science today. Grafting is now done with fruit trees, with ornamental flowers such as roses, and with plants such as tomatoes. The process is similar in all cases: a healthy branch is joined to another plant, and the result is production that the host plant was incapable of previously.

Our lesson today relies on the awareness of grafting as a common practice among those who cultivated orchards. One of the most important and valued trees of Paul's world was the olive tree. The readers of the book of Romans were familiar with orchards of olive trees in the countryside as well as the remarkable and valuable practice of grafting. Paul used these common sights and experiences to illustrate an important truth.

B. Lesson Background

In Romans 9, the apostle Paul began to discuss a situation that distressed him greatly: the unbelief of his fellow Jews. In last week's lesson we saw him recap the scriptural history of Israel to demonstrate that God controlled the nation's future. While we may not understand why God chooses certain nations and people as his instruments (Isaiah 7:18-20; etc.), Paul warned against considering God to be unjust in those decisions (Romans 9:14).

In the text just preceding that of today's lesson, Paul asked and answered two questions concerning Israel. First, "Did God reject his people?" No, Paul said, that cannot possibly be true (Romans 11:1). He supported his conclusion with a theme common in the Old Testament prophets: that God had preserved a "remnant" of faithful Israelites (Romans 11:5; compare Isaiah 10:21). Paul considered himself to be part of that remnant.

Second, why didn't more Jews believe in Jesus, as Paul did? His answer was that God had "hardened" many of the people of Israel in a way that precluded belief (Romans 11:7, 8). The apostle pointed out that this was nothing new for the people of Israel, and he quoted Scriptures to show this historical pattern of unbelief (a mixing of Deuteronomy 29:4; Psalm 69:22, 23; and Isaiah 29:10). All this led up to a further question, the one that begins today's lesson.

I. Holy Root, Holy Branches
(ROMANS 11:11-16)
A. Jews and Jealousy (vv. 11, 12)

11a. Again I ask: Did they stumble so as to fall beyond recovery? Not at all!

Paul uses a metaphor all will recognize: stumbling while walking. We have all done this—tripped on something like an uneven sidewalk and staggered for a few steps. Sometimes we regain our balance; sometimes we go down. Paul pictures those of unrepentant Israel (*they*) as if in the

HOW TO SAY IT

Abraham	*Ay*-bruh-ham.
Barnabas	*Bar*-nuh-bus.
Gentiles	*Jen*-tiles.
Isaac	*Eye*-zuk.
Nehemiah	*Nee*-huh-**my**-uh.
patriarchs	*pay*-tree-arks.

middle of the stumble. They have been tripped up by their unbelief and rejection of Jesus. Will their stumbling result in a complete fall? Paul uses strong language to answer: *Not at all!*

> **What Do You Think?**
> What is most likely to make you stumble in your faith walk? How do you resist or recover when it happens?
> *Talking Points for Your Discussion*
> - Regarding temptations of behavior
> - Regarding temptations of the tongue
> - Regarding temptations of thought

11b. Rather, because of their transgression, salvation has come to the Gentiles to make Israel envious.

Paul speaks as one who earnestly desires his fellow Jews to come to faith in Jesus. In this regard, he sees a useful purpose in *their transgression.* (Note: the Greek noun behind the word *transgression* in this half-verse and in verse 12 is elsewhere rendered "sin[s]" or "trespass[es]"; see Matthew 6:14, 15; Romans 4:25; 5:15-20; etc.) The long-simmering hostility toward Gentiles on the part of Jews is due to the latter's self-image as being favored as God's covenant people. As despised Gentiles now flock into the church and accept the Jewish Messiah as theirs, the result will be that Jews are made *envious.*

The apostle predicts that this envy will eventually serve as a wake-up call for his fellow Jews, causing them to reevaluate their unbelief (compare Romans 10:19, quoting Deuteronomy 32:21). That unbelief is therefore a temporary rather than a final and ultimate rejection of Jesus.

12. But if their transgression means riches for the world, and their loss means riches for the Gentiles, how much greater riches will their full inclusion bring!

Paul moves to an *if/then* argument using parallel phrases. *If [the Jews'] transgression* (which = *[if] their loss*) is resulting in *riches for the world* (which = *riches for the Gentiles*), then *how much greater riches will their full inclusion bring!*

In other words, Jewish unbelief has been the Gentiles' gain. Given that the parallel if-phrases

Visual for Lesson 12

As you discuss verse 22, use this visual to challenge learners to list ways God has been good to them.

describe reality, Paul is marveling at how much greater still the benefits would be if all Jews were to join Gentiles in faith. Just think of how much greater the riches of God would be for the entire world if all Israel decided to include itself in the family of faith in Jesus!

Paul knows that the spiritual blessings of God are not limited. There is an abundance of grace available, plenty for all believers. How blessed the entire world would be if Gentiles and Jews—everyone—named Jesus as Lord!

B. Rejection and Reconciliation (vv. 13-16)

13. I am talking to you Gentiles. Inasmuch as I am the apostle to the Gentiles, I take pride in my ministry

Paul leaves no doubt regarding the identity of his audience at this point. Although the church in Rome consists of both Jewish and Gentile believers, he is speaking specifically now *to you Gentiles*. He claims special authority to do this, because he is *the apostle to the Gentiles*—a status that the Roman church knows about even though Paul has not yet visited Rome (see Acts 13:46; 18:6; Galatians 2:8). No one else is described this way, and Paul is using his unique status as a megaphone.

14. in the hope that I may somehow arouse my own people to envy and save some of them.

Paul lays bare his plan: he will do anything to gain the attention and therefore the faith of his fellow Jews. We can see how awkward and strange

Paul's ministry must appear to them: a learned rabbi (Acts 22:3) who associates with "unclean" Gentiles and accepts them as beloved brothers and sisters in faith. Even so, that does not mean he has ever stopped loving those of his *own people* —his Jewish kinfolk. If his ministry to Gentiles results in Jewish *envy* and brings some to faith, that is good. Paul wants as many Jews as possible to be saved.

15. For if their rejection brought reconciliation to the world, what will their acceptance be but life from the dead?

Paul now pictures the desired outcome as he uses three more *if/then* statements across this verse and the next. First, if Jewish unbelief (*rejection*) has allowed the reconciling message of the gospel to be extended to the Gentile world, then the reception of the gospel by the Jews will be like a resurrection *from the dead*. That would be a miraculous work of God every bit as marvelous as the inclusion of the Gentiles into his people.

16a. If the part of the dough offered as first-fruits is holy, then the whole batch is holy;

Second, if in the process of making bread the part that is offered as *firstfruits is holy*, then the *whole batch* of dough *is holy*. This is a reference to the Jewish practice of giving a part of the grain harvest to the priests, a firstfruits offering (see Numbers 15:18-21). This firstfruits offering was given as an act of worship to the Lord, thus making it holy. Paul reasons that if a large batch of dough is created, enough for a dozen loaves, and a couple of the loaves become an offering, then all the loaves are sanctified because of their common source.

16b. if the root is holy, so are the branches.

Paul's logic is similar in the third *if/then* statement. If the foundational part of a tree (its root system) *is holy*, then it makes sense that *the branches* thereby produced are also holy. The apostle is expressing his hope that believing Israel (including himself) will have a positive, sanctifying effect on larger, unbelieving Israel. The example of believing Jews such as Paul, Barnabas, and Peter is to be a catalyst to bring Paul's beloved nation to faith in Christ.

This reminds us of last week's lesson concerning the history of the patriarchs Abraham, Isaac, and

Jacob. The promises and blessings they received still rest on Israel. We note, however, that the concept of *holy* as Paul uses it here does not mean "set apart for salvation," but means "set apart" in a general way for passing along the promises of God.

What Do You Think?
How can we let God's holiness be evident in our lives without projecting a sanctimonious "holier than thou" aura in the process?
Talking Points for Your Discussion
- At work or school
- At home
- In the church
- In public (at the mall, restaurants, etc.)
- Other

II. Wild Branches, Cultivated Tree
(ROMANS 11:17-24)

A. Breaking and Boasting (vv. 17-21)

17. If some of the branches have been broken off, and you, though a wild olive shoot, have been grafted in among the others and now share in the nourishing sap from the olive root,

Remember that Paul is addressing Gentiles in this section. In that light, he takes his final analogy a little further, narrowing the focus from a generic tree to an olive tree. Olive groves abound in the land of Israel, in Greece (where Paul is while writing this letter), and in the Roman countryside. Olives themselves serve as food, but more importantly they yield olive oil, a mainstay of Roman households. Paul knows how to paint a word picture that will connect instantly with his readers.

Imagine a cultivated olive tree. As the one who tends the orchard prunes off certain branches, he also grafts in branches he has cut from *a wild olive* tree. When these wild branches engage with the established tree, they begin to flourish. They receive nourishment from the tree's root system and produce olives. In this parable-like analogy, the tender of the tree is God. He has removed *some of the branches* of the cultivated olive tree, a reference to unbelieving Israel. In their place, he has grafted in foreign branches, a reference to the Gentiles. These Gentiles now benefit from the heritage

of the Jewish nation as they too become people of faith like Abraham or Paul himself (compare Ephesians 2:11-22). This sets the stage for a warning.

18. do not consider yourself to be superior to those other branches. If you do, consider this: You do not support the root, but the root supports you.

Gentiles must not see themselves *to be superior* because they have placed faith in Christ while many Jews have not. The Gentile readers are to remember that their faith is dependent on the faith heritage of the Jews (*the root*). The root is not dependent on the branches. Without the root, the branches would not exist.

This is a warning to be heeded yet today. Our faith is dependent on the examples and promises of the Old Testament and the biblical nation of ancient Israel (compare 1 Corinthians 10:1-13). Paul sees faith in Christ without Jewish roots to be an impossibility. We neglect the heritage of Old Testament Scripture at our peril! "Everything that was written in the past was written to teach us, so that through the endurance taught in the Scriptures and the encouragement they provide we might have hope" (Romans 15:4).

What Do You Think?
How do you use the Old Testament?
Talking Points for Your Discussion
- In private devotional times
- In Scriptures you memorize
- In discussions with fellow Christians
- Other

19, 20. You will say then, "Branches were broken off so that I could be grafted in." Granted. But they were broken off because of unbelief, and you stand by faith. Do not be arrogant, but tremble.

Paul's warning to Gentile believers continues. It is simplistic to think that the Jewish *branches* have been *broken off* from the tree merely so that Gentile branches can take their place by the grafting process. Everything revolves around faith and lack of faith (*unbelief*). When this is realized, the result should be humility (*not . . . arrogant*) and reverential awe (*tremble*; compare Philippians 2:12).

❧ *Honoring God's Treasure* ❧

I remember that, as a child, I sometimes heard people speaking ill of other nations that our country had been at war with in the past. These people seemed still at war. I wondered how their biases could coexist with our Sunday school song: "Red and yellow, black and white—they are precious in his sight. Jesus loves the little children of the world."

Annette, a new friend of mine, lived in the northwestern U.S. until her family moved to Iowa. Her attitude toward her new church family is *every person here is someone I can learn from*. Although she is busy finishing a college degree while raising several children, she acts on her belief by inviting people to coffee and meals. She honors the God-treasure she finds in each person she meets.

Our current church family has members from other regions of our country and other nations, so comparisons are inevitable. It seems just human nature to think of one's own way of life as "correct." But if we resist the urge to rank one way of doing things above others and, like Annette, have a heart to seek the God-treasure in people from other backgrounds, then we create a welcoming community. Let us marvel at what God is doing in each person so that we remain free to love them, their families, and their nations. —V. E.

21. For if God did not spare the natural branches, he will not spare you either.

Using another *if/then* statement, Paul expresses the ultimate guard against Gentile pride over Jews: God has proven his willingness to break off branches that do not expect it. The ancient Jews (*the natural branches*), because of their status as the covenant people of God, never expected to be cut off from their promised land—but it happened when God sent them into captivity in 586 BC. Arrogance and faith are not easy companions. Even as we remember God's mercy, we should fear his wrath no matter our background.

B. Goodness and Grafting (vv. 22-24)

22. Consider therefore the kindness and sternness of God: sternness to those who fell, but kindness to you, provided that you continue in his kindness. Otherwise, you also will be cut off.

Paul now uses the olive-tree analogy to reveal some profound things about God's nature. A tree tender might be seen as a kind giver of life when grafting and a severe judge when pruning (see Matthew 3:10; Luke 13:6-9). God displays both *kindness and sternness*. He rewards those who are humble and faithful (Genesis 15:1; Proverbs 22:4) and punishes the arrogant and unfaithful (Nehemiah 1:8; Proverbs 16:5). He is kind and gentle, yet consistently intolerant of those who misuse his mercy. If we preach the goodness of God but neglect to mention his severity, we give an incomplete picture of him.

23. And if they do not persist in unbelief, they will be grafted in, for God is able to graft them in again.

The Gentile readers are further warned to temper any arrogance. They should remember that God, the great grafter, is perfectly capable of grafting the broken-off branches back into the olive tree. This will happen if Jewish unbelievers *do not persist in unbelief.*

This is an important counterbalance to the verses that speak of God's hardening people against faith. Our faith is not wholly dependent on the actions of God. We play a part too. To continue in unbelief is a personal choice; so is yielding to God in faith. Just as the Gentiles in the church in Rome had chosen to become believers, so too may the many unbelieving Jews of their city.

❧ *Family Plans, Individual Billing* ❧

Even as we grow weary of advertising blitzes, it's hard not to be amused at various marketing attempts. At the time of this writing, a well-known company is offering lower per-line rates for cellular service for customers having 7 to 10 in their group. Of course, not all families are that large. But by billing lines separately (thus eliminating the need for a shared budget), the plan invites potential customers to recruit neighbors, coworkers, and acquaintances in order create a "family" and reap greater savings. The commercials illustrate the possibilities by depicting people who don't seem to have much in common.

Sometimes churches may feel like that. On the one hand is the "group aspect" of people from diverse backgrounds having a common allegiance to Jesus Christ. On the other hand is the "individual aspect," where each is accountable for his or her own faith in trusting that Jesus has paid the bill for sin. More people joining the kingdom of God is better for everyone, since he gifts each of us in ways that we can be a blessing to others. Today's lesson text reminds us that God's invitation to join is open to all. We dare not take upon ourselves the authority to determine whom God can and cannot include. —V. E.

24. After all, if you were cut out of an olive tree that is wild by nature, and contrary to nature were grafted into a cultivated olive tree, how much more readily will these, the natural branches, be grafted into their own olive tree!

Paul sums up his thoughts with a straightforward analysis that reveals his hope for his people. From a historical Jewish perspective, the inclusion of Gentiles into the people of God without requiring them to become Jews first is outrageous (compare Acts 15:1). The Jews see themselves as privileged heirs of the covenant of their ancestor Abraham. Their men bear the sign of this covenant: circumcision. Their faith has become systematized and ritualized through their food laws. Gentiles are not just outside the covenant, they are a filth that causes Jews to be "unclean" (Acts 10:28).

Yet the God of Israel, in his great wisdom and mercy, has included Gentiles in the new covenant people of God. Their inclusion is based on their faith. Paul's point is that since God is so surpris-

ingly gracious toward these Gentiles, why would we not expect him to be patient and gracious toward unbelieving Jews who reverse course and come to faith in Jesus? Even the broken branches of Israel can be grafted back into the tree and its rich root if they believe in him.

> **What Do You Think?**
> How can we do a better job of welcoming "grafted branches" into our churches?
> *Talking Points for Your Discussion*
> - Regarding adjustments to our attitudes
> - Regarding adjustments to our actions

Conclusion

A. Where to Focus

A controversial topic in some churches concerns the position of Jewish people today in relation to the will of God. For some Christians, this question centers on the modern state of Israel, established in 1948 in historic territory in Palestine. Some Christians teach that this nation's existence is an expression of God's will, a sign that he has not forgotten Israel. Others wonder about the Jews in their own cities, questioning whether faithful keeping of Torah and the old covenant is still a valid way to serve God and find his favor. Various interpretations of Romans 11:26 ("all Israel will be saved") stoke the flames of controversy.

We must not allow the importance of that topic —and it is indeed important—to overshadow what Paul is saying to his readers about the basis of their faith and their attitude toward it. That basis is faith in Jesus, and the proper attitude is fear in the sense of reverential awe.

B. Prayer

Heavenly Father, we pray for Jewish people of today who believe in you but have rejected your Son. May their hearts be softened to hear the truth about Jesus, who wants to be their Savior, as we take the gospel to them. May we speak that gospel humbly. We pray in Jesus' name. Amen.

C. Thought to Remember

God can graft in—and prune away—anyone.

INVOLVEMENT LEARNING

Enhance your lesson with NIV® Bible Student (from your curriculum supplier) and the reproducible activity page (at www.standardlesson.com or in the back of the NIV® Standard Lesson Commentary Deluxe Edition).

Into the Lesson

Conduct an interview with someone in your class or congregation who is skilled in horticulture. Give the interviewee a list of the following interview questions in advance: 1. How would you use a cutting to grow a new plant? 2. What is the purpose of pruning? 3. What is grafting? 4. Under what circumstances would you perform a grafting?

After thanking your interviewee, say, "In today's lesson, the apostle Paul uses the ancient technique of grafting to illustrate an important truth."

Alternative. Bring to class a large seed (such as a peach pit), a cutting from a plant in water, two small branches, and a jar of olives. Use these as visual aids as you give a mini-lecture on the lesson's "Grafting Branches" introduction.

Into the Word

Divide the class in half, designating one half as the *Gentile Wild Branch Group* and the other half as the *Jewish Olive Tree Group*. Distribute handouts of the questions below for in-group discussions. (*Option 1:* Leave off the italicized verse references to compel closer examination of the text at the cost of requiring more time. *Option 2:* If your class is larger, divide the halves into smaller subgroups and give the subgroups fewer questions.)

Gentile Wild Branch Group. 1–How did the fact that Jews stumbled over believing in Jesus benefit Gentiles? *(vv. 11, 12)* 2–What special connection did Paul have with Gentiles? *(v. 13)* 3–How were Gentiles benefitting from the holiness and "nourishing sap" of the olive tree? *(vv. 16, 17)* 4–Why did Paul tell Gentiles "do not consider yourself to be superior" and "do not be arrogant"? *(vv. 18-20)* 5–What is the basis of Gentiles' standing with God? *(v. 20)* 6–In discussing God's goodness, what warning did Paul give Gentiles? *(vv. 21, 22)*

Jewish Olive Tree Group. 1–Why was Paul trying to make the Jews jealous? *(vv. 11, 14)* 2–What special connection did Paul have with Jews?

(v. 14) 3–Why did Paul refer to the root of the olive tree as "holy"? *(v. 16)* 4–Why were some of the branches of the olive tree broken off? *(vv. 19, 20)* 5–What hope did Paul hold out for the olive branches that had been broken off because of unbelief? *(vv. 15, 23)* 6–Why was it more natural for formerly unbelieving Jews to receive God's grace than it was for the Gentiles? *(v. 24)*

Alternative. Distribute copies of the "Behind the Headlines" activity from the reproducible page, which you can download. Have learners work in pairs to complete as indicated. (This exercise will be more time consuming than it appears at first glance.)

After calling time under either alternative, have groups or pairs present their findings in whole-class discussion. Use the commentary to correct misconceptions.

Into Life

Write on the board *Attitudes / Actions / Speech* as the headers of three columns. Then write *To Do or Have / To Avoid* as the designations of two rows that extend across the three columns. Conduct a whole-class brainstorming session by challenging learners to suggest ways to continue in the Lord's goodness—to not be broken off of the tree into which they have been grafted. The column headings and row labels should prompt learner responses; jot responses on the board at the appropriate intersections of columns and rows. Request learners be specific. (For example, follow the general response "to have a good attitude" with the question "About what, specifically?") Use Luke 13:1-8 and/or John 15:1-8 to establish further the importance of the discussion.

Option. Distribute copies of the "Part of the Same Tree" activity from the reproducible page. Have learners complete it individually before discussing conclusions in small groups. Instruct that not all boxes need to have entries.

LOVE FULFILLS THE LAW

DEVOTIONAL READING: Deuteronomy 13:15-20
BACKGROUND SCRIPTURE: Romans 12:1, 2; 13:8-14

ROMANS 12:1, 2

¹ Therefore, I urge you, brothers and sisters, in view of God's mercy, to offer your bodies as a living sacrifice, holy and pleasing to God—this is your true and proper worship. ² Do not conform to the pattern of this world, but be transformed by the renewing of your mind. Then you will be able to test and approve what God's will is—his good, pleasing and perfect will.

ROMANS 13:8-10

⁸ Let no debt remain outstanding, except the continuing debt to love one another, for whoever loves others has fulfilled the law. ⁹ The commandments, "You shall not commit adultery," "You shall not murder," "You shall not steal," "You shall not covet," and whatever other command there may be, are summed up in this one command: "Love your neighbor as yourself." ¹⁰ Love does no harm to a neighbor. Therefore love is the fulfillment of the law.

KEY VERSE

Let no debt remain outstanding, except the continuing debt to love one another, for whoever loves others has fulfilled the law. —**Romans 13:8**

Photo: Heath Doman / Hemera / Thinkstock

TOWARD A NEW CREATION

Unit 3: Life on God's Terms

LESSONS 8–13

LESSON AIMS

After participating in this lesson, each learner will be able to:

1. Summarize the relationship between being a "living sacrifice" and living with the continual obligation to "love one another."

2. Understand why neighbor love is the underlying assumption behind the ethical commandments.

3. Help prepare a worship service that is focused on the theme of being a living sacrifice.

LESSON OUTLINE

Introduction
  A. Metamorphosis
  B. Lesson Background
I. The Surrender of Self (ROMANS 12:1, 2)
  A. Living Sacrifice (v. 1)
    The Perfect Gift
  B. Renewed Mind (v. 2)
    The Path of Most Resistance
II. The Law of Love (ROMANS 13:8-10)
  A. Ongoing Obligation (v. 8)
  B. Key Commandment (v. 9)
  C. Underlying Assumption (v. 10)
Conclusion
  A. Living and Sacrificing
  B. Prayer
  C. Thought to Remember

Introduction

A. Metamorphosis

One of the most remarkable phenomena we observe in nature is the change of a caterpillar into a butterfly. The caterpillar is a wormlike creature with many feet, eating leaves as it crawls among plants. It sheds skin as it grows larger, eating continually. Finally, it spins a cocoon around itself and seems to go into hibernation. After many days, this creature emerges from the cocoon. It looks nothing like the caterpillar it once was, for now it is a six-legged insect with glorious wings. Formerly limited to waddling around on plants and trees, it can now fly, for it is a butterfly. Scientists call this transformation from caterpillar to butterfly *metamorphosis*.

The word chosen by scientists for this process is actually an ancient Greek term that means "to change form." This is radical transformation, though, like going from a slug-like larva to a beautiful winged creature capable of flight. This Greek word occurs four times in the New Testament. It is translated "transfigured" in Matthew 17:2 and Mark 9:2, as "transformed" in 2 Corinthians 3:18 and Romans 12:2. As we study the latter verse this week, we are to think of drastic change—a personal transformation so profound that we can hardly remember what it was like to be a spiritual caterpillar.

B. Lesson Background

The book of Romans was written by Paul to Christians living in a city he had not yet visited. Although he knew some people there (see Romans 16), most did not know him personally.

The book itself (actually, a letter) is well organized. The sequence of thought in the first 11 of its 16 chapters begins with an exposition of the origin and scope of sin, follows with an explanation of the remedy for sin, and wraps up with a discussion of the fate of the unbelieving Jewish nation. Due to the nature of their content, these first 11 chapters are often referred to as *the doctrinal section*, meaning that they present teaching that is foundational to our understanding of the Christian faith.

In Romans 12, the apostle Paul moves to what is often called *the practical section* of the letter. Here we see concerns for how the great truths of the church are to be worked out in the lives of its members. Paul instructs in such things as the use of spiritual gifts (12:3-8), how to relate to governing authorities (13:1-7), and the dangers of judging others (14:10-13). These closing chapters are characterized by key summary statements such as "Do not be overcome by evil, but overcome evil with good" (12:21) and "Accept one another, then, just as Christ accepted you" (15:7). Today's lesson examines two texts drawn from this rich practical section.

I. The Surrender of Self
(ROMANS 12:1, 2)
A. Living Sacrifice (v. 1)

1a. Therefore, I urge you, brothers and sisters,

In reading the Bible, we should always pay careful attention to the word *therefore*. Paul uses this word here as a marker to signal that he is moving from the *what* and *why* of Romans 1–11 to the *how* of chapters 12 and following. It is as if Paul is saying, "Since you have listened to all the things I have said up to now, here's how your lives should be affected." Stated another way, Paul is about to say how Jesus' victory over sin and the Father's proving of his love should influence behavior.

The phrase *I urge you* that accompanies the word *therefore* indicates that what comes next rises above a quiet, logical presentation for the apostle. What he has to say next he does so with great insistence.

1b. in view of God's mercy,

This phrase highlights Paul's urgency. The word translated *mercy* here is used frequently in the Greek translation of the Psalms to supply context for urgent requests made to the Lord (see Psalms 25:6; 40:11; 69:16). In the case at hand, Paul is imploring the Christians in Rome (rather than God himself) by reminding them that the Lord is the God of great mercy. This, in some ways, sums up the character of God as revealed in the first 11 chapters of the letter (compare Romans 9:16, 18, 23; 11:30-32).

1c. to offer your bodies as a living sacrifice, holy and pleasing to God—this is your true and proper worship.

Paul now turns to the vernacular of the temple, of presenting *sacrifice*. The language of sacrifice depicts the act of offering an animal in the Jerusalem temple (or even in a pagan temple). Such language is also used by the Jews when they "present" a firstborn son at the temple (see Luke 2:22-24); this is part of the ritual of "redeeming" the firstborn according to Jewish law by offering a sacrifice in the child's stead (compare Exodus 13:2, 12, 13; Numbers 18:15).

The offering Paul has in mind, though, is not an animal or an animal substitute such as grain. Rather, he urges the Romans to present their *bodies*, their very selves. They are to be *living* sacrifices, not lambs or goats who do not survive the sacrificial act.

It has often been noted that there is a problem with a living sacrifice: it keeps crawling off the altar! A dead sacrifice is much more practical, since it won't move. Paul's striking imagery reminds us of Abraham, who bound his son Isaac and placed him on an altar to be sacrificed. Isaac was alive when his father laid him there (Genesis 22:9). That altar had dry wood that was ready to be set on fire. Abraham intended to kill his son and burn his body, being convinced that that was what God wanted him to do (22:2).

God's plan, however, was to test Abraham, not to witness and accept Isaac's death (Genesis 22:12). Isaac was of much more use to the Lord alive. As Paul relates in Romans 9, Isaac was to be the instrument of promise, a son chosen to be a key figure in building a future great nation. God will test our willingness to sacrifice our lives for him. But except in the cases of martyrdom, he wants to use those holy lives in his service.

What Do You Think?
How can you be more of a living sacrifice in the week ahead?
Talking Points for Your Discussion
- As an individual Christian
- As part of a wider group of Christians

Paul describes this as our *true and proper worship*. The word translated *true and proper* is the source of our word *logical*. The word translated *worship* is rendered "service" in the *King James Version*, and this is where we get the idea of a "worship service" (compare John 16:2). When we worship God, we are serving God. When we serve God, we are worshipping God.

This is all tied to Paul's "therefore" that introduces this section. Given all the territory the apostle has covered in explaining the great love, mercy, and grace of God, the willing sacrifice of ourselves is the only true and proper response. Would we spit in God's eye in ongoing rebellion when we realize all he has done for us? Paul does not think so!

✄ THE PERFECT GIFT ✄

I recall the summer of our twenty-fifth anniversary. Although we had agreed not to buy each other anything, my husband actually polled his coworkers for gift ideas. Some suggested candy. He knew that was not something I would want. His advisers were sure he was mistaken when he said I would not like a pricey bauble from the jewelry store either.

So he stuck to his knowledge of me, and what he chose was a wonderful surprise: a portable CD player. (This was a few years and a few technological advances ago!) He knew I loved to be outside, but I also liked to listen to music. I was warmed to realize that he had actually heard me say something about my no-way-to-have-music-outside dilemma and that he cared enough to formulate a solution.

Heartfelt, thoughtful gifts are a wonderful way to express love and appreciation. So, how can we not want to give something to God? But what do you give someone who has everything (Psalm 50:10)? Listening to what he says he desires will give us the key: he wants us as living, holy sacrifices. We give our lives to God moment by

moment, choice by choice. It is this that he desires —and deserves.
—V. E.

B. Renewed Mind (v. 2)

2. Do not conform to the pattern of this world, but be transformed by the renewing of your mind. Then you will be able to test and approve what God's will is—his good, pleasing and perfect will.

How do we perform this true and proper service of worship to God? Paul uses vibrant words here to explain further.

The Greek word translated *conform* is the source of our English word *schematic*—a drawing that details the plan for a device such as a smartphone. Once the schematic is created, thousands or millions of identical devices can be produced from it. It is as if Paul is saying, "Don't follow the world's schematic diagram!"

If we are following the world's *pattern*, then we are not doing the right sort of service for God. The world tells us that greed is good and that we should look out for ourselves most of all. Serving God, however, means that we love others and give to those in need, even if it cramps our own lifestyle and desires.

What Paul is *not* saying is that we are to be nonconformists in everything. The command *do not conform to the pattern of this world* is not a license to break rules. Every teacher labors to train children in ways of conformity that are beneficial for everyone. When youngsters are asked to line up, the little boy who can never seem to do so is not a person serving God by being a nonconformist. Rather, he is a rebellious soul that needs to learn basic discipline and how to follow rules.

Christians have sometimes used Paul's *do not conform* exhortation as an excuse to refuse to do things they don't want to do. This is far from Paul's intent (compare Romans 13:1, 2). The idea, rather, is that we don't follow the rules of the world when they conflict with *what God's will is* (compare Acts 4:19; 5:29; Colossians 2:8, 18-23). Our schematic for living is the Word of God, not the selfish souls we see in popular media.

The flip side of conforming is being *transformed* (see discussion of the word *metamorphosis* in the

HOW TO SAY IT

Isaac	*Eye*-zuk.
metamorphosis	*met*-tuh-**mor**-fuh-suss.
rabbi	*rab*-eye.

Introduction). This verb is in the passive voice, meaning that we do not transform ourselves; rather, we allow ourselves to be transformed by the power of God. Paul refers to this as *the renewing of your mind,* meaning this is not a physical transformation. This is not losing weight and working out at the gym to tone our bodies (compare 1 Timothy 4:8). It is instead a spiritual transformation, a mental renewal, a new way of thinking, a new orientation to the world.

We do not despise the world, but we are not controlled by its corruption either. This is a transformation by the Holy Spirit into being a servant who is pleasing to God. In a sermon on this passage, Dr. Martin Luther King Jr. described this as being "transformed nonconformists." Christians should never become adjusted to certain things that are acceptable in popular culture. King also noted that "There are some things in our world to which men of goodwill must be maladjusted."

True transformation is a one-way process. If we have been changed by the Holy Spirit, we should not relapse into old ways (compare 2 Timothy 4:10a). Nothing is the same for us. Our priorities are different. Our goals are different. Our ambitions are different. Our lives are renewed, transformed. Our guiding star is God's *good, pleasing and perfect will.* Our renewed souls are ready to know it and follow it (compare Ephesians 4:23).

❧ THE PATH OF MOST RESISTANCE ❧

Neuroscience has shown that our brains switch to a more meditative, suggestible state while watching television. I may not have felt overly alarmed from learning of that study had I not experienced the effects personally.

I remember watching a certain prime-time series over the course of a season. As I grew to know the backstories, endearing quirks, and hopes and dreams of the characters, I found myself cheering on the growing romance of two figures in the drama. I found myself hoping that by season's end they would declare their love for each other. Then I realized they were married to other people! This wasn't something I agreed with at all!

I won't blame television completely. The story line drew me in, and I allowed myself to enjoy

the drama. I was not watching in order to critique the morality of the message, but merely as entertainment. But therein lies the rub. If we do not hold tight to the command God gives us to take every thought captive (2 Corinthians 10:5), we can find our values eroding into whatever the culture suggests.

Anti-Christian messages lurk everywhere. The admonition "do not conform" requires active awareness and resistance on our part.   —V. E.

What Do You Think?
  What are some things this world offers that tempt us to conform? How do we resist these?
Talking Points for Your Discussion
  ▪ Within Christian contexts (worship, etc.)
  ▪ In our daily activities and interactions with unbelievers

---

II. The Law of Love
(ROMANS 13:8-10)
A. Ongoing Obligation (v. 8)

8. Let no debt remain outstanding, except the continuing debt to love one another, for whoever loves others has fulfilled the law.

Our lesson now shifts to Romans 13, a chapter full of practical instruction for Christian believers. Paul's injunction here combines financial advice with moral advice. A surface reading of the first phrase, *let no debt remain outstanding,* has sometimes been understood to prohibit Christians from borrowing money under any circumstances. This is not Paul's intent and would not be in harmony with other Scriptures (example: Matthew 5:42).

What is being said, rather, is that debts must be repaid. The wise person will borrow as little and as infrequently as possible (compare Proverbs 22:7). Pay your debts, Paul says. This is not a surprising or controversial piece of advice, especially for those of a Jewish background. Financial integrity is a desirable quality. But Paul uses this fact to move to his more important point, something that is undoubtedly surprising to many. We do have a continuing debt that requires constant payment. This debt will never be retired. It is the obligation *to love one another.*

The context of this command does not limit it to love for fellow Christians. Paul is pushing beyond the church, to our obligation to the community at large. We are to love those with whom we have any sort of relationship. This is to be unconditional love, not love that is conditioned on receiving love in return.

It is disappointing to hear voices in the public arena that claim to be Christian but are filled with invective. We live in angry times, and unquenchable anger toward others is hardly compatible with Paul's command. This does not mean we must wink at evil, but may God protect our hearts from losing sight of the obligation to love others (Galatians 5:14).

What Do You Think?
How do you pay your love-debt to humanity?
What about "missed payments"?
Talking Points for Your Discussion
- When dealing with "easy to love" people
- When dealing with people you don't like

B. Key Commandment (v. 9)

9. The commandments, "You shall not commit adultery," "You shall not murder," "You shall not steal," "You shall not covet," and whatever other command there may be, are summed up in this one command: "Love your neighbor as yourself."

Paul now does something that is very compatible with his identity as a Christian of Jewish background and as a trained rabbi who is steeped in the Law of Moses: he lists several of the Ten Commandments (compare Exodus 20:3-17; Deuteronomy 5:7-21). The ones cited are sometimes referred to as "ethical commandments" in that they give divine requirements for human relationships. We are to honor marriage boundaries (see Matthew 5:27, 28, 32; Hebrews 13:4). We are to guard the sanctity of human life (see Matthew 5:21, 22). We are to respect the possessions of others (see Luke 3:12, 13). We are to be satisfied with our own possessions (see Luke 12:15). With these we may compare the descriptions in Revelation 21:8; 22:15 of those excluded from eternal life.

What Do You Think?
What helps you overcome the temptation to covet?
Talking Points for Your Discussion
- Regarding others' possessions
- Regarding others' accomplishments
- Regarding others' jobs
- Regarding others' relationships

All of these are products of the heart determined to love others. If we are controlled by love, none of these will be a problem for us. How can we commit adultery with another person's spouse if we want what is best for other people? How can a loving heart commit murder? How can we steal from those created in the image of God as we are? How can we jeopardize our attitude toward others by being jealous of what they have?

All of this is covered in the great commandment of neighbor love (Matthew 22:39). We must love our neighbors (all whom we have contact with) as we love our own selves. We do not want to be victims of infidelity, murder, theft, or jealousy. If we love others, we do not want to be the perpetrators of any of these either.

C. Underlying Assumption (v. 10)

10. Love does no harm to a neighbor. Therefore love is the fulfillment of the law.

While other parts of the book of Romans are addressed specifically to Gentiles in the congregation (Romans 11:13; etc.), here Paul seems to be speaking especially to his fellow Jews. They have been raised to love the Law of Moses, and an essence *of the law* is to care about others. Loving others includes doing *no harm to* them. Relationships will be concerned with a neighbor's best interests. Therefore Paul's Jewish readers are to relax on giving undue attention to the specifics of the law. If relationships are controlled by love, then adherence to the law will take care of itself.

This is an important insight on Paul's understanding of the Jewish law. In Romans 7 he portrays the law as a tyrant that rules over humanity. This is not because the law is evil or ill intended, though. It is because some teachers of the law use it as a club to bludgeon their followers into conformity. The law itself is a good thing (see Romans 7:12). The rigid keeping of the law based on fear and/or with the expectation of earning God's favor is not fulfilling the intent of the law.

We should not be motivated to keep God's commands out of fear, for fear is a short-term emotion that eventually fades. We should not be motivated to keep the commandments as a way of earning God's favor, because that is futile (see Galatians 5:4). We should be motivated by love.

Love is a characteristic rooted in the nature of God himself. He has proven his love for us by giving his Son to die on our behalf (Romans 5:8). God has promised that we will never be cut off from his love (8:38, 39). God's demonstration of his great love is sufficient motivation for us always to act with love first in our relationships.

Visual for Lesson 13. *Start a discussion by turning this statement into a question as you ask, "Exactly how does love fulfill the law?"*

> ### What Do You Think?
> When, if ever, would a harsh act be appropriate and proper if it were intended to benefit the other in the long run?
>
> *Talking Points for Your Discussion*
> - Regarding a Christian "neighbor" (considering Acts 15:37-40; 1 Corinthians 5:13; etc.)
> - Regarding an unbelieving "neighbor" (considering Luke 9:5, 52-55; Acts 13:9-12; etc.)
> - Regarding the "tough love" concept
> - Other

Conclusion

A. Living and Sacrificing

Although only five verses total, our lesson text is packed with imperatives that resonate in our lives today. We are centuries removed from Paul and his Roman audience, yet these verses are great examples of the living Word, affecting every generation of Christians.

How much are you willing to sacrifice for God? How deep does your desire to serve him really go? We normally think of sacrifice as foregoing things and activities that people typically enjoy. But it is no sacrifice for me personally to say, "As a sacrifice, I will not drink beer," because I do not drink beer anyway (my personal choice). Similarly, our claims of sacrifice are often shallow and painless in

that we tend to give up things we don't care much about anyway. So the question remains: How and what are you willing to sacrifice for God?

Paul is not telling us to give up beloved things. He is not advising us to make our lives more painful and less enjoyable as a sign of spiritual maturity. He is urging us to *be* a sacrifice. If we do this, we hold nothing back. All our possessions, actions, attitudes, abilities, relationships, etc., are surrendered to God's will. This is what it means to be a living sacrifice. To be a sacrifice means we are ready for God's transforming power as we consider how best to live as his servants among his servants (1 Corinthians 8:13; etc.).

We cannot transform ourselves. If we try to achieve godliness through conforming, we will fail. We must allow the great transformer—God working through his Holy Spirit and his Holy Word—to change us.

B. Prayer

Lord God, you are the great transformer of souls! Mold us according to your perfect will so our service will be acceptable. May our relationships be a reflection of your own love for us. We pray these things in the name of your Son, Jesus, who showed us how to love and follow you in all things. Amen.

C. Thought to Remember

Transformation reveals itself in love.

INVOLVEMENT LEARNING

Enhance your lesson with NIV® Bible Student (from your curriculum supplier) and the reproducible activity page (at www.standardlesson.com or in the back of the NIV® Standard Lesson Commentary Deluxe Edition).

Into the Lesson

Ask who has been the victim of either a robbery or burglary. Allow volunteers to share experiences briefly in that regard. Then ask, "If the person who stole from you tried later to convince you that they really loved you, would you believe them? Why, or why not?" After a response that is along the lines of "love and stealing don't go together," say, "In today's lesson, Paul will help us understand the close connection between loving people and keeping God's commandments."

Alternative. Place in chairs copies of the "Clear as Mud?" activity from the reproducible page, which you can download, for learners to begin working on as they arrive. After discussing results, say, "People of Paul's day, being familiar with dead sacrifices as they were, must have been startled by the idea of a *living sacrifice*! Let's take a closer look at that phrase and its implications."

Into the Word

Form learners into three small groups to work on the assignments below, which you have reproduced on handouts.

Living Sacrifice Group. Read Romans 12:1 and give reasons why you agree or disagree with the following statements. 1–"God is less concerned with what we do with our bodies than he is with the condition of our souls." 2–"In some ways it's easier to be a dead martyr than a living sacrifice." 3–"Paul's reference to God's mercy is the same as that in Romans 9:16-18 (lesson 11)."

Renewed Minds Group. Read Romans 12:2 and give reasons why you agree or disagree with the following statements. 1–"It's important that we be radically different from other people in the world, so we don't conform to their way of doing things." 2–"If you want to change the way you act, ask God to help you change the way you think." 3–"No one can really know what God's will for him or her is."

Love One Another Group. Read Romans 13:8-10 and give reasons why you agree or disagree with the following statements. 1–"Being in any kind of financial debt is sinful since the Bible says 'let no debt remain outstanding.'" 2–"If we all loved our neighbors as ourselves, we wouldn't need to have any laws." 3–"You have to feel the appropriate emotion in order to love others and fulfill the law."

After calling time, have spokespersons from groups read their statements and responses in the ensuing whole-class discussion. Explore whether conclusions are the result of group consensus or if there is a "minority report" to consider. Encourage members of other groups to evaluate the conclusions and the reasons for them. Use the commentary to correct misconceptions.

Write this equation on the board: *living sacrifice = loving one another = keeping the law*. By show of hands, ask who agrees and disagrees with the equation, which proposes that these concepts are interchangeable. Ask why learners agree or disagree. For those disagreeing, ask, "If the equal signs are not appropriate, what would be a better way of showing how these three concepts are related?"

Into Life

Brainstorm ways for a worship service to be based on the theme *living sacrifice*. Depending on the size of your class, you can use small groups or whole-class discussion to propose how to reflect the theme in music selection, Scripture reading (in addition to Romans 12:1), communion and offering meditations, a skit, prayers, etc. Record ideas for submission to your church's worship planner(s).

Option. Distribute copies of the "Words of Wisdom" activity from the reproducible page. Form learners into pairs to consider one or both of the scenarios. Challenge learners to use today's lesson text as a basis for the counsel they would offer to either "Beth" or "Sam." Allow time for pairs to share their responses in whole-class discussion.